The Roots of Dependency

Richard White

The Roots of Dependency

Subsistence, Environment, and

Social Change among the

Choctaws, Pawnees, and Navajos

University of Nebraska Press

Lincoln and London

Publication of this book was assisted by a grant
from the National Endowment for the Humanities.

The paper in this book meets the guidelines for
permanence and durability of the Committee on
Production Guidelines for Book Longevity of
the Council on Library Resources.

Library of Congress Cataloging in Publication Data

White, Richard, 1947–
The roots of dependency.

Bibliography: p.
Includes index.
1. Choctaw Indians – Economic conditions.
2. Choctaw Indians – Social conditions.
3. Pawnee Indians – Economic conditons. 4. Pawnee
Indians – Social conditions. 5. Navaho Indians –
Economic conditions. 6. Navaho Indians – Social
conditions. 7. Indians of North America – Economic
conditions. 8. Indians of North America – Social
conditions. 9. Human ecology – United States.
10. Subsistence economy – United States. I. Title.
E99.C8W6   1983   306'.08997   82-11146
ISBN 0-8032-4722-2

To Beverly, and Jesse, Teal, and Colin

Contents

Maps & Tables

Acknowledgments

The research for this book began during a year's fellowship at the Center for the History of the American Indian at the Newberry Library, and its completion was made possible by grants from the American Philosophical Society and Michigan State University. I am grateful to all of these institutions.

I have also benefited from the criticism, warnings, and encouragement of numerous people who have read all or parts of this manuscript. Willy Dobak, Paul Stuart, Richard Aquila, and Clyde Milner all gave assistance and criticism in the early stages of the project. Clyde also later shared with me his own research on the Pawnees, which opened up areas I had neglected. Marty Zanger, acting director of the Indian History Center the year I was there, both encouraged the project and has been a patient and perceptive critic of the manuscript from its earliest stages. Susan Vehik read early drafts on the Pawnees and saved me from blunders in the archaeological record. Patricia Galloway read the final drafts of the Choctaw chapters and shared with me her own extensive knowledge of early Choctaw history. John Aubrey's help in using the collections of the Newberry Library was invaluable, and Robert Kvasnicka guided me through the often confusing collections of the National Archives. Without the help of both of them, I would have missed crucial sources. Other sources, too, might have gone unexamined without the aid of my brother, David White, who assisted me in gathering Navajo materials. Peter Iverson read the chapters on the Navajos and corrected numerous errors. Ray DeMallie and Kenneth Philp heard an earlier synopsis of the Navajo sections, and their criticisms led to necessary changes. Bill Derman, with whom I have taught for several years, not only gave parts of the manuscript a perceptive reading but also has raised questions in the classroom which eventually found their way into this work. Peter Levine, Peter Vinten-Johansen, and David LoRomer have repeatedly read drafts of sections of this book and regularly provided my best information as to what made no sense at all in the text and how I might fix it. Finally, Beverly Purrington, always my most perceptive critic, retained her ability to ask telling questions throughout the writing of this book. Many parts of the final result bear her influence. The stale caveat that, despite the efforts of all these people, the shortcomings and errors which remain in this work all belong to me, of course, applies.

Finally, there are people who have influenced this book without ever reading it. The Bridges, Franks, and other families of the fishing rights struggles on the Nisqually and Puyallup rivers of western Washington first allowed me to realize the quite different ways Indian peoples can have of perceiving and organizing the world, and how tenacious and creative seemingly powerless people can be in fighting to maintain a way of life. It is a lesson reinforced by later experience with Indian communities in Michigan and elsewhere.

My son Jesse could not even read when this book was begun, and now his literary tastes run to quite different things. Yet he has influenced my writing deeply by providing the countless distractions and interruptions which daily reminded me that the events written about here were not abstractions but affected the lives of human beings who once also had children they loved and had hopes for.

Introduction

Most twentieth-century Americans link Indians and the environment almost automatically. The connections are simple and largely symbolic—Indian peoples serve as a sort of environmental conscience for the larger society. This ubiquity of the Indian as environmentalist unfortunately tends to reduce most research about Indian peoples and the land to briefs for and against the recent canonization of Indians into environmental sainthood. Such arguments have outlived their usefulness. By considering the actions and concerns of Indian peoples only in terms of the controversies of the late twentieth century, they trivialize and distort native societies. They also obscure larger historical questions by failing to examine why and how human societies have influenced the environment, and what the social consequences of human induced environmental change have been.

These larger issues are the concern of this book. Indians, like all peoples, live in a physical world which is not only natural but also historical—a creation of their ancestors and themselves. Environmental constraints set certain boundaries on human creations, but they only limit; they do not dictate. Ideally, such human-dominated ecosystems produce food and shelter for human beings without degrading the natural systems upon which the society depends. Often, however, degradation occurs; a human environment breaks down and the society which created it faces crisis, change, and perhaps extinction.

Such crises have occurred repeatedly in human history; they occur now and will occur again. Too often they are dismissed as merely environmental or biological failures—failures of skill, of luck, or of environmental sense. Surely this may explain some crises, but such explanations ignore the larger web of political, social, cultural, and economic relations which have shaped human actions on the land. Far more is often involved than bad luck or lack of skill. Certainly this is true for the American Indian peoples who are the subjects of this book.

Mixtures of hunting, gathering, and horticulture typified the subsistence systems of numerous Indian nations from the eastern woodlands to the margins of the Great Plains and down into the desert Southwest. The lands and cultures of these peoples differed enormously, but their strategies for getting a living from the earth resembled one another in broad outline. Their subsistence systems also resembled each other in their final result: at varying rates and at different times this aboriginal mix of horticulture, hunting, gathering, and, later, herding failed. Peoples who had once been able to feed and clothe themselves with some security became unable to do so. Environments that had once easily sustained Indian populations underwent increasing degradation as familiar resources could not support the peoples who depended on them. The question, again, is why.

This study is designed to answer that question by examining in depth three Indian nations: the Choctaws, horticulturalists, deer hunters, and later cattle raisers of the southeastern woodlands; the Pawnees, horticulturalists, buffalo hunters, and later horse raisers for the prairies and Great Plains; and the Navajos, horticulturalists, hunters, and later shepherds for the southwestern deserts and mountains.

A study of the collapse of aboriginal subsistence systems may seem perverse since it refuses to accept the obvious cause: the military superiority of the more numerous and better-armed whites led to practical domination of the Indians. That two of these nations, the Pawnees and Choctaws, were never defeated by whites is, admittedly, somewhat beside the point. If necessary, the Americans could have easily subdued these people during the nineteenth century, and the Indians knew it. There is no denying that the eventual threat of force from the whites is basic to the histories of these nations, but to use military strength alone as an explanation is faulty for two reasons. First of all, changes in the subsistence systems of these nations began well before white military superiority was well established. The

Navajos were the scourge of the Spanish and Mexicans in the Southwest for a century; the Pawnees destroyed or intimidated the expeditions sent against them from New Mexico and were relatively impervious to American threats until the 1830s; and the Choctaws were locally far more powerful than the French or English for much of the eighteenth century. Military inferiority evolved over time; it was not instantaneous. More significantly, even when white military superiority was well established, it, in itself, explains little. Force was rarely employed for its own sake; it served other interests. The threat of force merely expedited the working of more elementary factors—political, economic, and cultural. Force often explains how change took place; it does not explain why it took place.

A more fundamental cause which emerges from an analysis of the histories of these peoples is the attempt, not always successful or consistent, by whites to bring Indian resources, land, and labor into the market. This unifying thread not only stitches together the histories of these nations, but within these histories, it also connects the environmental and social changes of each of the individual societies. To assert this is to subscribe neither to economic determinism nor to a crude materialism. Market relations were the goal of some whites, not all. Such goals sometimes blended with other imperial, religious, or cultural aims; they sometimes clashed with them. Among Indians themselves, market relations were such a threatening and destructive development that all these nations resisted them, with temporary success, for generations. Culture here controlled economics. Understanding change involves, not finding the invisible hand of economic interests, but rather finding the reciprocal influences of culture, politics, economics, and the environment. For the Indians, the result of these changes was dependency.

The idea of dependency has become fashionable in the last fifteen years. First developed by Third World scholars working in or on Latin America and Africa, dependency theory gradually became more and more influential among social scientists, particularly political scientists, who were attracted by its emphasis on international relations. Historians from the West have not been prominent in this development, although dependency theory relies on history for much of its explanatory power. Ironically, during a period in which some historians publicly wondered about the relevance of history in the modern world, a major school developed in other disciplines which turned to history to explain current conditions. The centrality of history in dependency literature has forced Western historians to notice it and to come to terms with the increasingly influential works of its adherents. For historians probably the most significant of these works have been the first two volumes of Immanuel Wallerstein's *The Modern World System*.[1]

As Wallerstein's title indicates, the central concern of the literature on dependency is the process by which peripheral regions are incorporated into the global capitalist system and the "structural distortions"—political, economic, and social—that result in these societies. Within this system, the capitalist core regions tend to benefit significantly from international transactions while the peripheral regions become underdeveloped. Dependency theorists tend to regard nation-states themselves as the scenes of social conflict, not as unitary actors, and they tend to speak not of capitalist countries but rather of capitalist systems. The lack of homogeneity in the literature contained in this rather broad framework has created a confusion which has only intensified the criticism that dependency theory predictably has encountered. Conservative scholars and politicians often have not bothered even to confront the analysis offered by writers on dependency, but instead have simply dismissed dependency as a "sophisticated form of scapegoating." Other scholars have, however, raised more serious and worthwhile objections. These critics contend that the elements of dependency often are not clear, that either the concept is not open to empirical statistical testing or its assertions fail when it is tested, and that, in the hands of some, arguments for dependency become excessively reductionist and ignore cultural factors and social relations.[2]

Often such criticism of the literature on dependency is not without merit, but, as Raymond Duvall and James Caporaso have argued, much of it results simply from a lack of clarity about the concept itself. Duvall particularly distinguishes between dependence and dependency. The concept of dependence closely resembles our everyday meaning of the term, denoting reliance on others. In this sense most modern countries are dependent on one another for technology, resources, and cultural exchanges. When such exchanges are roughly symmetrical, there is interdependence. When such exchanges are unequal, there is dependence. This, however, is not the sense in which dependency theorists talk about dependency even though they, too, often use the word "dependence."[3]

Third World scholars developed the idea of dependency (or dependencia) as a general context for inquiry. They are specifically interested in the "differentially or asymmetrically structured reflections of the processes of capitalist production and reproduction on the international level" and the social transformations that occur along with them. Dependency theorists then look at the conditioning of one economy by another. Dependency exists first as a general context of historical inquiry. Within this framework there is no single symptom of dependency, but rather a syndrome of social, political, and economic characteristics which deny some countries the ability either to expand or to be self-sustaining. Dependency thus has no single measurement but is instead an amalgamation of factors; empirical tests of the reality of dependency theory must take this into consideration. Dependency theorists emphasize a constellation of concepts: the extent to which economic activities within a region only reflect factors essentially controlled outside the area; the lack of economic diversification and choice; and domestic distortions—social and political, as well as economic—within affected societies. To quote the most frequently cited definition of dependency by Theotonio Dos Santos:

> By dependency we mean a situation in which the economy of certain countries is conditioned by the development and expansion of another economy to which the former is subjected. The relation of interdependence between two or more economies, and between these and world trade, assumes the form of dependence when some countries (the dominant ones) can expand and be self-sustaining, while other countries (the dependent ones) can do this only as a reflection of that expansion, which can have either a positive or a negative effect on their immediate development.[4]

The Dos Santos definition is aimed at the present world economy, but dependency theorists insist that present conditions are historically derived and must be historically explained by looking at the growth and consolidation of the present world system. It is the growth of this world system which affected the specific North American Indian

CHAPTER 1

The Choctaw Landscape

Today most Choctaws live far from their original Mississippi home-land. The American government removed the majority of the nation across the Mississippi River into Indian Territory in the 1830s. In doing so they halted a series of Choctaw adaptations which in the space of a century and a half had altered both the people and their land. This severing of the Choctaws from their homeland was such a brutal and dramatic act that for scholars it has overshadowed the rest of Choctaw history. Historians have studied the removal of the Choctaws repeatedly, but they have written little about the rest of their history east of the Mississippi.[1]

In the centuries after European contact, the Choctaws, like other Indian peoples, faced biological invasion and ecological change, new technologies and new political realities. In these changes the Choctaws saw opportunity as well as disaster; the new elements of their world did not remain entirely beyond their ability to manipulate them. The Choctaws adjusted to and, to a surprising degree, actually shaped the new world that followed contact. Dependency came, but the decline of the nation was neither automatic nor unresisted; and once dependent, the Choctaws rebelled. A few sought new regions where old ways could survive, but most of the nation chose to remain on ances-tral lands. There, in Mississippi, reluctantly and with enormous fric-tion, the nation embarked on a process of planned acculturation. Although removal aborted this process, the Choctaws of the early nineteenth century—the period just prior to removal—nonetheless represent a significant native attempt to modernize. An elite con-sciously hoped to achieve between land and people and among the people themselves a new relationship that involved dismantling, not preserving, an older way of life.

The descent of Spanish predators upon the Gulf Coast in the sixteenth century initiated this long cycle of change. In search of treasure and slaves, various expeditions, led by Juan Ponce de León, Pánfilo de Narváez, and Hernando de Soto, looted, pillaged, murdered, and raped their way through the Southeast from Florida to the Mississippi. Most of these expeditions ended in well-deserved catastrophes, but they left behind them a legacy of death and destruction that would permanently alter the region.[2]

Culturally, many of the peoples these Spaniards plundered and slaughtered were Mississippians. These peoples were mound-building horticulturalists who lived in populous towns arranged around central plazas. They made elaborate ceramics, had definite class structures, and dominated much of the Southeast between 900 A.D. and European contact. Among these Mississippian groups were the Muskogeans, lineal ancestors of the historic Choctaws, Creeks, and Chickasaws.[3]

According to tribal origin myths, the Choctaw nation moved into central Mississippi in company with the Chickasaws, with whom they then formed one people, however, when the Choctaws settled Nanih Wayia near the Pearl River in central Mississippi and began erecting the large temple mound there, the Chickasaws continued their migration, and the nations separated. The early connection between the Choctaws and Chickasaws is undoubted; linguistically and culturally, the two peoples were quite similar. Yet for the Choctaws the separation was more significant than the connections. They regarded Nanih Wayia as their birthplace. It was the emotional, although not the geographical, center of the nation. The term "nation" here is a fitting one for the Choctaws. It does not signify the existence of a centralized political unit but rather denotes the linguistic, cultural, and kin connections which made the Choctaws a people. Nanih Wayia, which contained a large and prominent temple mound, was probably the site of a particularly important Mississippian chiefdom, rather than the capital of any prehistoric Choctaw state.[4]

The Spanish invasion of the Southeast was catastrophic for the Mississippians, even for chiefdoms such as Nanih Wayia, whose people probably heard only second-hand accounts of the passage of de Soto up the Tombigbee valley and through the Chickasaw towns. Most people escaped Spanish swords; they did not escape the exotic diseases introduced by the invaders. The inevitable pioneers of European expansion, these diseases depopulated the Southeast. Probably beginning even before de Soto's expedition, the inroads of disease deepened after his coming. The late Mississippian and early historic period witnessed a catastrophic decline in population estimated by some to be as high as 80 percent. Many Indians died; others abandoned the towns and temple mounds of the valley, accelerating a migration which, for unknown reasons, appears to have begun even earlier. These first epidemics reduced populations, but they did not empty the river valleys entirely. When the French arrived to establish colonies along the Gulf Coast, the Yazoos, Tunicas, Biloxis, Pascagoulas, Mobiles, Tohomes, Houmas, Natchez, and other groups inhabited the valleys from Mobile and the Tombigbee River in the east to the Yazoo and Mississippi rivers in the west.[5]

French exploration and settlement in the late seventeenth century and the simultaneous advent of English slave raids from the east renewed the onslaught of disease. Once more Indians died in staggering numbers. In his journey up the Pascagoula River in 1700, Le Moyne d'Iberville passed through a virtually empty country of deserted, but still standing, villages. He found that most of the once-numerous Biloxis had succumbed to European diseases within the past two years and that only a few more of the neighboring Pascagoulas had survived. Farther east, disease reduced the Chaouachas on the Mobile from a "populous nation to only forty men" by 1725, and the Mobiles themselves to only sixty men. For mutual protection from slavers, the French had settled various immigrant tribes near Mobile Bay early in the century; their populations plummeted just as drastically. North of the Mobile on the lower Tombigbee, a disease identified simply as the plague arrived in a French ship in 1704 and ravaged the Tohomes. The Great Tohomes had 300 men in 1700; by 1725 they had 30. During the same period disease reduced the Little Tohomes from 500 to 60 warriors. The abandonment of villages along the Mobile and Tombigbee rivers and the drastic drop in Indian population were not solely the work of disease. By 1702 Creek slave raids promoted by the English had driven the Indians of the rivers from many of their towns. Indeed, the high mortality rate

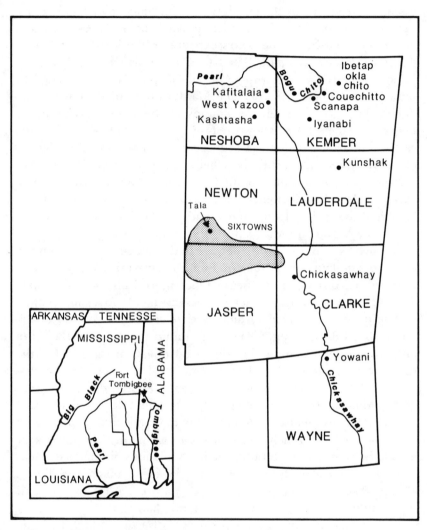

2. Choctaw Towns and Districts

which the French attributed to disease is unimaginable without corresponding social and political disruptions that interfered with agriculture and hunting. The raids left their victims desperate, malnourished, and vulnerable to infection.[6]

The smaller tribes of the Mississippi fared just as badly. They too
succumbed to the deadly combination of disease and slave raids and
by 1725 had only remnant populations. Governor De Bienville summarized the destruction of the peoples to the west of the Choctaws in
his "Memoir on the Indians of Louisiana" in 1726:

It is known that this country is one of the finest climates of
America and that it was formerly the most densely populated with
Indians but at present of these prodigious quantities of different
nations one sees only pitiful remnants that have escaped from the
fury of the continual wars they have had among themselves and
which were still lasting in the year 1699 when we made the discovery of those nations. Several have been entirely destroyed and of
about fifty others that are scattered along the Mississippi and
along the banks of different rivers that are tributary to it and
water the continent. There are, properly speaking, only the
Choctaws who can give us any ideas of what the Indians formerly
were. The others are feeble remnants which are diminishing every
day because of the different diseases that the Europeans have
brought into the country and which were formerly unknown to
the Indians.[7]

The Choctaws were hardly exempt from this destruction, but, as
the passage indicates, they did fare far better than neighboring
peoples. Although estimates vary widely, until the end of the
eighteenth century the Choctaw population usually fluctuated between 3,000 and 5,000 warriors (or a total population of 20,000 to
30,000 people); these figures indicate that they had attained some
demographic stability. Epidemics came among the Choctaws and
caused great losses, but their population never got caught in the grim
descent to oblivion which claimed so many Indian peoples. After the
epidemics the Choctaws recovered and restored, at least in part, their
losses.[8]

The ability of the Choctaws to maintain a relatively stable population cannot be separated from their political power. Although many

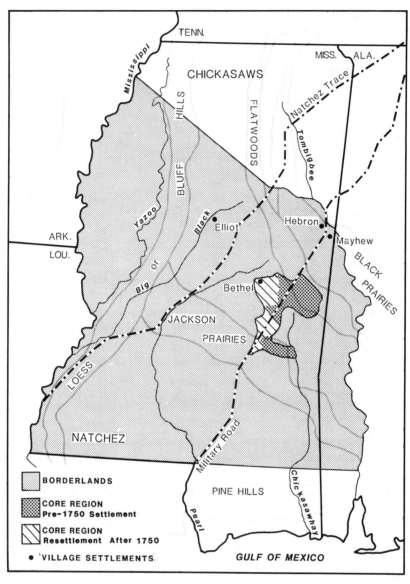

3. Choctaw Country

of their towns were virtually inaccessible by water, an isolation that
gave them some protection from disease, clearly some disease did
eventually reach them. Exotic diseases, striking virgin populations,
inevitably killed large numbers of people, but when epidemics struck
a malnourished, poorly sheltered, and socially disorganized people,
losses rose precipitously. A people, for example, who could repel slave
raiders and protect their homes and food supplies suffered fewer
losses to epidemics than those whose crops were burned, stolen, or
never planted at all. The simple ability to feed and nurse the sick was
critical. In the chaos of the late seventeenth and early eighteenth
centuries, only the strongest nations in the Southeast could protect
their resources and maintain their subsistence systems. They not only
survived in disproportionate numbers, they also absorbed the remnants of weaker groups.[9]

These surviving nations created a new landscape in the Southeast.
As the survivors first of the Mississippian towns and later of the historic nations abandoned the river valleys, they altered both the
human geography and the ecology of the region. Such movements
and their concomitant ecological changes were probably gradual and
incremental; they were similar, perhaps, to the process by which hundreds of Choctaws left Mississippi in the early nineteenth century and
moved west. Probably, as in the later period, the intention was to save
a way of life, not to change it. The movement of the people out of the
river valleys preserved many of the forms of Mississippian settlement,
but it changed their site.

Both the Mississippians and the historic nations structured the
natural landscape into two master categories: cultivated fields and
uncultivated borderlands. The Mississippians had built their towns
and grown their crops largely on the broad terrace lands of the
Southeastern rivers. These valleys, heavily settled and extensively
cultivated, were clearly the cultural creations of human beings.
Stretching beyond the fields was another landscape that was less obviously human. The wooded hunting lands formed a borderland
abounding in game that separated the areas of Mississippian settlement. It is tempting to dismiss such lands as wilderness that humans
entered and exploited only as predators and foragers more efficient
than their wild counterparts. Certainly this is how the first Spanish
invaders viewed them. The Gentleman of Elvas, a member of the de

Soto expedition of 1539 to 1543, wrote of traveling through a "desert" or wilderness for five days after he left the towns of the Tombigbee valley (probably Choctaw) and marched north toward the Chickasaws. Leaving the Chickasaw towns in the west, he passed through a similar "desert."[10]

The deserts the Spanish described consisted of widely varied landscapes. In the south, stretching from the Gulf of Mexico inland almost to the southernmost Choctaw towns, the borderlands were longleaf pine *(Pinus palustris)* forests. To the north the forest became mixed loblolly pine (P. *taeda*)—hardwood, with the hardwoods a complex mixture dominated by oak *(Quercus falcata, Q. stellata,* and others) and hickory *(Carya* spp.) but containing numerous other species. As one moved north, the amount of pine in these forests decreased. To the west the composition of the forest changed again at the belt of loessal hills in western Mississippi. The composition varied according to the thickness of the loess layer, but here the still abundant oaks and hickories were outnumbered by sweet gum *(Liquidamber styraciflua)*, basswood *(Tilia* sp.), beech *(Fagus grandifolia)*, and gum trees *(Nyssa sylvatica)*. A final change in the landscape occurred just to the northeast and east of the Pearl River in the region whites would later call the Black Belt—an arc of land twenty-five miles wide and several hundred miles long extending from central Alabama into northeast Mississippi. From one-quarter to one-third of this region was natural prairie, 10 to 15 percent was dense forest, and the remainder was parkland—widely separated trees surrounded by grasses. These "deserts" were borderland hunting grounds and, to a significant extent, they, like the river valleys, were cultural creations.[11]

Because of the dense horticultural populations of Mississippian peoples and their heavy reliance on wild meat, particularly white-tailed deer, there must have been substantial pressure on wild game. Choctaw traditional accounts both substantiate the tendency toward overhunting and indicate at least one of the reasons why it did not result in the destruction of game. The Lincecum manuscript—an account based largely on the origin legends of the Choctaws gathered by Gideon Lincecum from an aged informant, Chata Immataha, early in the nineteenth century—records how the Choctaws first killed deer in the lands immediately north of the Pearl River. Hunting out the game in the immediate vicinity of their towns, the hunters soon had to operate from temporary camps set up in the woods, where they gradually emptied more and more land of deer. They moved farther and farther north until they encountered the Chickasaws. This intrusion on Chickasaw hunting grounds provoked a war that drove the Choctaws entirely out of the borderlands. The Choctaws responded by sending out small parties to "hunt down the enemy and scalp them wherever they may be found."[12]

It appears, therefore, that one cultural mechanism used by the Mississippians to maintain borderland hunting grounds was warfare. Hunts took place peacefully until deer populations fell. When the number of deer declined, Indian groups intruded on their rivals' hunting grounds. This action prompted warfare that rendered the disputed region dangerous to all hunters and allowed game populations to recover. Such a version of hunting and borderland warfare fits well with the earliest written records of the region. The description by Garcilaso de la Vega of the warfare of the people de Soto encountered aptly summarized the borderland warfare not only of the Mississippians, but also of the Choctaws and Chickasaws two centuries later:

> Since, as we have seen, almost all of the provinces that these Spaniards traversed were at war with each other, it will be appropriate to describe here the kind of warfare that was waged. One should know that this was not a conflict of force against force with an organized army or with pitched battles, except in rare instances, *or a conflict instigated by the lust and ambition of some lords to seize the estates of others. This struggle was one of ambushes and subtlety in which they attacked each other on fishing or hunting trips and in their fields and along their roads wherever they could find an enemy off guard.*
> . . . But the hostility among these Indians amounted to no more than the harm they inflicted upon their persons with deaths, wounds, or shackles, *for they made no attempt to seize estates.* If sometimes the battles were more heated, they went so far as to burn towns and devastate fields, but as soon as the conquerers had inflicted the desired damage, they regathered in their own lands *without attempting to take possession of the land of others. . . . Moreover a cacique does not carry on warfare with just one of his neighbors, but with all who share his boundaries, for whether there be two, three, four or more, all wage war upon each other.* [Emphasis added.][13]

Warfare continued to prevent overhunting of borderland game into the historic period, but by the eighteenth century the number of animals in these borderlands had increased significantly. Three factors contributed to this rise: the opening of prime lands to the white-tailed deer, the maintenance of browse by burning, and the migration of bison into the region.

The gradual depopulation of the Big Black, Pearl, Tombigbee, and Yazoo river valleys by disease and slave raiding opened the bottomlands, once densely inhabited by humans, to deer. Bottomland hardwood forests were "the best of all southern forest habitats for white-tailed deer," with a carrying capacity of one deer to 13 acres, compared with one deer to 30–50 acres in the next best habitat, loblolly pine-hardwood. Not only were the best lands being made available to large numbers of deer, they were being surrendered in a condition best suited to the deer's needs. These lands were cleared fields, openings in the forest that provided the diversity of landscape and the proliferation of edge habitats the deer needed to obtain the variety of food sources necessary for their well-being.[14]

In time, this advantage would have been lost as the clearings reverted to forest and the forest matured, had the Indians not kept the lands open by burning. Indian hunters burned for many reasons: as a hunting technique, to clear the land of debris, and perhaps consciously to maintain the deer population. In all cases, the burning of the openings, the prairies, and the old fields was particularly common. In January of 1730, for example, De Lusser, a French emissary traveling with an escort of Choctaws, came to a prairie: "The Indians would not go on, no matter what I was able to say to them, without hunting in a prairie which they set on fire and in which they killed three deer." By retarding or halting normal successional patterns, such fires maintained the old fields that dotted the aboriginal Southeast.[15]

Burning also made the forests, albeit unevenly, a better habitat for deer. In the upland pine–hardwood forests that dominated much of the Choctaw homeland, burning stimulated prolific sprouting from understory plants, permitted more light to enter the forest and thus encouraged herbaceous growth, and improved the nutritional content of plants. Because some undesirable browse species such as sweetgum, red maple (*Acer rubrum*), and bayberry (*Morella pensyl-*

vanica) were particularly susceptible to fire, burning encouraged better browse species and improved yields of fruits, fungi, grasses, and
herbaceous plants. Only in the longleaf pine forests of the southern
part of the nation did burning prove detrimental to deer. There fire
gave a great advantage to longleaf pines, which concentrated their
growth in their root systems for the first five years of life and could
survive the periodic fires which killed off deciduous seedlings and
saplings. The top growth of the pine regenerated quickly after burning and this, coupled with its fire-resistant bark and the protection
afforded its growing tip by a dense tuft of green needles, gave the
pine an immense advantage over other species. Because of fires,
longleaf pines dominated a region that otherwise would have been
oak-hickory forest with a higher average carrying capacity for deer.[16]

It seems almost certain then that deer populations rose substantially following contact. They had favorable ecological conditions and
the biological potential to respond quickly. Deer were quite prolific
with a high reproductive potential (the rate at which a species could
reproduce under ideal conditions and in the absence of mortality).
The reproductive potential of a single pair of deer could, at a carrying
capacity of one deer to 40 acres, populate a section (640 acres) to near
capacity in only four years, and twelve sections in ten years.[17]

Depopulation also appears to have had a second notable effect on
the big-game population of the region: relaxation of hunting pressure
allowed small herds of buffalo to penetrate the Southeast. Bison appear to be only a very recent addition to the southeastern ecosystem.
De Soto and other early Spanish raiders never actually saw any buffalo in the Southeast, and bison apparently entered the region only
after they departed. Even in the eighteenth century buffalo herds
remained small. Europeans reported buffalo "abounded" in the
prairies, but when they gave specific numbers, they were talking of
herds of only several hundred animals each. Nevertheless, the arrival
of bison further enhanced the supply of game available to surviving
peoples.[18]

By the eighteenth century this environmental and demographic
transition in response to new disease patterns and European invasion
was well underway. The elimination of the Natchez, Yazoos, and
smaller nations during the wars of the 1730s climaxed the depopulation of the western river valleys and created even larger hunting

grounds with more abundant game. The Choctaws, in a sense, now operated in a new world in which farmlands had become hunting lands and hunting lands had become farmlands, and in which wild game populations had grown.

This historical process created the paradox of eighteenth-century Choctaw settlement. The Choctaws claimed land within four major soil regions of the Southeast: the Coastal Plain; the Black Belt Prairies; the brown loam, loessal soil belt of western Mississippi; and the Mississippi delta region (here defined as the alluvial plain of the Mississippi and Yazoo rivers south from Kentucky). Together the brown loam belt, the Black Belt Prairies, and the alluvial plain comprised the premier agricultural region of the Southeast. Yet the historic Choctaws did not settle these fertile lands until a decade or two before their own removal in the 1830s. Instead, they built their towns largely on lands of the Coastal Plain (and uplands) whose podzolic soils developed from marine sands and clays and were usually acid in reaction and frequently of low fertility. In short, they confined their agricultural settlement to one of the poorest groups of soils they claimed. The most fertile lands they reserved for deer.[19]

This is not to say that all the borderlands were prime farm lands. The southern pine forests were infertile: the heavy clay soils of the flatwoods and sections of the Black Belt could not be easily cultivated with digging sticks and hoes, and the Black Prairie as a whole suffered from drought too often to be a dependable agricultural region for the Choctaws.[20]

To the west and northwest of the Choctaw homeland, however, lay the loessal soils and delta soils of the Mississippi and Yazoo rivers, lands far more fertile than those the Choctaws farmed, lands well suited to their technology but unsettled. And to the east lay the Tombigbee valley, only periodically occupied by the Choctaws between 1690 and 1800. Only history explains the lack of settlement there. In these valleys lay the depopulated lands whose occupants had been destroyed or driven away by the epidemics, slave raids, and turmoil that began with European contact and continued through the 1730s when the French and the Choctaws destroyed the Yazoos and Natchez. Settlement there often became suicidal as epidemics, slave raiders, and war parties rendered the areas dangerous and left the valleys of the Pearl, the Big Black, the Tombigbee, and the Yazoo the home of deer, not human beings.[21]

The abandonment of the river valleys meant the Choctaws had to subsist in an environment with significantly more deer and significantly less fertile land, but the basic horticultural-hunting adaptation remained possible. The Choctaws did not migrate back into the fertile river valleys in any numbers for more than a century after contact because these lands remained dangerous and because there was no need to. The valleys produced deer, and as long as sufficient arable land remained available around their villages, the Choctaws could grow the crops they needed. So they remained in the hill country of east central Mississippi building virtually all their early historic towns in present-day Neshoba, Kemper, Newton, Lauderdale, Jasper, and Clark counties. They built only Yowani farther south, in Wayne County, and other settlements to the east in Alabama in times of peace. They were content to remain in the hill country from the time of French contact until early in the nineteenth century.

Within this rather narrow homeland the Choctaws often built their towns on the terraces of the streams that flowed into the Pearl, Tombigbee, and Chickasawhay rivers rather than along the rivers themselves. The rivers and streams formed these terraces when, as they flooded, they deposited their coarser particles first and thus formed ridges along their borders. Along the Mississippi these natural levees were up to 25 feet high and 3 miles wide, but they were proportionately smaller on other rivers and streams. These terrace soils were fertile loams that usually supported a mixture of dense canebrakes and oak-hickory forests. Cane lands for both whites and Indians meant fertile lands.[22] The affinity of Choctaw towns with the cane lands is readily apparent in their names: Kunshak (Cane Town), Kunshak chito (Big Cane Town), Kunshak bouleta (Round Canebrake), West Kunshak (West Cane Town), Kunshak osapa (Canebrake Field), Kunshak tikpi (Canebrake Knob), East Kunshak chito (East Big Cane Town), Oskelagna (Yellow Cane), and Escooba (Canebrake). Many other towns also neighbored cane lands, although their names did not reflect it.[23]

The Choctaws were not confined to the terrace soils with their extensive canebrakes; the correlation was not magical. Choctaws farmed the terraces because they represented concentrations of loam soils–either silt loams or sand loams—ideally suited to hoe and digging stick cultivation. The coupling of such soils with easy access to water fulfilled the major requirements of the horticultural village or town. While this combination usually was found on the terraces, it also existed in some sections of the uplands.[24]

It is presently impossible to correlate precisely all Choctaw towns with soil type and topography. Not only has archaeological excavation of historic and protohistoric town sites been minimal, but soil scientists have not surveyed the two counties, Kemper and Neshoba, which contained the densest Choctaw settlement. Nevertheless, some estimation of the possibilities and limits of Choctaw settlement and agriculture may be obtained by examining Newton County, an area which has been surveyed and which contained at least eight eighteenth-century Choctaw towns of both the southern and western divisions of the nation.[25]

In Newton County during the eighteenth century the Choctaws settled only one town, Tala, on the terrace soils, which form 5 percent of the county's area. They settled two more towns, Chunky and Oka Hullo, on upland ridgetops whose Nacogdoches loam soils, easily tilled, friable, and fertile, formed 2 percent of the county. The locations of two other towns, Oni Talemon and Coatraw, are uncertain but they also appear to have been on ridges. Loam soils, not terrace soils per se, were the key to Choctaw settlement. When in the late eighteenth and early nineteenth centuries settlement expanded, it continued to be on the upland ridges. Oka Kapassa, Okhatatalia, and Bissasha all were built on upland Ruston fine sandy loam or Nacogdoches loam soils.[26]

The location of Newton County towns eliminates for the Choctaws two models of aboriginal agriculture and society proposed for the Southeast. Some scholars have tentatively proposed a system of "riverine agriculture" similar to that of Egypt. Periodic flooding supposedly replenished the fertility of old fields and farming took place on the same tracts for centuries. Upland agriculture renders such a model implausible simply because such lands did not flood. It also eliminates an alternate vision of the aboriginal Southeast that describes a people who are confined to small tracts of terrace land and are inexorably pushed by population growth either to expand into new areas where additional terrace land is available or else to compete for the old fields. The movement onto the uplands contradicts this model as thoroughly as it does the riverine explanation. The Choctaws could and did settle the uplands (as presumably their

Mississippian predecessors could have). Indeed, in Newton County, the Choctaws actually seem to have preferred certain upland areas and left large amounts of stream terraces unsettled. In short, geographical models do not fully explain Choctaw land-use patterns. Only history does.[27]

The conclusion that historical factors such as new epidemics and slaving expeditions altered Choctaw subsistence so that old practices took place on new lands still tells us little about the practices themselves or how the food system as a whole operated. Subsistence is more than a question of locale; it also includes production, distribution, and cultural preferences for certain kinds of food. How people feed themselves and protect themselves against famine, and how and why their food systems change over time, are significant historical questions in their own right. They, too, must be examined for the Choctaws.

CHAPTER 2

Choctaw Subsistence

The Choctaws were as close to a nation of farmers as any Indians north of Mexico. So concluded Bernard Romans, who visited the Choctaws in 1770. As he saw it, they really had little choice except to farm since their country possessed virtually no game and almost half the men had never killed either a deer or a turkey in their entire lives. Romans's description of the evolution of Choctaw economy fits quite well with many popular and certain scholarly assumptions about the relationship between hunting and agriculture: agriculture will necessarily expand as game disappears; the elimination of game is the surest way to produce pure farmers from groups previously dependent on a mixture of horticulture and hunting. Since, in such a view, game inevitably declines as a result either of improved hunting techniques or of population increases (the two often being related), agriculture will tend to expand or to intensify to make up the losses. If technical or environmental limits stand in the way of such intensification or expansion, people starve. Romans's Choctaws, who were now armed with guns, seem to have been acting in a predictable manner. If later in the century they repeatedly faced famine, then it is clear that they had simply reached the edges of subsistence once more and further intensification was in order.[1]

Implicit in this view is the idea that any mixed hunting-horticultural economy is merely a transitional step between full hunting and gathering and full agriculture. In the standard materialist scenario, agriculture develops because of the depletion of game and, once developed, encourages larger populations which in turn put greater pressure on the remaining game animals. This population growth also necessitates a further expansion of agriculture until eventually game is only a minimal part of the diet or a luxury food. The transition then of Romans's Choctaws from hunting-horticulture to agriculture merely represents the last step in the predictable evolution of their subsistence system.[2]

Although this theory makes the evolution of the Choctaws comprehensible, much of it simply is not true. The factual problems began with Romans. Until quite recently, Romans's characterization of the Choctaws has endured remarkably well, although only one other independent observer of the Choctaws, Horatio Cushman, who relied on his boyhood memories as a missionary's son in the nation during the 1820s when game undoubtedly had largely vanished, made equivalent claims for their agriculture. Nevertheless, John Swanton, the major ethnologist for the Southeast, accepted Romans, and so have virtually all the ethnologists and historians who have followed Swanton. Since Romans described horses which shared with their Choctaw masters the peculiar inability to swim and so sank like stones in any deep body of water, one may read his account skeptically. In the case of hunting and agriculture, skepticism may be especially suitable because many of Romans's observations contradict his conclusions. For men who never killed anything larger than a squirrel, Choctaw hunters displayed an astonishing, and presumably mindless, persistence in tramping through the forest after game. Romans himself reported that one quarter of the Choctaw men were in hunting camps during his visit to the nation, and the major hunting season had yet to begin. Also, Romans's own proficiency as a hunter must have excited wonder among the Choctaws. After a lifetime of failure, what could that half of the nation who had never killed a deer or turkey have made of a man whose party shot two deer and five turkeys in two days in the southern borderlands? And in the northern borderlands, Romans's presence must have endowed Choctaw hunters with unheard-of luck and skill since he obtained deer and turkeys from the Choctaws there with little trouble.[3]

The glaring discrepancies between Romans's conclusions and his experience arose from his failure to understand the physical division of the Choctaw lands into agricultural, settled regions and borderland, hunting regions. When he reported that he never saw a deer in the settled regions, there is no reason to doubt him. When he concluded that there were, therefore, no deer in the nation, he contradicted his own experience in the borderlands. Likewise, his claim that he rarely tasted venison in the towns is perfectly credible. He traveled before the deer-hunting season was well underway at a time of year when venison was not regularly part of the Choctaw diet. It does not follow that the Choctaws rarely ate venison in other seasons.[4]

Despite the obvious inconsistencies of Romans's account, his portrayal of Choctaw subsistence has only recently been questioned. William Willis noticed that Romans was the sole authority for making the Choctaws a preeminently farming people before extensive white settlement took place around them, and that there was much evidence which contradicted him on this point. Willis's interpretation of the Choctaws, however, created problems of its own.[5] In his zeal to discredit Romans, Willis simply transfered Choctaw ineptitude from the forest to the field. The Choctaw's farming, according to Willis, was inferior to that of most of the nations around them. They lacked the skill and the technology to live by farming alone. Although both Romans and Willis are helpful in explaining the Choctaw subsistence system, their accounts, read literally, do not so much convincingly describe a subsistence cycle as excite wonder that so many people could have possessed so few skills and yet survived so long with so little to eat.

The problem with both accounts is, finally, conceptual. Each author was interested in determining which part of the system provided more food, agriculture or hunting. Such arguments are inevitable as long as the mixed hunting-horticultural system is perceived as a transitional stage instead of a long-lasting, stable system in its own right. If the mixed hunting-horticultural system is a transitional stage, it is hard to interpret the prehistoric and early historic periods in the Southeast where the hunting-horticultural mix goes back at least to 1000 B.C. and probably earlier. For a long time the Mississippians were presumed to represent the transition to an almost purely agricultural economy, but it now appears that they, like the people who came before and after them, also depended heavily on wild game for food. This means that the full transition from hunting to agriculture took at least 2,800 years and, far from evolving "naturally" in the region, came only as the result of massive foreign intrusions.[6]

In the Southeast it is far more profitable to consider the

economies, like the Choctaws', based on the mixture of horticulture and hunting as stable systems in their own right and to try to understand how they functioned and why they endured. Choctaw hunting and agriculture are not comprehensible as a zero-sum game where the decline of one is compensated for by the expansion of the other. Among the Choctaws, agriculture and hunting must be considered as a dynamic whole, part of an interrelated system where the expansion of agriculture (no matter what skill or lack of skill the Choctaw possessed) could never, under aboriginal conditions, make up for the demise of hunting. To examine the system in this light removes basic difficulties inherent in the accounts of Romans and Willis. It explains why Choctaws could be the skilled horticulturalists Romans described, yet also face repeated crop failures and, finally, famines as Willis asserted. It also explains why the system stood and fell as a coherent whole and not as a temporary compromise between two very different ways of procuring food.

The bulk of the Choctaw diet came from agriculture. At contact, they raised four of the usual staple crops of the American Indians: corn, beans, squash, and pumpkins. These crops themselves had largely replaced an even earlier agriculture based on squash, pumpkins, sunflowers *(Helianthus annua)*, sumpweeds *(Iva ciliata)*, chenopodium *(Chenopodium* sp.), pigweed *(Amaranthus* sp.), and knotweed *(Polygonum* sp.). Besides squash and pumpkins, the only plant of this old Eastern Agricultural Complex which retained much importance for the Choctaws was the sunflower.[7]

By the eighteenth century the Choctaws had considerably refined the original varieties of their staple crops. The earliest European commentator on Indian agriculture in the region, Le Page du Pratz, listed the basic Indian corns as a flour corn with a white, flat, shriveled surface, four kinds of "hominy corn," and a small early corn that ripened so quickly that the Choctaws got two crops of it in a season. In addition to these varieties, the Choctaws, by their own account, possessed a popcorn, a variety of the original tropical flint corn. The Choctaws also grew a wide selection of beans, but they had not developed new varieties of either pumpkins or squash.[8]

Following contact, the Choctaws adopted additional plants from the Europeans, but none of them would rival the native crops in importance. The most significant introduction was the sweet potato, which was usually referred to simply as the potato. The Choctaws were growing sweet potatoes at least by 1730 when French visitors feasted on it, and traditional Choctaw accounts indicate they adopted the watermelon, of which they were passionately fond, even more quickly. The Choctaws also added hyacinth beans and two varieties of guinea corn *(Sorgum Drummondii* and *Panicum maximum)* introduced from Africa, as well as leeks, garlic, and cabbage. Finally, the Choctaws had obtained peaches from the Europeans, and peach orchards certainly thrived around their towns. It is not clear if they domesticated other fruits. Grapes and plums also grew near their villages, apparently because the Choctaws spared wild nut and fruit trees and vines when clearing the fields. In any case, orchards only supplemented the continued gathering of wild fruits and nuts.[9]

In spring and fall, Choctaw agriculture involved virtually the entire able-bodied population of the towns, but women had the primary responsibility for the crops. In early March the people of a Choctaw town began preparing the fields. Traditional accounts emphasized that clearing and planting involved a combined effort of men, women, and children, and early French reports substantiate this. In late May of 1732, for example, Regis du Roullet could not obtain all the assistance he needed in building pirogues from the men of Bokfoka (Bouck fouca) "on account of their planting." Among the Choctaws and Chickasaws the initial labor took place on at least two, and perhaps three, different kinds of fields. Each family planted small truck gardens of beans and corn on suitable land close to their cabin, but they located their main fields in larger communal tracts of loam surrounding the village. As the Chickasaws told Adair, such a system allowed them to farm only the most fertile and productive lands around their towns, maximizing the yields from the labor they invested. In addition to these fields there was, at least among the Chickasaws, a third type of field planted only in pumpkins.[10]

By the early nineteenth century most Choctaws had specific fields marked out within the communally prepared town lands although they still did not own their lands. A family belonging to a town could take any uncultivated land they thought suitable and hold it as long as they used it. Yet even in the 1820s a vestige of what might be older, communal-farming patterns survived in the Sixtowns, where census-takers found several families cooperating in the tillage of common fields.[11]

This preparation of the fields in the spring regularly involved the subjugation of new land. The Choctaws first girdled the trees by hacking away a strip of bark all around the tree to kill it, and then cut and burned all the cane, brush, and saplings which covered the area. They repeated this process of clearing on the field each year, removing any new growth of brush and cane and burning the dead trees as they fell until the land was completely cleared. This method of land clearing returned substantial amounts of calcium, phosphorus, and potash to the soil. In a sense, burning the trees compensated for the leaching caused by the rainfall, since as they grew, the trees drew potash up from the subsoil where it had been washed by the rains and then released it as they burned. Burning, of course, was far more effective in the first years of cultivation when large amounts of debris were consumed.[12]

Although clearing the land began as early as late winter, the Choctaws did not put in their garden plots until late April or early May, and they did not plant their main fields until May or June, when the first wildfruits were ripe enough to attract the small animals and birds that might otherwise have eaten their seeds. As the Choctaws planted, they crowded and mixed their crops. They planted corn in hills three feet apart and with it placed beans. At the edges of the fields and between the hills they planted squash, pumpkins, and sunflowers. After planting, the women took over the agricultural work until harvest, but they did not begin cultivation right away. Instead, they allowed weeds to grow until, as the Europeans commented, the fields were rank with them. Europeans credited this neglect to lassitude, but this was not the reason behind the Choctaw failure to hoe. The Indians preserved the weeds because they too were a crop. Among the early successional growth in land disturbed for agriculture was chenopodium, once the basis of southeastern horticulture. Immediate, clear cultivation would have eliminated such edible plants along with the inedible weeds. The women hoed the crops several times during the summer and built up the hills around the corn each time. As the crops ripened, they stood watch in the fields, frightening off birds and animals.[13] In August the Green Corn Dance—a time of both feasting and fasting—signaled the approaching end of the agricultural year as well as the beginning of the Choctaw new year. The feast took its name from the green corn that the celebrants ate. Not until fall would the main harvest be gathered in. Then, once more, all would return to the fields to take in the crops and store them in raised wooden cribs in the towns.[14]

Europeans remained largely unimpressed with this agriculture and characterized it as slothful and inefficient. James Adair's denunciation of Indian farming summarized the European objections. The Indians crowded their fields. They planted their corn hills too closely and excessively filled up the land between the hills with other crops. They then compounded the problem by allowing the weeds to grow densely before the first hoeing. Adair attributed all this to the Indians' desire to have "multum in parvo," which, while true enough, he insisted on identifying with laziness. He was therefore perplexed by the abundant yields he admitted they usually obtained. This he dismissed as evidence of the extraordinary fertility of their soils.[15]

The soils were not extraordinarily fertile, however, and more than bountiful nature was involved in the productivity of Choctaw agriculture. Adair was right when he recognized that Indians sought as much food from as little land as possible. Land clearing, even with metal tools, remained tedious work, which gave the Choctaws much incentive to minimize their need for land. So they cleared only the best lands within their settled areas and then planted that land very densely. Adair obviously believed that this should not have worked, yet he admitted that it did.[16]

Dense planting and infrequent hoeing by the Choctaws does not seem to have harmed yields. The failure to cultivate early may have checked the initial growth of corn somewhat, but the yields from wild plants probably compensated for part of the loss. Nor does the overcrowding of corn appear to have hurt yields. The white farmers who succeeded the Choctaws on the lands of central Mississippi in the 1830s and 1840s initially spaced their corn crops far more widely than the Indians had, but experience soon demonstrated to them that closer planting on the better lands greatly increased their yields. Perhaps the most critical of all their practices in increasing yields and maintaining fertility was the refusal of the Indians to till an entire field or to farm hillsides, the lands most susceptible to erosion. They dug up only enough land for their corn hills, and these were then covered with a dense crop of corn and beans. Most of the Choctaw field remained relatively undisturbed and covered with plant growth. This limited the erosion so destructive to Mississippi agriculture after white settlement. Erosion loosened and floated away the organic matter rich in nitrogen and necessary for a heavy feeding crop like corn in a region like the warm Southeast, where organic nitrogen is already relatively scarce.[17]

The crops themselves also contributed to maintaining fertility. The corn-bean-squash triad basic to Indian agriculture was mutually complementary. The corn stalks provided poles for the beans to climb upon while leaving the ground free for the squash to spread. And although corn was a heavy feeder which demanded an ample supply of nitrogen, beans and squash were not so demanding; thus direct competion between the plants was limited. Indeed, beans, as a legume, actually returned some nitrogen to the soil through the bacteria on their root nodules. Intercropping certainly helped prolong the productivity of Choctaw fields, but its contribution should not be overrated. It did not make the bean-corn-squash combination a closed cycle with corn withdrawing nitrogen and beans restoring it. Depending on conditions, a reasonable estimate is that beans prolonged the life of a Choctaw field by 20 to 50 percent or, given a ten-year "normal" life, by two to five years. Choctaw agriculture was of necessity a shifting agriculture, with new fields brought into production as old ones gave out.[18]

The yields of this agriculture were sizable. Romans estimated corn yields at from 40 to 60 bushels an acre, with the richer river lands capable of producing 50 bushels. White settlers in Mississippi obtained yields of 60 to 70 bushels an acre on terrace lands during the first years of cultivation, and even in the hill country, farmers considered 30 bushels an acre average for corn after the first few years of production. Erosion and lack of fertilization took a heavy toll from these lands under white farming practices, however, and yields fell off precipitously after ten or twenty years, with many fields producing only 10 bushels or less of corn an acre. Modern agricultural scientists are often skeptical about yields of 40 bushels or more an acre for corn agriculture before nitrogen fertilizers, but contemporary estimates of the productivity of Indian agriculture are consistent and widespread, and it must be remembered that this agriculture was confined to the best soils. When yields fell, fields were abandoned and new ones cleared.[19]

Extrapolating the significance of agriculture in Choctaw subsistence from these data is difficult and risky, but a rough estimate can be made. In 1830 in the core of the Southern District, the most traditional area of the nation, the average household of seven people cultivated about five acres of land. If, to be conservative, Romans's estimate of corn yields is slightly reduced to 40 bushels an acre, then each household obtained about 11,200 pounds of corn a year or about 1,600 pounds for each person. Assuming an average requirement of 2,500 calories per person per day, corn alone could have provided about two-thirds of the total calories the Choctaws needed. Farming then could provide a substantial proportion of the Choctaws' nutritional needs; therefore, it was not the inevitable poverty of their agriculture or their lack of skill which led them to continue to hunt, fish, and gather.[20]

Since these figures also assume that the Choctaws were farming only their best lands, some calculation which takes into account the extent of this land as well as the necessity for fallow lands is also necessary. An examination of the town of Tala, regarded as densely settled in 1795, with its population of 343, is instructive. With seven people in a household, Tala had forty-nine families in 1795 and required between 122 and 245 acres in cultivation at any given time. Although there is no record of either how long Choctaw fields lay fallow or how long they were cultivated, if a ten-year productive life for a farm plot is taken as a minimum and a fifty-year fallow period is borrowed from New England Indian agriculture, then the minimal land requirement for a village the size of Tala was 612 to 1,225 acres. A visual estimate from soil maps indicates that there are roughly 160 acres of terrace land for each section cut by the principal creeks of Tala town. Thus, if the Choctaws farmed four sections along Bogue Falema Creek and five along Bethel and Parlow creeks, they would have had 1,440 acres of terrace land available for cultivation. This land was, of course, not concentrated but scattered along the creeks, and the Choctaws scattered to use it. As long as its population remained stable, Tala possessed sufficient land. If its population grew, new towns would have to form.[21]

This presumed pattern of fallowing, clearing, and abandoning is quite consistent with eighteenth-century descriptions of the Choctaw landscape as a mixture of "prodigious straggling towns" with houses and cornfields extending for miles along a creek or ridge, second-growth forest, prairies, and old fields. Going through several towns in the Northeastern District in a single day, Romans reported he "travelled chiefly through cornfields." When he resumed his journey going to Yanatoe in present southwestern Kemper County, he passed through a patchwork of woodland, cultivated land, and abandoned fields. Resuming his journey from Abeka to Chickasawhay, he went "chiefly through fine improved and many of them rich fields, and a large number of considerable towns of the savages." There is no need to believe Romans exaggerated the number or the extent of the fields he saw. Traveling from town to town along the creeks and rivers or upland trails, he would have passed lenghwise through the ribbons of cornfields and abandoned fields which wound through the nation. Leaving one town, he would have almost imperceptibly entered another. When Lieutenant Ford, a British army officer, traveled through the nation several years before Romans and plotted the locations of the larger Choctaw towns and their dependencies, he revealed how extensive these patches of settlement were. For example, four "contiguous and dependent" towns lay within a mile of Chickasawhay, two more were within two miles, and three more were within four miles. The houses of these towns were so dispersed, except on the frontiers, that according to Adair "a stranger might be in the middle of one of their populous extensive towns without seeing half a dozen of their houses in the direct course of his path," and Father Beaudouin, a French Jesuit missionary, contended that people living in the same town were sometimes strangers to each other.[22]

The ecological impact of this agriculture was considerable. Having avoided fertile, natural prairie regions and settled in forested lands, the Choctaws ironically created their own prairies. Many of the descriptions of Choctaw villages place them amidst open lands. De Lusser described Lukfata as a small village in a beautiful plain. Du Roullet reported that Yazoo was "situated in a great plain which lies on a height," Chickasawhay was "situated in a plain surrounded by hills," Couechitto was in a "small plain surrounded by very high hills," Kashtasha was "situated in a large plain, but in the middle of which there is a small hill," and Bokfoka was in a small plain. "Plain" is not necessarily synonomous with "treeless lands," but this seems to be the sense in which the French meant the word. In 1730, De Lusser reported that only inferior wood remained around Couechitto, and in 1764 when Lieutenant Ford visited Yazoo he reported that there was hardly a tree to be seen around the town.[23]

The prairies of the eastern and western Choctaw towns arose from the clearing and eventual abandonment of land over the long life-spans of the towns. Romans's description of the open and old fields he passed through is typical of the Southeast. It was precisely because such descriptions were so common that some geographers came to believe that there were no natural prairies in the region. It was an understandable error when the historical accounts of Indian-created prairies were so abundant.[24]

If cultivated crops provided roughly two-thirds of the Choctaws' diet, the other one-third in normal years came from hunting, fishing, and gathering. They procured part of this in the summer when they took large numbers of fish, gathered wild fruits, and hunted small game—squirrels, rabbits, and raccoons. The major hunting and gathering season, however, began in the fall and stretched through the late winter. From November until March the men stalked deer while women gathered both nuts and edible roots such as wild sweet potatoes *(Ipomoea pandurata)*, Jerusalem artichokes *(Helianthus tuberosus)*, and the various species of *Smilax*. Productive activities at this time centered on the borderlands, although all hunters and their families might not be absent for the entire period. The French and English always found some able-bodied men in the towns during the hunting season, but they discovered that it was virtually impossible to summon substantial numbers of Choctaws to councils as long as the hunt continued.[25]

Like so many aspects of the subsistence cycle, the deer-hunting season was a carryover from Mississippian times. Both archaeological materials and the traditional accounts of the Choctaws indicate a fall and winter "venison season" that antedated European contact. Because of the heat and heavy forest foliage of southern and central Mississippi, large-scale hunts were not very practical before November, when the weather moderated and the leaves fell. By late fall, especially in years of abundant acorn crops, the deer were fat and in full flesh and their "blue" or winter coat almost fully developed. Both for meat and skins, this was the prime time to hunt.[26]

The timing of the hunt had advantages that went well beyond the condition of the deer, however. In the fall, when mast became their primary feed, not only deer but also turkeys were concentrated in greater numbers and in more predictable areas than at other times of the year. And deer were not only more concentrated, they were far less wary and more vulnerable. Although exact estimates of dates differ, the mating season or rut for deer began in December in northern Mississippi and in January in southern Mississippi. While they were in rut, bucks were at their most reckless and unwary. Venturing out in daylight in search of does, they were taken more easily than at any other time of the year.[27]

Although this scheduling of the hunt seems to have favored the taking of bucks, a system which served to maintain higher rates of reproduction than if more does had been taken, the remains of deer at Mississippian sites indicate that roughly even numbers of males and females were killed there. Choctaw patterns may have been similar. Even so, winter hunting still served to maintain populations at higher levels than if hunting had taken place earlier in the year. Most fawns in Mississippi who lost their mothers to hunters in October or November were simply too young to survive the winter; the death of the doe usually meant her fawn died soon after. By December or January, however, the fawns were old enough to survive the loss of the doe. Doe hunting at that time was not, therefore, a double blow to the deer population.[28]

There is of course no direct evidence that the Choctaws realized all these advantages in scheduling their hunt, but with or without conscious Choctaw rationale, the advantages remained, and the hunters benefited from them. Such hunting practices, coupled with Choctaw maintenance of the deer habitat, meant that the Choctaw hunt did not hurt deer population unless excessive numbers were taken. If the Choctaws hunted out their own deer, however, they would be forced to impinge on other peoples' hunting grounds and thus spark the borderland wars which themselves could curtail hunting and bring about a recovery of game populations. Yet even without such a check, the Choctaws possessed great incentives to maintain adequate numbers of deer. Venison was not only a normal winter food, it was also the most important component of a secondary food cycle as critical to Choctaw well-being as the primary food cycle.

The agricultural yields of the Choctaws as previously estimated do not indicate that the nation needed any deer to meet its subsistence needs during years of good harvests. Corn was their staple food, and this crop plus small game, fish, and the products of gathering probably was sufficient to feed them if necessary. Unfortunately, however, no people survive by virtue of their best years; it is the worst years which create the limits of their subsistence system. And abundance among the Choctaws was not an annual occurrence; crops did fail.

Paradoxically, in a land of abundant rainfall, moisture was the critical limiting factor for Choctaw agriculture. In Mississippi, summer droughts are common, and in the eighteenth century they seem to have occurred with some frequency. The French reported continuous crop failures on the coast in 1711, 1712, and 1713. Two of these failures resulted from flooding and probably did not affect the inland Choctaw, but the third, which resulted from drought, may very well have. During this period, other factors contributed to failure. In 1717 intertribal wars disrupted harvests. These wars may have been confined to the coast, but certainly the earlier slaving wars had similar effects on the Choctaws. In 1732 a hurricane caused widespread crop damage, but whether it reached the Choctaws is not known. In 1734 the Choctaw corn crop definitely failed from drought, and in 1737 it was very poor because of worms and hot winds. In 1760 the harvests among the Choctaws and Creeks were total failures, and in 1777 and 1778 harvests were also poor.[29]

The late 1770s was the beginning of a prolonged period of sporadically poor crops. They failed again in 1782 and 1792 when drought destroyed the crops of the Creeks, Chickasaws, and Choctaws. The 1793 harvest must also have failed since the Choctaws still lacked corn in the spring of 1794, and later in that year a final drought destroyed the corn crop before it even had a chance to grow. The nineteenth century opened no more auspiciously. By December of 1801 the Choctaws were reported to be hungry and without food. The immediate cause was lack of game, but they probably had to rely on game because of a crop failure. This list of droughts and other disasters, though long, is certainly incomplete, particularly for the first thirty years of the eighteenth century, when relatively few Europeans visited the nation.[30]

A summer drought had to last for only a few weeks to severely reduce yields if it occurred at certain times in the growing cycle. Corn is a crop especially sensitive to moisture stress. Experiments indicate that moisture stress that occurs prior to silking reduces corn yields by 25 percent, stress at silking reduces yields by 50 percent and moisture stress at ear stage, thirty days after silking, reduces yields by 21 percent. Longer droughts could, of course, destroy a crop completely, and Choctaw oral tradition contained an account of a drought of three years duration during the eighteenth century (probably the drought of the late 1770s or the early 1790s). Because droughts posed such a grave and repeated threat to Choctaw agriculture, rainmaking became an aspect of shamanism highly developed in the nation.[31]

The threat of these periodic crop failures critically influenced the subsistence cycle. The Choctaws had to be able to survive crop failures that could run for several years in a row. The productivity of their agriculture in good years resulted in stored surpluses that might allow them to survive a single crop failure, but there is no indication that their stored supplies could have furnished them with food for much longer than this. Yet remarkably in the early years of French contact there is no indication of starvation or famine despite the certainty that crop failures occurred. It was the Europeans who in the first years of settlement had to beg from the Indians when crops failed. This is not to say that the French got corn from the Choctaws; they were too far away and too far removed from the main river routes to make this feasible. The French instead obtained corn from closer, smaller tribes. Famines did not occur because the Choctaw subsistence system guarded against them. Despite the productivity of their agriculture and its ability to meet virtually all their caloric requirements in good years, they never placed full reliance upon it. Instead, they maintained the mixed system of agriculture, hunting, and gathering which protected them from the famines that a complete dependence on agriculture would eventually bring.[32]

To counteract crop failures the Choctaws reverted to their secondary food cycle, which shared many elements of the primary cycle but differed enough to warrant its being distinguished. Drought not only disrupted crop yields, it also hurt other food sources of the settled areas. Since fish were particularly vulnerable to drought, they would be eliminated from the Choctaw diet if the streams and ponds dried up entirely. Deprived of both fish and crops, the Choctaws faced starvation if they remained in the towns. To survive they had to migrate, and the "Early Account" of the Choctaws reveals how, when their crops failed, they moved en masse from the towns into the borderlands: "In the years of scarcity when the corn crop has failed, all the savages leave the villages and go with their families to camp in the woods at a distance of thirty to forty leagues, in places where bison (boeuf sauvage) and deer are to be found, and they live there by hunting and on (wild) potatoes."[33] In the 1770s, when Romans visited them, remnants of this early cycle still survived.

> In the failure of their crops, they make bread of the different kinds of Fagus (now including merely the beeches, but then in addition the chestnut and chinaquapin) of the *Diospyros* (persimmon), of a species of *convolvulus* with a tuberous root found in the low cane grounds (wild sweet potato), of the root of a species of *Smilax* (Choctaw Kantack; Creek Kunti—China Briar) of live oak acorns, and Canna (imported probably from the West Indies); in summer many of the wild plants chiefly of the Drupi (plum) and Baccifeorus (berry) kind supply them.[34]

The addition of the seed of a species of wild cane, young roots of the longleaf pine, lizards, snakes, frogs, and various other reptiles and insects to the preceding list, gives a clear, if not complete, idea of this secondary drought food cycle.[35]

Obviously not all the foods described here were absent from the normal Choctaw subsistence cycle. Their increased reliance on deer, nuts, persimmons, and wild berries did represent in part an intensified use of normal foods. Major differences, however, stand out between the normal subsistence cycle and the back-up cycle. In location, timing, and food sources the differences outweigh the similarities.

In the secondary cycle, deer ceased to be primarily a winter food. The Choctaws now left their villages and extended their normal deer-hunting season at both ends. The change incurred a real environmental cost: the deer taken weighed far less; their hides had little value; fawn mortality probably increased; and the total number of deer in the borderlands was reduced. Since, however, such hunts were only an emergency measure, the species probably recovered quickly. On these extended hunts Choctaws also greatly increased their dependence on buffalo. In ordinary years the Choctaws hunted buffalo primarily for their skins; this situation prompted Adair's complaints of the vast waste of meat when the Indians took only the skins, tongues, and marrow-bones and left the rest of the animal to rot. During the secondary food cycle, however, they surely wasted less of the animal. Transportation of meat back to the town and the labor necessary for preservation were not now problems, and the buffalo could become a significant element in the Choctaw diet. With a crop failure the nation then remained away from the towns for most of the year and thus used familiar game animals such as deer at new times and added other animals not usually relied on for food to the subsistence cycle.[36]

During famines, wild plants, especially Indian potatoes and wild cane (when available), which were not ordinarily important parts of the primary food cycle, also assumed great importance. In years of normal harvest the Choctaws apparently made little use of wild potatoes. One native name for the Northeastern District, Ahepat Okla, can be translated as "Potato-Eating People," but H. S. Halbert is the only authority who contended that the wild potato was an important part of the daily diet. None of the food-gathering references in the traditional materials assembled by Gideon Lincecum referred to the wild potato as an everyday food, and Adair and Du Pratz mentioned the potato only as a hunting and famine food.[37]

In their pristine forms described here, both the primary and secondary food cycles of the Choctaws were balanced and dependable. When Romans saw the harvest of a good year, he rightly found it impressive. His mistake was believing that such harvests could regularly be depended on and that in any year the Choctaws could live solely on them. They could not. The Choctaws had to survive the worst years—the years when hot winds blew and no rains came, the years when the crops withered and died. To expand their agriculture to meet these years would have been difficult and probably futile. To produce and store surpluses on a scale necessary to survive two or more bad years in a row would have involved greater population dispersal, more land brought into production, more pressure on the limited arable lands, and far more labor. The resulting yields would have to have been stored not from season to season but perhaps for years—a difficult task in warm and humid Mississippi. An easier security could be gained not from expanding agriculture but rather from limiting it.

The borderlands provided security. Maintained by warfare and normally used for deer hunting, these lands had an important secondary function: they were the resort of the nation in starving times. That these same lands were potentially far more fertile than the lands the Choctaws farmed made little difference in this context; historical and technological factors limited their use. But beyond this they served the needs of the nation well as they were.

Maintaining enough deer in the borderlands to support the nation when crops failed remained critical to Choctaw well-being. Any prolonged overhunting of the borderlands to procure deerskins for trade would deplete the numbers of deer and eventually bring disaster. In a world without Europeans, Choctaw conservation practices and the sporadic aboriginal borderland warfare might have preserved adequate numbers of deer, but in the eighteenth century as commercial hunting appeared, these were no longer sufficient. To maintain deer populations the Choctaws would not only have had to regulate their own hunting, they would also have had to banish from the region the hunters of rival peoples who were more heavily involved in commercial hunting than they were. The only available means of accomplishing this banishment, given the political systems of the people involved, was warfare. And indeed among the most common reasons that the Indians of the lower Mississippi, including the Choctaws, gave to justify war was that another nation had "disturbed them in their hunting country coming thither to steal their game as they call it."[38]

Precisely because the subsistence patterns of the Choctaws were not dictated by their environment but rather were historically derived and culturally maintained, the arrival of the Europeans, with their own cultures and their own ambitions, created new possibilities for ecological and social change. The fall in human populations, the rise in deer populations, and the narrowing of the region of Choctaw settlement during the sixteenth and seventeenth centuries all formed the prelude to the second, more sustained, stage of Choctaw-European contact. The very abundance of deer aroused the cupidity of Europeans, who saw the deer as a source of wealth, not food, and moved to exploit them. Ecology and demography, themselves already historical as well as "natural," created the arena of contact, but ecological and demographic factors did not determine what followed. These events are understandable only in terms of the cultures and social systems of the Choctaws and the French and English whom they met.

CHAPTER 3

The Evolution of the
Choctaw Play-off System

The rise in deer populations would probably have remained merely a biological event, historically insignificant, if it had not been coupled with the appearance of French and English traders and settlers who came from societies which were themselves in the midst of tension, conflict, and change. Although these traders came to the Choctaws most obviously to offer manufactures in exchange for deerskins, commerce was only a single motive and not always the dominant one. Religion brought the Jesuits, and imperial ambitions heavily tinged with older ideas of honor and glory often overwhelmed the purely commercial ambitions of English and French military officers and officials. While these motives were not merely masks for purely material impulse, it is fruitless to ignore the deepening thrust of commercial relations into the southeastern interior during the eighteenth century. This commercial bias was particularly true of Choctaw-English relations. England as a whole was more commercial in outlook during this period than was France, and the immediate representatives of the English among the Choctaws until 1763 were almost all traders—men whose overwhelming motive for coming among the Indians was material gain.

The real differences between the English and French, however, pale before the differences between the Europeans and the Choctaws, to whom commercial exchange was largely foreign. They did not rush to the forests to slaughter deer when Europeans appeared in their midst offering manufactures for deerskins. The process by which commerce changed from a relatively unimportant adjunct of the

Choctaws' lives to the most significant and destructive force in the nation was quite complex and consumed half a century. The change did not come without resistance. Europeans found it difficult to persuade the Choctaws that to truck and barter, to seek unlimited personal gain should be the end of their labors. Before they achieved even partial success, the Choctaws had tried to incorporate the French and English into a quite different system.

The Choctaws at first were themselves only commodities in European commerce. Roughly between 1690 and 1710, South Carolina slavers and their Creek, Chickasaw, and Yamasee allies repeatedly attacked the Choctaws, burned towns and crops, and marched thousands of people to South Carolina as slaves. The heaviest blows from these slaving expeditions fell upon the eastern and northern borders of the Choctaw nation, especially upon the chiefdoms of Kunshak and Chickasawhay. Warriors from these chiefdoms, armed only with native weapons, faced slave raiders armed with muskets. Supposedly the Choctaws lost more than 2,000 men to the slavers, who reduced the chiefdom of Chickasawhay from ten towns to one. Eventually the people of both Chickasawhay and Kunshak had to abandon their previous territories and move west to their historic locations. Further north, the slavers destroyed the town of Scanapa, whose name translates as "the unfortunate ones," and in many other towns which escaped destruction the slavers ravaged fields, took captives, and caused severe economic disruption.[1]

In 1699 the French arrived on the Gulf Coast in the midst of these English slave raids. They immediately proclaimed their own benign intentions and began arming the surrounding nations. As Pierre le Moyne, Sieur d'Iberville, told the Choctaws in 1702, the French, unlike the English who loved only blood and slaves, wanted to stop the slave wars so that the Indians might return to the hunt and accept French merchandise in exchange for their buffalo, deer, and bear skins. This desire for peace sprang less from scruples than from self-interest. Since the English already dominated the slave trade, the French, stumbling into the bloody chaos brought by the English slavers, sought peace in order to promote a new and possibly lucrative exchange in furs and deerskins. They also sought an end to the slave raids, which sometimes reached to the outskirts of Mobile and threatened to hamper the Indian agriculture upon which the colonists depended for food.[2]

The French, too, held slaves but, on the whole, restrained their slaving activities and only rarely indulged in excesses comparable to those of the English traders. The French found Indian slaves expensive and troublesome: they escaped to neighboring tribes and often induced black slaves to accompany them. The slave owners could not eliminate such losses, however, by selling or trading Indians to the West Indies. Because of the high mortality of Indian slaves from European diseases, both merchants and plantation owners usually refused to trade blacks for Indians, even at the rate of two for one. French interest in the slave trade thus remained casual; they preferred peaceful exchanges of manufactured goods for corn and deerskins.[3]

The French trading policy was reasonably successful as long as deerskins did not bear the cost of transportation back to Charleston and the English sought only slaves. Under these conditions, the French not only controlled exchanges with the Choctaws but also briefly lured the Chickasaws out of the English orbit. From the beginning, however, cultural differences hindered the growth of trade. What the French sought was commerce. What the Choctaws offered them was participation in a gift-alliance system. The result was not so much the triumph of one or the other, or even a compromise, as a series of exchanges which took place in the interstices between the two cultures. Physical objects—deerskins, muskets, blankets—passed between Choctaws and Europeans, but the import of the objects themselves and the meaning of the exchange remained a source of contention and confusion for a long time.[4]

In a real sense the recorded history of the colonial Southeast began with cultural ambiguity, with common acts interpreted in different contexts. Only gradually did the Choctaws, French, and English learn the meanings and significance of each others' actions. Then, in time, the boundaries of the European and Choctaw worlds blurred, the interstices between them filled; the two worlds became a common, mutually coherent region, although one initially more Choctaw than European. At first, however, cultural ambiguity pervaded the political dealings between the Choctaws and the French.

In the early years of the eighteenth century the French mistook the chiefs who stepped forward to meet them as the petty royalty of petty states—a primitive nobility who should act like so many counts in skins. The chiefs, who received the gifts the French offered and gave them deerskins in return, came from a far different society. They were important men, but not in the way that the French imagined.[5] The Choctaw nation that emerged into the historic era was a collection of chiefdoms. The Choctaw word *okla* can be translated as "chiefdom" as well as "town" or "people." In a sense "chiefdom," "town," and "people" were all synonymous. There were between forty and fifty Choctaw settlements large enough to be called towns by Europeans during the early eighteenth century, as well as "many little places of two or three cabins." Not every town identified by the Europeans, however, was an independent chiefdom, or *okla*. Many were attached to larger towns as dependencies. In 1729, for example, the French emissary Régis du Roullet listed sixteen chiefdoms ranging in size from Tala with 30 warriors to Oskelagna (Okelagana) with 500, and the next year Joseph de Lusser submitted a slightly different classification with nineteen chiefdoms in which powerful towns like Scanapa, Couechitto, Oskelagna, and Kunshak had four to six dependent towns each. Gradually this system of dominant and dependent towns declined, but another political and geographical division of the nation maintained itself much longer: the district.[6]

In the early eighteenth century, five district divisions seem to have existed. Two were made up of single chiefdoms and their dependencies: Kunshak and Chickasawhay. These, although still important, were only remnants of what once had been much larger districts. The other three divisions were more purely geographic, although borders varied and towns upon the borders could and did belong to different districts at different times. The largest group of towns was Okla Falaya, or "the Long People," which comprised the western part of the nation and would eventually come to be the Western District. Bordering these towns and taking in the northeastern corner of the nation was the Okla Tannap, or the "People of the Opposite Side," which eventually became the Northeastern District of the nation. The final division was the Sixtowns, which lay to the south of the other two divisions. The Sixtowns became the core of the nineteenth-century Southern District (Okla Hannali), which included Yowani, the southernmost Choctaw town, and Chickasawhay and its dependencies, as well as the Sixtowns proper. These divisions were not only geographical and political, they were also to an extent cultural. There were dialectal differences between the speech of the various divisions, and the Sixtowns in particular were culturally distinct in a variety of manners and practices.[7]

Towns, chiefdoms, and districts were one level of social organization among the Choctaws, but other forms of organization at once subdivided these political and geographical units and united the nation as a whole. All Choctaws belonged to one of two great moieties: the Inhulahta and the Imoklasha, or Kashap okla. The moieties governed marriage and burial rites. The Choctaws were exogamous—one had to marry a member of the opposite moiety—and when a Choctaw died, members of the opposite moiety buried him. The Inhulahta was known as the war party among the Choctaws, while the Imoklasha was the peace party, but the actual connections of these groups with war and peace are hazy.[8]

Each moiety (sometimes called *iksas* among the Choctaws) was subdivided into nontotemic clans which were also called *iksas*. How many *iksas* there were in the nation is unclear. Nineteenth-century missionaries listed three or four for each moiety, or six to eight for the nation as a whole. In all probability the numbers were not stable, with some *iksas* dying out and others being added as remnant peoples were adopted into the nation. Swanton, for example, tentatively lists twenty-four possible *iksas* among the Choctaws. Each *iksa* claimed descent from a common ancestor, and *iksa* connections therefore resembled family connections. *Iksa* members were obligated to aid each other and to obtain blood revenge for the killing of one of their members. The moiety and the *iksas* were basic units among the Choctaws, who told American Board missionaries that they "considered that the nation could not exist" without them.[9]

The political relationship of the *iksas* to the towns and chiefdoms is problematical. Originally each *iksa* may have been restricted in locale since some *iksa* names listed by Swanton, such as Kunshak and Sixtowns, are also the names of chiefdoms, but any such homogeneity had vanished by the late eighteenth century and probably far earlier. More than likely, each town contained one or more *iksas*, with each *iksa* dominating a few towns and having members scattered through many more.[10]

Below the *iksa* the basic unit was the family. Among the Choctaws, descent was matrilineal, specifically what anthropologists classify as the Crow kinship system. Given exogamy, this type of descent meant that a father and his children would belong to different *iksas* and moieties and, as a result, have widely different social obligations. Among the Choctaws, therefore, the mother's oldest brother, who was of the same *iksa* and moiety as his sister's children, took responsibility for the children's upbringing, while their actual father was in turn more concerned with the education and training of his sister's children. This does not mean that the relationship between a father and his children was nonexistent, only that it was not the dominant one.[11]

Although each Choctaw belonged to an *iksa* and moiety, a town and chiefdom, these alliances alone did not fully define the male's social place. Men were also arrayed in a social hierarchy best described in the so-called Early Account of the nation: "They (the people) are divided into four orders, as follows. (The first are) the grand chiefs, village chiefs, and war chief; the second are the Atacoulitoupa or beloved men (hatak holitopa—holy or beloved men, hommes de valleur); the third is composed of those whom they call simply tasca or warriors; the fourth and last is atac emittla. They are those who have not struck blows or who have killed only a woman or child."[12]

The pioneer ethnologist for the Southeast, John Swanton, overemphasized the egalitarianism of the Choctaws, and this has led to a neglect of the status and power of the chiefs. Early French accounts stressed their power; one in 1716, for example, reported that the Indians had "a very exact subordination and great respect for their chiefs whom they obeyed spiritedly."[13] Choctaw chiefs were men set apart by birth. The French emissary, Regis du Roullet wrote in 1732 that the great chief of Couechitto ruled by "right of birth," and although this statement may be dismissed as French cultural prejudice, the civil chiefs themselves stressed the same thing in council. Albimanon Mingo informed the English, for instance, that he ruled by right of "birth and long experience." This idea of hereditary chieftainship (much weakened in practice) continued into the nineteenth century. Nathaniel Folsom, a trader of the late eighteenth and early nineteenth century, refers to the family of chiefs as does his mixed-blood son Israel Folsom. The word "family" as used by the Folsoms indicates connections between chieftainship and *iksas* rather than the existence of a single family of chiefs. The word *iksa*, or "clan," was often translated as "family" because of the supposedly common descent of all clan members from a single ancestor.[14]

Normally the brother of the oldest son of the elder sister of a chief would be his logical successor, but the position was not automatically his if he seemed unsuited for it. The French governor Jean-Baptiste de Bienville cited an instance of this in 1734: "One man distinguished by birth but little esteemed because he had never liked war . . . had caused his village to choose another than him to take the place of his brother who was chief."[15] Here birth alone was not enough. A candidate also needed experience, which he usually obtained by serving as *Tichou-mingo* (*Tishu minko*, or "servant chief"), who "arranges for all of the ceremonies, the feasts, and the dances. He acts as speaker for the chief and makes the warriors and strangers smoke. These Tichou-mingo usually become village chiefs."[16]

Apparently these civil chiefs could come from either the peace or war moieties. As De Bienville's remarks show, a chief could be expected to be a war leader or at least distinguished in war, and many civil chiefs of the towns were. But a civil chief from the peace moiety had at least some obligation to try to avoid wars. When De Lusser visited the Choctaws to solicit their aid against the Chickasaws in 1730, for example, he ran afoul of a calumet, or "peace chief" who argued against war and took the issue "very much to heart."[17]

These civil leaders were not the only officials to operate at the town level. There were also men who were solely war leaders: a town war chief, whose title was translated as "red shoes" by the Europeans, and his two lieutenants, or *taskaminkochi*. The route to these offices was open to anyone who achieved distinction in combat. These chiefs could be quite influential. In time of war they gained great influence and prestige in the towns, but in the early eighteenth century when the Choctaws were at peace, their influence dwindled.[18]

Below the civil chiefs and the war chiefs were other leaders who led the *iksas* that composed the town. As Gideon Lincecum described the nation in the early nineteenth century, "each district was subdivided, with but little system, into Iksas, or kindred clans, and each of these *Iksas* had its leader." Originally, these leaders, too, were often called chiefs by the Europeans (usually chiefs of the second class) but gradually they became known as captains. It appears that each *iksa* with an adequate population had a captain, and thus that each town could have several captains in addition to its civil and war chiefs.[19]

While all these offices brought with them prestige and status, most of all they brought obligations, the most important of which was generosity. A chief's practical influence in large measure depended on what he gave away. As the French traveler Bossu noted in 1759, a chief's prestige depended on "how liberal he was with his possessions." Such a pattern is typical of many chieftainships.[20]

Choctaw chiefs gave generously because such an obligation initially was indistinguishable from chieftainship. Aboriginally the chiefs redistributed food resources by alloting the proceeds of communal hunts and common grain reserves to the people. Although there are no complete accounts of communal hunts among the Choctaws, before the nation obtained the gun, they appear to have hunted by surrounds as well as individually. Large groups of men would encircle an area and, yelling and shouting, converge on a preconstructed trap where the game would be cornered and slaughtered. The French observed a vestigial version of such a hunt among the Natchez in which the hunters presented the deer they had killed to the Great Sun, or Head Chief of the Natchez, for redistribution. Choctaw chiefs probably had parallel duties when their people hunted by surrounds. Similarly, various southeastern peoples either cultivated a common field for the chiefs, made donations to a public granary, or gave the chiefs food for public purposes as the occasion demanded. The chiefs were also responsible for redistributing this surplus to sustain the people in need and to provide for visitors. The eighteenth-century naturalist William Bartram described this system among the Choctaws, Creeks, Chickasaws, and Cherokees. After the harvest

there is a large crib or granary, erected in the plantation, which is called the king's crib; and to this each family carries and deposits a certain quantity, according to his ability or inclination, or none at all if he so chooses; this in appearance seems a tribute or revenue to the mico; but in fact is designed for another purpose, i.e. that of a public treasury, supplied by a few and voluntary contributions, and to which every citizen has the right of free and equal access, when his own private stores are consumed; to serve as a surplus to fly to for succour; to assist neighbouring towns, whose crops may have failed; accommodate strangers, or travellers, afford provisions or supplies, when they go forth on hostile expeditions; and for all other exigencies of the state; and this treasure is at the disposal of the king or mico; which is surely a royal attribute, to have an exclusive right and ability in a community to distribute comfort and blessings to the necessitous.[21]

Choctaw chiefs thus were primarily redistributors. They maintained power not by hoarding goods but rather by giving them away. As it operated aboriginally, redistribution was coupled with another concept: reciprocity, or the obligation eventually to return certain gifts of goods, labor, services, and favors. Together, redistribution and reciprocity governed the exchange of goods in Choctaw society. There was no market. Instead, economic exchange was deeply embedded in the larger cultural framework of kinship, religion, and politics. Ideally, material goods did not divide Choctaw society; they served to unite it. For generations the Choctaws found any other way of governing production and use of goods inconceivable. As the English trader James Adair reported of the southeastern Indians in general: "Most of them blame us for using a provident care in domestic life, calling it a slavish temper: they say we are covetous, because we do not give our poor relations such a share of our possessions as would keep them from want. There are but few of themselves we can blame on account of these crimes, for they are very kind and liberal to every one of their own tribe, even to the last morsel of food they enjoy."[22]

Redistribution and reciprocal exchange were inseparable from the daily round of Choctaw life. The numerous dances were also feasts where the chiefs supplied food to all in attendance. In each Choctaw house a pot of *tan fula*, a thick hominy soup, stood by the entrance and each visitor ate of it upon entering. When a fish pond was dragged, the surplus had to be sent to neighboring people; when deer were killed, the meat was shared with neighboring camps. In times of widespread shortages, the chiefs supplied the needy using the town's surplus, and when this failed, as Adair indicated, all remaining personal stocks were distributed. In war, when the Choctaws took booty in raids, the war chief redistributed it among his warriors and the relatives of those killed in the fighting. In the nation there simply was neither power nor responsibility without generosity. Choctaw politics, social life, and economics were inseparable, and reciprocity and redistribution made up the glue holding them together.[23]

The Choctaw chiefs who met with the French believed that they were establishing an alliance based upon the obligations of generosity and reciprocity that ordered their own society. Like brothers, the two allied nations should meet each other's needs—the Choctaws providing the French with the land and deerskins they required, the French allowing the Choctaws the manufactured goods they needed. Later, French officials fumed at what they regarded as the Choctaw arrogance of believing that the French king owed them annual tribute. The Choctaws looked on these annual gifts, however, not as tribute, but rather as a proof of French friendship which affirmed the alliance that allowed the French to remain in Louisiana and made peaceful intercourse between the nations possible. Without generosity there was neither friendship nor alliance; peaceful contact would give way to bloodshed and theft.[24]

Trade itself took place only within this context of amity and alliance. Initially, the chief supervised his warriors' exchanges with the traders. This exchange proceeded almost ritually and involved no bartering. Instead, a fair price (in anthropological terms, a "balanced reciprocal exchange") was agreed to by the chiefs, and then the goods changed hands. The earliest French account of the commerce revealed how little it partook of the market:

> When a Frenchman wishes to go trade among them, he usually chooses the time when they return with their presents. He asks of the chief of the band the number of savages he needs to carry his goods, for they go by land and every evening he must lie down under the open sky and on the earth. . . . When one has reached the village he is conducted to the house of the chief, where, having entered without uttering a word, he is seated on a cane bed raised about three or four feet above the ground, for fear of the fleas. Then they throw you a pipe called calumet with the pouch full of tobacco which you smoke. It is to be noticed that all this is done without speaking, after which the chief says to you, "You are come then?" Having answered that he has, one tells him the object of his journey and the kind of merchandise which he has brought to sell to his warriors. The next day he [the chief] informs all the people of the arrival of the Frenchman at his house, what he has brought, and what he asks for it. Each one comes to his ship, and takes away his goods, and when he [the trader] desires to return he informs the chief, who has the payments which he has agreed upon with his warriors brought to him.[25]

This account, dating from the 1730s, shows the power that the chiefs then retained in exchanges a generation after contact. Earlier, their power may have been much greater because, although they redistributed virtually all the goods they received from the Europeans, the chiefs retained control over one very significant aspect of European technology—the gun. There was some aboriginal precedent for the chiefs' initial monopoly on firearms. Guns, Choctaws may have reasoned, were necessary for their survival as a people. Only guns could turn back the slavers. In its protection of the people, the gun resembled the ceremonials and the "medicine" of the town. Both of these remained under the control of the chief and his *tichou-mingo*. The town's medicine in this context seems to have referred to both various sacred objects enclosed in a holy bag or bundle and a mixture of "herbs and roots of trees boiled together," apparently similar to the famed black drink of the Creeks. The sanction of this bundle was considered necessary for warfare, and the Choctaw version of the black drink was indispensable for maintaining the purity or freedom from pollution which every Choctaw sought. If guns were classified originally as part of the "medicine" of the town, their natural guardian was the chief. In any case, the gun and ceremonial knowledge were the only productive goods of the Choctaws that were limited in number and controlled by an elite.[26]

This monopoly of the gun by the chiefs had practical effects. Guns did not remain solely weapons of war; they also transformed the hunt. The only traditional account of the changes the gun made in the Choctaws' hunting practices dates from the early nineteenth century. Chahta Immataha told Gideon Lincecum that "in the course of two or three winters, all the hunters had guns, and it changed the nature of the hunt entirely. In place of the large companies and laborious running, surrounding, and driving, men would sneak out alone and could accomplish more than twenty men could with the bow and arrow, and never go out of a walk. Besides it did not frighten off the game like the old way of yelling and driving."[27]

The accounts of the zeal with which Choctaw hunters adopted the gun and of the transformation of the hunt from a group to an individual activity are both probably correct, but Chahta Immataha exaggerated the rapidity with which the weapon spread throughout the nation. In 1798 Nathaniel Folsom, an English trader who married a Choctaw woman, recalled having been told that the Choctaws had received from the French only four guns for each town in the early days of the Chickasaw wars. James Adair, another English trader, also insisted that during much of the early French period the Choctaws possessed relatively few guns. If, however, Chahta Immataha's account meant that within a few years most Choctaws hunted with guns, and not that most Choctaws owned guns, these other sources corroborate him rather than contradict him. The hunters received these guns through the chief. Nathaniel Folsom described how the system worked:

> One little small smouth bore gun, for only one gun was given to one Town, and very small shear of powder and ball, new for a great hunt, one captan or chef for one town was pointed out to lead them to the chace after dere or to ware by turns ten or twelve men all must hunt with that one gun, one gose out a hunting, most not stay long, about an our, come in wat he killed be this dere the bare or any kind of game he delivers it to the captan and the captan gave it to one his warers delved the mit only the skin the Capton takes & good portion of the best met, but the next hunter is gon to hunt for his luck come on quick, no time to be lost and he returns about the sam time. Whit his lode, be it much or little, he does the sam with it as the other did, the Captaon turns and so they kept on hunting with one gun till the small quantity ammunition is gone, then comes home[28]

What Folsom described is still a redistributive system with similarities to the communal hunt the French witnessed among the Natchez. The hunters gave the deer to the chief; the chief redistributed the deer to the hunters. The significant difference here seems to be that the chief retained the majority of the kill. The English trader James Adair contended that the owners of the guns (the chiefs) "hired" out the guns, but Adair was probably translating the transaction into market terms he and his European audience could readily understand. What the chief had gained was not wealth but a marked increase in the dependence of warriors upon him. Most of the meat and hides the chief retained would be returned to the hunters in the form of European goods. Control over the gun thus further increased the power of the chief in exchanges with Europeans.[29]

The chiefs' monopoly on presents and their initial domination of the new technology of the hunt did not lead to a permanent change in the nature of their offices. Exchange with the French did not mark the beginning of the evolution of the chiefs into an elite that would grow increasingly wealthy and powerful. Culture was too strong. Instead, the gun and the French presents remained simply a new way of obtaining the goods necessary to validate the chiefs' traditional status. The chiefs redistributed their goods.

The chiefs' dedication to redistribution and generosity did not, however, mean that they possessed enough European goods to give them to all Choctaws. After their initial contact, the French gave relatively small gifts to the Choctaws. Governor De Bienville estimated that he had given out less than 10,000 livres' worth of presents to all the nations around Mobile in the decade before 1711, and between 1712 and 1720 the French budget for gifts was only 4,000 livres annually. The exchanges with traders which followed gift-giving did not produce substantially more goods since the Choctaws, who had limited access to other European traders, gave many skins for relatively few manufactured products. French traders in the 1730s routinely realized 200 percent profits, and profits were probably even higher in earlier years before competition with the English arose.[30]

With the relative scarcity of European goods, the nature of Choctaw redistribution changed. Chiefs no longer only redistributed the food that they had received from the people to those who needed it. Now, they also distributed relatively scarce European manufactures to a select group of kinsmen and followers who had first claim on their generosity. While the chiefs gave away goods, they did not grow rich; but many Choctaws, without reliable access to the goods the Europeans brought, did grow relatively poor. They lacked what others had, even though their basic subsistence needs continued to be easily met. The French system of gifts and the chiefs' method of redistribution thus divided the nation into two distinct groups: the chiefs and their immediate kinspeople and partisans, who shared in French gifts; and the bulk of the warriors and their families, who did not. The chiefs, to secure the tranquility and maintain the redistributive system of the nation, needed more goods.

It is important to emphasize here that the demand of the Choctaws for European goods was not unlimited. They needed guns, but relatively few sufficed to turn back the slavers. They adopted metal axes, knives, and kettles relatively quickly, but these were durable goods and the demand for them remained inelastic. Woolens and cotton clothing which were also in demand, were less durable, but in the early years cloth was not a necessity. The problem was not that Choctaw demand was high and insatiable. It was that the French could not meet even the limited demand of a populous nation. The French lacked the ability to supply Indian goods quickly and cheaply, the transportation network to deliver them reliably, and the home market to consume large numbers of deerskins.[31]

Ironically, the French failure to supply the Choctaws became critical only because French muskets had enabled the Choctaws to turn back the English slavers. In the early eighteenth century the cost of taking Indian slaves from western nations armed by the French seems to have risen considerably. This, coupled with the high death rate of Indian slaves as compared with Africans, led to the increasing displacement of Indian slaves by blacks in South Carolina. By 1708 there were signs that the English had begun to switch the emphasis of their western trade from slaves to deerskins. In 1707 the English counted the Chickasaws among those western tribes participating in the Carolina deerskin trade, although the number of skins traded probably remained few. The cost of transportation to the Atlantic coast was too high to support an extensive trade.[32]

The English initially responded to this problem of declining profits in the slave trade and excessive transportation costs in the deerskin trade with grandiose, imperial schemes. They sought either to lure French Indian allies to areas nearer South Carolina where the deerskin trade could be pursued with profit or, failing this, to destroy the western Indians and drive the French from Louisiana. Central to both these plans were the Choctaws, who were the heart of French strength in the Southeast.[33]

All the imperial dreams that emanated from South Carolina failed, but their failure was nearly as dangerous to the French as their success would have been. The English as a result had no choice but to rely on trade to profit from the western tribes, and in commerce the English possessed advantages that they would maintain for half a century. The English offered higher prices for deerskins, traded in higher quality goods, and usually seemed to possess these goods in abundance. They maintained these advantages because the British leather industry paid a considerably higher price for deerskins than did that of France and because the English manufactured Indian trade goods at a lower cost than did the French. British merchants brought these goods into South Carolina with a regularity the French never matched in Louisiana. The reliability of British transatlantic commerce contrasted markedly with the chronic supply problems of the French, who rarely seemed to have enough trade goods on hand. Together, these advantages eventually offset the high transportation costs English traders faced in packing their skins back to Charleston.[34]

The staple items of this Indian trade were duffels or coarse woolen goods, liquor, clothing of wool and cotton, blankets, guns, metal tools, and jewelry. In woolen goods, tools, jewelry, and guns the English had the clear advantage of better products at a cheaper price. The French did, however, have an advantage in two critical areas of the trade. They provided more and better powder and bullets which, because of their bulk and low value, the English could not transport conveniently by pack train. They also accepted the skins of the smaller deer common in the pine forests of the southern part of the Choctaw country. The English took these skins only at a substantial discount, if at all.[35]

The English first made their advantages felt about 1715 when they entered the nation at the invitation of Conchak Emiko, an important northeastern chief. Giving gifts and offering cheap and abundant goods in trade, they quickly won over the northeastern and western towns. English goods, however, could not entirely erase the memory of twenty years of slave raiding, and the French played upon the Choctaw hatred of the English to recruit the virulently anti-English warriors of Kunshak and Chickasawhay to expel them. Armed with French guns, these warriors fanned out into other sections of the nation and overawed the remaining Choctaws, who were not nearly as well armed. With the support of these war parties and the promise of French presents, Chicacha Outlacta, the chief of Couechitto and Con-chak Emiko's brother (probably an *iksa* relative), assassinated the pro-English chief. Because Chicacha Outlacta was of the same *iksa* as his victim, the murder was probably closer to an execution, and the obligations of blood revenge did not come into play. Chicacha Out-lacta brought Conchak Emiko's head to the French and expelled the English.[36]

These events made it clear to the French that they could no longer automatically assume Choctaw loyalty or commercially compete with the English. If English traders won over the Choctaws, the Indians would either claim neutrality or form an alliance with the English. In either case, Louisiana would have lost its main defense against the Chickasaws, Natchez, Creeks, and English. Therefore, the English had to be kept out of the Choctaw nation; once they gained entrance, the erosion of Choctaw loyalty would begin.

To keep the English out, the French involved themselves directly in the politics of the nation: by attempting to centralize power among the Choctaws with an hierarchical system of chiefs, and by propagating virtually constant warfare among the Choctaws and their neighbors. First they created the office of Great Chief of the Choctaw nation, a position held initially by Chicacha Outlacta, chief of the town of Couechitto and assassin of Conchak Emiko. To make this new office effective, the French planned to funnel all their gifts to the nation through this head chief. He would then distribute them to the other civil chiefs and thereby, theoretically, make them his dependents. They, in turn, would use the goods to consolidate their power in the towns. In theory the Great Chief would be dependent on the French, the other civil chiefs would be dependent on him, and French control of the nation would be absolute. Jean Baptiste Le Moyne de Bienville, the architect of this strategy, was also its strongest asset. He treated the chiefs with deference and grace, spoke Choctaw, and by entertaining visiting chiefs in his own house, initiated a custom later governors came to greatly resent. All of this was politic and should not be confused with affection, but it did help attach the chiefs to the French.[37]

Even De Bienville's skills and an increased number of gifts could not, however, secure the kind of centralization the French desired. The Choctaws refused to accept subordination to either the French or the Great Chief. The French saw the presents as proof of their power and a means of reducing the Choctaws to dependency. The chiefs insisted on regarding the presents as merely their due: the French gave them presents to renew the alliance that allowed the French to settle the coast and protected them from their enemies, both Indian and white. The chief of Couechitto was an important, but not paramount, figure in this alliance. The great chieftainship remained largely an honorific title rather than a powerful office. As Father

Beaudouin, the Jesuit missionary who lived among the Choctaws and knew them well, reported in 1732. "As regards the authority of the Great Chief of the Choctaws it is not one of the most absolute and his power is far from being despotic in his nation. All the villages are like so many little republics in which each one does as he likes."[38]

Beaudouin blamed this situation in part on the French failure to channel all presents through the Great Chief, but there is little evidence that, even when the French did use the Great Chief to distribute presents, his power was as great as the French intended. Mingo Tchito, who was the nephew and successor to Chicacha Outlacta and who apparently claimed the title of head chief from the 1720s into the 1740s, never showed much inclination to rule all the nation. His ambitions centered on the chiefdom of Couechitto and such alliances with neighboring chiefdoms of the Northeastern District as seemed beneficial. Far from inept, Mingo Tchito was often a masterful factional leader, but never an autocrat. Repeatedly he proved unable to control even his own town; he, in no sense, ruled the entire nation. In times of crisis for the French, the chiefs remained more likely to seek their own advantage than to rally to the aid of the Louisiana colonists. As a tool to manipulate the Choctaws, the office of Great Chief was badly flawed.

The failure of gifts to make of the Choctaws pliant tools threatened the second aspect of French strategy: the involvement of the Choctaws in chronic warfare with the Chickasaws and other neighboring nations. Such wars, De Bienville believed, would prevent the safe penetration of English traders into the nation while they simultaneously weakened the dangerous and powerful nations surrounding the French. Eventually Louisiana would no longer have any need of the Indians, who would then be the mere shells of once powerful peoples. As De Bienville explained the policy to the Council of Louisiana in 1723, putting "these barbarians into play against each other is the sole and only way to establish any security in the colony because they will destroy themselves by their own efforts eventually."[39]

Such logic held a lasting appeal for French officials. They often preferred Choctaw-Chickasaw warfare to a Chickasaw alliance with the French. If the Chickasaws yielded, allied themselves to the French, and renounced the English, the eventual effect would be only to demonstrate French poverty and impotence. The French could not supply the Chickasaws as effectively as the English already did. English traders would inevitably return to the Chickasaws and use the peace to enter the Choctaw towns and win that nation over, too. The French therefore feared peace. They sought it only when they believed they possessed sufficient goods to compete with the English. More often they agreed to it only when they could no longer persuade the Choctaws to continue the war.[40]

One governor, Périer de Salvert, questioned the utility of this approach, but De Bienville maintained the policy during his term as commandant general for the Company of the Indies and his administration as governor. Together, these gave him primary responsibility for French-Indian policy from 1717 into the 1740s, with a break only in the late 1720s and early 1730s. In 1742, for instance, while encouraging new Choctaw attacks on the Chickasaws, he defended his policy to his superiors in France by arguing that "the mutual enfeebling of the belligerent nations . . . is the greatest advantage we can derive from the expenditures these wars occasion." Carrying the policy even further, the French court advised Governor de Vaudreuil in 1751 to encourage divisions and civil war among the Choctaws in order to weaken and destroy them. De Vaudreuil had no moral objections to this policy, but he thought that in practice it made the Choctaws aware of French zeal for their national suicide and thus served to alienate them.[41]

The French often secured warfare; they more rarely secured their larger aims. Recruiting Choctaw warriors proved expensive, and, once begun, French involvement in Choctaw politics did not produce the ordered hierarchy they desired, but rather a complex factionalism in which war chiefs and warriors became increasingly prominent. In the early eighteenth century hatred of the Chickasaws, who had played a major role in the slave raids, often secured Choctaw allies for the French in their wars with that nation. When some of their honored men fell in battle, blood revenge added further incentive for Choctaw participation in the war. Blood revenge, however, hardly guaranteed indefinite retaliations. The Choctaws possessed and frequently used other cultural means of responding to the deaths of townspeople and kinspeople. Blood revenge could be deflected by suitable gifts "to cover the dead."[42]

Even with demands for revenge stirring the nation, the chiefs exacted a price for their support of the French. As a war—begun in 1718 to avenge the death of a French officer and supported by the Choctaws—went against them, the Chickasaws and their English allies offered sizable presents to make peace and cover the Choctaw dead. The French, to keep the Choctaws at war, had to offer gifts of their own. The cost of presents rose precipitously. In the fifteen months preceding September 1723 the French spent 26,652 livres on the Choctaws and smaller allied nations. These gifts went directly to the civil chiefs, but the French found it also necessary to make direct payments to the warriors. French officials offered individual warriors separate bounties of a gun, a pound of powder, and two pounds of bullets for a scalp, and 80 livres' worth of goods for a slave. This combination of gifts and bounties pushed French ambitions beyond French means. By 1724 French supplies had failed, and the Choctaws, after swearing the year before that they would never do so, accepted a calumet of peace from the Chickasaws. With the acceptance of the calumet, the Chickasaws gave presents to cover the dead and end the war.[43]

The French did not recognize it in the 1720s, but their bounties to the warriors became the crowning contradiction in a series of contradictions which eventually enfeebled their control of the Choctaws. Their own commercial weakness had forced them to rely on gifts and war to combat the English, but to secure war they soon found themselves forced to provide more gifts and bounties. They sought a centralized hierarchy to manipulate the Choctaws, but expediency forced them to bypass the very civil chiefs whom they sought to strengthen and to offer direct scalp bounties to the warriors. In doing so, they unwittingly increased the importance of war leaders who could use the goods acquired from the French to build their own followings and become, at least potentially, rivals of the civil hierarchy the French supported. Later, in the 1730s, fearing such centrifugal tendencies, the French sporadically sought, without success, to curtail or reformulate the bounty system.[44]

The significance of the war leaders as a counterforce to the civil chiefs evolved in the context of a nation already divided by sectional interests. Within the Choctaw hierarchy, the French naturally sought to act first through their Great Chief, Mingo Tchito, and his subordinate chiefs in Okla Tannap. Because of their proximity to the Creek and Chickasaw trading paths, however, these men were the most susceptible of all Choctaws to English overtures when French gifts and supplies failed. The distance from Mobile and New Orleans to Okla Tannap made it unusually difficult for the French to supply these towns and counter English offers of peace and trade. The Sixtown and Chickasawhay districts, on the other hand, lay much closer to Mobile than they did to the English trading outposts; the towns of Okla Falaya, because of their proximity to the Pearl River, the most practical water route into the nation, received supplies and gifts from the French more regularly than other districts. In a crisis these towns would not commit themselves to the English until satisfied that the pack trains of the traders could reach them as regularly as the *bateaux* of the French.[45]

In the late 1720s supply failures dangerously weakened the French hold on Okla Tannap. And in 1729 when the Natchez drove the French from their territory, French officials, despite initial Choctaw aid against the Natchez, became alarmed by English overtures made to the civil chiefs of Okla Tannap suggesting peace with the Natchez and the Chickasaws who sheltered them.[46] To counter the instability of their northeastern allies, the French increasingly relied on the civil chiefs of powerful towns outside of the district. By 1732 the chiefs of Chickasawhay, Kunshak, and Kashtasha were listed along with Mingo Tchito as great medal chiefs. This multiplicity of chiefs was only the onset of the collapse of De Bienville's hierarchy. By 1733, 111 chiefs—apparently civil chiefs of all ranks, captains or heads of *iksas* within the towns, and perhaps even some war chiefs— received presents from the French, and 39 town and village chiefs received additional presents for redistribution. The cost of presents climbed accordingly, reaching 50,000 livres a year by the mid-1730s. The centralized system De Bienville had imagined had become a mockery of itself.[47]

The complicated political maneuvering of the French and civil chiefs created new opportunities for war chiefs who yearned for the privileges, status, and power which fighting as French allies had brought them in the first half of the 1720s but which peace had denied them in the second half of the decade. In peacetime, war leaders apparently received their share of French presents from the chiefs, but when French supply failures occurred and the chiefs had no goods to redistribute, the war leaders suffered along with the rest. There were two ways out of this dilemma: the war chiefs could act as agents of the chiefs in negotiations conducted with the English to secure a new source of goods, or they could hope for renewed warfare as French allies.[48]

In fact, the most famous war leader of the period, Shulush Homa, or Red Shoes (the war leader) of Couechitto, the town of the French Great Chief, tried both approaches during the years that followed the end of the first Chickasaw war. With Mingo Tchito's consent, he accepted English gifts and negotiated with English traders in the Chickasaw towns in the late 1720s. Later, he helped lead a large Choctaw force that attacked the Natchez in alliance with the French. In both these instances he played a traditional role; he acted as the agent of the civil chiefs.[49] Red Shoes's conservative course ended in 1731 when, at the instigation of the French, he secretly organized a war party that attacked the Chickasaws in their hunting camps. His men killed six Chickasaws and captured eleven more. Red Shoes had made the path red; the Chickasaws would now revenge themselves on the Choctaws. War had begun.[50]

The civil chiefs of Okla Tannap were outraged. Their own negotiations with the English were now as dead as Red Shoes's victims, but what was worse, "the sentiments of an ordinary warrior had prevailed over that of the chiefs." The French rewarded Red Shoes with a great medal, like those of the leading civil chiefs, which entitled him to presents equal to theirs. Such a thing was unprecedented and the civil chiefs refused to recognize the war chief's right to either the medal or equality with them. Red Shoes was not of the proper birth to be a medal chief.[51]

The French thought they had created a pawn, but the civil chiefs knew better. Backed by his own iksa, which dominated ten towns, and supplied with French goods to redistribute, Red Shoes was now a very formidable figure. Even the civil chiefs, however, probably did not realize how formidable Red Shoes would become or how fully he would take advantage of his position to subvert both the French and the civil leadership.[52]

The rise of Red Shoes marked the beginning of two decades of factional strife, warfare, betrayals, murder, and theft. On one side were the French who, with the return of De Bienville to office in 1733, tried to restore an ordered hierarchy to the "ill-disciplined government" of the Choctaws. On the other side were the English, usually represented by Carolina traders who dreamed of a lucrative trade in the Choctaw towns but occasionally represented by colonial officials of Georgia and South Carolina with imperial and commercial ambitions of their own. Both sides sought to woo and control a nation increasingly divided by sectional interests, factional jealousies, class differences between warriors and chiefs, and personal rivalries. The master figure in this maze—switching from English alliance to French alliance and back again, challenging the civil chiefs and then cooperating with them, rallying the warriors and losing them—was Red Shoes.[53]

Throughout the 1730s, sometimes in alliance with the civil chiefs, sometimes in opposition to them, Red Shoes shifted his loyalty between the French and English. Rivalries between the civil chiefs and sectional divisions helped thwart attempts to control him, but beyond both of these sources of faction lay a newer division between warriors and chiefs. In 1734 Sieur Le Sueur had reported to De Bienville that the response to the latest English overtures to the Choctaws varied according to status. The chiefs and old men wished to continue fighting on the side of the French, "but the young men openly declared themselves for peace with the Chickasaws and for free trade with the English as well as with us." Their leader in these demands was Red Shoes.[54]

Free trade with the English and the French promised to benefit the warriors more than the existing alliance with the French did. In the words of Red Shoes in 1735, it was "the way to lack nothing. The English will take our large skins in exchange for cloth and guns which are not so dear as those of the French, and we shall keep the small ones to get from the others, powder, bullets, and other small merchandise." The discontent of the warriors simmered within the nation, yet De Bienville believed that the chiefs, with French support, could suppress it.[55]

De Bienville was wrong; the civil chiefs never shared French assumptions about their duties or their powers within the French hierarchy. The chiefs continued to redistribute presents to suit their own purposes, not those of the French. In 1738, for example, De

Bienville had persuaded a large number of Choctaws to attack the Chickasaw towns. He intended to reward them during the annual congress in Mobile where each participant would get gifts according to his "rank or services," but De Bienville became ill and left the distribution to his subordinate, Diron D'Artaguette. D'Artaguette, however, gave the gifts directly to the chiefs and left redistribution in their hands. Each chief then ignored most of the warriors and war leaders who had actually fought for the French and shared the presents only "with his relatives or his partisans." The warriors felt betrayed—not by the chiefs who had acted as expected, but by the French who had failed to reward them as promised—and grew more willing to listen to peace overtures from the English and Chickasaws.[56]

Fiascoes such as this, coupled with French defeats at the hands of the Chickasaws and continued shortages of goods, kept Red Shoes a potent force in the nation. In 1735, 1736, and 1738 he introduced English traders into the nation. In 1738 when the English gave him a medal and proclaimed him king of the Choctaws, when all the towns but Chickasawhay backed him, he seemed the most powerful man in the nation.[57]

The foundations of Red Shoes's success were, however, precarious. Despite his challenges to the civil chiefs, despite his alliance with the English traders, culturally Red Shoes remained fully a Choctaw. No matter how much he or the warriors who followed him desired English goods, they expected gifts and reciprocity, not greed and hard bargaining. Exchange could take place only with friends, and the evidence of friendship was generosity. Like other woodland Indians before and after them, they would be very disappointed with the English.

The collection of knaves, murderers, rapists, and all-purpose reprobates who traded in the southern forests consistently alienated the Indians they dealt with. Years later the Board of Trade admitted that "the many flagrant frauds and abuses which have too frequently been committed in our commercial dealings" had harmed English relations with the southern nations.[58] And in 1763 when the English victory over the French finally made them preeminent among the Choctaws, Albimanon Mingo, then the oldest and most powerful of the Choctaw civil chiefs, felt compelled to warn English officials of the danger the traders presented to friendly relations both because "they lived under no Government and paid no respect to either Wisdom or Station" and because of their treatment of Indian women: "often when the Traders sent for a Basket of Bread the Generous Indian sent his own wife to supply their wants instead of taking the Bread out of the Basket they put their hand upon the Breast of the Wives which was not to be admitted, for the first maxim in our language is that Death is preferable to Disgrace."[59]

As significant as the commercial and social abuses of the English were, however, they were subordinate to an even more basic conflict that plagued the trade. The Choctaws saw commerce as an extension of reciprocity, not as hard bargaining for personal advantage. The English acknowledged this concept of trade by giving the Choctaws gifts, but they hoped eventually to eliminate these presents.[60] They desired to trade, not to exchange gifts—an ambition which brought from Edmond Atkin, the southern superintendent of Indian affairs, lectures to the Choctaws on the distinction between "begging" (gifts) and trade.

> My king wants nothing of the Red People; but he is disposed to be kind to them, because they are poor—He gives what he pleases to his Friends; and whatever it is they ought to be thankful for it. The Reason why I mentioned this, I am going to tell you like a Friend—The Traders who carry Goods to the Indian Towns buy those Goods, & must pay for them. Your people have a way of begging Goods different from other Nations, which is like taking them away—This discourages Traders; and it is the Business of the Headmen to make their People behave otherways; And unless you can do that & keep your People in Order, I don't see how you can keep the Trade. . . . I don't want to buy the Trade.[61]

Closely connected with the problem of reciprocity and commerce was yet another block to English ambitions. The Choctaw market was relatively inelastic. They needed limited quantities of quite specific durable goods—blankets, metal tools, cloth, and clothing—as well as a rather narrow range of luxury items such as beads and silverwork. They remained quite indifferent to many of the products Europeans brought and rejected goods that did not meet their needs or were of poor quality. Although the major problem of the French was an inability to satisfy this limited market, the problem of the English seems to have been quite different. They wanted to increase Choctaw consumption and with it the volume of the trade.[62]

The Choctaws did not want enough. Once the hunters satisfied their need for European goods, they lacked further incentive to hunt. Their own subsistence agriculture and the seasonal yield of venison kept them well fed. The account by James Adair of the metamorphosis of the Choctaws from unproductive and unskilled hunters in the 1740s to skilled hunters in the 1760s and 1770s was merely an Englishman's version of the introduction of the Choctaws into the market economy. They were not better hunters in the 1770s than they were in the 1740s; they were merely more fully engaged in the market. Choctaw hunters killed relatively few deer annually between 1720 and 1740, in large part because they needed relatively few deer to meet their limited demands for European goods. At a time when the Creeks produced over 100,000 skins annually for the deerskin trade, the Choctaws could be depended on for only 15,000. They wanted European goods, but only in limited quantities, and their devotion to commerce was weak.

In this context the English traders' insistence on introducing and maintaining the two great banes of the Indian trade—the credit system and the traffic in liquor—becomes understandable. Both practices were outlawed, but both remained basic to stimulating the trade. If the Choctaws hunted only to satisfy their own needs, they killed relatively few deer. The traders, to prosper, had either to encourage or to force Choctaw hunters to kill more deer.[63]

Since the Choctaws refused to develop the proper appetite for European goods on their own, the English proceeded to force feed them. For this they needed rum. Alcohol was an ideal commodity for Indian commerce. Since it was consumed quickly and the English discovered that Indian appetites for it could be constantly stimulated, liquor presented a means both for luring Indians into the forests to hunt and for keeping them endlessly in debt. The French were not above using liquor; however, since they needed the Choctaws as relatively disciplined allies and the Jesuits consistently opposed its distribution to the Indians, they hesitated in their sales. The English shared no such inhibitions concerning liquor and the Choctaws. Rum allowed them to undersell the French by even greater margins and to induce the Choctaws, at least temporarily, to increase their kill of deer.[64]

Liquor almost inevitably produced debt, and debt was the basis of the credit system, which brought abuses of its own. Earlier in the century during the slaving period, when hunters could not or refused to meet their debts, the traders seized their children and female relatives to sell as slaves. Although the Yamasee War and the decline of the slave trade had largely ended such measures before they affected the Choctaws, the traders continued to seize chickens, hogs, crops, or other property of the various nations as payment for their debts. Edmond Atkin asserted that the credit system bore a major share of the blame for the failure of the English to hold Choctaw loyalty before 1763.[65]

The English use of credit and liquor to secure more deerskins thus tended to alienate the very people who were their initial partisans within the nation. Once the warriors had satisfied their basic demand for blankets, pots, or axes, the traders were merely belligerent creditors, men without generosity who refused to bestow gifts and cheated them of deerskins. The rules of the market which the English took as natural, the Choctaws rejected. They saw no reason, for instance, why the price of English goods in their towns should not be the same as the price in the Creek towns, despite the longer distances the traders had to travel. The object of trade was not profit; instead, two peoples, like brothers, should meet each other's needs. What did distance have to do with this? When the English refused to conform to these concepts of exchange, when the goods the Choctaws expected to receive as gifts, were sold to them on credit instead, when the English demanded large numbers of deerskins to satisfy the Choctaw debts, the discontent of the warriors rose.[66]

It was this basic cultural conflict, coupled with an aggressive French response to English inroads, which rapidly undermined Red Shoes' triumph. When adequate English gifts did not arrive, the chiefs looked once more to the French. And as the warriors of Okla Tannap fell into debt to the traders, they too saw little to lose from the expulsion of the Englishmen. The French persuaded the Chickasawhays, always their most loyal allies in the nation, to attack the Chickasaws and bloody the paths. When Chickasaws died under attack, partisans of Red Shoes rashly, if ineffectually, attacked the Chickasawhays. The French adroitly played on the possibility of civil war and the horror of Choctaws' spilling each other's blood over the death of Chickasaws. The promise of French presents won back the ten towns nearest Fort Tombigbee; Albimanon Mingo, the civil chief of Kunshak, openly backed the French; and war parties went out to kill Englishmen and Chickasaws. Thus the trading paths were closed entirely.[67]

While all this transpired, Red Shoes himself was absent. He was in Charleston seeking the necessary gifts from the English. He returned bitter over their parsimony and what he regarded as their betrayal of the alliance. He made no attempt to restore the trade but instead looted the English warehouses himself to secure gifts for his followers and to try to regain the favor of the French. In the end, De Bienville contended, only his own *iksa* remained behind him.[68]

The balance of power in the nation had once more overtly shifted to the French and the civil chiefs, but in the complex calculus of Choctaw politics a far more fundamental shift had occurred. The presence of Fort Tombigbee, built and garrisoned during the mid 1730s, had enabled the French to win back the northeastern towns and close the Creek paths. After 1739 Okla Tannap would not remain the center of warrior discontent; it was no longer geographically iso-lated from the French. French presents and trade goods reached Okla Tannap far more regularly than they had in the past. The new fort was not, however, the only reason for this reversal of allegiance. The neighboring Alabamas had now, for reasons of their own, taken a pro-French position. This not only made the northeastern towns less accessible to the English traders who used the old Creek trading paths, it also threatened those same towns with bearing the brunt of war if the French succeeded in soliciting the Alabamas' aid against the pro-English Choctaws.[69]

In the west, loyalty shifted in the opposite direction. Peace with the Chickasaws in 1738–39 had opened up new trading paths from the Chickasaw towns and had given the Choctaws of Okla Falaya a taste of English abundance. Since the number of traders who reached them was less than the number of those operating in the northeast, the abuses were correspondingly fewer. Peace, too, had freed Okla Falaya from the Chickasaw raids that had forced the abandonment of border towns such as Bok Chito and Oklatanap. These Choctaws were not eager to resume the Chickasaw wars, as the French demanded. The west after 1739 succeeded the east as the area most susceptible to

English overtures. The southern towns, isolated from the English, remained largely pro-French.[70]

The consequences of this shift in loyalty lay dormant for a number of years, however, because in 1739 the Chickasaws slaughtered a peace delegation sent them by Red Shoes during yet another unsuccessful French expedition against their towns. Cultural demands for blood revenge then forced the war chief to launch his own war against the Chickasaws, even though the French made peace and withdrew. This war cost the Chickasaws dearly; to maintain it De Bienville once more recognized Red Shoes as a medal chief and rewarded him with substantial presents.[71]

This reconciliation did not outlast De Bienville's governorship. His successor, the Marquis de Vaudreuil, sought in 1743 to restore a centralized civil hierarchy to the Choctaws and to break Red Shoes, that "polite and dissembling" chief whom officials warned him about. The governor underestimated the Choctaw leader. Plans to use the civil chiefs to lure the Chickasaws out of the English alliance failed when a new war with England broke out which closed down French supply lines to Louisiana and created shortages of Indian goods. Without sufficient presents, the Choctaw civil hierarchy itself began to crumble, and Red Shoes saw his opportunity.[72]

In 1745 Red Shoes opened negotiations of his own with the Chickasaws and the English. When the French secured the murder of members of the Chickasaw peace delegation visiting the Choctaw towns, Red Shoes retaliated by having his warriors kill three Frenchmen. The civil chiefs, shocked at these first murders of Frenchmen in the nation, told De Vaudreuil that Red Shoes had gone mad, but Red Shoes said that he made no more of the affair "than if he had killed the wood rats which ate their hens."[73]

Red Shoes now stood fully committed. The French demanded his head. There would be no turning back. Once more he sought to rally the nation behind him, and once more he directed his appeal for peace with the Chickasaws and trade with the English directly at the warriors. He and the English traders argued that "the French were liberal indeed, but to whom and for what: They gave presents to the headmen and the most eloquent speakers of their country to enslave the rest."[74]

Outmaneuvered, short of goods, demanding Choctaw heads in

retribution for their own dead, the French saw their influence in the nation virtually collapse. Warriors went over to Red Shoes en masse, English traders moved into the nation once more and reached even into the Sixtowns, an area where they apparently had never traded before. Isolated and intimidated by wandering bands of Red Shoes's warriors, those pro-French chiefs who were not won over by the promise of English presents had to mute their opposition. By 1747 Red Shoes had secured as solid a consensus in favor of the English as had ever existed in the nation.[75]

The English promptly dissipated their advantage. Rivalry among South Carolina officials and traders for a monopoly in the Choctaw trade prevented the arrival of necessary gifts and delayed adequate supplies of trade goods in some areas, while in other regions, particularly Okla Tannap, English traders soon had Choctaw hunters deeply in their debt. The French were not idle in the face of English bungling, and in 1747 they retaliated against Red Shoes; a paid assassin murdered him as he escorted an English supply train into the nation. The fortuitous arrival of a supply ship enabled the French to distribute gifts among the Choctaws, and much of Okla Tannap, in debt to the English and with little to gain from further allegiance, reverted back to the French. Okla Falaya, now under the leadership of Red Shoes' "brother" Little king, (probably an *iksa* relative), continued to trade with the English. When the French urged their allies to evict the traders and avenge the dead Frenchmen, civil war broke out.[76]

Between 1748 and 1750, when the civil war was at its bitterest the pro-English party was centered firmly in Okla Falaya. Of the northeastern towns, only Couechitto persisted as an English ally. It paid a high price for this. In 1748 pro-French Choctaws destroyed it along with two western towns, Abeka of the West and Kunshak Osapa (Neskuobo). With the destruction of Couechitto the nation fought largely along sectional lines. Kunshak, Chickasawhay, Okla Tannap, and most of the Sixtowns fought against Okla Falaya and Sinasha and Tala in the Sixtowns. The French offered their allies double scalp bounties and methodically singled out towns for punishment, adding Chunky, Oka Hullo, and Oni Talemon to their list in 1748. The pro-English Choctaws got little aid. Supplies failed to arrive, and the warriors were reduced to shooting beads and clay balls instead of bullets. By 1750 only two of the largest western towns, Kashtasha and Kafitalia, remained pro-English. With their submission to the French that year, the civil war ended.[77]

It had been a bitter and complicated struggle. Even as the war raged, smallpox had swept the nation, probably killing more people than had died in the fighting. In all, 800 scalps from the pro-English towns were laid at De Vaudreuil's feet for the bounties he offered. In the end, warriors from the west fought warriors from the east largely because of the switch in trade patterns. But this change was only part of the logic of the alignment. The towns dominated by Red Shoes's *iksa* followed him until his death and then apparently followed Little King. Once killings had begun, the *iksa* demands for blood revenge inevitably fueled the bitterness of the fighting.[78]

Section and clan, however, were not at the root of the civil war no matter how much they influenced final loyalties. These divisions had always existed among the Choctaws. The civil chiefs themselves indicated the deeper cause when they delivered a postmortem on the disaster for the French. Their account of the war was at once an analysis and a warning. The rebellion was, they said, largely the work of war leaders "who although they admittedly had no right to annual gifts from the French, nevertheless needed trade goods; the peace chiefs [civil chiefs] satisfied in their own needs by French gifts, had no right to oppose the warriors justifiable hope of obtaining their necessities by resorting to the English who had goods and were willing to supply them."[79] The warning was well placed. The bloodshed had changed nothing; if the French failed to supply the warriors, the nation would inevitably turn to the English.

Large gifts thus remained essential if the French were to retain the loyalty of the Choctaws. By 1749 such gifts cost 62,000 livres a year, and they remained at approximately this level until 1763. In exchange for the presents, the French received reciprocal gifts of deerskins worth about 32,000 livres a year. The hierarchy De Vaudreuil had tried to create was at this point little more than a memory. By 1763 the French listed 601 Choctaws, exclusive of medal chiefs, entitled to receive annual gifts.[80]

Although warfare with the Chickasaws resumed at the end of the civil war, the failure of the French to meet their commitments for gifts and trade lessened Choctaw enthusiasm considerably. By the late

1750s many Choctaws were once more disenchanted with the French. Complaining of their poverty, they opened peace negotiations with the Chickasaws and the English. French control was no more absolute than it had ever been.[81]

Superficially, Choctaw factionalism with its bloody denouement in the civil war seems precisely the kind of internal division which, historians have often asserted, made it impossible for Indians to resist European manipulation and conquest. The reality is, however, more complex. Certainly, the Choctaws paid a high price for their factional divisions, but they might have paid a far heavier price without them.

The conflicting interests and loyalties of the various parts of Choctaw society came to be the best insurance the nation had against European domination. Chiefs remained important but not at the cost of becoming French puppets presiding over a centralized client state. Warriors desired English goods, but they did not become helpless debtors of the English who emptied the forests of deer. Within their own factional, sectional, iksa, and status divisions, the Choctaws achieved a tenuous balance—economically, ecologically, and socially—which preserved their independence for more than half a century.

Choctaw independence was maintained not through unity, but through divisiveness. Factionalism created the parties that maintained the necessary exchanges and contacts with both the French and English without leading the nation into complete dependence on either. Such factions arose naturally from the existing divisions of aboriginal society with its towns, iksas, and chiefdoms. And, indeed, the whole world view of the Choctaws, with its emphasis on balance and its demands that humans play off the forces of the upper and nether worlds in order to secure peace and plenty, sanctioned the playoffs, divisions, and balances which dominated their relations with Europeans.[82]

The precise form which Choctaw factionalism took resulted from the economic and political pressures colonial powers put on an already decentralized, premarket society. Since chiefs never controlled the means of production in agriculture and did not long retain their monopoly of the gun, factions did not evolve into classes in Choctaw society. The economic interests of Choctaw factions were not based on a struggle to control the means of production within the society;

rather, they sprang from the quest for access to goods that originated outside the society. Since the suppliers of these goods, whether French or English, fundamentally threatened Choctaw well-being however, the permanent success of any Choctaw faction and its European ally of the moment could be fatal. The genius of Choctaw factionalism lay in its ability to avert such dominance and turn the internal divisions of the Choctaws to the nation's advantage.

The French had often succeeded in securing intertribal warfare, but they had not achieved their larger ends. Louisiana did not become the prosperous colony the French had hoped for, nor was Choctaw strength destroyed by French machinations. By 1763 the Chickasaws had been bled white, and the French were about to vanish from the region. The Choctaws alone remained a significant power when the English came to Mobile.

English machinations had proven no more successful. The Choctaws continued to insist on gifts instead of trade and had successfully avoided dependence on the traders. When their indebtedness had mounted, when they had become victims of chicanery and greed, they had expelled the traders and renounced their debts. Faced with twin evils, the Choctaws had played them off against each other.

Choctaw factionalism was the basis of Choctaw independence not only in a political sense but also in a material sense. Factionalism, war trade, and subsistence were subtly but inextricably entwined. To a surprising degree, factionalism itself served to maintain the subsistence system. The wars the Choctaws fought were certainly not designed to keep their subsistence system intact, nor was the maintenance of the existing subsistence system in any materialist sense their real cause. Nonetheless, the preservation of a balanced and successful subsistence system was one result of the wars. It was an example of the blending of material and cultural life which makes historical change so complex.

The Choctaw-Chickasaw wars severely affected the hunting of both peoples. At its most effective, warfare consisted of raids made by small parties on hunting camps and on women working in the fields. Red Shoes began the Chickasaw wars of the 1730s by attacking hunters, and attacks such as these harassed the Chickasaws in the 1740s and 1750s so continuously that they contemplated abandoning their homeland. The Chickasaws, with their fortified towns and abundance of guns, invariably defeated large French and Choctaw expeditions, but as English traders among the Chickasaws reported, Choctaw attacks on their hunting camps cost the Chickasaws dearly.[83]

In the course of these attacks the Choctaws seem to have concentrated on purging an area of all hunters, not just Chickasaws. They repeatedly "mistook" for Chickasaws Creek or Shawnee hunters who entered into lands normally hunted by the Chickasaws and Choctaws. Such warfare very effectively curtailed hunting. In 1740, for example, the Chickasaws told the English that Choctaw war parties had prevented them from hunting; in 1754 the Chickasaws sent word to the Creeks that the Choctaws had harassed them so much that they had "not been able to stir to hunt." This was not the first time Choctaw pressure had so crippled the Chickasaws. The warfare of the late 1730s and early 1740s had also disrupted their economy, caused some of them to move into the Creek nation, and forced some Englishmen to abandon the deerskin trade. The crippling effects which warfare had upon hunting were clear to all southeastern Indians. Later, during the Creek-Choctaw wars, the Creeks told the English that if fighting continued, the traders would suffer because when hunters could not "hunt in safety they could not pay their debts."[84]

This warfare had similar effects on the Choctaws. As early as 1723, French merchants complained that the Chickasaw wars interfered with the deerskin trade of the Choctaws. Chickasaw warriors could, after all, stalk Choctaw hunters just as effectively as the Choctaws stalked Chickasaws, and the Choctaws lost hunters even within the neighborhood of Fort Tombigbee. The civil war brought hunting almost to a halt, at least in the west. The pro-English Choctaws complained that "as the French and their Party make continual War upon them, they are very poor as they have not time to kill skins to buy ammunition or clothes for themselves." Warfare had become the de facto way of maintaining the animal populations.[85]

As long as the French-English rivalry continued, warfare not only preserved game but also gave the Choctaws another means of access to the material goods otherwise obtainable only through commerce. French gifts to the nation were necessary to keep the English out, and English gifts to the nation were necessary to make peace. These combined gifts amounted to a rather sizable subsidy. In 1754, for instance, when De Vaudreuil's successor Governor Kerlerec made gifts worth 62,000 livres to the Choctaws and received in reciprocal gifts 30,000 livre's worth of skins, the result was a net payment of 32,000 livres to the Choctaws. This represented the amount of goods the nation would otherwise have had to obtain through the hunt. It is difficult to estimate the number of deer the Choctaws would have had to kill to obtain these goods because of the fluctuating value of the livre in Louisiana, but a crude calculation is possible. Between 1743 and 1746 deerskins brought 30 sous a pound in the colony. A generous estimate of the average weight of a Choctaw deerskin is 2.5 pounds. Therefore, 32,000 livre's worth of gifts equaled 21,333 pounds of deerskins, or 8,533 deer, at Mobile prices. If the French continued to mark up prices by 200 percent at the Choctaw towns as they did in the 1730s, then the actual number of deer the Choctaws had to kill to get these goods was roughly three times this. In other words, gifts on this scale represented an alternative to the killing of 8,500 to 25,000 deer annually by the Choctaws.[86]

The failure of such subsidies sporadically brought the English back into the nation and increased pressure on the borderland. Such incursions, however, were relatively brief because the demands of the English traders for a fully commercial system alienated the Choctaws.

The effects of this political and economic cycle upon the deer of the borderlands were critical. Wars helped confine the settlements of the nation to a relatively small area surrounded by unoccupied borderlands. While they were allied to the French, the Choctaws severely restricted hunting in these borderlands. The hunting lands could not be used in safety because of Chickasaw, and sometimes Creek, war parties. In any case, trade was limited because of the relative shortage of French goods. When the alliance collapsed, as it did sporadically because of the inability of the French to supply sufficient goods, the Choctaws made peace with the Chickasaws and intensified their hunting of the borderlands. Now deer were taken in much greater numbers not only by Choctaw hunters, but also by Creek, Chickasaw, and Shawnee hunters. If the Choctaws had been fully adapted to the market, they would have been lured into taking more and more deer to buy greater and greater quantities of English manufactures. Since they were not, however, English trade abuses, coupled with the Indians' own limited demands for goods and the ravages of credit and liquor, eventually allowed the chiefs and the French to regain the advantage. Warfare flared again, and hunting pressure declined.

This system was, of course, fraught with danger. It meant not only playing off the French and English, but also balancing the demands of the various subdivisions of the nation. External wars could not be allowed to get out of hand and escalate from the skirmishes of small parties to costly military campaigns. Neither could the factions be allowed to solidify into bitterly antagonistic parties. The nation had to remain divided, but not too divided. The distinctions between chief and warriors; among Okla Tannap, Okla Falaya, Kunshak, Chickasawhay and the Sixtowns; between gifts and trade served them well only so long as a deeper consensus united the nation. When this failed, the tensions and divisions of the nation tore it apart. The civil war represented the failure of the system—a failure that both sides tried to repair with only partial success in the 1750s.

The deterioration of this system that began in the Choctaw civil war greatly accelerated after the French and Indian War. In order for the system to work, the Choctaws needed at least two European powers in the region, and one of these had to require from the Choctaws something other than trade. The Choctaws needed both the French and the English, or their equivalents. They could no longer easily do without Europeans since, as they themselves freely admitted, they relied on the English and the French for some of their clothing, their blankets, guns, ammunition, pots, knives, hoes, and other manufactured items. There was no going back to a pre-European technology. Unless some Europeans, like the French, relied on the Choctaws for military aid, however, this desire for European goods exposed them to inevitable exploitation. When in 1763 the French ceded the Choctaws' homeland to the English and it became part of the English colony of West Florida, a pillar of Choctaw economic, political, and ecological balance disappeared overnight. Great changes in the nation and its land became inevitable.

CHAPTER 4

Liquor and Deerskins: Consequences of the Market Economy

In 1763, after three-quarters of a century of contact with Europeans, the well-being of Choctaw society rested on a series of well-defined internal oppositions and balances. The Choctaws juxtaposed peace and war; trade and gifts; civil leaders and war leaders; the towns of Okla Falaya (the west), Okla Tannap (the east), Okla Chito (Kunshak and dependencies), and Okla Hannali (the Sixtowns); Englishmen and Frenchmen; and hunting and fighting to achieve a tenuous balance between land and people. These oppositions were, after all, natural for a people who divided the world into dualistic categories and whose organization at contact revolved around the mutual obligations of the moieties. When the coming of the Europeans with guns and the deerskin trade, with disease and depopulation, confronted the Choctaws with a new set of problems, they solved them with a new set of polarities. But the new balances were precarious and dangerous; they often rested on open rivalries where the older opposition had softened into mutual obligation. The civil war both conclusively demonstrated the danger and, by merging the chiefs and war leaders, began to defuse it.

Because the Choctaws no longer fully controlled change in their world, however, such internal solutions never proved fully effective. In 1763 France ceded the Choctaw homeland to England, and immediately the equilibrium based on the opposition of Englishmen and Frenchmen, gifts and trade, war and peace, which had steadied Choctaw society, went out of kilter. Technically this series of balances governed only the external relations of the nation, but such a distinction is too neat for the realities of Choctaw life. The repercussions of this imperial transfer touched the Choctaws politically, socially, and economically and eventually affected even the land itself. In the ceremonies that transferred Fort Tombigbee and Mobile from Frenchmen to Englishmen, the Europeans were solemnizing not only the transfer of sovereignty, but also the destruction of the white-tailed deer, its habitat, and the way of life it helped to support. However, neither the Europeans nor the Choctaw hunters who sought the deer and killed them knew this. No one foresaw such changes in 1763. The alterations in the land would be a consequence of the European peace, but not a direct one. The Choctaws had to change before the land changed. In human-dominated ecosystems cultural change—which appears unrelated to the land, its flora, and its fauna—often precipitates environmental change. This type of change would occur among the Choctaws.

In 1763 the survival of the white-tailed deer was linked, more closely than anyone knew, to the interests of the chiefs, headmen, and beloved men of the nation. To these men came the gifts of the Europeans, and to their kinsmen and followers goods they otherwise would have paid for with deerskins. But more significantly, the French gifts, by encouraging Choctaw warfare against the Chickasaws, maintained the borderland wars, which preserved the habitat of the deer. When the status of this elite changed, therefore, changes in the forest might soon ensue.

The arrival of the English posed a direct threat to the civil chiefs, although they did not realize it at the time. To them little seemed to have changed. The Spanish would not take effective control of Louisiana until 1769 and throughout the period French traders continued to visit the nation, particularly the Sixtowns. One of these traders informed the Choctaws that the French had merely lost the country for three years at a game of chunky (the national game of Choctaw gamblers); they would soon return. The chiefs, meanwhile, gladly took up English offers to negotiate an end to the Chickasaw wars and looked forward not only to peace but also to the abundance of trade goods which the Choctaws had lacked for many years.[1]

English goods might be abundant, but English gifts proved hard to secure. After some delay, John Stuart, the Indian superintendent for the Southern District, dispatched to Mobile the Choctaw's share of the gifts from an Indian congress held in Savannah that the chiefs had been unable to attend. Major Robert Farmar, the English officer in charge of West Florida, found the gifts so meager that he feared they would only insult the Indians. He therefore refused to distribute them at all. English colonial officials, however, had no intention of providing substantially greater gifts. Among the first instructions sent to Stuart was a letter from Sir Jeffrey Amherst recommending "the utmost economy and frugality" in his conduct of Indian affairs. When faced with a similar shortage of goods, French officials had resorted to hospitality to soothe the feelings of the Choctaws and extend their patience; English officers, both at Mobile and Tombigbee, however, received Choctaw visits with bad grace, complaining of the "vile custom" that compelled them to entertain the medal chiefs at their table and provide food for visiting warriors.[2]

The English had a certain logic in their actions; their frugality and bad manners were only incidentally intended to insult the Choctaws. The English were primarily interested in instructing the Choctaws in the niceties of the market. Under the French, exchanges of gifts, not trade, had been the rule. Now trade, market values, and hard bargaining, not gifts, generosity, and reciprocity, would govern the exchanges. Trade supposedly would make the Choctaws prosperous, but in practice the English traders brought chaos to the entire nation. Peace had allowed a flood of what Stuart called "low traders" to enter the Choctaw towns. The competition among these men for Choctaw deerskins brought the worst trading practices of the English to the fore. They used short weights, downgraded skins, brought immense quantities of liquor up the trading paths, insulted Choctaw men, and seduced or raped the women. The Choctaws, in turn, robbed them of their goods, stole or killed their horses and other livestock, and assaulted them.[3]

With the nation sinking into chaos and discontent during 1764, it became more and more apparent to British officials in and near the nation that the Choctaws would have to be either conciliated or fought. They feared that the Choctaws might soon join in Pontiac's rebellion to the north, but Major Farmar realized that, because of sickness, real English strength in the area amounted to no more than a company and sought to avoid fighting. Military subjugation of the Choctaws seemed far more costly and difficult than simply purchasing their loyalty with the gifts they requested. As a result, Farmar's demands for goods for the Choctaws grew increasingly insistent. By May of 1764 John Stuart wrote to General Thomas Gage that, while he agreed in principle with the decision to end presents, he thought an "immediate change of system in that particular, dangerous with regards to the Choctaws." Farmar, however, had already gone far beyond Stuart's modest proposals. He had promised the Choctaws annual gifts equal to what the French had given them.[4]

Reconciliation of a sort between the English and Choctaws came at the Mobile Congress of 1765, but with the British gifts came some disturbing requests and assertions. The British not only asked the Choctaws to cede them part of the nation's eastern and southern hunting lands, but they also claimed that the medal chiefs served only at English pleasure. The cession caused controversy in the nation, but the chiefs pushed it through. In part they did so because the major areas ceded—along the coast and on the Mobile and southern Tombigbee rivers—were not ancestral Choctaw lands but had come to the nation as they absorbed the remnants of the coastal tribes and those of the Mobile River—the Mobiles, Naniabas, and Tohomes. The chiefs appear to have seen the cession of relatively unproductive pineland and land shared (and disputed) with the Creeks more as a gift to the English than a sale.[5] Tomatly Mingo of Siniasha (Ceneacha) clearly stated the Choctaw reasoning behind the cessions: "as it is acting the parts of Brothers Mutually to Supply each others wants, we are determined amongst ourselves to give you Lands which you may plant."[6]

The Choctaws expected in return annual supplies of goods to satisfy their wants, just as crops from the land annually supplied English needs. When it became apparent to them that the English thought a single payment of goods completed these transactions, they reacted angrily. The Indians' reasoning, based on reciprocity, led them to later deny the validity of this and later cessions.[7]

The chiefs made the cession, but they refused to make further concessions to the British. Particularly, they denied English pretensions to the right to determine medal chiefs. Stuart intended to use the medals to create a set of pliable leaders who would aid him in regulating the trade, which he still believed would eventually render the Choctaws content. The English would simply reward their friends in the nation by conferring "Influence and Power" upon them, and effective management of the Choctaws would automatically follow.[8] The Choctaws, both directly and indirectly, challenged this assumption throughout the congress. In speech after speech the medal chiefs asserted their right to leadership in Choctaw terms. "It is the custom of the Red Men to take Precedence [sic] according to their Seniority," declared Tomatly Mingo, medal chief of Siniasha (Ceneacha) in the Sixtowns. Then he added "I am of the Race of Imongeltcha [Imoklasha, the Peace moiety] and in consequence the Second in Rank in the Choctaw Nation. The Race of Ingholata [Inhulahta, the war Moiety] is before me, but on this day being Invested by the Consent of the Chiefs with the Authority of the Pipe and other ensigns of Peace, I now take the place of Alibamo Mingo. Altho I acknowledge him to be my Superior [sic]."[9]

The chiefs declared their right to determine their titles and to speak in Choctaw terms—the terms of age and experience, of moieties and *iksas*, and of consent and recognition. Such things, they believed, were beyond the reach of the English, and the chiefs expected the English presents only to confirm the status quo. As Albimanon Mingo told Stuart, "I cannot Immagine the Great King could Send the Superintendent to deceive us. In case we deliver up our French Medals & Commissions we expect to receive as good in their place and that we Should bear the Same Authority & be entitled to the Same presents."[10]

The chiefs knew well and admitted their dependency on presents, but they resented the English perception of presents as mere bribes. They explained presents in terms of kinship—of fathers and children, of brothers supporting each other. On this reciprocity the chiefs depended. As Nassuba Mingo said, "I expect my people will receive presents in greater abundance [than from the French], and if we do not, it must proceed from want of Ability, I do not Speak for myself but for my Warriours, their Wives & their Children, *whom I cannot Cloathe, or keep in order without presents*" [emphasis added].[11]

The congress settled little. The chiefs accepted British presents worth about $3,360 but not the English premises that lay behind them. The Choctaws, however, did not obtain all they had expected. They left Mobile with what they felt were promises of annual congresses like those held by the French. Stuart meanwhile departed the congress believing it had rescued the situation among the Choctaws and won them over. He cautioned his superiors that, since the French had accustomed the Choctaws to large annual presents, they must not only regulate the traders but also continue granting gifts until the Indians could be reduced to complete submission. Before six months had passed, however, pressure from above caused Stuart to apologize for the expenses of his superintendency and promise greater economy in the future. The English did not convene a second congress until 1772.[12]

The niggardliness of English officials in the years between 1765 and 1772 caused the tenuous political balance of the nation to deteriorate. The English badly undercut the power of the civil chiefs. At Mobile, Nassuba Mingo, the pro-English great medal chief of Chickasawhay, had frankly told the English that he had to have gifts to keep his warriors under control. The failure of the English to heed this warning cost Nassuba Mingo his life. The Chickasawhays had assimilated the remnants of the Tohomes, Mobiles, and Niniabas, whose land the Choctaws had ceded at Mobile. These people probably formed a core of opposition to the cession and the chiefs who engineered it. And in the Sixtowns many chiefs remained pro-French, unmoved by Nassuba Mingo's pro-English arguments. Without gifts, Nassuba Mingo could do little to counter this growing anti-English feeling. In 1766 the pro-French party murdered him and threatened the lives of three other medal chiefs connected with the English. The southern towns closest to the French, and later the Spanish, at New Orleans were angry over the cession and jealous of the western towns, where pro-British feeling had centered since the civil war; they would remain disaffected for the remainder of the English occupation.[13]

The death of Nassuba Mingo represented an extreme result of English policy; the deterioration of most chiefs' power was incremental. Under English hegemony the chiefs were unable to redistribute goods, maintain order in the villages, or act as effective intermediaries with the Europeans. Their power diminished accordingly.

The major blow to the chiefs, of course, was their loss of annual gifts. They resented this loss bitterly and campaigned for restoration of the presents. Just as important as their inability to make these presents to their followers, however, was their failure to secure peace in the towns. Except for a brief period between 1766 and the summer of 1768, the English traders remained entirely unregulated by English officials. The result was social chaos as liquor became the major trade item among the Choctaws.[14]

At the second congress in Mobile in 1772, Mingo Emmitta of Ibetap okla chito (Bouktoucoulouchito), the nominal Great Chief of the nation, complained that "when the Clattering of the Packhorse Bells are heard at a Distance our Town is Immediately deserted young and old run out to meet them Joyfully crying Rum Rum; they get Drunk, Distraction Mischief Confusion and Disorder are the Consequences and this is the Ruin of our Nation."[15] By 1770 Charles Stuart, John's brother and his agent to the Choctaws, estimated that liquor made up 80 percent of the goods sold in the nation. The trade in liquor created a turmoil in the towns which the chiefs were powerless to stop. Drunken frays led to murders, which were then inevitably followed by revenge killings. Order and peace vanished, and the prestige of the chiefs declined.[16]

The cessation of gifts and the disorder of the towns both reflected a third failure: the chiefs were no longer effective intermediaries with the whites. Despite their promises, the English never secured gunsmiths to replace the ones the French had maintained at Mobile and Fort Tombigbee for years. Indeed, they could not even keep open Fort Tombigbee—the source of provisions, entertainment, and small gifts since the 1730s. The English abandoned it as a military post in 1764 and then as an administrative center in 1768. Within their own towns the chiefs were no more successful in their dealings with the British. Warriors complained of shoddy goods and inflated prices. "What can our White Brethren think of us by giving us such narrow Flaps they don't cover our secret parts and we are in danger of being deprived of Manhood by every Hungry dog That approaches us," Mingo Emmitta asked at Mobile. The warriors demanded intercession with the traders, but the chiefs were helpless and without influence. "My warriors reproach me," Illepotapo, the great medal chief of Chickasawhay, told Stuart plaintively, "and ask why I who am their chief do not obtain Justice for them this makes me ashamed and diminishes my Consequence in the Nation." The older medal chiefs had no goods to redistribute, they could not keep liquor out or maintain the peace of the towns, and they no longer succeeded as intermediaries of the Europeans. For them, the coming of the English had proved disastrous.[17]

English policies weakened the civil aspects of chieftainship, but they simultaneously strengthened the importance of the chiefs as war leaders. The distinctions between war chiefs and civil chiefs had been blurring since the time of Red Shoes. Civil chiefs led their towns to war, and war leaders had become medal chiefs. The English accelerated this shift toward the war leaders by making even friendship and alliance a commodity. Instead of annual gifts, the English paid for services rendered. When Choctaws served English troops as scouts or auxiliaries, their leaders were paid for their services. As a result, prominent war leaders such as Red Captain of Scanapa and Franchimastabe of West Yazoo procured goods for their followers when other chiefs did not. In 1765, for example, both chiefs helped escort English troops up the Mississippi and secured in return payment for their warriors. Such men became both firm British allies and influential leaders in the nation. Red Captain had remained an English partisan throughout the 1750s, and the British looked to him for aid when they obtained West Florida. After his death in 1767, Stuart called him "one of the best and bravest Indians I ever knew," adding that "he was the principal support of our interest in that nation, it will not be an easy matter to replace him."[18]

Payment for direct service to the English, however, became but a small part of the support the British gave war leaders. The exigencies of English Indian policy in the Southeast by the mid-1760s had induced the British to incite and encourage what would be a decade of warfare between the Choctaws and Creeks. Unwilling to meet the price of annual presents, unable to govern their own traders, faced with dangerous discontent among the Choctaws and even more serious discontent among their neighbors the Creeks, the English emulated the tactics of the French. They encouraged intertribal warfare to weaken powerful nations and divert them from their problems with the Europeans. Since the English had taken possession of West Florida, a series of borderland murders had upset relations between the Creeks and Choctaws.[19] The situation had not yet degenerated into war, but the potential was there. With a logic derived from a crude ethnography, British officials recognized the opportunity. As General Gage, Stuart's immediate superior in North America, wrote in 1764:

And we are now in that happy situation to the Southard to be courted by all the Nations, from the quarrels they have with one another. Their Education and the whole Business of their lives is war and hunting and it is not possible for us to divert that active spirit inherent in them as well as the rest of Mankind, to occupations which are more innocent and more industrious. The Savage Nations, therefore, can never be a longtime at peace & if we have not the dexterity enough to turn this rage for war from ourselves and direct it to other objects. I fear we shall often feel the ill effects of it.[20]

When the Mobile Congress of 1765 failed to fulfill Stuart's expectations of conciliating the Choctaws and the superintendent simultaneously found himself confronted with the threat of conflict between the Creeks and Georgia frontiersmen, Stuart and Governor Johnstone of West Florida set about turning Gage's ethnographic musings into actual policy. The English used a series of revenge killings between the Choctaws and Creeks to incite a war. James Colbert, an English trader, apparently acting under orders from Governor Johnstone, persuaded the Choctaws to reply to the last killing not with another murder but with numerous war parties.[21] These Choctaw war parties killed six Creeks, and the two nations were at war. Johnstone could not help gloating:

> The present Rupture is very fortunate for us more specially as it has been effected without giving them the least possibility of thinking we had any share in it. It was undoubtedly our interest to foment the dispute between these Nations. But considering the strong propensity mankind possesses for divulging what they know, it was difficult to bring matters to this point without appearing an accessory. Though I claim some merit in this transaction, yet certainly their own Passions chiefly operated to produce the Effect we wished. I am of the opinion we should now feed the war.[22]

To "feed the war" the English often supplied and provisioned Choctaw war parties at a time when little other English aid entered the nation. War leaders had access to goods denied others. The English hoped the new war would chastise the Creeks and "bring them to their senses," and they strove assiduously to prevent the two tribes from making peace. When the Creeks, angered by the English instigation of Choctaw attacks, killed two traders, Johnstone even dreamed of an alliance of all the southern tribes with the English to crush the Creeks completely. Stuart, however, wished to avoid an expensive war and was content to let the Choctaws and Creeks dominate the bloodletting.[23]

These wars increased the influence of war leaders but came at a cost. During the 1760s the fighting went badly for the Choctaws. The dependent villages of the Chickasawhay on the Tombigbee had to be abandoned, along with some of the border towns of the Northeastern District. All but the far western towns lived under threat of attack. By 1771 each nation had lost about 300 people. Perhaps a sign of how important the wars had become for chiefs trying to maintain their influence was the large number of medal chiefs who died in them. Red Captain was the most famous casualty, ambushed and killed in 1767 after most of the 800-man army he led decided to return home. Although the war went better for the Choctaws in the 1770s, more medal chiefs lost their lives. Tattoully Mastabe, the great medal chief of Kunshak (Cousas), died with five other members of a war party in 1773, and that same year two more medal chiefs also died, apparently casualties of the war. In 1774 Pya Houma, Red Captain's nephew and successor, also lost his life in the fighting.[24]

As they had done so often before, the Choctaws divided over the war, this time along roughly geographical lines. The western towns and many of the northeastern towns wanted peace, but the southern towns—Chickasawhay, Yowani, and especially the Sixtowns—insisted on war. Their formal rationale for war was vengeance, but traders indicated that this was only part of the reason. The war itself seems to have reinvigorated the hunting grounds of the lower Tombigbee by banishing hunters from them, and this area became a prize which neither the Lower Creeks nor the Sixtowns—the two groups who claimed them—wished to surrender. Only the coming of the American Revolution and the need of the British to obtain aid from both the Creeks and the Choctaws induced the English to help end the war.[25]

In the little more than a decade between 1763 and 1776, the new mixture of trade, liquor, and war brought by the English corroded those parts of Choctaw society that rested on the older hunting economy. There was a new tone to the speeches of the Choctaw leaders who gathered for the second congress with the English in 1772, a recognition of dependency that was almost painful. In 1765 the chiefs had challenged the English, asserting reciprocity against the demands of the English for purely commercial dealings, arguing for their native right to rule against English assertions of power. In 1772 most of these arguments were absent from the discussions. Speakers at the council confessed their need for white goods. While a familiar element of Indian speeches, rarely had this need been put with such abjectness. They acknowledged as well their own ignorance and helplessness. "We are poor and Incapable of making Necessaries for ourselves," lamented Illepotapo, the great medal chief of Chickasawhay; Captain Ouma of Siniasha (Seneacha) seconded him, asserting that the Choctaws were "Ignorant and helpless as the Beasts in the woods Incapable of making Necessaries for ourselves our sole dependence is upon you." [26] This tone of self-abasement had been missing from earlier requests for goods.

At least in part, the abjectness of these confessions of dependency came from the real vulnerability of the men who made the speeches. The old chiefs were almost all dead. Mingo Emmitta of Boktokolo chito (Bouktoucoulouchito) began his speech in 1772 by noting that since the last congress five great medal chiefs, as well as other leading men, had died. Captain Ouma prefaced his remarks by informing the English that he alone of the leading chiefs of the Sixtowns still lived. The death of so many chiefs during a time of great social turmoil undermined the basis of the Choctaw hierarchy. When old chiefs could hardly maintain the prestige of chieftainship except through war, how could new chiefs validate their power? Aspirants could claim the medal chieftainships by right of birth or by right of their prominence in war, but they could legitimate their claims only by receiving goods to redistribute. To further complicate matters, the English created more claimants to leadership by capriciously bestowing medals on men whom no Choctaw felt were entitled to chieftainship. In 1770, for example, Charles Stuart complained that Lieutenant Governor Monfort Brown of West Florida had bestowed "a medal on the most worthless fellow without knowing his Character and only from some information he gave him, which would have been better paid with a keg of rum." [27]

The critical factor, however, remained trade goods. Without goods no claimant to power could validate his right to a medal or to chieftainship. A medal became meaningful only when it gave the bearer access to the goods necessary to maintain a position of leadership. With the English refusing annual gifts, some Choctaws turned to the Spanish, who had finally assumed power in New Orleans, for the necessary gifts, but abundant presents would not be obtained from the Spaniards until after the beginning of the American Revolution. Without goods and without power except in war, and with war itself taking heavy toll of recognized chiefs, chieftainship weakened; no consensus emerged in the towns. As a result, when the English finally convened the congress in 1772, they found themselves beseiged by candidates for office.[28] These men needed the English goods, which, when properly distributed, alone could assure their position. As Stuart reported: "The Choctaws have been so accustomed to obey chiefs made by the French and us that they have lost all idea of choosing rulers for themselves. . . . I filled up the vacant medals with persons well attached to us, and in other Respects good men—It would surprise your excellency to see the competition and anxiety of the Candidates for these Honors."[29]

Stuart not only selected the chiefs, he also stressed to the Choctaws the new basis of the chiefs' power and their new duties. Annual presents would not be given the Choctaws; instead, the English would pay only for services provided. The French, Stuart contended, had given the Choctaws annual presents only because of Choctaw services as soldiers; the English did not employ them as such and thus did not have to pay them. Instead, he argued, the English gave the Choctaws abundant trade, which was far more valuable than presents. That the Choctaws did not kill enough deer to take full advantage of this was their own fault. The superintendent then proceeded to denounce the chiefs for not adequately protecting the traders; he announced that in the future presents would be given only to those who protected Englishmen in their towns. In the ceremony bestowing the medals, he reiterated the new conditions of chieftainship. The medals went to such "of you Red men as have appeared to deserve them."[30] Stuart urged the recipients to do "their Duty and recommended to them the Strict observation of Treaties, doing Justice protecting their Traders and restraining Licentousness of their young Warriors & he afterwards presented them to their People as their Governors and told them That all Messages or Orders from the King through his officers would be Directed to the Medal Chiefs enjoyned obedience to them as the only means of obtaining Honors or being Taken notice of by him."[31]

Stuart appointed the chiefs, and the chiefs distributed the presents, but the number of honors Stuart bestowed only revealed the fragmentation of power in the nation. There were now nine great medal chiefs, seventeen small medal chiefs, and sixty-five gorget chiefs, or captains. All of these chiefs received personal presents. In addition the English specified, almost certainly in consultation with the chiefs, a large number of other leading warriors and headmen entitled to a share of the presents. On this English list were 223 men in the Sixtowns, and 239 in the Northeastern District. The fragmentation of power which the French had fought but finally acknowledged had, if anything, grown worse. Leadership was almost entirely competitive; the old criteria of birth, age, and performance had lost much of their force. By the 1770s the medal chiefs, more than ever before, had become chiefs simply because Europeans had given them medals. Their traditional functions were in shambles; their real power was often virtually nonexistent. In a conference between the Sixtowns and the English in 1778, Mingo Ouma Chito, a warrior of Tala (Talpa), stood up and gave a "long & manly" denunciation of the chiefs for not keeping better order and protecting the traders. Charles Stuart rewarded him with a gorget and recommended the Indian to his brother, the superintendent, for a medal. With such ease could a warrior now embarrass the chiefs and gain a chieftainship for himself.[32]

In the late 1770s, with Choctaw leaders already numbering in the hundreds, Spanish attempts to win over the nation created even more contenders for power. James Colbert reported in late 1779 that, thanks to Spanish efforts, there was "hardly a Blackguard in the Sixtowns but has Medals, Gorget, & Red Coats given them." As Red Topknot of Oskelagna (Yellow Cane) explained, he had received from the Spanish the presents and a gorget which the English had denied him. "Two people loves us," he told Colbert, "whoever gives us the most will be the most Regarded." In the Sixtowns especially, as the older patterns of leadership collapsed, Europeans were reduced to courting the allegiance not of the nation or districts or towns or factions or *iksas*, but rather of individuals.[33]

A similar fragmentation took place in the internal organization of the nation. Until 1764 enumerators of Choctaw towns sometimes divided the nation into dominant and dependent towns. When Lieutenant Ford journeyed through the nation in 1764, he recorded this pattern and listed Chickasawhay, West Yazoo (Yarso), Kunshak (Couses), Scanapa (Escannapaw), Iyanabi (Yannaby), Ibetap okla chito (Beetapucculo), and Tombeckbe as the leading towns. The number of towns and villages subordinate to each, at least in European eyes, ranged from eighteen for West Yazoo to none for Tombeckbe. Ford is the last man to record this pattern. In the English, Spanish, and American censuses that follow, towns are listed individually. The multiplication of chiefs and warriors entitled to presents and the weakening of the medal chiefs seems to have been paralleled throughout the nation by a growing independence of smaller towns and villages.[34]

English policy had greatly accelerated the fragmentation of power and the decline of chieftainship that had been underway for decades, yet when Stuart and other officials acted high-handedly, they thought they were only duplicating earlier French policy. That they could so rapidly undermine the position of the chiefs shows how much chieftainship depended on the play-offs—peace-war, English-French, gifts-trade—that the imperial cession had rendered obsolete. The chiefs' attempts to replace these play-offs with new ones either failed or came too late. A Spanish-English rivalry comparable to the French-English rivalry did not arise until the late 1770s. The Creek war did not bring the amount of goods into the nation that the Chickasaw war had. Trade replaced gifts as the dominant form of material exchange.

Because of the close ties between Choctaw politics, economics, and environment, the political chaos of the nation had repercussions in the forest. Presents limited the amount of goods the nation as a whole had to obtain through trade and thus also limited the number of deer that hunters had to kill. The absence of presents meant either a cutback in European manufactures or an increase in hunting. Liquor insured that hunters would procure far more deerskins than the number necessary to exchange for the goods no longer received as gifts. Liquor was the only commodity that the Choctaws desired not in finite amounts, but in virtually infinite amounts. Liquor immensely increased the potential volume of the deerskin trade and thus the potential pressure on deer. The growing political failure of the chiefs left the hunters increasingly dependent on traders for guns, tools, and clothing, while the introduction of liquor led them to waste the proceeds of their hunt on rum. The old political and economic balance was clearly failing, and as it declined, it destroyed the ecological balance of the woodlands.

The older structural check of warfare could no longer prevent this. Before 1763 the cessation of presents and the introduction of liquor probably would have had fewer environmental consequences because for most of the century the Chickasaw wars had reduced hunting pressure on the most productive hunting lands of the nation by simply making it too dangerous to hunt them. In 1763, however, when the English made a lasting peace between the Chickasaws and Choctaws, members of the two nations intermarried and began sharing the borderland hunting grounds equally. Indeed, relations between the nations became so close that Ibetap olka chito (Ebilipougoulochio) and three other northern border towns actually moved to affiliate themselves with the Chickasaws. Both nations were now English allies, and the English could mediate disputes which previously might have brought war.[35]

The Chickasaw wars had cost the Choctaws dearly, but peace was not to be an unmixed blessing. For more than a generation the major restraints upon hunters in these lands had been external—the threat of foreign war parties. With this threat gone, the Choctaws had to rely on internal sanctions to regulate hunting. The maintenance of such sanctions, however, was aborted by the arrival of the numerous unregulated English traders in the nation and the liquor they brought with them.

It is the interaction of liquor, peace, and trade that shaped the Choctaw environment of the 1760s and 1770s. Together they proved a volatile mixture, one deadly to the white-tailed deer of the forests. The key ingredient was liquor. The absence of Chickasaw war parties and the appearance of English traders alone were not sufficient to bring on overhunting; there was a limit to the number of guns, blankets, hoes, kettles, beads, and other goods the Choctaws desired. In time, the cessation of presents and the end of the Chickasaw wars by themselves probably would have made significant inroads into the deer population, but the massive introduction of liquor makes this mere supposition. In fact, rum controlled the pace of hunting.

Why the desire for liquor became so strong among the Choctaws—and most other Indian peoples for that matter—has never been adequately explained. The Choctaws themselves sometimes put it in almost biological terms. As Captain Ouma, a small medal chief of Nashobawenya (Nahhoubawayna) in the Sixtowns, explained in council, rum was like a woman; "when a man wanted her—and saw her—He must have her." Biological explanations seem faulty, however, simply because liquor did not immediately become a problem in the nation. The French had used small amounts of brandy in trade with the Choctaws since the turn of the century; they regarded the practice as dangerous, but there had been no disastrous consequences for the Indians. In the 1730s the French described the Choctaws as a temperate people. In addition liquor did not undermine every nation that it touched. The Pawnees, as will be discussed in the next section, resisted its inroads for generations. The eruption of liquor as a major social problem among the Choctaws after 1763 seems inextricably combined with other elements of social change that created unacceptable levels of individual stress. The continuous warfare, the civil war, the smallpox epidemic of the late 1740s, the poverty of the late French period, the arrogance of English officials, and the abuses of English traders, probably all combined to create widespread stress in the nation and exposed it to the relief and the ravages of liquor. Many Choctaws seem initially to have seen liquor as an actual social good and praised its benefits. One Choctaw man, for example, credited rum with saving his children from smallpox. In any case, once rum drinking became prevalent, it, in turn, aggravated the very social problems that had induced people to drink and so became part of a vicious and unbreakable circle.[36]

The environmental consequences of the rum trade stemmed both from the incredible Choctaw demand for it and from the deleterious effects it had on older methods of social control. Both should be looked at in turn. Charles Stuart's estimate of 1770 that liquor comprised 80 percent of the Choctaw trade has already been noted; he never had any reason to revise it downward during the remainder of the decade. In 1776 John Stuart condemned anew "this Destructive Commerce," asserting that "for one skin taken in exchange for British

Manufacture, there are five gotten in exchange for liquor; the Effect of which is that the Indians are poor wretched, naked, and discontented." In three months he claimed 30,000 gallons of rum had been traded out of Pensacola. Choctaw towns seemed awash in rum. Bernard Romans thought the amount of liquor the Indians drank incredible. When Charles Stuart visited the nation in March of 1778, he found that those who had returned from hunting "were very unfit to be spoke with being constantly drunk." This incident was not merely an isolated spree by returning hunters. In May of 1778, nearly three months after the end of the winter hunt, Stuart visited the Sixtowns to hold a council. It was repeatedly delayed because so many Choctaws were drunk.[37]

The Choctaws, quite simply, hunted for liquor. Drunkenness was the final product of their hunt. At times the quest of the hunters for rum was intentional; more often, as Captain Ouma explained, the Choctaws simply succumbed to their craving for alcohol once the traders offered it to them. Choctaws who fully intended to trade for clothes or tools ended up getting drunk instead. In early 1770 at Natchez, for instance, Choctaw hunters traded away the skins taken during their winter hunt for rum and woke up to find that the entire proceeds of months of labor was a collective hangover. In this case, and in others like it, the warriors' frustration and resentment led to violence. Under such circumstances the Choctaws could take more deer than ever before and yet grow steadily poorer and more abject.[38]

Liquor not only introduced a commodity that the Choctaws could be induced to trade for in almost infinite quantities, it also reduced the chances that any order could be maintained in the hunt. The best evidence for this is indirect: the breakdown of social order in the villages. Like most woodland peoples, the Choctaws at contact had virtually no problem with violence within their towns. Fear of witchcraft and the certainty of revenge from the victim's *iksa* seem to have been very effective checks.[39]

All of this changed with liquor. By 1772 many Choctaws were conspiring to expel the English for "bringing so much rum among them and thereby causing great disturbance," but the trade remained, and Charles Stuart chronicled the result in 1777. In a letter to his brother he reported that as "I came thro' their Towns I saw nothing but rum Drinking and Women Crying over the Dead bodies of their relations who have died by Rum." The next year Stuart reemphasized the turmoil liquor brought, asserting that it was "the cause of their killing each other daily, it is the Cause of every disturbance in the Nation . . . and of this Town's [Mobile] being constantly in an Uproar." In 1777 one chief claimed the liquor trade had cost the lives of 1,000 Choctaws in eighteen months. If liquor could so thoroughly demolish the restraints that kept peace within the nation, if men, when drunk or seeking drink, men murdered each other and thereby sentenced themselves or their relatives to virtually certain death at the hands of their victim's *iksa*, then it is unlikely that these same men restrained themselves from overhunting when seeking deer to trade for liquor.[40]

Although the new combination of liquor, trade, and peace made overhunting a possibility, game disappeared at different rates in different sections of the nation. To begin with, game was not uniformly abundant in the borderlands. At the end of the French and Indian War in 1763, the old Chickasaw borderlands of the west, north, and northeast were full of deer that had been protected by years of warfare. The hunting grounds of the Chickasawhay and Sixtown Choctaws along the Amite River and Lake Pontchartrain had also remained productive partly because these regions had lacked access to English traders for most of the French period. Most of the rest of the coastal and southern borderlands was pinelands and normally held few deer. On the eastern border Choctaw settlement had expanded into the Tombigbee valley earlier in the century, and this expansion, along with the presence of Creek hunters who traded with the English, had put substantial pressure on game populations. The evidence that game actually had declined in this region by 1763 is largely inferential. When, during the hunting season of 1764, Lieutenant Ford visited Chickasawhay, the large town whose best hunting grounds were in the floodplain of the Tombigbee, he found most of the men still present in the town instead of out hunting. A shortage of game may have kept them at home. That the town suffered from a depletion of deer is also suggested by its reputation as a collection of stock thieves and later, more positively, as a center of stock raising in the nation.[41]

The northeastern and western towns thus controlled a disproportionate share of the nation's game in the 1760s, and English settlers further hurt the position of the Sixtowns by moving into the Amite and Bienville river areas and threatening the last secure and productive southern hunting ground. With the increased deerskin trade, the southern towns—the Sixtowns, Chickasawhay, and Yowani—increased hunting pressure on a region less able to sustain it than the northern borderlands. This made the Tombigbee hunting grounds, disputed with the Creeks and reinvigorated by war, even more crucial to the Choctaws.[42]

While competition for deer prolonged war on the southern borders by the late 1760s, signs of game depletion began to occur in the rest of the nation by the early 1770s. At the Mobile Congress of 1772 Choctaws complained of white hunters' taking their game and thus revealed a growing concern that deer were decreasing. Perhaps similar concerns over the decline of game convinced Bernard Romans in 1770 that game had already vanished. It was not merely the arrival of white hunters that caused the decline. The Choctaws themselves, under pressure from the traders, appear to have extended their hunting season at both ends. Romans stayed in the nation only until early November, but already a quarter of the Choctaw men were absent in the woods. To have so many men in the woods so early in the season indicates an earlier start to the hunting season and thus greater pressure on the deer.[43]

The evidence for the growing depletion of deer in the 1770s, except for Romans who badly overstated it, is inferential; clear and convincing evidence of overhunting did not appear until the 1780s. In any case, the shifting European politics of the region during the 1770s probably made the consequences of declining deer populations seem manageable to the Choctaws. Indeed, for a time, it appeared that with new imperial rivalries the old balances might yet be restored.

The American Revolution renewed competition between different groups of whites for control of the Southeast. The English then sought Choctaw aid against their own Anglo-American colonists; when the Spanish entered the war as allies of the colonies, they too bid for Choctaw favor. Once again the Choctaws could play Europeans off against each other, and they did so with their usual skill. The nation splintered into factions, largely by district, with the Sixtowns showing the most interest in Spanish solicitations and the other districts more often remaining pro-English. The existence of such factions ensured that both Spanish and English gifts flowed into the nation. Once again the Europeans denounced the Choctaws as the "meanest of all mercenaries"—the kind of language that could mean that the whites once more had to deal with the nation at least partially on its own terms.[44]

For six years, from 1776 to 1781, congresses and meetings occurred annually, and each brought the customary presents. Gifts had once again asserted their primacy in Indian diplomacy. Farquhar Bethune, the British subagent among the Choctaws, informed his superiors that "Reason and Rhetoric will fall to the ground unless supported by strouds and duffells. Liberality alone with the Indians is true Eloquence."[45] And this was expensive eloquence. Alexander Cameron, who after John Stuart's death took over half his old responsibilities—the western nations of the southern superintendency, justified his heavy expenditures by explaining, "The Indians in General have been long accustomed to receive large gratuities even when their services were not immediately called for, and they now consider it their due." If the English did not meet Choctaw demands, Cameron warned, the Spanish would and thus gain the allegiance of the nation. Spanish gifts to the Choctaws and neighboring nations were impressive, and their value rose precipitously after 1778. In 1779, 1780, 1782, 1783, and 1784, Spanish officials noted extraordinary expenses connected with Indian presents.[46]

Congresses and councils represented only part of the gift-giving. When individual Choctaws visited Mobile, each received presents according to his rank and importance; when the agents visited the nation, they also distributed gifts. Such visits and gifts became so common that supposedly every warrior among the Sixtowns had received some token of British affection in 1779, and these people still felt relatively deprived in comparison with the warriors of the Northeastern and Western districts. Besides these gifts, the British gave goods and supplies to those Choctaws who actually assisted them in the defense of Mobile, Natchez, and Pensacola. The various warriors who gathered at Pensacola in the spring of 1781 received £6,000 alone.[47]

Theoretically these gifts reduced pressure on the deer since the goods Choctaws received as presents would not have to be obtained through the hunt and trade. The maintenance of the liquor trade during these years, however, renders this problematical. It is more likely that hunting pressure and trade continued at relatively high levels. Deerskins which were not needed for manufactured goods could still be used to purchase liquor, and indeed the gifts themselves could be traded for liquor. Despite British and Spanish gifts, a British official described the Choctaws in 1780 as "a poor ragged Sett without Horses or other Effects." As long as the liquor trade continued unabated, even the restoration of gifts did not insure prosperity or a decline in commercial hunting.[48]

Probably, only military recruitment, by reducing the number of hunters, and the changing fortunes of war, by interrupting the supply of trade goods, had any significant effect on hunting pressure, and even this was sporadic. In February of 1781, for instance, 744 Choctaws who normally would have been hunting deer were helping to defend Pensacola from the attacking Spaniards. That same year Spanish victories finally severed English supply routes to the Choctaws. Since the Spanish and French traders who operated out of New Orleans bought their goods from the English, they were in no position to take up the slack. As a result, in 1782 Choctaw hunters took fewer deer primarily because they lacked the powder and ammunition to hunt for them.[49]

Although this shortage of ammunition kept up the enthusiasm of some western Choctaws for a return of the British, the English cause was hopeless by this late date, and in 1784 the Spanish and Choctaws came to terms. Fifty-eight towns attended the huge Indian congress held in Mobile in 1784, and there each town was feasted and received lavish gifts and promises of a well-regulated trade in English goods to be supplied by the British firm of Panton and Leslie. The Spanish had little choice in granting to Panton and Leslie a trading concession, which included exemption from duties. Not only did the Indians prefer English manufactures, which the Spanish could not otherwise obtain, but also the Spanish had no home market for the deerskins the Choctaws secured. The Spanish needed trade goods to hold Choctaw allegiance, and to obtain trade goods they needed Panton and Leslie. Since their whole policy in West Florida, an area whose exact boundaries were in dispute with the United States, depended on using the Indians as a bulwark against the advancing Americans, they had to surrender much control over the trade to secure the goods they required.[50]

Superficially this new Spanish-American rivalry seemed to offer the possibility of duplicating the French-English play-off which had protected the borderlands and preserved Choctaw autonomy earlier in the century. The Choctaws, for their part, certainly tried to establish such a play-off. As before, the nation split into factions, with the Sixtowns and other southern towns becoming predominantly pro-Spanish while various groups in the western and northeastern towns wavered between the Americans and the Spaniards. The Choctaw goal was to facilitate the flow of gifts into the nation and to do this, the Indians had to convince both the American and Spanish that they had friends within the Indian nation. The Americans, whose land hunger the Choctaws recognized, were dangerous, but they could be useful in reminding the Spanish of the need for presents to retain Choctaw loyalty. It was a lesson the Spaniards learned well; as Governor Gayoso de Lemos of Natchez phrased it: "Whilst you bestow on Indians they are devoted to you, but as soon as their avarice leads them to think they will do better elsewhere, they forget your bounties without the least return of gratitude."[51]

Gayoso may have cherished the illusion held by colonial administrators that Europeans never forgot a favor and always acted selflessly for the best interests of the Indians, but the Choctaws did not share that belief. They were intent on using the Spanish-American rivalry to protect their own interests. When the Spanish, after their large distributions at the Mobile Congress, cut back their presents in 1785, the western Choctaws countered by threatening an American alliance. Choctaw overtures to the Americans continued through the 1790s, peaking between 1792 and 1794, when there were numerous congresses. These meetings centered on American attempts to recruit allies against the northern Indian confederation and Spanish plans to create an anti-American confederation of their own in the south.[52]

By the late 1790s, however, the United States had far less incentive to conciliate the Choctaws than they had earlier in the decade. The defeat of the northern confederation at Fallen Timbers in 1794 and the agreement by the Spanish, in the Treaty of San Lorenzo in 1795, to surrender all claim to lands north of the 31st parallel had strengthened the American position considerably. Although American officials in Natchez found the lack of presents a constant source of embarrassment, since importunate Choctaws demanded that they fulfill their earlier promises of gifts and denounced them as liars, their discomfiture meant little to national leaders. Even when funds for annual presents were finally allotted, the governor of the Mississippi Territory found them so inadequate that he proposed simply telling the Choctaws that the United States would give them no presents and that if they molested the whites, the Americans would destroy them. The actual message, delivered by Agent John McKee, lacked this bravado, but the immediate implications were the same. He told the Choctaws to look to agriculture, not presents, for their well-being. After the Spanish withdrew from the ceded area in 1797, their presents too diminished. The Spaniards later made some gifts to the Choctaws during times of crisis, but these were neither as sizable nor as regular as those before 1795.[53]

This new system of gifts, even while it lasted, unfortunately fulfilled the internal political needs of the chiefs far better than it did the larger needs of the nation. Playing off the Spanish and the Americans did allow the Choctaws to retain their political autonomy, but it did not stop their relentless slide into economic dependence. Gifts alone could no longer do that. Choctaw demand for European commodities was no longer finite; the liquor trade had rendered it literally infinite. Goods obtained as gifts no longer meant a roughly equivalent decline in the amount of goods that had to be obtained through trade. Presents merely allowed the Choctaws to divert even more deerskins into the liquor traffic.

Choctaw commercial hunting had resumed on a large scale as soon as the Spanish agreement with Panton and Leslie made it possible. In 1786 Governor Miro moved to procure $120,000 worth of goods to supply the trade of the Choctaws and Creeks out of Mobile. In 1792 the Americans estimated the total commerce of the Choctaws and Chickasaws at $100,000 a year and it is doubtful if this included the entire liquor trade. Since the Choctaws far outnumbered the Chickasaws, the preponderance of this trade almost certainly belonged to them. How much liquor added to this trade is problematical. The Spanish called Franchimastabe's town of West Yazoo a village of drunkards in 1792. Liquor continued to be heavily traded, but now apparently whites sold liquor only for deerskins; they did not give credit. Thus a Choctaw hunter might obtain goods from a trader on credit, but on the way home meet another trader with liquor and give him his deerskins instead. In such a situation liquor did not so much add to the value of the trade as make it difficult for some traders to collect their debts. Part of the large sums eventually owed Panton and Leslie arose from transactions such as this. Since competition among the small traders—most of whom were supplied by Panton and Leslie—often became cutthroat, the Choctaws had numerous opportunities to run up sizable debts.[54]

Under such conditions the pressure on deer remained relentless. If the Choctaws paid for $50,000 worth of goods a year and their deerskins brought an average of $.50 each, then Choctaw hunters had to kill at least 100,000 deer a year. Since there were between 4,000 and 5,000 hunters during this period, each one would have had to kill a minimum of 20 to 25 deer a year, and, as shall be discussed later, there are indications that the kill was much higher. If these crude calculations are correct, therefore, the annual Choctaw kill of deer had increased sixfold since De Bienville estimated a trade of 15,000 skins annually in 1725.[55]

By the 1780s the depleted borderlands could no longer absorb hunting on this scale. Normally this situation would have increased tensions between neighboring nations and eventually provoked intertribal warfare, yet in the 1780s it did not do so. Since the whole purpose of Spanish gifts was to preserve intertribal peace and present a united front against the Americans, the Spaniards not only pledged the tribes to peace but also intervened in incidents that once might have led to borderland warfare. Ready to compensate the kin of murder victims and negotiate settlements, the Spanish quieted quarrels east of the Mississippi and encouraged the Choctaws and other eastern nations to seek game west of the Mississippi.[56]

The depletion of game affected the Sixtowns first, but gradually it reached all sections of the nation. Unable to take from their old hunting grounds the number of deer that the trade required, the Choctaws crossed the Mississippi and began wintering in the Red and Arkansas river valleys, hunting for deer and buffalo. Hunters from other sections of the nation joined them there. During the 1790s commercial hunting in the Tombigbee River area and other eastern areas grew increasingly more difficult; little large game survived there by the turn of the century. Game remained more abundant along the Yazoo River in the west, but even here not enough remained to fill the needs of all the hunters of the western towns. They, too, crossed the Mississippi in the late eighteenth and early nineteenth century.[57]

This movement across the Mississippi allowed Choctaw men to persist in the hunt long after the productivity of their own hunting lands had declined, but inevitably it involved them in war. The Caddos, the Osages, and the small nations of Louisiana and Arkansas did not yield their hunting grounds to the Choctaws willingly. From the 1780s on, Choctaw warfare centered in the west, and virtually its sole motivation was to gain access to trans-Mississippi hunting grounds. In the west Pushmataha, the leading chief of the Sixtowns and the most famous nineteenth-century Choctaw chief, first gained prominence in the wars against the Caddos and Osage. As warriors from other parts of the nation crossed the river to hunt, they too became involved in warfare. In 1794 warriors of the eastern towns were engaged against the Osage; in the fall of 1798 large war parties departed against the Caddos; and in 1807 warriors from the western towns were also engaged in fighting across the Mississippi. Final peace with the Osages did not come until the 1820s.[58]

The trans-Mississippi hunting grounds were worth fighting over, especially for a society where hunting and fighting had proved to be complementary and productive enterprises for nearly a century. In the early years the hunts seem to have proved quite lucrative. In 1793 Galiot la Fleche, a Frenchman traveling on the Mississippi, met a party of twenty-five Choctaw men and their families returning home from the hunt. They had fifteen horses "laden with pelts" and two pirogues full of skins. If all the hides La Fleche mentions were deerskins, as is likely, then the horses were each carrying 150 pounds, and the pirogues 500 to 700 skins. Since each deerskin traded by the Choctaws averaged 2.5 pounds, the pack animals carried 900 skins, and in the boats there were an additional 1,000 to 1,400. This averages out to a minimum kill of seventy-six deer for each hunter in the party. Yields of this size seem to have brought substantial amounts of goods into the nation in the 1790s.[59]

These incursions across the Mississippi, however, did not so much salvage the old hunting economy as postpone its collapse. There were no longer any means of protecting game or the ecological systems on which the hunt depended. Only a shadow of the political, social, and economic balance that had brought environmental stability to the

Mississippi forests for a century remained. Warfare no longer served to regulate the hunt; rather, it supported an effective and relatively well-organized form of piracy. The Choctaws were invading other people's lands. As large as the temporary yields from this invasion might be, stability was impossible. The Choctaws, lured into the market by liquor, were now its prisoners. As game declined and Choctaw debts rose, they were forced to hunt farther and farther west until game beyond the Mississippi also declined. As a response to changed conditions, expansion to the west proved abortive, but it was not without its effects on the nation.

As the trans-Mississippi hunting grounds grew in importance, small hunting groups began to identify their interests more with the western lands than with their homeland. Since the hunting grounds were now so far away, the Choctaw hunters spent far more time away from the towns. Some decided to settle permanently on the other side of the Mississippi. The villages there probably originated from hunters and their families who remained at a hunting encampment and planted corn instead of returning to their town. Eventually such villages might evolve into permanent Choctaw settlements, or else their inhabitants might leave to settle other sites in the region.[60]

Choctaws who moved across the river were attempting to recreate the older agricultural-hunting life of their homeland in the lands west of the Mississippi. Forced to choose between familiar places and familiar ways, they chose to retain the way they had lived over the place they had lived in. This became an increasingly popular response to the shortage of game east of the river. In 1805 John Sibley, the American Indian superintendent for the Orleans Territory, reported that 80 Choctaw warriors, who with their families would have represented several hundred people, had settled west of the Mississippi. By 1816 estimates of the number of Choctaws in the trans-Mississippi country had increased to 1,500.[61]

Many other people hunted in the west but never settled there, and dislocation for them became in some ways more profound than for those who actually moved their homes. In the early nineteenth century new descriptions of the Choctaws as a restless, wandering, "gypsy-like" people began to occur in the literature. Sibley mentioned "rambling hunting parties scattered all over Louisiana" in 1805 and claimed the Choctaws were disliked by both native nations and whites.

Many of these roving parties dispensed with returning to their native towns for several years at a time, and when game declined west of the river, they became frontier beggars and stock thieves.[62]

For the majority of the Choctaws, however, the hunt remained only a temporary excursion away from their towns. It preserved something of the social role and status of the warriors, and it gave them continued access to the European goods, but the price of this dislocation during the nineteenth century was growing indebtedness and poverty. In an age where the word had not yet even acquired its economic meaning, the Choctaws were becoming underdeveloped.[63]

Choctaw indebtedness to Europeans and Americans had become sizable by the early 1800s. The easily obtained credit of the flush hunting years of the 1790s had put the Choctaws $16,091 in debt to Panton and Leslie by 1796. This figure rapidly grew to $48,000 by the turn of the century. This was only part of the Choctaw debt. When the American government took over the trade and opened a factory, or government trading house, on the Tombigbee in 1803, Choctaw hunters returning from the west added the government to their list of creditors. In 1806 Indian debts—largely Choctaw—at the trading house amounted to $4,000 and climbed to over $12,000 by 1822. Since Choctaws also traded at the Arkansas post west of the Mississippi, this represented only part of what they owed to the United States government. Panton and Leslie bought up, at sizable discounts, the debts of many small traders, but the outstanding claims against the Choctaws held by the rest drove their total indebtedness still higher. Proceeds from the hunt made no inroads into this mounting burden of debt. Game was declining and many, perhaps most, of the skins the Choctaws did obtain were traded away for liquor.[64]

As long as the Choctaws remained a significant force in the balance of power between Spain and the United States, this growing economic weakness could be offset by political strength. Neither the United States nor Spain pressed debt claims or cut off trade as long as they valued the Choctaws as potential allies. Although the Choctaws suffered from poor terms of trade, the consequences were postponed; the whites took no drastic actions that might alienate the nation.

When the growing weakness of the Spanish after 1797 crippled the effectiveness of their play-off policy, the Choctaws lay exposed to the full consequences of their depleted forests and economic dependence. The American tactic, advocated by Thomas Jefferson, of encouraging the Indians' indebtedness to expedite land cessions, thrived among the Choctaws. The Americans used the Choctaw debts owed to Panton and Leslie—later John Forbes and Company—to arrange for the cession of a huge swath of land along the southern border in 1805. The money paid for the lands did not go to the Choctaws but rather to the traders to pay the Choctaw debts. By the nineteenth century it was becoming clear that the price of the maintenance of the hunt was indebtedness and that the end result of such indebtedness would be the continued alienation of the Choctaw homeland.[65]

Even before the turn of the century, chiefs such as Franchimastabe realized that the hunt was doomed. By 1820 awareness that continued reliance on hunting was unacceptable and dangerous seems to have become universal among the Choctaw elite. Hunting could not be maintained in the face of increasing poverty, powerlessness, and the loss of the land itself. The chiefs renounced the hunt in the early nineteenth century in large part because of the political and commercial consequences of the depletion of game, but the decline of deer also posed a threat to the subsistence system. By altering Choctaw subsistence patterns, this decline became a powerful force driving further ecological and social change within the nation. Changes in subsistence paralleled the decline of commercial hunting, but for a long time they were obscured by it. Although the roots of change in the Choctaw food production extend deep into the eighteenth century, the extent and consequences of this alteration became readily apparent only in the nineteenth century.[66]

CHAPTER 5

The Collapse of the Traditional Economy

The rapid growth of the deerskin trade among the Choctaws was the prelude to dependence. The English, believing the Indians to be lazy beggars, regarded commerce as the natural road to wealth and urged the Choctaws to escape their poverty through trade. The English insisted that like all human beings, except those few of high birth, the Choctaws must either work or starve; the English policy of promoting the hunt and replacing gift exchanges with market exchanges, however, was in fact an ultimatum to work and to starve. Commerce not only diminished the wealth of the Choctaws but also wrecked their subsistence system and left them hungry and vulnerable.

Trade spawned overhunting, and overhunting eventually destroyed the secondary food cycle of the Choctaws, but the first changes had come earlier during the Choctaw-Chickasaw wars. As late as the 1730s, crop failures had promoted peace between warring nations since both then needed unimpeded access to the deer of the borderlands in order to survive. The successful peace overtures made by Red Shoes to the Chickasaws in 1734 and 1737, for instance, coincided with Choctaw crop failures. Peace allowed the Choctaws to leave their towns and hunt the buffalo and deer they needed.[1]

If the French wanted consistent military aid from the Choctaws, they could not allow this secondary food cycle of the borderlands to continue. The French probably began to provision the Choctaws during bad years in the 1740s. In ceding the region to the English in 1763, the French pointedly reminded the Choctaws that they had supplied food and seed "when your Nation has been in want of provisions. You know this has often been the case."[2]

Conditions changed little under the English, even after the end of the Creek wars. In 1779 John Stuart blamed his excessive expenditures on his need to provide for the Indians during the "great dearth" that had prevailed in surrounding nations during the previous two years.[3] By then, of course, the Choctaws and neighboring nations were allies of the English against the American revolutionaries and the Spanish. The English could not allow the Indians to scatter in search of food for if they did, not only would they be useless as allies, but they would also be far more receptive to Spanish offers of aid. Abandoning their earlier injunctions for self-sufficiency, the English gave the Indians food.

The end of intertribal wars and the most bitter phase of colonial rivalries in the 1780s did not mean a reversion to the older secondary subsistence cycle, however. It was too late for that. The introduction of liquor and the thorough entanglement of the Choctaws in the commercial deerskin trade made the return to old patterns impossible. By then the number of deer east of the Mississippi had dwindled drastically and the buffalo were gone entirely; there was little point in moving into a secondary food cycle whose resources had been so badly depleted. Instead, the Indians petitioned, demanded, and, if need be, stole from the Spanish to get the food necessary to live. Needing the Choctaws as allies against the Americans and faced with the alternative of losing their cattle to starving Indians, the Spanish too gave them food. The Choctaws descended on Spanish coastal settlements in 1782 to beg and steal goods when their crops failed, and in both 1792 and 1794 the Spaniards had to provide them with food. To relieve themselves of the burden of this support and to increase the volume of skins, the Spanish encouraged the Choctaws to undertake more hunts west of the Mississippi.[4]

When the Americans took over Natchez in the 1790s, they discovered that hungry Choctaws now regularly descended on the cattle herds of whites as they had once descended on deer. Repeated crop failures in the 1790s reduced them to a desperate state, and white farmers paid the price. The Choctaws stole cattle, pigs, and horses; they moved into fields and took the crops for themselves. In the normal years the governor of Mississippi merely described them as "great pests"; in the worst years, when the Indians facing starvation took all the stock and crops of white planters, the governor could consider war. For the Choctaws all these depredations were justified; gifts of food from Europeans had become their standard recourse in times of want. Since the United States government refused to meet its obligation, the responsibility, in Choctaw eyes, descended on its individual citizens.[5]

In the space of half a century the Choctaws had been reduced to dependence on Europeans, not just for manufactured goods but for food itself. They had lost the ability and the resources to cope with recurrent drought and crop failures without outside assistance. The escalating involvement of the Choctaws first in European rivalries and later in the market had initially disrupted the secondary food cycle and then destroyed it. By the droughts of the end of the century they were pathetically dependent on Europeans for the food necessary to sustain life.

This destruction of the dual subsistence cycle east of the river and the end of colonial and intertribal warfare combined to render existing patterns of Choctaw settlement obsolete. Fertile borderlands empty of game and a relatively infertile core area crowded with towns no longer made either environmental or social sense. Yet new adaptations did not necessarily come quickly, no matter how pressing the need, nor did they come without great cost. The movement of Choctaws into the borderlands at once fueled and was the result of major social changes in the nation.

In the late eighteenth century after Choctaw hunters had virtually eliminated deer from large sections of the borderlands, stockraisers began refilling the forests and prairies with cows, horses, and pigs. This restocking of the borderlands constituted a species replacement equivalent to the depopulation of much of the area at European contact and the subsequent growth in the number of deer.

These domesticated animals made a new way of life possible; they did not make it inevitable. The Choctaws, after all, had possessed chickens, horses, and hogs for years before the migration began, but as long as their own subsistence cycle maintained its productivity, swine and domesticated fowl remained peripheral to their economy. Until the end of the French regime in 1763 they raised some chickens and a few pigs, but they largely reserved these for exchange with the Europeans. They initially refused to eat either chicken or swine themselves because these animals ate filth, but eventually the Choctaws consented to eat pork and chicken at French feasts. Not until the permanent settlement of English traders among the Choctaws in the 1760s and 1770s did the number of hogs increase significantly in the nation. The Choctaws had, on the other hand, eagerly sought horses. After the Natchez war the Indians traded to the French for mares the black slaves they recaptured from the Natchez. By the 1730s horses had become abundant, and raids on the Chickasaws increased their numbers. The Choctaws rarely rode these horses and never used them for war; they employed them instead as pack animals and later as sources of food.[6]

The rejection of pigs and chickens and the enthusiasm for horses both make sense in view of Choctaw beliefs. The religious life of the Choctaws was posited upon a series of balances of mutually opposed categories that had to be kept distinct. Animals that overlapped two categories were abominations and so normally not fit for food. Thus bats—four-footed animals that flew—were taboo, as were carnivores—four-footed animals that ate flesh instead of vegetation. In such a system the chicken—a bird that did not fly—and the pig—an omnivore—presented immediate problems. Apparently the Choctaws initially classified the pig with carnivores instead of its near relative, the bear, which formed a unique category of its own. The horse—a four-legged animal which ate grass—presented no such problem and could be assimilated into the Choctaw diet quite readily.[7]

What made the Choctaws' adoption of the horse even easier was the existence of readily available ecological niches around the Choctaw towns. Choctaw environmental practices, particularly burning, had created a suitable habitat for grazing animals by clearing the forest floor and encouraging the growth of grasses, but such areas were devoid of game. Thus in the vicinity of the towns, horses could move in without threatening any existing herbivores. As the horses multiplied around the towns, they could, unlike deer, be retrieved without the danger often inherent in an expedition into the borderlands. The horse thus fit into Choctaw ecology and economy as nicely as it fit into their symbolic system. There were no bars to its acceptance.

Because of the Choctaw fondness for horsemeat and the advantages the animal possessed, it would seem natural for the horse to replace the deer in the subsistence system as game disappeared. Yet this did not happen simply because the same forces destroying the deer also destroyed the horse. When the English assumed sovereignty, they promoted a trade in horses with the same methods and the same zeal as they promoted a trade in deerskins. In a nation innundated with rum, the trade soon became merely an exchange of horses for liquor, with a Choctaw horse bringing a 4-gallon keg of rum half diluted with water. Not content with robbing the Indians, the Englishmen began robbing each other as traders encouraged the Indians to steal pack animals from their European rivals to trade for additional whiskey. The Choctaws pursued this trade in horses so enthusiastically that the animals Romans described as plentiful in 1771 had greatly diminished by 1780, when Alexander Cameron described the Choctaws as "a poor Ragged Sett without horses." As a result of this trade, when the years of dearth came upon the nations in the late 1770s and 1780s, the Choctaws had only depleted herds to fall back on, and eating these left them the people Cameron described— poor and without horses.[8]

The old economy was in a shambles by the 1780s. The Choctaws, impoverished and desperate, persisted in attempting to reestablish the old balance by making the lands across the Mississippi serve as a new borderland. Such a response was understandable, conservative, and, in the long run, doomed. Liquor, the market, and dependence would destroy western resources as surely as they had destroyed those in the east. Yet during the 1780s, the yields from the hunt may have enabled the Choctaws to rebuild the horse herds destroyed in the 1770s. The animals were then, if anything, more critically necessary since the Choctaw hunters had to carry their deerskins long distances from the hunting grounds to their homeland or to the trading houses.

Even a replenishing of the horse herds and the trans-Mississippi hunt could not have long maintained the old economy in the face of the continued inroads of market hunting and the liquor trade. Disaster, however, was not gradual, but sudden. In the early 1790s not only did drought destroy the Choctaw crops, but an unidentified disease swept through the horse herds and carried off so many horses that the traders could not even transport deerskins out of the nation. Bereft of deer, horses, and crops, the Choctaws killed Spanish cattle; only these animals and the aid the Spanish gave them to stop further depredations on their herds preserved them from starvation.[9]

The significance of this latest disaster was not lost on at least some of the Choctaw chiefs. To Franchimastabe of Yazoo, the titular head chief of the nation, the drought, the decline of game, and the loss of horses underlined the vulnerability of the Choctaws and the inevitability of change. The Spanish emissary, Stephen Minor, who visited Franchimastabe in 1792, approached him on private business: the sale of some lands between the Natchez line and the Pearl River where he hoped to graze his own cattle. Franchimastabe refused. The time of "hunting and living by the Gun" was nearly over, he replied, and the Choctaws needed these lands to live like white men. For Franchimastabe, living like the white men of the Mississippi region meant cattle raising, not farming. This was the main rural occupation of the region.[10]

When Franchimastabe spoke, Choctaw settlement was already spreading out, but it had not yet penetrated the borderlands. Beginning in the 1750s and 1760s with the end of the Chickasaw wars, Choctaws dispersed and moved away from the fortified towns. Refugees from older towns destroyed during the wars settled towns such as Sahpetchito and Kunshak Osapa, which grew into substantial places in their own right. Other new settlements were probably only satellite villages of older towns that had grown short of land while constricted by the wars. Such villages might be reabsorbed by the spread of the old town, be abandoned as the lands gave out, or grow into permanent towns themselves.[11]

Such a process of expansion was general in the nation during the 1750s and 1760s, but in the late 1760s the outbreak of the Creek wars checked it in the east and south. Romans, on entering the nation from the east in 1771, had to pass through the deserted towns of Osapa issa and Itokchako before he reached the first inhabited settlement, East Abeka, and he later mentioned deserted towns along the Tombigbee. The end of the Creek wars, in turn, opened the way for renewed expansion particularly in the south and east. The Spanish census of 1784, the first detailed enumeration of towns since Romans's list of 1771, revealed four new settlements in the south, two in the east, and two in the west.[12]

The Choctaws continued to settle new towns in the 1790s and the early nineteenth century, but at that time the direction of settlement shifted considerably. Of the towns appearing for the first time in the censuses and treaty conferences between 1794 and 1804, fourteen were in the northeast, five were in the west, and only one was in the south. The creation of new towns in the south during the late 1770s and early 1780s probably represented the dispersal of people previously confined by the Creek wars. The south, bordered by pinelands and with less arable land than any other district, reached its environmental limits relatively quickly, however. In the 1790s and early 1800s its people would not take up new lands within the district except within the established towns; instead, they migrated across the Mississippi to settle new villages where game was still abundant and the old economy could be reestablished in toto.[13]

In the northeastern and western districts, however, no such environmental constraints existed. Their borderlands were not pinelands but rich loessal and prairie soils. Still, the mere existence of these lands explains nothing. Northeastern and western Choctaws faced the same crippling of the subsistence cycle as the southern Choctaws; more fertile farmland could not stop droughts and could not bring the deer back. They needed more than rich land if they were to escape continued dependence. People still devoted to the traditional hunting and farming economy did not move into the borderlands in great numbers; they moved west of the river.

Livestock became important only in the context of this larger economic and social breakdown. Those people who first moved into the borderlands were not traditionalists. The pioneers of this new settlement were the intermarried whites and the mixed-bloods, and they came not to reestablish the old economy but to raise cattle as Franchimastabe predicted the whole nation must do. Many full-blood Choctaws settled with them in the borderlands, and gradually the way of life and the interests of these people would diverge from their kinsman in the old towns.

White men had first settled extensively among the Choctaws and intermarried with them in the years preceding the Revolution. These men, who were French, American, and English, largely traders and ex-traders, recognized in the borderlands surrounding them an excellent cattle range. The prairies, the open forests with their grassy floors, and the canebrakes all promised abundant forage.[14]

Intermarried whites first introduced cattle among the Choctaws sometime around 1770, but initially the animals seem to have remained largely the property of the traders and their families—the Perrys, LeFlores, and Folsoms. A report to the American government in 1789 stressed that the Choctaws, far more than the Creeks and Chickasaws, remained hunters and possessed few, if any, cattle.[15]

The traders themselves, however, rapidly expanded the cattle range. In the 1780s the LeFlore brothers and Lewis Durant, with their mixed-blood families, drove cattle onto the land along the Yazoo River well within the western borderlands. In the northeast, Noah Wall received permission from the Choctaws to settle along the Natchez Trace on the Chickasaw border sometime in the late eighteenth or early nineteenth century, and at roughly the same time Nathaniel Folsom settled his family at Pigeons Roost on the Natchez Trace. John Pitchlynn, too, moved north to Hush-ook-wa in present Noxubee County.[16]

The disasters of the 1790s insured that this migration did not remain solely a movement of intermarried whites and mixed-bloods. Intermarried Frenchmen and their families settled French Camp along the Natchez Trace, for instance, but numerous full-bloods took up land around them. Such migrations moved slowly at first, but by 1819, when missionaries noted the migration of seventeen mixed-blood men together with their families into the then unsettled Yalobusha River region, stockraising had reached the northern boundaries of the Western District. The next year Adam Hodgson, an English traveler, found one of these families—a mixed-blood Choctaw man and his Chickasaw wife—settled along the river. Their herd numbered fifty to sixty horses and "more than two hundred very fine cattle."[17]

While these people moved northwest, others moved southwest, into the lands Franchimastabe had sought to preserve, and northeast toward the prairies. Puckshenubbee, a leading chief of the western towns, settled in the western borderlands in the early nineteenth century. Other full-bloods settled near him and made the region important enough to become the site of the first American Indian agency among the Choctaws. In the northeast most Choctaws continued to avoid the prairies because of their deficient summer rainfall until the prosperous missionary stations established there proved settlement feasible; then in the 1820s full-blood families settled around them.[18]

The Choctaw herds fueled this expansion and then symbiotically grew because of it. By 1805 John Pitchlynn's property consisted mainly of livestock. His children and other mixed-bloods grew to adulthood not as hunters but herdsmen; their earliest duty was watching their parents' cattle and horse herds. The full-bloods' herds, stocked in part with animals stolen from the Americans who had settled along the Mobile and lower Tombigbee rivers, and in part with animals acquired from the herds of intermarried traders, grew at a considerably slower rate.[19]

Livestock did not enter just the lands of the Choctaws; it entered their culture as well and made pastoralists of many who had been hunters. When George Gaines went to a Choctaw feast in 1813, he was fed on beef and pork not wild game. Choctaw burial ceremonies were now, on occasion, completed with a slaughter of the favorite horses, cattle, and dogs of the deceased. Since the Choctaws did not bury their dead, but rather placed them on platforms until their flesh rotted and their bones could be gathered and placed in the charnal houses located in each town, these animals too were presumably not buried but consumed at the feast that accompanied a Choctaw funeral. By the end of the nineteenth century authorities referred to the custom among the "ancient" Choctaws of giving to each child at birth a mare and a colt, a cow and a calf, a sow and pigs, and preserving the increase to give the child at marriage. The custom was real enough, but it is hard to see how it could have become widely prevalent before the rapid growth of stockraising in the early nineteenth century.[20] By the 1820s the movement into the borderlands, at that time actively encouraged by American Indian agents and farmers who urged the Choctaws to expand their farming and take up stockraising, had become rapid and sustained. In the late 1820s these American agents provided the first relatively precise, if limited, accounts of the extent of Choctaw stockraising. A poor and wondering *iksa* of 313 people that migrated into the northeastern borderlands in the late 1820s soon possessed 188 horses, 511 cattle, and 353 hogs. Such holdings were apparently common in the northeast and in the west, where virtually everyone owned some livestock. By 1829 the 5,627 people of the Northeastern District enumerated in a missionary census possessed 11,661 cattle, 3,974 horses, 112 oxen, and 22,047 hogs.[21]

These animals and the people who owned them lived predominantly in the borderlands. The extent of the population shift can be measured only in 1830 when the Americans took a census of the nation prior to removal in 1831, but by then it was formidable. The clearest migration and the sharpest social divisions were in the Northeastern District. Migration had reduced the old town core to 30 percent of the population; the households here were both larger and cultivated less land than those elsewhere in the district. The bulk of the Choctaws lived in the old borderlands, and one small segment of these people deserves singling out. Those households along the Tombigbee River and near the government factory located there had markedly smaller households and more cultivated acreage than elsewhere (see Table 1).[22]

Table 1. Settlement Patterns and Cultivated
Acreage in the Northeastern District, 1830

Northeastern District Households	Number	Percentage of District	Mean Cultivated Acreage	Mean Household Size
Old Core	223	30	4.3	6.9
Border	491	66	7.3	6.3
Tombigbee/Factory	31	4	13.4	4.7

SOURCE: National Archives, Record Group 75, Records of the Bureau of Indian Affairs, Armstrong Census.

Although in the west migration was also heavy, the area shows no similar sharp divisions between sections. Western towns had always been more dispersed, and the fertile lands of the Pearl River valley on the edge of the old core region were open to settlement. As a result, the older towns were not sharply distinguished from the newly settled borderlands. The Yazoo River valley, the home of the LeFlores and other mixed-blood planters, did have the largest cultivated acreage per household, but the smallest mean cultivated acreage of any section was also in the borderlands. If accurate livestock records were available, sharper distinction between the old core area and the borderlands might emerge (see Table 2).[23]

Table 2. Settlement Patterns and Cultivated
Acreage in the Western District, 1830.

Western District Households	Number	Percentage of District	Mean Cultivated Acreage	Mean Household Size
Old Core	312	27	7.7	7.4
Pearl River borderlands	176	15	8.9	7.0
Natchez Trace borderlands	417	36	5.4	5.3
Yazoo	162	14	13.9	6.1
Yalobusha	99	8	8.4	6.5

SOURCE: National Archives, Record Group 75, Records
of the Bureau of Indian Affairs, Armstrong Census.

Finally, in the Southern District the vast majority of settlement remained within the old town core, although the towns themselves had largely dispersed. The only settlement that might be called borderland was made up of a few households along the Tombigbee below those of the Northeastern District. These households differed predictably from the core settlement in having more cultivated land, but they also surprisingly had more members (see Table 3).[24]

This substantial shift in population, with the resulting shift in land use from hunting to grazing and increased agriculture, was not the result of population pressure. It sprang from the disruption of the old economy. According to Nathaniel Folsom and the missionaries who got their information from him, during the period from the Revolution until removal Choctaw population declined from 30,000 people in 1775 to 20,000 in 1831. More than likely this decline represented a pattern of depopulation caused by smallpox and measles, exacerbated by liquor and the famines of the 1780s and 1790s, and followed by a gradual recovery of population during the early nineteenth century. The total decline here probably was less dramatic than Folsom indi-

Table 3. Settlement Patterns and Cultivated
Acreage in the Southern District, 1830.

Southern District Households	Number	Percentage in District	Mean Cultivated Acreage	Mean Household Size
Old Core	731	97	4.8	6.7
Tombigbee	23	3	9.9	8.1

SOURCE: National Archives, Record Group 75, Records
of the Bureau of Indian Affairs, Armstrong Census.

cated since he apparently took no account of the sizable migration
across the Mississippi during this period. Choctaw population probably fluctuated around 20,000 people, as it had in the past.[25]

The cultural patterns of the Choctaws were in part responsible for
their controlled growth. Infanticide was widespread in the nation, but
it was a practice about which little is known. Which children the
Choctaws killed and why remains unclear. Though certainly not designed as a population control device, the custom could clearly function to keep population down. Since, as George Cowgill has argued, it
takes only a relatively small alteration in birth spacing or marriage age
to slow or halt population growth, infanticide, by increasing the
spacing of children, could have stabilized population.[26]

Certainly the Choctaws did not have to produce more food for a
growing population. What they needed was not more abundant food,
but rather a more secure food supply for those years in which agriculture failed entirely. This is what they had lost; this is what livestock raising provided.

This transition from the hunt to livestock occurred neither evenly
nor easily. In the Sixtowns with their more limited forage, the new
grazing economy remained only partially developed. The old pattern
of agriculture and winter hunts, now, of course, largely hunts across
the Mississippi, continued until the eve of removal. As game across
the Mississippi too began to decline, the southern Choctaws instituted
strict hunting rules designed to limit and equalize yields. *Iksa* captains
now dictated the amount of game to be taken. Such conservation

practices are often cited as a primeval custom among the Choctaws, but actually the only evidence for them is among the remnants of the southern Choctaws who eventually refused to leave Mississippi. These Choctaws changed the place of the hunt and then the methods of the hunt, but they maintained the hunt itself. The American missionaries who came to the Choctaws in the 1820s correctly regarded them as the most conservative part of the nation.[27]

In the west and northeast, stockraising eventually triumphed, but some hunters remained, particularly in the older settled areas. Conflict between the pastoralists and hunters occurred, especially in the early years of the transition when the cattle owners were whites or mixed-bloods and the hunters, most often hungry and desperate, were full-bloods. When the LeFlores introduced their cattle on the Yazoo, the immediate danger was that Choctaw hunters would treat the animals as wild game. And as game decreased, many hunters began to do so. Early in the nineteenth century a Choctaw hunter killed some of the cattle George Gaines introduced along the Tombigbee, and in 1815, when the decline of game was virtually complete, intermarried whites appeared in council to complain to the American agent and the chiefs of the killing of their cattle. Cattle grazing the old hunting grounds, whites insisted, could not be treated as feral animals available to any hungry man. Such animals, no matter what their number or their distance from the owner's home, were personal property.[28]

The complaints by stockraisers only underlined the existence of a new and dangerous condition in the nation: there were now identifiable rich families and identifiable poor families. Such a situation had never existed before among the Choctaws. In the eighteenth century there had been differential access to scarce European goods, but goods continued to be redistributed. The complaint of the warriors then had been not that the chiefs were rich while they were poor, only that the chiefs benefited from their privileged access to a supply of goods that was not large enough to be distributed to the whole nation. The warriors did not challenge the chiefs' right to presents; they simply demanded a large total supply of goods so that redistribution could reach them. In any case, no one went hungry in the eighteenth century unless everyone did.

This general equality of condition did not persist into the

nineteenth century. The rise of property holding on a significant scale was a direct result of both intermarriage with white traders and the ecological shift that put human residences in areas once reserved for game. Domestic animals like the horse and pig, and especially the cow, belonged to specific owners. They replaced wild animals that had "belonged" to whoever, within a recognized hunting territory, could take them. The multiplication of cattle, unlike deer, benefited only their owners. With this shift to livestock raising, relatively permanent distinctions in wealth and well-being appeared in the nation for the first time.[29]

The numerous conflicts and divisions involved in the economic transition from the hunt to livestock of necessity spilled over into both the internal politics and the diplomatic negotiations of the nation. The nature of the Choctaw dilemma was clear by the first years of the nineteenth century. The persistence of the hunting economy meant a constant accumulation of debt that the declining revenues of the hunt were unable to offset. The obvious solution was a land cession, such as the one made at Mt. Dexter in 1805, to pay off the debts, but to cede land threatened the new expansion into the borderlands and the accumulation of livestock that sparked it. In 1805 the Choctaw chiefs had circumvented this problem by reneging on a promise to cede the rich western borderlands the Americans coveted, ceding instead a broad strip of pinelands to the south. Thomas Jefferson, who supported the mutually contradictory policies of encouraging the acquisition of livestock to "civilize" the Choctaws while simultaneously attempting to strip them of their best grazing lands, was so angered by this piece of diplomacy that he refused to submit the treaty to the Senate for over two years. Eventually, however, the need to strengthen the Spanish border induced him to accept the cession.[30]

The hunters' increasing indebtedness threatened the stockraisers' resources, and the resulting tension arose in a political system in the throes of transition. Status gained by right of birth had not entirely disappeared. Choctaws remembered the chiefly lines and sometimes even acknowledged the eldest son of the chief's eldest sister as heir apparent, but more often they did not. Even the chiefs themselves increasingly disregarded the old criteria. Franchimastabe of Yazoo, for instance, conspired with the Spanish to secure a minor chieftainship for his son and chosen successor.[31]

Warriors now dominated the Choctaw hierarchy. The warriors sometimes publicly threatened the civil chiefs, and war chiefs acted as de facto civil chiefs. The two most powerful chiefs of the early nineteenth century—Pushmataha and Mushulatubbee—gained their positions because they were prominent war leaders in the fighting in the west against the Osages, and Caddos. Mushulatubbee, the son of the important chief Homastubbee, became chief instead of his cousin, the supposed heir, because of these war exploits. Pushmataha rose by the same means, though he lacked even Mushulatubbee's claim to chieftainship. His common parentage, in fact, remained a matter of some comment among the Choctaws, and of sensitivity to him. On one occasion, when Americans innocently inquired about his right to chieftainship, Pushmataha first replied it was none of their business and then told them he had no human parents.[32]

Men like Pushmataha and Mushulatubbee initially took their places among the welter of war chiefs and various civil chiefs—both Spanish and American—of the towns and villages throughout the nation. This very profusion of chiefs made the Americans long for some order, as had the French and Spanish before them. Beneath this confusion a substantial reordering of political power was taking place. In the early nineteenth century the break-up of the towns further eroded the power of the towns' civil chiefs. These chiefs did not disappear, but their effective power in daily affairs passed to the captains of the iksas that settled each neighborhood. This further diffusion of power, however, was only preliminary to a new centralization, based not on the old towns and chieftainships but in three districts—the Western, the Northeastern, and the Southern, which consisted of the Sixtowns, Yowani, and Chickasawhay. The district chiefs of these regions, each recognized by the Americans with a medal, emerged as the most powerful men in the nation. Pushmataha in the South and Mushulatubbee in the Northeast became district chiefs.[33] How they rose can be pieced together from missionary accounts:

> a high chief, called Mingo, often translated king, presided over each district. These three mingos appear to have been equal in power and rank. So far as can be learned, they rose gradually to this station by the consent of other leading men, but without any formal election. In each village, or settlement, a head man was

appointed, whose rank is indicated, in our language, by the word captain. There are about thirty of these in the northeast district; and perhaps nearly the same number of each of the others. The captains were raised to this office by the consent of their neighbors and of the Mingo; but all appointments appear to have been confirmed in a council of chief, captains, and warriors; meaning by the word warriors, all the common men. The councils were held at irregular periods, and were usually called by the chief.

Elsewhere the missionaries specifically identified the captains as heads of *iksas*, and Cushman, the son of a missionary, asserted that one of the major criteria of status was prestige gained in war.[34]

The Americans both encouraged and capitalized on this trend, not only by giving gifts and medals to the district chiefs but also by giving them control over distribution of the annuities the Choctaws received for their land cessions. When Pushmataha and Mushulatubbee persuaded the Choctaws to reject Tecumseh's call for a vast pan-Indian union against the Americans and instead led many of them into the War of 1812 as allies of the Americans against the British and Creeks, the strength and effectiveness of the district chiefs was demonstrated and fortified. Gradually the presents given to the "principal chiefs" evolved into annual salaries bestowed by the Americans. This arrangement pleased both parties. The chiefs could rely on a regular supply of goods, while the Americans believed that presents to the chiefs were the best way to secure land cessions.[35]

The Americans, for their own purposes, clearly sought to encourage the centralization that the growth of the district chieftainships represented, but their success was not complete. The national council they promoted was not achieved until the mid-1820s, and then it actually served as center of anti-American politics in the nation. Nor did the American salaries, any more than earlier French gifts, reduce the chiefs to puppets. Although they were not beyond manipulation, internal politics, not external bribes, usually determined their actions.[36]

The new leadership that was evolving during the early nineteenth century had to deal with both increasing American pressure for land and Choctaw indebtedness. The Choctaws ceded their claims to the lands east of the Tombigbee in 1816, but since few people lived in the district and it was largely devoid of game, the cession provoked little controversy. Far more critical were the demands the Americans began to make in 1818 for further cessions.[37] In 1818 three American commissioners arrived in the nation both to secure more land and also to broach the question of eventual removal west of the Mississippi. The Choctaws stubbornly refused both proposals, and Pushmataha and Mushulatubbee wrote the president that "our land is so small, we could not spare any." White settlers in Mississippi were hardly satisfied with such answers, and congress soon applied pressure. Late in the fall of 1818 a Mississippi representative, George Poindexter, pushed through the House Committee on Public Lands a report which asserted that the Choctaws west of the Mississippi were actually trespassing on American lands acquired under the Louisiana Purchase and had no right to be there, either permanently or on winter hunts. Since Poindexter believed that the eastern Choctaws would never agree to land cessions, much less to permanent removal, as long as they could keep their eastern lands and have free access to those of the west, he desired to use the western lands to gain cessions in the east.[38]

When in 1819 the United States prepared for further negotiations, Andrew Jackson was among the treaty commissioners appointed by Secretary of War Calhoun. Jackson knew the Choctaws from the War of 1812 and was quite prepared to exploit their divisions. He informed the Choctaws that a failure to negotiate would result in the expulsion of the trans-Mississippi Choctaws from their lands and a ban on future western hunts. The Sixtowns would then be in danger of starvation and would have no choice except to abandon their homes and join some other tribe. The result would be the end of the Choctaw nation. The Choctaw agent John McKee shared Jackson's assumption that the Sixtowns—the people most devoted to the hunting economy—would not only agree to a cession but would also willingly remove to lands west of the Mississippi.[39] Both McKee and Jackson underestimated the Choctaws. When McKee presented the American arguments for a cession to a general council of the nation, Pushmataha disavowed any Choctaws who crossed the Mississippi. Pushmataha declared: "Those of our people who are over the Mississippi did not go there with the consent of the nation; they are considered as strangers; they have no houses or places of residence; they are like wolves; it is the wish of the council that the President would direct his agents to the west to order these stragglers home, and if they will not come, to direct them where he pleases."[40]

Behind the chiefs a coalition of young mixed-bloods, the people most devoted to the expansion of the Choctaw herds, united to denounce both the western lands and any proposal of removal. Despite this inauspicious beginning, the United States convened the treaty council in October of 1820 at Doaks Stand on the Natchez Trace and proposed granting the Choctaws title to lands west of the Mississippi in exchange for a cession of part of their lands east of the river.[41]

Resistance appeared immediately. Puckshenubbee, the head chief of the Western District and himself a herdsman and resident of the western borderlands the Americans coveted, refused even to take American rations. Pushmataha, apparently fearing that Sixtown hunters might agree to a cession in order to secure hunting lands across the Mississippi, tried to keep southern warriors from the treaty ground and to confine negotiations to the captains. The commissioners countered this tactic by using James Pitchlynn and Edmund Folsom, themselves mixed-bloods but also salaried agents of the government, to persuade the Sixtown Choctaws to attend the council. There the commissioners posed as advocates for the poor full-blood hunters, beggared by liquor and lack of game, who "died in wretchedness and want" while the selfish mixed-bloods grew wealthy. A cornucopia awaited the full-bloods across the Mississippi if only, with the aid of the United States, they could escape the manipulations of their mixed-blood tribesmen and seize it. Andrew Jackson would use such arguments in dealing with southern tribes throughout his career, and he employed them with good effect at Doaks Stand. The commissioners expertly played upon the division between the hunters and the herdsmen, assuring the Choctaws that only a small cession of land would insure them a vast hunting ground in the west. To refuse the cession, they threatened, was to risk the Choctaws' very existence as a nation.[42]

As a political tactic Jackson's approach was brilliant; as a realistic assessment of the condition of the nation it was badly flawed. He recognized correctly the growing wealth of the mixed-bloods, but he ignored the concurrent, if slower, switch of many Western and Eastern District Choctaws to herding and their movement into the bor-

derlands. These people were no longer hunters, and the sale of grazing lands threatened their interests as well as those of the wealthy
mixed-bloods. Puckshenubbee was representative of such people, and
he was the most vocal and stubborn foe of the treaty. Jackson also
badly underestimated the depth of the Choctaws' attachment to their
homeland and the desire of even the Sixtown Choctaws to remain
after the game had vanished.

For three days the Choctaws considered the American proposals
and threats. They reached no decision. The council then reconvened
with the American commissioners to hear the specific proposals for
the boundaries of a cession. The United States asked for a large
section of the southwestern borderlands that Franchimastabe had insisted on retaining in 1792 and Jefferson had unsuccessfully sought in
1805. In exchange they offered a much larger tract of land in the
west, a school fund, and assistance for anyone wishing to migrate
west. This, they promised, would also be the last land cession they
would ever seek from the Choctaws.[43]

The Choctaws renewed their deliberations with resistance at this
point now centered, logically enough, in the Western District whose
lands comprised the cession. On October 15 Puckshenubbee met with
the commissioners and informed them that they had asked for too
much land. He received a chilling reply. If the Choctaws refused the
treaty, the Americans would go to the emigrants west of the river and
negotiate with them. These people "might be found to be a majority
of the nation, and would make an exchange that might not suit those
living here." When Puckshenubbee continued to block the cession, the
commissioners repeated the threat to the entire council with even
greater force. If the Choctaws refused to cede the land, they would
forfeit any American obligations toward them, and such a rejection
might be "a measure fatal to your nation." The carrot the Americans
coupled with this stick was an offer of an additional $1,000 a year in
annuities.[44]

In the face of such threats the districts unaffected by the cession
swung against Puckshenubbee, and even the old western core regions
now apparently favored the treaty. Puckshenubbee, unable to agree
with the emerging consensus, took the only alternative available, in
anger and frustration the district chief left the council. The next day
the draft treaty was submitted to the Choctaws, and on October 19

they signed it. By doing so the Choctaws ceded 6 million acres of their best land in exchange for a much larger tract west of the Mississippi. To conciliate Puckshenubbee, the Americans gave him a private grant within the ceded area.[45]

On the surface the treaty seemed a defeat for the mixed-blood herdsmen and a victory—if it was a victory for any Choctaws—for the hunters. Those who sought to maintain the traditional economy and the traditional ways in which it was embedded had received a large grant in the west while the herdsmen had lost prime grazing land. In fact, the meaning of the treaty within the nation was far more complex. Virtually all the mixed-bloods not in the direct employ of the American government opposed the cession, and this opposition, while immediately ineffective, raised their standing in the nation immensely by quieting the doubts about the patriotism of these "sons of white men."[46]

The group of young mixed-bloods whose opposition to the treaty had so outraged Andrew Jackson were patriots, but they were also much more. In a manner similar to the politics in contemporary developing nations, they became at once modernizers, destroyers of traditional ways of life, and ardent nationalists. They believed not only that change was necessary for the Choctaws but that it was good. In a society where courage, kin obligations, generosity, and the leisure to deliberate, talk, play in ball games, and participate in ceremonies were the governing social values, at least for males, these young mixed-bloods urged the substitution of thrift, sobriety, accumulation, and hard work. These values served their interests well, and they were never men to doubt that their best interests and those of the nation coincided. They never hesitated in attempting to transform the life of the nation, to change, in effect, what it meant to be a Choctaw.

They were, for all their patriotism, different from their countrymen. Their interests and attitudes reflected their position as the children of white fathers, the settlers of the borderlands, the owners and heirs of the cattle herds and later the cotton plantations. The Choctaws regarded the fathers of many of these mixed-bloods as rich men, and Jackson had used this wealth against them in the treaty councils. Accumulation of wealth and rights of property were divisive issues among the Choctaws in 1820. As the poaching of the herds of the intermarried whites and their mixed-blood children demonstrated,

Choctaw traditional beliefs offered no sanction for the accumulation of property on such a scale, particularly when others were in desperate need. The intermarried whites, however, shared none of the Choctaw concern with reciprocity and redistribution. Obligations of kinship, *iksa*, and town weighed lightly upon them. They held onto their property and justified themselves by their own values, which they imparted to their children.

The general equality of the nation was melting away. The new wealth remained illegitimate in traditional terms, but it did not disappear. Conflict between values and reality had developed which tradition could neither resolve nor halt. The mixed-bloods' solution to the dilemma was simple enough: dispense with tradition. They were people of property, and their concerns were with property. The letters of the intermarried British trader John Pitchlynn to his son, Peter Pitchlynn, a chief of the Choctaws following removal, were those of a substantial farmer to a young man rising the world—full of news of planting, herding, and the condition of Peter's cattle. These were the concerns the mixed-bloods carried into national life which introduced an interest in gain and accumulation foreign to the thinking of most Choctaws.[47]

The mixed-bloods took the individual pursuit of wealth and accumulation of property for granted in a manner their countrymen did not. This ambition was the sun around which their other values orbited, and they desired that their countrymen's values resemble their own. Their first step, in many ways a far more significant one than their later opposition to land cessions, came when they and their fathers invited Protestant missionaries to come into the nation in 1818. The Folsoms, the Brashears, the Nails, the LeFlores, the Pitchlynns, all these mixed-blood families were sympathetic to Christianity but often not actually church members themselves. Their interest in religion was only incidentally a concern with salvation. They wanted the missionaries to come primarily as "propagandists for industry and farming," for values and practices which they as much as the missionaries themselves identified with Christianity, and which they felt were critical for reforming the nation.[48]

In response to this invitation the American Board of Foreign Missions sent out Cyrus Kingsbury. Kingsbury established Eliot Mission on the Yalobusha River in 1818 and founded a second mission at

Mayhew in the Northeastern District in the fall of 1821. Other stations followed, most like their predecessors built in the fertile borderlands still being settled in the 1820s rather than in the old settled core of the nation.[49]

The missionaries immediately formed a strong alliance with the mixed-bloods. They built their stations among them and followed their advice over that of the full-blood chiefs—a practice that would greatly speed their alienation from the traditional leadership. It is hard to see how a mixed-blood–missionary alliance could have failed to form; the secular values of the two groups were already quite close. The Protestant Christianity of the American Board missionaries was largely undifferentiated from a devotion to hard work whose end was the acquisition of material wealth. The mission farms, the carpentry and blacksmith shops, the schools, the herds of cattle, and the droves of swine, all reflected the missionaries' zeal for material improvement and for accumulation, so much so that many Choctaws immediately suspected that their real motive was speculation in Indian lands. The missionaries, however, were not so much interested in wealth for themselves as in persuading more Choctaws to desire wealth. In a sense they wished to be envied, then they could use the envy to make the Choctaws more like themselves.[50]

This social transformation so ardently desired by the mixed-bloods and their missionary allies was inextricably tied to resistance to the Americans. By 1818 David Folsom was arguing that the hunt was dead, the old support gone. With the old economy deteriorating, the only question that remained was whether the result would be complete social collapse, dependence, and the wresting away of even more of the nation's land, or a new, revitalized nation led by a mixed-blood elite. The nationalist resistance which the mixed-bloods envisioned could never succeed if the Choctaws continued their slide into economic dependence. The nation needed to be self-sufficient, but this was impossible as long as traditional values and practices persisted. Thrift and accumulation had to be encouraged, respect for property inculcated, and, equally important, sobriety instituted and the liquor trade banned. Although these changes also served their personal interests, protected their wealth, and guaranteed them status and power, the nationalism of the mixed-bloods was real nonetheless. Without the missionaries' intending it or even realizing how it was happening, Christianity became a vehicle for a strain of Choctaw nationalism, and the American Board missionaries themselves protested until the end against removal.[51]

The missionary–mixed-blood alliance gained its first political victories in 1820 at the Treaty of Doaks Stand, which seemed to symbolize the mixed-bloods' defeat. Outside of their bitter differences over the cession, the young mixed-bloods found that there was much they and the Americans could agree on. For quite different reasons, both sought acculturative programs and values—education, respect for property, and the encouragement of sobriety—the mixed-bloods because they believed it would strengthen the nation, the Americans because they believed it would promote eventual assimilation. Both were ready to write appropriate measures into the treaty.

The mixed-bloods needed American aid because the initial enthusiasm of the chiefs and many full-bloods for the missionaries was already waning in 1820. The chiefs, with mixed-blood encouragement, had originally agreed to turn over a portion of their annuities to pay for mission schools—a promise that had caused considerable resentment among many Choctaws. The treaty solved this budding crisis by providing both additional school funds and additional annuities to assuage the discontented. It thus preserved the mission schools, which served as a major acculturative institution among the Choctaws. The treaty hardly stopped at this. It also prohibited the illegal liquor trade in "order to promote industry and sobriety amongst all classes of Red People, in this nation, but particularly the poor," and it created a police force called the Choctaw Lighthorse in each district to be funded by the United States. The force was to see that "good order may be maintained, and that all men, both white and red, may be compelled to pay their just debts." Imbedded in the terms of the treaty, then, was the possibility of major acculturative change: the implementation of education, sobriety, thrift, industry, and the sanctity of property.[52]

As the treaty stood, however, all this was merely a possibility; results depended not only on the efforts of missionaries and mixed-bloods but also on the cooperation of the chiefs and the willingness of the mass of Choctaws to accept such purposeful change. In 1820 the mixed-bloods, while rising quickly in the nation, were in no position to compel obedience to their program. They could influence chiefs and captains, but as yet only David Folsom was even a captain among the Choctaws. Initially, however, the chiefs appear to have given them some freedom in implementing the new program.[53]

Young mixed-bloods dominated the Choctaw Lighthorse. Joel Nail headed the force in the Sixtowns; David Folsom did the same in the Northeast; and Peter Pitchlynn, on his return from school outside the nation, took over the Northeastern force in 1824. The laws they enforced were very often not traditional. With missionary aid they managed to secure a series of district and local ordinances directed against liquor, theft, and traditional cultural and religious practices. In the Northeastern District the council outlawed the trade of liquor, provided for the elimination of infanticide, and secured provisions for the collection of debts and punishment for the theft of cattle and hogs. In the Southern District the council refused to go so far, but even there the mixed-bloods led by Joel Nail succeeded in getting at least part of the Sixtowns to ban the whiskey trade, outlaw polygamy and infanticide, and order the destruction of the crops of any family where women rather than men planted corn. A cooperative captain, Ahoha Kullo Humma, also outlawed cattle theft, a practice still common among the hunters, proclaiming: "The Choctaws formerly stole hogs and cattle and killed and ate them. I have organized a company of faithful warriors to take every man who steals, and tie him to a tree and give him thirty-nine lashes." This new emphasis on the sanctity of property and the obligation of Choctaws to repay debts instead of treating them like gifts to be reciprocated on a future date when the recipient was able, hit hard at established values.[54]

Besides serving as protectors of property, the Lighthorse could also be used against liquor sellers, a use of the police force both the missionaries and many of the mixed-bloods ardently desired. Whiskey remained the bane of the Choctaw nation. Missionaries reported that they never saw violence between Choctaw men unless the participants were drunk, but then the affrays became murderous. Liquor did not kill most Choctaws, however; it merely impoverished them. Reports were that they bartered "for Whiskey at an exorbitant price, their horses, hogs, skins, fowls, blankets, and indeed all they have." Nathaniel Folsom, in his old age, cited cases of families' trading virtually all they possessed for liquor and he thought that more than anything else it had rendered many Choctaws destitute.[55]

Temperance, which in fact meant prohibition, was critical on two levels to the new order of the mixed-bloods. On an individual level the cultivation of the new virtues of thrift and industry depended on it, and on a national level it formed the point of departure for any program designed to reduce dependence and indebtedness to the Americans and promote national development. Temperance was not merely a moral issue; it was a critical part of the political program of the mixed-bloods, and they pushed it vigorously.

This political element of temperance can be overlooked amidst the missionary calls for moral reform, but it was basic. Without temperance, accumulation was impossible. If all of a family's possessions were periodically dissipated in an orgy of whiskey drinking, then the gradual accumulation of wealth that the mixed-bloods urged would be impossible. And since the mixed-bloods thought of accumulation as merely the logical result of diligence and probity, it formed a universal mark of virtue that had to be protected. If there was no accumulation, there would be no means of encouraging the cultivation of the more basic values of industry and thrift. The treaty's linkage of "industry and sobriety" was no accident. The long fight for temperance was in many ways inseparable from the simultaneous battle for the sanctity of property rights—a battle in which the mixed-bloods and intermarried whites, as the largest property holders in the nation, took particular interest.[56]

The individual reform sought through temperance was, in turn, tied to the still larger national goal of self-sufficiency. Ever since the trade in liquor had lured the Choctaws into the market, whiskey and growing dependence had remained inextricably connected. Like horses and deer before them, cattle had become commodities in the trade that threatened stockraising with the same ruin it had earlier visited upon deer hunting and horse raising. In the Sixtowns, hunters continued to barter deerskins from across the Mississippi for liquor, but in the other districts livestock dominated the trade. The liquor trade thus continued to siphon off essential Choctaw resources without offering anything in return except a brief release from the very poverty the market system engendered.[57]

The American government condemned the trade and refused to sell whiskey at their factories; nevertheless, the government, as much as its citizens who sold the whiskey, was prime beneficiary of the trade.

American efforts to combat the use of whiskey consisted of little more than periodic lectures by the agents on the evil of drink. On any important occasion, such as a land cession, such exhortations could be dispensed with, and the American government gladly provided enough whiskey to lubricate Choctaw negotiators. Indeed the very willingness of the Choctaws to negotiate was a result of their increasing poverty, which was itself a result of a system of commerce that made whiskey a major commodity. The Americans took few real steps to suppress a trade whose results, while appalling, served their own interests so well.[58]

The liquor trade thus made a travesty of any Choctaw attempt to reduce their dependence on the Americans. Although the Choctaws needed both cotton and wool cloth, hoes, pots, and pans, the resources they had to obtain these supplies went for liquor. Many full-blood chiefs had shown increasing interest in cotton cultivation, cotton cards, spinning wheels, and looms in the years just before and after the War of 1812, and some Choctaw women had become accomplished spinners and weavers by the early 1820s. Amidst the general blight of liquor trade, however, this interest meant little. Trade and the annuities the Choctaws received for their cessions remained their main source of goods. Annuities compensated for some of the goods lost to the liquor trade, but the cost was immense—the constant reduction of the Choctaw homeland. And when actually distributed, the individual benefits of the annuities were few; the amount of goods any family received was quite small. The mixed-bloods were hardly the first Choctaws to recognize the disastrous effects of this cycle, but they were the ones to attack it the most directly.[59]

The grave weakness of these constant exhortations to industry, sobriety, and thrift as a political program was that they constituted not only a call for independence but also an assertion of Choctaw inferiority that the chiefs and many full-bloods found infuriating. The self-righteousness of the missionaries could be particularly grating. In council in 1822 the usually polite and genial Mushulatubbee could bear it no longer, and he assailed the missionaries: "I can never talk with a good man without feeling displeased. The first thing I hear is about the drunkenness and laziness of the Choctaws. I wish we were travellers & then we would see whether we are worse than everybody else."[60]

Although the chiefs agreed to the Lighthorse, to the laws, and in principle to the necessity of temperance, their hearts never accepted the full-scale repudiation of the old ways that such programs involved, and their support soon slackened. The Lighthorse briefly suppressed the whiskey traffic, but the trade quickly recovered. The new laws went unenforced except in the areas around the mission stations where sympathetic captains, increasingly of mixed blood themselves, cooperated with the police.[61]

Nowhere did the full-blood chiefs' repudiation of the mixed-blood program show up more clearly after the Treaty of Doaks Stand than in education. Education to the missionaries involved far more than literacy. Its aim was the inculcation of hard work, thrift, and Christianity to be achieved through a liberal regimen of land clearing and training in trades and domestic arts, along with a generous dose of corporal punishment. The mixed-blood children who attended missionary schools usually outnumbered the full-bloods, but initially the schools enjoyed the support of the chiefs. Inevitably, however, this dour regimen of work and harsh discipline, the sickness too often prevalent in the schools, and the isolation of the children from their families produced a reaction against education itself.[62]

The missionaries' arrogant disregard of Choctaw norms only compounded the problem. Visiting Choctaw parents were not only upset by the complaints of their children but also appalled by the conduct of the missionaries. In a society where generosity still reigned as the primary virtue, the missionaries seemed greedy misers. The Protestants refused to feed the visiting parents, an act of inhospitality so alien and repugnant to the Choctaws that it caused a furor in the nation. The only consistent defenders of the missionaries were the mixed-blood families who provided so many of their students. An 1829 letter in defense of the schools was probably typical of their attitude. Signed by members of prominent mixed-blood families—the Brashears, Turnbulls, and McKenneys—the letter offered the warm thanks of these families to the missionaries, insisting that "the improvement of the children in every instance has fully equalled our expectations, and in many instances altogether surpassed our most sanguine hopes." Such letters did not reflect majority opinion in the nation. If the missionaries and their allies had not taken the precaution of writing into the Treaty of Doaks Stand a guarantee of funding from the annuities as promised by the chiefs when the missionaries arrived in the nation, the schools would have been eliminated.[63]

By the early 1820s the progress of the mixed-bloods had evaporated in the face of opposition from the district chiefs, and by the middle of the decade their missionary allies were fighting discouragement. The schools were in trouble, and the missionaries at least privately admitted that they were to blame. They had seriously misjudged the Choctaw character. Their old faith in the universal human love of gain had dwindled considerably. As late as 1829 they would report that "the more enlightened love of gain may perhaps influence a few to become industrious, but the distant prospect of riches acquired by honest industry presents too feeble a motive to the great mass of this people to overcome the combined influence of their habits and prejudices." Many of the old values seemed to be holding.[64]

The mixed-bloods themselves did not despair so easily. Their direct assault on Choctaw customs and habits had momentarily failed, but the vulnerability of the Choctaws to American demands had not decreased. Removal remained the pivotal issue. If the district chiefs weakened in resisting American overtures for further cessions, then the mixed-bloods would be ready to challenge them for the leadership of the nation. The mixed-bloods, in the name of saving the Choctaws, might yet transform them.

Their great opportunity came in 1825 when the American government invited a Choctaw delegation to Washington to renegotiate the Treaty of Doaks Stand. The Americans had discovered that part of the land west of the Mississippi that they had ceded to the Choctaws had already been settled by their own citizens. The roles of 1820 had been neatly reversed; Americans were now illegally living upon Choctaw lands. The Americans, however, saw no irony in the situation; they only wanted the land back. And they got it, although to do so they had to provide immense amounts of whiskey to the negotiators and make substantial concessions. The Choctaw chiefs ceded the land but increased their annuities and rejected further cessions east of the Mississippi. The district chiefs also secured provisions that seriously weakened the American Board's monopoly over Choctaw education.[65]

The nation, however, was outraged by the cession. Two of the district chiefs who had led the delegation—Puckshenubbee, the chief of the Western District, and Pushmataha, the chief of the Southern District and the most renowned and powerful Choctaw leader—had died while on the mission to Washington. Therefore, Mushulatubbee of the Northeastern District, had to confront the anger of the nation alone. On his return, Mushulatubbee faced a national uproar orchestrated by David Folsom. Folsom, himself a member of the Choctaw treaty delegation, had recognized that any treaty ceding land to the Americans was bound to be unpopular. Even before the delegation left Washington, he had begun undermining the chiefs by writing letters to the missionaries denouncing the drinking of the chiefs during the negotiations. Folsom accused the chiefs of weakening before American demands for removal. Mushulatubbee attempted to divert his warriors with a two-month moratorium on the ban on whiskey drinking, but this action only spurred more intense mixed-blood antagonism to the treaty.[66]

Riding a wave of resistance to the treaty and fear of eventual removal, the mixed-bloods adroitly moved to depose the chiefs and achieve what David Folsom frankly called a revolution in the affairs of the nation. Confident enough now to attack the district chiefs in council, the mixed-bloods in the spring of 1826 deposed Mushulatubbee in the northeast and replaced him with David Folsom, then repeated their success in the west by replacing Robert Cole, a full-blood whom the Americans had recognized as chief of the Western District, with Greenwood LeFlore. The mixed-bloods eventually extended their control to the south by securing the elimination of the last full-blood district chief, Pushmataha's nephew, Tapenhahamma, on charges of intemperance and immorality and replacing him with another mixed-blood, John Garland. At the end of the "revolution" the mixed-bloods were the most influential group in the nation. As Agent William Ward reported, of the three district chiefs, "two of them [were] ¾ white and one a half-breed."[67]

The basis of this new political power was opposition to removal. The mixed-bloods, who promised never to cede any part of the Choctaw homeland, claimed that the full-blood chiefs were unlearned and unable to defend Choctaw rights. Such an assessment was not entirely unfair; there were signs that the district chiefs' resolution was weakening. Although in March of 1826 Mushulatubbee had asserted that the Choctaws would "sell no more land on any terms," the American agent William Ward and American treaty commissioners all continued to believe that a removal treaty could have been negotiated with the full-blood chiefs. The danger of the chiefs' agreeing to a cession seemed real enough for the Choctaw council to approve the death penalty for any person selling his country for a bribe.[68]

In 1826 any political program based on resistance to removal was virtually guaranteed success because the Americans greatly escalated their pressure upon the Choctaws for a cession of all remaining lands east of the Mississippi. Although the Indians flatly refused to consider any more cessions, Congress authorized and the president dispatched a new set of treaty commissioners to the nation. They arrived to find not the whole nation assembled in council as they expected, but rather three new district chiefs, all young and "without years and experience," and thirteen treaty commissioners appointed by the nation in council, a majority of whom were also young men. "The government," they lamented, "seems to be in the hands principally of half-breeds and white men." This Choctaw delegation was pledged to resist further cessions, and the Americans could not budge them. The American negotiators blustered and threatened. They ran through the whole negotiating repertoire that had succeeded so well in 1820: they demanded the entire nation be assembled; they accused the rich mixed-bloods of defrauding the poor full-bloods; they threatened to negotiate with the Choctaws west of the Mississippi; they said the Americans were determined to force removal if they had to, they asked for a smaller cession. None of it worked. The new mixed-blood elite stood firm, and their prestige within the nation was greatly enhanced.[69]

Their success in defeating the removal treaty now gave the mixed-bloods the chance to implement the rest of their political program. For these men retention of their homeland and greater acculturation continued to be linked; now they could turn their ideas into an effective political program. They had already successfully argued that the nation needed educated, bilingual leaders familiar with American ways and laws if the Choctaws were to hold onto their homelands. They could now credibly extend this and assert that the Choctaws themselves would have to acculturate rapidly if they wished to remain in Mississippi. The Americans wrapped removal in a mantle of benevolence, arguing that they only wished to rescue starving hunters from impoverishment and degradation. Even the full-blood chiefs recognized that the strongest counterargument was that the Choctaws were not hunters but farmers and herdsmen rapidly adopting American manners. The mixed-bloods pushed the same argument with far more enthusiasm and sincerity.[70]

The convictions of this dominant and relatively wealthy mixed-blood elite were reflected in the constitution they drafted for the nation in 1826 and in subsequent laws they passed. The Americans had long encouraged the Choctaws to form a strong government, one that "should possess a strong coercive power sufficient to punish crimes and compel justice." The Constitution of 1826 strove to achieve this end. It was clearly only a beginning, however, since the combination of three elected district chiefs serving for four years provided only a weak executive, and the national council seems to have consisted in fact of the captains of the nation—the local leaders whose strength lay in their *iksas*. Nonetheless, the mixed-bloods were hopeful; they believed a Christian, westernized nation would emerge from these still quite traditional roots. As George Harkins, later chief of the Western District, wrote Peter Pitchlynn, the time was not far off when the Choctaws, at that time in a "state of darkness and superstition," would become "one of the most enlightened nations upon the face of the earth."[71]

The new elite was neither reticent about attacking traditional ways nor tactful in the pursuit of their ends. Their new laws renewed the ban on polygamy and infanticide, effectively enforced the ban on whiskey traffic, provided for inheritance through the male line—a crippling blow to both the *iksa* and the control of women over property, set new guidelines for the settling of estates, provided for the lawful enclosure of fields, and prohibited trespassing. In the Western District, LeFlore banned traditional burial ceremonies, long opposed by the missionaries as an occasion for feasting, drinking, and ball playing, and as a diversion from the pursuit of industry and thrift. In addition, the new chiefs renewed the old drive for self-sufficiency. They successfully encouraged cotton cultivation and weaving. By 1828 there were 530 spinning wheels and 124 looms in the Northeastern District alone, and many families manufactured enough cloth to be self-sufficient in that old staple of the trade. The chiefs also diverted annuity money to stock blacksmith shops built by Choctaw labor and staffed them with people trained in the mission school and with outsiders.[72]

This dual assault on Choctaw customs and Choctaw dependency was possible because of the continuing threat of removal but also because of what might be called an incipient Choctaw middle class in the borderlands—families with small herds, increasing amounts of land under cultivation, and a growing involvement in producing a surplus for the market. This group arose from the continuing migration of Choctaws outward from the old town core. Whole *iksas* of destitute full-bloods settled in the borderlands, acquired livestock and came under the influence of the mixed-blood captains of the area. Men such as David Folsom purposefully sought out impoverished hunters to form settlements. As these people prospered, they often became their captains' political allies, far more sympathetic than most Choctaws to calls for education, sobriety, and thrift. Together the removal issue and the growing prosperity of some borderland Choctaws gave the elite the power to push forward what otherwise would have been an impossible program of modernization.[73]

The program surged forward on a volatile and emotional mix of Christianity and fear for the future, which manifested in a massive Christian revival that swept across the nation in 1828. Folsom, Le-Flore, Garland, and other leading mixed-blood chiefs continued, of course, to cooperate closely with the American Board missionaries, but by the late 1820s these missionaries had been joined by Methodists. At a Methodist camp meeting in the Western District during the summer of 1828 the Christian revival began. Significantly, the initial converts were captains. In 1828 such men were under unprecedented pressure. Local leaders who realized the depth of their people's opposition to removal served with district chiefs who told them that to be effective this opposition had to involve the destruction of the same traditional system that sustained the captains themselves. To survive, the Choctaws had to become new men, and the captains faced a staggering array of mixed-blood proposals designed to reorder their world. More than any other people in the nation, these men bore the burden of crisis and change, and in 1828 at a summer camp meeting five or six of them broke down, wept, and appeared to be "new creatures." By October the revival was general in the west, and during the winter it moved not only into the Northeastern District but also to the south. Captains led and organized meetings at which the district chiefs as well as the missionaries spoke. By the winter of 1830 missionaries estimated that one-quarter of the nation, including many town chiefs and captains, were "anxious inquirers after Christ."[74]

This outpouring of Christian enthusiasm paralleled new American efforts at removal. In the spring of 1828 just before the revivals began, a bill to force the removal of the Choctaws passed the House of Representatives but failed in the Senate. At the time revivals began, a Choctaw exploring expedition was leaving the nation, persuaded by the government at least to look at the "goodly" land in the west. The revival spread as word of the election of Andrew Jackson reached the nation and as the Mississippi's jurisdiction over the Choctaws—a law which presaged the future but which, as yet, had little effect. In September of 1829, as the revival solidified and Choctaws actually became members of the Christian churches, the American agent Colonel William Ward brought before the Choctaw Council of the Northeastern and Southern Districts new government proposals for removal. The Choctaws, especially their captains, obviously had much to disturb them as they flocked to "the anxious seats" of the camp meetings. In large part the Choctaws were translating anxiety over their lives and land into anxiety over their souls. John Pitchlynn, who favored removal, sourly described the chiefs' message: "Join the church and keep your country."[75]

Conversion did serve the political ends of the nation; it was not only a religious phenomenon, but also a political, cultural, and economic one. It is fitting that in the vicinity of the American Board stations the revival began among Choctaws who had originally gathered not to prepare the way for Christ but to prepare the way for a blacksmith by cutting wood and building a shop. For the remainder of the revival, religious and secular ambitions would remain similarly intermingled in the minds of both Choctaws and missionaries. As the missionaries were quick to point out, the results of the revival were as much economic as religious. Seeking salvation and raising cotton, for instance, proved to be complementary endeavors. In 1829 many Indians took up cotton raising for the first time and the Choctaws raised 124,000 pounds in the vicinity of Eliot Mission alone. Missionaries, who reported that the Indians cultivated more land in a better manner (i.e., like the whites) than ever before, unabashedly measured their success in material as well as religious terms, citing "an increase of industry, and a consequent advance in dress, furniture, and all the comforts and conveniences of civilized life."[76]

In such an atmosphere the mixed-blood elite could push cultural change more harshly and more forcibly than they had in the early 1820s. The penalties invoked for crimes against property such as theft were draconian—50 lashes for the first offense, 100 for the second, and death for the third—but beyond that the new Christian order made the punishments virtually a religious ceremony. Horatio Cushman's eyewitness account of the punishment of a man for theft during the 1820s at the mission station of Hebron illustrates both the physical and religious force thrown behind this new sanctity of property.

Before the hour appointed the neighborhood assembled around the church which stood about forty rods distant from the missionhouse [sic], where they indulged in social conversation and smoking; never, however, mentioning, or even hinting the subject which had brought them together. The culprit was as gay and cheerful as any of them, walking with an air of perfect indifference, chatting and smoking with the various groups sitting around on blankets spread upon the ground. Precisely at the moment designated, the lighthorse [police] would appear. The crowd then went into church, closed the door, and commenced singing a religious hymn, taught them by the missionaries, which they continued until the tragedy outside was over. At the same time the culprit shouted "Sa mintih!" (I have come!) then ejaculated "Sa kulle!" (I am strong) He then elevated his arms and turned his back to the executioner and said: "Fummih" (whip). When he had received fifteen or twenty blows, he calmly turned the otherside to the Fummi (one who whips); and then again his back, uttering not a word or manifesting the least sign of pain. As soon as the whipping was over, the church door was opened and the whole assembly came out and shook hands with the "Fummsh" (whipped) thus reinstating him to his former position in society, and the subject was then dropped, never to be mentioned again, and it never was.[77]

The old warrior ideal obviously persisted here. Just as a man surrendered himself for retribution under blood law, he surrendered himself here, taking punishment with stoicism and dignity. But now the punishment went to protect the unevenly divided property of the nation, not life; and as significant as the ferociousness of the penalty was the simultaneous attempt to sanctify the punishment as a Christian action.

Such marked signs of acculturation had great political value since the Americans contended that the Choctaws were already being reduced to a mass of drunken and impoverished hunters. The mixed-blood chiefs like Folsom countered such arguments by pointing to the marked reduction in the liquor trade, the rise of stockraising, and the growing influence of Christianity. This acculturation, however, had not proceeded evenly. The borderlands appear to have provided the bulk of Christian converts (this is where most of the missions were) and the core of support for the mixed-blood chiefs. These borderland converts were the people Folsom and the missionaries pointed to with pride as the most prosperous and fastest growing segment of the nation.[78]

While the population of the borderlands had become increasingly Christian, pastoral, agricultural, and relatively prosperous, the core areas changed more slowly. There available resources were fewer; the amount of cultivated land was smaller, most people owned only a cow or a few hogs; and, especially in the Sixtowns, the remnants of the old horticultural-hunting economy lingered on. As long as the mixed-blood leaders presented the nation's best hope of preventing removal, chiefs such as Folsom and LeFlore could draw support from these regions despite their own hostility to traditional ways. This the Americans refused to recognize, even as they correctly insisted that the economic interests of the mixed-bloods differed fundamentally from those of these poorer Choctaws.

The emigration to the borderlands had resulted in very real economic differences among the Choctaws. A portion of the nation had expropriated the richest Choctaw lands. Once the borderlands had provided food and deerskins for all Choctaws; now they were monopolized by the mixed-bloods and the increasing number of full-bloods who joined them there. Those Choctaws who remained in the old core area, whether they hunted or grazed a few animals, now

Table 4. Classification of Agricultural Lands, Northeastern District

	Land Classification		
Households	Good	Tolerable	Poor
Old Core area:			
Number	2	47	130
Percentage	1	26	73
Borderlands:			
Number	131	223	200
Percentage	24	40	36

NOTE: Land quality is not noted for all households in the district.

SOURCE: National Archives, Record Group 75, Records of the Bureau of Indian Affairs, Armstrong Census.

operated within a subsistence cycle which had been badly truncated. The borderlands, once an integral part of the subsistence system, had been removed from their control. These lands might now produce more; however, not all of the pork, corn, beef, and even cotton they yielded went for subsistence. Part of it was now diverted into the market for the benefit of those Choctaws who insisted on their right to retain, not redistribute, all the fruits of their labor (or their slaves' labor) on these lands.

The existence of commercial agriculture, the rise of the wealthy mixed-bloods, and the persistence of the older economy in core areas are all reflected in the Choctaw removal census of 1830. The census is largely agricultural; it does not reflect Choctaw possession of livestock since the special agent in charge of enumerating the Choctaw herds died in the nation before his work was complete. The document, however, still gives a sense of the condition of the nation in the late 1820s as long as it is interpreted in the light of Mushulatubbee's statement that the Choctaws were herdsmen, not farmers. As Table 4 shows, the households in the borderlands farmed much more fertile lands than those in the core areas of the northeast.[79]

Although the majority of this agriculture remained subsistence hoe agriculture, both the plow and commercial agriculture had made substantial inroads into the borderland areas. By 1829 there were 360 plows in the Northeastern District alone, or a plow for almost every other household if they were distributed evenly (which they almost certainly were not). Most families with plows probably used them only to lighten the labor involved in putting in their traditional plots of corn, beans, and squash, but some families began raising new crops and produced a small surplus for the market.[80]

This market agriculture, however, took place on two vastly different scales. A very few intermarried whites and mixed-blood Choctaws undertook large-scale cotton cultivation with slave labor, while a much larger group of people, both full-bloods and mixed-bloods, produced a small surplus of corn which they sold to the mission stations, to the government factory, or to travelers. In 1830 Stephen Ward, the son of the agent, wrote that he had bought hundreds of bushels of corn along the Natchez Trace, and his father William Ward reported that the Choctaws had become major suppliers of beef and pork to the surrounding white settlements.[81]

Whites and mixed-bloods clearly contributed the bulk of this new agricultural commerce. Whites who had spent their lives in trade could not help regarding their growing herds as marketable commodities, especially when just to the west along the Mississippi ready markets for livestock existed. These markets grew steadily as Americans settled around the nation and moved through it in increasing numbers.

The large-scale cultivation of commercial crops in the nation began relatively late. In 1801, for example, only about a dozen people grew cotton at all, and the Choctaws rejected entreaties by some of the traders and mixed-bloods that they accept an American offer of a cotton gin for the nation. By the 1820s, however, many of the intermarried whites and their mixed-blood children had begun full-scale plantation agriculture. In 1830 in the Western District, Greenwood LeFlore had 250 acres under cultivation and his cousin Benjamin had 100. In the Northeastern District, David Folsom had 150 acres under cultivation; John Pitchlynn, the intermarried white interpreter, had 200 acres, part of it farmed by a white tenant; and Peter Pitchlynn had 90 acres. There was less large-scale commercial agriculture in the Southern District, but even there Joel Nail had 140 acres under culti-

Table 5. Households with Twenty or More Acres
under Cultivation ("Commercial" Farmers)

	Southern District	Northeastern District	Western District	Total
Intermarried whites	4	11	8	22
Choctaws with English names	4	30	75	110
Choctaws with native names	11	8	26	45
Total	19	49	109	177

SOURCE: National Archives, Record Group 75, Records
of the Bureau of Indian Affairs, Armstrong Census.

vation and Allen Yates, an intermarried white man, also farmed 140
acres. Although figures are not available, it appears that a substantial
portion of the acreage of these men was devoted to cotton. These
wealthy whites and mixed-bloods were only the largest farmers; many
others in the nation had 20 or more acres in cultivation. As Table 5
shows, most of these people were Choctaws, not intermarried whites;
but in all probability many of the Choctaws with white names were
mixed-bloods.[82]

As among the neighboring Americans, in the Choctaw nation
cotton cultivation on a large scale was conducted by slave labor. Only
about sixty-five households, or 2 percent of those in the nation, held
any slaves, and these households were headed disproportionately by
intermarried whites and by mixed-bloods. Intermarried white households, for example, comprised only 2 percent of the nation, but they
held 15 percent of the slaves. Mixed-bloods are not identified as such
on the census, but since 94 percent of the slave-holding households
were headed by people with English names (including intermarried
whites), probably the vast majority of the slaveholders were people of
mixed-blood. An examination of the census reveals that the leading

slaveholders were rich mixed-blood planters. Greenwood LeFlore, for instance, owned thirty-two slaves, Della Brashears had sixteen, Cornelius Kearney had twelve, Rubin Harris had twenty, George Turnbull had nine, Joseph Perry had twenty-one, David Folsom had seventeen, and Joel Nail had eight. John Pitchlynn, an intermarried white, owned more slaves than anyone else with fifty.[83]

Distinguishing the smaller commercial farmers who raised a few extra acres of corn or cotton for the market from the purely subsistence farmers is far more difficult than identifying the slaveholding elite. Since no records on the marketing of crops are available, the problem is one of defining commercial agriculture in terms of acreage. The Sixtowns can, perhaps, serve as a base. Here, in the least acculturated section of the nation, the average household cultivated a mean of 4.8 acres of land, which is substantially below the national average of 6.7 acres. A normal subsistence acreage would thus appear to be about 4 or 5 acres for a household, a figure that falls within the range of 1 to 10 acres for subsistence cultivation given by a visitor to the Choctaws soon after emigration. To be safe, however, a household engaged in raising a small surplus for the market will be defined here as one cultivating 10 or more acres of land. Under such a standard, only 20 percent of the nation was involved even marginally in market agriculture in 1831. The distribution is indicated in Table 6.

Like stockraising, market farming appears to have been greatest in the borderlands and among those who had English names. Mixed-bloods and those Choctaws most exposed to American culture, probably through the mission schools, seem to have participated disproportionately, but there remained a substantial participation in small-scale market agriculture by those Choctaws who retained native names and presumably some native culture. After all, 60 percent of the Choctaw commercial farmers did not have English names and thus were probably neither mixed-bloods nor mission educated. Although such farmers and their families formed only a small percentage (16 percent) of all households headed by Choctaws with native names, they reveal how pervasive the new economy was becoming. Taken together, the full-blood and mixed-blood market farmers formed a critical transitional segment of the nation, one that increasingly dominated local as well as national positions of authority. More and more, captains in the Western District and the Northeastern Dis-

Table 7. Choctaw Captains, 1830

District	Number with English Names	Number with Native Names	Number with ten or more Acres in Cultivation
Northeast	5	25	20
West	9	21	19
South	0	30	8

NOTE: There were 30 captains in each district.
SOURCE: National Archives, Record Group 75, Records of the Bureau of Indian Affairs, Armstrong Census.

been decisively breached. The *iksa* had been stripped of its control over property, which now descended through the male line; criminal punishment, once dominated by the blood revenge of the *iksa*, had now become the responsibility of the embryonic Choctaw state; the towns, the old center of the *iksa* and community life, were broken up; the ritual duties of the *iksa* such as the burial of the dead had virtually vanished; and, perhaps most significant of all, exogamy was weakening. Within a few years after removal to the west, the *iksas* themselves would begin to disappear as the prohibitions about marrying within them were disgarded. The change was a profound one for a people who had told the missionaries that the nation itself was unimaginable without the *iksas*.[85]

The old nation had been a collection of towns, families, and *iksas*; the new nation was becoming a collection of individuals whose well-being was determined not by communal obligations and resources but by the goods they could personally command on the market. The new nation was markedly divided by the distinctions in wealth, which the mixed-bloods defended as a social good. They did not see their growing wealth as the result of a market ethic which they had adopted but which their countrymen rejected, and of their expropriation of resources that had once been communal. In their eyes their superior wealth was solely the product of their superior industry, and, conversely, the poverty of their countrymen was the result of their lazi-

ness and lack of thrift. Even land had entered the market. A few of
the mixed-bloods such as John Pitchlynn and Robert Folsom had
begun leasing land to white tenants. This practice was in itself unimaginable in the nation just a few years before when only kinship and
personal use gave a right to the land. Others, however, had already
gone beyond this. They were buying and selling the land itself.
Greenwood LeFlore, for instance, in 1830 had bought 30 cultivated
acres for his son from a man named Roebuck and retained title to it,
although his son neither lived nor worked on the farm.[86]

Property and commercial exchange had achieved a preeminence
in the nation that they had never known before. Many categories of
men and women either previously unknown or very rare among the
Choctaws—trespassers, debtors, and thieves—became enshrined in
the new laws. All reflected a concern with protecting property. The
mixed-blood chiefs patronized their "poor blind brothers," as Greenwood LeFlore called them, and told them that their only salvation was
to imitate the Americans who oppressed them.[87]

Amidst such tensions, only the continued widespread belief in the
mixed-bloods' ability to prevent removal could keep the nation whole.
Once the Choctaws' perception of their effectiveness or determination weakened, there was little to prevent the nation from dissolving
into political chaos. The deposed chiefs were willing and ready to
capitalize on this situation.

Mushulatubbee had soon regretted his decision to relinquish the
chieftainship of the Northeastern District. He contended that he was
chief for life and still the legitimate leader of the northeastern Choctaws. Nitakechi in the south and Robert Cole in the west had joined
him in opposition to the new chiefs. Allied with them were the Pitchlynns, the prominent mixed-blood family related to Mushulatubbee.
John Pitchlynn served as a United States interpreter and thus was on
the American payroll. The Pitchlynns, wealthy and acculturated, had
been one of the few mixed-blood families in favor of removal; hardly
traditionalists, they shared the general mixed-blood enthusiasm for
westernization, but they were bitter political rivals of the Folsoms.
And it was the Folsoms, especially David Folsom, along with Greenwood LeFlore in the west and John Garland and the Nails in the
south, who led the mixed-blood opponents of removal. In 1828,
against the advice of John Pitchlynn, the United States government

had stopped paying Mushulatubbee and Robert Cole the $300 salary promised them for life, on the grounds that neither was any longer a chief. Mushulatubbee had complained that this was illegal and had insinuated that if his salary was restored and a fair treaty offered, he would lead a movement to remove. He went so far as to suggest in the fall of 1829 that "a few men" be invited to Washington to discuss removal. If the "proper means" were employed, he said, emigration was possible.[88]

That same fall, as Mushulatubbee offered his cooperation in removal, the government agent William Ward, put new United States proposals for removal before a joint council of the Northeastern and Southern districts. David Folsom argued against the proposals at the council, but he and Garland asked for time to reply in writing since LeFlore and the Western District were not represented. When the reply came in November, the chiefs reasserted their opposition to removal. They admitted that they alone could not stop the threatened extension of Mississippi's laws over the nation but called on the United States to protect Choctaw sovereignty under existing treaties. If the United States would not honor its existing obligations, why should the Indians have faith in any guarantee made in yet another treaty? Ward obviously expected such a reply and, in collaboration with John Pitchlynn, had already concocted a scheme by which the United States would recognize Mushulatubbee as chief, appoint another chief in the south, and negotiate with both of them.[89]

In December, Mushulatubbee called his own council and set his plan in motion. At the council he came out for removal and reported to Ward that the majority of the captains in the Northeastern District had elected him chief. Ward, contending that few captains had attended the counter-council called by Folsom (one which had elected him chief for life), now argued that Folsom and the other mixed-blood leaders were only "self-made chiefs." Folsom and the missionaries in turn contended that Mushulatubbee was unfit to be a chief and had virtually no popular support—arguments which, whatever their validity, were totally peripheral to Ward's concerns. He proposed that a treaty be negotiated with Mushulatubbee's faction.[90]

In December of 1829 the approaching political battle appeared to be a clear conflict between proremoval and antiremoval forces, a battle that Mushulatubbee and his allies could never legitimately hope to win. By March, however, the situation had changed dramatically, and mixed-blood control was doomed. Two events marked the change. In January, Mississippi extended her laws over the Choctaws and eliminated the nation's sovereignty by fiat. A $1,000 fine and a year in prison awaited any Choctaw who challenged the state's authority. In addition, sometime during that eventful fall or winter Greenwood LeFlore visited the Cherokee nation and returned convinced that the Methodist missionaries, who unlike the American Board missionaries saw removal as unavoidable, were correct: the Choctaws had no choice except to leave Mississippi. In March of 1830 he summoned Folsom and Garland to a council attended largely by people from his own Western District. Folsom and Garland used the occasion to promptly and publicly resign their offices, apparently fearing imprisonment under Mississippi law. LeFlore, now intending to support removal, had no such fear of prosecution and had himself elected head chief of the nation by those present. He then explained the dire effects which the actions taken by Mississippi would have on the nation; they left the Choctaws no choice but to remove. LeFlore then produced a manuscript removal treaty written in the hand of one of the Methodist missionaries, and those present, including Folsom and Garland, approved its terms and signed the document. LeFlore's coup was complete: in one move he had obliterated two of the nation's three divisions, had caused himself to be named as head chief, and had secured a removal treaty which included generous remuneration for himself and other leading men.[91]

LeFlore now presented the treaty to Mushulatubbee and argued that it offered far more than anything the Americans would produce on their own. Disassociating himself from Folsom, LeFlore offered to recognize Mushulatubbee's supporters as the true captains of the old Northeastern District if Mushulatubbee would in turn recognize him as head chief. Mushulatubbee, already involved in his own conspiracy with the Americans, was in danger of being totally preempted. He could not very well refuse to sign a removal treaty without alienating the Americans who backed his return to power, and, besides, he too regarded removal as inevitable. Yet to go along totally with LeFlore was to be coopted.[92]

Mushulatubbee extricated himself from this dilemma by igniting the smoldering social tensions of the nation. He quietly accepted and signed the removal treaty, but he simultaneously attacked LeFlore as a tyrant who had betrayed the nation to the Americans and arbitrarily eliminated the ancient divisions of the Choctaws. In this action, said Mushulatubbee, were the real fruits of acculturation and mixed-blood leadership—removal, betrayal, and the extinguishing of two of the three council fires by the fiat of a despotic, mixed-blood chief. Once he had signed the treaty, Mushulatubbee disavowed it—an action both safe and politic—and with Nitakechi convened a council of the Southern and Northeastern districts where he capitalized on antiremoval feeling to denounce the treaty and attack LeFlore's pretensions to the head chieftainship. He simultaneously went out of his way to let Agent Ward understand that he did not object to removal treaties *per se* only to LeFlore's treaty.[93]

Mushulatubbee had adroitly and effectively stymied his rivals. He had at once convinced the Americans that he would cooperate in removal and capitalized on the antiremoval sentiment aimed at LeFlore. He had tapped the deep resentment felt by many Choctaws against mixed-blood leadership. By April the Southern and Northeastern districts openly revolted against LeFlore and asserted their traditional autonomy. Throughout the nation Choctaws turned on the Christians, deserted the churches, and blamed missionaries and their converts for the nation's fate. The reaction was most pronounced in the south, always the most traditional area, where the Choctaws deposed Christian captains, repealed recent Sabbath laws, and promoted ball playing, feasts, and ceremonies. Even in the west, however, it appears that churches and schools were burned and Christians denounced.[94]

LeFlore's response was clumsy, heavy-handed, and ineffective. As early as April he threatened to use force against his full-blood rivals, but this threat only fortified his reputation as a tyrant since Mushulatubbee had already branded LeFlore, Folsom, and their followers, the Despotic Party. LeFlore did no better with the Americans. In May, with estimates of the ultimate cost of the settlement running around $50 million, the United States Senate rejected the treaty. Mushulatubbee welcomed news of the rejection and offered to negotiate a mutually more acceptable agreement.[95]

Outmaneuvered and politically embarrassed, LeFlore resorted to tactics born of desperation. He and Folsom gathered 400 warriors and marched against Mushulatubbee and Nitakechi, who were supervising the distribution of annuities. LeFlore asserted that he marched to halt Mushulatubbee's attacks on religion and education and the arson they provoked. His followers were apparently Christians from the borderlands angered by church and school burnings; they marched while singing Christian hymns. Folsom drew his support from the borderlands too. Mushulatubbee said only Christians and his relatives now followed Folsom, and white observers agreed that his support centered on the Christian northern, or borderland section, of his district. Mushulatubbee and Nitakechi armed their followers and prepared to resist, but LeFlore backed down. He got only token concessions and retreated with nothing accomplished.[96]

By August the nation had been reduced to almost complete turmoil and confusion. The mass of Choctaws both rejected removal and feared the impact of Mississippi's laws. They supported Mushulatubbee because he opposed the "despot" LeFlore and the mixed-blood leadership, who now seemed to many to have both oppressed and betrayed them. In reality, however, these people were leaderless. All the major factional leaders—Mushulatubbee, the Folsoms, the Pitchlynns, and LeFlore—were ready to negotiate with the Americans. All they refused to do was negotiate together. The opposition to removal felt by most of the nation was politically irrelevant. The council of the Western District reported that any captain or headman who negotiated for land was in danger of losing his life, but LeFlore still was ready to sign a removal treaty. Little Leader, a prominent town chief, reportedly promised to kill any man who signed a removal treaty, but all the district chiefs were ready to cooperate with Mushulatubbee in securing such a treaty.[97]

The Americans confidently pressed forward with treaty preparations. LeFlore and Folsom threatened to boycott any negotiations held with their rivals, but American officials correctly recognized that they would have to attend "in self-defense." On September 18, 1830, the final treaty council that the Americans held with the Choctaws in Mississippi convened at Dancing Rabbit Creek in the Northeastern District. Whiskey dealers, prostitutes, and gamblers flocked freely to the grounds, but the commissioners for the United States banned the antiremoval American Board missionaries. Predictably, the council opened with factional fighting between LeFlore and his full-blood rivals, but after a compromise settlement, which gave LaFlore's supporters half the positions on a negotiating team headed by Peter Pitchlynn, discussion of the treaty began. The Choctaw negotiators talked with the Americans and considered their proposals for five days; however, camped around them were 6,000 of their countrymen and countrywomen, who dominated the early negotiations. The Choctaw negotiators informed the Americans on September 23 that they had decided not to accept the offers for their land. "It is the voice of a very large majority of the people here present not to sell the land of their forefathers."[98]

This Choctaw refusal did not end negotiations, however. It only began them. Thousands of Choctaws left the grounds believing the council was over, but Eaton forcefully reminded the Choctaw commissioners that the alternative to removal was the enforcement of Mississippi's laws. The Choctaws' commission asked him to remain a few days and on September 25 accepted the major American proposals. On the twenty-seventh the removal treaty was signed. The leadership, for whom the Americans had included lucrative land grants, had accepted removal; the mass of the nation did not. The missionaries reported that in the Sixtowns only one chief signed the treaty although he eventually brought three or four captains to support it, and similarly in Chickasawhay only a single captain and a few warriors were in favor of the cession. Shock and despair spread throughout the nation as the Choctaws received news of the treaty. Opposition, which the government blamed on the missionaries, was immediate, and enemies of the treaty deposed those leaders of both factions who had supported it. In the Western District opponents of the treaty deposed LeFlore and elected George Harkins; in the Northeastern District Folsom, who had also signed the treaty, nevertheless led a rebellion against Mushulatubbee; and in the Southern District Joel Nail succeeded Nitakechi.[99]

As an effective tactic against the treaty, the attack on these leaders was meaningless. Not only did the Americans refuse to recognize the new chiefs, but the leaders themselves betrayed their cause. Nail and Folsom themselves had signed the treaty and were only turning the massive opposition to it to their own factional advantage. In fact, of the new chiefs, only George Harkins does not appear to have signed. Likewise Jerry Folsom and Peter Pitchlynn, the two men who led the fight for the repudiation of the treaty, had both signed it. Their opposition, too, had as much to do with factional maneuvering as with sincere opposition. Folsom quickly gave up his opposition, but Pitchlynn would eventually emerge as the leader of the migration and head chief of the nation.[100]

Real opposition centered in the mass of the nation who were leaderless. These were the "hundreds of ignorant Indians . . . daily councilling among themselves," desperately trying to overturn the treaty. These "ignorant Indians" deposed LeFlore, in part for selling his country but also because his laws were "oppressive and degrading." These charges David Folsom believed weighed even more heavily against LeFlore than did his signing of the treaty—an act in which virtually the entire leadership of both factions was implicated.[101]

The real helplessness of the poor who opposed the treaty was not only political, it was also social and economic. Although social divisions and factional quarreling continued in the nation into 1831, the economic vulnerability of the poorer Choctaws had crippled the opposition to the treaty by the fall of 1830. In 1830 Choctaw crops failed in a drought. The mixed-bloods and chiefs like Mushulatubbee worried about their herds; the poor worried about their lives. The secondary subsistence cycle was gone, and the rich Choctaws had abandoned any responsibility for redistribution. The poor emigrated in search of food, the factional leaders quarreled over the spoils of the treaty. Even for those who remained, access to food and goods rivaled removal as a political issue. By spring, political fighting in the south centered on a quarrel among Kunshak, Chickasawhay, and the Sixtowns over the distribution of annuities.[102]

The Choctaws fought through the last months before removal with social and factional divisions splitting them on a welter of issues. Eventually the nation achieved a tentative and unstable unity behind Peter Pitchlynn. He was a mixed-blood but also a nephew of Mushulatubbee and a man with a family history of political opposition to LeFlore and the Folsoms and thus acceptable to their enemies. Since he was also pro-Christian and proacculturation, however, he was acceptable to their followers, the Christian borderland Choctaws. Finally, since he had led both the commission that negotiated the treaty and the national opposition to the same treaty, he was unimpeachable on the removal issue.

One of the old factional leaders, Folsom, would remove, but the years of his greatest political influence were over. He died in 1847, proud to the end of his role in transforming the Choctaws. The inscription on his gravestone reads: "To the memory of Colonel David Folsom, the first Republican Chief of the Chahtah Nation, the promoter of industry, education, religion, and morality." LeFlore remained in Mississippi, retained his plantation, lived the life of a Southern planter, and eventually was elected to the Mississippi Legislature. Mushulatubbee, his enemy and rival, also removed, and settled a separate district with his followers and banned missionaries from it. Mushulatubbee died of smallpox in 1838 but until the end displayed passive resistance to further acculturation. Under Pitchlynn the mixed-bloods continued to dominate the nation, which grew more Christian. As the concern with property increased, the old ways and values that conflicted with the new order declined.[103]

The continuing evolution of the Choctaw nation took place in Indian Territory while behind them in Mississippi Americans settled their old homeland. It was a land that for hundreds of years had been shaped by the Choctaws. Its small prairies, its longleaf pine forests, its animal populations—all of these the Choctaws had created or influenced, and all in turn had had reciprocal influences on the nation. As the Choctaws started west, driving their cattle, horses, and swine before them, they left a much altered land. The deer were virtually gone; the old hunting grounds were farms and plantations; the once prosperous interior was impoverished with its old clearings returning to forest. All of these physical changes were the legacy of Choctaw social change.

Purely biological change resulting from European contact had also influenced the nation, but its influence must not be overestimated. European diseases, European animals, and European crops were all important, but none of them in and of themselves transformed the nation. Disease, for example, had cut population, but the Choctaws had succeeded in halting the decline and preventing either demographic or social collapse. Likewise, domestic animals affected the Choctaws, but only within the changing social context of the nation. Pigs, cattle, and cotton, for example, were virtually ignored for generations but became quite significant in the late eighteenth and early nineteenth century as settlement spread to the borderlands. Pigs, cattle, and cotton, in this sense then, did not transform Choctaw culture; rather Choctaw culture controlled them by relegating them initially to the periphery of Choctaw life before bringing them to the center. Yet these elements indicate a change in Choctaw culture and society and raise the question of what initiated this change.

If any single factor is to be isolated as critical for understanding the fate of the Choctaws, it is market. The market and liquor emptied the forests of game; they brought into the nation the white traders who intermarried, pushed cattle herds into the borderlands, and started cotton plantations. The market forced land sales; it created distinctions of wealth unknown in the older order which it crippled. And when removal came, the market was well on its way to reducing Choctaw land and labor—once inseparable from other social relations—to mere commodities to be bought and sold.

The market was not "natural" for the Choctaws. It was an alien way of allocating goods, and they resisted it for generations. The play-off system, their own self-sufficiency, and their military strength made their resistance successful, but when the French vanished and the English employed credit and liquor effectively, the Choctaws' resistance collapsed, and they were trapped. Even those Choctaws who adopted market values most enthusiastically showed some ambivalence about their consequences for the nation. They adopted a new vision of self-sufficiency to combat the dependency that eroded their homeland through cessions to the Americans. This vision of self-sufficiency, which was coupled to the mixed-bloods' own search for wealth, was not achieved. For the Choctaws as a whole, trade and market meant not wealth but impoverishment, not well-being but dependency, and not progress but exile and dispossession. They never fought the Americans; they were never conquered. Instead, through the market they were made dependent and dispossessed.

CHAPTER 6

The Pawnees

At the beginning of the thirteenth century a drought greater than any
during the recorded history of the area came to the Great Plains. As
the rains failed year after year and the crops withered in the fields,
the hunters and horticulturalists who lived along the rivers of
present-day western Nebraska and Kansas (whom archaeologists have
called the Upper Republicans) abandoned their small earthlodges on
the central plains and moved east. Behind them the incessant winds
covered the deserted villages with 10 to 20 inches of fine loess, a mute
testimony to the severity of the climatic change that had forced the
occupants away.[1]

The drought was an environmental catastrophe. It set numerous
peoples in motion, rearranged the social and political geography
of the plains, and temporarily increased warfare among groups
competing for the now scarce resource of arable land. As previously
separated cultures came together, they shared as well as fought;
archaeologists have demonstrated that people exchanged various material techniques, objects, and probably beliefs. Yet what is surprising is
how little these cultures responded specifically to the drought. Any
force that prompted large-scale migrations and cultural contacts might
have been expected to produce roughly the same changes that the
drought did. Crudely stated, the people's locations changed, not their
habits.

The drought points up the dangers of regarding environmental
alterations alone as the mainspring of historical evolution. The evi-

dence suggests that on the central and northern plains the cultural response to environmental disaster was increased competition for scarce resources rather than technological innovation. When the land no longer yielded to their customary techniques, the plains horticulturalists moved to lands that would. Their culture was not clay in the hands of some environmental potter; it changed little. On the middle Missouri River in South Dakota there are some indications of short-term adjustments in the horticulturalists' subsistence patterns; they stayed in one place for shorter periods, and they may very well have been forced to rely more on hunting and gathering and less on horticulture because of lessened rainfall. But here, too, it appears that their reaction was to push northward to better watered portions of the Missouri valley and reestablish older patterns. When cooler, moister conditions returned with the Neo-Boreal period of the sixteenth century, the technology and subsistence patterns of the villagers were essentially what they had been before the droughts of the thirteenth century.[2]

The Pawnees originated from the earthlodge villagers of the central plains. Horticulturalists had reestablished themselves along the Loup River by the fifteenth century when the climate of the plains ameliorated. Archaeologists, by tracing the evolution of ceramic designs and by other cultural comparisons, have established that these returning farmers, the people of the Loup Focus, were ancestors of the Pawnees. The precise descent of the Pawnees from these people is not clear.[3] The basic division of the nation into the Skidis on the one hand and the South Bands (the Grands [Tsawi or Chaui], the Republicans [Kitkehaxhi], and the Tapages [Pitahawirats]) on the other is an ancient one. The Pawnees claimed that this division antedated the nation itself. The Skidis asserted original kinship with the Arikaras, who lived farther north on the Missouri River, while the South Bands claimed that they were once the Kawarahkis, a single group who had migrated north with the Wichitas.[4]

Whatever the origins of the two groups, the union of the Skidis and the South Bands was often a factious one. The two tribes disagreed on who had created and who dominated the nation. According to traditions of the South Bands, the Skidis were already present in the Loup valley when they arrived, and the Kawarahkis "conquered" the earlier tribe and made them a subject people. This conquest the Skidis denied, asserting instead that they were the most powerful and important Pawnee tribe. In any case, long after the formation of the nation—or more accurately, confederation—the Skidis remained distinct from the three South Bands. They spoke a separate dialect, maintained unique traditions and ceremonies, went on separate buffalo hunts, and, as recently as the late eighteenth century, even engaged in armed battle with the other tribes.[5]

By the early sixteenth century the initial movements into the Loup valley had ended, and the constituent elements of the Pawnees had established themselves along the river. The Skidis occupied a series of villages in the vicinity of Beaver Creek, while the Kawarahkis, or South Bands, settled near Shell Creek. By the early seventeenth century the Kawarahkis had expanded southwest and built their villages on the south bank of the Platte, while the Skidis remained on the Loup. All these villages, especially those on Beaver Creek, covered large areas, taking in from 15 to 100 acres. Their builders located them on bluffs and hilltops seemingly with an eye for defense and in a few cases fortified the villages with walls and ditches. Edwin James, who visited the area with the Long expedition of 1820, even wrote of ancient remains of large forts in the vicinity of Beaver Creek near the center of the Skidis' villages.[6]

This concern with defense could have been a product of the invasion of Skidi territory by the Kawarahkis, or it could have resulted from clashes with the Apaches of the Dismal River culture farther west. But these attacks, whoever made them, were serious and on occasion quite costly, as archaeological remains seem to testify. At the Wright Site above the Beaver Creek valley, archaeologists found fifty human skeletons on the floor of one burned lodge, presumably the victims of a successful assault and evidence to the violence of the conflict.[7]

Despite signs of war, the two centuries that followed Pawnee settlement on the Loup and Platte appear to have been, on the whole, prosperous and fruitful. The Lower Loup Focus sites are distinguished not only by their large areas but also by the number and size of their storage, or cache, pits. The village economy seems to have produced large, storable surpluses, and in the round earthlodges the elaborate culture of the Pawnees flowered. The Skidis and Kawarahkis built their villages according to ritual requirements often neglected by the historic Pawnees. In Lower Loup villages, for instance, the earthlodges had only four center posts, and the entrances

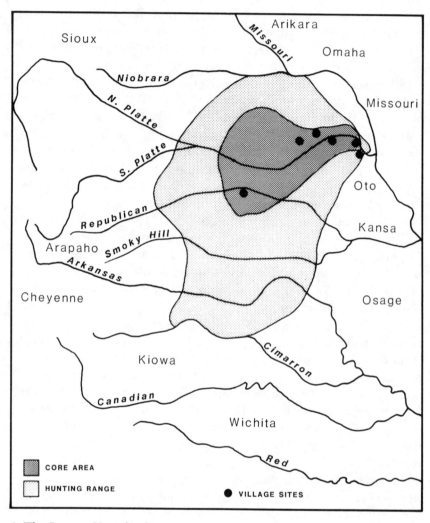

4. The Pawnee Homeland

to the lodges invariably faced east—requirements remembered but often not practiced during the nineteenth century.[8]

The decline of the Pawnees in the nineteenth century represented the failure of a horticultural-hunting system, which was centuries old, in the face of new competition and changed conditions. Here, simple material forces—disease, horses, new technologies—only seem an adequate explanation for social change. Undeniably they were crucial elements, but Pawnee culture was an equally important component of the nation's nineteenth-century history. The relationships between environment, production, and demography on the one hand, and the cultural "superstructure" on the other are complex. One is not merely derivative of the other. Culture itself shapes environments, limits the uses to which technology can be put, and governs the intensity of production. These material forces are not truly independent. Both symbolically and materially, culture shapes the natural world.

Natural events, no matter how significant, do not affect people directly. Culture mediates between people and the natural world. This is not to deny the obvious. Smallpox kills humans and humans starve when crops fail repeatedly, regardless of their culture. But just as clearly, historical change is not merely the product of smallpox epidemics or crop failures. Dead people do not make history. The survivors must interpret the meaning of their experience and act accordingly, and they do this only within a given cultural context. It is from their interpretations and actions, which are in turn the result of their previous history, that cultural change comes.

The problem of change thus becomes quite complex. The meaning human beings give to their world and the order they create for it must be considered along with material factors affecting production. Pawnee material life is important, but it is historically meaningful only when placed within its proper cultural context.

When the first Europeans arrived in the central plains during the sixteenth century, the Pawnees seem to have been in the midst of a great creative burst of cultural and tribal organization. This owed nothing to European influences. Even if the Pawnees were the Harahay who met Coronado at the Wichita villages in 1540, the contact was fleeting and unimportant. After Coronado, Europeans visited the plains only intermittently for more than a century, and the cultural evolution of the Pawnees continued virtually unaffected by the white presence elsewhere on the continent. They concentrated their villages on the Loup and Platte, usually bordering the rivers themselves rather than on their tributary streams, and each summer and winter they moved west to hunt the buffalo. Eventually they claimed a hunting territory that stretched from their villages to the region between the forks of the Platte and then south to the Kansas River and, less firmly, to the Arkansas.[9]

The Pawnees did not have exclusive claim to this territory. To the west the Apaches, dog nomads who followed the buffalo herds, occupied the core of the old Upper Republican territory and blocked further Pawnee expansion. By the end of the seventeenth century a portion of the Apaches had taken up limited horticulture in the stream bottoms west of the 98th meridian and adopted an economic pattern very similar to the older Upper Republican system. The Apaches would remain enemies of the Pawnees until they were in turn pushed south during the eighteenth century by the invading Comanches, who inherited not only the Apache's territory but also their wars with the Pawnees.[10]

During the eighteenth century the shape and context of this warfare began to change. As the effects of European settlement to the east and southwest rippled outward in the form of guns, horses, and disease, tribal conflicts on the plains may have intensified. Tribes strengthened by the acquisition of horses and guns preyed upon more isolated peoples. Like the Choctaws, the Pawnees became victims of slave raiders.

Although slave raiding became endemic on the plains, historians have probably overemphasized its impact on the Pawnees. The very word "Pani" came to mean a slave taken from the plains by tribes allied to the French, but the Pani slaves of the French were usually not Pawnees at all. Indeed, the Pawnees seem to have continued to prosper and expand during this period. When to the south of them Siouan tribes such as the Kansas displaced the Wichitas, the Pawnees too moved southward to take over new territory. The Republicans and Tapages first joined the Skidis (Panimaha) and Grands (Pani) in the historical record during the mid and late eighteenth century when they split off from the Grands, perhaps violently. The Republicans established villages on the Republican River and the Tapages built their lodges on the Smoky Hill and Blue rivers. With the creation of these tribes and their movement south, the Pawnees reached their maximum historic territorial limits. Such an expansion seems unlikely among a people ravaged by slave raiders.[11]

The Pawnees, by moving into Kansas, came into increasing conflict with the southern prairie tribes, particularly the Kansas and Osages. By the early nineteenth century, warfare with these peoples had grown serious enough to induce first the Tapages and then the Republicans to retreat north into the Platte valley. During the 1820s the Republicans returned to Kansas and rebuilt at least one village on the Republican River, but in the 1830s they relinquished the region for good, although they continued to hunt along the western Republican until they removed to Indian territory in the 1870s.[12]

To the east of the Pawnees, the Otoes, Omahas, and Missouris, dispossessed by Sioux expansion, peacefully moved into the Missouri valley and the lower Platte during the eighteenth century. The displaced tribes lived, the Pawnees claimed, under their protection and on the whole the relationship among these tribes appears to have been friendly, marred only occasionally by raiding and fighting.[13]

The Pawnees faced their most formidable enemies on the mixed-grass plains to the west. The Spanish, however, seem to have remained more a potential than an actual threat. A half century after Coronado's visit a second Spanish expediton penetrated the plains where it was met and destroyed by Indians, perhaps the Pawnees, in 1593. By the early 1700s the presence in New Mexico of the Spanish with their horses and trade goods had lured Pawnee warriors south where they became feared raiders, first of the Spanish settlements and later of the Sante Fe Trail. In response, the Spaniards sent at least two more expeditions against the Pawnees. The first of these, a force of over 100 led by Pedro Villasur, the Pawnees and Otoes destroyed on the upper Platte in 1720. The second expedition, which arrived at the Pawnee villages just before Zebulon Pike's American exploring expedition of 1806, concluded a peace with the tribe. But, since the Skidis ratified the agreement by stealing most of the Spaniards' horses, the treaty apparently imposed few real controls on Pawnee raiders.[14]

The Comanches, who drove the Apaches from the Great Plains between 1720 and 1750 and moved steadily south toward the source of horses in New Mexico, represented a much more immediate and formidable threat to the Pawnees than did the Spanish. The Pawnees raided the Comanches to acquire horses and fought them over western hunting grounds until the 1840s. They feared these nomadic horsemen above the rest of their enemies until they experienced an abrupt and simultaneous increase in pressure from the Americans and Sioux in the mid-nineteenth century. The Pawnees had had contacts with both these groups for decades, but only in the 1830s did they become immediate threats to the tribe. The Americans pushed in from the east, and although they never fought the Pawnees, and in fact were usually at least their nominal allies, they weakened the villagers by introducing disease and slaughtering the buffalo along the Platte. The Sioux came down from the north and west and steadily conquered Pawnee hunting grounds, raided and destroyed villages, and defeated Pawnee war parties. By the 1870s the Pawnees surrendered; against the wishes of their American agents they moved south, out of their Nebraska homeland, into Indian territory.[15]

Pawnee population throughout these years fluctuated as much as their political fortunes. From their settlement on the Loup until the mid-eighteenth century the Pawnees probably maintained or increased their numbers. A rising population appears to have contributed to the steady spread of their villages from the Loup valley into the Platte valley, and to the creation of the Tapage and Republican villages on the banks of the Smoky Hill, Republican and Blue rivers. Eighteenth-century references to the number of Pawnees were vague and unreliable, but Europeans consistently described the tribe as very numerous, inhabiting from ten to two dozen or more villages of indeterminate size. Furthermore, the internal organization of the Skidis was based on a confederation of thirteen villages (with two other villages remaining independent). Since the Skidis inhabited only a single village during the nineteenth century, the surmise of a larger eighteenth-century population seems warranted. A population of 20,000 people is a reasonable estimate for the Pawnees before the arrival of epidemic diseases in the mid-eighteenth century.[16]

When these epidemics arrived, the rise in Pawnee population ceased. The decline in the estimates of Pawnee warrior strength during the late eighteenth century probably reflected the inroads of European diseases on the tribe. Smallpox and measles epidemics struck the Grands in the 1750s and in the 1790s the Pawnees suffered dreadfully from smallpox. If they sustained the same fatalities as other village tribes during this period, at least one-third to one-half of them died. This population decline was not permanent, however, and between 1800 and 1830 the Pawnees appear to have increased once again. Zebulon M. Pike estimated the tribal population at a little over 6,000 in 1806, but he actually saw only one Republican village. His count did not include the Tapages at all, and he only estimated the number of Skidis and Grands, the two largest tribes. The actual population of the Pawnees in 1806 was probably closer to 8,000 or 10,000 people.[17]

By all indications the Pawnee birth rate continued quite high during the early nineteenth century. When George Sibley visited the tribe in the summer of 1811, he remarked on the high proportion of women, girls, adolescents, and children in comparison to men and thought the Pawnees were increasing in numbers. In 1823 Paul Wilhelm, the Duke of Wurttemberg, visited the Pawnees and reported that they were proud of their great numbers. The head chief, Scharkerul-leschar, told him that "the Pawnee nation counted as many heads as the stars in the sky, so that they could not be counted." This is hardly the kind of statement made by the leader of a people in decline. Estimates of population during the 1820s clustered around 10,000 but, again, because these figures were not usually based on actual observation, it can be assumed that the real population may have been significantly higher.[18]

In 1831 smallpox returned to the villages for the first time in three decades and killed, according to the Pawnees' American agent, half the population. Yet even after the epidemic his estimates of tribal population continued to be about 10,000 people (which indicates a considerably higher population during the 1820s). It was after this epidemic the Republicans permanently abandoned their villages in Kansas and returned to the Platte. In 1838 smallpox struck once more, and this time 2,500 people, mostly children, died. By 1840 the Pawnee population had declined to 6,244 by actual count. Although their birth rate continued high for some time, steady contact with whites made diseases such as syphilis, dysentery, and tuberculosis virtually endemic, and epidemics of influenza, smallpox, and cholera continued to sweep sporadically through the villages. In addition, as will be discussed later, the Pawnee subsistence system was in shambles.

Their children suffered most from these diseases, but people of all ages died, and Pawnee population declined as steadily as did their political power. By the 1870s the Pawnees numbered only 3,000 people, and at the turn of the century fewer than 1,000 tribal members remained.[19]

Up until the 1830s, then, the Pawnees seem to have maintained, with brief exceptions, a minimum population of 10,000 people in a core territory that stretched along the Platte valley from the mouth of Skull Creek north to an area around Hordville in present Hamilton County, Nebraska, and in the Loup valley from the mouth of that river to an area just north of Cottonwood Creek. This region was the site of their permanent villages and fields, and only during periods of increasing population did they move beyond it to settle the river valleys of Kansas.[20]

Within this region, however, a definite progression in settlement patterns appears to have taken place during the eighteenth and nineteenth centuries. Increasing warfare brought about both the fortification of villages and their consolidation within a narrowing territory. Lodges, once spread over a wide area, now were crowded together within fortifications. These villages took up less space than their predecessors, but they probably contained larger individual populations, becoming in fact small towns of 2,000 to 3,000 people. After the mid-eighteenth century the number of Pawnee villages declined, a result not only of diminishing population but also of the gathering of smaller villages into larger, more compact settlements for defense. During the nineteenth century two or three large villages might be located within a 20- or 30-mile stretch of river bottom.[21]

In addition to this river valley area, the Pawnees claimed hunting grounds that stretched across the mixed-grass plains from the north fork of the Platte south to the Kansas River and its tributaries. They successfully maintained their claim to this region west and south of their earthlodge villages until the late 1830s, but after that Sioux competition increasingly narrowed their hunts to lands within the drainage of the western Republican and Kansas rivers.[22]

CHAPTER 7

Natural and Cultural Order

The relationship of the Pawnees to their natural environment was never simple. They lived in and united three very different ecosystems: the tall-grass prairies, the river valleys, and the mixed-grass plains. These environments created the parameters of the Pawnee world and put certain constraints upon it, but the physical world itself was not immutable. The Pawnees did not passively accept the plants and animals these ecosystems made available; the villagers often both actively shaped their environments and used each ecosystem to escape limits the others put upon them. The Pawnee world was a created world, not only in a physical but also in a cultural sense. The Pawnees believed that they annually recreated and renewed the earth and maintained its existence through their ceremonies. In their eyes and in their world, nature and culture exerted reciprocal influences.

The Pawnees built their villages, planted their crops, and spent roughly half the year in the river valleys. The ecology of the Platte, Loup, and Republican valleys where they lived was significantly different from the Missouri River and the smaller rivers farther east, and indeed different from their own tributary creeks. Because these rivers were sandy streams with shifting beds, cottonwood *(Populus deltoides)* and willow *(Salix* sp.), the only broadleaf trees that preferred a sandy soil and high water table, along with a few elm *(Ulmus* sp.) dominated their banks. Over large areas, trees did not grow along the rivers but were confined to the numerous islands of the Platte. Only in some of the smaller, less sandy feeder streams or in sheltered ravines could other species—principally green ash *(Fraxinus lanceolata)*, American elm *(U. americanus)*, black walnut *(Juglans nigra)*, box-elder *(Acer negundo)*, and hackberry *(Celtis occidentalis)*—survive and dominate.[1]

In the absence of forest, several other plant communities dominated the bottomlands of the Platte and Loup. On the first bottom or flood plain and on some creeks, numerous swamps and marshes supported bulrushes *(Scirpus validus)*, cattails *(Typha latifolia)*, and other reeds, as well as sedges and many forbs. On slightly drier lands, tall coarse grasses such as prairie cordgrass *(Spartina pectinata)*, switchgrass *(Panicum virgatum)*, and Canada wild-rye *(Elymus canadensis)* became numerous before yielding to Indian grass *(Sorghastrum nutans)* and, much more commonly, to big bluestem *(Andropogon gerardi)* communities on the higher and better drained second terraces. Wild fruit trees and shrubs grew along ravines and streams or where bluffs afforded shelter. Sumac *(Rhus glabra)*, hazel *(Corylus americana)*, wolfberry *(Symphoricarpos occidentalis)*, buckbrush *(S. orbiculatus)*, wild plum *(Prunus americana)*, and prairie roses *(Rosa suffulta)* were especially common.[2]

When they selected village sites in these river valleys, the Pawnees sought both fertile corn lands and available supplies of timber. But sufficient amounts of timber became hard to find, especially as the villages grew larger through the recombination of bands or as the Americans confined the tribe to the reservation on the Loup. The Pawnees needed firewood for cooking, heating, making pottery, and drying corn. Cooking utensils and bowls came from black oak, post oak, and elm. Tipi poles, usually of cottonwood, required more timber, but the earthlodges represented the greatest drain of wood supplies. On the Republican the Pawnees apparently used oak for building, while on the Platte and Loup they preferred elm but often had to resort to cottonwood, a tree poor in both strength and durability. The Grands in their village on Skull Creek used cedar for their lodge poles—perhaps going well up the Platte to obtain it.[3] By the 1830s the Pawnees often cut wood for the earthlodges at Grand Island and floated it downstream. By 1835 the demand for wood at the Skidi village now identified as the Palmer Site (25 HW 1) had so depleted the trees that women were forced to go seven or eight miles to secure firewood and timber to repair the lodges. Missionaries and Indian agents thereafter regularly reported timber shortages here and elsewhere.[4]

This lack of wood imposed restraints upon the Pawnees that both they and early white observers clearly recognized. In 1811 George Sibley visited the Republicans in their town on the Loup River near present-day Fullerton, Nebraska, and noted that the "shrubbery [wild plum bushes] and the few scattering forest trees appear to be very carefully husbanded & preserved from injury by the Pawnees." Much later, during the 1850s and again in the 1870s, the Pawnees repeatedly worried over timber supplies. They complained bitterly and threatened to resort to arms because white settlers stole timber from their lands.[5] Just as the search for timber drew the Pawnee women away from the village sites and farther out into the river valleys, so did their search for agricultural lands. If during the seventeenth and eighteenth centuries Pawnee villages were smaller and more numerous, women would have been close to their fields. But by the nineteenth century the proximity of the large Pawnee towns made long journeys to the fields mandatory. Visitors to the Pawnee towns described them as surrounded by cornfields or, more accurately, small plots of corn.[6]

The Pawnee women planted their corn, beans, melons, and squash in plots of one to three acres assigned them by the village chief. A woman was entitled to her field year after year for as long as she wished to use it, but it reverted to the village as a whole for reassignment at her death. This land was highly valued. The women planted only plots of disturbed soil—most often found in the creek bottoms near the mouth of ravines—since such lands could be brought into production without the arduous work of breaking the sod with scapula hoes. To find such lands the women had to go seven or eight miles from the village, often locating their fields near natural springs.[7]

The range of crops these women planted had changed little from those of the Upper Republicans. The Pawnees appear to have added potatoes to their fields, but outside of this they cultivated the usual staples of native American agriculture: corn, beans, pumpkins, watermelons, squash, and sunflowers.[8] But if the range of crops was relatively narrow, the variety of each crop was impressive. As late as the end of the nineteenth century, Pawnee women maintained seven varieties of pumpkins and squash, eight of beans, and ten of corn which represented a decline from fifteen or more. The Pawnees favored the flour corns, which, being all soft starch, were largely deficient in protein, but "could be easily crushed or ground and was much softer than flint when eaten parched."[9]

The planting of corn and other crops seems to have taken place on the same land year after year without either fertilization or any rotation beyond the annual relocation of hills within the field. In the spring men and women, working together, cleared the plots of weeds and burned the debris to mellow the soil. The women hoed only the soil in the corn hill itself (and even here the hoeing went only to a depth of about two inches) and planted five to seven kernels of corn in hills 1½ feet in diameter scattered irregularly over the fields about a step apart. They next planted beans among the corn and finally pumpkins, squashes, and watermelons in separate patches located between the different varieties of the corn; they thus inhibited cross-pollination and preserved the breeds. By the nineteenth century some of these garden plots were protected by being "literally fenced in by sunflowers, curiously woven together." These sunflower fences were supported by stakes, and the women gave the fields further protection from birds and small animals by erecting small platforms on which they stationed watchwomen.[10]

After the tribe departed on the summer hunt, no one touched these garden plots. The crops had received two hoeings, which gave the broad-leafed crops the advantage they needed to tower over and smother most competing weeds. Men, women and children on their return from the hunt, again accompanied by the necessary ceremonies, harvested the squash and beans first and dried them for storage; next they harvested a portion of the corn crop while it was still green or in milk. Although this corn was usually specified as sweet corn by the whites, actually the initial harvest was of flour corns; indeed, sweet corns were allowed to ripen on the stalk and were harvested last. George Will has suggested that harvesting a portion of the crop while green was a significant innovation that allowed the Indian horticulturalists to get in a portion of the crop even in years when drought and grasshoppers might destroy the corn left to ripen in the fields. The parching and drying of this initial harvest took days, and while it continued, the harvesters began gathering and drying the pumpkins. The Pawnees gathered the ripe corn in a definite order, proceeding from the small-kerneled varieties to the larger kerneled corns, and deliberately selected the best cobs for the seed supply of the next year. The villagers put great value on this corn, carefully husbanded the entire crop, and condemned any sort of wastefulness.[11]

Many aspects of this horticultural system have been seriously misunderstood; not the least of these is the role played by the women. Early American observers judged the Pawnee women to be little better than drudges for the men. According to Samuel Allis, an early missionary, they were the most "industrious women I think I ever saw & perform more hard labor than any women I have seen of any description" while the men "eat, smoke, sleep, attend their feast, sing, gamble, go to war & steal horses." But Allis, like many mid-nineteenth century white Americans influenced by the "cult of domesticity," was predisposed to consider any hard physical labor by women outside the home as degrading; what he wanted was to place the Pawnee men in the fields and to make the women Christian housewives. There is no more reason, however, to believe that the Pawnee women saw their work as degrading merely because it was hard than to think that nineteenth century American farmers did. There is no question that the work was arduous. George Will had watched the work of women of horticultural tribes similar to the Pawnees since childhood and, as both an anthropologist and a plant breeder, had come to know and respect their work and skill. He found them to be proud and enthusiastic horticulturalists. As the numerous varieties of crops testify, the women knew their work and their crops well and took great pride in them. The commencement of spring and the return to the fields, as well as the harvest, were times of pleasure and rejoicing.[12]

How much corn the Pawnees produced annually is difficult to determine. Zebulon Pike wrote that the nation raised only enough corn "to afford a little thickening to their soup," and their agent similarly downplayed the importance of Pawnee agriculture in 1838. The missionaries who lived among the Pawnees in the 1830s and 1840s, and who knew them far better than did the agents who lived in Council Bluffs and rarely visited the nation, said, however, that the Pawnees raised "an abundance of corn." Neither the missionaries nor the agents give any precise figures on the actual acreage planted. The earliest estimate is by an agent who in 1837 reported that the Pawnees had planted about 400 acres which yielded 10,000 bushels of corn with an abundant supply of beans and squash. This estimated yield of 25 bushels an acre is below George Will's estimate of 40 bushels an acre for Mandan agriculture in a good year.[13]

Another way of estimating the crop is to allow one-half to one acre for every woman in the tribe who worked the fields. In 1840 Dunbar counted 2,085 women over ten years old. If two-thirds of these women actually farmed, their work produced 695 to 1,390 acres in cultivation, and if each of these acres yielded 30 bushels of corn, they produced a total crop of from 20,850 to 41,700 bushels. Given the distances women had to travel, such an acreage would be feasible. In the mid-1860s on upland plots, Pawnee women cultivated an average of 1,200 acres with hoe agriculture even with a reduced population, and in good years produced large crop surpluses, which they sold to settlers and traders. Such acreage hardly seems to indicate declining dependence on horticulture.[14]

How long the necessary resources of fertile soil and timber upon which the villagers depended could be maintained under traditional Pawnee land use is no easier to determine than their yields, but again estimates are possible. Prior to 1840 those village sites on the Platte and Loup rivers that were sheltered from outside military pressures showed surprisingly long periods of occupation. The Pawnees— either one band or a series of bands—occupied with only brief interruptions three village sites on the Loup—the Palmer Site (25 HW 1), the Horse Creek Site (24 NC 2), and the Cottonwood Creek Site (25 HW 5)—for times ranging from twenty-two to thirty-five years respectively between 1800 and 1842. On the Platte the Grands occupied a village near present-day Linwood in Butler County, Nebraska (24 BU 1), continuously between about 1777 and approximately 1806, and the Clark Site (25 PK 1) from around 1830 until the early 1840s.[15]

The length of these occupations indicates that the Pawnees conserved basic resources near their villages for considerable periods of time. By the time the Skidis abandoned the Palmer Site in the early 1840s, timber had become very scarce, and three or more decades of occupation may also have begun to deplete the fertility of the garden plots. In 1839 the Skidis considered moving away entirely to a new site in the Platte River valley where their chief said the soil was fertile. Yet what is striking is not that the amount of timber declined, or that unfertilized garden plots diminished in productivity, but that these resources survived for well over thirty years.[16]

Early white observers, as noted, often attributed village relocations to the exhaustion of timber, but the decline in timber supplies was gradual. In 1839 Capot Blue and his band built a village of twenty-nine lodges just four miles above the major Grand village at the Clark Site. The Grand village of some 2,000 people had already been inhabited for almost a decade, and yet even if Capot Blue's band obtained the timber for their twenty-nine lodges from Grand Island, enough trees still remained around the village to supply its firewood and other timber requirements.[17]

For the Pawnees, timber and the loose, fertile patches of soil along the ravines and creek bottoms formed the essential resources of the river valleys. Of lesser importance, but still significant, were the wildlife and wild plants of the bottomlands. Large animals did not occur in great numbers near the Pawnee villages even before extensive white immigration. Beaver, waterfowl, and game birds seem to have been relatively abundant, and perhaps even increased during the wet and cool Neo-Boreal period of the eighteenth and early nineteenth centuries. And elk too seem to have been common, although the herds were hardly sizable; bear and deer populations, however, were small. Certainly in the early nineteenth century, when there had been little or no hunting by whites, game alone could not sustain a sizable group traveling up the Platte until they were 100 miles above the Pawnee villages. Sibley reported the Platte and Loup valleys had but few deer in 1811, and in 1820 the Pawnees informed Stephen Long that his expedition could not hope to feed itself off game while moving up the Platte. Long disregarded this advice, and his command was reduced to unsuccessful hunts for prairie dogs. In 1825 William Ashley similarly found that the areas around the Pawnee villages "afforded little or no game."[18]

The Pawnees adjusted comfortably to this situation and relied on the woodland animals of the river bottom for moccasins and minor items of dress far more than for food. When they hunted deer, elk, beaver, and small mammals such as raccoons, otters, and skunks, they ate what they killed, but it was the skins of the animals they really wanted. With the number of people who had to be fed, the nation could not have afforded to depend on local game for meat. Substantial populations of browsers such as deer and elk did not inhabit the Platte and Loup valleys simply because there was not an adequate food supply for them. Any attempt by the Pawnees to rely on browsers for food would almost inevitably have ended in the depletion or disappearance of the animal population and the starvation of the nation. Furthermore, hunting elk without guns was so difficult that hunters armed largely with bows, as the Pawnee were until the 1860s, would have spent vast amounts of time and energy killing very few animals. Such tactics would make little sense when cooperative hunts could result in large kills of buffalo with far less time and labor. Most woodland animals were never hunted methodically, at least before the early nineteenth century, and indeed some, such as quail and prairie chickens, were left to the boys of the tribe who hunted them with long poles. The one place where these conditions of scarcity did not apply was Grand Island—the 20-mile-long island in the Platte above the Pawnee villages. There, provided with an ideal environment, woodland animals prospered, and apparently the Pawnees took advantage of this situation to secure fresh meat on their way to the buffalo hunts.[19]

The wild plants of the bottomlands played a more prominent role in the Pawnee economy than did the game animals of the tall-grass river valleys. Like most Indians, the Pawnees had no trouble combining the symbolic meaning attached to natural objects with a precise and sophisticated understanding of the natural world. In 1809 John Bradbury, collecting plants along the Missouri River, found that the Omahas could identify and name all the specimens he had gathered. They invited him into their lodges, eager to discuss the plants with him, calling him "physician" and showing him the greatest respect. Over one hundred years later Melvin Gilmore, an anthropologist who worked with Pawnee informants while compiling an ethnobotany of the Missouri basin tribes, found them close observers of the natural world who "showed keen powers of perception of the structure, habits, and local distribution of plants through a wide range of observations thus manifesting the incipiency of phytogeography, plant ecology, and morphology." In his informants he found a knowledge of what he called the meager beginnings of taxonomy and an awareness of the relation of species to species.[20]

Gilmore recognized that Pawnees had studied and imposed an order on their surroundings. When a Pawnee informant showed Gilmore minute differences in not only the fragrance but also the structure of the stem of four varieties of a mint (*Monarda fistulasa*) used to perfume lodges, it became obvious that his, and his fellow villagers', observation of plant life was close and subtle.[21] But what Gilmore with some condescension regarded as "the beginnings of a system of natural science which never came to maturity" was in fact an elaborate and successful ordering of knowledge about the natural world. This ordering did not proceed from white assumptions, and its assumptions and explanations of causes, while logical, were not scientifically persuasive. However, in the quality of observation, in the logical construction of similarities and differences, and in the very attempt to relate and order the world, there was much that might strike observers such as Gilmore as belonging to science.[22]

This Pawnee interest in the natural world did not spring solely from economic concerns. The religious, medicinal, and magical uses of plants entitled them to high importance in Pawnee culture, and in the sheer variety of species collected, Pawnee doctors and priests probably outgathered the women. Yet economically it was undeniably food plants that absorbed most Pawnee attention and labor. Gathering of wild foods, of course, was not confined to the river valleys, nor did its yields compare with those of the cultivated crops or the buffalo hunt. Instead, gathering complemented the hunt and the cultivated fields; and when the buffalo and corn failed, as they did with discouraging frequency after 1840, gathering sustained the tribal economy for short, but critical, periods.[23]

The Pawnees integrated much of their gathering into the seasonal journeys to and from the hunting grounds on the mixed-grass plains, but barring disastrous hunts, the gathering cycle usually began at the villages in March or early April, after the ground had thawed. Although men hunting deer in spring regularly collected substantial amounts of milkweed (*Asclepias syriaca*) and mushrooms (probably *Morchella escalenta*), women did the bulk of the gathering, and the Indian potato (*Glycine apios*) was by far the most important plant collected.[24]

According to the missionaries, the Pawnee women secured "hundreds of bushels" of these potatoes every spring, but only at the cost of immense labor. A day's work with a mattock along the banks of the Loup yielded no more than a peck of the root, and the supply the Pawnee women gathered every spring resulted from a season of work that began in March and continued into May and the planting of the crops. But the advantages of the plant offset the amount of labor required to obtain the relatively low yields. Indian potatoes were abundant. They grew all along the river valleys particularly along the Loup, on Grand Island in the Platte, and along the Republican River. Women could dig the roots in early spring when there was no other essential work to perform and when few other foods were available; they could gather them again on their way to the summer and winter hunts. Finally, in late fall, the stay-at-homes who wintered on Grand Island made a final collection to carry them through the cold season and to supply returning hunters.[25] Ideally, the plant only supplemented other food supplies, but in emergencies Indian potatoes sustained the entire nation. If they became the sole resource for thousands of people for any length of time, however, the supply might fail, and the Pawnees would face starvation.[26]

In addition to Indian potatoes, the Pawnees eagerly sought water chinquapin *(Nelumbo lutea)* in the marshes near the villages for both its seeds and tubers, the wild onion *(Allium* sp.), wild cucumbers *(Micrampelis lobata)*, and lamb's-quarters *(Chenopodium album)*. They also collected wild plums *(Prunus americana)* and chokecherries *(P. virginiana)*, which they dried and preserved, and harvested a variety of rushes and grasses such as bulrush and cattails for mats, and cut porcupine grass or Spanish needle *(Stipa spartea)* for brushes. The year's final round of gathering took place in the fall as they prepared to move up the Platte valley on their way to the winter hunt. During this season a second wild food of the bottomlands, ground beans *(Falcata comosa)*, joined Indian potatoes as a staple food. These beans, which grew in dense masses near timber, were gathered and cached by wood rats and voles, and Pawnee women raided the caches to gather a supply. The women also dug Jerusalem artichokes *(Helinanthus tuberosus)*, but because this tuber could not be preserved, it remained a minor element in the diet. Although these were the important river valley plants of the Pawnees of course this brief list does not name all the plants they used for one purpose or another.[27]

The last major resource of gatherers, and the only real resource provided by the Platte and Loup rivers, was shellfish. The Pawnees fished, but shellfish appear to have been a more considerable food source. The Indians used the meat of two species, *Proptera alata megaptera* and *Lampsilis ventricosa occidens*, for food and the shells as tools. The use of these species, both clams (Unio) of sandy or muddy rivers like the Platte and Loup, probably indicates that the gatherers' needs were satisfied by local populations of clams and that the villagers did not seek out additional supplies of shellfish on the smaller streams.[28]

This Pawnee exploitation of the river valleys through agriculture, hunting, and gathering was itself part of a larger system. The harvests of fields and wild foods provided sustenance for the tribes on their journey to the buffalo herds of the plains. A household of eight people took enough dried food on the summer hunt to feed them for a forty-seven-day journey. In the 1860s such a supply amounted to about 10½ bushels of dried corn, 5 bushels of beans, three 2-foot square mats of dried pumpkin, and dried buffalo meat. A greater amount of corn and beans might have been taken on the hunt before the 1860s, since during the final year in Nebraska traditional supplies were complemented by wheat flour and other trade goods. During the winter the families took substantially the same supplies, although the winter hunt lasted much longer. The villagers supplemented these dried supplies with foods gathered on the march, whatever deer and elk the hunters might bring in, and, of course, the buffalo themselves.[29]

The Pawnees, in essence, expended the products of the valley—corn, grass, Indian potatoes, ground beans, and woodland animals—to reach the Great Plains hunting grounds—the mixed-grass lands of the Great Plains, the home of the immense buffalo herds. The transition from the true or tall-grass prairie to the mixed prairie took place in a 100- to 150-mile-wide area centerd on the 98°30′ longitude or in the general vicinity of Grand Island in the Platte above the Pawnee villages. South of the Platte in this area, blue grama and buffalo grasses gradually became intermixed with little bluestem (*Andropogon scoparius*), while big bluestem (*A. gerardi*) and other tall grasses were restricted to the moist bottoms of ravines. Farther west, blue grama (*Bouteloua gracilis*) and buffalo grass (*buchloë dactyloides*) formed nearly complete stands in some areas, and in others they formed an understory to side-oats grama (*Bouteoua curtipendula*), needle-and-thread (*Stipa comata*), and other mid-sized grasses.[30]

In their travels between the rivers and high plains the Pawnees largely ignored the tall-grass prairies and the transition zone. The bluestem prairies, the core of the grasslands for later white agricultural economies, remained largely a peripheral area to the Pawnees. These lands were rich in grass but, oddly enough, usually poor in grazers. The buffalo herds never inhabited the region in the huge numbers that have often been supposed. Early travelers, later historians, and some ecologists have assumed that the huge herds were never found in the tall-grass prairies simply because they had been driven west by immigrant tribes from the east and by white settlers. Small numbers of buffalo had, after all, penetrated almost to the Atlantic in certain areas, and the tall-grass lands did offer huge amounts of grass, far more than the mixed-grass lands of the Plains. It seems reasonable to suppose that the buffalo must have inhabited these areas in at least the numbers that existed on the high Plains.

There is a basic logic to this position and in certain areas, such as the upper Missouri River valley in the Dakotas, historical evidence shows a movement of the buffalo westward. But the idea of immense herds in the bluestem prairies of the central Plains lacks any kind of historical verification. The buffalo did diminish and retreat, but the movement took place within the mixed-grass prairie. Historians and geographers have chosen to deal with the buffalo in terms of a false boundary, the Mississippi River, instead of a true one, the transition to mixed-grass prairie around 98°30' longitude. Consequently they have confused the history of the species itself and that of the Indian peoples who depended upon it.[31]

Most American immigrants on the Oregon, California, and Mormon trails usually first spotted the large buffalo herds around the forks of the Platte far to the west of the 98th meridian. Yet they assumed, as did earlier explorers, that the range of these large herds (as distinct from smaller groups such as those found east of the Mississippi until the nineteenth century) had until quite recently extended much farther eastward. The buffalo were supposedly not only diminishing but rapidly retreating westward.[32] Although everyone who reached the tall-grass lands supposed these huge herds had only recently departed, no one actually cited previous travelers who had seen them there. Such sightings of buffalo as occurred in the area were of single animals or small groups. John Bell reported one bull below the Skidi villages in 1820; Sibley reported herds of buffalo and elk between the Kansas and the Pawnee villages in 1811; another account reported the killing of single animals near the mouth of the Platte in the 1820s.

When even the earliest travelers reported their own encounters with large herds of thousands of animals, however, they too met them in the mixed-grass region near 98°30' longitude. In 1540 when Coronado first visited the Wichitas, they were four days west of their villages hunting buffalo on the Arkansas River. When Lieutenant Wilkinson of the Pike expedition of 1806 met the herds whose size "surpassed credibility," he was near present-day Hutchinson, Kansas, around the 98th meridian. On the Platte itself virtually all the initial sightings of the large herds were along or west of Grand Island. In the early nineteenth century, migration of the buffalo below this point was a cause of amazement. In 1813, a date well before either extensive migration into the area by whites and Indians or the beginning of a large trade in buffalo robes, Robert Stuart found that during the previous winter the buffalo had come into the transition zone between the mixed and tall-grass prairies near Grand Island. He regarded the descent as so unusual that he theorized that an exceptionally bad winter must have forced them down. When the buffalo descended into the vicinity of the Pawnee villages in the winter of 1820, the Indians considered it equally unusual. The previous spring the Pawnees had warned the Long expedition that buffalo could not be procured below the forks of the Platte. Finally, in the winter of 1835 the buffalo once more moved into the transition area between the tall-grass prairies and the mixed-grass plains, coming as low as the villages themselves. This occurrence the Pawnees viewed as little short of miraculous and gave credit to the white missionaries who had come to live with them because it had not happened for twenty years.[33]

If during the early nineteenth century Indians and whites viewed the movement of the buffalo into margins of the tall-grass prairies near the Pawnee villages as rare and marvelous, then theories about millions of the animals, inhabiting the tall grass prairies east of the villages just prior to this era seem hard to maintain. Furthermore, if the animals occurred in such areas, why did the tribes invariably move west to hunt, even at the time of their first contacts with whites? The theory of huge herds on the bluestem prairies appears to have arisen from a misinterpretation of a real and observable phenomenon—the retreat of the bison from heavily traveled American trade and migration routes such as those along the Missouri, Platte, and Arkansas rivers. On the Platte the buffalo herds began to avoid the river and the Oregon Trail during the late 1830s, but not in serious numbers until the large migrations of the 1840s and afterward. By the mid-1840s the Pawnees were making numerous and direct complaints about the dearth of buffalo along the Platte and fixed responsibility on the Americans. In 1845 Old Soldier, a Skidi, complained in council, "For a long time . . . the buffalos were plenty on the Platte. But now the whites have gone before us and will scare all the buffalo away." The next year a chief of the Grands rejected the usual presents paid by travelers for passage across Pawnee lands on the grounds that they did not compensate for the damage the migrants did to the herds. The Pawnees denied that the whites had the right to pass through their country and imperil their whole economy. They did not, however, contend that the travelers drove the herds westward, only that they drove them away from the Platte.[34]

Recent ecological studies have provided further evidence that the buffalo was predominantly an animal of the mixed-grass region. Not only does the buffalo depend far more on warm-season grasses such as blue grama, buffalo grass, red three-awn *(Aristida longiseta)*, and sand dropseed *(Sporobolus cryptandrus)* than cool-season grasses such as little bluestem and forbs, but it also has the ability to digest these grasses far more completely than cattle and thus get more nourishment from a given short-grass range. Cattle, on the other hand, prefer cool-season grasses and forbs and are better at digesting these plants. Cattle actively seek out low swales where greater moisture allows the taller grasses and forbs to survive, while buffalo prefer the drier hillsides where the warm-season short grasses predominate.[35]

The tall-grass lands, then, were of minor importance to the Pawnees. Archaeologists have expressed wonder that the Pawnees never expanded eastward toward the Missouri into the rich agricultural lands the Americans would so value. Such amazement arises only from the lack of clarity about how the Pawnees used this land and what it contained. The bluestem grasslands yielded few economic resources important to the Pawnees. They contained plants for medicinal and ritual uses but few important food plants. Even the apparently desolate Sand Hills north of the Loup yielded more sources of wild food than the lush tall-grass prairies. In the Sand Hills the Pawnees could obtain wild rice and sand cherries—wild foods more important than anything the prairies back from the rivers offered. The Pawnees could easily afford to let smaller tribes occupy eastern Nebraska; what the Pawnees valued lay elsewhere.[36]

The main object of the journey to the western plains was of course buffalo, but the land yielded other foods to the Pawnees. The hunters took some antelopes, but since like deer these were hunted mainly for their skins, the Pawnees did not kill them in great numbers. As the tribe moved onto the high plains during the summer hunt, gatherers went along the route searching for prairie turnips, or pomme blanche (*Psoralea esculenta*). A plant of the dry prairies, pomme blanche had to be dug in late June or early July while its foliage marked the edible root's location. Later in the summer the foliage would have dried, broken off, and blown away, and the roots would have been impossible to find.[37]

The Pawnees planted their crops, gathered wild foods, and hunted buffalo in a definite seasonal cycle. Planting came during April and May; then the women hoed the crops twice—first early in June and again later in the month before their departure for the buffalo hunt. The Pawnees spent July and August on the plains hunting buffalo. They returned to their earthlodge villages about the first of September to begin the harvest, which was followed by the most elaborate ceremonial cycles of the year. Between the tenth and fifteenth of November the villagers began their second migration to the buffalo plains. They usually tried to hunt quickly in late fall and early winter before severe cold and snow set in. The tribe secured a supply of meat and then moved from creek bottom to creek bottom to camp. The Pawnees returned to the permanent villages in March when soon the cycle began again.[38]

This seasonal cycle certainly followed natural rhythms, but culturally the Pawnees regarded these rhythms as their own work, their own ceremonial creations. They ordered their world, and the cultural order they created shaped their work and their political order and helped to determine how the goods they produced during their seasonal cycle were distributed. The symbolic soul of the cultural order of the Pawnees resided in their medicine bundles. Each lodge had its own bundle, as did each village and each warrior and each dancing society, but within each of the four tribes there was an hierarchy of bundles, with the most important tribal bundles controlling the ceremonies.[39] Such a tribal bundle, viewed in the 1830s, contained "a buffalo robe, fancifully dressed, skins of several fur bearing animals . . . the skull of a wild cat, stuffed skins of a sparrowhawk . . . and the swallow-tailed fly catcher, several bundles of scalps and broken arrows taken from enemies, a small bundle of Pawnee arrows, some ears of corn and a few wads of buffalo-hair, such as may be found in wallows where the animals roll when moulting."[40]

These objects both symbolized and contained power. And while all power originated with *tirawahut*, the "pervasive ocean-of-power investing the universe," the power of the bundles was more specific. In Pawnee cosmology, for example, the stars served as intermediaries between *tirawahut* (heaven) and earth. *Tirawahut* gave certain stars the power to create the human race and instructed the stars to give the Pawnees their holy bundles.[41] The bundles, derived from the stars according to *tirawahut's* command, gave the Pawnee universe its symbolic structure; they governed the rituals that insured fertility, abundance, and success on the hunt. For the Pawnees the medicine bundles created the ceremonial cycle which in turn shaped the orderly annual round of the village year.[42]

It was the ceremonies that ensured that the corn grew and the buffalo could be hunted. For the Pawnees' world to prosper, the power of the sky had to vitalize the earth to produce life and plenty. All the rituals surrounding agriculture and the hunt reflected an attempt to procure this life-giving contact. Sacred corn kernels were kept in the sky bundles and ritually planted each year. One of the young plants, ceremonially picked, became Young Mother Corn, who would watch over the tribe and insure the harvest.[43]

In the captive girl sacrifice, the opposition between the Morning Star (male, light) and the Evening Star (female, dark) dominated. The ceremony returned the first woman, created by the Morning Star's conquest and mating with the Evening Star, to the sky power, Morning Star. In the ceremony the Skidis actually sacrificed a young, captive girl (sometimes in the ceremony's final years, a boy) so that the Morning Star could take back the first human placed on earth, and, in return, would continue to protect the people and provide life and fertility.[44]

Similar rituals governed the buffalo hunt. When the chiefs assumed responsibility for the hunt, they literally became the sky powers on earth. The buffalo, an animal of the earth, nonetheless became sacred by having its meat, which was necessary for every ceremony, pledged to the bundles. Buffalo indeed came to "signify the entire ceremonial life."[45] After Pawnee scouts located the herds, days might pass before the hunt began. The Pawnees' concern that ritual signs were auspicious before beginning the hunt confused and irritated whites who accompanied the tribe on the plains, but to the Pawnees such rituals were as basic a part of the hunt as the shooting of arrows.[46] The hunt was not just a subsistence activity; it was also a sacred activity and the signs had to be right. The hunt, like other practices, had to bend its immediate exigencies before the deeper order of their world.[47]

Power in the Pawnee world was thus the power of the bundles. This power ordered their society as clearly as it did the rhythms of the natural world. The power of the bundles was available only through the intercession of the chiefs and priests, whom the Pawnees regarded as stars on earth, "the earthly reservoirs of a power which enabled them to be the fathers and protectors of their children, the people."[48] These men passed their standing on to their sons so that the chiefs and priests formed an hereditary elite. Their rank as chiefs was a birthright; their actual power within the nation, however, depended on their knowledge and behavior.[49]

Meaningful political power in the society came only to those of the proper rank who either displayed knowledge of the bundles or manifested the power embodied in them. A strict distinction between Pawnee chiefs and Pawnee priests is artificial. Although all priests did not rule as chiefs, a chief could often be a priest, or he might only possess a bundle and leave its care and ceremonies in the hands of a priest. The necessary knowledge of the bundles was not easily acquired. To gain it, the aspiring priest had to serve a long apprenticeship to another priest, usually a kinsman, to whom he gave gifts in exchange for knowledge. The older priest, however, always held back some of the secrets of the bundles and communicated them only when ready to die.[50]

The chief, too, depended on ceremonial knowledge, but more important for him was his bearing, conduct, and wisdom, which were taken as manifestations of the power of the bundles. Preston Holder has cogently summarized a proper chiefly personality.

> They were men to whom violence was a stranger; they were quiet and secure in the knowledge of their power. Their voices were never raised in anger or threatened violence. The image was one of large knowledge, infinite quiet patience, and thorough understanding. There was no outward show of authority; such was not needed . . . These were secure, calm, well-bred, gracious men whose largess was noted and who had no need to shout of their strength.[51]

To fail to display such traits was to demonstrate one's lack of real authority, even though hereditarily one held chiefly rank.[52]

Once acknowledged as a ruling chief by the people, a leader possessed much greater power than was possible among most North American Indian peoples. Early travelers and missionaries and, later, agents, testified to the respect accorded the recognized chiefs and their ability to take decisive action even when opposition existed within the tribe. If need be, a Pawnee chief could authorize the village *nahikut* ("brave" or "soldier"), whom he appointed, to use the *raripakusus* (literally "fighting-for-order"), or village police, to punish or, in extreme cases, even kill anyone who seriously threatened a custom or policy agreed to by common consent.[53]

Below the elite families of chiefs and priests was another small group of families from whom the chiefs drew their braves, and below this, making up the bulk of the village, were the families of the common people. Since most Pawnee men could not attain the hereditary office, they sought to distinguish themselves in other ways. They might become members of the three-man *raripakusus* or war leaders. They might become warriors by performing the number of sacrifices required to gain power from heaven or doctors, shamans, by mastering the curing rituals and techniques whose power came not from the sky bundles but rather from animals and the earth. The Pawnees identified the priests with life and regeneration, but they connected the doctors with death. During the curing ceremonies the doctors held death at bay, but they were equally capable of unleashing it through magic or witchcraft. Commoners, too, might join one of the dancing or warrior societies open to the mass of the people and, by rising in it, obtain status. If not a doctor, soldier, war leader, warrior, or prominent member of a village society, a Pawnee man remained a "boy," a person who hunted and defended the village but who possessed only low status within the nation.[54]

The results of this status system among commoners determined the composition of the various village and tribal councils. Only men of recognized standing could participate in these chief's councils, although, if the meeting was not secret, anyone could attend as a spectator. Council membership was a coveted distinction, and within the council rank, seniority, and personal prestige determined the order in which members spoke. When in council, members were addressed as *a-ti'-us* (fathers) and deliberated for the benefit of their children—the people. At the close of the meeting the first chief stated what he felt was the consensus of the council, and his herald communicated the decision to the people.[55]

The language of the council (the chiefs and council as fathers, the people as children) reflected the Pawnee conception of politics as kinship. Because each village traced its descent back through the female line to a single ancestor, all villagers were theoretically kin.[56] The village, in this sense, was the largest kin unit, and outside the kin group Pawnees "assumed that people must be mean, unreliable, and treacherous."[57] If men dominated in the fictional kin group of the village, women exerted real influence within the actual kin group of the family. Although chiefs inherited status from their fathers and bundles descended through the male line, descent among the Pawnees was otherwise matrilineal and the mother-child relationship was the foundation of the whole kinship system. A father had only married into the family and might leave to return to his mother's or sister's lodge if a marriage broke up. The real center of the Pawnee family and lodge was the senior woman. The occupants of a lodge consisted of the woman, her husband, her unmarried children, her married daughters and their husbands, sometimes her married sons, her grandchildren, and more distant kin. Here the Pawnees organized the productive activities of the village; here the center of everyday life was fixed.[58]

The kinship and status relations both created the political organization of a village and controlled the distribution of the goods that the Pawnees obtained from agriculture, the hunt, raiding, and outside exchanges. As in many pre-state societies, politics and culture dominated the economic system and geared individual ambitions toward redistribution rather than the accumulation of wealth. The sharing of goods began within the family where all goods were shared, but extended to the village, theoretically a collection of kinspeople, where necessities of life were never denied to another.[59]

Kinship created a horizontal, reciprocal exchange of food and goods, but the status distinctions created another vertical exchange. It was the mark of chiefs to give to their people. When able, they gave freely, and it was their particular duty to provide personally for the destitute. Accepting the gift of a chief did not normally involve an obligation to reciprocate. The only instance where those who took gifts clearly came under personal obligation to the chiefs involved the "boys," or low-status men, who lived in the chief's lodge and were fed by him. In return for his generosity, these boys acted "very nearly like servants."[60]

Reciprocal giving between chiefs and people would have been redundant in Pawnee society since the whole structure of the village channeled goods upward. They flowed toward the bundles and those who controlled the bundles. During the major ceremonial feasts of the year, the people gave gifts to the celebrants—the priests and chiefs—whose knowledge of the bundles brought prosperity to the people. The power that chiefs and priests derived from the medicine bundles greatly ramified the occasions for giving. Gifts came to the chiefs and priests as a payment for knowledge, as thanksgiving to the powers for success in war or the hunt, and as part of numerous other occasions in daily life. At feasts, the first invited were the chiefs and priests. Even in times of dearth, as another white missionary Samuel Allis complained, "if there was anything to eat in the villages the old imposters [priests] got it."[61]

From this constant upward flow of goods, the chiefs acquired the presents that they gave to the people. Most wealth paused only briefly at the top of the Pawnee hierarchy; a chief's unwillingness to give would have meant his loss of influence since his greed would have violated the very code that assured him of his power. As wealth filtered back down, however, the best goods—those which possessed highest quality or which gave symbolic status (such as flags after the arrival of Europeans)—remained with those of the highest social standing. Redistribution was thus in practice uneven; the highest got the best. All of this was integral to the social order. The ceremonies upon which Pawnee existence depended demanded the maintenance of chiefs and priests whose status and role, in turn, both dictated and depended on the constant vertical flow of goods.[62]

This ancient Pawnee world, now, in the words of Gene Weltfish, a lost universe, was for the people who inhabited it a secure and comprehensible place. Culture embraced and controlled the natural world; it explained and ordered its growth and decay and gave its various elements human meaning. Culture and environment were linked, not in any simple determinist sense but rather through an intricate net of reciprocal ties. The fates of Pawnee chiefs and the buffalo, of Pawnee priests and women and the cornfields were intertwined. The evolution of both the grassland environment and the Pawnee nation could not fail to be connected.

CHAPTER 8

Social Change and
Environmental Change

The seasonal cycle of the Pawnees and the cosmology that ordered their world have a certain timelessness about them. Standard ethnographies, including the best one, Weltfish's *Lost Universe*, reinforce this impression of practices begun in time out of mind and repeated annually in an inevitable rhythm. As even the cursory account of Pawnee history already given here emphasized, however, flux and change, conflict and migrations characterized Indian history. Tribes and villages were human creations; their organization and economy were the products of human actions. The particular adaptations of the Pawnees resulted from human decisions and values that evolved and changed through time. What existed in the eighteenth and nineteenth centuries when the whites first met them had not existed from the moment the Pawnees built their earthlodges on the Loup. The best example of change involves the horse, although most studies of the influence of the animal on Indian cultures have focused on the nomadic tribes of the plains, not on horticulturalists such as the Pawnees.[1]

Before they acquired the horse, the only domestic animal the Pawnees possessed was the dog. Early explorers indicated that originally the dog was far different from the various mongrels that Pawnees kept during the mid and late-nineteenth century. Then, it was a distinct breed, carefully maintained to carry tipis, food, and equipment on the hunt. This role the horse eventually took away. Even after the acquisition of the horse, the dog remained a secondary pack animal used on the hunts as late as the 1830s, but gradually the animals came to serve only as watchdogs and as a ceremonial and emergency food supply.[2]

The Pawnees probably did not possess horses until the end of the seventeenth or the beginning of the eighteenth century. The successful Pueblo Revolt of 1680 put large numbers of the animals into Indian hands and made the rapid diffusion of the horse nearly inevitable. By 1690 horses had reached the Red River, and by 1719 two villages of the Wichitas in present-day Oklahoma possessed a herd of 300 animals. The Pawnees may have acquired horses from the Wichitas, or they may have obtained them in raids on the Apaches along their western border. In either case, they certainly possessed the animal before 1714 when they were referred to as good horsemen.[3]

The villagers quickly assimilated the horse into the buffalo hunt. In 1720, when members of the Villasur expedition met the Pawnees who would destroy them on the upper Platte, the tribesmen were mounted and on their summer hunt. The Pawnees' link with the source of horses in the Southwest remained tenuous and fragile, however, for some time. In 1724 the chief of the Skidis informed De Bourgmond that his people wanted peace with the Apaches in order to secure a steady supply of horses "which will help us to carry our belongings when we move to our winter grounds, because our wives and children die under the burden when we return." What peace failed to secure, however, warfare often obtained, and the Pawnees raided the Spanish, the Apaches, and later the Comanches to maintain an ample supply of horses. Until well into the nineteenth century the Southwest remained the main source of horses. The South bands traded with the Wichitas, the Skidis occasionally raided them and all the bands raided the Spanish and Comanches for "great numbers of horses and mules." In turn, the Pawnees traded these horses to the Omahas, Arikaras, Otoes, and Missouris and lost them in raids to the Sioux, Cheyenne, Kansas, and other tribes.[4]

The number of horses in the Pawnee herds varied considerably according to the Indians' fortunes in war and their losses during the rugged plains winters. In the early nineteenth century the tribe as a whole maintained a herd of from 6,000 to 8,000 head, but by the 1860s declining village population, Sioux raids, and lessening access to the source of horses on the southern plains contributed to a general decline in the number of Pawnee horses.[5]

For the Pawnees, horses always remained preeminently animals of the buffalo hunt. Horses carried the villagers, their equipment, and supplies to the hunt; the men rode on horses during the hunt; and horses transported the meat and hides back to the villages. By the late eighteenth century participation in the buffalo hunt required horses, and without the buffalo hunt individual and communal security and plenty were unattainable. Families without horses had to either remain at home or else play a peripheral and less rewarding role in the hunt.[6]

The horse, in a sense, took its place as a peculiar form of property among the Pawnees. Far more than any other outside addition to their material world, it became essential for production. The Pawnees required horses for the hunt, but they also needed them as gifts to give to the priests and chiefs for the ceremonial knowledge and blessings that the Pawnees regarded as essential for success. Horses, too, formed the bride price necessary for marriage. In a way no other possession did, horses began to denote wealth and created the beginnings of a social standing somewhat apart from the older distinctions of birth, knowledge, and skill. Horses were personal property, and they remained unevenly distributed. A rich family might have twenty or more, while a poor family had two, one, or none. A Pawnee, of course, would seek status by giving away some of these horses at the ceremonials, but he was unlikely to give away a significant portion of his herd. The very vulnerability of horses to raids and to the cold and other rigors of the winter hunt made them an especially unstable form of property. One always needed a surplus on hand to feel secure because if a family lost their horses, they lost much of their access to the hunt. Even at the begging dance where gifts of horses were part of the ceremony, the missionaries noted that it was only poor and mediocre animals which were given away.[7]

The horse did not restructure the hierarchical standards of Pawnee society, because existing forms still served to channel many horses upward to priests and chiefs. Possession of horses thus roughly conformed to possession of knowledge and diluted somewhat the contradiction between the two as marks of status. Still, socially and environmentally, the horse introduced into the society undeniable tensions that had to be either resolved or tolerated.[8]

Quarrels over horses often disrupted the family, the basic productive unit of the society. Men owned the horses, but women and boys often had to take care of them. The result was the friction Samuel Allis described: "There are more broils, jealousy, and family quarrels caused by horses than all other troubles combined. The horse frequently causes separation between man and wife, sometimes for life."[9] Such a conflict is understandable. Within the riverine economy, the horse represented something of an anomaly. It was an economic asset which threatened timber and cultivated crops, the basic resources the valleys had offered the Pawnees and their predecessors for centuries. Since these resources were the domain of the women and horses were owned by the men, numerous possibilities for conflict emerged. And with the addition of the women's responsibility for the animal—a duty which in the village made their lives harder—the quarrels Allis mentions became virtually inevitable. The horse, important as it was, was never totally reconciled with previous adjustments and existing environments.

The horse posed serious ecological problems as well. Horses failed to increase the production of any of the staples of the bottomlands and river terraces, and they directly threatened some of them. The Pawnees could not allow horses to graze freely around their villages. Since unwatched animals would obviously be in danger from Sioux or other raiders, boys and young men were detailed to watch the herds. By the 1830s and 1840s this watch had been elaborated into a system of sentinels posted on the bluffs surrounding the valleys. During the night, the men confined the animals in corrals within the villages. The main object of this watchfulness was obviously defense, but a secondary object was to keep the animals out of the fields where, unrestrained, they could wreak havoc. The Pawnees became acutely aware of this drawback of domestic animals; like other prairie tribes during the 1820s they refused American offers of pigs and cows since they realized (as did the Americans) that any domestic animal that could not accompany them on their hunts posed a direct threat to their fields and established economy.[10]

The Pawnees lived in a country of seemingly limitless grass, yet paradoxically feeding their horses came to be a major problem. A scarcity of feed might seem to visitors inconceivable in late spring or early summer when the grasses of the valleys were waist and chest high, but from late summer to early fall, especially during droughts, the problem of feed was acute. Since most American expeditions came through the Pawnee country in spring or early summer, they did not find animal fodder a problem, but in September of 1844 Major Clifton Wharton came down the Loup from the Skidi villages and with some relief found wild pea vines in the stream valleys "of which they [his horses] stood much in need after their bad fare in the vicinity of the Pawnee towns." Even if tall-grass species remained abundant after the grazing of the Pawnee herds, by the fall they had dried in the summer sun and lost most of their nutrients. The difference between the nutritive qualities of dry tall-grass and dry buffalo grass, which retained most of its nutrients year round, was so marked that John Charles Frémont noticed that his animals "began sensibly to fail as soon as we quitted the buffalo grass" and entered the tall-grass prairies.[11]

Because of the nature of the tall-grass prairies, the difficult times for the Pawnee horse herds ranged from fall until mid-spring. During this period the grasses of the bottomlands remained virtually worthless as food since the plants stored their nutrients underground in the rhizomes for the winter. Cutting the grass in mid- or late summer and storing it as hay seemed the obvious solution to contemporary whites, and even as astute an ethnologist as Weltfish expressed some surprise that the Pawnees did not begin to do so until the 1860s. But to harvest hay in mid- or late summer the Pawnees would have had to disrupt their whole economy. The tribe was absent on summer hunts until early September and, on returning, both men and women labored in the fields for several weeks. There was no opportunity to cut hay while it still had value as feed unless they abridged their summer hunt, and this hunt was, after all, the economic rationale for the horse.[12]

As the herds grew in size, the Pawnees faced a serious problem maintaining their horses during the fall, winter, and early spring. They tended to face the problem seasonally, adopting different solutions for each part of the year. In the fall, when they returned to their villages after the summer hunt, many families sent young men and boys with the horses to Grand Island where the grass remained green long after it had dried in the areas surrounding the village. There the horses grazed and mated. Those families who kept their horses near the villages in the fall often had to give them supplemental feeding of the small nubbin ears from the corn harvest. And if snow fell before the tribe left the villages for the winter hunt, the women went to the creek bottom where the grass was the freshest to hand cut hay to feed the animals of the men.[13]

Despite these attempts to strengthen the herds, early winter remained a dangerous time for the horses. They were worked hard in the late fall on the tribal hunt, and if storms during November and December were severe, losses to the herd could be serious. When William Ashley and Jedediah Smith visited the Pawnees in winter quarters in 1824, early snows had made severe inroads into the Skidi horse herds.[14]

There is some evidence, admittedly often circumstantial, that the winter hunt itself may have been an adaptation which resulted from the problem of supporting horses as well as human beings through the winter. The Pawnees probably never spent the entire winter in their earthlodges before they obtained horses; they, like the horticultural tribes farther north, probably sought the bottomlands where forests could shelter them from the storms and provide abundant firewood. In the Pawnee country the most suitable region for such winter villages was Grand Island and other islands in the Platte. In the summer of 1720 the Villasur expedition reported "a very large settlement of Indians of the Pawnee nation" on "an island in the middle" of "a very full coursing river." What they might have seen was the occupation during the summer hunt of a relatively permanent winter village site. Furthermore, the reference in De Bourgmond's diary to a move "to our winter grounds" could refer to the move to a winter village site, not the series of moves typical of a winter hunt. Likewise, the meager references to pre-horse winter buffalo hunting in Pawnee tribal stories could easily refer to limited expeditions near the islands, especially since one of them specifically referred to driving the buffalo out onto a frozen river. Even in historic times a portion of the Pawnees—usually those too poor, too old, and too sick to accompany the tribe on the hunt—continued to spend each winter in camps on Grand Island.[15]

Only with the acquisition of thousands of horses would such winter villages become ecologically unmanageable. Without large supplies of well-cured, nutritious hay, which as we have seen was impossible to obtain, there was simply no way to maintain 6,000 to

8,000 horses in one locale during an entire winter. The Pawnees and other plains tribes did discover a substitute for hay in cottonwood bark and small branches, which the horses ate readily even in preference to grass, but repeated winterings in a single site would rapidly deplete cottonwood. Among the Sioux, who wintered in much smaller bands, this happened around their regularly used winter campgrounds. From necessity, the Pawnees moved repeatedly during the course of a winter, until by the nineteenth century white observers regarded the winter buffalo hunt as much an adjustment to the needs of their horse herds as a search for meat. On the western streams the Pawnees could cut cottonwood bark and boughs, and on the uplands, when they were clear of snow, the horses could eat the nutritious buffalo and grama grass.[16]

The coming of spring and the return to the villages did not end the time of danger for the horse herds. Already weakened by an arduous winter, the horses had to move the tribe back to the permanent villages during March or early April when the grasses had as yet made little growth. Obviously, any way in which the Pawnees could encourage the early growth of prairie grasses had significant benefits for the tribe and its horse herds.

For the Pawnees and other prairie tribes, fire provided the means for securing feed for their horses in early spring, the time of critical need. The role which fires set by the Indians played in creating and maintaining North American grasslands in general, and the Great Plains in particular, has generated an immense and thriving literature. In much of this writing it is assumed that the plains and prairie peoples, like the woodland peoples, burned to maintain open land and increase the population of large grazing or browsing mammals. There are, however, serious problems in applying this rationale to the Pawnees and similar tribes. Burning would not increase the population of deer and elk in the already open woodlands of the Pawnee country. Indeed, if trees and shrubs were destroyed and grasses encouraged, the browsers would lose sources of food and probably decline in numbers. Nor would burning assist the bison, since these animals inhabited the short-grass plains and only relatively small numbers were found in the tall-grass prairies most often burned by the Pawnees. Occasional fires were set by hunters to trap or control game, but the systematic burning of the tall-grass lands carried out by historic tribes would seem to have little relation to the needs of local game animals.[17]

This burning did have a direct relation, however, to the needs of the horse herds. A series of ecological studies carried out in Kansas and Nebraska have demonstrated that burning has a marked effect on the initial growth of prairie grasses. By eliminating the previous year's growth and excessive ground mulch, fire allows the sun to warm the earth more quickly, with the result not only that, in spring, growth comes weeks earlier, but also that yields are significantly higher from March to July, exactly the period when the Pawnees needed the grass. In one experiment, burned lands had by June yielded twice the grass of unburned excessively mulched land.[18]

The difference in the rate of growth on burned and unburned land was noted by early travelers through the Pawnee country. According to Lorenzo Sawyer, who journeyed through the Platte valley in mid-May of 1850, "Those portions of the valley which have been burnt over, are covered with fresh, though short grass, giving them the appearance of smooth shaven lawns, while the portions still covered with old grass resemble thick fields of ripe grain waving in the breeze and just ready for harvest." Visitors realized that travel in the spring through unburned prairies would result in scarcity of feed, and it is not surprising that the more knowledgeable observers such as George Catlin understood that the purpose of these Indian-set fires was not so much to provide for game as to assure feed for the Indian horses.[19]

The Pawnees appear to have regularly burned the prairies in the fall, with less frequent burning in the early spring. They set these fires both in the vicinity of their earthlodge villages and along the routes—the Platte, Republican, Blue, and Smoky Hill valleys—to their hunting grounds. The operation involved some skill, and whites who witnessed it were impressed by the way the Indians took advantage of the winds to burn the grass around the villages without touching the surrounding cornfields. Even when confronted with natural fires or fires set by other tribes, the Pawnees could often control their courses through backfiring. But no matter how great the villagers' skill, uncontrolled prairie fires presented great dangers, and men and women often lost their lives in them.[20]

The area covered by these fires could take in hundreds of square miles, for, if no rain fell, they could burn for days at a time. While the Long Expedition was camped at Council Bluffs in 1819, Edwin James witnessed a fire that burned from October 24 to November 10, and Captain Howard Stansbury reported that in 1850 a 300 mile long region on the Platte had been completely burned over by autumn fires. The kind of total destruction Stansbury reported was unusual, however. Winds and topography usually shaped the course of fires so that patches of irregular shape and size escaped burning in any given year. Contemporary descriptions suggest that although the Pawnees did not burn all of their territory annually, few tall-grass areas escaped at least one burning in any two- or three-year period.[21]

As necessary as these annual fires became for the maintenance of the horse herds, they meshed poorly with older Pawnee ecological adaptations. Although the Indians might carefully protect trees in the immediate vicinity of the villages, the fires exacted their price in the more distant groves. During the early nineteenth century missionaries and explorers reported extensive annual losses of timber in prairie fires and the destruction of large numbers of trees each fall. Later, the first white settlers in the region complained vehemently about the losses of scarce timber that Indian-set fires caused. When the Americans wrested control of portions of the old Pawnee homeland from the tribe, a resurgence of tree growth along the streams and ravines often marked the change in sovereignty.[22]

The price paid to keep the horse was large, but it was more than balanced by the benefits the animal brought. The conflict between the horse and horticulture was not complete; in important ways the horse helped tie the river valleys and the plains together in a cultural knot that survived all but the final ecological and political catastrophes that confronted the Pawnees. The horses, by providing transportation to the plains as well as becoming tools of the hunt itself, more than compensated for the problems they created in the villages. During their hunts, the Pawnees appeared to be little different from the nomadic tribes they encountered and often fought. Each summer and winter they lived in skin tipis and traveled surrounded by their thousands of animals. During the early nineteenth century the summer buffalo hunt for the Pawnees was, in George Sibley's words, a "season of enjoyment." Once they located and reached the herds, plenty was assured. But, paradoxically, this season of enjoyment was also the time of the greatest social discipline.[23]

The hunt took place under the direction of specially appointed police. Members of one of the many Pawnee bundle societies or other tribal organizations made up the hunt police. Directly under the chief selected to lead the attacks on the herds were two soldiers, or braves, as they were often called by the whites. The soldiers in turn commanded the tribal police. The soldiers and police rode ahead of the mass of hunters, who assembled behind them. When the horsemen had come as near as possible to the buffalos without alarming them, they arranged themselves in a single line so that all would have an equal chance, and the signal was given for the attack. The penalties for not obeying the directions of the tribal police were severe: anyone who attacked the herds before the signal was given, and thus endangered the whole hunt, would be unmercifully beaten and perhaps killed. Neither position nor prestige could save a man from this beating, but if later the tribe decided that the whipping had been unjustified, the bundle society that inflicted it could be barred from serving as police on any future hunt.[24]

While whites called the Indian hunting technique a surround, it was rare that the herd was actually surrounded, although hunters might approach from several directions. Whether the hunters, armed with bows and arrows and mounted on their best horses, descended on the herd from a single direction or from several directions, the hunt usually ended as a chase across the plains. The Indians generally disdained the rifle as a buffalo hunting weapon both because a gun was difficult to reload and aim on horseback, and also because a buffalo supposedly could run much farther with a bullet in its body than with an arrow. The hunters did not kill animals indiscriminately; they selected their prey as they rode into the herd and preferred either young animals under 2½ years of age or else cows. They rarely took mature bulls because they found the meat tough and distasteful.[25]

The dead buffalos were apportioned according to who had killed them, but here once more the horse produced inequities. A single well-mounted hunter might kill three or four animals while a man poorly mounted or on foot might kill none at all. The Pawnees compensated for what would have been a dangerous unequal distribution of necessary food supplies by allowing any man who butchered an animal killed in the hunt half of the meat while giving to the hunter the other half of the meat and the hide. An unmounted or poorly mounted Pawnee, stopping to butcher buffalos while hunters pursued the fleeing herd, could get significant amounts of meat since the skill of the Pawnees at butchering animals was astonishing. Observers claimed, probably with some exaggeration, that in fifteen minutes a single Indian could skin, cut up, and pack a dead buffalo on waiting horses. Like the nomadic tribes, the Pawnees used the entire buffalo—the hides for tipis, robes, and trade; the horns for spoons, the scapula for hoes (and other bones, cracked or boiled, for their marrow); and the meat and entrails for food. As the hunt continued, the villages came to resemble outdoor factories with the women stretching and tanning skins and slicing and drying meat. During the summer the women used the skins of the shedding animals for making tipis; in the winter the hides were turned into robes. The bulk of the meat in both seasons was dried and with care it "could be preserved without apparent deterioration for years." Since much of this meat was dedicated by the hunters to ceremonies, it was distributed throughout the village during the feasts.[26]

In any given hunt approximately four major attacks were made on the herds. According to missionaries who accompanied the tribe during the 1830s, a successful attack on a herd of from 1,000 to 1,200 animals netted from 300 to 500 buffalos and thus yielded the hunting group 1,200 to 2,000 animals a season. With two hunts a year, the group thus killed 2,000 to 4,000 buffalo. They hunted in two groups—the South Bands in one, the Skidis in another. During this period the total annual yield of the hunt was between 4,800 and 8,000 animals, but the yields of earlier hunts when the Pawnees were more numerous were probably greater. Finally, during the 1860s when the Pawnees hunted as a single group, 1,600 animals per hunt or 3,200 per year was considered a good yield.[27]

The horse brought change to Pawnee society: it created new forms of wealth, increased the productivity of the hunts, exaggerated the differences in productivity between individual hunters, increased warfare and raiding, threatened the fields of the valleys, and increased the environmental alterations made by the Pawnees through burning. Yet the horse posed no unresolvable challenge to the Pawnees. It took on meaning only within Pawnee culture. Although the horse increased certain tensions within Pawnee society, it did so along certain preexisting fault lines. It did not overwhelm culture and force drastic new adaptations to the plains and prairies. It did not demand nomadism.

A far more fundamental challenge to the Pawnee's culture and society presented itself very soon after their acquisition of the horse. The challenge was trade—market exchanges—but this, too, the Pawnees met quite successfully. Traders made initial contacts with the Pawnees in the early eighteenth century, and by the 1720s the Pawnees were making exchanges with both the Spanish and French. In 1724 they promised De Bourgmond an abundant traffic in beaver pelts if he could secure them a steady supply of trade goods, specifically firearms, which they may have needed for defense against European-promoted slave raids. This trade with the Spanish and French continued throughout the century, but it was never large. A Spanish compilation made in 1777 showed that the Republicans traded 3,200 livres' worth of beaver, buffalo, otter, and deerskins while the Grands traded thirty-six packs of beaver, buffalo, and otter valued at 5,500 livres. The bulk of this trade was presumably in beaver because of the high value attached to such a small supply of furs.[28]

During the early nineteenth century as Americans moved into the trade, the Pawnees ceased trapping beavers in any numbers. By 1802 the total Pawnee trade had increased to 450 packs, but it was primarily in buffalo robes and barely equaled, or was actually less than, the trade of much smaller Missouri River tribes such as the Omahas and Otoes. Traders reported that beavers remained numerous in the Pawnee country, but the hunters refused to trap them. The tribe now dealt mainly in buffalo hides that the women dressed superbly and handsomely ornamented with paint and porcupine quills. The procurement of buffalo hides, unlike beaver, called for no great alteration in tribal hunting patterns since the hides were a natural product of the semiannual hunts, but the preparation of these robes did put another heavy economic burden on the women who prepared them for the trade. Robert Stuart's figures, compiled in 1813, demonstrated this new commercial concentration on bison. According to these statistics the average annual production of the Grands was 120 packs of buffalo robes and 12 packs of beaver and of the Loups was 80 packs of buffalo robes and 5 packs of beaver.[29]

Neither the Pawnees nor the traders were satisfied with the state of the trade in the early years of the nineteenth century. The Pawnee trade was so small that merchants did not even arrive every year, despite Pawnee solicitations to the Americans to send them. Requests for commerce strengthened the hopes of the traders that the Pawnees would trap more assiduously if they had regular, guaranteed exchange. Such optimism was misplaced. The Pawnees wanted only limited goods even if they wanted them regularly. Their general attitude toward European commerce comes down in a traditional, and probably apocryphal, story told to James Murie, an American-educated Pawnee, by Curly Chief in the late nineteenth century. When Zebulon Pike arrived among them in 1806, the Pawnees supposedly took from the medicine bundle sticks to rub together to make fire, a flint arrow to kill a buffalo, and corn to give them food. These they showed Pike to demonstrate that they need depend on the Americans for nothing. The same scorn for trade was expressed by a Pawnee priest during the visit of Paul Wilhelm, the Duke of Wurttemberg, in 1823. In language probably much embroidered by the duke, the priest told him: "You have not come into our country to trade with us, and to give all sorts of useless trash and poisoned drink for our best property, as so many do, and to enrich yourself with our poverty."[30]

By the 1820s the Pawnees were seeing traders regularly, but their trade did not increase materially. White trappers now hunted out much of their beaver and thus further diminished commerce with the Pawnees. In 1831 Joshua Pilcher, a fur trader and American agent for the Upper Missouri, reported that the value of American trade with the Pawnees and neighboring tribes had "greatly diminished with the last ten years, and in a short time will scarcely be worth attending to." American hunters "almost exclusively" trapped the beaver, while Indian productions consisted of buffalo robes and dried meat to supply the Americans.[31]

This tendency of the Pawnees to devote only cursory attention to the fur trade is both interesting and significant. The Platte was too shallow to serve as a major artery for the fur trade, but this fact does not really explain the Pawnees' disinterest in commerce. In the 1820s and 1830s, at least, traders reached them annually and often wintered with them. The opportunity to trade existed. Logistics hindered the trade, but cultural factors were more basic to its failure to expand. The traders were simply unable to stimulate demand. The Pawnees' pride in their self-sufficiency was not misplaced. Bows and arrows were better buffalo-hunting weapons than guns; buffalo supplied clothing; and buffalo and corn insured plenty. Metal goods did replace pottery and stone, but these were durable and the demand limited. The Pawnees wanted little of what the Europeans offered; the trading of relatively few skins met their needs.[32]

The normal commercial recourse in such a situation was, of course, to introduce liquor. The Pawnees, however, remained a remarkably temperate people, and their abstinence was widely remarked upon on the plains. The Pawnees' refusal to accept liquor explains in large part their ability to avoid commercial subordination and market relations. But what explains their rejection of liquor? Much of the answer lies in the ability of the chiefs to retain control of the trade, and this was culturally determined.[33]

The chiefs appear to have dominated trading relations from the very beginning, when they probably were regarded as gift exchanges. Early accounts are not definitive on this point, only suggestive. When Pedro Vial visited a Republican village in 1793, for example, he was immediately met by the first chief and escorted into the village. The chief, speaking as if these items were gifts, praised the Spanish for sending the Pawnees guns, powder, and balls so they could defend themselves against their enemies, and Vial himself distributed gifts, apparently through the chiefs, before he left.[34]

The missionary accounts of the 1830s gave much clearer indications of the chiefs' domination of commerce. In the 1830s visiting traders often resided in and apparently always traded in the lodge of the chief. The chief jealously guarded this monopoly. When in 1843 the Indian agent refused to restrict traders to the main village and even allowed them to trade "in the lodges of persons who were not considered as chiefs," the chiefs delayed coming in for annuities and conferences because "they were displeased and felt they had been lowered in the estimation of their people and others were enjoying privileges which belonged exclusively to them."[35]

In view of the authority of respected chiefs, their insistence on personally overseeing the trade is significant. Unlike, for example, Choctaw chiefs, they could have their soldiers use force to stop measures they regarded as being clearly against the common good. A Pawnee who persisted in willful insubordination toward a chief, it must be remembered, could be beaten and, in extreme instances, sometimes killed. By combining supervision of the trade with their authority within the village, the chiefs could, and apparently did, control Pawnee access to liquor and thus limit the extent of trade itself.[36]

The critical element in this control was the chiefs' supervision of the traders. It is not accident that in the early 1840s when traders left the lodges of the chiefs, they also attempted to make liquor the staple of the trade. In the late winter of 1842 Samuel Allis complained of growing intemperance among the Pawnee, and that summer the agent seized whiskey from traders returning from the Pawnee villages. That the agent seized whiskey from *returning* traders shows that the thirst of the Pawnees was as yet hardly insatiable, and the chiefs acted to make sure it did not become so. The complaints the chiefs made against the traders the next year almost certainly reflected their concern over liquor as well as prestige. By the 1850s the chiefs had secured a total ban on liquor in the villages, which lasted through the 1860s.[37]

The failure of the fur trade among the Pawnees temporarily preserved game within their lands, but all around them furbearers and woodland animals disappeared. The hunters of neighboring tribes, those of Indian nations from the east, and intruding whites, killed off the beaver, the otter, the elk, and the deer. Because of this slaughter, the tribes of the lower Missouri River who depended on such game far more than did the Pawnees faced disaster. By 1834 the territory of both the Otoes and the Omahas was reportedly empty of game, and these people suffered accordingly. The Pawnees did not suffer nearly as much as these neighboring peoples; their dependence on such animals had never been great, and the fur trade had not succeeded in appreciably increasing it.[38]

The first century of sustained contact—the acquisition of the horse, the slave raids, the advent of the fur trade, the coming of epidemic diseases—had not shattered the Pawnee world. To them it still seemed a coherent and controlled place, and they remained a powerful people. The physical world of the early nineteenth century bore their cultural mark.[39]

In agriculture, of course, the Pawnees made the first and most fundamental alteration in the natural communities of the plains.

They introduced new plant species onto the prairies, eliminated native communities in localized areas, and then transformed the species they themselves had introduced by creating new varieties of corn, beans, and squash. Change was not, however, confined to agriculture. At least five plants found in or near the old Pawnee homeland occurred only in small, local communities hundreds of miles away from their normal range. The Pawnees highly valued two of these plants, *Acorus calamus* and *Lobelia cardinalis*, whose Nebraska range was a small area near the Pawnees' villages. The Pawnees used *Acorus* for medicinal and religious purposes and red *Lobelia* as a love charm. Certainly the introduction of these plants, and probably their preservation, was due to the actions of the doctors who needed a small but certain supply. This same kind of cultivation and preservation of wild plants occurred on a much greater scale when white land use threatened the natural supply of valued plants, and the Pawnees took to planting and harvesting the species needed for medicinal and religious use. When the tribe departed Nebraska for Indian Territory, the Pawnees took with them seeds of native plants to cultivate in their new homes.[40]

Besides introducing plants and creating local environments where they could survive against the competition of native communities, the Pawnees expanded the natural range of other plants. Amaranths or, as the settlers called it, pigweed or hogweed surrounded the Pawnee villages in the 1830s. Amaranths, which thrived in disturbed land such as that around a village, were among the earliest domesticated food plants of the American Indians. The Pawnees may have encouraged the communities around their villages and harvested them for food, even though by the time Gilmore made his ethnobotanical collections in the early twentieth century the plant no longer had any economic significance in the tribe. Like amaranths, lamb's-quarters (*C. album*) was an early and significant component of American Indian agriculture that was later abandoned for the corn-squash-bean complex. Lamb's-quarters, too, is an invader of disturbed lands. The Pawnees continued to use the plant as a green throughout the nineteenth century, but archaeological excavations indicate that the plant earlier was raised for its seed and formed a more significant part of the Pawnee diet.[41]

Other wild plant populations bear the marks of Pawnee manipulation. White travelers were struck by the size and abundance of the wild onions found in the vicinity of the Pawnee villages. According to Edwin James in 1820, the roots were about "as large as an ounce ball" and very plentiful near the streams. Twenty-six years later William Clayton wrote that the area around the Pawnee villages was "full of wild onions which appear far richer and larger than any wild onions I ever saw." The mention of these plants by both these men coincided with their entry into Pawnee territory. But what is as interesting as the size and range of the onions is their abundance over a twenty-six year period. One of the few environmental effects granted plains gatherers by some ecologists is the diminution of local populations of edible plants through overgathering. This clearly did not happen to the wild onion and, what is more significant, it did not happen to the wild potato, the staple of the gatherers. Even though in some years the Pawnee women dug virtually every potato they could find, the plant remained abundant until the end of the Pawnee period.[42]

The continued abundance of these plants may have been due simply to the reproductive capabilities of the onions, potatoes, and also ground beans, but the combination of size and abundance in wild plants could also have been the result of gathering practices. Part of this was accidental—the loss or splitting of roots during gathering or the scattering of seeds by the gatherers—but part may also have been purposeful replanting and selection for size. If during the late nineteenth century the Pawnees carefully preserved populations of wild plants needed for medicine or religion, it seems likely that they would have also preserved other wild populations upon which their economy relied. Furthermore, there is evidence that when such care was not taken, wild populations did decline in the face of extensive harvesting. The Pawnees and other tribes collected quantities of water chinquapin for food and apparently, as crop failures put unusual pressures on the plant, took insufficient steps to insure its reproduction. The result was a marked decline in local chinquapin populations that F. V. Hayden blamed on over-harvesting by Indians.[43]

Direct evidence of the establishment and maintenance of a wild plant population can be found in the case of wild plums. The Pawnees harvested this fruit and dried it with the pit still inside. When the pits were discarded, shrubs sprouted around the village and were in turn protected from the fires that might destroy them. The abundance of wild plums around Pawnee villages then was not a natural occurrence. When the tribe moved to Oklahoma, they took the wild plum with them, and once more it marked their village sites. In a similar manner either accidental or purposeful planting by gatherers may explain the abundance of sand cherries near the rivers and streams along which the Pawnees traveled on their way to the hunts.[44]

The most substantial alteration of the Plains environment by the Pawnees did not come from gathering practices, however, but from their care of the horse herds. The Pawnees and other peoples had almost certainly burned the plains for centuries as a hunting technique, but if, as seems apparent, Pawnee burning became far more extensive with the acquisition of the horse, Indian-set fires probably should not be credited with the creation of the grasslands.

These fires did, however, have marked and significant effects on the woodlands bordering the rivers. Within the woodland communities repeated burning tended to encourage poplars (*Populus grandidentale*) and those oaks (*Q. macrocarpa, Q. coccinea,* and *Q. borealis*) which can endure considerable burning without injury or, if injured, can resprout from stumps. But more than altering species composition within woodlands, these fires restricted the area covered by forests. Although without fires trees would hardly have covered the grasslands, their range would have been far greater. After the Pawnees left Nebraska for Oklahoma and the burning ceased, there was a significant regrowth of cottonwood along the Platte in the 1870s. These trees very probably were only reoccupying areas from which the fires had driven them, and the large areas of wolfberry reported by Hayden on the Great Plains during the 1850s may have been relicts of previous woodlands destroyed by fire.[45]

The consequences of Indian set fires did not stop with the restriction and destruction of forest communities and the enlargement of the grasslands. The nature of the grasslands themselves was influenced by these fires. The whole rationale for Pawnee burning in the historic period, after all, was that it encouraged earlier growth of grass and insured a larger yield of forage during the crucial spring months. But the consequences of burning went beyond earlier growth. Occasional fires (every two to three years) help renovate the prairies and usually prove quite beneficial. Such fires, by eliminating accumulated debris, allow the soil to warm more quickly and give an advantage to small earlier grass species that otherwise tend to disappear into pure stands of big bluestem. Over much Pawnee territory, burning in two- to three-year intervals seems to be exactly what took place. Although descriptions of most early travelers were not precise, those who traveled in the spring and early summer remarked that the flora was varied and poor in neither grass species nor the number of forbs.[46]

But in some areas, especially meadows of the second river terraces near the villages, burning probably occurred nearly every year. Here the consequences of burning may have been different. One grass that almost certainly benefited from burning was fittingly enough called Indian grass (*Sorghastrum nutans*). This tall grass of the prairies greatly increases its range with regular fires.[47]

Although burning probably had the most widespread effect upon the prairies of any Indian action, their horse herds too, at least locally, shaped the grasslands. The complaints of early visitors concerning the amount of forage near the Pawnee village indicates that while local grazing land was virtually limitless during late spring and summer, the actual available land was severely limited by the danger from Sioux horse raiders. The horses had to remain fairly close to the villages. Most grazing apparently took place on the prairies of the second river terraces. Certain consequences of the Pawnee grazing pattern can be predicted, but they are very hard to verify. Since the Pawnees were most interested in obtaining early grasses for their horses, probably the plants whose main season of growth is in the spring were the most heavily grazed. Since both big and little bluestem do not begin growth until mid- or late-spring, such palatable early grasses as needlegrass (*S. spartea*) would probably become very liable to overgrazing under the Pawnee pattern. The horses would eat them before they had a chance either to seed or to store food in their rhizomes. If this kind of grazing continued year after year, these plants would gradually cease to be an important component of the local ecosystem.[48]

It is, however, from surviving accounts of the flora of the Pawnee territory hard to see if such a pattern actually occurred. Many of the accounts of the 1840s and later were from travelers along the Oregon and Mormon trails, and the vegetation in the immediate vicinity of these trails showed the effects of white as well as Indian use. But even early accounts or accounts by those who avoided heavily traveled white routes rarely named the actual plants observed and thus cannot be used to check for indicators of overgrazing. Furthermore, even when botanists did travel through the country, they were more plant collectors than ecologists. Although they listed species, they only rarely provided even rough figures on the abundance of the plants collected. There were mentions of plants that can be indicators of overgrazing; Frémont mentioned that asters were conspicuous along the Platte in 1843, and Hayden identified dock (*Rumex venosus*) and wooly vervain (*Verbena stricta*) in the Platte and Loup valleys in 1858. But since precise quantities are not given, the evidence from these plants alone is too meager to establish overgrazing.[49]

On the high plains the methods of hunting employed by the Pawnees had, in time, repercussions for the herds. The selective killing of young animals and cows certainly never helped maintain the breeding population of the buffalos, but in the eighteenth and early nineteenth century this depletion of breeding stock made little difference. When the kill of a large tribe such as the Pawnee amounted to only 20,000 animals annually at the most, the buffalo population was in no serious danger at a time when estimates of their annual reproduction ran to 3,240,000 animals. But when this disproportionate slaughter of breeding animals took place in herds that white hunters had already drastically thinned, the buffalo declined more precipitously. As early as the 1830s John Dunbar reported what he took to be an excessive proportion of bulls in the buffalo herds.[50]

The Pawnees realized the danger that whites represented to the herds and attempted to halt the slaughter that threatened them with ruin. They complained to their agents of the damage whites were doing to their hunting grounds as early as 1832, but the government did nothing to stop the slaughter. During the 1840s the Pawnees made attempts to police the plains themselves, so that in 1847 the trader at Fort Laramie warned members of the Mormon battalion returning east that they might have trouble with the Indians if they attempted to kill buffalo. But as American immigration mounted and as the Sioux forced them off the upper Platte, such threats became impossible to enforce, although the Pawnees never surrendered their claim to the buffalo.[51]

As the number of buffalo steadily decreased, plains tribes began to attempt to control buffalo migrations so as to confine the animals within hunting grounds safe from both the whites and other Indians. But the Pawnees became more the victims of this kind of environmental manipulation than the instigators. There were two major ways of controlling the buffalo: herding and the burning of the grass lands. Both were used by the Sioux to deprive the Pawnees of buffalo.

By the 1850s some Sioux bands treated the buffalo almost as a semidomesticated, pastoral animal. The band would locate a group of buffalo, literally herd them through their range, and kill only isolated bulls so as not to disturb the main body. They protected their buffalo from all other hunters, both white and Indian. Only when the herd had fattened and their skins were suitable for robes did the major hunt take place.[52]

The second technique was less elaborate and depended on the destruction of grazing lands to steer the animals away from other peoples' hunting territories. By the 1850s this tactic had apparently become very common; soldiers and Indian agents mention its being successfully employed against the Pawnees in 1854 and again in 1862. Thus by the 1850s the peoples who preyed on the herds had begun to manage and manipulate their natural migration patterns.

Until the very end of their history in Nebraska, the Pawnees continued to shape the natural world around them. As a people, they were neither impotent nor passive. They made choices; they took action. A stubborn, proud, independent nation, they avoided the snares of the market that humbled other Indian peoples, but as their subsistence system too failed, they became dependent on Americans nonetheless. This ultimate failure, combining as it does political, cultural, and environmental factors, deserves closer consideration.

CHAPTER 9

The Pawnee Decline

The decline of the Pawnees in the face of the Sioux and the Americans and their reduction to starvation and dependency formed part of a larger historical process taking place all over the plains in the nineteenth century. Everywhere horticultural villagers steadily lost ground, first to the nomadic buffalo hunting tribes, then to the Americans.

Two rather sweeping explanations have been offered for these developments. White contemporaries and later white scholars have assumed the Pawnees starved and suffered in the mid-nineteenth century because they had always starved and suffered; such conditions, they have assumed, merely reflected the exigencies of the Indian economy. If this were so, however, the Pawnees and other horticultural tribes could never have survived as long as they did. Early missionary accounts noted the general dependability of crop yields under traditional Pawnee agricultural methods. Although they do mention starving times, these are the result of Sioux attacks or the plundering of Pawnee stores by other tribes while the Pawnees were away on hunts. The crop failures and famines of the 1840s, 1850s, 1860s, and 1870s resulted from the historical conditions that verged on chaos, not from any inherent shortcomings of the Indian economy that forced them to rely on whites as soon as white aid became available.[1]

The second explanation is more historical. Archaeologists and anthropologists sometimes seem to arrange the history of the grasslands so that the introduction of the horse both allowed the flowering of nomadic culture and simultaneously sounded the death knell of the horticultural villagers of the plains and prairies. In the words of John Ewers, the horticulturalists found themselves "surrounded and largely at the mercy of the mounted nomads." Implicit in Ewers's evaluation and in that of numerous other anthropologists is the idea that the horse changed the material condition of plains life so drastically that nomadism became a much more suitable adjustment than life in permanent horticultural villages had been. Tribes like the Pawnees became cultural reactionaries, throwbacks to earlier days and older conditions. Much more than the horse was involved, however (as anthropologists do often admit).[2]

As the case of the Pawnees demonstrates, the horse, for all the problems it presented, did not represent an insurmountable difficulty for the village horticulturalists. Indeed the villages very often became centers for the diffusion of the horse through trade and raiding. The Pawnees maintained herds of 8,000 animals during the 1820s, a time when the Sioux were poor in horses. For generations the Pawnees successfully resisted the incursion upon their hunting grounds of numerous nomadic as well as eastern emigrant tribes.

Tribes did not wander unrestrained in search of buffalo. Tribal groups hunted specific territories. These might be shared with other peoples but not with all peoples. If unauthorized nations entered their buffalo grounds, the Pawnees resisted, as the Americans discovered when they gave emigrant tribes from the east access to the mixed-grass plains. The Pawnees had fought the Comanches for a century and then in the 1820s repulsed Cheyenne and Arapaho inroads upon the lands they claimed on the plains. They resisted the Delawares in the 1830s as they had resisted the others. As their agent John Dougherty wrote William Clark in 1832: the Pawnees "have ever considered their hunting lands intruded on by other tribes if found there and in most cases have treated other Indians when found hunting on those lands as enemies except such of the small neighboring tribes who obtain permission of them and accompany them on their hunts." Pawnee resistance to the Delawares and others forced the Americans, who had created the conflict, to intervene and negotiate a peace. Forty years later the Pawnees still claimed ownership not only of a hunting territory but also of the herds themselves. Petalesharo, the first chief of the Grand Pawnees, complained to

Barclay White, head of the Central Superintendency, that white hunters had no right to kill buffalo since "our fathers owned both the land and the animals feeding on it. We sold the land to the whites, but reserved the buffalo."[3]

The conquest of the Pawnees came only at the hands of the last and most powerful of the nomadic confederations—the Sioux and their allies. In the late 1830s the Tetons expelled the Skidis from the region above the forks of the Platte and forced them to hunt near the South Bands on the Republican and Kansas rivers. By the 1840s, as the Platte hunting grounds declined in the face of American emigration, not even the Republican and Kansas valleys remained secure as the Oglalas and Brules began to move south. For decades the Pawnees struggled to maintain themselves, but the slaughter of one of their hunting parties at Massacre Canyon in 1873 ended their centuries-old hold on the region.[4] Even this defeat, however, antedated by only three years the final defeat of the Sioux themselves by the Americans.

In their warfare with the Sioux there is no doubt that the Pawnees' horticultural-village way of life, their cornfields and their earthlodges, made them vulnerable to attack in ways the nomadic Sioux never were. The nomads murdered Pawnee women in the fields, burned and trampled their corn, and robbed their food caches. The Pawnees returned from hunts to find their earthlodges destroyed and the old people who had remained behind dead. It is no wonder that in desperation they sometimes threatened to abandon their villages forever and become nomads themselves. Yet they never did.[5]

The Pawnees remained horticulturalists and hunters, but under pressure the form and locale of the hunt began to change. The Pawnees now had to travel farther to get meat. What started as a week-long journey to the Platte hunting grounds became a three-week search for buffalo along the Republican, Kansas, Blue, Solomon, and Smoky Hill rivers. As the journey lengthened, the amount of meat the Pawnees consumed simply in making the trip and conducting the hunt increased, so that in some years missionaries reported they ate most of what they killed merely in getting to and returning from the hunting grounds. When poor hunts were coupled with agricultural failures or the looting of cached foods by other tribes, the Pawnees resorted to emergency hunts, undertaken only by young men, to secure food supplies. By the late 1840s not even these extra hunts could compensate for other losses, and the tribe repeatedly faced starvation.[6]

Even under intense pressure from nomadic warriors, the advantages of village life over nomadic life were enough to maintain old ways. Few village groups on the plains willingly became nomads during historic times—the height of the nomad's dominance. The Sioux briefly drove the Arikaras, Poncas, and Omahas into nomadism, as they had the Cheyennes and perhaps the Crows before them, but all these tribes except the Cheyennes and Crows eventually returned to their villages. The starving times that nomads faced when the hunt failed and they had no other substantial resources to fall back on held more fear for villagers than nomadic attacks.[7]

What the mixed economy of the hunt and farming offered the villagers above all else was security. This was the great strength of the horticultural-hunting subsistence system here, as elsewhere. The Pawnees explicitly recognized it and valued it above the real, but often sporadic, plenty of the hunt alone. The hako ceremony gives an explanation of why the turkey was deposed as protector of the children of the human race:

> Both the turkey and the woodpecker desired to be the protector of the human race, and there was trouble between them on that account. One day the woodpecker was flying about looking for its nest when the turkey chanced that way and the woodpecker called out: "Brother where are my eggs?" The woodpecker talked of his eggs, but he meant the children of the people on earth and the turkey knew that was what he was talking about.
>
> "They are not your eggs (offspring); they are mine," said the woodpecker.
>
> "They are mine to take care of," answered the turkey; "for in my division of life there is great power of productiveness. I have more tail feathers than any other bird and I have more eggs. Wherever I go my young cover the ground."
>
> "True," replied the woodpecker, "but you build your nest on the ground, so that your eggs are in constant danger of being devoured by serpents, and when the eggs hatch the young become prey to the wolves, the foxes, the weasels; therefore, your number is continually being reduced. *Security is the only thing that can insure the continuation of life.* I can, therefore, claim with good reason the

right to care for the human race. I build my nest in the heart of the tall oak, where my eggs and my young are safe from the creatures that prey upon birds. While I have fewer eggs, they hatch in security and the birds live until they die of old age. It is my place to be a protector of the life of men."[8]

The mixed economy gave the Pawnees a security the nomads lacked. The failure of the buffalo hunt meant suffering, but as long as the Pawnees maintained their agriculture, it did not mean death. A bad winter hunt for the Pawnees in 1838, for example, meant only that the tribe lived on corn. Starvation came only if both halves of the subsistence system repeatedly failed.

In Pawnee eyes, of course, such practical reasons for maintaining the life of the village never stood alone. The richness and meaning of their lives, as well as their physical security, were too deeply entwined with the ceremonials and cosmology of the earthlodge village. For priests, chiefs, and women, the abandonment of agriculture must have seemed unimaginable. It would have left both their daily lives and the meaning of their world in a shambles. Yet mere resistance to change could not remove the problems which the Pawnee faced. And in time pressure from the nomads added internal tensions within the nation to the external pressures. Why maintain a subsistence system whose great advantage is security when the system itself becomes insecure? And no matter how rich the symbolism of a cosmology, how long can it and the social structure it justifies be maintained when it no longer adequately explains the conditions of everyday life that it promises to control? Indeed, how long can the patterns of daily life be maintained when they yield only hardship and scarcity? These were questions the Pawnees grappled with for more than a generation.

The incursions of the nomads and the problems they presented for the Pawnees were themselves related to another set of new conditions on the plains: the arrival of whites with their new technologies and their eagerness for trade. Like most Indian peoples, the Pawnees had readily engaged in a certain kind of technological substitution. Metal pots replaced pottery; metal knives replaced those of stone, metal hoes replaced those of buffalo scapula. The woolen trade blanket entered the Pawnee wardrobe, and the skin blanket was dropped. Only firearms represented a distinctively new kind of tool, and these played only a minor productive role. Technological innovations such as these were undoubtedly more efficient, but because they demanded so little change in accustomed ways of doing things, they too failed, in and of themselves, to substantially alter Pawnee life.[9]

Nonetheless, the possibility for dependence now existed simply because the Pawnees received essential goods from whites. Dependence, however, was a political condition, not purely a material condition. The mere exchange of goods hardly represents dependence. What brought dependence to the Choctaws, for example, was not woolen goods or hoes or guns in and of themselves but the penetration of the market economy, heavily dependent on liquor, which resulted in the destruction of native subsistence. Among the Pawnees the market never took hold, and the reasons were largely cultural.

Because the institution of the market is so disruptive and poses such a threat to the group cohesiveness and stability, resistance, not receptivity, is the usual reaction. The major tool that the whites used overcoming such resistance among Indian peoples was liquor, which both created unlimited demand and allowed whites to dictate the form of exchange. Yet the success of liquor was not automatic. Among the Pawnees, the chiefs successfully continued to block its introduction.

By definition men of peace who derived their power from the bundles, the chiefs, whose goal was the harmony and stability of the group, could hardly welcome liquor. Whiskey brought turmoil and replaced distribution through the chief with direct trade with the whites. Liquor threatened both the status and power of the elite, but because of the standing they derived from the bundles, the chiefs had the power to blunt the threat. Pawnee chiefs controlled the traders by the simple expedient of protecting them and confining the trade to their own lodges. Their cultural power and standing enabled them to maintain such an arrangement; in a society whose culture did not sanction such power, this control could not have been maintained. The result was that the liquor trade remained small or nonexistent, and the Pawnees remained outside the market economy. As late as the 1870s Pawnee chiefs expected gifts from the traders who lived among them and secured their expulsion when the presents were not forthcoming.[10]

The Pawnees' successful resistance to market relations, however, merely reoriented white influence; it did not remove it. As carriers of exotic diseases, allies against the Sioux, and proselytizers for extensive agriculture and Christianity, whites remained quite significant to the Pawnees. Always, however, their influence has to be understood in relation to the pressures exerted by the Sioux and other nomads. The Pawnees, faced with two alien groups that threatened established ways, rejected both of them and tried to keep both at a distance. Only when the Sioux incursions became unbearable did they move—both literally and metaphorically—closer to the Americans.

In part, then, the decline of the Pawnees is inseparable from the changing military and political relationships on the plains, and these deserve closer examination. One of the major reasons the Pawnees grew weaker was the great depletion of their population caused by epidemic disease. Yet disease alone is an unsatisfactory explanation for their downfall. It is important to remember that the Pawnees always rebounded from epidemic losses until the 1838 smallpox epidemic, when population decline became steady and, at times, precipitous. The date is quite significant, because after 1838 both Sioux pressures and American contact, via the overland trails, increased considerably.

It is tempting to offer a straightforward biological explanation for this population decline and the parallel decline in political power. Increased contact with Americans brought increased exposure to disease, which reduced population and weakened resistance to Sioux attacks. This situation, in turn, led to the concentration of population in fortified villages where the survivors met even greater chances for contagion; the consequence was still higher death rates. Indeed, there is some truth in this formulation, but contemporary descriptions indicate that the actual course of events was more complex. Politics, disease, and culture served to create a more seamless web of causation.[11]

It is not just disease that reduced Pawnee population. As scholars writing of extraordinary death rates in both native and colonial societies have emphasized, the loss of 70, 80, or 90 percent of a population in relatively short periods is not the natural result of a disease or complex of diseases, no matter how virulent. To achieve death rates of this magnitude, other factors must be involved. The two most common are malnutrition and the loss of what is, in the vernacular, known simply as the "will to live." In the Pawnee case, disease, subsistence failure, and cultural breakdown—a loss of spirit as John Dunbar, who had known them for years, phrased it—all contributed to their population decline and growing military and political weakness. Their decline was more than just a biological event.[12]

The failure of Pawnee subsistence was the result of both conditions beyond their control and decisions they made under duress, which, no matter how understandable, resulted in disaster. On the plains the slaughter of the buffalo by the Americans and emigrant tribes increased Indian competition for the diminished herds. The normal precariousness of the hunt was multiplied many times over as Sioux attacks distrupted the Pawnee seasonal migrations and their burning of the prairies denied buffalo to the Pawnees. After the Civil War the Americans so diminished the buffalo that no tribe could be assured of enough.

To the Americans, the meaning of these events seemed quite clear: since the buffalo would soon be gone, the Pawnees must raise more crops and depend on cattle for meat. The Pawnees disagreed and tried to explain why they persisted in hunts that were increasingly dangerous and unrewarding. As Petalasharo explained to Samuel Janney, the buffalo was a sacred animal; its meat, dedicated to the ceremonies by the hunters, in a sense fueled the whole Pawnee world. If they did not hunt buffalo, they could not offer meat at the ceremonies; if the meat were not offered, then *tirawahut* would be offended, crops would fail, and the Pawnees would suffer even more. They had to hunt until the buffalo were gone.[13]

The Pawnees persisted in the hunt until the end, but increasingly they had to rely on their agriculture for food. The Sioux struck here, too. They killed women working in the fields and destroyed their crops. The Pawnees, at the urging of the Americans, decided to concentrate their agriculture on the upland fields plowed for them by the agents and this action made political and economic sense. Here warriors could better protect the women. The upland fields, however, not only were less well watered than those by the creeks and ravines, but the Pawnee movement onto them coincided with a climatic cycle which brought a disastrous series of droughts and grasshopper invasions. What crops the Pawnees did produce and store, they often could not protect. The Sioux raided these supplies, and as the Americans decimated the game of the Missouri bottoms and the Sioux denied the plains to all but the strongest tribes, smaller village peoples such as the Omahas, Otoes, and Missouris—now themselves often near starvation—took to looting the Pawnee stores of food while the tribe was absent on the hunt. The agriculture the Pawnees struggled to maintain became less and less reliable.[14]

When disease came, therefore, the Pawnees were often malnourished and weak, sometimes actually near starvation. In 1844 they had both poor hunts and poor crops; in 1848 the chiefs reported they were starving to death, and officials described the Pawnees coming in like "hungry wolves"; in 1849 their trail back from the winter hunt was marked by the corpses of those who had starved to death; and in 1854 Captain H. M. Wharton said their sufferings would "seem beyond belief of anyone who had not been an eyewitness to them." Disease alone was not responsible for their staggering death rates; the epidemics bit into an already malnourished and desperate people.[15]

Deprived of hunting lands, sporadically horseless, often hungry, the Pawnees were literally fighting for their lives. The warfare they waged was real, not some dangerous game, and their losses reflected its severity. Scores of warriors died at a time in the battles for the Platte hunting grounds and in defense of the villages. And warfare with the Sioux, involving as it did the loss of hundreds of horses, spurred increased raids to the south to restore the reduced herds. Large numbers of men now went south not only to raid for horses but sometimes because the villages lacked the food to feed them if they stayed. Because these Pawnee horse stealing parties departed on foot, they were extremely vulnerable to entrapment on the prairies if they were discovered. As the number of raids increased, so did the Pawnee losses, and the Indians were accordingly motivated towards even greater warfare for revenge. Battle losses in the south were heavy. Sometimes a hundred or more warriors would depart and never return. The various censuses, incomplete and crude as they are, reflected the result. When Pike visited the Pawnees in 1806, he counted about the same number of men and women—1,973 men and 2,170 women. In 1859 Agent William Dennison listed 820 men and 1,505 women. Warfare may not have accounted for all of the difference, but it clearly took its toll.[16]

For a nation whose cultural ideal was peace and security, this endless warfare, disease, death, and starvation had to have cultural consequences, which in turn influenced further Pawnee adjustments to the changes taking place around them. People were dying, but so too were basic elements of a cultural order. Because of the special mechanisms for communicating sacred knowledge, increasing death rates deprived the Pawnees of knowledge itself and the hierarchy it controlled. Sacred knowledge could only be legitimately acquired from a priest or chief in exchange for the proper gifts. Thus when a priest died before communicating all his wisdom, the knowledge died with him even if, in fact, survivors who had witnessed a ceremony for years could have recreated much of it. When the knowledge involved was that of sacred bundles, a cultural catastrophe was in the making since the bundles maintained and ordered the Pawnee world. By the end of the century the Pawnees had lost much of their legitimate knowledge of the sacred bundles. The bulk of this loss probably occurred after the nation fled to Indian territory, but it began in Nebraska.[17]

A whole world was dying. When in 1880 John Dunbar described the Pawnees as "completely broken-spirited," he attributed their staggering death rate in large measure to despair. Dunbar gave an example of how disease, despair, and cultural loss all combined. Skurararesha, the second chief of the Skidis, came down with malaria a year after removing to Indian territory. He recovered, but

> soon after his convalescence was well established his wife and two sons were attacked by the disease. The death of his wife, which occurred within a few days, was a bitter blow to him. In less than a week the older son, aged about twelve, succumbed. The aggravated sorrow bore heavily upon him, and when the younger son too was taken away he broke down entirely. On returning from the grave of this child he remarked that he could not live any longer and the next morning was dead, apparently dying of grief.[18]

Such evidence is certainly shaky, but the conditions it describes are not historically unknown.

Epidemics and other diseases cut deeply into the ranks of Pawnee leadership and diminished sacred knowledge, but the surviving chiefs and priests (and the bundles they controlled) must have seemed increasingly ineffectual as the hunts and harvest failed. The natural world resisted the elite's powers, and so too did the Americans and Sioux. The Americans refused to help the Pawnees despite promises to supply guns and arbitrate disputes. The United States neither curbed the Sioux nor honored Pawnee requests for guns. When some Pawnees under Chief Siricharis abandoned the villages north of the Platte and returned south of the river where they raided and exacted tribute from American travelers, the United States prepared to send troops against them. By 1847 the chiefs who had supported the American alliance were rapidly losing influence.[19]

The eventual response of Americans to such resistance from traditional chiefs was to name new ones. In earlier times such an attempt would have been ludicrous; by the 1860s it was a significant threat to traditional social organization. The increasing poverty of the Pawnees as their subsistence base failed made them dependent on the annuities that the Americans paid them for their land cessions. The goods for redistribution that once originated within the society now came from without. Without the Americans, the chiefs found it difficult to fulfill their customary role as redistributors. To alienate the Americans would be to lose the goods a chief needed to affirm his status and fulfill his obligations.[20]

In a nation plagued by increasing poverty, however, redistribution, which had once bound the people together, now accentuated their differences. The chiefs did not distribute the annuities equally. Those with the highest status got the best goods. Money, in particular, was defined as a status good, so that, while all the Pawnees might get clothing, money only went to the elite. The chiefs hardly got rich. They got eighty dollars each, the priests somewhat less, and so on, but even this stood out amidst the glaring poverty of the nation. Such a system angered the Pawnees' Quaker agents. As Jacob Troth reported at the 1870 distribution, "The result was as usual, the poor and aged got little or nothing." Throughout the early 1870s the chiefs and soldiers argued vehemently for their right to redistribute annuity goods, but it was a losing battle. Their Quaker agents put the chiefs and soldiers on salary and took over the distribution of the remaining annuities themselves. They expected that in exchange for their salary, chiefs and soldiers would act as government employees; the soldiers, for example, were now reduced to truant officers who secured students for the school. This American interference in tribal government weakened the authority of the chiefs and sometimes resulted in a dual system, with many Pawnees acknowledging one man as chief and the government and other Pawnees another.[21]

The chiefs themselves grew discouraged and dissatisfied; recognizing the erosion of the old world, they were unsure of their position in the new. Likitaweelashar, or Captain Chief, of the Skidis told John Williamson in the 1860s: "If the white men had staid on the other side of the big water we Indians would have been better off for we are neither white men nor Indians now. For the Great Spirit had given us all this land and plenty provided [sic]."[22] The chiefs' ties to the Americans and the need for defense against the Sioux pulled the Pawnees toward the new world, and a few even became modernizers of sorts, but for most a profound cultural inertia made them view change with sadness and regret.[23]

During these last years in Nebraska, as Sioux raids made neither life nor property secure, the prestige and authority of warriors appears to have risen at the expense of that of the chiefs. Indeed, the chiefs themselves now often had to fight. Lalahwahlerasharo, or Sky Chief, the first chief of the Republicans, died at the hands of the Sioux, and Petalesharo, the first chief of the Grands, said he had to sleep with "my head on my revolver for the safety of my life and property."[24]

With the chiefs themselves forced to fight, the status of warriors rose considerably, and by the 1860s and 1870s these warriors entered combat under new conditions. In the Pawnee Scouts recruited by the Americans, well-armed and mounted Pawnee warriors fought the Sioux with considerable effectiveness, albeit for American ends and on American terms. Such men, fighting under American officers, operated outside the normal bounds of Pawnee society; to a large extent they were beyond the control of the chiefs.[25]

The growing status of the warriors perhaps emerged most clearly in the Pawnees' migration from Nebraska. Soon after more than one hundred Pawnees died in the disastrous Sioux attack on the buffalo hunting expedition at Massacre Canyon in the fall of 1873, two braves, Big Spotted Horse and Frank White, decided to join the Wichitas in Indian territory and advocated the move in council. When they prepared to leave by themselves the next spring, hundreds of Pawnees joined them. The chiefs, who were ambivalent about a move south, disavowed it in council with the agent; they were, however, powerless to stop it and later requested American permission to migrate. It is significant that the decision did not originate with them and that their opposition to it did not stop it. The social hierarchy of the Pawnees was becoming as tenuous as the people's subsistence.[26]

No single element, therefore, emerges as the master factor of Pawnee decline. The crisis in subsistence came quickly, but it came from various directions. The Pawnees might have resisted any of the material ingredients of their defeat individually, just as the Upper Republicans centuries earlier had resisted and survived the drought and their subsistence crisis with a culture largely intact. The Americans surely would have subdued the Pawnees, but they would not have necessarily reduced them to dependency. Trade had failed to do so, and mere political supervision, unless accompanied by direct and forceful efforts to dismantle their economy and society, would also have failed. The decline of the buffalo herds was a crippling blow, both as a symbol and for subsistence. But if Pawnee agriculture had remained viable, the Pawnees might have gradually replaced buffalo with cattle just as the Choctaws replaced deer with cattle. And if the Pawnees had remained well nourished and secure, they might have resisted the Sioux as they had the Comanches, Arapahos, and Cheyennes before them. Even disease, with the Pawnee subsistence system intact, might have been endured. Pawnee population would probably have recovered from the epidemics that came after 1838 just as it had recovered from those which came before. But all these things did not come separately; they came virtually simultaneously in a volatile and disastrous mix. Pawnee culture was not indestructible. It broke, but its breaking was not inevitable. Its strength stood out even in its decline.

Removal itself, despite its novel origins, despite the breakdown which prompted it, was ironically a conservative response—a defiant affirmation of and attachment to the old culture that even in a sadly changed world still exerted an irresistible appeal to the Pawnees. In the 1870s men and women still lived who remembered the security the villages had once provided. They believed the old life might still be possible, if not in Nebraska, then somewhere else. When the Pawnees decided to leave the Loup Valley, it was in the hope that to the south in Indian territory lay a land where they could hunt the buffalo, grow corn, and let the old life of the earthlodges flower beyond the reach of the Sioux and American settlers. Such a land had disappeared forever.[27]

CHAPTER 10

The Navajos

By the twentieth century the relationship between environmental change, subsistence changes, and social change among most Indian peoples had become relatively insignificant. They were a subjugated people, driven into dependency and deprived of control over much of their own lives and their land. The great exception was the Navajos or, as they called themselves, the Diné or People. A farming and sheepraising nation, they remained largely self-supporting and isolated from whites on a large reservation straddling Arizona, New Mexico, and Utah. In their own eyes and in those of government officials, their greatest wealth lay in their livestock—in their horses, in their goats, but especially in their sheep.

The ancestors of the Diné were Apachean hunters and gatherers of the Athapascan language group who 600 or 700 years ago moved into the Southwest after a long migration from the north. Although most Athapascan groups still remain in Canada or Alaska, the ancestors of the Navajos halted only when they reached the upper Chama and San Juan drainages of northern and central New Mexico—Dinetah, or old Navajo land. This was the country of the creation of the Diné, the place where they cite the beginnings of their earliest clans, where they perhaps first acquired corn from the Pueblos. By the time of the arrival of Spanish colonists in 1598 they were already distinguished from other Apaches as the *Apaches de Nabahu*, or "Strangers of the Cultivated Fields." They were then already a horticultural people.[1]

With the Spanish came sheep and horses, and by the early seventeenth century the Navajos had begun to acquire these animals. They got some in raids and others from the Pueblo sheepherders who, when forced to work for the Spanish, fled to the Navajos with their flocks. In 1680 the Pueblos revolted and drove the Spanish from New Mexico; when the Spanish returned in 1692, refugees from the Pueblos fled to the Navajos. Some refugees stayed only briefly, but others stayed much longer. Over the next three-quarters of a century Pueblos intermarried with the Navajos and greatly influenced their culture. Increasingly, as Pueblo contributions grew, the culture of the Diné deviated from that of their Apachean neighbors and allies.[2]

The return of the Spanish meant the renewal of raids. For more than a century the Navajos alternately raided and lived at peace with the Spanish. Peace with the Spanish, however, meant wars with others whom Navajo raiders turned upon to secure the slaves the Spanish coveted. The Navajos were victims as well as perpetrators of such attacks. By 1740 the Utes had driven some of the Diné south to the Puertocito and Canoncito region where, increasingly isolated from their kinspeople, they became known as the Alien or Enemy Navajos and formed a distinct subgroup within the nation. The mass of the Navajos moved too, but they went west toward Canyon de Chelly and Cebolleta into the "lands between the four mountains" which became and remains their homeland. The Spanish then counted five distinct groups of Navajos—"San Matheo, Zebolleta, or Canon, Chusca, Hozo, [and] Chelli"—who had begun restoring their herds with captured animals, looking after them "with the greatest care and diligence for their increase." By the end of the century the Spanish reported that the Navajos no longer coveted their sheep since their own were innumerable.[3]

As the herds grew, the Spanish and Navajos remained at peace during the last years of the eighteenth century. This was the last period of prolonged peace the two nations would enjoy. There was a short bitter war in 1804–1805 and then in 1818 Spanish incursions into Navajo lands brought fighting that remained virtually constant thereafter. Each side raided the other for livestock and slaves. Thousands of Navajos became Spanish slaves; lesser numbers of Spaniards became Navajo slaves. The Mexican Revolution and independence from Spain changed nothing; the raids continued. If anything, the Navajos grew stronger. Lords of the Soil, Men of the Mountains were what the Mexicans and Pueblos called them, and many Navajos for the first time grew wealthy, with their herds numbering in the thousands. The territory of the Diné grew with their herds and they expanded south into southwestern Colorado and southeastern Utah, and west to the Colorado and Little Colorado rivers. By the 1850s the Navajo country stretched from the Rio Grande River in the east to the Colorado River in the west and from approximately the 37th parallel in the north to the Zuni River in the south.[4]

This period of warfare and raiding was nearly half a century old when the Americans won New Mexico from Mexico in 1846. They promised the New Mexicans peace and protection, but it was nearly twenty years before they accomplished anything of the sort. The raids continued as before since raiding was now too critical to Navajo well-being to be dispensed with lightly. Intervention by the Americans only added them to the list of Navajo enemies and their stock to the list of Navajo targets.[5]

The end of this phase of Navajo history came quickly and unexpectedly. In 1863 Kit Carson with nine companies of volunteers—three of them unmounted, moved against the Navajos. Short of horses, ammunition, and supplies, they were not an imposing force, but Carson rarely used them for fighting. His troops killed less than fifty Indians during the campaign; he left the killing to the Hopis, Zunis, and Utes, who had their own scores to settle and Navajo horses, sheep, and slaves to take. Navajo traditions recorded the result: "The corn fields came not be attended to . . . the sheep and the horses had become annihilated . . . the several trails leading to the open flats had become impassable."[6]

Carson's troops merely followed the raiders, destroying Navajo crops and cutting down their orchards. He fed those he took prisoner, treating them kindly and taking them with him when he retired to Fort Defiance, where he waited while starvation forced the vast majority of Navajos, who had escaped him, to come to terms. As delegations came in, he told the headmen to get their people. They would not be harmed, but they would have to leave their homeland and go south to Bosque Redondo in southern New Mexico. Over 8,000 Navajos, a large majority of the nation, eventually surrendered to the Americans and marched south. In Navajo history this march is the Long Walk, their entrance into captivity. It was an experience seared into their memory which colored all future dealings with the government. It would be four years before the Diné returned to their own country—four years in which the government tried to make them settled villagers farming irrigated tracts, four years of humiliation, suffering, death, and near starvation.[7]

The Bosque Redondo experiment was a disaster, but, more pertinent to a government accustomed to disasters in Indian affairs, it was an expensive disaster. As a result, in 1868 the Indian Bureau changed its policy and decided to release the Navajos. The treaty that they signed that year gave them as a reservation an area a fraction the size of their previous country, but it allowed them to return home, and it gave them sheep to replace those Kit Carson and his allies had seized and killed. The government issued 14,000 sheep and 1,000 goats to them in 1869 and 10,000 more three years later. These sheep, with the remnant flocks of those who had managed to hide in the mountains and escape the exodus to Bosque Redondo, formed the nucleus of future Navajo herds. Despite continued suffering as crops failed in recurrent droughts, the Navajos rebuilt their way of life. By 1880 the number of Navajos was approaching preconquest levels, and the size of their herds was increasing. Once more the Navajos were stockraisers and farmers.[8]

Between 1880 and 1930 far-reaching changes took place among the Navajos. The raids and the wars were over, and if most outsiders, including their agents, knew the people at all, it was only as herdspeople, the makers of blankets, rugs, and silver jewelry. Yet quietly and unobtrusively changes came to the Navajos and to their land. The relationship between these changes in the culture and economy of the Diné (particularly alterations in their subsistence system, the growth of their sheep herds, their own increase in population, and their involvement in the commercial production of rugs, wool, and, later, lambs) and the changes in their land (the beginning of a new erosion cycle in the Southwest) is not a simple one, although it would later seem so to conservationists and American officials in the 1930s. The coincidence of the start of a new erosion cycle at the time of the stocking of the Navajo range disguised this complexity; all changes in the land seemed to spring from the relentless foraging of the sheep, goats, and horses. Changes in land and changes in people came simultaneously, but this does not mean that one caused the other.

The number of Navajos, the size of their herds, and the extent of their reservation, all increased dramatically after the return from Bosque Redondo. The Bureau of Indian Affairs, eager to have the Indians self-sufficient, encouraged the growth of Navajo herds and forbade the selling of breeding stock so that the flocks might attain maximum productivity. The Indians obeyed willingly, but in doing so they scattered far beyond the reservation boundaries to graze their animals on the land which they had occupied since their movement out of Dinetah in the eighteenth century. Reservation boundaries had little immediate impact on Navajo life.[9]

There were initially few Americans to contest their de facto repossession of their old homeland. Indian agents saw the exodus from the reservation as a legitimate exercise of the Navajos' treaty right to hunt the unoccupied public domain. If anything, the agents were astonished at the Navajos' ability to get any living from such a land. In 1883 one described the reservation as over "10,000 square miles of the most worthless land that ever laid out doors" and the next year added that "three quarters of it is about as valuable for stock grazing as that many acres of clear sky."[10]

Officials in Washington also recognized that their original reservation of about 4 million acres was woefully inadequate for the maintenance of the Navajos, and they added to it by creating by executive order reservation lands in 1876, 1880, 1882 (the Hopi Reservation), 1884, 1900, and 1901. These executive order reservations were the unilateral creations of the president and raised serious questions as to who held title, but through them the reservation tripled in size. The expanded reservation still did not equal the old homeland in size and did not solve the problem of the off-reservation Navajos. In the 1870s and early 1880s more than half the Diné lived outside the reservation; in 1888, when the major additions to the reservation had been made, one-quarter to one-third of the people remained outside reservation boundaries.[11]

By the turn of the century further expansion of the reservation to coincide with actual Navajo occupation had met formidable obstacles, the most frustrating of which were the checkerboard or railroad lands which bordered the reservation to the west, south, and east. Navajos had reoccupied this country at their return from Bosque Redondo, but their claims meant little when legal title had devolved to the railroads and white cattlemen began showing interest in the land.[12]

The original railroad grant of alternate sections of forty sections per mile—twenty above and twenty below the right of way—had been made to the Atlantic and Pacific Railroad in 1866. A long, complicated series of forfeitures, sales, and reassignments had followed so that by the end of the century three companies—the New Mexico and Arizona Land Company (a subsidiary of the St. Louis and San Francisco Railroad Company), the Atchison, Topeka, and Santa Fe Railroad; and the Aztec Land and Cattle Company—controlled the old grant. The northern portion of these company lands overlapped both executive order grants made to the Navajos and public domain lands on which many Navajos lived. The resulting pattern of railroad sections alternating with either public domain sections or executive order reservation lands was known as the checkerboard.[13]

The checkerboard would have been more of a legal problem than a practical one if white stockraisers had not expanded into the area. Although conflicts began as early as 1885, they became very serious in 1900 and 1901 after the discovery of artesian water in lands east and southeast of the reservation brought white cattlemen who threatened to monopolize traditional Navajo grazing areas. As the whites leased railroad lands and took up public domain lands, the Navajos pleaded for another expansion by executive order of the reservation in New Mexico to protect them. They failed to get such an expansion. Instead, in 1907 the bureau tried to secure for the Indians control of permanent water in the area through the allotment process of the Dawes Act, but normal Bureau of Indian Affairs bungling and incompetence and bitter opposition from whites rendered the whole plan unworkable.[14]

Attempts to consolidate checkerboard lands in Arizona initially seemed more promising. Here the Santa Fe agreed to exchange their checkerboard lands for other lands in the public domain, but the solicitor of the Department of the Interior vetoed the transfer on legal technicalities in 1913. In both Arizona and New Mexico further reservation expansion would remain effectively blocked for nearly twenty years. Eventually, substantial consolidation of checkerboard lands would take place in Arizona, but expansion of the reservation—except for relatively small purchases in the late 1920s and 1930s—remained impossible in New Mexico. There, approximately 8,000 Navajos lived on the public domain by the 1930s.[15]

The failure of their reservation to encompass all their traditional

grazing lands had profound implications for the Diné. The boundaries of the reservation were widening, but the actual land area available for Navajo use was shrinking, as some of the best off-reservation grazing lands fell into the hands of Anglo cattlemen and Mexican-American sheepmen. Superficially, reservation boundaries appear to have expanded as Navajo population and herds expanded; in reality, an increasing number of Navajos had to subsist on a dwindling amount of land. As early as 1885 the government had begun efforts to get the Diné back on their actual reservation.[16]

Throughout this period Navajo population increased steadily. The best estimate indicates that there were from 10,000 to 12,000 Navajos at the time of their return from Bosque Redondo (this includes prisoners, those held as slaves, and those who had escaped captivity). By the 1890s the Navajos certainly numbered over 20,000, and their population continued to rise until the first reliable counts yielded a figure of nearly 40,000 for 1930. Between 1870 and 1957 the Navajos sustained a remarkable average annual rate of increase of 2.34 percent.[17]

Agents had only a hazy idea of how much livestock the Navajos held between the late nineteenth century and the 1930s. Estimates, often just guesses, began with 15,000 to 20,000 head of sheep in 1869. After that the number of sheep and goats grew rapidly, both from natural increase and from the Navajo practice of trading virtually all their annuity goods to the whites for livestock. The severe winters of 1873–74 and 1882–83 reduced the herds, but their numbers quickly recovered. It seems safe to assume that the Navajos possessed nearly 1 million head of sheep and goats by the mid 1880s, as well as numerous horses.[18]

This period of relative prosperity came to a halt in the early 1890s when a succession of very dry years brought widespread loss of livestock. The severe winter of 1894–95 killed even more stock, and yet another bad winter in 1898–99 cost the Navajos an estimated 20 percent of their sheep. These disasters were followed by renewed drought. In 1900 the animals of the Diné were weak and dying, and the agent feared the Navajos could lose half their herds that winter. The drought lasted until 1903 when at last the rains came. Hundreds of thousands of sheep and horses died. In light of the virtually unrelieved gloom of agency reports from the early 1890s until 1903, the drastically reduced estimates of Navajo stock holdings for the early twentieth century may not be as far-fetched as some scholars think. The agents estimated sheep and goats at only 400,000 to 500,000 head between 1901 and 1904, and in 1907 an enumeration based on counts made at dipping stations on and off the reservation estimated sheep and goat holdings at 640,000 head.[19]

The renewed increase in livestock after 1905 was rapid but uneven. The flocks of many off-reservation Navajos in competition with the whites for land and water actually declined. Despite these local losses, Navajo sheep and goat herds as a whole once more surpassed 1 million head during the 1920s, but estimates of by how much varied wildly, ranging from 1.1 million head to 1.8 million. Counts became more reliable about 1930, and between 1930 and 1932 the Navajos possessed between 1 million and 1.37 million head of sheep and goats.

In part, a fairly steady reduction in the number of Navajo horses compensated for this increase in sheep and goats. Estimates of Navajo horse herds ranged as high as 250,000 head in the 1880s and as low as 118,298 in 1891. Agents repeatedly complained of an excessive number of "useless" ponies and of the damage they did to the range. Many of these horses died or were eaten during the long droughts, and unlike sheep and goats they never recovered their former numbers. In the early 1920s there were still an estimated 100,000 horses, but an epidemic of dourine—a contagious disease resulting in paralysis and death—made severe inroads into the horse population. Further reduction came from the sale of some horses for manufacture into chicken feed. By the end of the decade the estimates of Navajo horses ran from 40,000 to 80,000. Considering even the maximum figure, this represents a net decline of almost 39,000 animals from the low estimate of 1891 and of 170,000 animals from the high estimate. Since a horse eats five times the forage a sheep does, the removal of 39,000 horses made way for an increase of 155,000 sheep.[20]

These figures are admittedly crude, but they do illuminate several quite important aspects of Navajo stockraising. A rough plateau in livestock holdings was reached sometime during the 1880s. At that time the number of sheep and goats the Navajo owned was slightly less than in the 1920s, but the number of horses they owned was greater. Livestock numbers were not constant, however; a serious and

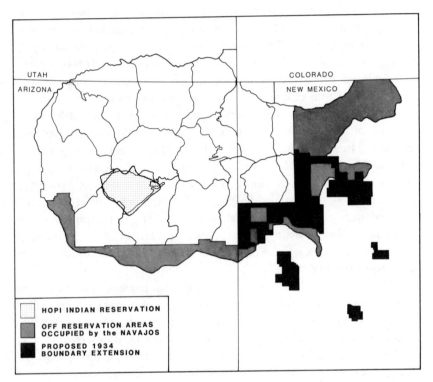

6. The Navajo Reservation and Land Management Units during the 1930s.

sustained reduction took place in the bad years between 1890 and 1903. After that, herds increased to earlier levels with a shift in emphasis toward sheep and goats.

The increase in Navajo herds thus was not sustained, while that of their population was. The implications of this imbalance are obvious. Per capita holdings declined after 1890. Based on a population figure of 20,000 for the late 1880s and livestock estimates of roughly 1 million head, there were roughly 50 sheep and goats for every Navajo man, woman, and child. After the drought, positing a population of 25,000 for the 1905–1910 period and sheep and goat holdings of 640,000 head, the per capita holdings had shrunk drastically to 25.6 animals. The widespread distress reported by the agents substantiates this decline. Thereafter conditions improved. An estimate for the Southern Navajo reservation gives per capita holdings at from 38 to 43 head in 1915, but the leveling off of the growth of the herds coupled with increasing population lowered the per capita figure to between 25 and 33 head by the early 1930s. Thus per capita holdings peaked in the 1880s, recovered somewhat in the early twentieth century and then began a slow decline.[21]

The Navajos did not, however, depend on livestock alone for their subsistence. Most Navajos considered themselves farmers as well as herders. Only in portions of the western reservation was stockraising overwhelmingly dominant, and this was offset by other regions such as the Canyon de Chelly or the Canyon del Muerto, where geography severly restricted sheepherding and agriculture dominated.[22]

The first detailed figures on sources of Navajo income and subsistence were not available until the mid-1930s when the human dependency surveys were conducted by the Soil Conservation Service. Since by this time wage work under government programs had become a major source of income for the Navajos, the figures for the 1930s are far different from those of earlier periods. Nonetheless they give some idea of the balance between agriculture and stockraising. Although stockraising regularly provided a higher percentage of total income than agriculture, it is important to note that in noncommercial or subsistence production, agriculture was more important than stockraising.[23]

So important was agriculture that the Navajos centered their annual economic cycle on their crops rather than on their sheep. Regardless of the misconceptions of their agents or early twentieth-century observers, the Navajos were not nomads following their herds across the desert. They were people with permanent, mutually recognized holdings. All Navajos might not herd sheep, but virtually all of them farmed.[24]

Navajo agriculture was not as impressive as that of their Pueblo neighbors, but nineteenth-century agents admitted that their farming techniques were better adapted to wringing a crop from the arid lands than were those of the whites. The primary concern of Navajo farmers was water rather than soil. They judged lands by their access to water, and they concentrated their fields and their homes around the perennial or intermittent streams, which were almost invariably the best guide to population concentrations.[25]

The Navajos needed this water for floodwater irrigation. They located their fields where natural floods would inundate the crop, but sometimes the farmers placed dikes across arroyos to divert floodwater onto the fields. After the return from Bosque Redondo, some Navajos, often with government assistance, adopted ditch irrigation, but this remained a minority practice.[26]

The agricultural cycle and the economic year began in April with the preparation of fields which averaged about 6 acres for each residence group. Planting took place from May to late June, depending on location. Farmers cultivated the usual Indian staples—melons, beans, squash, and the most important, corn. The Navajos had several varieties of corn. All of them had very short stalks and large root networks to provide the plant with scarce water and were therefore especially adapted to the harsh conditions of the land.[27] The Navajos easily incorporated exotic crops into this system. Although they grew wheat and potatoes, the most noticeable addition was peaches. Peach orchards were located in the Canyon del Muerto, the Canyon de Chelly, and Nazlini. The people here kept large orchards and exchanged the fruit widely, initially for game, later for sheep.[28]

The Navajos took few steps to maintain the fertility of their lands. They neither rotated their crops nor fertilized their fields. As in other American Indian systems, the land benefited somewhat from the corn-bean combination, but this alone could not extend productivity indefinitely. It probably did not have to. In many years drought brought enforced fallows, and later erosion compelled the abandonment of agricultural lands before their productivity had otherwise ceased. The Navajos contended that they never knew a farming plot to become exhausted.[29]

The care of sheep revolved around this care of crops. Since the Navajos selected spring and summer homesites because of their access to water and fields, sheep were not necessarily grazed on the best pasture lands. When pasturage or water failed in summer, the resident group moved the sheep to more distant pasture, but only a few members of the group went with them. Most remained behind to tend and harvest the crops. Once the crops were harvested, the resident group often moved to their winter hogans. These hogans could be located within a few miles of their summer homes if the wood and shelter the Navajos sought were available, but sometimes a group might winter on lands 40 to 60 miles away.[30]

The daily herding practices of the Navajos had even greater effects on the range than these seasonal movements. Women and children provided most of the actual care for the sheep, or rather for the mixed herds of sheep and goats which dominated the Navajo country. The herder released the animals from the family corral before sunrise, and then the goats—bolder and more intelligent animals than sheep—largely determined the course and pace of grazing. Since the goats grazed faster than the sheep, the flocks moved far more rapidly than they would have if they had contained sheep alone, and this movement increased the trampling of the range and the destruction of the grass. At mid-morning the herder returned the flocks to the corrals since otherwise, if caught in the heat of the day, the animals would stop and refuse to move, and force the shepherd to remain out all day. On cool days the herder sometimes did not actually pen the animals but only drove them back to the immediate vicinity of the hogans. To make this return movement easier, the Navajos did not allow the flock to spread out, and this close herding both decreased the potential feed and increased the damage done by the animals' hooves. In the afternoon the same pattern was repeated; the herder released the sheep when the heat had subsided and returned them to the corral by nightfall. No Navajo willingly remained out on the range with the flock at night. The fear of ghosts and witches was too strong. The result of this system of herding was intensive grazing of the lands within a five-mile radius of the hogans and degradation of the range.

The only break in the pattern came when the sheep needed water. Even then, however, the rapid driving of the herd to the nearest spring or waterhole led to further trampling and the convergence of herds on water, which made grazing around springs and wells as intense as that around the hogans.[31]

The Navajos grazed their animals on the lands they had occupied since their movement out of Dinetah in the eighteenth century. Their reservation proper was roughly the size of West Virginia, but the Navajo country (the region occupied chiefly by Navajos) came closer to 28,000 square miles, an area larger than Ireland. A beautiful, austere, and varied country, it seemed to many a "bewildering array of scattered mesas, buttes, isolated ridges, and towering spires, among which dwindling streams followed their torturous path," but essentially it was a plateau, part of the larger Colorado Plateau into which streams had cut their canyons and above which mountains rose. Most of the land lay between 4,500 and 7,000 feet, but around the mouth of the San Juan River in the north the altitude dropped below 4,000 feet only to rise abruptly to over 10,000 feet at the crest of Navajo Mountain only eight miles away. Navajo Mountain and the Carrizo Mountains were laccolithic in origin and towered like domes over the surrounding country, but the other mountains of the Navajo country—the Chuska Mountains of the New Mexico–Arizona border, Black Mesa in the central reservation, and Segi Mesa in the north— were, as their names suggest, modified mesas bordered by cliffs.[32]

Except for a small portion of the eastern reservation whose waters drained into the San Jose River and then flowed to the Rio Grande, virtually all the surface water of the Navajo country eventually fed the Colorado River through the Little Colorado and San Juan rivers. The contribution of the reservation to these rivers was, however, intermittent since most of the streams on the reservation were dry for much of the year. Water flow was unpredictable: a summer rain could turn a wash into a river and a rill into a stream.[33]

Above all else this was an arid land. While the mean precipitation ranged from 8 inches to 20 inches a year, the lands in the west were drier than those in the east, and areas of lower elevation were more arid than the higher regions. The rainfall was seasonal. Almost 40 percent of all precipitation occurred in July, August, and September, but a whole month's total could fall in a brief, torrential downpour. At other times the humidity could be so low and the heat so great that the water of a sudden summer storm would evaporate before reaching the ground. These were the conditions in average years. When drought came, as it seemed to do every three to eight years, twenty to twenty-five months might pass without measurable rain or snow.[34]

The vegetation of the country varied largely with topography and rainfall. At the higher elevations rains were sufficient to support forests of Douglas fir *(Pseudotsuga taxifolia)* and Western yellow or Ponderosa pine *(Pinus ponderosa)*. Below the forest zone in the steppelands which lay between 6,000 and 7,000 feet, were a combination of pinon *(P. edulis)* and juniper *(Juniperus osteosperma, J. monosperma)* woodlands intermixed with sagebrush *(Artemisia tridentata)* and grassland, largely blue grama. At 5,000 to 6,000 feet, sagebrush and grass became dominant, lesser amounts of pinon, juniper, bluestem, and greasewood *(Sarcobatus vermiculatus)* grew in the alkaline washes. Below 5,000 feet where sagebrush-grassland dominance continued, all vegetation was sparse and in the spectacular but desolate areas such as the Painted Desert was virtually nonexistent. In the 1930s botanists classified the reservation as 35 percent woodland (pinon-juniper), 25 percent brushland, 5 percent grassland, and 5 percent forest. Less than 1 percent was suitable for farming, and much of this would not be considered farmland under "usual standards."[35]

This was a harsh land in the best of years, but sometime just after the middle of the nineteenth century a change took place which made it far harsher. Streams that had long been aggrading the canyons through which they flowed began cutting into them instead. Erosion increased dramatically with accompanying gullying, and the water table began to drop. This phenomenon was not novel; periods of aggradation and cutting had alternated in prehistoric times, but there does not seem to have been a period of such significant gullying since the twelfth and thirteenth centuries. It was this earlier cutting that had led the Puebloan group to abandon the large population centers at Kayenta, Chaco, Mesa Verde, and La Plata and thus create a vacuum into which the Navajos later moved.[36]

The new phase of gullying began relatively slowly, only to accelerate during the early twentieth century. Streams like Laguna Creek, which once created a series of small lakes, had trenched and drained the last of them by 1900. Ganado was once a valley covered with reeds that were supported by a small stream. By 1930 it was cut by a deep wash which was usually dry but sometimes became a "raging torrent." The reeds had vanished and were replaced by snake weed (*Gutierrezia Sarothrae*). Exising arroyos such as Oraibi Wash deepened and grew. Oraibi in the Hopi country was only 20 feet across and 12 feet deep in 1897; by the 1930s it was, on the average, 150 to 300 feet across and 30 to 35 feet deep. The Keams Canyon Wash did not even exist in 1880, by 1930 it was 25 feet deep. Gullies cut into and across trails and forced the Navajos either to abandon them or to alter their course annually.[37]

For a people dependent on floodwater farming, this trenching was disastrous. The gullies carried away prime farmland and lowered the water table so that farming the remaining land was impossible. Sometime about 1884 entrenching began in the Tsegi region; farmlands and lakes vanished because, the Navajos said, the region had been bewitched. In 1894 Indians cultivated the flat alluvial valley of Walker Creek; in 1913 the stream had cut itself a trench eighty feet below the old terraces. The land abandonment forced by this cutting had been going on for at least twenty years by 1913 and continued for at least twenty more. By the late 1930s gullying forced the Navajos of Ramah, a region outside the reservation, to abandon traditional floodwater farming entirely.[38]

Year by year the gullies grew. After the melting of winter snows in the spring or after summer downpours, incredible amounts of water rushed through the washes, tearing away banks and carrying away trees and blocks of soil. It was dangerous even to stand on the bank of a gully after such a storm; the waters might undercut it and send earth and observer hurtling into the torrent. Little could stand before these floods. The agent reported in 1888 that dams to collect water in the arroyos were a waste of time and money; they inevitably washed out.[39]

The blame for this destructive erosion was originally put on livestock, especially sheep. There seems to have been no marked climatic change, and the beginning of the erosion cycle clearly coincided with the introduction of large herds of livestock. The herds which overgrazed the vegetation weakened or killed it; water, instead of percolating into the ground covered with grasses and other perennials, rushed over a soil practically denuded of vegetation, cutting gullies and destroying the country. Or so the theory ran, and it remained dominant into the 1930s.[40]

Not everyone accepted this model. Herbert Gregory, the most thorough student of the geology of the Navajo country in the early twentieth century, did not doubt that livestock contributed to erosion, but he did not believe that the herds were the primary cause. Sections of the reservation ungrazed by Navajo flocks exhibited the same kind of erosion patterns as those heavily grazed. Channels cut lands covered with grass just as they did denuded lands. A single heavy flood brought gullying and erosion while twice the total rainfall spread out more evenly did little or no damage. Simply measuring annual amounts of rainfall was not enough; the distribution of rainfall and the character of storms must also be judged. Gregory's caution was vindicated in the 1950s when archaeologists discovered the first evidence of the prehistoric gullying that drove the Pueblos from the region in the thirteenth century. Sheep and goats could not take the blame for these earlier episodes of cutting and trenching.[41]

Following these discoveries, two mutually contradictory theories arose to explain gullying. One suggested that arroyo cutting corresponded with periods of drought when the vegetation cover was weakened, whereas alluviation and healing of the trenches corresponded with wetter phases. This theory was based on evidence drawn largely from the study of tree rings of the thirteenth century. In this model, increasing aridity took over the role once given to livestock or decreasing vegetation cover.[42]

Other scholars, however, suggested that gullying came not from increased aridity, but from greater humidity. According to them, an increase in the high-energy storms of summer was the key factor in erosion. They dismissed dendochronological data as measuring only winter precipitation, and relied instead on the pollen record, which they contended showed no decrease in vegetation but instead an increase during periods of gullying. Studies of modern gullies seem to support this second theory, although the evidence is far from conclusive. Numerous instances exist, as Gregory noted earlier, of sudden and severe gullying following unusually heavy storms. The kind and severity of gullying differ according to location of headwater, stream gradient, normal rainfall, and other factors, but in all cases there appears to be a correlation between intense rain or heavy runoff and gullying.[43]

Although explanations of gullying are as yet tentative and unproven, a simple correlation between the erosion cycle of the late nineteenth and early twentieth century and the increase in livestock cannot stand. In some areas erosion began before livestock was introduced; in other areas prehistoric gullying was far worse than that which followed the introduction of livestock. Navajo herds cannot be blamed for initiating the gullying and accelerated erosion that afflicted the reservation. This does not mean that the range was not being overgrazed, only that severe gullying would have occurred with or without sheep. Overgrazing hurt the land, hurt the sheep, and hurt the Navajos, but it was only a secondary cause of gullying and erosion.[44]

Because government officials in the 1930s tended to blame all erosion on livestock, it is difficult to determine precisely when overgrazing began in the Navajo country. Leonard Fonaroff and David Aberle date overgrazing from the 1880s and 1890s, but this seems too early. The reports of gullying and poor vegetation they cite seem more clearly related to the beginning of the erosion cycle and the drought of the 1890s. Gullying occurred independently of overgrazing and the Indian agents do not seem to have regarded other damage to the range as permanent; when adequate rains returned, they reported that the vegetation recovered quickly. In 1903 enough grass grew for the Indians to harvest wild hay.[45]

One of the first clear mentions of serious overgrazing came in 1905 when the agent for the Western Navajos reported that the concentration of stock around permanent water during the drought had so denuded the land that it would take years for the vegetation to recover. Heavy concentration of flocks around permanent water and virtual exclusion of sheep from areas without springs or perennial streams had long been a feature of Navajo sheep husbandry. Large areas of the reservation remained virtually empty. In 1886 the agent had reported that he had ridden for days without seeing an Indian and in 1880 another agent estimated that Navajo sheep grazed only one-third of the reservation. This concentration of livestock on a small portion of the range was dangerous, but the Navajos had largely avoided its repercussions by spreading out far beyond the reservation proper to take advantage of all permanent water. Increasing competition with whites limited this option in the late nineteenth and early twentieth centuries, but then the reduction of Navajo herds by drought had cut the pressure of their livestock on the range and only limited overgrazing occurred. Nevertheless, the potential for serious overgrazing remained latent, ready to emerge whenever the Navajos began to rebuild their herds if whites restricted their access to off-reservation lands.[46]

The invasion of the checkerboard region by Anglo cattlemen precipitated the crisis. In this situation allotments solved nothing, and the Navajos increasingly lost control of water and land. Overgrazing occurred, and the Navajos were its victims. Anglo cattlemen and Mexican-American sheepmen too had resources the Navajos could not match. The 6,000 or so Diné living in the checkerboard area of northwestern New Mexico sold off some of their sheep for the high prices they brought during World War I, but they had already lost many more in the bad winter of 1915 when the overgrazed range weakened their herds and provided little food when the snows fell. The Anglos moved their animals out to winter ranges or trucked in feed. The Navajos could do neither, and they watched their sheep die. Still they persisted. They leased railroad lands, but when the cost of such leases doubled and even tripled, the Navajos could not meet the price. The Anglo stockmen responded to attempts to extend the reservation by demanding that the Diné themselves be removed to the existing reservation. The off-reservation Navajos, now defenseless, endured disaster after disaster on the impoverished range. During the 1920s and early 1930s the flocks in the Pueblo Alto region—a representative district—shrank from 100,000 to 37,000 head. The animals of Anglo stockmen replaced them.[47]

By the 1920s a crisis in the affairs of the off-reservation Navajos, and indeed all the Navajos, had clearly arrived, but it was not simply a Malthusian crisis of increasing population and increasing Navajo herds as officials of the Bureau of Indian Affairs later tended to present it. Although Navajo population had increased dramatically, Navajo herds, which had also increased since 1900, did not greatly surpass predrought levels. If Navajo holdings in 1886 are translated into sheep units (a measurement of grazing pressure in which one horse equals five sheep or goats and one cow equals four), the livestock of the Diné amounted to 2,354,200 units. This is probably a high estimate, and therefore the number of horses should be cut from 250,000 to 125,000, or roughly the low estimate of the early 1890s. With this recalculation the estimate is still 1,725,000 units. In 1928 the highest estimate of Navajo holdings in the twentieth century gave them 1,862,500 units, and the more accurate 1930 count gave them 1,111,589.[48]

If these statistics are anywhere near accurate, the crisis the Navajos faced was not the result so much of a pronounced increase in livestock, as of a decrease in grazing land that stemmed from Anglo cattlemen's successfully restricting Navajo access to traditional off-reservation ranges. The animals which in the nineteenth century had been spread over the entire Navajo country now were concentrated in the narrower bounds of the reservation. Since in 1885 the agent estimated that one-half of the Diné lived outside the reservation, it seems fair to assume that roughly one-half their stock also grazed off the reservation. By the late 1920s a smaller percentage of Navajos lived off the expanded reservation, and their proportional livestock holdings had decreased even more. Now the overwhelming proportion of Navajo livestock was on the only slightly enlarged reservation. Without any great, absolute increase in Navajo herds over the numbers of the late 1880s and early 1890s, the grazing pressure on the reservation proper had increased significantly. This was the root of the overgrazing that began to occur after 1900.[49]

As restocking after the drought began and available grazing lands narrowed, local officials were not blind to the danger. They recognized that there were limits to how many more sheep the reservation could support. In 1907, William H. Harrison, a reservation official, told the commissioner of Indian Affairs: "I believe that the Indians own numerically all the sheep that they have permanent range for and to increase the number of head of stock very materially is deliberately to invite wholesale disaster to their main industry, the one from which 80 percent of these Indians gain their living and derive their prosperity."[50] Warnings alone could not stop the rapid rebuilding of the Navajo herds nor the relentless invasion of off-reservation lands by whites. By 1911 the Franciscan missionary to the Navajos, Father Anselm Weber, citing inspectors from the Board of Animal Industry, reported that overgrazing both on and off the reservation was "notorious." After 1911 complaints of overstocking became a recurrent feature of official reports.[51]

By the fall of 1922 Superintendent Peter Paquette believed that the final limits of the reservation's ability to support livestock had been reached. He described range conditions as deplorable and predicted a disastrous loss of stock. Heavy rains in the spring saved the situation, but reservation officials warned Washington once more that the range was fully stocked and that the number of animals should not be increased.[52]

The Navajos did not remain passive in the face of changed conditions. They replaced many horses with sheep. They improved their shearing methods, which had once consisted of merely hacking off wool with a sharpened tin can, to increase the wool yield of their flocks. None of this altered the inescapable fact that they had too little land to support the sheep they needed for subsistence. To change this situation they had to rely on the Bureau of Indian Affairs.[53]

The major initiatives of the bureau revolved around reservation expansion, stock improvement, and stockwater development. All of these had been staple recommendations of reservation officials for years, but water development had been blocked by lack of funds, stock improvement by lack of Indian interest, and reservation expansion by Anglo and Mexican-American opposition. All made limited progress in the 1920s.[54]

More land remained the preferred, if the most ineffectual, solution to both Navajos and reservation officials. Herbert Hagerman, appointed special commissioner to the Navajos in 1923, regarded their need for more land as a "matter of great importance." His initial plan to consolidate holdings in the checkerboard would have added over 1 million acres to the reservation, but New Mexican officials succeeded in blocking it in Congress. Similar plans to consolidate lands in the west got through Congress but came to nothing when the Santa Fe Railroad changed its earlier position and refused to negotiate. Only oil, which had been discovered on the reservation in 1922, gave promise of relief from this impasse. In 1927 Hagerman worked with the tribal council, a body created to approve oil and gas leases, to set aside for land purchases 25 percent of oil and gas revenues up to a maximum of $1.2 million. A bill authorizing this expenditure squeaked through Congress, and small purchases began in 1930, but they provided little immediate relief.[55]

While attempts to get more land continued, bureau officials

sought to make each animal on the existing reservation more productive. In the 1920s they undertook a scabies eradication program that achieved some success. Since this disease of sheep could cut the wool production of an infected animal in half, to reduce scabies was to increase wool production. Bureau officials, however, were not satisfied with this. They also sought to introduce improved breeds of sheep on the reservation and to eliminate nonproductive animals, particularly horses. They believed such a program would mean producing more meat and wool without increasing the size of the herds.[56]

The renewed push for stock improvement in the 1920s was well-intentioned, but it was illconceived. In the thirties far more careful breeding programs showed some respect for the tough, longhaired sheep of the Navajos and their ability to survive harsh conditions, maintain body weight, and produce a fleece excellent for weaving rugs. Researchers then made the native animal the base of a new breeding program. In the 1920s officials merely sought to replace the animal. They introduced Rambouillet and Lincoln rams to breed with the Navajo sheep and succeeded in persuading owners of some herds, both large and small, to use them. The results were disastrous for subsistence herders. The imported sheep were ill suited to their new environment and deteriorated rapidly. Interbreeding with the Navajo sheep meant only that the native sheep lost their uniformity, their hardiness, and the desirable characteristics of their wool. Navajo women soon discovered that they could not weave with the wool of the "improved" sheep.[57]

The most successful of the bureau's programs was the attempt to increase stockwater on the reservation, but even it remained small scale. Permanent water supplies could open up otherwise ungrazable lands and offset somewhat the loss of off-reservation areas. Congress first gave sizable appropriations for this purpose in 1916, and reservation officials supplemented these appropriations by getting oil companies to agree to turn wells over to the Navajos for the cost of the casing if they struck water instead of oil. By 1928 the bureau had drilled 304 wells for the Navajos, of which 147 were in production, and they had developed more than 200 springs.[58]

These programs met with little Navajo resistance. The Diné might, as events would show, disagree about the causes of range deterioration and quarrel about what was an "unproductive" animal, but the tribal council at least was readily willing to admit the reality of the degeneration of the range in 1928. It had been a dry year, and the herds were in bad shape. The councilmen gave government livestock and range experts a respectful hearing. They welcomed plans for more stockwater improvement and agreed that more horses would have to go. J. C. Morgan, the councilman from the northern Navajo area around Farmington and later one of the most prominent figures in the stock reduction controversies of the 1930s, even suggested that Navajo dependence on sheep had become too great and that it was time for a renewed emphasis on farming.[59]

At the 1928 council meeting, bureau officials introduced the first plans for stock control. They suggested a grazing tax of fifteen cents a head for all sheep over 1,000 head which an individual owned with the proceeds to go for stockwater development. On this point they ran into opposition: many councilmen pointed out that such a tax, if passed, would be totally ineffective since no individual owned all the sheep in a family herd. Ownership was divided among husband, wife, and children, and no one's share came to over 1,000 head. The bureau insisted, and the council passed the tax by a 7 to 5 vote. This was an unusually close vote for the Navajo council, where consensus and unanimity were sought. It was a warning of the divisiveness and volatility of the issue. As the councilmen had predicted, the tax was ineffective and neither yielded revenue nor reduced the number of sheep.[60]

Officials of the Bureau of Indian Affairs had reason to be hopeful, if hardly sanguine, as the 1920s drew to a close. With Navajo cooperation, they had succeeded in achieving substantial horse reduction and had even obtained acceptance, at least in principle, of the right to assess grazing fees. Stockwater and stockbreeding programs were underway, and oil royalties promised finally to make reservation expansion a reality. The peacefulness and cooperation of Navajo-government relations was, however, in a sense illusory. Away from the agencies, government programs still affected most Navajos relatively little; they neither knew of nor participated in the proceedings at Leupp in 1928. Yet for these people, too, a far-reaching transformation had begun. They would not bear it quietly.

The government approached the sheep herds as basically a technical problem. Officials sought an ideal land/sheep ratio that would halt erosion and an ideal sheep that would yield a maximum amount of meat and wool. Bureau of Indian Affairs policies were based on the assumption that all Navajos would come to see stockraising as a primarily commercial activity to be engaged in for profit. Yet only a few Navajos were engaged in rationalized market production. Some of these people were, predictably, the most enthusiastic about herd improvement and water development. These men were *ricos*, large owners like Chee Dodge and the Lynch brothers. Not all *ricos* were commercial operators, but those who were had operations indistinguishable in many ways from those of non-Navajo stockmen. Chee Dodge, the son of a Navajo mother and a Mexican-American father, became the most prominent Navajo leader of the 1920s and much of 1930s. He developed his own sources of stockwater, and since the pumps and windmills which brought the water up belonged to him alone, he controlled the surrounding range in much the same manner as off-reservation Anglos controlled the public domain. Dodge employed his poorer kinsmen to tend his flocks, he moved his sheep from summer to winter grazing lands; and the care his herds received was more like that given to Mexican-American or Anglo herds than Navajo. As a result he could make far better use of improved breeds and other technical developments than most Diné, and he adopted them quickly.[61]

The bureau envisioned a Navajo nation made up of a series of miniature Dodges. With proper education and instruction they would change the breeds of their sheep to develop an animal more suited to the market, get rid of unproductive stock, and change their herding practices. In short, they would rationalize their operations to secure the largest possible cash income. The Americans regarded existing Navajo practices as simply a product of ignorance; they were unwilling to grant validity to techniques divorced from market rationality. Their attempts to rationalize Navajo stockholding in order to save the land while obtaining more wool and mutton from fewer sheep led to twenty years of turmoil, transformed the Navajo subsistence system, and furthered the transformation of Navajo society which the loss of their traditional homeland and the commercialization of off-reservation land had begun. Understanding this turmoil involves understanding the Navajo conception of economy, sheep, and society which livestock reduction threatened.

CHAPTER 11

Navajo Culture and Economy

By the 1920s Navajo sheepherding had become a partially commercial activity but not one that operated on American terms. Navajo economy and land use were deeply embedded in Navajo culture; to abstract them from the culture is to distort them. Yet it is also something of a distortion to describe the Navajos, as a single undifferentiated group, which they certainly were not.

As a conceptual system, Navajo culture sought to order or structure the natural and social universe of the Diné. Within this universe the Navajos themselves made no sharp distinction between society and nature. Nature for them was "an all-inclusive organizing device, a fusion of natural, supernatural and human or social elements." The Navajo cultural ideal was *hozho*, a concept embodying harmony and order. All trouble, particularly sickness and strife, grew from disorder, and for a cure the Navajos tried through their ceremonies to "recreate and restructure the universe." In these ceremonies material objects became symbolic objects associated with a supernatural order.[1]

For the Navajos all events were controlled by the "thought and will of intelligent or thinking beings." In and of themselves "things, beings, events and conditions, processes and power are neither good nor evil, or are potentially both good and evil." Intelligent thought and speech ordered the world. Evil was simply disorder. To create good was to restore order, and order is achieved through ritual.[2]

When order was achieved, a state of universal harmony or *k'e* existed. *K'e* is a verbal prefix meaning love, kindness, peacefulness, friendliness, and cooperation. In Navajo social life *k'e* was symbolized in motherhood which pervaded Navajo culture and provided the patterns and sentiments which ordered Navajo social life. Motherhood and the *k'e* it embodied were not limited to people, for "the earth is called mother, the sheep herd is called mother, corn is called mother, and the sacred mountain soil bundle is called mother." Motherhood, in this sense, was not just metaphorical. The earth gave life and sustained life, and for the Navajos this life giving quality was the essence of motherhood. As Gary Witherspoon suggested, "Maybe it is the earth who is really mother, and human mothers merely resemble the earth." The concepts of *k'e* and *hozho* thus extended into the natural world, but human beings were faced with the necessity of killing plants and animals in order to live. Ideally, they did so only when justified by clear and present need, and "a prayer must be said to the plant or animal explaining one's need and asking pardon or indulgence." Often, however, such practices were honored more in the breach. The Navajos killed many small animals indiscriminately and without ceremony, but earlier practices may very well have been different.[3]

Just as in practice the ideal of *k'e* extended more to some animals than others, so too did it extend more to some people than others. The Navajo word *diné* means simply people, but Navajo categories extended far beyond this.

Diné are subdivided into two important categories; (1) diyin kine'i—the supernaturals or the holy people . . . ; and (2) nihokaa dine'e—the naturals or the earth surface people. The earth surface people are further subdivided into the diné (the Navajo) and the ana'i (the non-Navajo). The ana'i are further subgrouped into various kinds of foreigners or non-Navajo; the diné are further subdivided into more than sixty matrilineal clans, called dine'e—a particular kind of diné.[4]

One's closest relationships—those where *k'e* is most fully realized—were with one's matrilineal relatives and clanspeople. The further out one went from such kinspeople, the less reason there was for security and trust.

The concepts of *k'e* and the idea of motherhood dominated actual Navajo social relations. The largest kin unit was the clan, which originated, at least mythically, in an ancestral mother. Although members of the same clan could not marry and had obligations to provide assistance in ceremonials, it was on the family level that the importance of motherhood was clearest. This relationship was not just a reflection of the biological relation between mother and child. It was culturally derived; people other than a Navajo's biological mother, indeed even men, could be mother to him. Motherhood in Navajo culture was symbolic; that which gave life and sustained life was mother. This was the basis of kinship.[5]

In the light of these concepts, Navajo social organization was actually quite simple beneath the surface complexity of kin terms and kin relations. The fundamental unit of Navajo society was the resident group organized according to the relationship of the members to a head mother. This household most often consisted of the mother, her husband, her children, her children's spouses, and their children. Married couples could live either with the wife's mother, the husband's mother, or as an independent household, but in practice they lived most often with the wife's mother. This subsistence residence group was the primary unit of production and consumption, and it controlled, through use rights, certain definitely bounded agricultural and grazing lands. Within the group, individuals owned personal property and possessed certain inheritance rights, but in actuality production and consumption were largely communal, the function of kin relations.[6]

A subsistence resident group always had a single sheep herd, although everyone from the head mother to the grandchildren might own individual animals. The sheep herd was fundamental to the group. It was the focus of their cooperative activities and the "symbol of the life, wealth, vitality, and integration of the subsistence residential unit." The sheep fed the Navajos, but they also were, and remain today, an important symbolic and emotional center of the lives of the Indians. All members of the group might do as they wished with their sheep since no one would think of telling them what to do with their property. Conversely, and to whites paradoxically, the owners were expected to use most of the income for the welfare of the group. The sharing of food within the group was the primary symbol of this kinship solidarity. To refuse to share food within the unit was "an anti-social act of enormous proportions."[7]

The only productive unit larger than the residence group was the outfit, which appears to have atrophied considerably in some parts of the nation. It was a cooperating kinship group on what were often contiguous landholdings whose component residence groups traced descent from a common head mother, usually deceased. The more remote the connection through the head mother, the weaker was the cooperative bond; thus such relationships rarely went back for more than two generations. The outfit cooperated on special occasions or for special tasks—for ceremonials, planting or harvesting, sheep dipping, and, in the nineteenth century, defense. Its directly productive role probably shrank considerably after the 1930s.[8]

Within the residence group, the head mother's husband most often functioned as a political leader or headman in dealing with outside groups. The only larger political community was a loosely organized union of all families in a locality led by a *nat'ani* or peace chief. Selected by consensus, his power lay in exhortation and persuasion, and locally his influence could be great. In the reservation period the Americans attempted to build local political units or chapters with elected officers upon this older community base. Neighboring *nat'anis* consulted and cooperated. Before Fort Sumner there may even have been large councils which brought together significant numbers of the nation, but overall the Navajos had little organization above the local community and did not have any tribal government until the Americans created the Tribal Council in the 1920s.[9]

The Navajo emphasis on kinship is reflected in their organization of production. Traditional Navajos distrusted nonrelatives and those who are not of their clan, their father's clan, or affiliated clans, that is those who had no obligations of sharing or reciprocity. The cooperation which typified activities within the extended family often vanished outside of it, where Navajos were wary and distrustful. This productive system was geared toward subsistence rather than the market.[10]

Specific Navajo values resembled those of Anglo-Americans, but they cannot be confused with economic individualism. The Navajos, for instance, held hard work and thrift (which was defined in terms of preserving one's possessions) in high esteem. Traditionally, these values were the subjects of endless homilies, injunctions, and stories. They recurred again and again in *Son of Old Man Hat*, the classic autobiography of a Navajo recorded by Walter Dyk in the 1930s. At one point Old Man Hat tells his children:

If you want to learn about the horses, sheep, cattle, and properties, if you want to have all these things, you don't want to be lazy, you don't want to go to bed early at night and get up late in the morning. You have to work hard for all these things. . . . Everything is hard to get, even little things. If you're lazy you can't get anything. If you do nothing but sleep and lie around you won't get anything, you'll starve to death.[11]

Hard work alone, however, was not enough for success. Taking care of stock demanded knowledge, and no sharp line was drawn between ritual knowledge and "practical" knowledge. Old Man Hat's daughter asked him for "medicine that one uses for sheep and horses, so that I can raise them. I haven't got any medicines for them. I haven't anything so I am not strong." He gave her medicine and sent her to her oldest brother to learn the proper songs for horses, sheep, and property. Ceremonial knowledge, practical knowledge, and hard work all had to be fused to fulfill the basic commandment of the Navajo economy: maintain the herds.[12]

The fear of losing property was deeply ingrained in Navajo culture, and all things which threatened the stock had to be resisted. Sheep, goats, and horses are the subject of most injunctions to maintain property. To quote Old Man Hat again: "The herd is money. It gives you clothing and different kinds of food. You know that you have some good clothing; the sheep gave you that. And you've just eaten different kinds of food; the sheep gave that food to you. Everything comes from the sheep."[13] When Old Man Hat said the herd was money, his meaning must be understood in terms of other injunctions; it cannot be simply equated with a white business outlook. He also told his daughter that the sheep and goats were her mother and father, and this emotional identification with the herd ran deep in Navajo society. Sheep were killed and sheep were eaten but sheep were also "loved," and this statement must be taken seriously.[14] In such a system animals were wealth, but they were not simply assets subject to commercial cost accounting. The emotional links were equally as strong as financial ones. What threatened the sheep, threatened the family in a deep and profound way.

Implicit in these injunctions to hard work and the general concern with maintaining one's property and herds was a fear of poverty. This fear, however, was coupled with a distrust of riches and rich men. Both the rich and the poor were open to ridicule and social

opprobrium—one for stinginess, the other for laziness. And traditionally both were open to accusations of witchcraft, which sometimes
was punished with death. Indeed, great riches were often taken as
proof of witchcraft.[15]

The goal of hard work and thrift then was not riches; it was security and respect. Navajos considered people good if they were hard
working, possessed enough property to be comfortable and secure,
had ceremonial knowledge, spoke well, and helped people. Generosity was the mark of a good person, and people should respond to
requests for help as they were able. Within the family sharing was
assumed; outside the family, gifts brought reciprocal obligations, and
rich men could presume some returns in the form of labor.[16]

The Navajos' emphasis on generosity, reciprocity, the need for
harmony and a ceremonial system which served to promote them,
they did not insure economic equality but did contribute to a measure
of general economic security. The first detailed account of the distribution of stock among the Navajos, presented in a census for the
Southern Navajo Reservation in 1915, revealed that 24 percent of the
resident groups owned no sheep, 42 percent possessed under 100, 18
percent had from 101 to 300 (a subsistence herd), 14 percent had
from 300 to 800, and 4 percent had over 800. Since in 1897 the agent
had reported that one third of the adult population owned no property, this inequality had existed for some time. The poor, however,
did not starve. As the agent reported in 1897, those without livestock
depended on wealthier neighbors, "it being the custom among them
to share the necessaries of life with each other, even to the last meal in
the house." If people refused to share, ridicule and supernatural
sanctions were brought against them. Navajos shared to avoid the
stigma of witchcraft, and to avoid community resentment rich men
were coerced into sponsoring expensive ceremonials, at which all who
attended were fed.[17]

Although trade was largely peripheral to this domestic economy,
the nature of trade began to change significantly in the late
nineteenth and early twentieth centuries. Since the Spanish period,
the Navajos had exchanged wool in the form of blankets for manufactures, but this exchange increased in both size and significance
after the return from Bosque Redondo. Its evolution is, however,
somewhat complex.

The first exchanges between the Americans and the Navajos after Bosque Redondo involved sheep and manufactures, but it was the Navajos who possessed the manufactures and the New Mexicans the sheep. The phenomenal growth of Navajo herds in the 1870s resulted, in part, from their trading an estimated 90 percent of their annuity goods for sheep. Once their herds were built up, trading became a much more sporadic endeavor. Their agent in 1871, William Arny, persuaded some of them to bring in wool to trade to the sutler at Fort Defiance, but for most families commerce was a by-product of sheep raising, not its focus.[18]

Exchange with outsiders was irregular and followed much older patterns of occasional journeys to the Hopi, the New Mexican Pueblos, or the Utes when exotic goods or horses were needed or when emergency food supplies had to be secured. Such commerce was peripheral to daily existence, and often it was not trade at all. Ideally, a Navajo trader, who qualified for his task largely by possessing ceremonial knowledge, had a trading partner or "friend" among the people with whom he dealt. In the early days he gave gifts of hides or baskets to this friend; later the gift was almost always blankets. The friend reciprocated by giving horses if he were a Ute, or foodstuffs, pots, or turquoise if he was a Pueblo. When such gift exchanges were mutually satisfactory, the "friendship" of families and traders might endure for generations. Gift exchanges which involved no barter at all were the Navajo ideal. When, as often happened with the Pueblos, some bartering took place, the Navajos resented it and thought the Pueblos "greedy."[19]

The first American traders quickly learned that small gifts facilitated trading, but they, no more than earlier European traders, were content to make commerce merely exchanges of gifts. As a result no special trading relationship seems to have developed, and the Navajo approach to such exchanges shared as much with attitudes appropriate to raiding as they did with older trading practices. Seeking to get goods from the Americans, they stuffed wool sacks with rocks to increase their weight and forged credit slips; the traders resorted to short weights, low prices for wool, and shoddy goods. The traders, the Navajos complained, were like gamblers; they tried to "beat" everybody. This trade too remained peripheral to Navajo survival. Sometimes Navajos went to the Pueblos, sometimes to the Utes, sometimes to the Americans; in all cases such exchanges remained closer to those of the preconquest period than they did to the later trading post era.[20]

The American traders were, however, already altering the older system. They began with liquor—the standard means for bringing Indian assets to the market and increasing Indian consumption of European manufactures. Liquor traffic became a serious problem and a mainstay of the agents' correspondence in the 1870s and 1880s. The agents' attempts to check liquor were often ineffectual, but among the Navajos its tendency to dissipate personal property (which was its great appeal for white traders) brought into play native moral sanctions that checked its inroads. Drunkenness was not wrong; the dissipation of property was. Liquor remained a problem—a source of poverty and a link to the market—but it did not devastate Navajo society on the scale it did Indian societies elsewhere. For whites it might bring short-term speculative profits; it was not, however, the basis for a reliable commerce.[21]

A more stable trade became possible with the arrival of the transcontinental railroads in 1881. Now eastern manufactured goods could penetrate the Navajo country at greatly reduced prices, and, more significantly, traders could send Navajo wool and blankets to eastern markets at profit. The significance of the possibility of large-scale trade, however, should not be confused with the actuality of trade itself. By 1890 there were still only nine trading posts on the reservation; there were, it is true, thirty more off it, but how many of these were merely short-term specultive operations dealing in liquor is hard to say. The real expansion of trading did not begin until 1890 and did not grow rapidly until after 1900. Too many accounts simply assume that the Navajos, like other Indians, only awaited the opportunity to acquire European manufactures and engaged in commercial dealing with the same enthusiasm and for the same reasons as other Americans. Trade and market dealings, however, were hardly natural and inevitable.[22]

The Navajos desired some European manufactures—especially metal goods and cotton cloth—but their demands were not insatiable. In the 1870s they sold manufactured items to obtain sheep and for years afterward many of them got along with very few American goods. Why then did they begin trading on a larger scale in the 1880s, trading over 1 million pounds of wool and 240,000 sheep pelts in

1886, increasing this to over 2 million pounds in 1890, and expanding the amount thereafter? The beginning of an answer can come from examining what they traded for.[23]

Like many other aspects of Navajo life, the first reliable statistics on Navajo consumption date from the 1930s and the human dependency surveys. These reveal that the Navajos overwhelmingly traded for foodstuffs—flour, sugar, coffee, and canned goods. These products formed 68 percent of the trade goods the Navajos used in 1940. The percentage had increased during the 1930s, but old traders reported that the basic pattern had existed from the dawn of the trading post era. It was not manufactures then that brought about Navajo trade. Although the Navajos consumed manufactured goods in limited quantities, such goods formed only a minority of exchanges.[24]

The Navajos entered the market to obtain food and became partially dependent on commerce for their subsistence. The question is why? The answer is that they probably did it for the same reason they had initially traded manufactures for sheep: to secure a reliable subsistence base in a harsh and variable land.

Before Bosque Redondo the Navajo subsistence economy had stood, like their sheep or horses, on four legs—agriculture, livestock, hunting and gathering, and raiding. In good years agriculture provided the bulk of their food, but the whole economy was designed to accommodate the numerous bad years when frost, drought, or grasshoppers killed the crops or when bad winters or prolonged droughts killed their sheep. In these years other activities carried the Diné through. After the return from Bosque Redondo, however, the Americans truncated this economy. Raiding disappeared and this contributed to the decline of hunting.

Large-scale raiding and large sheep herds had grown up simultaneously in the late eighteenth and early nineteenth century. Sheep herding in the years before the Carson campaign had to adapt to a political climate of chronic warfare where Utes or New Mexicans might descend on Navajo herds nearly as expertly as the Navajos descended on the herds of others. If studies of the western Navajo lands are applicable to all sections of the Navajo country, one Navajo adaptation to these raids was to confine settlement to secluded and defensible upland sites where forest and scrub lands provided some shelter for hogans and sheep, and where raiders could be spotted at a distance. Ninety-five percent of all western Navajo sites between 1750 and 1867 were in or adjacent to woodlands.[25]

This settlement pattern tended to preserve game habitats. The widely scattered Navajos left the grasslands of the valleys and the desert shrub zones to the antelope, and deer survived in the higher mountains and in the unsettled transition zones. The Navajos ritually hunted both animals to obtain seasonally important sources of meat, and in times of famine wildlife became the major source of food. Parties of four to ten men commonly killed up to 100 deer during a two-week hunt.[26]

With the end of raiding, the absolute dominance of upland sheltered settlement sites came to an end. There was no longer any reason to avoid the open grazing and agricultural lands, and between 1868 and 1900 the purely woodland sites of the Navajos fell from 49 percent to 22 percent of the whole. Although 70 percent of the sites remained in or adjacent to woodlands, the remaining 30 percent represented a sizable shift to open land, especially in view of increasing population. Such a shift threatened game lands, particularly those that supported antelopes since these animals now had to compete with sheep. At the end of the century both the growth of population and the increasing concentration of settlement on the reservation further magnified the problem.[27]

In and of itself such a shift could be expected to have significant effect; when coupled with Navajo poverty and persistent crop failures, it was disastrous. The rapid growth of the Navajo herds after 1870 is evidence enough of where their priorities lay: they sought to restore their depleted flocks as quickly as possible. To do so they could not rely on the animals so extensively for food that they endangered their increase. In large part they turned to the government for food, but they also retained their dependence on wild foods.[28]

Deer and antelope eventually vanished from Navajo lands. Visitors reported abundant game in the early 1870s, which casts doubt on the earliest estimates of depletion in the 1870s. The Navajo agent reported no game left in 1884, and it is probable that the 1880s or, at the latest the 1890s witnessed the elimination of game as an important source of food. Except for bears, which were protected by taboos, the Navajos had hunted out virtually all the large game animals by the 1890s. Gathering suffered a similar decline. Only pinon nuts remained an economically significant product. In earlier days, raiding would have taken some pressure off these wild animals and plants, and the flocks would have been large enough to supply food. Now deer and antelope had to die so that sheep might increase.[29]

The shift in Navajo settlement and the increase in their flocks thus came at a price. Subsistence, once government rations were withdrawn, stood on two legs, not four. Two of the Indians' buffers against crop failures—wild game and raiding—were gone; only the herds remained. It was into this truncated and unusually precarious economy that the traders moved in the years after 1880.[30]

In this light, Navajo trading patterns begin to make more sense. Trade gave them a way of restoring some of their lost security. Through wool and blankets, sheep could be turned into food without actually being killed. By the 1880s the flocks themselves were a regular and important source of food, of course, but the demands put on the herds varied from year to year, depending on the fate of the crops. If in bad years the Navajos had not engaged in trade, they would have been forced to deplete their herds at a far greater rate than they did.

This integration of trade into the subsistence system also begins to explain an otherwise anomalous development: the accelerated increase in the number of Navajo trading posts and the rise of blanket and rug trade in the 1890s during a period when drought sharply reduced the number of Navajo sheep. This increase makes sense if trade is considered as part of a reorientation of the subsistence system that was most useful in bad years. As crops failed repeatedly, as sheep had to be eaten in increasing numbers, and as others froze or starved to death in the 1890s, the Navajos needed a way to turn dwindling amounts of wool into increasing amounts of food. The trade in blankets and rugs fit both their needs and those of the trader, who found a waiting market in the East.[31]

With the rug trade, the trading post economy began to take full shape. Navajos took wool and rugs and traded them for food; indeed, in the 1890s even those who lacked or had lost their sheep could obtain yarn from the trader and make rugs from it. Only the introduction of credit transactions remained to make the system complete, and by 1900 traders were extending credit to weavers to insure the production of blankets, in what briefly became a competitive business.

At the turn of the century not only the traders sought Navajo rugs but also the Fred Harvey hotel chain and the Hyde Exploring Expedition of 1899–1903 (which attempted to monopolize the trading post system and rug trade). The Hyde Exploring Expedition alone had $125,000 to $175,000 worth of goods out on credit to the Navajos when it went bankrupt.[32]

Together the decline of game and raiding, the bad years of the 1890s, the rise of the rug trade, and the extension of credit made trade necessary and a permanent part of the subsistence system. The return of better years after 1900 did not significantly alter the new adaptation. Flour, coffee, canned goods, and sugar continued to absorb a good portion of Navajo trade while surpluses were converted into whites' manufactured goods or more often into status items such as clothing or jewelry that might be pawned later. The decline of the rug trade after World War I meant only that the raw wool trade increased. This acceptance of trade made the Navajos even more dependent on seasonal production and thus rendered credit even more of a necessity. Since the trading posts had now evolved into stable operations seeking to secure a guaranteed protected market, they were quite willing to grant credit and settle with their customers at shearing time.[33]

The trading post had become a necessary supplement to a subsistence system based primarily on agriculture, sheep, and goats. One more source of food should be mentioned, however, because it became a *bête noire* to officials of the Bureau of Indian Affairs—the horse. Complaint about excessive numbers of useless and worthless horses began in the 1880s and continued through the 1930s. To Indian agents a horse, which ate approximately five times as much forage as a sheep, represented a mere squandering of scarce range and water resources. The Navajos kept horses for reasons other than for transportation; indeed, many of the animals were either too old or too wild to ride. Although large horse herds were the clearest possible mark of wealth and prestige, horses were not an economic resource per se. They were, for example, almost never traded; they were exchanged only as a bride price.[34]

What most agents ignored was that the Navajos ate their horses and liked horsemeat as well as mutton, beef, or goat meat. Horses seem to have been a famine food par excellence because their ability to travel greater distances to water allowed them to survive better than sheep. In good times such as the 1880s they multiplied while serving as a mark of prestige and wealth. In the drought years of the 1890s they served as food; some families lived on them for weeks at a time. In 1903 during the last year of the drought, the agent told the poor Navajos coming to him for rations to kill the excess horses of richer men. They did so readily, and the agent reported few complaints from the owners since the Navajos were "very philanthropic when it comes to a matter of hunger." Until the 1930s horses remained a reserve food supply in times of drought.[35]

This new subsistence system was largely in place by the turn of the century. The economy based on it was, by white standards, uneconomic. It did not maximize the returns possible from the land, nor was land use efficient. The Navajos had merely adapted the old economy to new conditions, with trade filling the gap left by the decline of the hunt and raiding. As yet the Navajos were only marginally oriented toward the market.

This Navajo subsistence system was clearly in danger by 1930. The Navajo homeland had been narrowed; Mexican-American and Anglo sheepherders had expropriated the best off-reservation grazing land; an erosion cycle was cutting away the land; and much of the reservation suffered from overgrazing. At the same time Navajo population continued to rise, but the older Navajo response to rising population—dispersion into new areas—was blocked by powerful interests in the larger society. A crisis was at hand. An understanding of the government's response to this crisis, and the failure of that response, rest upon three basic points. The government misunderstood the erosion cycle and its causes and blamed it largely on Navajo herds; the government acted initially not so much to benefit the Navajos as to protect the economic development of the Southwest; and, finally, until late in the 1930s the government knew little about the social and cultural basis of the Navajo economy it sought to transform.

The Navajos had escaped disaster before but they were now caught in a catastrophe, largely because they were a colonial appendage of American society and their interests had been subordinated to those of dominant groups. Stock reduction was merely another manifestation of this basic relationship; it was begun to save huge federal and private investments. Even though those immediately involved in running the program often came with the best intentions and with real sympathy toward the Diné, their actions were nevertheless destructive. The tragedy was that a group that had weathered previous crises and changes with substantial ingenuity and success was never given a chance to develop its own programs and responses. Instead, the government forced the Navajos into a position of desperate and finally sterile opposition.

CHAPTER 12

Southwestern Development and
Navajo Underdevelopment

For millennia the Colorado River has drained an immense slice of the American West, carrying silt and water toward the Gulf of California. When the river reached sea level, its waters slowed and deposited much of this silt to form a vast delta near the Gulf of California. Eventually this delta became the Imperial Valley of southern California, a farming region of unsurpassed richness. Americans diked, irrigated, and cultivated the valley, but their actions did not stop the larger geological processes. Partially confined between levees, the river continued to deposit the silt, which aggraded its bed, and forced farmers to build a constantly higher and more elaborate series of levees to hold the waters back. In 1906 the river broke through the dikes, diverted its entire flow into the valley, and inundated it. Incredible effort and millions of dollars were expended before the Colorado resumed its old course. There it remained a constant danger, a threat to the valley it had created.

While the people of the Imperial Valley feared flood, the inhabitants of Los Angeles insatiably sought water. In the 1920s the city had commandeered the waters of the Owens River, destroying the farms of the Owens Valley in the process, but this had only temporarily allayed its thirst. Los Angeles still lacked sufficient water to meet its projected needs after 1940. The Colorado River beckoned to the west, but not even California, let alone Los Angeles, could unilaterally allocate its waters.

In 1928 Herbert Hoover, then secretary of commerce, moved to solve both problems at once. He secured from Congress authorization for the Colorado River Project, whose main component was Boulder Dam, later renamed Hoover Dam. When completed, the dam was capable of holding back two years' flow of the Colorado and creating a lake 150 miles long. The dam both protected the Imperial Valley and made possible a greatly improved irrigation system. It also guaranteed water to Los Angeles and southern California; as an added benefit, it generated enough electricity to supply the entire Southwest.[1]

Boulder Dam, rising well to the west of the reservation, seemed remote and unconnected with the Navajos as it progressed from planning toward construction in the late 1920s and early 1930s, but the connections between the two were there. They floated with the silt suspended in the river. In 1929 the United States Geological Survey estimated that the San Juan River, which contributed 14 percent of the Colorado's water, supplied almost half her silt and that the contribution of the Little Colorado was roughly proportional. The implication was clearly stated somewhat later: "Briefly in the main Colorado system, the Little Colorado and the San Juan are major silt problems, while within each of these basins the Navajo Reservation's tributaries are the major silt problem. The fact is the . . . Navajo Reservation is practically 'Public Enemy No. 1' in causing the Colorado Silt problem."[2] Too much silt was coming down the river from the reservation; it would pile up behind the dam and destroy its usefulness.

To alter the landscape of California, it now seemed necessary to preserve the landscape of the Navajo country. Since to American officials overgrazing and gullying were synonymous, overgrazing had to be halted quickly and decisively. As the Soil Conversation Service reported the situation in 1936:

> The physical and geological processes which have occurred *within the reservation*, if unchecked must ultimately have an important effect on areas outside the reservation principally through the vastly increased deposit of silt in the Boulder Reservoir. If erosion continues unchecked, ultimately the entire alluvial fill of most of the valleys of the Navajo reservation will be deposited behind the dam, thus threatening the enormous Federal, State, municipal, and private investments involved in, or directly or indirectly dependent on, the maintenance of the storage capacity of the reservoir.[3]

The urgency which came into the attack on overgrazing during the New Deal was a direct result of this growing perception of a threat to the economic development of the whole region. The dam was the catalyst that prompted drastic stock reduction. The government saw itself not only as saving the Navajos from themselves but also as saving much of California, and indeed the entire Southwest, from Navajo herds. The Diné were, in spite of themselves, drafted into the huge scheme for economic growth which Boulder Dam represented. Unfortunately while others reaped the benefits, the Navajos were called on to make the sacrifices.

Concerted efforts at stock reduction were not, then, the result of a simple recognition of overgrazing. This recognition had been present for years, yet government fervor for stock reduction had mounted very slowly before the New Deal. A watershed of sorts was reached in 1930 when William Zeh, a forester of the Bureau of Indian Affairs, made what was until then the starkest and most detailed report on overgrazing in the Navajo reservation. Zeh reported 1.3 million sheep and goats on less than 12 million acres of arable land, or an average of 9 to 10 surface acres a head. On the Navajo Reservation this was only one-half to one-third the amount needed to maintain a sheep or goat without damage to either the land or the animal. And, Zeh added, he had entirely left out the Navajo horses and cattle from his calculations. The results of this overstocking were everywhere apparent to the trained eye—trampled and denuded lands around water holes and hogans; juniper and yellow pine trees cropped as high as a goat could reach; a growing scarcity of palatable grasses; increasing sheet erosion.[4]

The problem was compounded by Navajo grazing practices, which included mixed flocks, close herding, and preponderance of unproductive animals that took away food from ewes and lambs. The lack of permanent stockwater, which forced long trailing of the herds to reach water, caused a serious loss of forage from trampling. The concentration of stock in the vicinity of water during the summer and the practice of bedding the herd in a corral by the hogans each night and midday led to severe cropping of grass in narrow areas. Unable to grow enough food to store in their rhizomes or produce seed, the grasses died out.[5]

Zeh's report was more detailed than prior surveys, but his recommendations differed relatively little from those policies already in effect. He commended efforts to enlarge the reservation, urged the continued elimination of excess horses, suggested improved breeds of sheep and goats and a gradual reduction in the total number of goats, and stressed the need for more permanent stockwater, which would open new summer ranges and allow the old ones to be used as winter ranges and thus recover. To these suggestions he added a program of rodent control to eliminate the prairie dogs, which competed with sheep for feed, and a program to educate Navajos in better methods of stock handling. A second report, prepared by Donald Harrison, the forester for the Southern Navajo Reservation, detailed the same conditions but suggested more drastic measures: the elimination of goats by fiat and the institution of regulations controlling the maximum number of stock and mandating new methods of herding.[6]

Neither Zeh's nor Harrison's report produced drastic changes in policy. At an Indian Service conference in February of 1931, William Post, the newly appointed director of irrigation, pushed for immediate draconian reductions, but the superintendents were more sanguine. They approved of a plan prepared by Zeh and H. C. Neuffer, the supervising engineer for the reservation, which called for an intensive survey of reservation conditions and focused on water development, irrigation, and rodent control as the preferred solutions to the problem.[7]

When a subcommittee of the Senate Committee on Indian Affairs held hearings on the reservation in April and May, reservation officials complained of range conditions and requested more land and water, but such requests and complaints differed little from those of the previous decade. The hearings served largely as a forum for the senators to lecture the Navajos on market rationality and to display their ignorance on an impressive array of cultural and economic matters. An indication of things to come, however, appeared in Senator Burton Wheeler's repeated admonitions to Navajo witnesses to get rid of their goats and horses, despite testimony by the superintendents that the Navajos had few, if any, surplus horses, and the patient insistence of the Navajos themselves that goats were basic to their subsistence. When Wheeler pressed Donald Harrison on the possibility of reduction, he replied that if Navajo sheep were reduced, the Indians could not make a living.[8]

The possibility of more forceful policies, however, persisted in "An Economic Survey of the Range Resources and Grazing Activities on Indian Reservations," a larger report, solicited by the Bureau of Indian Affairs in 1930 and finished early in 1931. It estimated that there were 113,699 excess animal units on the reservation (in this tabulation a unit equals one horse, one cow, five sheep, or five goats). The report pointed out that on the Navajo Reservation the Indian Service had never enforced its standard grazing regulations which provided for a maximum of 500 sheep, 100 cattle, 50 horses, or their combined equivalent for each owner. It recommended doing so, thus forcing an immediate reduction of 51,110 units in cattle, sheep, and goats alone. Officials, however, hesitated to initiate so drastic a step.[9]

Meanwhile, conditions on the range continued to deteriorate, and the market for Navajo lambs collapsed. In the winter of 1931–32 deep snows covered the reservation and obliterated even the sagebrush. Temperatures fell to −20F, and around Ganado rains fell on top of the snow and then froze, creating a thick sheet of ice. Sheep and goats starved by the tens of thousands. In Washington John Collier, then secretary of the Indian Defense Association but soon to be Roosevelt's commissioner of Indian Affairs and the man most responsible for stock reduction, vigorously lobbied Congress for relief. He obtained $150,000 to help feed and replace Navajo stock and, in the process, was appalled by the opposition of Indian Service officials who told him the snows were a godsend that could cut down livestock numbers and save the range from overgrazing. He publicly condemned these officials, an action he would later repudiate.[10]

The next winter severe weather struck again. The blizzards were unprecedented. Once again with their forage buried beyond reach, sheep and goats starved by the tens of thousands. Not even retention of much of the lamb crop could make up the losses. The total number of sheep units grazing on the reservation stood at 1,178,372 in 1931, fell to 1,053,498 in 1932, and to 999,725 in 1933. The number of sheep and goats did not rise over 1 million again during the 1930s.[11]

The Navajos staggered out of these terrible winters into the arms of a series of drought years and the New Deal. In early 1933 Franklin D. Roosevelt named John Collier, the most prominent opponent of a federal Indian policy, as head of the Bureau of Indian Affairs. A trenchant and effective critic of the assimilative policies of the Indian bureau, Collier was a cultural pluralist who not only wanted to permit Indian societies to survive but also sought to encourage and help them to do so. As he conceived it, his program had "three chief objectives": "Economic rehabilitation of the Indians, principally on the land. Organization of the Indian tribes for managing their own affairs. Civil and cultural freedom and opportunity for the Indians." It was a generous and sincere policy, and in the Navajos—culturally whole and as nearly self-sufficient as any Indian group in the nation—it should have found its logical supporters. Yet for most Navajos John Collier became not a savior but a man who stubbornly, unreasonably, and finally successfully sought to take away their sheep, goats, and horses. He did so because the believed that conditions left him little choice. Zeh's ominous report was in the files and was cited repeatedly by the bureau. In 1932 an engineer's report concluded that silt from the reservation would, if unchecked, destroy the usefulness of Boulder Dam.[12]

The Zeh reports and the engineering reports on Boulder Dam were enough to convince Collier of the need for stock control and range rehabilitation, but it took the emergency measures of the New Deal to give him the means for doing so. Eventually money for the Civilian Conservation Corps (CCC), the Soil Conservation Service, and other programs brought more funds into the Bureau of Indian Affairs than it received from its own appropriations. Congress passed the Emergency Conservation Work Act even before Collier took office, but by May he had stepped into the planning process for the Navajos. Essentially these early programs were rushed into effect to provide jobs for the Indians virtually impoverished by two bad winters and the beginning of drought, but the work undertaken was also aimed at implementing the recommendations of the Zeh report. By far the most generous allotments went to water development, erosion control, rodent control, and the construction of trails to grazing land and water.[13]

On the whole the Navajos welcomed the Civilian Conservation Corps camps and the work they provided. Rumors that joining the CCC actually meant joining the army circulated among the southern Navajos, but once these were dispelled Navajos rushed to the agencies for jobs. The work enabled them to liquidate much of their debt to the traders and redeem the jewelry they had deposited to secure credit for the coming winter. Despite their enthusiasm and gratitude for the program, there was, however, some discontent. Some Navajos resented the first poisonings of the prairie dogs which had served them as an emergency food source. Others complained that Navajo advice was ignored, that they had spent a summer building check dams in the arroyos which they correctly assured their supervisors would wash away in the first flood. These objections, however, were minor compared with the enthusiasm the program generated. This was not the first penetration of the wage economy into the reservation, but it was the most significant and most welcomed.[14]

Even before the shoddiness and poor planning of much early CCC work had been revealed by the floods, Collier had realized that the Indian Service alone did not possess the expertise to supervise a conservation program among the Navajos. The total range personnel consisted of three men in the forestry division. For the experts he needed, Collier turned to the Department of Agriculture. Meetings were held in Washington, and by late June a joint Conservation Committee for the Navajo Reservation headed by H. H. Bennett, "the father of soil conservation," had been formed and was ready to depart for the Navajo reservation.[15]

After years of relative inaction and delay, the program for range rehabilitation suddenly became a juggernaut. The Indian Service and the Soil Erosion Service agreed to develop a central experiment station on Indian land in the Southwest for the study of erosion, and Collier arranged for Bennett's committee to make their examination of conditions and attend the Navajo Tribal Council meeting in July. Under such conditions Bennett's survey of conditions and his report could only be cursory. The committee reached Gallup on June 26 and prepared a report by July 2; Bennett himself addressed the Navajo council on July 7.[16]

The tone of Bennett's report was far more alarmist than Zeh's. The committee members announced that the "very life of the Navajo Nation" was at stake and that erosion had to be halted. To do so they recommended the establishment of an erosion control station that would not only determine conservation techniques best suited to the reservation but also train Indians in erosion control. Bennett envisioned restoring the land through a combination of terracing, subsoiling, and furrowing, construction of check dams and diversion dams, and limitations on range use.[17]

In presenting this plan to the council Bennett stressed not only the emergency the Navajos faced but the need for government-Indian cooperation. He told the council that the government would never dictate a program to the Navajos and that without Navajo cooperation little could be accomplished. Collier repeated this pledge to the council and asked it to set aside a 5-by-20-mile strip near Mexican Springs for the experiment station.[18]

Such a proposal posed a terrible dilemma for the councilmen. Called into existence by the government to ratify oil and gas leases, the council enjoyed little standing among the Diné as a governing body. Navajos regarded the council as yet another agency of the federal government and the councilmen as employees of the government. As one later study phrased it, "The councilman's function, as he and the community see it, is not to represent Shonto at the seat of government, . . . but to represent government at Shonto."[19] The council thus reacted uneasily when presented with what promised to be unpopular or controversial programs. In council meetings, members often denounced government programs, tried to dissuade government officials from implementing them, and then dutifully voted for them. When faced with opposition to these same programs on their return home, councilmen just as readily disavowed them and denied any responsibility for their passage. Given the councilman's conception of his job as an advisor to the government and federal representative to the Navajos, all of this was perfectly consistent. The councilmen were obligated to communicate decisions, not to take responsibility for them or even support them.

What complicated matters even more was the intense factional conflict that wracked the council. Perceived by most Navajos as essentially an alien institution, its offices were often filled by those who had had the most experience in dealing with Anglos. One faction led by Chee Dodge was called the traditionalists, but such a label is more confusing than enlightening. Dodge himself was a rich mixed-blood Catholic who favored Buick touring cars and who moved easily in white society. He was hardly a traditional Navajo. In practice his faction favored cooperation with federal officials and avoidance of conflict. He was traditional largely in comparison to J. C. Morgan, who led a faction centered on the northern Navajo jurisdiction. Northern Navajo opposition to Dodge rose originally from disputes over the control of oil reserves located in their region. The northern

Navajos wanted to monopolize leasing arrangements and accused Dodge of being a tool of the oil companies. The rise of Morgan, the councilman from Farmington, partially transformed this opposition into a progressive faction centered on students returned from Indian boarding schools. Morgan, who became a Protestant missionary, favored assimilation of the Navajos into white society but at the same time was far more willing than Dodge to challenge federal programs and openly oppose reservation officials. Morgan, the assimilationist, therefore would be ideally, if ironically, suited to capitalize on opposition that arose from federal attempts to change traditional Navajo practices.[20]

The council instantly recognized that Collier's and Bennett's proposals were potentially dangerous. Suddenly the government officials were asking the council to consent to programs which went far beyond the oil leases and timber sales that were their usual topics of discussion. Councilmen sensed the opposition the programs could raise but, given the conception of the council, felt powerless to oppose them. The council approved the station, but many councilmen who had voted for it immediately joined a campaign to force its abandonment.[21]

At the end of October Collier returned to the Navajo country to attend another council meeting at Tuba City, Arizona. In his opening speech to the council he stressed the need for more land, proposed a new arrangement for the reservation centered on a unified jurisdiction rather than on six superintendencies, and then came to erosion control. In the ordinary course of events, Collier told the council, erosion control might not have been a major issue in 1933, but government officials had realized

> that down there on the Colorado River is the biggest, most expensive dam in the world, the Boulder Dam now being built which will furnish all Southern California with water and with electric power, and the Boulder Dam will be filled up with your fine agricultural soil in no great number of years if we do not stop erosion on the Navajo reservation. This reservation, along with the other Indian reservations on the Colorado River, is supplying much more than half of all the silt that goes down the Colorado River, which will in the course of a comparatively few years render the Boulder Dam useless and thereby injure the population of all Southern California and a good deal of Arizona also.

If erosion continued at the present rate, Collier warned, within fifteen or twenty years the Navajos would be homeless, a people stranded helplessly in a desert. The Indian bureau had decided to "save your soil and thereby save your life." Collier did not pause to explain why, if the threat to Navajo well-being was so imminent, it had taken a threat to Boulder Dam to trigger action but instead went on to promise the Navajos greater control over the administration of their reservation.[22]

Collier liberally sweetened the program he presented at Tuba City by attaching erosion control to a wide array of relief and development programs, but at the core of it was stock reduction. He promised an extension of Emergency Conservation Work and the wages it brought into the reservation, which, in addition to the wages paid the Navajos at the Mexican Springs station, totaled nearly $800,000. In all, he promised wages equal to six times the amount to be lost in livestock income. Beyond this he committed the bureau to nearly a million dollar's worth of new irrigation projects, the acquisition of land in the checkerboard, and seventy new day schools. None of this, however, would be possible without erosion control. It was not sensible to commit funds to a reservation that was washing away and to acquire new land only to supply more silt to Boulder Dam. Erosion could be stopped, but erosion control depended above all on range control, and this demanded livestock reduction. The reduction would be temporary—four or five years—but the rest of the program was contingent upon it. Collier was, in effect, threatening the Navajos with abandoning them to their fate in the midst of drought and depression, but as he had in July, he disavowed any intention to coerce them. As long as he was commissioner, he promised, the bureau would "never use compulsion on the Navajo tribe."[23]

In proposing reduction, which as a reformer he had opposed only two years earlier, Collier faced cruel dilemmas of his own. In 1933 he spoke at once as commissioner of Indian Affairs and as the most prominent critic of prior Indian policy. Previous reformers committed to Protestant civilization and convinced that they knew what was best for Indians had with the best of conscience shredded dozens of Indian cultures. Collier's career had been based on recognition of the havoc they had wreaked; he brought with him to office a real respect for Indian cultural traditions and a genuine belief in Indian self-determination. Collier, however, also believed in conservation, in science, and in progress. Because of his deep commitments to these programs and values, Collier found himself coming to the Indians to tell them what they must do for their own good. Higher government officials might act only out of concern for Boulder Dam, but Collier's concern for the Navajos was real and the conflict he faced, more acute. In a way Collier would refuse to admit he was offering the Indians an old choice: to submit to white programs or be destroyed. His agency of destruction—erosion—was impersonal, but so too had been the "inexorable push of civilization" friends of the Indian had conjured up in the nineteenth century. They too had opposed what they regarded as brute force; the army was their *bête noire*.[24]

Collier was offering the Navajos a choice that was no choice at all just as the assimilationist reformers he had attacked had offered illusory choices. When Indians had refused to buckle under forced acculturation, earlier reformers had always resorted to compulsion—withheld rations, forcible seizures of school children, and, if need be, military force. Collier sincerely hated such policies; in 1933 he could only disavow them even as he began to use them.

The irony of all this was not lost on the Navajos. After two days of talk on saving the Navajo nation and on self determination, Jim Shirley, a delegate from the Southern Navajo, demanded to know when the Navajos were going to get to say something. "This is the second day at the meeting which is supposed to be our meeting. It seems that the officials are taking most of the time in discussing the way this work should be done. We know something about that by nature because we were born here and raised here and we knew about the processes of nature on our range." Shirley then went on to ask the government not to interfere with the livestock industry for it was the only thing the Navajos knew. Other delegates joined him. Henry Taliman asked Collier not to push "the hardest question that has ever been brought before the Navajo council."[25]

That evening the council met in executive session with Collier. The commissioner got everything he wanted. Taliman, who had opposed reduction on the council floor, the next day sponsored a resolution supporting it. Apparently Collier won his and other councilmen's support with renewed promises of reservation expansion, development, and wage work. The resolution passed with J. C. Morgan in opposition. Immediately after the council, Collier made arrangements to buy 100,000 head of sheep from the Navajos.[26]

Collier, the Indian Service, and the Soil Erosion Service entered 1934 with a certain naive and blind optimism. They mistook council approval for Navajo consent and cooperation. In exuberant language that betrayed his past as *Sunset Magazine* editor, Walter Woehlke, an Indian Service field representative, described rows upon rows of blanketed Navajos listening to Collier's words, debating them around campfires at night, and finally accepting the commissioner's program. This was the sheerest fantasy, but it was typical of the euphoria that gripped officials. The Navajos would be a model to the nation.[27]

By March the Soil Erosion Service and the Bureau of Indian Affairs had a working plan for the Navajo Project. It was a confident, ambitious document and a humane one. Officials meant to restore Navajo lands to their "maximum productivity" by stopping erosion, conserving water, and regulating grazing. To do so they proposed three to six more demonstration areas as well as extensive range, soil, forest, erosion, agricultural, and biological surveys. Despite the ambitious technical objectives of the program, officials eschewed narrow technical approaches. Land use would be integrated with the other "arts, occupations, and problems of the Navajo people, with the interest of their permanent economic and social welfare." Social scientists would study their manners, traditions, customs, economy, and social structures as closely as scientists studied their land. The ends sought from this knowledge could hardly be questioned. "The ultimate aim is the highest practicable use of each unit of land and the greatest possible welfare of the Indians with full preservation of their self-respect and tribal integrity." By the end of the month orders had gone out to reservation officials that all further Emergency Conservation Work projects would have to be cleared by the Soil Erosion Service.[28]

While great expectations were building in Washington, the first stock reduction of 100,000 head of sheep was already proceeding in the Navajo country. It was as haphazard, illconceived, and arbitrary as the Navajo Project outline was well-planned and well-intentioned. Prices were set by the relief administration and they were exceptionally low: $1.00 to $1.50 for ewes, $2.25 to $3.00 for wethers. Chee Dodge warned officials that unless better prices were offered for breeding stock, the large owner would sell only culls—barren ewes and old wethers—and thus leave the breeding potential of the herds unchanged. Dodge prophesied accurately; although 90 percent of the 100,000 quota was quickly met, no significant change in the herds took place since the potential lamb crop was largely unaffected and could quickly make up the loss.[29]

Biologically ineffective, the first reduction was socially disastrous. Large owners refused to bear the burden of reduction. Negotiations in the Western Navajo Reservation produced an agreement that every owner should sell 10 percent of his herd, 75 percent of which should be ewes, the balance wethers. This agreement soon spread over the entire reservation. While the big owners sold their culls, the small owners lost stock that they needed for subsistence. In remote regions of the reservation many Navajos were astonished and angered to discover that there even was a tribal council that could order reductions.[30]

The reduction of 1933–34 was barely completed before Collier returned to the reservation for a March meeting of the Tribal Council at Fort Defiance. The meeting followed the pattern set by the two earlier council sessions. Once more officials linked extension of the reservation, relief programs, and physical improvements to stock reduction. They asked for sizable additional reductions: 150,000 head of grown stock, of which 100,000 head should be goats; castration of all remaining male goats; and the sale of at least 80 percent of the lamb crop every year. This, J. M. Stewart, the chief of the Land Division, promised, would be the last reduction.[31]

At this and two other meetings held in the next four months, the council reacted uneasily, but it did not move into active opposition. One delegate accused the government of reneging on promises made at Tuba City: additional land had not been obtained, and erosion control wage work was confined to Mexican Springs. Other delegates worried openly about the effect of reduction on the most vulnerable Navajos—the poor and those of the eastern checkerboard—and warned of widespread opposition to forced sales. They won some concessions. Government officials agreed to J. C. Morgan's suggestion that any Navajos who owned under 100 head be allowed to replace with sheep any goats they disposed of. The reduction would be paid for by the Navajos themselves out of their oil revenues. In the end the council unanimously passed a resolution approving of this last reduction despite the turmoil the members knew it would bring. As Albert Sandoval explained, there was "not . . . any other way out." They needed additional land and the government had firmly tied reservation extension to stock reduction. They rejected later attempts to weaken the resolution. Government officials reaffirmed that this would be the last reduction as long as 80 percent of succeeding lamb crops were sold, but their own estimates made such promises seem rash. In July of 1934 at Keams Canyon the council approved a contract with the secretary of agriculture which provided for the purchase of 150,000 goats, or half the Navajo holdings, and up to 50,000 sheep at one dollar a head.[32]

In the summer and fall of 1934 the reduction of goats began. To officials, goats were the long time ecological and economic nemesis of the reservation; goats, along with horses, seemed both the substance and the symbol of the "Navajo problem." Although officials believed goats were ecologically destructive, the major sins of the goats were economic, not ecological. They were scrubby, mixed-breed anir als that produced little marketable mohair or milk and each hide brought only a quarter. The Navajos raised them for meat, and the butchered goat had "practically no market value except among the Indians." They were a subsistence animal, not a market animal. Since a rationalized reservation economy would have to be based on the highest possible commercial yield per head, goats would have to be drastically reduced.[33]

Officials admitted this would be difficult since the Navajos retained "an affection for goats that is hard to understand." It was hard to understand only because officials held market rationality as the only standard of production. The goat was not an ecological demon to the Navajos; it was as crucial to their livelihood as sheep. When pressed at Senate hearings to exchange unmarketable goats for sheep, the Navajos had patiently explained that goats were not meant to be marketed. As Peter Price, whose medium size herd of 200 animals contained more goats than sheep, told the senators in 1931, he got as much use out of goats as sheep; goats gave him meat and milk for his children and for scrawny spring lambs which might otherwise die. Goats, Navajos such as Price insisted, were hardier than sheep; they survived the winters better. Goats were critical especially for owners of small herds since they could eat their goats and save their sheep. To take their goats was to threaten them with starvation; to castrate the billies was to deny their children their birthright.[34]

The actual reduction of goats which took place in the fall of 1934 deeply shocked the Navajos. It was never forgotten by those who lived through it; only the Long Walk equaled its emotional impact. This reduction was the first direct governmental intervention in Navajo lives, the first use of large-scale coercion since Bosque Redondo. In reducing the herds the government touched a nerve of Navajo culture. As details of the plan became known in the spring, the Navajo women, who largely owned the goats, moved into open opposition in chapter meetings. Even some reservation officials urged caution, sympathizing with what became the refrain of the next ten years: if you take our stock, how shall we live?[35]

The second reduction not only repeated, it compounded, all the errors of the first. Once more, quotas were assigned to the various reservation jurisdictions, and once more the herds were reduced horizontally by taking a straight percentage of each. As a result, the bulk of the 148,344 goats and approximately 50,000 sheep actually eliminated came from small and medium sized herds. Because goat reduction disproportionately affected the poor and took a subsistence rather than a commercial animal, the second reduction hurt those people Collier later contended he was trying to protect.[36]

The poor sold from a mixture of fear, compulsion, and need. The amount of coercion used was always hotly disputed. Collier later admitted that compulsion had been employed in the eastern jurisdiction, but he insisted that elsewhere Navajos freely surrendered their goats. The Navajos challenged this. Many believed that their CCC jobs depended on reducing their goats, or they believed that the government would replace their goats with sheep. Others said officials threatened them with jail or that policemen simply seized their goats. Collier apparently denied responsibility for such tactics because those using them were often not white employees but rather Navajo policemen who told stockowners that the orders came from Washington. As Mary Jumbo's mother-in-law later recalled: "We were so scared. Everybody was bossin. It is hard to tell who it was. Maybe it was a common Indian tellin us we had to do a certain thing. And we did it. We were so scared of everything."[37]

The poor apportioning of the cut was only one sign of federal bungling. The goats soon began to come in faster than the packing houses, which were to can them as food for those on relief, could process them. Officials then gave permission to the Navajos to slaughter some of the animals and dry the meat, but even this did not relieve the pressure. Goats continued to pile up, and with the drought there was not enough water available to move them or keep them. In Navajo Canyon 3,500 goats were slaughtered and left to rot. The Navajos contended similar slaughters occurred elsewhere. The mass purchases and the mass slaughters horrified the Navajos, and opposition to further reductions crystallized almost instantly.[38]

The testimony of Navajos and their traders indicates that the social consequences of goat reduction were profound. As even the government agreed, the herds of the poor were disproportionately affected because the provisions of the agreement for replacing goats with sheep were not observed; therefore, the herds of many small owners fell to dangerously low levels. Goat reduction was, according to one council delegate, "the great mistake. The poorest people owned goats—the easiest people to take away from. Big men held on. Each jurisdiction was given a quota. The pressure was so great the little fellow sold, everyone sold. A goat sold for one dollar. The money doesn't mean half so much to the family as having the goat to kill and eat for several days."[39]

Overnight the subsistence base of the poor was drastically impaired. In emergencies or simply to obtain daily food, the poor often had to eat more animals then their depleted herds could produce. They ate up their breeding stock. The traders asserted that many families never recovered from this, and their records reflect the result. The most immediate consequence of goat reduction was a rise in the Navajo cost of living of about 20 percent, according to the traders; at Toadlena the trader sold 30 percent more food, and at the Outlaw Post the trader reported a marked increase in his sale of meat.[40]

When many of the Navajos who had lost their goats began eating their sheep, the traders denied them credit at the stores. Many of these same people had obtained a larger cash income from government jobs than they had ever gotten from their herds, but since the traders could not control such income, they extended no credit to wage earners. Previously the traders controlled the marketing of Navajo wool, so they could extend credit knowing that when the Navajos sold their wool at the trading post, they could subtract the amount they had advanced to any customer from what they owed the family for the wool. They were assured of collecting their debts. Once government reforms stopped the practice of withholding debts to the traders from the paychecks of Navajo workers, however, the traders could not count on controlling wage income in a similar manner. As a result, they began dealing on a cash basis only. The number of Navajos who could obtain credit at the posts—a necessity during lean seasons or emergencies—fell drastically. This was not only a serious economic loss, it was also a cultural loss. As they cut credit, the traders began selling a wide array of treasured Navajo silverwork that they held as pawn.[41]

As significant as were the changes goat reduction brought to the reservation proper, they did not approach the disasters that ensued on the checkerboard lands of New Mexico. Collier would not even attempt to defend his policy in Senate hearings on this area; he acknowledged that the government's actions were unjustifiable. One of the promises Collier had made to the Navajos was to bring this region into the reservation, and the Navajo boundary bill pending in Congress was an attempt to do just that. He had repeatedly tied its success to the willingness of the Navajos to reduce their herds. The whole premise behind the original reduction quota for the eastern Navajo jurisdiction was that the people of the checkerboard would soon be within the reservation. By spring of 1934 it had become clear that the boundary bill was blocked in Congress; nevertheless, reduction went forward in the area. It made absolutely no sense as part of a conservation program since, as Navajo stock were removed, the cattle and sheep of white owners replaced them. The herds of the checkerboard had been dwindling for twenty years as their owners tried unsuccessfully to compete with Anglo cattle and sheep operations. The bureau at this point proceeded to reduce the Navajo herds still further through a combination of physical compulsion, lies, and threats. This reduction brought many families to the brink of starvation, and since they were outside the reservation, little relief work was available to aid them. A Soil Conservation Service investigation conducted in 1936 by Richard Van Valkenburgh found the destitution of the people around Torreon, Star Lake, and Pueblo Alto, incredible.

> The general situation is beyond belief. I have never seen on the reservation proper anything that could compare with the misery of these people. My interperter [sic] Danny Bia stated that he

never realized that Navajo's [sic] lived like this. Trachoma or similar eye afflictions is [sic] prevalent. It is conservative to state that 50 percent of the people over 60 years are blind or partially blind. Tuberculosis is widespread. In the Torreon region there were 12 cases of pneumonia at one time.[42]

The Navajos reacted to the insecurity and suffering which goat reduction brought both by moving into opposition to the New Deal and John Collier and by increasing the number of ceremonies in order to restore balance to a world seemingly dissolving into chaos. The second reaction, was, perhaps, more predictable than the first in a society that had not witnessed widespread political protest since the Long Walk, with perhaps the possible exception of earlier resistance to federal school policies.

The increase in the number of ceremonials taking place on the reservation following goat reduction partially reflected the extent to which "ritual and material sides of the culture . . . appear indistinguishable." With fear, worry, and, in the checkerboard region, actual malnutrition and disease rampant, an increase in the number of ceremonials, whose focus was on the curing of individuals and connected blessings for the people, was predictable. In 1938 Clyde Kluckhohn estimated, based on a study of the off-reservation community of Ramah, that Navajo men devoted one-fourth to one-third of their productive time to ceremonials and women one-fifth to one-third of theirs, and that the percentages had probably been higher in the recent past.[43]

Implicit in this stress on ceremonials were alternative Navajo explanations of why the range was in bad shape. Many, probably most Navajos did not deny that the range was in poor condition; they did deny, however, that range depletion came from too many animals. They contended that there was less grass because there was less rain. In 1934 in the middle of a drought this was a plausible assertion, and the Navajos believed that when the rains returned, so would the grass.[44]

For many of these Navajos, however, the onset of drought itself was only a sign of deeper problems. Some thought the Diné were suffering because of their neglect of proper ceremonials, while others believed that the drought was the result of an even more serious spiritual disharmony—incest among the Holy People. Such beliefs were real and significant, explaining partially the recourse to ritual, but they should not be seen as evidence of Navajo passivity in the face of nature or of a reluctance to tamper with natural systems.[45]

The Navajos quite explicitly depicted human beings as active agents of their fate. Their ceremonials reflected this, and so did their subsistence practices. They were quite willing to alter the face of the land—building reservoirs, constructing irrigation systems, and drilling for water—and hoped for government assistance in doing so. Officials who accused them of seeing range depletion as an act of God about which little could be done, for instance, also paradoxically emphasized the desire of the Navajos to press forward with water development.[46]

Another sign that the great increase in the frequency of ceremonials did not indicate passivity is reflected in its links to the growth of political opposition on the reservation. The ceremonies brought people together and promoted unity, cooperation, and an awareness of common values and ways. In such a harmonious atmosphere, common cause in the midst of common disaster became more likely. Navajos, worried and fearful of reduction, met constantly, and resistance was almost certainly solidified. Resistance was and remained local, organized in the chapters and local communities, not in the alien institution of the council, and this resistance tended to focus symbolically on a single man: John Collier.[47]

In view of the Navajos' conception of the causes of range depletion, Collier's actions made no sense. Droughts and bad winters brought their own reductions as animals died off. To purposefully and wastefully kill even more animals on top of this, as Collier had done, was dangerous and foolhardy. In promoting such a program Collier could only be acting from malevolence or ignorance. He was the real source of their troubles. John Collier became anathema to the Navajos. They questioned his premises, his actions, and his integrity. Collier had tricked them with his relief and development programs; they had been a ruse to take their livestock. When Collier, as he repeatedly did, argued that the Navajos themselves agreed in the council votes to reduction, he was making the narrowest possible defense. He would later admit that real consent had never been obtained.[48]

Collier and other federal officials tried to understand the attacks upon them, but they believed that these, like other Navajo actions, were simply the result of ignorance. Collier and other experts contended that materially the Navajos had never been better off, that federal programs had more than offset the losses in income suffered through livestock reduction, and that Navajo income as a whole had actually risen. In Collier's eyes the Navajos with their emotional attachment to their livestock were not accurately judging the costs and benefits involved in reduction.[49]

The technicians involved in the program were less able to understand the Navajo position, even when they were willing to try. Soil conservationists attempted to put themselves in the place of the Navajos, but the analogy they drew was to small businessmen, and this comparison only increased misunderstanding. The Navajos were not small businessmen. Their major concern was not in raising their profit margin. It was not even in acquiring wealth. They appreciated their new income from the New Deal, but to them it seemed totally extraneous to the issue of livestock and their way of life.[50]

Both Navajos and sympathetic anthropologists repeatedly tried to explain that the Indians did not equate livestock and wage income. Wealth was livestock, not money. Security came only from the herds. Wages went largely to young men and disappeared quickly. The old people, the children, the women—the residence unit itself—depended on the flocks. In time this attitude would penetrate the bureau, but its influence on actual policy remained slight.[51]

At the beginning of 1935 then, the reduction program was in shambles, and the euphoria of the previous year had vanished. The goat reduction had been achieved, but only at the price of mass discontent, and the other parts of the program had failed entirely. The Navajos had not castrated their remaining billy goats, and they had not sold 80 percent of the lamb crop. Such a sale, the bureau admitted, was impossible. There were no markets. Walter Woehlke, who had so exuberantly praised the Navajo Project a year earlier, now admitted that the government had a program hardly worthy of the name. The government did not know how many sheep were necessary for a minimum subsistence herd for the Navajos, and reduction had already come dangerously close to eliminating many small herders and "creating a Navajo proletariat" while increasing a "Navajo aristocracy." Successful reduction, Woehlke argued, depended on the redistribution of Navajo range lands. It was wealthy Navajos such as Chee Dodge who were really blocking reduction; they should be the targets of government action. He recommended unilateral federal action to implement grazing fees and grazing quotas.[52]

Woehlke's ideas gained a receptive hearing in Washington, for already the political consequences of goat reduction were shaping up on the reservation. The first casualty of the reaction against reduction was the Indian Reorganization Act, and the person who led the opposition to it would be J. C. Morgan, a man whose assimilationist ideals and Christian religion were far from the ideas and beliefs of the traditional Navajos who rallied behind him.

Most officials regarded the IRA—a measure that would reorganize tribes on the basis of constitutional tribal councils and establish tribal corporations for economic development—as entirely peripheral to reduction. The act did include a provision empowering the secretary of interior to issue grazing regulations and to regulate livestock numbers, but this provision was redundant since the secretary had such power anyway. The act, however, was a Collier measure and thus an ideal focus for Navajo resentment.[53]

Morgan's opposition to the IRA originally had little to do with stock reduction. He and his followers recognized that the complicated and confusing act, and the Collier program in general, was anti-assimilationist (at least culturally) and could serve as a means of returning power to traditionalists who now took little part in reservation governance. Morgan's distaste for the New Deal originally focused on the day-school program and Collier's policy of religious toleration, but the anti-Collier sentiment raised by livestock reduction gave his campaign against the IRA widespread support from traditional Navajos who had no sympathy with Morgan's larger aims. Since, to take effect on any reservation, the IRA, by its own terms, had to be approved in a plebiscite by the people residing there, the measure was vulnerable to antigovernment sentiment. Despite an extensive government campaign and attempts to disassociate the measure from herd reduction, in June of 1935 the Navajos voted by a narrow majority to reject the IRA. To have the largest Indian nation in the country reject the keystone to his entire reform program was a bitter and embarrassing defeat for Collier. It sprang directly from goat reduction.[54]

The defeat did not alter Collier's determination to pursue stock reduction. Immediately following the election he informed the new superintendent of the centralized Navajo Agency, C. E. Faris that reduction would go forward; the Navajos were sadly mistaken if they thought the vote would prevent further cutting of their herds.[55]

Even before the defeat of the IRA, Collier had recognized that a thorough revamping of the program was necessary. In May of 1935 a new program which centralized the existing work under a general superintendent and expanded the role of the Soil Erosion Service was announced. When later it became the Soil Conservation Service and was transferred into the Department of Agriculture, Collier quickly negotiated an agreement that allowed the Soil Conservation Service to continue work on the reservation.[56]

Collier tried to match administrative changes with much more substantial changes in both goals and methods. He promised to gather the economic and social information necessary to plan effectively. Under the new program the reservation would be subdivided into land management units based on watersheds, and these would be the units of administration, range control, and land use. Collier also reiterated the government's commitment to tribal cooperation and to reduction on a sliding scale that would affect big owners far more than small. Statements that range rehabilitation was largely the Navajos' "own responsibility and their own gain" and that permanent improvement was possible only through efforts by "the Navajo People themselves, encouraged and guided by [the] government" were hardly new, but in 1935 the government appears to have sincerely attempted to follow them. The bureau's third attempt at reduction in the late summer of 1935 was truly voluntary, without force or coercion of any kind and with no use of government personnel to bring in sheep or goats. The reduction was also a total failure. The voluntary purchasing plan aimed at securing 250,000 sheep and goats resulted in the sale of only 13,312 head of goats and 13,866 head of sheep.[57]

Given the widespread Navajo opposition to reduction, such an outcome was hardly surprising, but in light of the first reports of the Soil Conservation Service it was particularly disastrous. The service warned that the ongoing range surveys showed that Zeh's 1931 report had actually overestimated the carrying capacity of the reservation. The longer substantial reduction was postponed, the more severe it would be. Collier, who had originally promised the Navajos that the first two reductions would be sufficient and that in four or five years the range would be restored, was informed during 1936 that the first three reductions had not materially reduced grazing pressure and that the range was growing worse. The 1.3 million sheep and goats on the reservation in 1930 had declined to 944,910 by 1935, but much of this reduction had come from severe winters and in any case did not "keep pace with range depletion." Counting cattle, horses, sheep, and goats, the equivalent of 1,269,910 animals were grazing on a reservation that could carry an estimated 560,000. "This means that a further reduction of 56 percent would be necessary in order to reduce the stock to the carrying capacity of the range." Collier publicly admitted that, despite the disruption the reductions had caused, they had accomplished little, and that by implication the worst reductions still lay ahead.[58]

The failure of the 1935 reduction once more made voluntary reduction irreconcilable with the perceived urgency of the situation. Collier reacted by issuing special regulations for the Navajo range in November of 1935. The regulations did not fully abandon the principle of obtaining Navajo consent before acting, but they rendered the principle meaningless by opening the way for unilateral federal action if the Navajos refused to act. The regulations gave the commissioner power to establish land management districts and a maximum carrying capacity for each one. Responsibility for procuring reduction to the carrying capacity and establishing grazing regulations would still initially belong to the Navajos, but if the tribe failed in its duties, the "Commissioner with the approval of the Secretary of the Interior [would] take such action as he [might] deem necessary to bring about such reduction or to establish such management plans in order to protect the interests of the Navajo people."[59]

Collier hoped unilateral action could be avoided; he still hoped to bring about Navajo consent and cooperation. The government strategy saw two major avenues to attaining this cooperation. The first was primarily educational and involved the use of the demonstration areas and Soil Conservation Service personnel to show the Navajos that they could reduce their flocks while simultaneously, through improved practices, salvaging the range and improving their yields. The other was primarily political. The government now sought to put the burden of reduction upon the large owners by exempting entirely small herders with under 100 sheep and reducing medium sized herd owners only slightly. Since in most of the new range-management districts the majority of the owners would not have to reduce at all even though they benefited from government wage work, the big owners would become isolated in their opposition to stock reduction. Popular opinion and the threat of government compulsion could then combine to bring about a relatively painless reduction.[60]

Bureaucratic squabbling on the reservation between Indian Service and Soil Conservation Service employees hampered reinvigoration of Collier's program, but still the two main thrusts, educational and political, moved forward. They did not achieve the desired results. Much Soil Conservation Service work was experimental. Successful results took time while disasters were immediately apparent. Check dams on arroyos, for example, were impressive, but the Service soon discovered that they were expensive and relatively ineffectual. It moved away from large dams, which often washed out, to smaller structures designed to spread the water before it reached the arroyos. A washed out dam was a dramatic failure; successful waterspreading was an inconspicuous success. Likewise, early stockwater-development projects often failed when the water quickly drained through sandy soils; Navajo critics accused the Service of building reservoirs that filled with sand.[61]

Other Service activities were simply ill conceived and destructive. Some range management experts, for instance, advanced extravagant claims for the benefits from prairie dog eradication. They claimed that prairie dogs ate enough forage on two acres to support a sheep. According to such calculations, killing prairie dogs could have solved all the Navajos' grazing problems, but more restrained observers pointed out that there was no grazing land in the Southwest—prairie dogs or no prairie dogs—good enough to support a sheep on two acres. The government eventually restricted poisoning programs amid contentions that they were killing the birds that helped prevent insect damage to Navajo crops, but by then they had killed enough prairie dogs to eliminate one of the last emergency wild food resources of the Navajos.[62]

The demonstration areas became even more visible than other Soil Conservation Service projects and far more controversial. The Navajos initially reacted to them with hostility and suspicion, but by

June of 1936 the government had secured 191,488 acres for experimentation. The government planned to fence all of this land and remove Navajo livestock from it to allow the range to recover. As grasses returned, improved stock from neighboring Navajo herds would be reintroduced at reduced levels under the Service's management. Five areas—Mariano Lake, Ganado, Frazer, Klagetoh, and Kayenta—besides Mexican Springs, were in operation by June of 1936. The Service reported both dramatic recovery of the range and improved conditions of the animals in virtually all these areas and continued to report progress in succeeding years. At Ganado they found that the fleeces of ewes within the demonstration area weighed twice as much as those of comparable animals outside. The Soil Conservation Service hoped to use such dramatic increases in the productivity of individual animals to convince the Navajos that stock reduction could be more than offset by the use of improved breeds on improved ranges.[63]

Most Navajos remained unpersuaded. At Mariano Lake the decision to replace Navajo sheep with government-owned cattle got the project off to a disastrous start. The government seemed to be depriving the Navajos of grazing land only to raise cattle that wandered off the still unfenced project and destroyed Navajo fields. When Navajos refused even to consider cattle raising themselves, the herd was disbanded and the experiment ended in failure. At Mexican Springs and on the Frazer Demonstration Area, Navajo owners initially refused to put their sheep under Service control although the success of the Ganado project apparently persuaded many of them to cooperate. Cooperation remained grudging and narrow, however. The Navajos resented the fences, and they resented the fines they incurred when their stock broke through them. The Navajos, with their deep distrust of nonkin, resisted Soil Conservation Service plans to contract with them for management of their herds, and they resisted plans to merge small family herds into more efficient and manageable units for similar reasons. Resentment of the demonstration areas remained high enough in 1936 so that there were threats to rip down the fences and demands that the conservationists be fired.[64]

Some Navajos came to accept the Service's theories of overstocking and improved management, but for most Indians the demonstration areas proved little. This was not because, as some scholars have suggested, cause and effect was alien to Navajo culture; rather, it was because they rejected the conservationists' premises and controls. The Navajos complained (apparently inaccurately) that the government had taken the best land for demonstration areas and that was why it provided better grazing. Others, convinced that drought was the real cause of depletion, simply contended that it rained more in the demonstration areas. Navajo stock bordering the demonstration areas appeared inferior to the stock within, they contended, because the fencing of so much prime land crowded more animals on the remaining land.[65]

Obviously examples which conservationists took as convincing proof the Navajos reinterpreted in their own light. Demonstration areas might improve conservation techniques; they were not going to bring about reduction. The Navajos were at least partially correct when they claimed that the demonstration areas and the range were not comparable areas. In the demonstration areas the government operated with sophisticated equipment and relatively abundant capital. They could, for example, supplement the herds' food during severe weather. A subsistence herder could duplicate none of this.[66]

Necessarily, then, if the government sought to avoid reduction through sheer force, they were going to have to rely on a political strategy. This was not mere expedience. Collier's enemies, both within and without the tribe, were capitalizing on the inequities of reduction in order to attack him, but his own advisors had already pointed out the same inequities. Stockholding among the Diné was uneven, and horizontal reduction had hurt the poor, not the rich. But social justice was not the only reason for focusing on the rich, at least for some Indian Service theorists. As one official stated later in the year: reduction of the rich would save the government money. Reducing the herds of the poor would only put them on the dole.[67]

The immediate result of this strategy was the government's abandonment of the Navajo council, which Collier now perceived as a tool of the large stockowners and a danger to the entire conservation program. Thomas Dodge, Chee Dodge's son and tribal chairman, informed officials that if the council were convened, it would pass a resolution condemning the Soil Conservation Service. The bureau skirted this issue by simply not convening the council which, after the frenetic activity of the early New Deal, languished for eighteen months without a meeting. Some of Collier's aides urged him to disband the council and appoint a new one, but for the time being he hesitated to do this.[68]

Any further reductions based on the side of individual holdings and the carrying capacity of the range demanded accurate ownership records and surveys of the range management units. By 1936 the range, erosion, and agricultural surveys were substantially complete. Data on Navajo holdings were available from dipping records and from the first of the sociological, or human dependency, surveys. Use of this data in creating a new program, however, was blocked by Bureau of Indian Affairs–Soil Conservation Service feuding. In early 1936 Collier sought to restore momentum by dismissing Superintendent Faris, who was quarreling with Soil Service personnel, and appointing E. R. Fryer, who had already successfully supervised stock reduction among the Pueblos.[69]

After the appointment of Fryer, a redefinition and reorganization of the Navajo project designed to integrate Indian Service and Soil Conservation Service personnel in a unified program under the general superintendent took place. The new program created a special land-management division and subdivided the entire reservation into eighteen land management districts. Each had its own director and staff, with all of them subordinate to a land management-director.[70]

The new director of land management, W. G. McGinnies, went right to work and in May at the request of Fryer issued the most important report since Zeh's initial survey of the reservation. It was ponderously entitled "The Agricultural and Range Resources of the Navajo Reservation in Relation to the Subsistence Needs of the Navajo Indians," but it was the most forceful statement of problems and alternatives yet.[71]

Presenting the problem in Malthusian terms, McGinnies stressed that the basic Navajo problem was an increasing population on a declining resource base. The carrying capacity of the reservation stood at 560,000 sheep units and was declining rapidly. This meant a further reduction of 56 percent would be necessary to reduce existing stock to carrying capacity. This reduction, however, could be achieved without the economic destruction of the Navajos because their livestock economy was so inefficient. Improved animals, elimination of useless stock, and improved range conditions could actually raise the output of wool and meat after reduction. And this reduction need not be done at the expense of small owners. Of the 4,593 bands of sheep and goats dipped in 1935, 36 percent consisted of less than 100 head, but the total holdings of these bands made up only 10 percent of the sheep and goats in the reservation. The larger bands, which averaged 288 units, held 90 percent of the stock, and they could bear the brunt of reduction. Subsistence herds would not be touched.[72]

McGinnies did not, however, stop at this. For the first time he tried to define a subsistence income for the 10,000 Navajo families. Using the economic data compiled at that time, he put the average income of a Navajo family at $235 on a trading basis. He estimated that it took fifty-seven ewes or 6 acres of irrigated land to produce such an income. At proper stocking, therefore, 7,193 families could be supported at a subsistence income of $235 a year. This was slightly under the 7,500 families then dependent on livestock. An equal division of all available and potential irrigated farm lands among the remaining Navajo families would give them 7.7 acres each and a somewhat larger income. If all Navajo resources were divided equally, McGinnies continued, each family would probably earn about $317 a year.[73]

McGinnies's calculations, however, were based on the assumption that Navajo herds would soon consist solely of productive ewes. Since the herds in fact consisted of wethers, rams, and barren ewes as well as productive ewes, reduction without the substitution of productive for nonproductive animals would only drive the Navajos deeper into poverty. By 1940 the bureau still had failed to achieve the income goals McGinnies had projected. In that year, sheep owners in only four of the eighteen land-management districts which McGinnies had used as the basis of his estimates received the $4.10 average income from each sheep in their herds. The reservation average income for each sheep was $3.61, and eight districts received less than $3.00 from each animal. A herd of fifty-seven animals, in the poorest district, yielded an income of $106.59, not $235.00. McGinnies' estimate of $19.60 as the average income for each acre of agricultural land was equally flawed. Five districts met or exceeded this figure, but five fell below $15.00 and the reservation average was only $17.49.[74]

McGinnies could argue that with further stock improvement his average figures could be achieved, but regarding $235 as an adequate income was itself unfair. In 1940 income statistics were compiled according to residence (or consumption) groups rather than families, but a rough comparision with McGinnies's estimates is possible. McGinnies worked on the basis of 10,000 families; the 1940 figures enumerated 5,669 residence groups. Average family income in 1940 can therefore be crudely estimated to be 57 percent of the residence group income. On this basis the average group income of $556 breaks down to $317 for each family, well above McGinnies' $235 estimate. This figure includes the reduced-wage income of the late New Deal, and McGinnies did not include such wages in his calculation, but by 1940 virtually everyone admitted that such wage income was necessary to preserve the Navajos from absolute penury. Even with such income, 1940 was a year of widespread destitution on the reservation because of the drought of 1939. Without wage income, which comprised 28 percent of the total Navajo income, average family income would drop to McGinnies's figure. This, however, was not "bare subsistence" income; it was clear destitution.[75]

Such shortcomings in the McGinnies report were not obvious in 1936, and within the bureau the report was seized upon by those who wished to get the moribund reduction program moving again. Robert Marshall, the director of forestry and grazing, praised the report for going beyond the wishful fantasies of the preceding years, he recommended reduction at the rate of 210,000 head a year plus the natural increase of the herds for three years in order to save both Boulder Dam and the Navajos.[76]

With the McGinnies report provoking within the bureau calls for draconian reductions, it is astonishing that Collier released it to the New Mexican newspapers. When articles based on it were published in the Gallup press, they provoked shock and outrage on the reservation. The Navajos, like Marshall, read it as a call for the immediate reduction of their herds by 50 percent.[77]

J. C. Morgan, who had renewed his attack on reduction in March by testifying before the Senate committee on Indian affairs during its hearings on the now hopelessly stalled boundary extension, quickly capitalized on the report. At a meeting held at Ganado he vowed to end reduction, kill the day schools, and abolish the eighteen districts. At the same meeting, Chee Dodge, Morgan's bitterest political enemy, echoed the same sentiments. Among Navajo leaders only Henry Taliman defended the conservation program. In such circumstances the Senate hearings on the boundary bill held on, and near the reservation in August largely served as a forum for attacking reduction and the Collier administration. In August, Collier managed to persuade Chee Dodge, who hated Morgan, to support reductions. Although Dodge's testimony before the Senate committee was hardly an endorsement, he did make a strong statement in favor of reduction later on. Dodge's support, however, only served to make Morgan the most prominent opponent of reduction and thus increase his support accordingly.[78]

This new outburst of opposition embarrassed the bureau, but it did little to deter their program. Internal analysis of the Navajos' resistance to reduction showed flashes of real insight into the Navajo conception of economy and the inequities of early reduction, but finally such admissions carried little weight. After evaluating such motives, one report concluded that the "greatest cause of disturbance" lay in the "red herrings" brought forth by "religious zealots" (Morgan) and the resistance of large owners. How could the Navajos resist reduction unless they were being deceived and misled? The work programs had brought in income equal to that derived from 500,000 ewes, twice the number removed through government programs. Total Navajo income had actually grown, and the 1936 lamb crop and wool clip were the largest since 1930. To planners there was simply no objective reason for resistance.[79]

Such a position hardened in the fall of 1937. Any immediate steps toward reduction were impossible until the administrative structure of the new land-management districts were in place, but by the fall officials were raising the possibility of coercive action. The several hundred "rich" Navajo families would oppose reduction; the tribe would be unable to formulate grazing regulations; and action would depend on the government. "It would appear that on condition that the use of authority would be made successful, authority rather than democratic procedure should be used with regard to this particular matter." In fact this method had been dominant all along, but such frank advocacy represented a drastic departure from the rhetoric of the early Collier administration.[80]

Both Fryer and Collier still hoped that a representative body of

Navajos might agree to the conservation program. In November, Fryer set out to create such a body. By then the Tribal Council was a totally discredited institution, repudiated by both the government and most Navajos. Fryer, with the advice of Father Berard Haile, a Catholic missionary, linguist, and anthropologist, proposed abolishing the council and replacing it with another council made up of traditional headmen from the new grazing districts. These men were supposedly the natural leaders of the tribe who would unselfishly act in its best interest. To form this government Fryer proposed that the executive committee of the existing council and two former tribal chairmen, assisted by Father Haile, tour the reservation and appoint headmen as delegates to the constitutional convention. At a November meeting, the existing council agreed to its own demise almost with relief. Before adjourning, it passed a resolution approving the grazing districts and urging the Navajos to organize in each district to help draw up grazing regulations.[81]

The immediate result of this attempt to rescue the political strategy was chaos. Morgan, alleging he had never been properly notified of the council meeting, opposed the entire plan as an attempt by Collier to secure a "handpicked," subservient council of "longhairs." He now entered an alliance with Senator Chavez of New Mexico and Paul Palmer, a right-wing attorney from New Mexico identified with Anglo cattlemen's interests. Morgan now opposed boundary extension and thus abandoned the eastern Navajos whose cause he had championed; in exchange Chavez promised to exempt the Navajos permanently from the IRA, whose principles were being applied despite the Navajos' rejection, and to drive Collier from office. Morgan asserted that the grazing districts violated the 1868 treaty and that the government had no authority to proceed with further reductions. Once more he was popularly identified with resistance to reduction. Despite his opposition to the constitutional convention and provisional council, Morgan was appointed as a delegate, and in April of 1937 he attended its meeting long enough to denounce the whole process and walk out to the applause of the other delegates. After he had left the meeting, the chairman of the convention Henry Taliman appointed him head of the committee to draft the new constitution. Morgan boycotted the drafting committee's meetings. A new elective government was not formed until 1938, and then Morgan was elected tribal chairman.[82]

It was in the midst of this turmoil, that information from the numerous surveys underway since 1935 began to yield precise information on the specific ranges, fields, and forests of the reservation and on the economic and social conditions of the people themselves. The Soil Conservation Service admitted in 1937 that in the past it had proceeded with little knowledge of the economic life and needs of the Navajo but promised that in the future technical surveys and human surveys would be combined in the planning process. They were too sanguine. As Fryer later acknowledged, the government made the Navajos perhaps the most studied people on earth but largely ignored the information they gathered.[83]

The technical data was uniformly grim. Significant stock reduction had taken place (according to 1936 records, sheep and goats were down 35.5 percent from 1930), but over 80 percent of the reservation remained overused and badly depleted. Navajo sheepherding practices had not changed to conform to Anglo ideals except among a few of the large herdsmen, whose herds the bureau now hoped to reduce. Erosion and gullying continued, and in some overgrazed areas grasslands and brushland were being invaded by juniper and pinon trees, while, more commonly, lands once covered by blue grama grass now grew snakeweed, yellow bush, and Russian thistle. On the other hand, significant areas continued to be undergrazed because of the lack of permanent water.[84]

Damage extended beyond the rangelands and into the forests and woodlands. Herds feeding on the shoots of young pinon trees deformed or killed the seedlings, and their trampling hurt reproduction. In the mountain forests the herds compacted the ground, eliminated ground cover, and thus retarded percolation and increased runoff. As a result, ponderosa pines suffered from a lack of moisture that caused them to shed leaves and produce meager foilage. This, in turn, hurt their food production and made them vulnerable to insects and disease. No new trees replaced those that died since seedlings had no chance to grow in the hard, overgrazed ground. Foresters believed the Navajo forests were advancing toward extinction and instituted a permit system to guide wood use.[85]

The information available on farm lands was as gloomy as the rest. There was far too little agricultural land—less than an acre per capita—and what there was had suffered badly. Wind and water erosion continued to take their toll, and on the new irrigation projects failure to subjugate the land properly increased erosion while overirrigation rendered the land alkaline and unusable.[86]

The technical reports showed little that the Navajos did right, and predictably the foresters, the range experts, the agronomists, and the soil management people saw their task as one of conversion, of leading the Navajos to the proper road of conservation and efficiency. In such a situation a missionary-heathen relationship soon developed, and a spirit of zealotry pervaded the ranks of the Navajo Service. E. R. Fryer concluded the Land Management Conference held on the reservation in 1937 by admitting that "to me the Navajo Service is a fetish—almost a religion; to most of you it is also a religion. Having seen the complete good fellowship that has been present this week, I know that you are just as pleased as I." Such enthusiasm might have been harmless enough if it were not mixed with a tendency to see Navajo opponents of reduction as either ignorant or evil. As the senior soil conservationist for the project succinctly summarized the situation, there were four reasons for the opposition to stock reduction: "ignorance, blindness, laziness, and dishonesty."[87]

The Navajo Service in 1937 faced problems far too severe to be combatted with such zealotry. Stock reduction had already ripped the fabric of the Navajos' life and had begun to reduce them to dependency. The persistent Navajo question—"If you take our stock, how shall we live?"—deserved an answer. The bureau's own data indicated that its response so far had been glib and unrealistic.

As officials compiled the data on Navajo income made available by the first human dependency surveys, a shocking statistic emerged. Wage income—the bulk of it from temporary government work—constituted nearly 40 percent of the meager Navajo per capita income of $128 a year. Relief work, which under Collier's original plan was meant only to be an expedient to tide the Navajos over until the range was restored (a process then presumed to take four or five years), had become a mainstay of the Navajo economy. Planners clearly recognized the implications. Since the termination of the work projects would "seriously affect the Navajo level of subsistence," a new source of income must be found. Agriculture seemed the most promising alternative. The Navajos, to an extent the bureau had long ignored, were farmers. Farming in most areas, however, took place in conjunction with sheep raising, and as a result the government proposed to make more Navajos exclusively farmers. Officials reasoned that since many Navajo families lacked livestock anyway and since a significant proportion of the goods Navajos purchased at the trading posts were food items such as flour or oats that could be produced on the reservation, the ideal solution would be to have Navajo farmers raise these products. In this way the need for livestock income with which to purchase agricultural commodities would be reduced without any real loss in living standards.[88]

Planners for the Navajos, however, ignored basic conditions of Navajo society. Most Navajos insisted on being farmers *and* herdsmen, not farmers or herdsmen. And even those who only farmed would need owners of large herds who could give them sheep in exchange for crops. They tended to see the land-management units which barred them from moving their herds to lands they had always used as impositions on traditional grazing rights. The basic conditions of Navajo social organization could not be ignored without endangering the whole government program. The truth of this had already clearly emerged in another of the needless controversies that plagued the reservation: the dispute over the Fruitland Irrigation Project. In 1937 the Fruitland project was potentially the largest irrigation system on the reservation. When finished, the canals running off the San Juan River near Farmington would irrigate 5,000 acres of land. The Navajos had always been enthusiastic about the project and had pushed for it since 1930.[89]

The government and the Navajos agreed on the need for the project, but as it turned out they agreed on very little else. When the first 1,000 acres were ready for assignment, Fryer contended that the original plans called for the Indians to be farmers only. All who took allotments were to give up their livestock. Since as late as June 2, 1935, H. C. Neuffer, who was in charge of constructing the project, reported to Collier that at Fruitland "some of the family group will tend the flocks while others will be farming," Fryer's demand in 1936 that the allottees give up their stock came as a shock to the Navajos. What shocked them even more was Fryer's decision soon after taking office to reduce the size of the allotments to 10 acres instead of the 20 acres previously agreed on. The Navajos regarded this as a breach of trust, particularly since most of the allottees had contributed labor, and some had already fenced their allotments.[90]

Fryer argued that there simply was not enough land to go around. A twenty acre tract was a commercial, not a subsistence, plot and in any case, the Navajos were incapable of farming a 20-acre tract efficiently. At a meeting with the Navajos held at Shiprock in April of 1936, he insisted that "on the Navajo Reservation there is only 28,000 acres which can be put under water, and for the allottees to insist on twenty acre allotments was greedy and took food from other needy people."[91]

The Fruitland Navajos saw their position as realistic, not selfish. Within families and clans they were perfectly willing to share, but such generosity did not extend to nonkin whom they thought did not work hard enough. To them, what Fryer was asking ignored the reality of their lives. They contended they could not live on 10 acres. They were already irrigation farmers using a smaller existing system, and they knew that alkali would form on their lands and they would need a surplus of land to replace the fields they lost. They had been promised 20 acres, and they should get it. Just as they needed farm land, they needed sheep. Their whole concept of a proper economy was a diversified economy; in the desert no one could rely on a single source of subsistence. As Allen Neskahi tried to explain to the Senate Committee on Indian Affairs: "What I want to do is put very carefully before you that our Navajo people want to have a piece of land and some flocks so that they can fall back on their sheep. If they lose their sheep they can fall back on their farm. That is what our people want and what they need. That is what I am here for and what the rest of my friends are here for." This diversified economy focused on security and balance, not efficiency and maximum annual productivity; it had been basic to the Navajos for centuries. Irrigation changed none of this. Droughts lowered water levels, canals silted up, alkalai formed; therefore, one must have something to fall back on. Fryer's concepts of efficiency and equity seemed beside the point.[92]

The result of this argument was the usual stalemate. Fruitland became one of Morgan's leading issues, and most local Navajos refused to take allotments. By the fall of 1938 only twenty-three families had taken allotments totaling 250 acres, and they suffered from community scorn and threats of witchcraft. To accomplish the occupation of the allotments the bureau recruited vigorously from outside the Fruitland area, got many returned students, and settled the new families at Fruitland. These newcomers dominated the first set of allotments. When the second section of the project, Unit II, was opened up, a compromise settlement allowed families resident in the area to take up allotments larger than 10 acres and retain some livestock. The final section, Unit III, was given to resettled families.[93]

The results were illuminating. Yields were chronically low. In 1942 Navajos obtained less than one-quarter the yield per acre of Mormon farmers cropping equivalent land just across the river, despite the fact that the Navajo irrigation system was in every way superior. Erosion cut into the fields, and fertility declined annually. Part of the problem was the Navajos' maintenance of dry-farming techniques based on shifting cultivation on permanent, irrigated tracts. Problems also resulted from the continuance of a ceremonial system that kept Navajos away from their farms at critical periods. The Navajos refused to subordinate their cultural life to rationalized production schedules. But basically the problem went back to the whole organization of Fruitland.[94]

Those units which retained functioning kin and clan networks worked the best. In Units I and III isolated families had been resettled. The kinship grouping upon which the Navajo economy depended was broken up. As a result, there was no basis for cooperation in these units, and without cooperation irrigation agriculture was impossible. Farmers did not work out plans for rotating irrigation. They tended to open their gates at the same time, with the result that those of the end of the line did not get enough water. When a farmer shut his gate without warning, he increased the flow and flooded and eroded the fields of those beneath him. What made matters worse was that the original 10-acre plots in these units did turn out to be too small. Once introduced to a wage economy by New Deal relief work, farmers found they could meet their needs better by working for white farmers than farming their own lands.

The situation on Unit II was far better. Although distrust of the government was greatest here, a framework for cooperation and organization existed since resettlement had not taken place. Here, kin groups combined their holdings to form tracts larger than 10 acres, bought tools cooperatively, and farmed more efficiently and productively. Even here, however, the government's refusal to allow kin groups full control over their land caused resentment and uneasiness that, like sheep, their land too might be taken from them. In the face of such results the government gradually abandoned its original irrigation plans. In 1948 when government officials contemplated new irrigation projects, they proposed allotments of either 40 acres of Class I land or 60 acres of Class II land for each family. The experience at Fruitland showed that simple plans to relocate stockless Navajos on irrigation projects would not work easily.[95]

As government plans went awry, officials increasingly began to focus on the big stockmen and the Morgan faction as the villains of the reservation and the real cause of Navajo suffering. Such beliefs were far easier than the analysis of Navajo society officials promised but rarely indulged in. There was no doubt that the big stockmen did control a disproportionate share of the Navajo range, but there was much room for doubt that all their operations were equatable with those of white commercial operators or that a sharp line could be drawn between their interests and those of smaller herdsmen.

When 5 large family groups alone controlled 10 percent of the reservation while 2,500 families had no stock at all, the overall distribution was obviously badly skewed. Some right-wing Anglo and Chicano politicians thought this was as it should be; in their eyes this condition simply was a reflection of the advantages skilled and industrious sheepherders had over the lazy and backward. Formalist economists later also adopted basically the same position: under market competition efficient units of production were emerging; inefficient ones were being eliminated. The conclusions of New Deal officials sprang from the same capitalist market perspective. Only their value judgments differed. The big owners were "livestock barons," a "Navajo manifestation of the centralization of capital which has visited white culture with catastrophic results." Collier easily equated such people with white opponents of the New Deal and branded them "economic royalists" even though the total income of the residence groups to which they belonged was often only $1,000 to $2,000.[96]

Such analyses were hopelessly culture-bound and contradictory. It is true that some of the biggest owners such as Chee Dodge could be equated with Anglo commercial operators, but insofar as the New Deal sought rationalization of the Navajo livestock industry, there was a certain contradiction in penalizing the most efficient operators. Collier justified such action by claiming to uphold the subsistence economy. Dodge's success, he asserted, was achieved by the pauperization of a large portion of the reservation population. That Navajo impoverishment in fact sprang from Anglo competition off the reservation and the early reductions which hurt small owners, he ignored.

Collier, however, was not really interested in maintaining a traditional subsistence economy. He wanted to create a highly efficient but small-scale market operation. He admired Dodge's methods and asked other Navajos to imitate them, but he mandated that their market rationality and efficiency should have sharp upper limits. Navajos were to act as if they had all the market qualities and ambitions of the whites save one: getting rich.[97]

Collier's plans and perceptions ignored the traditional nature of virtually all livestock operations, large and small. Dodge was an exception. Most of the big sheepmen were quite traditional and often as unoriented toward the market as their neighbors with smaller holdings. The most isolated and traditional districts, not the most accessible and acculturated ones, were precisely the areas with the most *rico* residence groups. In such districts *ricos* operated amidst all the Navajo sanctions against wealth—traditional sanctions that mandated gifts of food and aid to poor relations, not New Deal sanctions for reduction. Many impoverished Navajos actually feared attempts to reduce the big herders. The poor herded their stock on shares and received food from them when in need. Reduction threatened to deprive the impoverished of this last resource. Formalist economic concepts are no more helpful in understanding this situation. The *rico* families' commitment to production for the market and their commitment to efficient production were quite uneven. A large stockman like Many Goats who ran over 150 "useless" half-wild horses on his range was not acting like a white businessman.[98]

The result of the surveys and the decision to concentrate on reduction of the rich became apparent in the Navajo-Hopi grazing regulations which Navajo Service officials wrote in conjunction with the grazing committee appointed by the old council and issued on June 2, 1937. These regulations provided for a reduction to carrying capacity in each district. Officials were to divide the total carrying capacity of the land-management unit as determined by the range surveys by the total number of stock owners in the district to derive the base preference number, or the amount of stock each owner would possess if the livestock were divided equally. Theoretically, each owner would have to pay a grazing fee for any animal he or she possessed over the base preference number, or for any nonproductive stock the owner held, even if the herd was under the base preference number. In practice, however, the government was uninterested in grazing fees; it was interested in reduction. The new rules allowed the superintendent to issue each owner a grazing permit for a limited number of animals, the total of which would equal carrying capacity, and to remove any stock in excess of the permit number.[99]

The regulations, while clear in their intention to eliminate unproductive stock and reduce the herds to carrying capactiy, were rather vague about how the reduction would be carried out. They left much leeway to the superintendent and were relatively inoperative until necessary information had been gathered. The carrying capacities were known; ownership of sheep and goats was determined at the 1937 dipping, and in 1937, too, the government began a careful program to ascertain horse and cattle ownership. Six districts—13, 9, 11, 14, 1, and 5—were selected, and beginning with number 9, Teec-Nos-Pos, government range riders and CCC personnel held roundups to determine the ownership of and to brand all horses.[100]

Once the ownership of the animals was determined, the land-management division began to set up individual grazing quotas for each owner in the district. Range specialists tabulated the number of sheep units in herds smaller than the base preference limit. They subtracted this total from the carrying capacity of the district and divided the result by the number of owners over the base preference list. The result was the "maximum limit," or the largest herd anyone in the district could graze. Everyone over the limit would have to reduce below it. Everyone below it would not have to reduce, but neither could they raise their herd size in the future.[101]

Officials acted as if the new regulations removed all the prior inequities of the program. They would not only reduce livestock to carrying capacity, but as Walter Woehlke—his optimism restored—told newspapermen, they would achieve a fair distribution of livestock among all Navajos. Collier himself reiterated this early in 1938 when he emphasized that the regulations would largely affect the large owners who dominated far more than their just share of the range. In fact, the actual situation was far more complex. Not only did the completed 1937 figures establish in some districts maximum permit levels which were economically ridiculous (seventy-seven sheep units for Unit 4 and seventy-nine for Unit 14) and freeze the herds of many small owners at levels below subsistence, but the regulations as a whole ignored the Navajo notions of how an economy should function. They threatened to destroy the entire fabric of Navajo social and economic life in the name of preserving it.[102]

CHAPTER 13

The Navajos Become Dependent

In 1937 and 1938, as the human dependency surveys were completed, the government began to realize for the first time the diversity
and complexity of the society they were remaking. The bureau had
imposed a relatively uniform plan on a people with marked regional
differences. Three land-management units—numbers 1, 18, and
11—reveal both the extent of this diversity and the variety of ways the
government's program to reduce sheep and increase farming
threatened the Navajos.

The Navajos of unit 1, on the western edge of the reservation,
were overwhelmingly shepherds whose harsh and arid land permitted
only limited reliance on farming. Physically isolated, they were among
the most traditional and conservative of the Diné. New Deal programs
had penetrated the area, but as yet wage work was relatively slight.
Such people differed significantly from inhabitants of land management unit 18 in the southeastern corner of the reservation. There,
government and tribal building programs at the new capital of Window Rock had given the unit the largest per capita income in the
nation ($247), over half of which was derived from wage labor. These
people were probably the most acculturated of the Diné. Finally in
unit II, roughly in the physical center of the nation, the people were
also quite traditional, but here they relied on agriculture (53 percent),
not sheepherding (37 percent) or wage work (5 percent) for the bulk
of their income. In each unit the government program would mean
different things, but in each it threatened to cripple the economy of
the people.[1]

Unit I was quite poor with a per capita income of $84 a year; the government program would make it substantially poorer. Over half the unit's income came from livestock which the bureau proposed to reduce by 39 percent. The government argued that reduction would affect only 76 of 347 stockowners, but since, in practice, the bureau issued only one stock permit for each residence group, 64, or almost half, of the 143 residence groups faced reduction. The maximum herd permitted would be 213 sheep units although officials recognized that an ideal subsistence herd for the region would be 500 sheep units. To make up the loss in income, the bureau proposed increased agriculture, but in the Kaibito Plateau, with its glaring sun and constant south winds, farming was very unreliable. When crops failed, they would only fail on a larger scale and the Navajos would have fewer sheep to fall back on. The government plan defied the logic of the Navajo economy. It offered them only the equity of starving together.[2]

In unit 18 the problems were different. There, overgrazing was largely confined to the agricultural districts around St. Michaels, Fort Defiance, Manuelito, Rocky Point, and Lupton. Increasing reliance on agriculture, therefore, would only concentrate more people and their sheep in these areas. This meant that mixed farming and sheepherding in the district would have to be virtually prohibited to allow the range to recover. In effect, a diversified economy would be impossible for most residence groups. This itself represented a serious threat to the Navajos, but the government also proposed ending the wage work that already supported most of these people. The shock to the district would be a double one: the people would lose not only the traditional security the sheep-farming mixture provided but also the higher standard of living the New Deal had briefly brought them.[3]

In unit 11 reduction posed still a different threat. There, too, the population concentrated in the best agricultural lands of Round Rock, Wheatfields, Tsaile, and Lukachukai, but around them were other residence groups with much larger herds. In the district as a whole there was an inverse relationship between stockraising and agriculture. The residence groups with large herds (over 150 sheep units) did little farming, while the small and medium sized owners (50–150 sheep units) relied more heavily on agriculture. Those who owned few or no sheep (up to 50 units) mixed rug weaving, wage labor, and a smaller amount of farming to earn a living. The unit could be brought down to carrying capacity by reducing only the largest owners 25 percent, but in fact this reduction would mean severe disturbances for all residents of the district. Reduction to a maximum herd size of 185 sheep units meant that exchanges between herdsmen and farmers would virtually cease. With only 185 sheep units a residence group could supply only its own needs for meat; it would not have a surplus for exchange. Farmers could, of course, still rely on their own small herds for meat, but this would mean eating up breeding stock. And if the crops failed, there would be no surplus animals anywhere in the district to fall back on.[4]

In 1937, despite the threats reduction posed to these Navajos and those of other districts, the government still hoped that the Diné would voluntarily consent to reduce their herds. When the Navajos refused to acknowledge either the justice or the necessity of reduction, reformers who sympathized with Collier reluctantly concluded that the Navajos did not know what was best for them.[5]

That Navajo resistance to reduction had, if anything, increased since goat reduction became clear as soon as the bureau tried to obtain figures on livestock ownership. In 1937 the annual dipping for scabies, by now an accepted practice on the reservation, became an issue when the Navajos understood it would form the basis for the government's ownership lists upon which reduction would be based. Morgan, already campaigning against the land use districts, the "hand picked" council, and the prospect of further reduction, rose to the height of his popularity and power. He now supplemented his alliance with Senator Chavez and right-wing Anglos off the reservation by forming a coalition with traditional Navajo medicine men or singers, long-time targets of his abuse. Foremost among these new allies was Tall Man, a widely respected and feared singer in unit 9.[6]

The growing uneasiness over new reductions did not, however, bring about mass noncompliance with dipping. The government decided to prosecute vigorously all those who failed to dip their sheep. Although this undoubtedly lessened overt resistance, it created new martyrs. With their usual ineptitude in such matters, reservation officials allowed the Navajo police to make an illegal arrest in Gallup and severely beat their prisoners in the process. One of their victims, arrested for failing to dip his sheep, was Hosteen Tso, Morgan's brother-in-law. This arrest coupled with widespread opposition to further reduction generated extensive publicity off the reservation, particularly when Paul Palmer, Morgan's white associate, falsely telegraphed Senator Chavez of New Mexico that hundreds were in jail and that the reservation was about to rise in armed rebellion. By August, Navajo discontent and the publicity it brought had clearly put the government on the defensive.[7]

In the face of this unrest even Collier's decision to proceed cautiously and to conduct the horse roundups a district at a time instead of on a reservation wide basis could not prevent further turmoil. In unit 9 Morgan and Tall Man united to oppose the roundup. Wild rumors spread that the government planned to shoot all Navajo horses as they had shot the goats, and government workers feared violence. Resistance, however, turned out to be more passive. Many hid their horses to stop them from being branded and counted, and when the government organized voluntary sales to dispose of excess horses, the Navajos refused to sell. The horse sales were an abject failure. The government persisted. The local supervisor attended a meeting to issue grazing permits and explain the regulations, but the Navajos threw the permits on the ground and only gathered them up when the supervisor left the meeting so they could dump them in the back of his pickup truck as he drove off. As Fryer explained to officials of the Indian Rights Association, "It is rather difficult to completely educate the people when this kind of attitude is expressed."[8]

The government, as usual, attributed all resistance to Morgan's agitation and the wild rumors circulating on the reservation, but there was a legitimacy to many Navajo complaints. They were not being duped or deceived by agitators. In February of 1938 Fryer met with Morgan, Palmer, and a group of headmen, including Tall Man, from the northeastern reservation. How, they wanted to know, could the Navajos live under the new regulations? Their holdings would be so small that the people could not kill enough sheep to eat and still maintain the herds. Sheep were their livelihood; they depended on them. The plan to reduce horses was also unfair. Large families needed numerous horses, and all many poor families had left after the early reductions were horses. They not only rode them; they ate them. The government seemed intent on reducing them to poverty. If this occurred, how, with their growing numbers, could they live?[9]

Many of the headmen's points were well taken. The only standard for the number of horses a family could retain was the condition of the range. In some districts four might be allowed, in others ten. The government correctly stressed that some Navajos still kept large herds for their prestige value, but it slighted the many Navajos who owned much smaller numbers of horses which they needed to survive in a reservation of vast distances and few roads. James Downs in his study of Navajo animal husbandry in the early 1960s pointed out that not all Navajo horses were available for use at a given time. Pregnant mares or those with foals, injured animals, young unbroken animals, all might count toward the quota but were useless. And beyond this, the Navajo herding practices which let the horses graze freely put other animals out of immediate reach. To get the minimum of two usable teams, families needed a total of more than four horses.[10]

Voluntary reduction had once more proven to be a failure, but Collier and Fryer believed that force would not work if applied to the reservation as a whole, and they resisted the increasing Soil Conservation Service pressure for immediate drastic reduction. Instead they continued to advocate gradual, district-by-district reductions. Excess horses would have to be removed ten days after the government issued permits in a district, but sheep reduction would be postponed until October 1, 1938.[11]

Collier returned to the reservation in January of 1938 to seek consent for the new program from the provisional Navajo council in session in Window Rock. In a way it was a quixotic gesture; the "hand picked" council was under nearly as much attack as reduction, and Morgan's followers boycotted the meeting. Nonetheless, using the same tactics which had worked so well in the past, Collier, obtained council approval for the new regulations. Chee Dodge had suggested a test case to ascertain the legality of the regulations, a course of action which Fryer approved, but Collier cautioned against it. He told the council they had two choices: approve the new regulations, or be put under the far harsher General Grazing Regulations for Indian Lands. Even if they successfully challenged the Navajo-Hopi regulations in court, he told them, the end result would be the application of the general regulations. Regulation and reduction would take place no matter what they did; only the severity would vary. Predictably, the council agreed to cooperate and appoint a grazing committee to consult with the government on modifying existing regulations, and they unanimously passed a resolution approving of efforts to remove "excess" horses.[12]

It is doubtful whether this council consent to the grazing program was either real or meaningful. As usual, the council acted under duress, and Fryer's explanation of horse reduction was very deceptive. In his presentation to the council Fryer had used unit 1 as an example. Here, the maximum number of horses allowed for a family was ten; Fryer did not indicate that other districts might have smaller quotas. When the council debated horse reduction, therefore, they focused on the number ten. This, most councilmen agreed, was the minimum number a family needed, but people with large families needed more. Some argued for fifteen horses a family; others argued for twenty. When they passed the resolution with its vague approval of reducing "excess" horses, they had no idea that the range management reports in some districts considered family horse herds of more than four or five animals excessive.[13]

Even as Collier sought council cooperation, he was backing off from the original plan for a new constitution and council. Oliver La Farge, the novelist and anthropologist whom Collier had persuaded to examine the entire situation on the reservation, had urged him to postpone action on the constitution and instead concentrate on a new election code to provide means for selecting a new council. By July the code was complete and approved by Taliman on behalf of the Navajo council and by Secretary of the Interior Ickes. The roots of this change in policy, which amounted to a significant concession to Morgan, dated back to the summer of 1937.[14]

That summer, during his visit to the reservation, La Farge had met with Morgan and came away believing that he might cooperate with the government. Morgan, La Farge insisted, did not oppose reduction per se, only the bureau's methods. Shortly afterward, in August of 1937, Fryer and Morgan met, and Morgan admitted the need for range management of some kind. He indicated that if the new tribal council and tribal chairman were elected by popular vote, he would back the program.[15]

Collier's abandonment of plans for a new constitution brought further moderation of Morgan's activities in 1938. At a private meeting held just after the council session he boycotted, he tentatively expressed a willingness to cooperate with the government, but his distrust had not vanished. When the new election code was issued, Morgan objected, protesting that supervision of the voting by land-management officials was an invitation to fraud. Nonetheless, elections proceeded, and Morgan's followers participated. Morgan won the chairmanship by a landslide. His election did not particularly disturb Fryer. Although Morgan lived adjacent to rather than on the reservation and was thus technically ineligible for office, Fryer recommended against disqualifying him. Morgan, he cautioned, would be far less dangerous as chairman of the council than as "a frustrated raving maniac on the outside." He could be reasoned with and flattered. To win Morgan was to lose Dodge, Fryer admitted, but Dodge would be lost anyway as soon as his interests were threatened. Fryer's assessment of both Morgan's and Dodge's future course was prophetic.[16]

Even as signs of a reconciliation between Morgan and the bureau mounted, the horse reduction remained stalled. The target districts refused to cooperate. Rumors were rampant. Navajos would be allowed only ten sheep each; the army was going to seize the reservation; Congress would suspend the regulations. As Fryer recognized, Dodge was moving back into opposition. He asked for a delay in reduction in February, before denouncing the whole plan as unfair and unworkable in a letter to Collier in late August. The Navajos, he asserted, could not live under Collier's plan. Collier in turn blamed the problem on Dodge and the 200 "big Navajo stockmen operating like yourself on a commercial scale."[17]

What gave Dodge's claims additional credence in 1938 was that the CCC programs that had given the Navajos so much wage income were being drastically cut back just when the heaviest reductions in livestock were contemplated. The government sliced CCC funding from $1,225,000 in 1937 to $600,000 in 1938 and mandated that one enrollee be employed for every $920 received. This allowed only a meager investment in equipment and supervisory personnel. To comply with the new guidelines and funding, Fryer cut his work force in half, abandoned many projects, and used many of his remaining employees largely for maintenance work. He concentrated virtually all of his new projects in units 10 and 11 because of the possibilities for subsistence farm development there, despite protests from Navajos elsewhere on the reservation that they were being neglected. These cuts were not restored, and CCC payrolls declined steadily until the demise of the corps on the reservation in 1942.[18]

The sharp curtailment of the CCC was only the first blow. In 1938 the Soil Conservation Service also began severe retrenchments on the reservation. By 1939 the expenditures of the Service had, according to Collier, declined from nearly $500,000 a year to a proposed $12,000 for fiscal year 1940–41. The total deficit in wages paid to Navajos in 1939 measured against the peak year was nearly $750,000. As reduction proceeded, the Navajos would be losing not one but two mainstays of their depression economy.[19]

Only one step was made toward enforcing meaningful stock reduction in 1938, and it involved a return to coercion. Faced with failure of voluntary sales, the Navajo Service had to choose between abandoning the program until Navajos were ready to cooperate or resorting to compulsion. Discussion continued for months until a consensus was reached that it was the large stockowners who were blocking the program and that "federal court action would clarify the situation and greatly weaken the political opposition to the enforcement of grazing regulations." Officials selected twelve cases, and the government filed injunction suits in the United States District Court in Phoenix to force thirty defendants to reduce the number of their horses. Collier claimed such suits would prove to the Navajos that the Navajo Service had both the power and the will to act. He insisted that this action was not the beginning of a policy of coercion, however. He merely wanted to show the Navajos he could club them into compliance; once he possessed the club he would lock it up and proceed by education and negotiation. Stock reduction came to a virtual halt while the cases progressed.[20]

During this renewed pause in reduction, the rapprochement between the government and Morgan continued. The publicity about turmoil on the reservation and the attacks on Collier by old line Indian reform groups had led to an independent investigation of conditions among the Navajos by Thomas Jesse Jones, educational director of the Phelps-Stokes fund, an organization dedicated to the improvement of race relations. His report, issued in 1939, commended the government's intentions while lamenting its excesses. The investigators blamed much of the resistance on large owners. Overall, they thought that "if the antagonisms which [had] resulted from the early errors and misunderstandings and from much subsequent propaganda could be removed, the problem of reduction would not be too difficult."[21]

As it stood in the report, this sentence might seem only a bland little homily. Jones, however, meant it as more than a platitude. He had known Morgan when the new chairman had studied at Hampton Institute, and he arranged new meetings between Morgan and Fryer in March of 1939. The two found that there was much they agreed on in their mutual concern with health, education, and economic development on the reservation. In Fryer's eyes, Morgan evolved from that "raving lunatic" to "one of the most responsible and intelligent of all the Navajo leaders with whom I . . . worked."[22]

The depth of this reconciliation became evident in the spring of 1939 when on May 13 the United States District Court in Phoenix ruled in favor of the government in the grazing cases and ordered the United States marshals to seize the horses if they were not removed within thirty days. News of the decision reverberated through the reservation. The ruling came just days before the opening on May 15 of a tribal council meeting where most Navajos believed Morgan would lead the opposition to the decision. He, as it turned out, did no such thing.[23]

The court decision clearly surprised and shocked the Navajos. To the councilmen it seemed gratuitous. Their bewilderment was evident in the questions they asked William Barker, the special assistant to the attorney general who had prosecuted the case. Who had brought the case to court? How could anyone who knew the Indians' condition bring such a case? Why were such regulations made? How, as Kit Seally (a singer and delegate from unit 9) asked, could the government want to take "the sheep, which is our heart, and the horse, which is our head, and goat, which is our tongue?" It was, he thought, because whites wanted to destroy his people and take the reservation "because of some valuable minerals that may be inside the land." Howard Gorman and other educated councilmen pressed Barker on violations of the treaty guarantee "to use and to occupy," but Kizie Yazzie Begay, one of the defendants in the suit, merely expressed his bewilderment at his prosecution for rules he could neither read nor understand, and a decision against him when he had never been able to say a word in his own defense. The whites clearly did not recognize what they had done. "It is only starvation for us."[24]

Morgan, for the most part, listened to the questions. When he spoke, he said he thought the decision unjust, but what followed was hardly a call to resistance. The lesson he drew was the need for education. "If 75% of our people had been educated, we would have been able to fight."[25]

Once the council grasped the impact and the immediacy of the decision—enforcement by marshals within 30 days unless a postponement was secured—Fryer stepped forward to explain once more how reduction would work. He offered the council a resolution approving the elimination of nonproductive stock which the court decision had made clear would now go forward no matter what the council did. The bait attached to the resolution was a promise that reduction in 1939 would be limited to horses. Discussion of the poorly understood regulations differed only slightly from that of preceding years. The Navajos emphasized the sheep they needed to survive; Fryer emphasized the limits of the range.[26]

Opposition to the resolution surfaced immediately, and the council voted to lay the resolution aside until they could consult their attorney on the prospects of an appeal. Guy Axeline, the attorney for the defendants in the case, then appeared before the council, and he too explained the decision. The grazing regulations stood and had the force of law. He was not encouraging about the prospects of an appeal. James Stewart, the land director of the Washington office, seized on Axeline's comments to point out to the Navajos that although the regulation stood whether they approved the resolution or not, they could by passing the resolution restrict the first year's reduction to nonproductive stock. On the final day of the session, the council passed a revised resolution supporting horse reduction and pledging support to the district supervisors in the implementation of the permit system. The standard scenario had been enacted once more; the government had framed the question so that the council did not choose between reduction and no reduction, but rather between immediate full application of grazing regulations with all the rigor the law allowed and a partial application with initially only limited reduction. The council's choice of a partial application for 1939 was then publicized by the government as support of the entire program.[27]

Fryer renewed the horse roundups almost immediately. Reaction over the reservation varied, but the court decision, coupled with Morgan's and the council's capitulation, vitiated effective resistance.

Navajos protested that renewed drought made their horses more necessary than ever and denounced their councilmen for voting for a reduction, but they complied. The low prices paid for the horses and the slaughter of many of them only increased their anger and resentment. By the end of the drive in 1939, 14,000 horses or one-quarter of all those the Navajos owned, had been sold, most for between two and four dollars a head. The government had met concerted resistance in only two northern districts, units 9 and 12. Unit 9, Teec-Nos-Pos, one of the original districts targeted for horse reduction, was isolated and strongly traditional with a history of active opposition to the government. Unit 12, centered on Shiprock, was far more acculturated and had previously been one of Morgan's main centers of support.[28]

In these districts the government resorted to the tribal courts to punish the resisters, and apparently some people who refused to have their horses rounded up and branded were jailed. In at least one instance the result of such enforcement was violence. In January of 1940 the trial of Kitty Black Horse and three others for refusing to brand their horses ended in an uproar when Black Horse and his sons disrupted the trial and armed supporters invaded the court. Black Horse himself escaped and went into hiding.[29]

When tribal courts failed to secure reduction, Fryer took the cases into the federal courts of Utah and Arizona. The government decided to single out the leaders of resistance for prosecution. None of them were large stockowners; most grazed from 200 to 600 sheep units. These were men who could live on their existing herds but who, if the government succeeded in reducing unit 9 to its maximum herd limit of 83 sheep units, would be forced below subsistence. Fryer admitted that from the "standpoint of equity" cases against these men would be hard to try, but he nonetheless considered them critical in the movement from *laissez faire* to conservation. The Arizona cases were filed in Phoenix on June 28, 1940, and went to trial in September, despite attempts by an armed band of Navajos to prevent the serving of notices to the defendants. The court decided in favor of the government, upholding reduction once more. When the defendants still refused to comply, the government instituted contempt proceedings.[30]

Although one defendant, councilman Kit Seally, then paid a fine,

Fryer suspected that he and other defendants still retained un-branded horses hidden on the range. The federal suit in Utah was delayed longer than the Arizona suit because the defendants went into hiding, but when the trial commenced in February of 1941, the ruling was the same. Reduction was upheld; the Navajos would have to reduce their excess stock.[31]

The prolonged resistance to horse reduction in units 9 and 12 quickly merged with the more widespread resistance that arose with the issuing of grazing permits elsewhere on the reservation during 1940. Fryer hoped to forestall opposition by promising no reduction in productive stock until the fall of 1941 if the Navajos accepted the permits. The idea was to create a "breathing spell" to allow the small owners who had sold horses to replace them with an equivalent number of sheep, preferably by buying them from the large owners.[32]

The permits, however, only created fear, confusion, and resent-ment. Many Navajos tried to avoid the employees who delivered them; others, including some councilmen, refused to accept them; still others burned them or threw them away. A whole new protest movement, at first diffuse and leaderless, began to gather strength.[33]

The new protesters now regarded Morgan as a traitor in the pay of the government. He reinforced such perceptions with his attempts to quiet the troubles around Shiprock, his denunciations of local pro-test leaders, and a proreduction speech he made over the radio in 1940. The movement was new only in that it was anti-Morgan instead of pro-Morgan; otherwise, its opposition to grazing regulations, per-mits, reduction, and grazing districts echoed older positions.[34]

The widespread opposition to the grazing permits left the coun-cilmen in an embarrassing position since a year earlier they had en-dorsed the permit system and promised to help in its acceptance. They had then, of course, in the usual manner of the council, re-turned home to denounce these same permits. At the next council meeting in June of 1940 many members denied they had ever offered to cooperate in issuing permits despite the passage of a resolution to that effect at the previous meeting.[35]

In the eyes of the councilmen, their constantly shifting position was not duplicity. As Tsehe Nota from unit 18 explained, it was all the government's fault: "Who calls the Council in and who proposed different things? It is the government who calls the Council in and lays down the program for the Council and the Council acts on these and approves a lot of things on account of that, and the government is to blame for all this. . . . We have not as yet made plans for our own people. It has always been the government making plans for us."[36] Tsehe Nota's position had much merit. It reflected the Navajo's concept of the council as a mere auxiliary of Washington, not as a Navajo governing body. The council never made real choices; the program would always go forward no matter what they did; their consent to programs was only a means of postponing more drastic action.

In the June meeting the council engaged in the usual ritual denunciation of the government program: the maximum herd sizes were too low, a family could not be supported on them; freezing small herders where they stood in 1937 was unfair; the grazing districts broke up traditional grazing lands; differences between districts were inequitable. How could they live? Once more they tried to persuade officials that the reduction threatened their very existence. The drought had brought suffering to the pinon country around Navajo Mountain, and relief supplies had been provided. But what would happen when there was no relief money and their stock had been taken away? Then when drought struck they would starve. When they were through, they voted 56–0 to renew their support for the issuance of grazing licenses. Even Kit Seally—soon to be prosecuted for his failure to reduce his horses—voted for it.[37]

The vote no more signified a commitment to reduction than had earlier ones; the Navajos indeed had more reason than ever to be fearful of the ultimate consequences of reduction. The relief supplies mentioned in the council debate were a result of the drought that had hit the reservation and deprived the Navajos of approximately one-half their 1939 corn crop. The government, despite allegations they were letting Navajos starve, had stepped in with relief that Fryer estimated would run at about $125,000, enough to provide over 2,500 families with basic foodstuffs for eight months. What had appalled the council was not the failure of aid, but the need for it. What good was increased agricultural land in a drought? The government reservoirs dried up, and floodwater irrigation failed. The Navajos then had to rely on their stock, but their stock was being taken away. They would soon be reduced either to abject dependence on the government or to starvation.[38]

The future seemed uncertain and dangerous to the Navajos, and even Fryer admitted that such a view was justified by the new economic conditions on the reservation. Fryer would later concede that the cuts in appropriations which had nearly halted the irrigation program and severely restricted Navajo employment left no livelihood for those Navajos who had lost their sheep. Morris Burge, a field representative for the American Association of Indian Affairs, visited the reservation in the summer of 1940 and stated the case even more strongly. With Navajo population rising and the stock permit system beginning to function, "more and more young Navajos will be left without sheep, and face a bleak and hopeless future." Since wage work had already dropped off, and any increase in income from range improvement would take years, the result would be the steady pauperization of the nation.[39]

The government plans, according to the American Association on Indian Affairs report released the next year, were not working. Farming was not supporting the people who were losing their stock; they were dependent upon the remnants of the wage work programs and direct relief. Nearly half the tribe was no longer supported by either farming or livestock. The result was an impasse. "If the vast majority of Navajo families were allowed to run flocks of sheep on the reservation large enough to ensure subsistence, the reservation would be destroyed, but no adequate substitute has yet been found to replace this means of livelihood."[40]

As government programs failed, unrest continued. New arrests springing from the Kitty Black Horse incident of January created more turmoil in July, which was publicized by a new right-wing, Anglo ally of the Navajo protesters, newspaper publisher George Bowra of Aztec. Morgan distanced himself even further from the resisters by denouncing all the protesters as "stubborn and dissatisfied" people who refused to abide by council decisions.[41]

By fall a new organization began to take form. Former tribal chairman Dashne Cheschillege organized the Navajo Livestock Owners Association, which was almost immediately transmuted into the Navajo Rights Association (NRA). The new group, committed to fighting reduction in the courts, gained immediate support in units 9 and 12 by enlisting Robert Martin, Morgan's old lieutenant, and Kit Seally, the medicine man and councilman from unit 9. In the western part of the reservation, however, many felt Martin and his associate Peter Begay were too headstrong and unstable. They talked about turning to Chee Dodge for leadership. Dodge was quite willing to cooperate with Dashne Cheschillege's group, and by winter they had begun to collaborate.[42]

Dodge's active opposition did not surprise Fryer; he attributed it to a conspiracy of large owners, but Dodge's plans frightened Fryer badly. Dodge intended to get an injunction against the government to halt the livestock program issued in the name of a medium sized owner who owned about 200 sheep units and had a large family in unit 14, where the maximum herd limit was then set at between 74 and 80 sheep units. Using such a person in a test case, Dodge and the Navajo Rights Association could contend that enforcement of the grazing regulations "would force privation on a large proportion of the Navajo population." The range, they would assert, was not as badly overgrazed as the government claimed. At the very least, Fryer feared Dodge's move would lead to a lengthy judicial examination of the range surveys, which could delay the conservation program indefinitely.[43]

The spring of 1941 was the ideal time to file such a suit. The drought had broken, and by February abundant rain and snow had turned the reservation into a bog. The Navajos expected more grass in 1941 than had been available in thirty years. Accordingly, the Navajo Rights Association proposed that, because of the abundant forage and the emergency brought on by the advent of war in Europe, the reduction scheduled for December 1 be postponed.[44]

The government countered with a dual strategy of its own and decided to go to court ahead of Dodge. The government would file suit in New Mexico against the largest owners in units 12 and 13 and thus avoid the embarrassment involved in arguing for reduction of an already small herdsman in a district with impossibly low limits. In addition, Woehlke advised Collier to postpone the reduction scheduled for December 1, 1941, by proclaiming a temporary special limit of 500 sheep. With abundant grass on the reservation, reduction would be even harder, particularly since irrigation development had virtually halted and left the government with no economic alternatives to present to the Navajos. If the government raised the limit, attention could be confined to the 110 owners with livestock in excess of 500 sheep units, and discontent might be minimized.[45]

The government, of course, did not wish to admit that the post-ponement was their reaction to an NRA proposal. Fryer accordingly suggested that the special limit be proposed by Morgan and Gorman as their own plan during a trip to Washington. That way "Morgan could return as a great leader who has accomplished things for his people, especially for the small owners," and Dodge and the NRA could be denied any credit for prompting the action.[46]

Lack of enthusiasm in the Justice Department for further suits against the Navajos caused Collier to drop plans for immediate legal action, but the second part of the plan was put into motion. The special limit was revised downward from Woehlke's original 500 to 350 sheep units for 1941 and 300 for 1942, a move which increased the number of owners affected to 272 in 1941, and 396 in 1942. This still allowed the removal of 77,000 sheep units from the larger owners over two years. Late in February Morgan and Gorman presented the proposal to Collier, who approved it subject to consent of the department's solicitor and Secretary Ickes.[47]

In April, at the next meeting of the Tribal Council, Morgan had the special-permit plan proposed as a council resolution and thus created an even greater illusion of official Navajo participation. Op-position was immediate. Kit Seally pointed out that this was only a temporary postponement and "we have seen in the past that just by having accepted such resolutions we have been deprived of our live-stock." Another councilman demanded abolition of the grazing reg-ulations. As usual in such debates Fryer pointed out that this was not possible. The choice was between a temporary alleviation of reduction and immediate reduction. When Bazhaloni Bikis, who owned 400 sheep, complained that people could not live on the 72 sheep units allowed by permits in his district, Collier, who was in attendance, intervened to tell him that the vast majority of Navajos get along on less.[48] Bazhaloni Bikis retorted: "I know the circumstances and how they get along, and that is they are people who come to us and ask us if we could not spare some meat. These people who have 70 sheep or up to 100 are hard up and are living on the doles of the govern-ment."[49]

Approval of the special limit now left officials free to concentrate on those who still had not complied with horse reduction, the larger owners and the protest organizations. This opposition was hardly united; indeed, in the spring and summer of 1941 it was rapidly factionalizing. The NRA, at least in its announced program, was a surprisingly moderate organization. Its leadership admitted the reservation was overgrazed but demanded that the government assist the Navajos in growing feed on irrigated lands instead of forcing reduction and consult with the Navajos more effectively before making major policy changes. Following the council's adjournment, the NRA held meetings in the northeastern reservation to denounce both the grazing program and the council and to collect money for sending a delegation to Washington. Fryer worried that such a delegation might be accorded official recognition by government officials, but as it turned out, another delegation led by an ex-missionary and reservation eccentric, Shine Smith, got the recognition and the publicity. Smith's group of backcountry Navajos—none of whom were previously prominent leaders—met with Ickes, Chavez, and others. And they were soon joined by another delegation from Shiprock led by Sam Ahkeah, a young Navajo leader who would eventually be tribal chairman. Both delegations met with Eleanor Roosevelt. That so many groups of Navajos were separately organizing delegations to Washington did not bode well for future unity.[50]

Opposition within the reservation itself threatened to be far more violent than within the delegations to Washington. On their return, one group supposedly held a meeting and asked for a vote on how many were willing to take up arms against Washington, but there were more overt acts of resistance than this. Once more some Navajos refused to dip their sheep; so their stock could not be counted.

In June an armed band of Navajos gathered near Aneth and camped on Montezuma Creek. They had come together to resist the serving of warrants for Selective Service evaders. The draft was unpopular on the reservation; as one Navajo had contemptuously declared at an NRA meeting, the government, not satisfied with reducing their livestock, now intended to reduce their young men. Nothing came of this protest, but in July fifteen Indians near Navajo Mountain attacked two government employees and forcibly removed a herd of unbranded horses they were holding for identification. Reports from the reservation now seriously mentioned the possibility of armed resistance. Both Fryer and Lucy Adams, the Bureau of Indian Affairs education director for the reservation, urged firmness and a demonstration of force in the Aneth and Navajo Mountain regions.[51]

After the Navajo Mountain attack, Fryer entered the area with a Captain Johnson, apparently a uniformed army officer. Fryer hoped that the mere presence of a soldier would lead the Navajos to conclude that, just as in the days of the Long Walk, the military might be brought against them. Johnson told the Indians that further resistance would only bring in the police or even troops, who would certainly shoot whatever horses they could not catch. The Indians responded to this threat by bringing in for branding the number of horses they were allowed under their permits and hiding the remainder in the canyons.[52]

Still, by early August Fryer thought the worst was over. Convictions of grazing violaters in federal and tribal courts seemed to be breaking resistance in the northern strip. At Shiprock convictions had induced leaders to bring in their horses, and only the people of Aneth, Navajo Mountain, and the north fringe of Monument Valley held out. There was little unity in their efforts. On August 8, Fryer took advantage of the increasing factionalism among Navajo opponents of reduction to attend an NRA meeting at Kayenta where he spoke for 2½ hours. The Indians were divided and disheartened by the arrests of their leaders, and Fryer thought the meeting was a turning point. They would at this point he thought, reduce their horses and their sheep. Even Navajo Mountain and Aneth would cooperate.[53]

Despite Fryer's mounting optimism that the Navajos had been coerced into compliance, Walter Woehlke and Collier now began to draw back from enforcing the 350 sheep-unit limit. The reservation was still 160,000 sheep units over capacity, but early frosts had killed the corn and thus increased the Navajo need for livestock, and the range was in better shape than virtually anyone could remember. Perhaps there was no need to push reduction immediately. Lorenzo Hubbell, the most prominent trader on the reservation, wrote Collier urging delay. Even Ward Shepard, a forester whom Collier consulted, agreed that reduction was not immediately necessary. The abundant grass that the rains had brought had gone to seed. Once the grass had seeded, Shepard explained, there was no need to preserve the plant; indeed not to graze it would be a waste. Woehlke suggested a compromise. The big owners would not have to reduce their flocks, only pay a grazing fee for each unit over 350.[54]

Collier, for the first time since reduction had begun, hesitated. Deciding on a new investigation, he asked Zeh, whose report of more than a decade before had helped spur reduction, and Frank Lenzie, another forester, to visit the reservation. It did not seem fair, Collier thought, to freeze the small owners at the ridiculously low levels of their 1937 flocks nor to deny the big owners the right to give their children the usual gifts of sheep without impoverishing themselves. He asked them for "something which would save the range and yet be less implacable, less emotionally hard on the Navajos then the existent plan."[55]

Zeh and Lenzie submitted their report a month later. Since it was also signed by Fryer, the head of the socioeconomic surveys, Solon Kimball, and range examiner Lyle Young, Zeh and Lenzie had presumably worked in conjunction with these reservation officials. They reported the Navajos "reconciled" to reduction and blamed unrest on the NRA, but they thought much discontent could be dissipated by a few reforms of the grazing regulations. They suggested that 350 sheep units be established as the maximum herd limit; that no further reductions take place after December 1; that the smaller owners be allowed to acquire some additional stock; and that means be created by making grazing permits transferable for young married couples to acquire livestock. Under no circumstances, however, should the reduction to 350 head by December 1, be postponed.[56]

Reduction did go forward. Chee Dodge and some other owners sold the excess stock in their once large herds outright. Hosteen Yazzi Jesus, the largest owner on the eastern reservation, arranged to buy or lease lands off the reservation, as did three other large outfits. Other owners distributed their stock on shares to Navajos in the checkerboard, but only a few gave their stock on shares to those small operators who had room on their permits because of their sale of horses. Fryer was elated; except for units 4 and 12, reduction was substantially complete.[57]

In 1942 Collier issued special permits which incorporated the suggestions made in the Zeh report. The 350 sheep unit maximum limit was not made universal, but it was applied to those districts whose existing limits were very low—units 4, 9, 12, 14, and 15 (the previous permit size in these districts ranged from 61 to 104 sheep units). The other districts were still required to reduce to the earlier maximum limits.[58]

The advent of World War II made the last years of livestock reduction at once possible and anticlimatic. Resistance never ceased. The Navajos elected Chee Dodge and Sam Ahkeah as chairman and vice-chairman of the Navajo Tribal Council in 1942. Morgan was not even nominated by his home district of Shiprock. Under Dodge the council actively sought to vitiate reduction by indefinitely extending the special permit limits of 350 for the whole reservation and thus allowing small owners to rebuild their herds above permit size, and by abolishing the demonstration areas. The council passed resolutions to this effect in 1942 and in 1943, Collier vetoed all of them. In 1943 and 1945, after the pause brought by the special permits, the government renewed its efforts to bring livestock numbers down to the required numbers and began making periodic cuts in special permit numbers. The government again prosecuted violaters in 1944 and again there was scattered violent resistance, most notably the kidnapping and beating of a district supervisor in unit 9. Among those eventually arrested and imprisoned for this was a tribal councilman. Although several districts remained badly overstocked, the amount of livestock on the reservation as a whole had by 1945 fallen below carrying capacity.[59]

Reduction continued without pauperizing the Navajos only because World War II provided unprecedented demands for Navajo labor. Approximately 3,000 Navajos fought in the war, and by 1945 another 10,000 were employed in war work of various types; others supplied labor on the railroads and became migrant agricultural workers. Wage work at this point now replaced sheepherding and agriculture as the major source of Navajo livelihood.[60]

The Navajos did not feel the full consequences of reduction until the war ended and the veterans and workers returned. Then there were few jobs and few sheep; annual family income plummetted from its high of $1,200 in 1945 to $400 in 1947, and the relief load on the reservation increased enormously. Once more the Tribal Council attacked grazing regulations and threatened to challenge them in court. There was no need to; the tribal attorney convinced the secretary of the interior that the mechanism for enforcement was illegal, and the punitive trespass provisions were suspended in 1948. The government then gave the Navajos themselves the chance to administer their own range management program and to revise the existing regulations to meet their own long standing objections. The Bureau of In-

Table 8. Sources of Navajo Income

Category	1936	1940	1958 (est.)
Livestock and agriculture	54%	58%	10%
Arts and crafts	6	9	1
Wages	34	30	68
Miscellaneous	6	3	0
Mineral leases			5
Welfare, benefits, railroad retirement			16

SOURCE: David H. Aberle, *The Peyote Religion among the Navajo*, Viking Fund Publications in Anthropology, no. 42 (New York: Wenner Gren Foundation for Anthropological Research, 1966), p.81.

dian Affairs did not, of course, relinquish control completely. It retained the right to veto any objectionable provisions the Navajos might insert in the regulations. The original deadline for revision was July 1, 1949, but the issue touched so deeply on Navajo fears and concerns that no quick resolution was possible. Not until 1956 was a mutually agreeable set of regulations established.[61]

By 1945 the government had transformed the Navajo economy. The Diné no longer relied on subsistence agriculture and livestock raising for the bulk of their income. They were no longer self-supporting people. Their reliance on wage labor and welfare increased throughout the 1950s. The Navajos had become dependent (see Table 8).

Stock reduction ultimately neither restored the lands of the reservation, revitalized the Navajo livestock economy, nor made the Navajos a predominantly farming people—all developments promised at one time or another by the government. Instead, it made them wage earners and welfare recipients—people who sold their labor and who operated increasingly in a cash economy rather than the older economy of credit, reciprocity, and redistribution, but people who nonetheless retained a partial subsistence base in sheep and agriculture. As a result the 1950s was a transitional period in which the people of some areas assimilated wage work into older ways of life, while the inhabitants of other regions drastically rearranged their lives to meet the demands of the market and to relieve the stresses reduction had brought. The changes that wage work, reduction, and development of the reservation wrought in the 1950s set in motion far more drastic changes in the 1960s and 1970s. Once the traditional economy was broken and the Navajos, no longer able to support themselves, were pushed into the market and onto welfare, development of other resources, no matter what the cost, became inevitable. The Navajo reservation today remains overgrazed, but on the reservation stripmining, radioactive rivers, and mines which cause cancer dwarf overgrazing as an environmental problem.

The population of the Navajos has doubled again since the 1930s, and Indian Service officials have insisted that their problem was always Malthusian: too many people pressing against too few resources. Such an interpretation abstracts the Navajo dilemma, however, and pulls it from its historic context. Overpopulation is meaningful only in comparison to a resource base. "Too many people" means too many people for existing resources and services. Navajo population was growing rapidly, but what is more significant is that Navajo resources were shrinking rapidly. By the 1930s the Navajo country had largely been confined to the Navajo reservation, a situation for which there was no historic parallel except for the confinement during the Long Walk period.

Comparing Navajo growth to the growth of the population in New Mexico and Arizona reveals the extent to which growth rates per se are an abstraction and disguise the issue of resource distribution. Between 1860 and 1930 Navajo population roughly quadrupled, rising from 10,000 people to approximately 40,000 people. During that same period the total population of Arizona rose by a factor of 67 from 6, 482 people to 435,573, while the total population of New Mexico increased from 61,547 to 423,317 or by roughly a factor of 7. No one, however, argued that Anglos or Chicanos in New Mexico had a problem of overpopulation. Non-Indians could secure adequate resources. They obtained part of them by commandeering traditional

Navajo grazing lands and water holes which forced the growing Navajo population to subsist on a severely restricted land base. The allocation of power and resources was more significant than population growth per se.

The Indian bureau itself recognized in its plans for reservation expansion the problem of dwindling Navajo resources but eventually recognized also that politically this expansion was impossible. Accordingly officials began to emphasize the growth in population as the real source of the problems facing the Navajos, while the Navajos emphasized the loss of land. More than mere biology was at work here; politics and power relations were crucial.

If nothing else demonstrated the political and colonial elements of the Navajo situation, the roots of reduction in the concern over Boulder Dam should. This was what gave livestock reduction its urgency. Livestock reduction has taken place on virtually all federal lands in the twentieth century, but the Navajo experience stands apart. On national forest lands, for instance, an economic interest group (livestock raisers) had to give up a virtual monopoly of resource use in the face of competing demands and the rise of bureaucratic planning. A whole culture was not threatened, however, nor was reduction precipitous; it averaged about 2 percent a year between 1908 and the mid-1950s and resulted in a net reduction of 40 percent in the number of sheep units grazing on national forest lands over half a century. In the Navajo case, when the whole economy of a people and a way of life was at stake, reduction was far more drastic and cut Navajo livestock on the reservation from 1,053,498 sheep units in 1933 to 449,000 sheep units in 1946 when active reduction ended, a decline of 57 percent in slightly more than a decade. The sincere belief of men like John Collier and E. R. Fryer that the existence of the Navajos themselves was at stake, still does not erase the origins of the program in the concern for Boulder Dam.[62]

Boulder Dam meant nothing to the Navajos; they received no benefits from it. It was a development program geared entirely to the larger society of which the Navajos were a colonial appendage. Yet the Navajos appeared to endanger the program because soil which eroded from their lands could fill in Lake Mead, the immense reservoir behind the dam. Another of the many ironies of stock reduction is that scientists themselves abandoned this simple version of the erosion problem. Overgrazing certainly aggravated the erosion cycle in the Southwest, but it did not cause it. By the 1930s, as stock reduction and range management got underway, gullying appears to have already been declining all over the region, both on lands where active measures had been taken to halt it and on untreated lands. By the 1950s, although 5 percent of the Lake Mead reservoir had already silted up, scientists were far more hesitant in attributing blame for the siltation than their colleagues in the 1930s. As Luna Leopold wrote in 1956: "The allocation of the sediment to various portions of the upper Colorado Basin can be made only roughly, and it is virtually impossible to ascertain what percentage of the measured sediment yield can be attributed to effects of land use."[63]

A new series of dams funded during the 1950s, including the Glen Canyon and Navajo dams, were designed, in part, to control siltation; emphasis on range management was relaxed. It was during this period that the government allowed the Navajo herds to increase far over carrying capacity once more. By the 1970s the rate of siltation in Lake Mead had indeed declined, but to attribute this to stock reduction when the Navajo reservation continued to be severely overgrazed and overstocked seems unwarranted.

The government had failed to restore the Navajo range, but this is a minimal statement of its failures. Coming to the Navajos with a program promising economic rehabilitation, Collier had crippled their way of life and accelerated the onset of dependency. Advocating Indian rule, the Bureau of Indian Affairs instead dictated policy. And in an administration best remembered for its championing of civil and cultural freedom for Indians, the Navajos felt the coercive power of the government to an extent unequaled since the Long Walk. That all of this had been done in the name of conservation did not make it any less disastrous and selfserving. The Navajos knew this. Few stated the consequences of stock reduction more eloquently than an anonymous Navajo in the mid-1950s:

That is the way we were treated. A great number of the people's livestock was taken away. Although we were told that it was to restore the land, the fact remains that hunger and poverty stood with their mouths open to devour us. Before the stock that remained could reproduce, people slit the animal's throats to satisfy

Conclusion

Early colonists and administrators in America rarely wondered why the peoples they conquered and colonized starved. The answer, to them, seemed all too apparent. They starved because they had always starved; starvation was simply the natural result of their dependence on the hunt or on primitive and inefficient agriculture. Such starvation formed part of the rationale for colonialism itself. Without colonists to aid and improve them, it stated, Indians would only continue to suffer and die. The fact that Indians actually starved because colonizers had come, that they died in such prodigious numbers from disease in part because colonizers had wrecked their subsistence systems, and that these subsistence systems themselves were inextricably intertwined with the political, social, and cultural relations colonizers set out to undermine subverted the more beneficent rationale that colonialism brought a better life to all. Colonialists, therefore, tended to prefer imaginary pasts and more benign presents.

It is only more recently that scholars have wondered why people starved, why subsistence systems failed, and why societies changed. Anthropologists have done much of the more forceful thinking on these questions, at least as they apply to ancient and colonial peoples. Their predominant approach has been materialist. Reducing culture to a mere superstructure, cultural materialists have created an engine of progress that would have horrified progressive historians of a generation or two ago. Cursed with inexorably expanding populations that continuously foul their nests and deplete their environments, human societies, according to the cultural materialist, must regularly adopt newer modes of production and organization that buy time until population once more catches up with the expanded possibility for subsistence. Materialists reduce most human history to the desperate attempt to cope with too many people and too few resources.

The histories presented here have addressed these questions, which colonizers failed to examine and which materialists have examined far too narrowly. The focus has been on the subsistence economy itself, but politics and culture have constantly intruded. To have focused too narrowly on subsistence and the environment would have meant depriving the study of its social context and reducing the issues to abstractions.

Among all these peoples, the goal of production was security. They not only did not seek to maximize production of resources, they often actively avoided it. Diversity of production and security were virtually synonomous for all these people, but there were cultural as well as ecological limits to their acceptance of new resources. The assimilation or lack of assimilation of livestock into the economy serves as a convenient example of the material and symbolic constraints at work. All of these peoples became enthusiastic stockraisers. The Choctaws accepted horses, and later cattle, but for years they rejected pigs; the Pawnees likewise accepted horses, but they raised neither cattle nor pigs; and the Navajos took sheep and horses, but, until relatively recently, they adopted neither pigs nor cattle. Much of this pattern of acceptance and rejection makes environmental sense—pigs are not suited to the arid Southwest; cattle and pigs left behind while the Pawnees hunted would threaten their crops—but material concerns do not explain all such adoptions. For instance, the Choctaw rejection of pigs (and chickens) as sources of food seems more clearly symbolic than ecological. These animals violated fundamental categories of classification and were thus taboo. Thus to understand the evolution of a subsistence system, one must appreciate symbolic culture and environmental conditions.

This intertwining of symbolic and environmental factors goes beyond subsistence. All these Indian peoples shaped their environments. At contact, wilderness—in the sense of a physical environment unaltered by human actions—did not exist over a large part of their homelands, for the Indians had already taken measures to mold an environment suitable to their needs. Most of these measures sprang from eminently practical concerns. With fire, for example, they cleared the debris from the forest floor and made travel easier, increased browse, brought earlier growth of grasses on the plains and prairies, and concentrated animals for hunting. Yet such practical measures do not exhaust the human actions that influenced the physical environment. Although cultural demands for blood revenge were not designed to keep game abundant, by stimulating warfare they often created borderland havens for game. They were therefore one element of symbolic culture that had to be circumvented by Europeans before large-scale commercial hunting could develop among the Choctaws. Likewise, some Navajo herding patterns, which did indeed often locally damage grasslands, evolved not from practical concerns but from a fear of the dead and ghosts. To avoid being abroad at night, Navajos always bedded their sheep in the home corral every evening.

Once established, the mixed hunting-gathering-horticultural system shared by all these people seems to have been remarkably stable. It was not a transitory or evolutionary stage forced upon them by declining faunal resources or growing population. Adequate means of maintaining game populations seem to have existed among all three tribes. The eventual depletion of game was instead the result of white contact, the growth of the market, and the political chaos the Americans and Europeans brought in their wake. Likewise, adequate means of controlling population also was at hand. Only among the Navajos was the intensification of production accompanied by a rapidly growing population, and their situation is hardly an ideal Malthusian example. More pertinent than demography in the Navajos' immediate fate and the changes in their economy, were their loss of traditional grazing lands and their victimization by a misguided reform program intended to benefit the large society of which they were a colonial appendage.

Yet despite their internal stability, all these economies succumbed. Their destruction was not the result of an evolutionary cycle brought on automatically by new technologies or eager imitation of whites. It was more complex. Two elements in particular stand out during the period of initial decline: epidemic diseases and market relations with Europeans and Americans.

The diseases which Europeans brought to the North American continent introduced an important new factor into the histories of these peoples. Among the Pawnees and Choctaws population losses were staggering. These losses, however, do not make disease alone a sufficient explanation of the direction the histories of these peoples took. To cite the obvious, the Navajos actually increased in population, and the Pawnees and Choctaws repeatedly recovered from the losses brought by epidemics. To demolish a society, disease had to do more than merely kill individuals; it had to be a part of a symbiotic interplay with subsistence, politics, and culture which destroyed the society's ability to produce and distribute food and care for the sick. As long as subsistence systems continued to function and cultures remained intact, native populations could, and often did, recover.

The subsistence systems themselves, however—precisely because they balanced a variety of cultural, environmental, and political factors—were very vulnerable to disruption from without. If such disruption, which came in various ways, crippled a subsistence base during a period of epidemics, it could be fatal.

The Pawnees, Navajos, and Choctaws all survived the first and more obvious assault resulting from white contact—the slave raids. The next disruption, however, was more subtle, and indeed superficially it was not a threat at all. It was the market. Europeans and Americans offered to exchange manufactured items for food, furs, and deerskins. The Indians accepted and actively sought many such manufactures. Axes, knives, posts, guns, woolen clothing, and other tools and goods made their lives much easier. But nearly all of this technological adoption took place strictly on a replacement level. Indians substituted European tools for native tools to perform a preexisting task more quickly and easily. Such exchanges were initially limited and took place as much on Indian as on European terms. They resembled gift exchanges more than trade. These initial exchanges, particularly with English traders, however, did not satisfy the European appetite for furs and deerskins.

This situation created a peculiar problem for the English and later the Americans. How could they increase Indian demand for European goods and thus stimulate Indian production of furs and deerskins? The answer was by offering liquor and credit. Liquor created exactly the insatiable demand the traders sought while loosening cultural restraints against overhunting. Credit put the Indians quickly into debt, and furthered the traders' control. When given full rein, the credit-liquor combination could lead to rapid overhunting, the loss of wild-food supplies, the institution of a market economy, the growth of market relations inside the society, eventual turmoil, and complete dependence on Europeans and Americans.

Because of its catastrophic possibilities, the triumph of the market was neither easy nor inevitable. Indians resisted it; at nearly every step they sought to maintain native norms of reciprocity, sharing, and gift exchanges against commercial values. The Choctaws did this relatively successfully for more than half a century. They used their political strength to secure gifts and kept trade a subordinate means of exchange. The Pawnees restricted trade and successfully banished liquor until they left Nebraska. Like the Navajos, they saw raiding as a method of securing goods which was far less dangerous than trading. The Navajos were perhaps the most successful of all. Because cultural sanctions against wasting property limited the liquor trade among them, the Navajos rejected commercial values and a commercial economy well into the twentieth century. Even in the early twentieth century their connections with the market through the trading posts were tentative and always subordinated to the demands of subsistence herding and agriculture.

Without the ability to resist entrapment in the market and the environmental and social catastrophe this engendered, political independence alone was often irrelevant. Political strength had to guarantee not only nominal independence but also the real ability to deal with Europeans on the basis of reciprocity rather than of market exchange. Some nations, like the Choctaws, maintained this type of political strength for significant periods of time. For other groups, like the Pawnees, however, the loss of this political power was the beginning of dependency. The Pawnees were defeated by the Sioux, not by the Americans; nonetheless, the origins of their downfall remain primarily political. In the 1830s they rejected trade, successfully maintained their subsistence system, and preserved their symbolic culture, but around them the native political world dissolved into a chaos that threatened their very existence. Native warfare eventually destroyed the Pawnees' ability to feed themselves, made them vulnerable to epidemics, and drove them into the arms of the Americans whose embrace proved as fatal as that of the Sioux.

Yet even conquest, when it came, did not always bring dependency if a subsistence base and social organization remained intact. Although many native peoples lacked an adequate land base once they were placed on reservations and needed the American rations to survive, the Navajos demonstrate that conquest and dependency were not always synonomous. The loss of traditional grazing lands and watering rights in the late nineteenth and early twentieth centuries certainly weakened the Navajo economy. They were a conquered and vulnerable people, but not until the 1930s did they become dependent. Disaster, when it came to the Navajos, arrived as it so often did for American Indian peoples, in the guise of reform. In a relatively few years and in the name of conservation and self-determination, they were stripped of their stock and made largely dependent on wages and various public programs for their living. It was a blow that they stagger from still.

If the routes that led these three nations to dependency were not atypical, they suggest that three limited choices were available to horticultural-hunting societies struggling to control their own destinies. First, Indian peoples could try to maintain their existing subsistence strategies and their social organization substantially unchanged. Since this attempt to maintain traditional values in their original homeland usually involved warfare which itself often altered subsistence and social patterns, paradoxically it often became necessary for Indians to leave their old land in order to preserve old ways. It was for this reason that the Pawnees and some of the Choctaws sought new lands.

A second strategy available to the Indians was a policy of incremental change within existing homelands. Without conscious planning, new elements could be slowly grafted onto preexisting cultural forms. The Navajos were, and to a degree still are, masters of this approach. Before and immediately after stock reduction they even succeeded in assimilating into their existing economy certain kinds of wage labor such as railroad work. The strategy of incremental change worked well when contact was gradual and coercion was limited, (ideally with a successful playoff system or a geographical location that whites found uninviting). When such conditions were absent—when, for example, whites forced rapid transformation of the core of Navajo economy and society during the stock reduction period—then the option of gradual, ad hoc change vanished, and overt resistance or capitulation became the only choice. It is possible that without stock reduction and with some expansion of their land base, Navajo dependency could have been averted. Change certainly would have come, but the Navajos had been changing for three hundred years. Rather than allowing them to adapt once more to a changing economy, however, government officials in the 1930s simply imposed their own wishes upon the society. In doing so, and with the best of intentions, Collier arrogantly disregarded the legitimate concerns of the Navajos.

The final alternative available to native societies was purposeful modernization, which involved the acceptance not only of modern technology but also of much of the attendant social organization and values of the larger society. The goal of this modernization was not assimilation, but rather the retention of an independent national identity by a group in control of its own destiny. This was essentially the goal of the modernizing elite of the Choctaws and appears to be the general intent of at least part of the present leadership of the Navajo nation. Its obvious parallel is the modernization programs of the elites of some Third World nations. This option almost inevitably resulted in internal strife as groups within the nation resisted the efforts of modernizers as strenuously as they did those of various white conquerers, traders, and reformers. Modernizers, for all their sincere nationalism and genuine concern for the poverty and exploitation of their nation, still represented yet another attempt to alter traditional society and create an economic man and economic woman where no such people existed.

This internal revolution in values was nearly as difficult when native elites forced it as when colonial powers did. In traditional society kinship, clan, and village relations determined economic decisions; no one sold land, and no one sold labor. These were natural or social elements, not mere commodities. With their subsistence systems intact, the older societies promised support for all. No one starved or went hungry unless everyone did. Material desires were culturally limited; generosity was the supreme economic virtue. When modernizers, native or alien, sought to make security an individual concern, not a communal one; when they sought to make the individual acquisition of wealth the sole end of economic endeavor; and when they sought to make the market the sole regulator of land and labor, then turmoil became inevitable. Very often their programs threatened to impoverish the mass of the people while enriching an elite.

Quite obviously the choices available to Indians in retaining or altering traditional social and economic forms were, and are, clearly related to the actions of the whites who encountered these societies. Yet with the center of attention on the Indian societies, it becomes apparent that the whites often had to adjust to Indian norms. European responses varied with the different political, economic, and cultural contexts. The French and Spanish, often short of goods and markets and wedded to imperial ambitions, adjusted trade to the preferred Indian framework of gifts and reciprocity far more readily than did the English. This adjustment was not because they were a more tolerant people. They readily engaged in slaving, exploitation, and extermination of recalcitrant nations whenever they were able to and whenever it suited their interests. They avoided market exchanges not because they did not desire wealth but because they often found they could not compete with the English on market terms.

The English and the Americans, too, sometimes subordinated trade to imperial, political concerns, but they usually preferred market relations with the Indians because it was their avenue to wealth and dominance. To facilitate their commerce, they sought to rip Indians from the land and the social web which bound them together. They wanted to "free" these people, particularly the men whom they regarded as lazy beggars, so that Indians too could fulfill their "natural," but inhibited, desire to seek gain. In time such aims became a species of commercial idealism, as soldiers, missionaries, reformers, and even some progressive Indians agreed that the ruthless destruction of traditional communal societies formed the necessary basis for progress.

Because John Collier spent much of his early career challenging such views and championing the values of the traditional societies, it is ironic that Collier himself should eventually have cooperated, no matter how unwillingly, in incorporating the Navajos into the market. Collier, to a degree traders, missionaries, and reformers never had been able to accomplish, made Navajo resources and labor commodities: the reservation and the labor of its people were for sale no matter what the social cost. He forced Navajo workers and Navajo resources and labor into the larger economy, and in doing so he defeated his own stated aims. Navajo society after the 1930s conservation program is not a revitalized traditional society, but an exploited dependent one. Collier himself probably would have been horrified at an economy where strip mines and uranium mines scar the land and destroy the people's health to an extent sheep never did, and where profits enrich multinational corporations, not Navajos.

As the Navajo example demonstrates, social change clearly has environmental consequences, but environmental change, in turn, also affects societies. The process is reciprocal. Large parts of the physical environment are cultural creations shaped by the people who live on the land. Nature, however, is not infinitely malleable. Changes in the physical world rebound back to affect the societies which initiate them. In hunting out their deer, in moving their agriculture to upland fields which were cleared and plowed, in eliminating game and increasing the number of sheep, the Choctaws, Pawnees, and Navajos respectively each made decisions which significantly altered their environments. All these decisions had political and social origins; all affected the natural world; and these changes in the natural world then, in turn, had further political and social ramifications. That environments do change as cultures change is important not only for understanding the environment, but also for appreciating the full complexity of social change itself.

Abbreviations in Notes

ASP: Indian Affairs — American State Papers. Indian Affairs, Documents, Legislative and Executive, of the Congress of the United States, from the First Session of the First to the Second Session of the Thirteenth Congress, Inclusive: Commencing March 3, 1789, Ending March 3, 1827. 2 Vols. Washington, D.C., 1832–34.

AHS — Arizona Historical Society, Tucson.

CRG — Allen D. Candler, ed. Colonial Records of the State of Georgia. 26 vols. Atlanta, 1904–26.

CRSC: Indian Affairs — William L. McDowell, Jr., ed. Colonial Records of South Carolina: Documents Relating to Indian Affairs. 3 vols. Columbia, S.C.: University of South Carolina Press, 1956–70.

CRSC: Journals . . . Assembly — A. S. Salley, ed. The Colonial Records of South Carolina: Journals of the Commons House of Assembly. 11 vols. Columbia: Historical Commission of South Carolina, 1951–77.

Carter, Territorial Papers — Clarence Carter, ed. The Teritorial Papers of the United States. 28 vols. Washington, D.C.: Government Printing Office, 1934–75.

Collier's Navajo Documents — National Archives, Record Group 75, Records of the Bureau of Indian Affairs, Office Files of Commissioner John Collier, Collier's Navajo Documents, 55.

EWT — R. G. Thwaites, ed. Early Western Travels. 32 vols. Cleveland: Arthur H. Clark, 1904–1907.

HD	U.S. Congress, House of Representatives. House Document [issue number varies].
Jacobs, *Atkins Report*	Wilbur R. Jacobs, ed. *The Appalachian Indian Frontier: The Edmond Atkin Report and Plan of 1755.* Lincoln: University of Nebraska Press, 1967.
KSHSC	*Kansas State Historical Society Collections.*
Kinnaird, *Spain in the Miss. Valley*	Lawrence Kinnaird, ed. *Spain in the Mississippi Valley, 1765–1794: Translation of Materials from the Spanish Archives in the Bancroft Library.* Annual Report of the American Historical Association for the Year 1945. Washington, D.C.: Government Printing Office, 1946.
McGinnies Report	NA, RG 75, BIA, CCF, 9055-36-344, Navajo, The Agricultural and Range Resources of the Navajo Reservation in Relation to the Subsistence Needs of the Navajo Indians, May 12, 1936, by W. G. McGinnies.
NA	National Archives
CCF	Central Classified Files
CCC-ID	Civilian Conservation Corps, Indian Division
CF, GSF	Central Files, General Services File
LMU	Land Management Unit
LR	Letters Received
OIA	Records of the Office of Indian Affairs
RG	Record Group
SCS, NS	Soil Conservation Service, Navajo Service
SW-IA	Records of the Secretary of War Pertaining to Indian Affairs
NSHS	Nebraska State Historical Society
NSHSC	*Nebraska State Historical Society Collections*
NSHST	*Nebraska State Historical Society Transactions*
PRO, CO 5, 80	British Public Record Office, Colonial Office, Series 5, vol. 80. Microfilm, Library of Congress, Washington, D.C.
Report of Commissioner, [year]	*Annual Report of the Commissioner of Indian Affairs for the Year* [varies]. Washington, D.C.: Government Printing Office, [annual].

Rowland, *MTA*

Dunbar Rowland, ed. *Mississippi Territorial Archives, 1798–1803, Executive Journals of Governor William Charles Cole Claiborne.* Nashville: Brandon Printing, 1905.

Rowland and Sanders, *French Dominion*

Dunbar Rowland and A. G. Sanders, eds. *Mississippi Provincial Archives: French Dominion.* Jackson: Mississippi State Department of Archives and History, 1927–32.

SD

U.S. Congress, Senate. Senate Document (issue number varies).

SDHC

South Dakota Historical Collections.

SED

U.S. Congress, Senate. Senate Executive Document.

Survey of Conditions

U.S. Congress, Senate, Subcommittee of the Committee on Indian Affairs. Hearings. *Survey of the Conditions of the Indians of the United States.* 74th Cong., 2nd sess. (part numbers vary).

UNML

University of New Mexico Library.

USDA

United States Department of Agriculture.

White-Tailed Deer

White-Tailed Deer in the Southern Forest Habitat: Proceedings of a Symposium at Nacogdoches, Texas, March 25–26, 1969. Southern Forest Experiment Station, U.S. Forest Service, USDA, in cooperation with the Forest Game Committee of the Southeastern Section of the Wildlife Society and the School of Forestry, Stephen F. Austin University. Nacogdoches, Texas, 1969.

Zeh Report

Soil Conservation Service, Navajo Service. General Report Covering the Grazing Situation on the Navajo Indian Reservation, by William Zeh. Special Collections, University of New Mexico Library.

Notes

INTRODUCTION

1. Immanuel Wallerstein, *The Modern World System: Capitalist Agriculture and the Origins of the European World Economy in the Sixteenth Century* (New York; Academic Press, 1974), and *The Modern World System II: Mercantilism and the Consolidation of the European World Economy, 1600–1750* (New York: Academic Press, 1980).

2. Two excellent discussions of this literature are in a special issue of the journal *International Organization* edited by James A. Caporaso and entitled *Dependence and Dependency in the Global System*. See James A. Caporaso, "Dependence, Dependency, and Power in the Global System: A Structural and Behavioral Analysis," and Raymond D. Duvall, "Dependence and Dependencia Theory: Notes toward Precision of Concept and Argument," both in *International Organization* 32 (Winter 1978): 13–43, 51–78. For a brief discussion of the reception of this literature among economists, see Alan Sica, "Review Essay: Dependency in the World Economy," *American Journal of Sociology* 84 (Nov. 1978): 728–30.

3. Caporaso, "Dependence, Dependency, and Power," pp. 18–26; Duval, "Dependence and Dependencia Theory," pp. 51–61.

4. Duval, "Dependence and Dependencia Theory," pp. 57, 61–67; Caporaso, "Dependence, Dependency, and Power," pp. 23, 25–26.

5. For an attempt to use a variant of dependency theory to analyze the situation of American Indian peoples, see Gary C. Anders, "Theories of Underdevelopment and the American Indian," *Journal of Economic Issues* 14 (Sept. 1980): 693–96.

CHAPTER 1

1. The major historical monographs on the Choctaws are Angie Debo, *The Rise and Fall of the Choctaw Republic*, 2nd ed. (Norman: University of Oklahoma Press, 1961); Mary Elizabeth Young, *Redskins, Ruffleshirts, and Rednecks: Indian Allotments in Alabama and Mississippi, 1830–1860* (Norman: University of Oklahoma Press, 1962); Arthur DeRosier, Jr., *The Removal of the Choctaw Indians* (Knoxville: University of Tennessee Press, 1970); and Patricia D. Woods, *French-Indian Relations on the Southern Frontier, 1699–1762* (Ann Arbor: UMI Research Press, 1980).

2. For an excellent synopsis of these expeditions see Carl O. Sauer, *Sixteenth Century North America: The Land and the People as Seen by the Europeans* (Berkeley: University of California Press, 1971), pp. 26–28, 36–46, 158–80.

3. For a brief recent review of prehistory in the area, see Don W. Dragoo, "Some Aspects of Eastern North American Prehistory: A Review, 1975," *American Antiquity* 41 (Jan. 1976): 20; also James B. Griffin, "Prehistoric Cultures of the Central Mississippi Valley," in James B. Griffin, ed., *Archaeology of the Eastern United States* (Chicago: University of Chicago Press, 1952), pp. 226–38, and James B. Griffin, "Eastern North American Archaeology: A Summary," *Science* 156 (Apr. 1967): 175–91. For the Muskogeans, see J. A. Ford and Gordon Willey, "An Interpretation of the Prehistory of the Eastern United States," *American Anthropologist* 43 (July–Sept. 1941): 351.

4. For the origin legends, see John Swanton, *Indians of the Southeastern United States*, Bureau of American Ethnology Bulletin, no. 137 (Washington, D.C.: Government Printing Office, 1946), pp. 777–78; John Swanton, *Source Material for the Social and Ceremonial Life of the Choctaw Indians*, Bureau of American Ethnology Bulletin, no. 103 (Washington, D.C.: Government Printing Office, 1931), pp. 5–37; Charles Hudson, *The Southeastern Indians* (Knoxville: University of Tennessee Press, 1976), pp. 202–3.

5. Sauer, *Sixteenth Century North America*, p. 171. William Haag, "A Prehistory of Mississippi," *Journal of Mississippi History* 17 (Apr. 1955):107. Ford and Willey, "Interpretation," p. 357.

6. Pierre Margry, *Découvertes et Établissements des Français . . . Mémoires et Documents Originaux* (Paris: Imprimerie D. Jouaust, 1880), 4:425–27, 512. "Continuation of the Memoir of De Bienville, 1726," in Dunbar Rowland and A. G. Sanders, eds., *Mississippi Provincial Archives: French Dominion* (Jackson: Mississippi Department of Archives and History, 1927–32), 3: 536–37. Alfred Crosby, "Virgin Soil Epidemics as a Factor in the Aboriginal Depopulation in America," *William and Mary Quarterly* 33 (Apr. 1976): 289–99.

7. "Continuation of the Memoir of De Bienville, 1726," in Rowland and Sanders, *French Dominion*, 3: 526–27.

8. "A Translation of La Harpe's Historical Journal," in Benjamin F. French, *Historical Collections of Louisiana and Florida*, 7 vol. (New York and Philadelphia: various publishers, 1846–75), 3:20. Swanton, *Southeastern Indians*, p. 123; Letter from Fr. Le Petit, July 12, 1730, in Reuben Gold

Thwaites, ed., *The Jesuit Relations and Allied Documents*, 73 vol. (Cleveland: Burrows Bros., 1896–1901), 68:195.
A partial list of population estimates is in Swanton, *Southeastern Indians*, p. 123. For the Folsom estimate, repeated in several sources, see Horatio B. Cushman, *History of the Choctaw, Chickasaw and Natchez Indians* (Greenville, Tex.: Headlight Printing House, 1899), p. 389. To my own and the reader's inconvenience, I have, in the course of research, also used an abridged reprint of this work issued by the Redlands Press of Stillwater, Okla. in 1962. Citations from this edition will be labeled Stillwater, 1962. Finally, see Crosby, "Virgin Soil Epidemics," pp. 289–99.

9. The only political upheaval after the slave trade and wars of the early 1730s that may have contributed to population decline was the Choctaw civil war, which will be discussed later. For the difficulty in reaching the Choctaws, see Du Roullet Journal, 1:52–53, De Lusser Journal, 1:81–84, both in Rowland and Sanders, *French Dominion*.

10. Hudson, *Southeastern Indians*, pp. 78–79. Theodore H. Lewis ed., *The Narrative of the Expedition of Hernando De Soto by the Gentleman of Elvas*, Original Narratives of Early American History, ed. J. Franklin Jameson (New York: Barnes and Noble, 1977, reprint of 1907 ed.), pp. 195–202.

11. This description of the native forest has been derived from Elsie Quarterman and Catherine Keever, "Southern Mixed Hardwood Forest: Climax in the Southeastern Coastal Plain, U.S.A.," *U.S. Ecological Monographs* 32 (Spring 1962): 167–85; and Donald Caplenor, "Forest Composition on Loessal and Non-Loessal Soils in West-Central Mississippi," *Ecology* 49 (Spring 1968): 322–31. For Black Belt, see Erhard Rostlund, "The Myth of a Natural Prairie Belt in Alabama: An Interpretation of Historical Records," *Annals of the Association of American Geographers* 47 (Dec. 1957): 392–411, who contended that there was no natural Black Belt prairie. Later research has proved him wrong. See Alice Simms Jones and E. Gibbs Patton, "Forest, Prairie and Soils in the Black Belt of Sumter County, Alabama in 1832," *Ecology* 47 (Winter 1960); 75; and H. Taylor Rankin and D. E. Davis, "Woody Vegetation in the Black Belt Prairie of Montgomery County, Alabama in 1845–46," *Ecology* 52 (Summer 1971): 716–18.

12. The Mississippian peoples were not as completely agricultural as once thought. They obtained a substantial amount of food from hunting and gathering. Bruce D. Smith, *Middle Mississippian Exploitation of Animal Populations*, Anthropological Papers, Museum of Anthropology, University of Michigan, no. 57 (Ann Arbor: University of Michigan Press, 1975), pp. 94–95. Swanton, *Choctaw Indians*, pp. 24–26.

13. Quotation taken from Jon L. Gibson, "Aboriginal Warfare in the Protohistoric Southeast: An Alternative Perspective," *American Antiquity* 39 (Jan. 1974): 130–31. The emphasis of my own interpretation differs from that of Gibson, who stresses the status function of warfare. This indeed may have been the function of warfare within the culture; here I am more interested in its environmental results.

14. For settlements in the Big Black Valley see, James A. Ford, *Analysis of Indian Village Site Collections from Louisiana and Mississippi*, State of Louisiana, Department of Conservation, Anthropological Study, no. 2 (New Orleans, 1936), pp. 115–28; for the Yazoo region, see Philip Phillips, *Archaeological Survey in the Lower Yazoo Basin, Mississippi, 1949–1955*, Papers of the Peabody Museum of Archaeology and Ethnology, Harvard University, vol. 60 (Cambridge: Peabody Museum, 1970); and for the Mobile River, see E. Bruce Trickey, "A Chronological Framework for the Mobile Bay Region," *American Antiquity* 23 (Apr. 1958): 388–96. For deer habitats, see J. J. Stransky, "Deer Habitat: Quality of Major Forest Types in the South," in *White-Tailed Deer in the Southern Forest Habitat*, Southern Forest Experiment Station, Forest Service, USDA (Nacogdoches, Tex.: Southern Forest Experiment Station, 1969), pp. 42–43; Joseph Larson, "Agricultural Clearings as Sources of Supplemental Food and Habitat Diversity for White-tailed Deer" in ibid., pp. 46–47; Lowell K. Halls and E. A. Epps, "Browse Quality Influenced by Tree Overstory in the South," *Journal of Wildlife Management* 33 (Oct. 1965): 1028–31; Daniel Lay, "Fruit Utilization by Deer in Southern Forests," ibid. 29 (Apr. 1965): 371–75.

15. "De Lusser Journal," Rowland and Sanders, *French Dominion*, 1:83. Rostlund, "The Myth of a Natural Prairie Belt in Alabama." Rostlund is wrong in his central contention that there was no natural Black Belt prairie, but he is correct in citing the abundant evidence for Indian-maintained grasslands. (See note 11, above.)

16. Gary Dills, "Effects of Prescribed Burning on Deer Browse," *Journal of Wildlife Management* 34 (July 1970): 540–44; Paul A. Shrauder and Howard Miller, "The Effects of Prescribed Burning on Deerfood and Cover," in *White-Tailed Deer*, pp. 77–80. H. H. Chapman, "Is the Longleaf Type a Climax?" *Ecology* 13 (Oct. 1932): 330–31. David Burch and Allen Bickford, "Use of Fire in Natural Regeneration of Longleaf Pine," *Journal of Forestry* 48 (Feb. 1950): 114–17. Quarterman and Keever, "Southern Mixed Hardwood Forest," pp. 167–69, 182. Stransky, "Deer Habitat," pp. 42–44. A convenient but dated summary on the literature on fire in southeastern forests is K. H. Garren, "Effects of Fire on Vegetation of the Southeastern United States," *Botanical Review* 9 (Nov. 1943): 617–54.

17. Walter Robertson, "Population Dynamics of White-Tailed Deer," in *White-Tailed Deer*, p. 5. Smith, *Middle Mississippian Exploitation*, pp. 23, 26; Antoine Simon LePage Du Pratz, *The History of Louisiana, or of the Western Parts of Virginia . . .*, 2 vols. (London: T. E. Becker, 1763), 1:267.

18. Erhard Rostlund, "The Geographic Range of the Historic Bison in the Southeast," *Annals of the Association of American Geographers* 50 (Dec. 1960): 395–407. For sightings of buffalo and Indian use, see Duclos to De Pontchartrain, Dec. 25, 1715, in Rowland and Sanders, *French Dominion*, 2:208–9; Du Pratz, *History*, 1:226–28; James Adair, *The History of the American Indians . . .* (London: E. C. Dilly, 1775), p. 415; Swanton, *Southeastern Indians*, pp. 325–27; "Historical Journal or Narrative of the Expeditions Made by Order of . . .

King of France to Colonize Louisiana under Command of M. Pierre Le Moyne d'Iberville," French, *Historical Collections*, 7:49,108.

19. USDA, *Soil: The Yearbook of Agriculture, 1957* (Washington, D.C.: Government Printing Office, 1957), p. 381.

20. Ralph Cross, ed., *Atlas of Mississippi* (Jackson: University Press of Mississippi, 1974), pp. 4–5. Rostlund, "Myth of a Natural Prairie Belt in Alabama, pp. 392–93, 408–11. Jones and Patton, "Forest, Prairie and Soils," p. 75. H. Taylor Rankin and D. E. Davis, "Woody Vegetation in the Black Belt Prairie of Montgomery County, Alabama in 1845–46," *Ecology* 52 (Summer 1971): 716–18. For the soils of the Black Belt, see *Mississippi Agricultural Experiment Station Bulletin* 731, "Normal Yields and Production Practices by Soil Types, Mississippi Black Belt Area," by Thomas Tramel, et al. (Oct. 1966): 1–4. For climate, see Warren Thornwaite, "An Approach toward a Rational Classification of Climate," *Geographical Review* 38 (1948): 55–94 (see map facing p. 94). For Choctaw problems with water in the Black Belt, see *Missionary Herald* 19 (Jan. 1823): 8.

21. For the abandonment of the Tombigbee valley during the Creek wars, see Bernard Romans, *A Concise Natural History of East and West Florida* (New York: printed for the author, 1775), pp. 328–29.

22. For the most complete published lists of Choctaw town locations, see Swanton, *Choctaw Indians*, pp. 59–75, and Henry S. Halbert, "Bernard Romans' Map of 1772," *Publications of the Mississippi Historical Society* 6 (Oxford, Miss., 1902): 415–39. For archaeological investigation of some of these towns, see John T. Penman, "Historic Choctaw Towns of the Southern Division," *Journal of Mississippi History* 40 (May 1978): 133–41; John T. Penman, *Archaeological Survey in Mississippi, 1974–1975* (Jackson: State of Mississippi Department of Archives and History 1977), pp. 236–93; Adair, *History*, pp. 284, 309; Romans, *Natural History*, p. 29; Du Pratz, History, 1:252.

23. For names, see Swanton, *Choctaw Indians*, pp. 59–75; Halbert, "Romans' Map," p. 124.

24. Clay and silt soils have slow water and air movement, becoming sticky when wet and cloddy when dry. Such soils cannot be tilled easily with hand tools. Sandy soils, on the other hand, while easily worked, have such poor water retention that they are ill suited for agriculture. Loam soils, a mixture of sand, silt, and clay particles, are both easily worked and possess good water retention. Trawick Ward, "Correlation of Mississippian Sites and Soil Types," *Southeastern Archaeological Conference Bulletin* 3 (1965): 42–43.

25. A. J. Brown, "Antiquities of New ton County, Mississippi," *Publications of the Mississippi Historical Society* 6 (Oxford, Miss.: The Society, 1902): 441–48, mentions nine towns in Newton County: Coatraw, Tala, Oka Kapassa, Oni Talemon, Chunky, Chunky Chito, Bissasha, Oka Hullo, and Okhata Talaia. Of these, French and English records of the eighteenth century corroborate the existence of all but Chunky Chito. Only Romans mentions Coatraw, however, and it is very probably a mangled form of another Choctaw word. It may have been an extension of Tala, which it supposedly adjoined. See Swanton,

Choctaw Indians, p. 69. USDA, *Soil Survey: Newton County, Mississippi*, ser. 1957, no. 1 (Washington, D.C.: Government Printing Office, Feb. 1960), pp. 54–57. 26. The amount of terrace soils is an estimate. Bottomland and terrace soils together make up 15 percent of the county. USDA, *Soil Survey: Newton County*, pp. 2, 9–25, 29; *Mississippi Agricultural Experiment Station Bulletin 562*, "Newton County Soils: Major Uses and Management," by L. C. Murphree (July 1958); p. 22. The Falena Site, 22-NW-508, may represent part of Tala—Penman, *Survey*, pp. 277–80: See USDA, *Soil Survey: Newton County*, maps, 29. Brown, "Newton County," p. 444, puts Coatraw in section 17, Township 4, Range 11 East. Neither Brown (p. 443) nor Swanton, *Choctaw Indians*, p. 63, gives a precise location for Oni Talemon, both merely placing it south of Pickney's Mill. Brown places Oka Kapassa in section 23, Township 8, Range 11 East—Brown, "Newton County," pp. 443, 445. USDA, *Soil Survey, Newton County*, sheet 9. Okhatatalaia has been excavated (it is the Little Laura Site, 22-NW-513), but it is the source of some confusion. Penman, in his archaeological survey, confused Okhatatalaia with the similar-sounding but much larger town of Okatalaia farther south. He rightly concluded that Okhatatalaia is too small to contain the 186 people credited to "Okatalaya" in 1795, not realizing that "Okatalaya" is Okatalaia, not Okhatatalaia. Penman, "Historic Choctaw Towns," p. 138.

27. Hudson, *Southeastern Indians*, p. 291; Ward, "Mississippian Sites and Soil Types," p. 44. This is not to deny that something akin to riverine agriculture did take place in some areas of the Southeast. The coastal tribes appear to have planted on lands annually inundated by floods. "Memoir of D'Artaguette on Louisiana, May 12, 1712," in Rowland and Sanders, *French Dominion*, 2:62–63.

CHAPTER 2

1. Romans, *Natural History*, pp. 71, 86. Romans gives the most detailed eighteenth-century account of the material life of the Choctaws.

2. See, for example, Marvin Harris, *Cultural Materialism: The Struggle for a Science of Culture* (New York: Random House, 1979), pp. 62–70, 87–88, 335–36.

3. Cushman, *History*, p. 251. Swanton, *Choctaw Indians*, pp. 46–47. Romans, *Natural History*, pp. 74, 86, 306–7, 323.

4. Romans, *Natural History*, p. 86.

5. William Willis, "The Nation of Bread," *Ethnohistory* 4 (Spring 1957): 125–49.

6. Hudson, *Southeastern Indians*, p. 293. Smith, *Middle Mississippian Exploitation*, p. 9.

7. T. N. Campbell, "Choctaw Subsistence: Ethnographic Notes from the Lincecum Manuscript," *Florida Anthropologist* 12 (1959): 17. Du Roullet Journal, in Rowland and Sanders, *French Dominion*, 1:146. Adair, *History*, pp. 405–7; Romans, *Natural History*, p. 361. Hudson, *Southeastern Indians*,

pp. 59–62, 294. For the origins of the Eastern Agricultural Complex and the diffusion of the new crops, see Richard Yarnell, "Aboriginal Relationships between Culture and Plant Life," University of Michigan, Museum of Anthropology, *Anthropological Papers*, no. 23 (Ann Arbor: University of Michigan, 1964), pp. 11–119, 147–48; Charles Heiser, "The Sunflower among North American Indians," *Proceedings of the American Philosophical Society* 95 (Aug. 1951): 435; Richard Yarnell, "Early Woodland Plant Remains and the Question of Cultivation," in Stuart Struever, *Prehistoric Agriculture* (Garden City, N.Y.: Natural History Press, 1971), pp. 550–54; Melvin Fowler, "The Hypothesis," in Struever, *Prehistoric Agriculture*, pp. 122–27; Stuart Struever and Kent Vickery, "The Beginnings of Cultivation in the Midwest Riverine Area," *American Anthropologist* 75 (Oct. 1973): 1197–1220. For remnants among Choctaws, see Halbert, "Romans' Map," p. 439; Hudson, *Southeastern Indians*, p. 61.

8. Du Pratz, *History*, 2:3, 7. Hudson, *Southeastern Indians*, pp. 292–93; Adair, *History*, pp. 407–8; Swanton, ed., "Early Account of the Choctaw Indians," *Memoirs of the American Anthropological Association* 5 (Apr.–June 1918): 57–58. Swanton, *Choctaw Indians*, pp. 47, 208. Romans, *Natural History*, pp. 84–85.

9. Both Romans, *Natural History*, pp. 84–85, and Henry C. Benson, *Life among the Choctaw Indians and Sketches of the Southwest* (Cinncinnati: L. Swormstedt & A. Poe, 1860; New York: Johnson Reprint, 1970), p. 33, who calls it a yam, clearly identify the potato as the sweet potato rather than the Irish potato. Campbell, "Choctaw Subsistence," p. 16. Swanton, *Choctaw Indians*, pp. 288–89. Romans, *Natural History*, p. 308. Romans cites the abundance of fruit around Pante. Sauer, *Sixteenth Century*, pp. 290–91.

10. Campbell, "Choctaw Subsistence," p. 17. Du Roullet Journal, in Rowland and Sanders, *French Dominion*, 1:146. This account is taken largely from Adair, who obtained most of his information from the Chickasaws, but since he was familiar with the Choctaws and purports to describe Indian agriculture in general, I have presumed that the same general pattern prevailed among the Choctaws. Adair, *History*, pp. 405–7, 430.

11. Adair, *History*, p. 430. NA, RG 75, OIA, Choctaw, Armstrong Rolls. Swanton, *Choctaw Indians*, p. 46.

12. Adair, *History*, pp. 405–6; Colin Clark and Margaret Haswell, *The Economics of Subsistence Agriculture* (New York: St. Martins Press, 1964), p. 35.

13. Campbell, "Choctaw Subsistence," pp. 10–11. Adair, *History*, pp. 405–8. Hudson, *Southeastern Indians*, p. 297. Du Pratz, *History*, 1:305.

14. Swanton, *Choctaw Indians*, pp. 221, 225–26. The best account of ceremony in the Southeast is in Hudson, *Southeastern Indians*, pp. 365–75. His account is a composite; there is no detailed account of the way the ceremony was performed among the Choctaws. For the harvest, see Campbell, "Choctaw Subsistence," p. 19; Swanton, *Choctaw Indians*, p. 48; and Hudson, *Southeastern Indians*, p. 299.

15. Adair, *History*, p. 408.

16. It seems that among the Choctaw what Alfred Metraux has called the revolution of the ax—the rapid transformation of a way of life with the introduction of metal tools—did not occur. Life certainly became easier and stone tools were quickly abandoned, but there is no evidence of huge in- creases in productivity or drastic reductions of labor. Alfred Metraux, "The Revolution of the Ax," *Diogenes* 25 (Spring 1959): 28–40.

17. John H. Moore, *Agriculture in Ante-Bellum Mississippi* (New York: Bookman Associates, 1958), pp. 116–17. Some of these farmers also fertilized their land, but since they did it regardless of the spacing, that alone does not account for the difference. For erosion, see USDA, *Soil: The Yearbook of Ag- riculture, 1957*, p. 93; G. Melvin Herndon, "Indian Agriculture in the South- ern Colonies," *North Carolina Historical Review* 44 (Summer 1967): 287.

18. Conversations with Sylvan Wittwer, Director, Agricultural Experiment Station, Michigan State University, and Vernon Meints, Crop and Soil Science Department, Michigan State University, May 9, 1979. Beans are not one of the legumes used as a green manure crop in modern agriculture simply because other legumes can fix up to 200 pounds of nitrogen an acre, five times the amount fixed by beans. USDA, *Soils: The Yearbook of Agriculture, 1957*, pp. 87, 93–94.

19. Romans, *Natural History*, p. 118. Moore, *Agriculture in Antebellum Mississippi*, pp. 58–59. For estimates of yields of 40 bushels an acre for New England, Pennsylvania, and areas of the Southeast, see M. K. Bennett, "The Food Economy of New England Indians, 1605–1675," *Journal of Political Economy* 63 (Oct. 1955): 391; and Herndon, "Indian Agriculture," p. 234.

20. I have used Bennett, "Food Economy," pp. 369–97, and Peter Thomas, "Contrastive Subsistence Strategies and Land Use as Factors for Understanding Indian-White Relations in New England," *Ethnohistory* 23 (Winter 1976): 1–18, for the estimates of necessary calories. I have calculated the caloric value of corn at 376 calories per pound as given in USDA, Ag- ricultural Research Service, *Agricultural Handbook 456, Nutritive Value of American Foods in Common Units* (Washington, D.C.: Government Printing Of- fice, Nov. 1975), p. 67. 2,500 cal. x 365=912,500 (total necessary calories in a year); 1,600 lbs. x 376=601,600 (caloric yield from corn).

21. If the Tala Choctaws used the Ruston sandy loams of the uplands, a far larger acreage was available to them. USDA, *Soil Survey: Newton County*, plates 27, 28.

22. Romans, *Natural History*, pp. 308–13. Ford to Stuart, Nov. 21, 1764, Gage Papers, vol. 49. Ford to Stuart, Nov. 24, 1764, Gage Papers, vol. 49. Adair, *History*, p. 282. Beaudouin to Salmon, Nov. 23, 1732, in Rowland and Sanders, *French Dominion*, 1:155.

23. De Lusser Journal, 1:92–93, and Du Roullet Journal, 1:52, 146–48 both in Rowland and Sanders, *French Dominion*. Ford to Stuart, Nov. 21, 1764, Gage Papers, vol. 49.

24. Romans, *Natural History*, pp. 309, 311. Rostlund, "Myth of a Natural Prairie Belt in Alabama," pp. 394–406.

25. For summer hunting and gathering, see Swanton, *Choctaw Indians*, pp. 48, 54–55; Campbell, "Choctaw Subsistence," pp. 10, 14; Swanton, *Southeastern Indians*, pp. 244–45, 343–44. For fall gathering, see Swanton, *Choctaw Indians*, p. 47; Hudson, *Southeastern Indians*, p. 285. For fall hunting, see Du Roullet Journal, in Rowland and Sanders, *French Dominion*, 1:35–36; Ford to Farmar, Dec. 10, 1764, Gage Papers, vol. 49.

26. Smith, *Middle Mississippian Exploitation*, pp. 36–37, 80. Campbell, "Choctaw Subsistence," p. 12. Robert Noble, "Reproductive Characteristics of the Mississippi White-Tailed Deer" (Ph.D. diss., Michigan State University, 1969), pp. 29–36, 121–22. Walter P. Taylor, *The Deer of North America: The White-Tailed, Mule and Black-Tailed Deer, Genus Odocoileus, Their History and Management* (Harrisburg, Pa.: Stackpole Press and Wildlife Management Institute, 1956), pp. 84–86.

27. Robert Noble, "Progress Report on White-Tailed Deer Productivity Studies in Mississippi," *Proceedings of the Fourteenth Annual Conference, Southeastern Association of Game and Fish Commissioners, 1960* (Columbia, S.C., 1960), p. 55.

28. Smith, *Middle Mississippian Exploitation*, pp. 32–33. Noble, "Mississippi White-Tailed Deer," pp. 119–20.

29. For droughts, see *Mississippi Agricultural Experiment Station Bulletin 466*, "Farm Practices and Organization in the Southern Sand Clay Hills of Mississippi" (Oct. 1949), p. 5; *Mississippi Agricultural Experiment Station Bulletin 650*, "Climatic Patterns of Mississippi" by J. C. McWhorter (Oct. 1962), pp. 113–14. During the growing seasons between 1931 and 1960, the mean growing season precipitation in the old Choctaw homeland was between 26 and 30 inches. Much of this was in the spring, however. During the summer an average of 12 to 13 inches of rain fell. For eighteenth-century droughts see Cushman, *History*, p. 260. For early crop failures, see Duclos to Pontchartrain, Oct. 25, 1713, in Rowland and Sanders, *French Dominion*, 2:80. Hubert to Council, Oct. 26, 1717, in ibid., 2:247; De Bienville and Salmon to Maurepas, May 12, 1733, in ibid. 3:594. For crop failures of 1730s, see De Bienville to Maurepas, Apr. 14, 1735, Dec. 20, 1737, in ibid., 1:257, 3:705. For mid-century, see Daniel Thomas, "Fort Toulouse: The French Outpost at the Alibamos on the Coosa," *Alabama Historical Quarterly* 22 (Spring–Summer 1960): 200. Stuart to Germaine, Jan. 11, 1779, PRO CO 5, 80.

30. Carondelet to De Lemos, Dec. 18, 1792, Lawrence Kinnaird, ed., *Annual Report of the American Historical Association for the Year, 1945, Spain in the Mississippi Valley*, 3 pt. (Washington, D.C.: Government Printing Office, 1946) 3:105. Maxent to Boulgny, Sept. 24, 1782, in ibid., 2:59. Delavillebeuvre to Carondelet, Sept. 5, 1792, in ibid. 3:77. Delavillebeuvre to Carondelet, June 9, 1794, and May 7, 1794, in ibid., 3:297–98, 280. R. S. Cotterill, *The Southern Indians: The Story of the Civilized Tribes Before Removal* (Norman: University of Oklahoma Press, 1954), p. 134.

31. O. T. Denmead and R. H. Shaw, "The Effects of Soil Moisture Stress and Different Stages of Growth on the Development and Yields of Corn," *Agronomy Journal* 52 (1960): 272–74, quoted in Carrol Wilsie, *Crop Adaptation and Distribution* (San Francisco: W. H. Freeman, 1962), p. 160. Cushman, *History*, pp. 366, 260–61. Swanton, *Choctaw Indians*, pp. 240–41.

32. Duclos to Pontchartrain, Oct. 25, 1713, in Rowland and Sanders, *French Dominion*, 2:80, 107–8; Dec. 25, 1715, ibid., 208–9; Hubert to Council, Oct. 26, 1717, ibid., 247.

33. Swanton, *Choctaw Indians*, p. 49.

34. Romans, *Natural History*, pp. 84–85. The quote given here is from Swanton, *Choctaw Indians*, p. 47, with botanical identification supplied him by Paul C. Standley and E. P. Killip.

35. Campbell, "Choctaw Subsistence," pp. 13, 15. De Bienville to Maurepas, July 26, 1733, in Rowland and Sanders, *French Dominion*, 1:212.

36. Adair, *History*, p. 415.

37. Henry Halbert, "District Divisions of the Choctaw Nation," *Report of the Alabama Historical Commission*, vol. 1 (Montgomery, 1901), pp. 377–78. Swanton, *Choctaw Indians*, p. 57. Romans, *Natural History*, p. 426. Campbell, "Choctaw Subsistance," pp. 15–16. Adair, *History*, p. 409. Du Pratz, *History*, 2:239. De Bienville to Maurepas, July 26, 1733, in Rowland and Sanders, *French Dominion*, 1:212. Other sources, such as Campbell, "Choctaw Subsistence," p. 5, mention chestnuts as a common food among the Choctaws.

38. Du Pratz, *History*, 2:242.

CHAPTER 3

1. Beaudouin to Salmon, Nov. 23, 1732, in Rowland and Sanders, *French Dominion*, 1:55–63.

2. Margry, *Découvertes*, pp. 517–18. La Harpe's Historical Journal, in French, ed., *Historical Collections*, 3:28, Louis XIV to De Muy, June 30, 1707, in Rowland and Sanders, *French Dominion*, 3:51. De Bienville to De Pontchartrain, Aug. 20, 1709, ibid., 3:136–37. Duclos to De Pontchartrain, Oct. 9, 1713, ibid. 3:129. De Bienville to De Pontchartrain, Feb. 25, 1708, ibid. 3:112, and June 21, 1710, ibid. 3:151.

3. Nancy Marie Surrey, *The Commerce of Louisiana during the French Regime, 1699–1763*. Studies in History, Economics and Public Law, no. 167 (New York: Columbia University Press, 1916), pp. 226–30. Perier to Abbe Raguet, May 12, 1728, in Rowland and Sanders, *French Dominion*, 2:573–74. Louis XIV to De Muy, June 30, 1707, ibid., 3:53. De Pontchartrain to De Bienville, May 10, 1710, ibid., 3:141. Abstract of Letters from De Bienville to Pontchartrain, 1706, ibid. 2:23. De Bienville to De Pontchartrain, Oct. 12, 1708, ibid. 2:37. Robert to De Pontchartrain, Nov. 26, 1708, ibid., 2:45–46.

4. De Bienville to De Pontchartrain, Oct. 27, 1711; Abstract of Letters from De Bienville to De Pontchartrain, 1706, both in Rowland and Sanders, *French Dominion*, 3:159–60, 23. N. Johnson et al. to Proprietors, Sept. 17,

1708, in A. S. Salley, ed., *Records in the British Public Record Office Relating to South Carolina, 1701–1710*, 5 vols. (Columbia, S.C.: Historical Commission of South Carolina, 1947), 5:209.

5. A sign of this is the common European reference to Indian kings. Hudson, *Southeastern Indians*, p. 202.

6. Du Roullet Journal, in Rowland and Dunbar, *French Dominion*, 1:41–44. De Lusser Journal, ibid., 1:115–17.

7. As Swanton, *Choctaw Indians*, pp. 55–57, makes clear, these classifications differ drastically in early French accounts. I have departed from Swanton in making Kunshak and Chickasawhay independent districts. Louis Le Clerc de Milford, *Memoir of a Cursory Glance at My Different Travels and My Sojourn in the Creek Nation,* ed. John F. McDermott (Chicago: Lakeside Press, 1956), pp. 197–200.

8. Swanton, *Choctaw Indians*, pp. 76–79. Fred Eggan, "Historical Changes in the Choctaw Kinship System," *American Anthropologist* 39 (Jan.–Mar. 1937): 34–52. Alexander Spoehr, "Changing Kinship Systems: A Study in the Acculturation of the Creeks, Cherokees, and Choctaws," *Anthropological Series, Field Museum of Natural History* 33 (Chicago, Jan. 17, 1947).

9. Swanton, *Choctaw Indians*, pp. 79–84, 104. Cushman, *History*, p. 367.

10. Swanton, *Choctaw Indians*, pp. 81–82.

11. For details of kinship, see Eggan, "Historical Changes," pp. 34–52. For patrilineal institutions, see William Willis, "Patrilineal Institutions in Southeastern North America," *Ethnohistory* 10 (Summer 1963): 250–69.

12. Swanton, ed., "Early Account," p. 54.

13. Hubert to Council, Oct. 26, 1716, in Rowland and Sanders, *French Dominion*, 2:249.

14. Du Roullet Journal, ibid., 1:153. Mobile Congress, in Dunbar Rowland and A. G. Sanders, *Mississippi Provincial Archives: English Dominion*, 1763–66 (Nashville, Tenn.: Press of Brandon Printing, 1911), pp. 239–40. Cushman, *History*, (Stillwater, 1962), pp. 329–31. Swanton, *Choctaw Indians*, p. 94.

15. De Bienville to Maurepas, Apr. 25, 1734, in Rowland and Sanders, *French Dominion*, 1:226.

16. Swanton, ed., "Early Account," p. 54.

17. De Lusser Journal, in Rowland and Sanders, *French Dominion*, 1:91.

18. Swanton, ed., "Early Account," p. 95.

19. Swanton, *Choctaw Indians*, pp. 81, 83. *Missionary Herald* 19 (Jan. 1824): 10.

20. Jean-Bernard Bossu, *Travels in the Interior of North America, 1751–1762*, trans. and ed. Seymour Feiler (Norman: University of Oklahoma Press, 1962), p. 164. See also Marshall Sahlins, *Stone Age Economics* (Chicago: Aldine Press, 1972), p. 205. The data on redistribution discussed here are not purely Choctaw. Many sources speak of southeastern Indians in general and anthropologists do the same. It seems almost certain, however, that Choctaw chieftainship functioned along the general lines described.

21. For hunt, see Hudson, *Southeastern Indians*, p. 311. For quote, see William Bartram, *Travels through North and South Carolina, Georgia, East and West Florida* (New York: Dover, 1955, reprint of 1791 ed.), p. 401.

22. Adair, *History*, p. 431.

23. Swanton, *Choctaw Indians*, pp. 1, 2, 54–55, 194–200, 221, 224–25. T. N. Campbell, "Choctaw Subsistence," pp. 17–18; Hudson, *Southeastern Indians*, p. 297. Bossu, *Travels*, p. 165. Swanton, ed., "Early Account," p. 61.

24. From De Bienville, Aug. 25, 1733, in Rowland and Sanders, *French Dominion*, 1:193.

25. For balanced exchanges, see Sahlins, *Stone Age Economics*, p. 194, and Swanton, ed., "Early Account," pp. 56–57.

26. Adair, *History*, p. 285. Folsom, "Discussion of Choctaw History, 1798," Peter Pitchlynn Papers, Thomas Gilcrease Institute of American History and Art, Tulsa, Okla. Swanton, *Choctaw Indians*, pp. 11, 163. Swanton, ed., "Early Account," pp. 63–64.

27. Campbell, "Choctaw Subsistence," p. 19.

28. Folsom, "Discussion of Choctaw History, 1798"; Adair, *History*, p. 285.

29. Adair, *History*, p. 285.

30. De Bienville to De Pontchartrain, Oct. 27, 1711, in Rowland and Sanders, *French Dominion*, 3:161. Patricia Dillon Wood, *French-Indian Relations on the Southern Frontier, 1699–1762* (Ann Arbor: UMI Research Press, 1980), p. 11, 34, 50. Swanton, ed., "Early Account," p. 51.

31. For the general outlines of the trade, see Verner Crane, *The Southern Frontier* (Durham, N.C.: Duke University Press, 1928), p. 115; Charles W. Paape, "The Choctaw Revolt: A Chapter in the Inter-Colonial Rivalry in the Old Southwest" (Ph.D. diss., University of Illinois, Urbana, 1946), pp. 16ff., 40–41; Surrey, *Commerce of Louisiana*, pp. 319–20, 340–42. For examples of French complaints of their commercial disadvantages, see De Bienville to Regent, Aug. 8, 1721, in Rowland and Sanders, *French Dominion*, 3:307; Du Roullet Journal, ibid., 1:172; De Bienville and Salmon to Maurepas, May 12, 1733, ibid., 3:596, Sept. 2, 1736, ibid., 3:690–91, Sept. 13, 1736, ibid., 3:692; Périer and La Chaise to Directors, Oct. 27, 1727, ibid., 2:537. Vaudreuil to Maurepas, July 18, 1743, Letterbook (English translation) LO 9, vol. 1 (2); Extracts from Marquis de Vaudreuil's Letterbooks, Jan. 28, 1752, LO 26; 67, Loudoun Collection, Henry Huntington Library. For an early example of the English realization of their corresponding advantages, see Letter of Thomas Nairne, July 10, 1700, Salley, ed., *Records in PRO . . . S.C.*, 5:98.

32. Surrey, *Commerce of Louisiana*, p. 340. A 3,000-man expedition against the Choctaws got few slaves and suffered heavy casualties in 1706. De Bienville to Pontchartrain, Sept. 14, 1706, in Rowland and Sanders, *French Dominion*, 3:34. A 2,000-man expedition yielded only 130 slaves in 1711. Crane, *Southern Frontier*, p. 96.

33. Crane, *Southern Frontier*, pp. 94–97. Letter of Thomas Nairne, July 10, 1708, Salley, ed., *Records in PRO . . . S.C.*, 5:193–94.

34. Crane, *Southern Frontier*, p. 115. Paape, "The Choctaw Revolt," pp. 16ff., 40–41. Surrey, *Commerce of Louisiana*, pp. 319–20, 340–42.

35. For a list of trade goods, see Du Roullet Journal, in Rowland and Sanders, *French Dominion*, 1:53; Surrey, *Commerce of Louisiana*, p. 352. For powder and bullets see Wilbur Jacobs, ed., *The Appalachian Indian Frontier: The Edmond Atkin Report and Plan of 1755* (Lincoln: University of Nebraska Press, 1967), p. 11. Notes Relating to the Management of Indian Affairs, Feb. 1756, LO 2476, Loudoun Papers. Du Roullet Journal, in Rowland and Sanders, *French Dominion*, 1:32; De Lusser Journal, ibid., 1:92; Perier to Maurepas, Jan. 25, 1733, ibid., 1:164. For small deerskins, see De Bienville to Maurepas, Sept. 19, 1735, ibid. 1:270–72, Apr. 23, 1735, ibid., 1:262. Noble, "Mississippi White-Tailed Deer," p. 112. Bartram claimed that throughout the Southeast deerskins of the interior weighed twice as much as those near the coast. Bartram, *Travels*, p. 186.

36. "Brother," here, probably meant that he was an *iksa* relation and thus could kill Conchak Emiko without starting a cycle of revenge killings between *iksas*. If warriors from Kunshak and Chickasawhay, men who presumably belonged to different *iksas*, had killed him, a civil war might have ensued. Beaudouin to Salmon, Nov. 23, 1732, in Rowland and Sanders, *French Dominion*, 1:156–58. Charles Gayarré, *History of Louisiana*, 4 vols. (New York: Redfield, 1854–66), 1:158.

37. Gayarré, *History of Louisiana*, 1:158. Crane, *Southern Frontier*, p. 104; Beaudouin to Salmon, Nov. 23, 1732, in Rowland and Sanders, *French Dominion*, 1:156–57. De Bienville on the Indians, May 15, 1733, ibid., 1:195. Duclos to De Pontchartrain, Oct. 19, 1713, ibid., 2:125–29. De Vaudreuil to Maurepas, Feb. 12, 1748, Letterbook 1, English Translation, LO 9, vol. 1 (2), Loudoun Papers.

38. From De Bienville, Aug. 25, 1733, in Rowland and Sanders, *French Dominion*, 1:193; Hubert to Council, Oct. 26, 1717, ibid., 2:250. Swanton, "Early Account," p. 55. For quote, see Beaudouin to Salmon, Nov. 23, 1732, Rowland and Sanders, *French Dominion*, 1:156. In what follows I am assuming that all the Mingo Tchitos mentioned in French documents are the same person. As those experienced in working with such documents know, this is not always a safe assumption.

39. For this and other early statements of the policy, see De Bienville to Council, Feb. 1, 1723, in Rowland and Sanders, *French Dominion*, 3:343; Minutes of the Superior Council, Aug. 3, 1723, ibid., 3:357–58; Extract from the Register of the Minutes of the Council, Sept. 18, 1723, ibid., 3:378–80.

40. Minutes of the Superior Council of Louisiana, Representation of M. de Bienville, July 23, 1723, ibid., 3:355–56; Extracts from . . . Minutes of the Council, Dec. 1, 1724, ibid., 3:457–58. Extracts from De Vaudreuil's Letterbooks, Dec. 28, 1744, Loudoun Papers.

41. Perier to Abbe Raguet, May 12, 1728, Rowland and Sanders, *French Dominion*, 2:573–74. Wood, *French-Indian Relations*, p. 41. De Bienville to

Maurepas, Mar. 28, 1742, in Rowland and Sanders, *French Dominion*, 3:767. Extracts from De Vaudreuil's Letterbooks, Apr. 20, 1741, LO 26: 56–57, Loudoun Papers.

42. Minutes of the Superior Council, July 23, 1723, in Rowland and Sanders, *French Dominion*, 3:355. For a discussion of blood revenge among the Choctaws, see Swanton, *Choctaw Indians*, pp. 104–10. For a more detailed account of a very similar system among the Cherokees, see John Philip Reid, *A Law of Blood* (New York: New York University Press, 1970). On the whole, anthropologists tend to credit more aboriginal warfare to vengeance than do historians. See Anthony Wallace, *The Death and Rebirth of the Seneca* (New York: Random House, 1972), pp. 101–2, and Hudson, *Southeastern Indians*, p. 239. For contemporary evaluations, see Reid, *Law of Blood*, p. 154; Duclos to De Pontchartrain, Sept. 7, 1716, in Rowland and Sanders, *French Dominion*, 3:210; D'Artaguette to Maurepas, Mar. 17, 1734, ibid., 245–46, Sept. 1, 1734, ibid., 1:252; De Bienville to Maurepas, Aug. 26, 1734, ibid., 1:230–31.

43. Swanton, ed., "Early Account," p. 55. Du Roullet Journal, in Rowland and Sanders, *French Dominion*, 1:43. De la Chaise to Directors of the Company of the Indies, Sept. 6, 1723, Duclos to De Pontchartrain, Oct. 25, 1713, ibid., 2:132. Minutes of the Council of Commerce of Louisiana, Mar. 5, 1721, ibid., 3:303. Minutes of the Superior Council, July 23, 1723, ibid., 3:335; Dec. 1, 1724, ibid., 3:457.

44. Over 400 scalps and 100 prisoners were given to the French for bounties in the winter of 1722–23 alone. De Bienville to Council, Feb. 1, 1723, in Rowland and Sanders, *French Dominion*, 3:343. De Bienville to Maurepas, Aug. 26, 1734, ibid., 1:236.

45. De Bienville to Maurepas, Feb. 10, 1736, ibid., 1:277; July 15, 1738, ibid., 3:718–19; Apr. 28, 1738, ibid. 3:712. De Bienville and Salmon to Maurepas, Sept. 1, 1736, ibid. 1:325; De Bienville, King's Paper, July 29, 1738, ibid., 1:367–68.

46. For Choctaw politics, see Paape, "Choctaw Revolt," p. 17, 40, 41; A. S. Salley, ed., *The Colonial Records of South Carolina: Journals of the Commons House of Assembley*, 11 vols. (Columbia: Historical Commission of South Carolina, 1951–77), Dec. 3, 1725, pp. 52–53; Minutes of the Superior Council of Louisiana, July 23, 1723, in Rowland and Sanders, *French Dominion*, 3:355–56; Du Roullet Journal, ibid., 1:17–20, 27–37, 48–52; De Lusser Journal, ibid., 1:110; Beaudouin to Salmon, Nov. 23, 1732, ibid., 1:158. For an account of the Natchez War by a French contemporary, see Du Pratz, *History*, 1:134–62. For a good, brief account of the war, see Jean Delanglez, "The Natchez Massacre and Governor Périer," *Louisiana Historical Quarterly* 17 (1934): 630–41. Choctaw complicity in planning this attack is not clear. The French invariably suspected the worst. Périer to Maurepas, Apr. 10, 1730, in Rowland and Sanders, *French Dominion*, 1:117–22, Mar. 18, 1730, ibid., 1:63–70. The above also contain accounts of the Choctaw attacks on the Natchez and the Choctaw refusal to return French slaves, but also see Du Roullet Journal,

ibid., 1:176–83, 187; D'Artaguette to Maurepas, Feb. 9, 1730, ibid., 1:59–61; Mar. 20, 1730, ibid., 79–80; De Lusser Journal, ibid., 1:88, 97–98, 100.

47. The first mention of medal chiefs as a rank among the Choctaws is in Régis du Roullet's journal of 1732, but medals as a mark of distinction were much older both in the Southeast and elsewhere, and they continued to be significant into the nineteenth century. See Du Roullet Journal, in Rowland and Sanders, *French Dominion*, 1:150–53; Jean Delanglez, ed., "Journal of Pierre Vitry, S. J.," *Mid-America* 28 (Jan. 1946): 51; Francis Paul Prucha, *Indian Peace Medals in American History* (Madison, Wis.: State Historical Society of Wisconsin, 1971). For the increase in medal chiefs, see From De Bienville, May 15, 1733, in Rowland and Sanders, *French Dominion*, 1:194–95; De Bienville to Maurepas, Mar. 15, 1734, ibid., 3:64.

48. Du Roullet Journal, in Rowland and Sanders, *French Dominion*, 1:33–34, 36.

49. Ibid., 1:33–34, 178.

50. Ibid., 1:185–87. Beaudouin to Salmon, Nov. 23, 1732, in ibid., 1:159.

51. Beaudouin to Salmon, Nov. 23, 1732, ibid., 1:159. See also De Vaudreuil's denunciation of Red Shoes, with the approval of the civil chiefs, for his lack of rank and his unworthiness to hold a medal. De Vaudreuil to Maurepas, Feb. 12, 1744, Letterbook (English Translation) LO 9, vol. 1 (2), Loudoun Papers.

52. De Bienville to Maurepas, Mar. 25, 1739, in Rowland and Sanders, *French Dominion*, 3:723.

53. From De Bienville, May 15, 1733, ibid., 1:195. De Bienville to Maurepas, Feb. 10, 1736, ibid., 1:277; Mar. 15, 1734, ibid., 3:634. Swanton, ed. "Early Account," p. 54.

54. Wood, *French-Indian Relations*, p. 111–46, gives a factual account of the events of these years, but her analysis of the motives and politics of the Choctaws is ethnocentric. The same events can also be followed in the letters of De Bienville in vol. 1 and 3 of Rowland and Sanders, *French Dominion*. A fuller account of the life of Red Shoes is in Richard White, "Red Shoes: Warrior and Diplomat," in David G. Sweet and Gary B. Nash, *Struggle and Survival in Colonial America* (Berkeley: University of California Press, 1981), pp. 49–68. For the quote, see De Bienville to Maurepas, Mar. 15, 1734, Rowland and Sanders, *French Dominion*, 3:633.

55. For the quote, see De Bienville to Maurepas, Mar. 9, 1735, Rowland and Sanders, *French Dominion*, 1:270–74. For De Bienville's belief in the chiefs, see From De Bienville, May 15, 1733, ibid., 1:195; De Bienville to Maurepas, Sept. 30, 1734, ibid., 1:237–41.

56. De Bienville to Maurepas, Apr. 28, 1738, ibid., 3:714–16.

57. Gayarré, *History of Louisiana*, 1:482–83; M. Dumont, "Historical Memoir" in French, *Historical Collections*, 5:112; De Bienville to Maurepas, June 28, 1736, in Rowland and Sanders, *French Dominion*, 1:305–8; De Bienville and Salmon to Maurepas, Sept. 1, 1736, ibid., 1:325; Diron d'Artaguette

to Maurepas, May 8, 1737, ibid., 1:338, 339; De Bienville to Maurepas, Dec. 20, 1737, ibid., 3:705, Apr. 28, 1738, ibid., 3:709–11. For the crisis of 1738, see *CRSC: Journals of . . . Assembly*, May 5, 1737, p. 285, June 1, 1738, p. 527, Sept. 12, 1738, p. 575, Jan. 17, 1739, p. 590, Jan. 19, 1739, p. 595. Copy of Col. Bull's Letter to the Lords of Trade, July 20, 1738, in Allen D. Candler, ed., *The Colonial Records of the State of Georgia* (Atlanta, 1913), 22:212–13. De Bienville to Maurepas, Apr. 28, 1738, in Rowland and Sanders, *French Dominion*, 3:709–12, 715–16; July 15, 1738, ibid., 3:718, King's Paper, May 29, 1738, ibid., 1:368; Louboey to Maurepas, July 11, 1738, ibid., 1:371; D'Artaguette to Maurepas, May 8, 1737, ibid., 1:338–40. Paape, "Choctaw Revolt," pp. 38–41, 50. De Bienville contended later that his subordinates exaggerated the crisis.

58. Board of Trade to Governors, July 1, 1756, LO 1278, Loudoun Collection.

59. Mobile Congress, in Rowland, *English Dominion*, p. 241.

60. De Bienville to Maurepas, Sept. 9, 1735, Rowland and Sanders, *French Dominion*, 1:272. Notes Relating to the Management of Indian Affairs, Feb. 1756, LO 24716, Loudoun Papers.

61. Conference with the Choctaws, beginning 25th October, 1759 . . . , Saturday, 27th October, Speech of Superintendent, in William Henry Lyttelton Papers, 1755–1760, William L. Clements Library, University of Michigan. James Adair also refers to the Choctaws as "great beggars," Adair, *History*, p. 304.

62. See, e.g., De Bienville to Salmon, May 11, 1737, in Rowland and Sanders, *French Dominion*, 1:349. Alfred Reynolds, "The Alabama-Tombigbee Basin in International Relations, 1701–1763" (Ph.D. diss., University of California at Berkeley, 1928), p. 136.

63. Adair, *History*, p. 309. Memoir of De Bienville (1726), in Rowland and Sanders, *French Dominion*, 3:538. De Bienville to De Pontchartrain, Sept. 1, 1715, ibid., 3:188.

64. Jacobs, *Atkin Report*, pp. 22–23; Périer and De La Chaise to Directors of the Company of the Indies, Oct. 27, 1727, in Rowland and Sanders, *French Dominion*, 2:612–13. Surrey, *Commerce of Louisiana*, pp. 358–59.

65. Surrey, *Commerce of Louisiana*, p. 343. Edmond Atkin, "Historical Account of the Revolt of the Choctaw Indians in the late War from the French to the British Alliance . . .," p. 53, original in British Museum, Lans. 809, copy in John Carl Parish Papers, University of California at Santa Barbara. Jacobs, *Atkin Report*, p. 23.

66. Conference with the Choctaws, Oct. 25, Oct. 30, 1759; Atkin to Hewitt, Sept. 21, 1759, enclosed to Lyttelton, Nov. 30, 1759, all in Lyttelton Papers. Atkin, "Historical Account," p. 53. Jacobs, *Atkins Report*, p. 23.

67. De Bienville to Maurepas, Mar. 25, 1739, in Rowland and Sanders, *French Dominion*, 3:722–30; May 20, 1739, ibid., 1:395–97. *CRSC: Journal of . . . Assembly*, Feb. 2, 1740, pp. 172–73. Edmond Atkin, "Historical Account," p. 53.

68. Louboey to Maurepas, June 3, 1739, in Rowland and Sanders, *French Dominion*, 1:398. De Bienville to Maurepas, May 20, 1739, ibid., 1:395–97. Reynolds, "Alabama-Tombigbee," p. 226. Paape, "Choctaw Revolt," p. 50. *CRSC: Journal of . . . Assembly*, Jan. 17, 1739, p. 590.

69. David Corkran, *The Creek Frontier*, 1540–1783 (Norman: University of Oklahoma Press, 1967), pp. 116–27. Paape, "Choctaw Revolt," p. 106. Representation of English Traders in the Creek Nation, Aug. 18, 1747, Loudoun Papers. De Bienville to Maurepas, Mar. 25, 1739, in Rowland and Sanders, *French Dominion*, 3:724–25.

70. See Du Roullet Journal in Rowland and Sanders, *French Dominion*, 1:148, for raids and fortifications. These conclusions about town occupations are based on a list of Choctaw towns drawn up to include all available references between 1702 and 1804. Many towns disappear from the list in the 1730s. For example, Du Roullet mentions Bok Chito in 1732, as does the Crenay Map of 1733, but after that it disappears. Du Roullet Journal, ibid., 1:151; Crenay Map in John Swanton, *Early History of the Creek Indians and Their Neighbors*, Bureau of American Ethnology Bulletin, no. 73 (Washington, D.C.: Government Printing Office, 1922). Likewise, Oklatanap is not mentioned again after being cited in the so-called Early Account. Swanton, "Early Account," p. 72. Swanton dates this about 1755, but I believe that the early 1730s is a more accurate date and that Fr. Beaudouin may be the author. Swanton, *Choctaw Indians*, p. 3. For change in western and southern towns, see Extracts in English from De Vaudreuil's Letterbooks, Mar. 6, 1748, pp. 40–45, Loudoun Papers: Paape, "Choctaw Revolt," p. 106; "De Beauchamps' Journey to the Choctaws in 1746," in Newton Mereness, *Travels in the American Colonies* (New York: Macmillan, 1916), pp. 263–64; Highrider to Glen, Oct. 24, 1750, in William L. McDowell, Jr., ed., *Colonial Records of South Carolina: Documents Relating to Indian Affairs*, 3 vols. (Columbia, S.C.: University of South Carolina Press, 1956–70), 2:38–39. Romans, *Natural History*, p. 72, badly muddles the divisions during the civil war.

71. For the murders and the response, see Salmon to Maurepas, Jan. 29, 1740, in Rowland and Sanders, *French Dominion*, 1:419–20; De Bienville to Maurepas, May 6, 1740, ibid., 1:453–54; May 8, 1740, ibid., 3:731–32. For Red Shoes's return to French favor, see De Bienville to Maurepas, Mar. 28, 1742, ibid., 3:765. De Vaudreuil to Maurepas, June 1743, Letterbook (English Translation) LO 9, vol. 1 (2), Loudoun Papers. Maurepas to De Vaudreuil, Oct. 27, 1742, LO 23, Loudoun Papers.

72. These events are full of complicated betrayals and maneuverings: De Vaudreuil to Maurepas, July 18, 1743, LO´, vol. 1 (2), Loudoun Papers. *The Present State of the Country and Inhabitants, Europeans and Indians of Louisiana . . . by an Officer at New Orleans* (London: J. Millan, 1744), pp. 36–38, 45. This is a letter of Mar. 1, 1744, from De Vaudreuil to his brother, which was captured and published by the English. Also see, Letter of De Vaudreuil, Feb. 12, 1744, Letterbook (English Translation) LO 9, vol. 1 (2), Loudoun Papers; De Vaud-

reuil to Maurepas, May 10, 1744, Letterbook 1 (English Translation) LO 9, vol. 1 (2), Loudoun Papers; Extracts from De Vaudreuil's Letterbooks, Sept. 17, 1744, pp. 15–16; Dec. 28, 1744, pp. 18–20, Loudoun Papers. Adair, *History*, pp. 314–15; Paape, "Choctaw Revolt," pp. 52–55, 78–83, 91. "Journal of De Beauchamp's Journey to the Choctaws, 1746," in Newton Mereness, *Travels in the American Colonies* (New York: Macmillan, 1916), p. 292. White, "Red Shoes," pp. 61–66. For De Vaudreuil's attempts to assert French hegemony across the region, see De Vaudreuil to Maurepas, July 18, 1743, June 1743, Feb. 12, 1743, all in Letterbook 1 (English Translation) LO 9, vol. 1 (2), Loudoun Papers.

73. Paape, "Choctaw Revolt," pp. 78–81, 84–86. *CRCS: Journal of . . . Assembly*, Jan. 25, 1745, pp. 309, 349. Extracts from De Vaudreuil's Letterbooks, Dec. 28, 1744, pp. 18–20; Oct. 28, 1745, p. 21; Apr. 1, 1746, p. 29; Nov. 20, 1746, pp. 31–32, Loudoun Papers. Atkin, "Historical Account," p. 64. Bossu, *Travels*, p. 175. Reynolds, "Alabama-Tombigbee," p. 242. The quote is from the "Journal of De Beauchamps," p. 262.

74. Adair, *History*, p. 317.

75. Paape, "Choctaw Revolt," pp. 84–85. Extracts from De Vaudreuil's Letterbooks, Nov. 20, 1746, pp. 21–32, Loudoun Papers. The most detailed contemporary English accounts are Atkin, "Historical Account" Governor Glen's report of 1751, Glen to Board of Trade, Dec. 1751, PRO, CO 5, 73: 177–88; and Adair, *History*, pp. 314–51. All the contemporary accounts have to be used carefully; they are all self-serving. Atkin is probably the most reliable.

76. For the murder of Red Shoes, see Paape, "Choctaw Revolt," p. 100; Extracts from De Vaudreuil's Letterbooks, Mar. 20, 1748, p. 39, Loudoun Papers. For subsequent events, see Paape, "Choctaw Revolt," pp. 106–19.

77. Paape, "Choctaw Revolt," pp. 119, 129, 132–34. Extracts from De Vaudreuil's Letterbooks, Jan. 1, 1750, p. 53, Loudoun Papers.

78. Extracts from De Vaudreuil's Letterbooks, Jan. 1, 1750, p. 55, Loudoun Papers. Paape, "Choctaw Revolt," pp. 106–13, 116–27, 158–59. Many of the scalps given to De Vaudreuil may have been taken from victims of smallpox, which raged during the war.

79. Paape, "Choctaw Revolt," p. 161.

80. Ibid., p. 75. Surrey, *Commerce of Louisiana*, p. 360. Names of villages of Choctaws, in Rowland, *English Dominion*, pp. 26–29.

81. Conference with the Choctaws beginning 25th of October, 1759 . . . , Lyttelton Papers.

82. For this aspect of the Choctaw world view, see Hudson, *Southeastern Indians*, pp. 120–28.

83. Memorandum of Jerome Courtance (1757), *CRSC: Indian Affairs*, 2:414–15. De Bienville to Maurepas, June 17, 1737, in Rowland and Sanders, *French Dominion*, 3:709.

84. Journal of John Buckles, Jan. 1, 1754, *CRSC: Indian Affairs*, 2:509. Extracts from De Vaudreuil's Letterbook, May 10, 1751, pp. 60–61, Loudoun

Papers. Message of Lieutenant Governor, Feb. 2, 1740, in *CRSC: Journals of . . . Assembly*, 2:172–73. Daniel Pepper to Lyttelton, Dec. 21, 1756, in *CRSC: Indian Affairs* 3:297. Paape, "Choctaw Revolt," pp. 52–53. Answer of Indian Chiefs to George Johnston, May 16, 1766, in Rowland, *English Dominion*, p. 529.

85. Minutes of Superior Council, July 23, 1723, in Rowland and Sanders, *French Dominion*, 3:355. D'Artaguette to Maurepas, May 8, 1737, ibid., 1:343. For typical assaults by the Chickasaws, see De Bienville to Maurepas, Apr. 28, 1738, ibid., 3:709. Also see De Vaudreuil to Maurepas, June 1743, Letterbook (English Translation) LO 9, vol. 1 (2), Loudoun Papers. Deposition of John Petterow before the Governor, Oct. 8, 1751, *CRSC: Indian Affairs*, 2:16.

86. Paape, "Choctaw Revolt," p. 75; Surrey, *Commerce of Louisiana*. pp. 360, 362. These calculations proceed from ibid., p. 210. Surrey gives the price French merchants paid traders for deerskins at Mobile. Aloysius Plaisance, "The Choctaw Trading House, 1803–1822," *Alabama Historical Quarterly* 16 (Autumn 1954): 407–8, 415, gives the average weight of Choctaw skins as 2.6 pounds. These figures, however, covered deer killed west of the Mississippi. The deer of Mississippi were probably smaller. There were 200 sous in a livre. For reports of a normal 200 percent mark-up, see Swanton, ed., "Early Account," p. 59.

CHAPTER 4

1. Council with the Choctaws by M. Dabbadie and Major Farmar, Nov. 14, 1763, in Rowland, *English Dominion*, pp. 83–93. Farmar to Gage, Sept. 17, 1764, vol. 17; Ford to Stuart, June 21, 1765, vol. 49, both in Gage Papers. Kinnaird, *Spain in Miss. Valley*, 1:xv. J. Stuart to Amherst, June 2, 1763, in Jeffrey Amherst Papers, 1758–64, Clements Library, University of Michigan, 3:51.

2. For gifts at Savannah, see Farmar to J. Stuart, Mar. 5, 1764, vol. 17; Farmar to Gage, Mar. 29, 1764, vol. 16; J. Stuart to Gage, Apr. 11, 1765, vol. 34, all in Gage Papers. For English Attitudes: Farmar to Secretary of War, Jan. 24, 1764, p. 13; Extract of letter of Lt. Ford, Dec. 3, 1763, p. 13, both in Rowland, *English Dominion*; Amherst to J. Stuart, June 17, 1763, Gage Papers, vol. 10.

3. See, for example, Stuart's speech at the Mobile Congress, in Rowland, *English Dominion*, p. 229; J. Stuart to Gage, Sept. 20, 1765, Gage Papers, vol. 43; Ford to J. Stuart, Nov. 21, 1764, Gage Papers, vol. 49. Clarence Carter, ed., "Observations of Superintendent John Stuart and Governor James Grant of East Florida on the Proposed Plan of 1764," *American Historical Review* 20 (July 1915): 830. Mobile Congress, in Rowland, *English Dominion*, pp. 219–20, 230, 238–39.

4. J. Stuart to Gage, May 20, 1764, vol. 18; Farmar to J. Stuart, Mar. 5, 1764, vol. 17, Mar. 29, 1764, vol. 16, Jan. 1, 1764, vol. 17, J. Stuart to Gage, May 22, 1764, vol. 18, all in Gage Papers. Memorial of Gov. Johnstone to

Board of Trade, May 30, 1764, in Rowland, *English Dominion*.

5. Mobile Congress, in Rowland, *English Dominion*, pp. 238, 240, 242, 248. J. Stuart to Earl of Hillsborough, Feb. 6, 1772, PRO, CO 5, 73:46–50. In the nineteenth century John Pitchlynn would assert that large sections of the Choctaw country had once belonged to "extirperated" peoples; NA OIA, LR, Choctaw Agency emigration, Terrell to Barbour, Mar. 25, 1826.

6. Mobile Congress, in Rowland, *English Dominion*, pp. 237–38.

7. Chester to J. Stuart, Sept. 10, 1771, PRO, CO 5, 72:353–54.

8. J. Stuart to Gage, May 22, 1764, Gage Papers, vol. 18.

9. Mobile Congress, in Rowland, *English Dominion*, p. 237. See Swanton, *Choctaw Indians*, pp. 76–77, for moieties.

10. Mobile Congress, in Rowland, *English Dominion*, p. 241.

11. Ibid., p. 242.

12. For costs and belief in annual Congresses, see J. Stuart to Gage, Aug. 2, 1766, vol. 55; Warrants for Jan. 3, 1765, vol. 106; J. Stuart to Gage, Dec. 19, 1766, vol. 60; C. Stuart to J. Stuart, June 6, 1767, vol. 67; J. Stuart to Gage, July 21, 1767, vol. 67; C. Stuart to J. Stuart, Aug. 6, 1770, enclosure with J. Stuart to Gage, Sept. 27, 1770, vol. 94; Extract for Report of Council on West Florida to Gov. Chester, Sept. 9, 1771, vol. 108; Declaration of John Stuart, Minutes of Council of West Florida, Oct. 1771, vol. 108, all in Gage Papers. For Stuart's changing policy, see J. Stuart to Gage, Sept. 20, 1765, vol. 43, Apr. 11, 1765, vol. 34, both in ibid. Report of Johnstone and Stuart, June 12, 1765, in Rowland, *English Dominion*, p. 187. J. Stuart to Board of Trade, Aug. 24, 1765, vol. 43; J. Stuart to Gage, Jan. 21, 1766, vol. 47, both in Gage Papers.

13. J. Stuart to Earl of Hillsborough Feb. 6, 1772, PRO, CO 5, 73:46–50. Ford to J. Stuart, June 21, 1765, vol. 49; J. Stuart to Gage, Dec. 19, 1766, vol. 60, both in Gage Papers. The victim of the assassination is identified only as a great medal chief "much in our interest," but since this is the language used earlier to describe Nassuba Mingo and the opposition to him, he appears to have been the victim.

14. Shelburne to J. Stuart, Sept. 13, 1766, Dec. 11, 1766, both in Gage Papers, vol. 60. J. Stuart to Gage, Dec. 26, 1767, Gage Papers, vol. 73; Abstract of Letter of John Stuart, Apr. 11, 1767, Shelburne Papers, 51:167. Corkran, *Creek Frontier*, pp. 261–69. J. Stuart to Gage, Mar. 3, 1770, vol. 60; Aug. 2, 1770, vol. 94, both in Gage Papers.

15. Eron Opha Rowland, *Peter Chester*, Publications of the Mississippi Historical Society, vol. 5 (Jackson, Miss., 1925), p. 148.

16. Abstract of Letter of C. Stuart to J. Stuart, Aug. 26, 1770, vol. 94; C. Stuart to Haldimand, Apr. 10, 1771, vol. 102, both in Gage Papers.

17. J. Stuart to Gage, Dec. 19, 1768, vol. 74; Sept. 26, 1767, vol. 70; Sept. 20, 1765, vol. 43; Farmar to Gage, Nov. 24, 1764, vol. 27, all in Gage Papers. For Mingo Emmitta, see Eron Rowland, *Peter Chester*, p. 148; for Illepotapo, see ibid., p. 150.

18. Ford to J. Stuart, June 21, 1765, July 11, 1765, both in Gage Papers, vol. 49. Mobile Congress, in Rowland, *English Dominion*, p. 247. For quote, see J. Stuart to Gage, Nov. 27, 1767, Gage Papers, vol. 70.

19. J. Stuart to Amherst, Nov. 10, 1763, Amherst Papers, 7:23.

20. Gage to Halifax, Jan. 21, 1764, Gage Papers, English ser., vol. 1.

21. J. Stuart to Gage, May 6, 1765, Gage Papers, vol. 35. Corkran, *Creek Frontier*, pp. 254–55. Corkran identifies Colbert as Stuart's agent, but Johnstone claimed the credit. See quote below in text.

22. Johnstone to Stuart, May 19, 1766, Gage Papers, vol. 55.

23. C. Stuart to J. Stuart, Oct. 29, 1767, vol. 72; J. Stuart to Gage, May 17, 1768, vol. 77; C. Stuart to Haldimand, May 12, 1774, vol. 119; J. Stuart to Gage, Aug. 6, 1760, vol. 55, Johnstone to J. Stuart, June 3, 1766, vol. 55; Abstract of Johnstone to Conway, June 23, 1766, vol. 55; Johnstone to J. Stuart, Sept. 13, 1766, vol. 55; J. Stuart to Gage, Jan. 7, 1767, vol. 61, all in Gage Papers. Corkran, *Creek Frontier*, p. 256.

24. C. Stuart to J. Stuart, Oct. 29, 1767, vol. 72; J. Hewitt to Traders in the Choctaw Nation, Oct. 16, 1767, vol. 72; J. Stuart to Gage, Dec. 26, 1767, vol. 73, all in Gage Papers. Romans, *Natural History*, pp. 73, 309, 329. For deaths of chiefs, see C. Stuart to J. Stuart, Oct. 29, 1767, vol. 72. Abstract of letter of C. Stuart to J. Stuart, Mar. 17, 1773, vol. 118, both in Gage Papers. J. Stuart to Sup., Dec. 12, 1774, PRO, CO 5, 77:69.

25. For divisions, see J. Stuart to Dartmouth, Aug. 2, 1774, PRO, CO 5, 75:165. For hunting lands, see Folsom, "Discussion of Choctaw History," Pitchlynn Collection. Abstract, J. Stuart to Hillsborough, Jan. 18, 1770, PRO, CO 5, 72:343. C. Stuart to Supt., Dec. 26, 1770, PRO, CO 5, 72:179. C. Stuart to Creeks, Dec. 12, 1770, PRO, CO 5, 72:167. For peace, see Corkran, *Creek Frontier*, p. 293. J. Stuart to Germaine, Oct. 26, 1776, PRO, CO 5, 78:109. Extract, Taitt to Supt., Aug. 3, 1777, PRO, CO 5, 78:47. Germaine to J. Stuart, Feb. 7, 1777, PRO, CO 5, 78:7–8.

26. Eron Rowland, *Peter Chester*, pp. 149–50.

27. Ibid., pp. 147, 160. C. Stuart to J. Stuart, June 12, 1770, enclosure with J. Stuart to Gage, Aug. 6, 1770, Gage Papers, vol. 94.

28. Governmental Expenses, 1767, in Kinnaird, *Spain in Miss. Valley*, 1:18.

29. J. Stuart to Gage, Feb. 16, 1772, Gage Papers, vol. 109.

30. Eron Rowland, *Peter Chester*, pp. 139, 157.

31. Ibid., p. 158.

32. Choctaw Towns and Those Receiving Presents—Headmen and Principal Warriors, PRO, CO 5, 73:380–81. Report of the Proceedings of the Hon. Charles Stuart . . . July 1, 1778, PRO, CO 5, 79:392.

33. C. Stuart to J. Stuart, Apr. 8, 1777, PRO, CO 5, 78:255. J. Stuart to Germaine, Oct. 9, 1778, PRO, CO 5, 80:7. For first quote, see Colbert to Cameron, Nov. 19, 1779, PRO, CO 5, 81. For second quote, see A Talk from the Six Towns . . . to Captain Colbert, Nov. 19, 1779, PRO, CO 5, 80:113.

34. Ford to Stuart, Nov. 21, 1764, Gage Papers, vol. 49.

35. Romans, *Natural History*, p. 66. Eron Rowland, *Peter Chester*, p. 151.

36. Stuart to Gage, May 20, 1764, Gage Papers, vol. 18; Swanton, ed., "Early Account," p. 61. For smallpox quote, see Adair, *History*, p. 339. For Captain Ouma, see Report of the Proceedings of the Hon. Charles Stuart . . . July 1, 1788, PRO, CO 5, 79:387.

37. J. Stuart to Germaine, Oct. 26, 1776, PRO, CO 5, 78:34. Romans, *Natural History*, p. 77. C. Stuart to J. Stuart, Mar. 4, 1777, PRO, CO 5, 78:251. Report of the Proceedings of the Hon. Charles Stuart, July 1, 1778, PRO, CO 5, 79:396.

38. Ford to Stuart, June 21, 1765, Gage Papers, vol. 49. Stuart to Earl of Hillsborough, Remarks (an extract), June 8, 1770; Stuart to Earl of Hillsborough, July 22, 1770, both in Gage Papers, vol. 108.

39. For peace of towns, see Adair, *History*, p. 429. The best discussion of how peace within woodland villages was maintained is in Irving Hallowell, "Some Psychological Characteristics of Northeastern Indians," in Hallowell, *Culture and Experience* (Philadelphia: University of Pennsylvania Press, 1955), pp. 125–50. Similar techniques and patterns probably obtained among the Choctaws.

40. Affidavit of Henry Le Fleur, Aug. 27, 1772, Gage Papers, vol. 115, and C. Stuart to J. Stuart, Apr. 8, 1777, PRO, CO 5, 78:255. Report of the Proceedings of the Hon. Charles Stuart . . . July 1, 1778, PRO, CO 5, 79:402. J. Stuart to Germaine, June 14, 1777, PRO, CO 5, 78:286. Such figures may be exaggerated, but they do reveal Choctaw perceptions of the extent, significance, and danger of the liquor problem.

41. Campbell to Farmar, Mar. 26, 1765, vol. 34; Ford to Farmar, Dec. 10, 1764, vol. 29; Ford to Stuart, Nov. 21, 1764, vol. 49, all in Gage Papers.

42. Campbell to Farmar, Mar. 26, 1765, vol. 34; Haldimand to Stuart, Mar. 1, 1768, vol. 74, J. Stuart to Gage, Aug. 2, 1770, vol. 94, all in Gage Papers. Abstract, Stuart to Hillsborough, Jan. 18, 1770, PRO, CO 5, 72:343. Adair, *History*, pp. 297–99. For hunting and war, see Bartram, *Travels*, p. 216. Folsom, "Discussion of Choctaw History," Pitchlynn Collection. Abstract, Stuart to Hillsborough, Jan. 18, 1770, PRO, CO 5, 72:343. Stuart to Hillsborough, Feb. 6, 1772, PRO, CO 5, 73:46–50.

43. Eron Rowland, *Peter Chester*, p. 157. Romans, *Natural History*, p. 74.

44. C. Stuart to Cameron, Dec. 20, 1779, PRO, CO 5, 81:95–97. For conferences, see J. Stuart to Germaine, Oct. 26, 1776, PRO, CO 5, 78:29. Congress at Mobile, May 26, 1777, PRO, CO 5, 81:36. J. Stuart to Germaine, June 14, 1777, PRO, CO 5, 78:286. Tait to Commissioners, Aug. 5, 1779, PRO, CO 5, 81:574–75. J. Stuart to Germaine, [spring] 1778, PRO, CO 5, 79:165. J. Stuart to Germaine, Oct. 9, 1778, PRO, CO 5, 80:7. Cameron to Germaine, Dec. 20, 1779, PRO, CO 5, 81:85.

45. Quoted in James O'Donnell III, *Southern Indians in the American Revolution* (Knoxville: University of Tennessee Press, 1973), p. 101.

46. For quote, see Cameron to Germaine, Sept. 20, 1780, PRO, CO 5, 82:177. For Spanish, see Statement of Expenses, May 31, 1787, Jeseph de Orue, in Kinnaird, *Spain in the Miss. Valley*, 2:209; "Financial Reports Relating to Louisiana," *Mississippi Valley Historical Review* 6 (Dec. 1919): 394–97.

47. For gifts, see Report of the Proceedings of the Hon. Charles Stuart . . . July 1, 1778, PRO, CO 5, 81:383–403; Account of Presents, 1st of Apr. to 31st of May 1779, PRO, CO 5, 81:609; G. Barnes, General Account of Goods . . . Apr. 1 to Sept. 30, 1779, PRO, CO 5, 81:607. For warriors, see Cameron to Clinton, July 18, 1780, 2:158–59; Receipts, 2:71, 77, 78, both in Historical Manuscripts Commission, *Report on American Manuscripts in the Royal Institution of Great Britain*, 3 vols. (London: Mackie & Co. and Anthony Bros., 1904–1907).

48. Return of Choctaw, Chickasaw . . . Remaining at Pensacola, Feb., 1781, PRO, CO 5, 82:288. Cameron to Germaine, Nov. 30, 1780, PRO, CO 5, 82:233–43. Even the outbreak of an unidentified epidemic that swept through the nation in 1779, killing many, probably had only a temporary impact on the hunt. Cameron to Clinton, Dec. 15, 1779, PRO, CO 5, 81:104.

49. For loss of English supplies, see Bethune to Germaine, Jan. 10, 1782, PRO, CO 5, 82:585–88; Bethune to Cameron, Sept. 4, 1780, PRO, CO 5, 82:193–96; Graham to Earl of Shelburne, Sept. 1782, PRO, CO 5, 82:823; Brown to Germaine, Aug. 9, 1781, PRO, CO 5, 82:508. For Spanish dependence on English goods and their failure to supply the Indians with enough goods, see J. Thomas to J. Stuart, Dec. 11, 1771, PRO, CO 5, 73:99; Report of New British Campaign, Mar. 9, 1783, in Kinnaird, *Spain in the Miss. Valley*, 2:71–73. For decline in hunt, see Maxent to Bouligny, Sept. 24, 1782, in Kinnaird, *Spain in the Miss. Valley*, 2:59; Maxent to Miro, Dec. 5, 1782, ibid., 2:67. Bethune to Cameron, Aug. 27, 1780, PRO, CO 5, 82:189. Bethune to Cameron, Sept. 4, 1781, PRO, CO 5, 82:193–96. Bethune to Cameron, Jan. 10, 1782, PRO, CO 5, 82:585–88.

50. For British partisans, see Graham to Shelburne, Sept. 1782, PRO, CO 5, 82:823; Trevino to Miro, Oct. 18, 1783, in Kinnaird, *Spain in the Miss. Valley*, 2:88–89; Favre to Tugean, Nov. 25, 1783, ibid., 2:92, John Douglas to Carleton, Jan. 20, 1783, HMC, Report on American Manuscripts, 3:334; O'Donnell, *Southern Indians in the American Revolution*, p. 129. For the Spanish alliance, see Lawrence Kinnaird, "Spanish Treaties with Indian Tribes," *Western Historical Quarterly* 10 (Jan. 1979): 41–48; Jack D. L. Holmes, *Gayoso: The Life of a Spanish Governor in the Mississippi Valley, 1789–1799* (Baton Rouge: Louisiana State University Press, 1965), pp. 142–43; Petition of Panton and Leslie and Company, July 31, 1784, in Kinnaird, *Spain in Miss. Valley*, 2:114–15; Jane M. Berry, "The Indian Policy of Spain in the Southwest, 1783–95," *Mississippi Valley Historical Review* 3 (Mar. 1917): 462–77. Kinnaird, *Spain in the Miss. Valley*, 2:xvi. Bouligny to Miro, Jan. 23, 1785, quoted in Gayarré, *History of Louisiana*, 2:162; Holmes, *Gayoso*, pp. 142–43.

51. Holmes, *Gayoso*, p. 159.

52. For negotiations of 1780s, see Cotterill, *Southern Indians*, p. 68; Holmes, *Gayoso*, p. 74; Treaty with the Choctaws, Jan. 3, 1786, 7 Stat. 21, Charles J. Kappler, *Indian Affairs: Laws and Treaties*, 5 vols. (Washington, D.C.: Government Printing Office, 1904), 2:11–14; Miro to Wilkinson, Apr. 30, 1789, in Gayarré, *History of Louisiana*, 2:282. For the American conference of

1792, see Secretary of War to Blount, Mar. 31, 1792, 4:131–32; Blount to Secretary of War, Aug. 31, 1792, 4:169, both in Clarence Carter, *Southwest Territory*, vol. 4, *The Territorial Papers of the United States*, 28 vols. (Washington, D.C.: Government Printing Office, 1934–75), pp. 1131–32, 169; Knox to Chiefs and Warriors of Choctaw, Feb. 17, 1792, Kinnaird, *Spain in the Miss. Valley*, 3:4–6; Blount to Choctaws, May 10, 1792, ibid., 3:7; Delavillebeuvre to Carondelet, Sept. 5, 1792, ibid., 3:74–77. For Spanish and American conferences of 1793 and 1794, see ibid., 3:xxxiii; Delavillebeuvre to Carondelet, June 9, 1794, ibid., 3:297–98; Message of Carondelet to Choctaws and Chickasaws (1793), ibid., 3:140; Proposal for Indian Congress, Feb. 26, 1793, ibid. 3:141–42. Holmes, *Gayoso*, pp. 152–53.

53. Sargent to Marshall, Aug. 10, 1800, p. 266; Sargent to McHenry, Aug. 3, 1799, pp. 163–64; Sargent to Pickering, Feb. 10, 1800, pp. 206–7; Sargent to McKee, Nov. 25, 1799, pp. 193–95, all in Dunbar Rowland, ed., *Mississippi Territorial Archives, 1798–1803, Executive Journals of Governor Winthrop Sargent and Governor William Charles Cole Claiborne* (Nashville: Brandon Printing, 1905). McKee to Choctaw Chiefs, Oct. 19, 1800, box 4, no. 137, McKee Papers, Library of Congress. For the decline in Spanish gifts, see Holmes, *Gayoso*, p. 236; Claiborne to Madison, July 9, 1803, in Dunbar Rowland ed., *Official Letterbooks of W.C.C. Claiborne*, 1801–1816, 4 vols. (Jackson, Miss.: Department of Archives and History, 1917), 1:260.

54. For estimates of trade, see Petition of Panton and Leslie, July 31, 1784, in Kinnaird, *Spain in the Miss. Valley*, 2:114–15; Gayarré, *History of Louisiana*, 2:174. An Estimate of the Annual Trade of the Chickasaws and Choctaws by Governor Pickens and Governor Blount, Aug. 1, 1792, Carter, *Territorial Papers: Southwest*, 4:293. For liquor, see Delavillebeuvre to Carondelet, Sept. 5, 1792, in Kinnaird, *Spain in the Miss. Valley*, 3:77; Franchimastabe to Lanzos, Apr. 22, 1793, ibid., 3:152–53; Edward Ross and Dawson Phelps, "A Journey over the Natchez Trace in 1792: A Document from the Archives of Spain," *Journal of Mississippi History* 15 (Oct. 1953): 255–66. For debts, see Delavillebeuvre to Carondelet, May 7, 1794, in Kinnaird, *Spain in the Miss. Valley*, 3:282; Traders of the Choctaw Nation to Lemos, June 28, 1794, Bolton Papers, Bancroft Library, University of California, Berkeley.

55. I have calculated the value of deerskins from the early nineteenth-century rate given by Plaisance, "Choctaw Trading House," pp. 408, 417.

56. Kinnaird, "Spanish Treaties," pp. 45–48. Henry White to Carondelet, July 6, 1793, Bolton Papers, pt. 1; Kinnaird, *Spain in the Miss. Valley*, 3:xvii.

57. Ruth T. West, "Pushmataha's Travels," *Chronicles of Oklahoma* 37 (Summer 1959): 167–70. For decline of game in the east, see D. Kirby to President, Apr. 20, 1804, Carter, *Territorial Papers of the U.S., Mississippi*, 5:319; Hawkins et al. to Dearborn, Dec. 18, 1801, "Letters of Benjamin Hawkins, 1796–1806," *Collections of the Georgia Historical Society* 9 (Savannah, Ga.: The Morning News, 1916), p. 410. For hunting in the west, see Sara Tuttle, *Conversations on the Choctaw Mission* (Boston: Mass.: Sabbath School Union, 1830), p. 74; Franchimastabe to Lanzos, Apr. 22, 1793, in Kinnaird, *Spain in*

the Miss. Valley, 3:151–52; Lanzos to Carondelet, Apr. 25, 1793, ibid., 3:152–53; National Archives, Records of the Secretary of War Pertaining to Indian Affairs, Letters Received Relating to Indian Affairs, M 271, Abstract of Letters from John Sibley, May 5, 1807; Ross and Phelps, "A Journey over the Natchez Trace," p. 271.

58. Delavillebeuvre to Carondelet, Oct. 27, 1794, in Kinnaird, *Spain in the Miss. Valley*, 3:367. NA, SW-IA, LR, M 271, Abstract of Letters of John Sibley, May 5, 1807. Sargent to Wilkinson, Oct. 16, 1798, Oct. 17, 1798, in Rowland, *MTA*, pp. 63–64. Cushman, *History*, pp. 393–94.

59. Log of Galiot la Fleche, Jan. 22, 1793, in Kinnaird, *Spain in the Miss. Valley*, 3:114. The carrying capacity of horses and pirogues is given in Daniel Thomas, "Fort Toulouse: The French Outpost of the Alibamos on the Coosa," *Alabama Historical Quarterly* 22 (Spring–Summer 1960): 173. The average weight of skins has been calculated from figures in Plaisance, "Choctaw Trading House," pp. 407–8, 417. White commercial hunters in the 1770s supposedly each killed up to 300 deer annually; Bartram, *Travels*, p. 329. Ross and Phelps, "A Journey over the Natchez Trace," p. 265.

60. Lt. Bowmar to Claiborne, Apr. 15, 1804, Carter, *Territorial Papers: Orleans Territory*, 9:224, NA, SW-IA, LR, M 271, Abstract of Letters, John Sibley, Apr. 30, 1807.

61. NA, SW-IA, LR, M 271, Sibley to Secretary of War, May 5, 1805; Report of John Jamison, Nov. 20, 1816.

62. Swanton, *Choctaw Indians*, pp. 160–61. NA, SW-IA, LR, M 217, Abstract Letters of John Sibley, Aug. 18, 1807. Joseph Hatfield, "Governor William Charles Cole Claiborne, Indians, and Outlaws in Frontier Mississippi, 1801–1803," *Journal of Mississippi History* 27 (Nov. 1965): 335. De Lemos to Delavillebeuvre, June 23, 1794, in Kinnaird, *Spain in the Miss. Valley*, 3:308.

63. I am not using "underdeveloped" here in the sense of some condition of unrealized potential for economic growth. Rather, I mean a condition of economic dependence that is the result of an intruding market system under the control of a metropolitan power. In such a system the metropolitan power exploits certain basic commodities while at the same time undermining the existing economy of the colonial region.

64. For debts to Panton and Leslie, see NA, SW-IA, LR, M 271, Abstract of Debts, Panton and Leslie, n.d. (reel 1, frame 227); Delavillebeuvre to Carondelet, May 7, 1794, in Kinnaird, *Spain in the Miss. Valley*, 3:282; Franchimastabe to Lanzos, Apr. 22, 1793, ibid., 3:151–52. For debts to the United States, see Plaisance, "Choctaw Trading House," pp. 403, 405, 423; Wayne Morris, "Traders and Factories on the Arkansas Frontier, 1805–1822," *Arkansas Historical Quarterly* 28 (Spring 1969): 32. For inability to reduce debts, see Franchimastabe to Lanzos, Apr. 22, 1793, in Kinnaird, *Spain in the Miss. Valley*, 3:151–52; Delavillebeuvre to Carondelet, Sept. 5, 1792, ibid., 3:77; July 7, 1794, ibid., 3:317; July 22, 1794, ibid., 3:328.

65. NA, SW-IA, LR, M 271, Dinsmore to Secretary of War, Aug. 19, 1803. Also see, Secretary of War to Dinsmore, Apr. 20, 1811, in Carter, *Territorial*

Papers of the U.S., Mississippi, 6:191; Simpson to Secretary of War, Oct. 19, 1810, ibid., 6:123–26; Dinsmore to Simpson, Apr. 25, 1809, ibid., 6:126–27. "Treaty with the Choctaws, 1805," in Kappler, *Laws and Treaties*, 2:87–88. For a map of the cessions, see Charles Royce, *Indian Land Cessions in the United States*, Bureau of American Ethonology, Eighteenth Annual Report, 1896–1897 (Washington, D.C.: Government Printing Office, 1899), Cession no. 61, pp. 672–73, maps of Alabama and Mississippi, nos. 1, 36.

66. Ross and Phelps, "A Journey over the Natchez Trace," p. 271. Folsom to Cornelius, July 16, 1818, quoted in Cushman, *History*, pp. 353–54. Quote of chiefs from Arthur H. DeRosier, Jr., "Pioneers with Conflicting Ideals: Christianity and Slavery in the Choctaw Nation," *Journal of Mississippi History* 21 (Jan.–Oct. 1959): 179.

CHAPTER 5

1. De Bienville to Maurepas, Apr. 14, 1735, in Rowland and Sanders, *French Dominion*, 1:257, 259. The willingness of Red Shoes to attack the English, mentioned in this letter, quickly dissipated and he actively sought peace. See De Bienville to Maurepas, Sept. 9, 1735, ibid., 1:270–74. De Bienville to Maurepas, Dec. 20, 1737, ibid., 3:705. De Bienville to Maurepas, Apr. 28, 1738, ibid., 3:709–17.

2. Mobile Congress, Nov. 14, 1763 in Rowland, *English Dominion*, p. 86.

3. J. Stuart to Germaine, Jan. 11, 1779, PRO, CO 5, 80:n.p. (letter no. 30).

4. Maxent to Bouligny, Sept. 24, 1782, in Kinnaird, *Spain in the Miss. Valley*, 2:59. Maxent to Miro, Dec. 5, 1782, ibid., 2:67; Carondelet to De Lemos, Dec. 18, 1792, ibid., 3:104. Delavillebeuvre to Carondelet, Sept. 5, 1792, ibid., 3:77. July 7, 1794, ibid., 3:317. Also see , ibid., 2:xvii.

5. For Choctaw poverty, see Sargent to Pickering, Mar. 1, 1800, Rowland, *MTA*, pp. 211–12. For thefts, see Sargent to Pickering, Aug. 29, 1798, ibid., p. 32; Mar.13, 1799, ibid., p. 110; Sargent to Dexter, June 1, 1800, ibid., p. 237. Claiborne to Madison, Dec. 12, 1801, in Rowland, *Claiborne's Letterbooks*, 1:12–14. Claiborne to McKee, Mar. 28, 1802, ibid., 1:60, June 29, 1802, ibid., 1:130. For Choctaw seizure of crops in place of presents, see Sargent to Pickering, Dec. 20, 1798, in Rowland, *MTA*, p. 91. For the reactions of the governors, see Sargent to Pickering, Dec. 20, 1798, ibid., p. 9, and Claiborne to Madison, Apr. 3, 1802, in Rowland, *Claiborne's Letterbooks*, 1:69–70.

6. For chickens and swine, see Swanton, "Early Account," p. 67; Romans, *Natural History*, pp. 84–85; Ford to Stuart, June 21, 1765, Gage Papers, vol. 49; Cushman, *History*, pp. 234–36, 390–91. For horses, see Adair, *History*, p. 133; Swanton, *Choctaw Indians*, p. 175. The "Early Account" is somewhat contradictory. It states that the Choctaws were rich in horses but then goes on to say that the scarcity of horses obliged them to use cattle to plow. Since the Choctaws not only did not plow until the beginning of the nineteenth century

(if not later) and did not possess cattle until the 1770s, this makes little sense. Even the French had few cattle in the early eighteenth century. Swanton, "Early Account," p. 71; Hubert to Council, Oct. 26, 1717, in Rowland and Sanders, *French Dominion*, 2:247; Perier and La Chaise to Council of the Indies, Mar. 25, 1729, ibid., 2:629; Folsom, "Discussion of Choctaw History," Pitchlynn Collection.

7. Hudson, *Southeastern Indians*, p. 318.

8. Romans, *Natural History*, p. 83. Clinton Howard, *The British Development of West Florida, 1763–1783*, University of California Publications in History, vol. 34 (Berkeley: University of California Press, 1949), p. 27. Cameron to Germaine, Nov. 30, 1780, PRO, CO 5, 82:233–43.

9. Delavillebeuvre to Carondelet, Sept. 5, 1792, in Kinnaird, *Spain in the Miss. Valley*, 3:77.

10. Ross and Phelps, "A Journey over the Natchez Trace," p. 271.

11. Many new towns appeared between the mid 1750s and the early 1770s. There are six major listings of towns during this period: "Treaty of Friendship & Commerce concluded on the Eighteenth day of July 1759 . . . [with] the Choctaw Nation . . ." enclosure with Atkin to Lyttelton, Aug. 18, 1759, in Lyttelton Papers. Names of Villages, Chiefs, and No. of Inhabitants of the Tchacta Nation in Rowland, *English Dominion*, pp. 26–29. Ford to J. Stuart, Nov. 21, 1764, Gage Papers, vol. 49. Return of the Names of Chiefs etc., enclosure with J. Stuart to Gage, Mar. 14, 1766, Gage Collection, vol. 49. Choctaw Towns, Those Receiving Presents (1771), PRO, CO 5, 73:330–81. Henry Halbert, ed., "Romans' Map." On these lists many towns are hard to classify because of the imprecise locations and the widely variant spellings. But when towns such as Tookfrio are mentioned only briefly and then disappear, the inference is that they were only briefly settled and then abandoned. (Of these six lists, Swanton used two in his compilation of Choctaw towns— Swanton, *Choctaw Indians*, pp. 59–75.)

12. Romans, *Natural History*, pp. 308–9.

13. Henry Halbert, "Okla Hannali: or the Six Towns District of the Choctaws," *American Antiquitarian and Oriental Journal* 15 (1893): 148. These calculations are taken from a list of towns compiled from the various censuses.

14. Adair, *History*, p. 304.

15. Cushman *History*, pp. 390–91, 403. Commissioners to Secretary of War, Nov. 20, 1789, *ASP: Indian Affairs*, 1:79.

16. Cushman, *History*, pp. 389–91, 403. NA, SW-IA, LR, M 271, Minutes of Council, Dec. 11, 1815.

17. *Missionary Herald* 16 (July 1820): 320. Adam Hodgson, *Letters from North America*, 2 vols. (London: Hurst, Robinson, 1824), 1:240. Tuttle, *Choctaw Mission*, pp. 60–61.

18. *Missionary Herald* 19 (Jan. 1823): 8.

19. George S. Gaines, "Gaines' Reminiscences," *Alabama Historical Quar-*

terly, 26:146. Charles Lanman, "Peter Pitchlynn, Chief of the Choctaws," *Atlantic Monthly* 25 (Apr. 1870): 486. Cushman, *History*, p. 403. McKee to Chiefs of the Choctaw Nation, n.d., box 4, no. 138, McKee Papers.

20. Gaines, "Reminiscences," p. 164. *Missionary Herald* 15 (Oct. 1819): 461. Cushman, *History*, p. 228. Tuttle, *Choctaw Missions*, 2:47.

21. *Missionary Herald* 25 (Mar. 1829): 153. Letter of Stephen Ward, *Niles' Register*, July 13, 1830. *Missionary Herald* 25 (May 1829): 152.

22. NA, RG 75, Armstrong Roll. This census has been tabulated by computer.

23. Ibid.

24. Ibid.

25. Folsom estimate from Cushman, *History*, p. 389. Also see *Missionary Herald* 25 (Nov. 1829): 350. Europeans quite consistently put the Choctaws at about 3,000 to 5, 000 fighting men during the mid-eighteenth century. See, for example, De Bienville to Regent, Aug. 8, 1721, in Rowland and Sanders, *French Dominion*, 3:307; Lusser Journal, ibid., 1:117; and Du Roullet Journal, ibid., 1:150–54. In the 1730s the "Early Account" estimates the warriors at 4,000, an estimate Bossu repeats in 1759 (*Travels*, p. 163). Adair estimates the warriors at about 4,500 in the 1760s, very close to another English estimate of 4,400 in 1771 (Adair, *History*, p. 282; J. Stuart to Germaine, June 14, 1771, PRO, CO 5, 78:288). Using the ratio of four women, children, and old men for each warrior, this yields a population range of from 16,000 to 25,000, and since the two low estimates—of Du Roullet and Lusser—probably did not give data for all the towns of the period, the actual population in 1729 and 1732 may have been higher. U.S. agents estimated the total Choctaw population at 20,000 in 1816 (NA, SW-IA, LR, M 271, McKee to Secretary of War, Nov. 28, 1816) and the removal census of 1830 put 19,554 Choctaws east of the Mississippi. Other figures go much higher and lower, but the clustering of such estimates between 15,000 and 25,000 over more than a century indicates that 20,000 people can be taken as a "normal" Choctaw population after the great losses of the early contact period. Swanton, *Southeastern Indians*, p. 123, collects a number of population estimates.

26. For infanticide, see Cyrus Kingsbury, Autobiography, manuscript in the Oklahoma State Historical Society, McBeth Papers, p. 15; Folsom, "Discussion of Choctaw History," Pitchlynn Collection; *Missionary Herald* 19 (Jan. 1823): 9. For a cogent discussion of population growth, see George Cowgill, "On Causes and Consequences of Ancient and Modern Population Changes," *American Anthropologist* 77 (Sept. 1975): 506–22. The current tendency to apply simple population growth intensification models to changes in environment, subsistence, and culture certainly does not fit in the case of the Choctaws. Two particularly influential studies of this type, although differing in their emphasis, are, Ester Boserup, *The Conditions of Agricultural Growth: The Economics of Agrarian Change under Population Pressure* (Chicago: Aldine, 1965), and Marvin Harris, *Cannibals and Kings: The Origins of Cultures* (New York: Random House, 1977).

27. *Missionary Herald* 25 (June 1829): 187–88. Swanton, *Choctaw Indians,* p. 34.

28. Cushman, *History,* (Stillwater, 1962), pp. 345–46. Gaines, "Reminiscences," pp. 178–79. NA, SW-IA, LR, M 271, Minutes of Council, Dec. 11, 1815.

29. Intermarried whites were already described as "rich" in 1819; see J. Pitchlynn to Calhoun, Mar. 18, 1819, *ASP: Indian Affairs,* 2:229.

30. For Jefferson's policy of encouraging the Indians to abandon hunting and raise stock, see "Message to Congress, Jan. 18, 1803," in ibid., 1:634; for the original offer to cede land along the Yazoo and Big Black in exchange for U.S. payment of Choctaw debts to Panton and Leslie, see Dearborn to Robertson and Dinsmore, Mar. 20, 1805, ibid., 1:700; for the treaty and Jefferson's subsequent actions, see Jefferson to Senate, January 15, 1808, and accompanying papers, in ibid., 1:748–52.

31. Willis, "Patrilineal Institutions," p. 256. Ross and Phelps, "A Journey over the Natchez Trace," p. 268. Cushman, *History,* p. 390.

32. John Edwards, "The Choctaw Indians in the Middle of the Nineteenth Century," *Chronicles of Oklahoma* 10 (Sept. 1932): 395. Cushman, *History,* pp. 362, 390. Halbert, "District Divisions," p. 379. Cushman, *History,* (Stillwater, 1962), pp. 64, 236–37, 262–64. Swanton, *Southeastern Indians,* p. 653.

33. Delavillebeuvre to Carondelet, Dec. 23, 1794, in Kinnaird, *Spain in the Miss. Valley,* 3:382. Secretary of War to Wilkinson, Apr. 16, 1803, Carter, *Territorial Papers of the U.S., Mississippi,* 5:212.

34. *Missionary Herald* 26 (Aug. 1830): 251. For captains, see Cushman, *History,* (Stillwater, 1962), p. 197. *Missionary Herald* 19 (Jan. 1824): 10.

35. For Tecumseh's visit to the Choctaws and Pushmataha's opposition to his plans, see Cushman, *History,* (Stillwater, 1962), pp. 243–60. At the outset of the war, however, the Americans and the chiefs themselves were worried that many Choctaw warriors would join the Creeks. Holmes to Secretary of War, Aug. 3, 1813, in Carter, *Territorial Papers, Mississippi,* 6:391. Choctaw participation was never enthusiastic because of American frugality with presents, but there were 795 warriors with Jackson during his campaign at New Orleans. McKee to Monroe, Nov. 12, 1814, McKee Papers, box 4, no. 222. For a summary of Choctaw participation in the war, see Cotterill, *Southern Indians,* pp. 182–85. For salaries, see Secretary of War to McKee, May 20, 1816, in Carter, *Territorial Papers, Mississippi,* 6:686–87; Mushulatubbee et al. to McKee, July 20, 1820, McKee Papers, box 2, no. 199; "Treaty with the Choctaws, Oct. 18, 1820," 7 Stat. 210, Art. 14, Kappler, *Laws and Treaties,* 2:194.

36. McKee to Chiefs, n.d., McKee Papers, box 4, no. 139.

37. DeRosier, *Choctaw Removal,* p. 37. "Treaty with the Choctaws, October 24, 1816," 7 Stat. 152, Kappler, *Laws and Treaties,* 2:137.

38. DeRosier, *Choctaw Removal,* pp. 46–48. NA, SW-IA, LR, M 271, Pooshemattaha and Mushulatubbee to President, Oct. 13, 1818. Emigration of the Choctaws . . ., Dec. 1, 1818, in *ASP: Indian Affairs,* 2:810–11.

39. Jackson to McKee, Apr. 22, 1819, *ASP: Indian Affairs*, 2:229. McKee to Jackson, Aug. 13, 1819, in ibid., 2:229.

40. Mushulatubbee and Pooshamataha to President, Aug. 12, 1819, in ibid., 2:230.

41. McKee to Jackson, Aug. 13, 1819, in ibid., 2:229. Calhoun to Commissioners, July 12, 1820, in ibid. 2:231.

42. Folsom to Commissioners, Sept. 13, 1820, in ibid., 2:232. Treaty Journal, Oct. 3, 1820, in ibid., 2:234–35. Oct. 10, 1820, in ibid., 2:235–37.

43. Treaty Journal, Oct. 14, 1820, in ibid., 2:238–39.

44. Treaty Journal, Oct. 15, 1820, and Treaty Journal, Oct. 17, 1820, in ibid., 2:239–40. Jackson and Hinds to Secretary of War, Oct. 19–21, 1820, in ibid., 2:242.

45. Jackson and Hinds to Secretary of War, Oct. 19–21, 1820, in ibid., 2:243.

46. *Missionary Herald* 25 (Aug. 1830): 252 and (Dec. 1829): 378.

47. John Pitchlynn to Peter Pitchlynn, Apr. 14, 1828, Feb. 15, 1828, Pitchlynn Papers, Gilcrease Institute.

48. Debo, *Choctaw Republic*, p. 42. D. Folsom to McKenney, Oct. 1, 1818, in *Missionary Herald* 16 (Jan. 1820): 27. Ibid. 14 (Nov. 1818): 509–10. Cushman, *History*, (Stillwater, 1962), p. 291.

49. For a summary of early locations, see *Missionary Herald* 20 (Jan. 1824): 2, 3.

50. Brief Notice of the Choctaw East of the Mississippi, McBeth Papers; *Missionary Herald* 16 (Aug. 1820): 365, 367. John Edwards, Historical Sketch of the Missionary Activities of the Presbyterian Church among the Choctaw Indians, 1818–1831, pp. 1, 12–13, MS in John Edwards Papers, Bancroft Library, University of California, Berkeley. For an example of the mixed-blood influence on the decision where to locate stations, see *Missionary Herald* 19 (Jan. 1823): 8. For material wealth, see *Missionary Herald* 20 (Aug. 1824): 252; ibid. 18 (Dec. 1822): 375; NA, SW-IA, LR, M 271, Kingsbury to Calhoun, 1823 (reel 4, frames 689–90).

51. Debo, *Choctaw Republic*, p. 42. Although missionary activity, in most cases, represents an imposition upon Native American cultures, it is important to realize that elements within Indian societies could turn Christianity and missionaries to their own use.

52. Treaty with the Choctaws, Oct. 18, 1820, 7 Stat. 210, Kappler, *Laws and Treaties*, 2:193. Jackson and Hinds to Calhoun, Oct. 19–21, 1820, in *ASP: Indian Affairs*, 2:242. *Missionary Herald* 16 (Jan. 1820): 27, and 16 (Aug. 1820): 365, 367–68.

53. *Missionary Herald* 16 (Jan. 1820): 27, and (Aug. 1820): 368.

54. Ibid. 18 (Apr. 1822): 103. John Pitchlynn to Peter Pitchlynn, Apr. 16, 1824, Pitchlynn Papers. Cushman, *History*, (Stillwater, 1962), pp. 88–89, 355. W. David Baird, *Peter Pitchlynn: Chief of the Choctaws* (Norman: University of Oklahoma Press, 1972), p. 21. *Missionary Herald* 19 (Jan. 1823): 9, 11. For quote, see Cushman, *History*, (Stillwater, 1962), p. 88.

55. *Missionary Herald* 25 (Feb. 1829): 61-62. Folsom, "Discussion of Choctaw History," Pitchlynn Papers.

56. Treaty with the Choctaws, Oct. 18, 1820, 7 Stat. 210, Art. 12, Kappler, *Laws and Treaties*, 2:193.

57. *Missionary Herald* 19 (Jan. 1823): 9. Thomas Nuttall, *A Journal of Travels into the Arkansas Territory* (Ann Arbor: University Microfilms, reproduction of the 1821 ed.), p. 228.

58. The government spent $2,500 on whiskey for the 1825 negotiations, or an average of $8.21 a day per delegate for a period of three months. National Archives, RG 75, Records of the Bureau of Indian Affairs, Letters Received, Choctaw Agency, M 234, Debts Contracted by the Choctaw Delegation, 1824. DeRosier, *Choctaw Removal*, p. 80.

59. NA, SW-IA, LR, M 271, John McKee, Estimate of Expenses, 1817, John McKee to William Crawford, Apr. 1, 1816. Secretary of War to Dinsmoor, Oct. 23, 1810, in Carter, *Territorial Papers, Mississippi*, 6:127. NA, OIA, LR, M 234, Choctaw Agency, Bakewell to Secretary of War, Sept. 2, 1824. NA, OIA, LR, M 234, Choctaw Agency, Memorandum of Goods for the Annuity for Topanahoma's District for 1826, and Memorandum of Goods for the Annuity for Mushulatubbee's District, 1826. *Missionary Herald* 18 (July 1822): 223, and 19 (Apr. 1823): 115-16.

60. *Missionary Herald* 18 (Dec. 1822): 378.

61. Ibid. 19 (Jan. 1823): 8; ibid. 25 (May 1829): 152-53; ibid. 26 (Aug. 1830): 251. Mushulatubbee was himself branded an opponent of religion and a lover of whiskey by the missionaries. Ibid. 26 (Aug. 1830): 252.

62. NA, SW-IA, LR, M 271, Cyrus Kingsbury to J. Calhoun, Jan. 15, 1823. *Missionary Herald* 19 (Apr. 1823): 115; ibid. 16 (Aug. 1820): 368. NA, OIA, LR, M 234, Choctaw Agency, Ward to McKenney, Dec. 2, 1825.

63. *Missionary Herald* 19 (Sept. 1823): 284-85. Treaty with the Choctaws, Oct. 18, 1820, 7 Stat. 210, Kappler, *Laws and Treaties*, 2:193. *Missionary Herald* 19 (Aug. 1823): 252. Ibid. 18 (Dec. 1822): 31. NA, SW-IA, LR, M 271, Kingsbury to Calhoun, Jan. 15, 1823, Oct. 30, 1823. NA, OIA, LR, M 234, Choctaw Agency, Ward to McKenney, Apr. 25, 1826. *Missionary Herald* 25 (Dec. 1829): 376-77.

64. *Missionary Herald* 23 (Sept. 1827): 280. NA, OIA, LR, M 234, Choctaw Agency, L. McDonald to McKenney, Apr. 25, 1826. For the quote, see *Missionary Herald* 25 (Feb. 1829): 62.

65. DeRosier pictures the treaty of 1825 as a triumph for the Choctaws. The chiefs did secure concessions from the Americans, but DeRosier ignores the Choctaws' own anger over the treaty and the subsequent reaction against it within the nation. The full-blood chiefs with the assistance of their mixed-blood allies, the Pitchlynns, used the 1825 education money to send students to the Choctaw Academy of Sen. Richard Johnson in Tennessee, a move which David Folsom and the American Board missionaries opposed. DeRosier, *Choctaw Removal*, pp. 78-83. Baird, *Pitchlynn*, pp. 23-24. For the treaty and accompanying documents see, Treaty with the Choctaws, Communicated

to the Senate, on the 27th of January, 1825, in *ASP: Indian Affairs*, 2:547–55.
66. Debo, *Choctaw Republic*. p. 5, 50; Treaty with the Choctaws . . . 1825,
Art. 10, in *ASP: Indian Affairs*, 2:548. Wm.Clark et al. to Sec. of War, Nov. 19,
1826, in ibid., 2:709. NA, OIA, LR, M 234, Choctaw Agency, W. Ward to
McKenney, Dec. 1825.

67. For the revolution, see NA, OIA, LR, M 234, Choctaw Agency, Folsom
to McKenney, June 27, 1826. McKenney himself would echo this assessment,
NA, OIA, LR, M 234, Choctaw Agency, McKenney to Secretary of War, Nov.
3, 1828. For political moves, see NA, OIA, LR,M 234, Choctaw Agency,
Letter of Secretary of Treaty Commission, Nov. 17, 1826; W. Ward to Barbour, Aug. 9, 1826; D. Folsom to McKenney, Oct. 14, 1828; Ward to McKenney, Oct. 11, 1828 (source of Ward quote); *Missionary Herald* 26 (Aug. 1830):
251–52. Tuttle, *Choctaw Missions*, 2:36–37.

68. NA, OIA, LR, M 234, Choctaw Agency, Ward to Barbour, Apr. 15,
1826; Mushulatubbee et al. to Barbour, Mar. 18, 1826, in *ASP: Indian Affairs*,
2:704. Clark et al. to Barbour, Jan. 19, 1826, in ibid., 2:709. NA, OIA, LR, M
234, Choctaw Agency, Ward to Barbour, Aug. 9, 1826. Treaty Journal, Nov.
11, 1826, in *ASP: Indian Affairs*, 2:710.

69. Clark et al. to Barbour, Nov. 19, 1826, in *ASP: Indian Affairs*, 2:709;
NA, OIA, LR, M 234, Choctaw Agency, Ward to Barbour, Aug. 9, 1826.
Treaty Journal, Nov. 10–16, 1826, in *ASP: Indian Affairs*, 2:710–17.

70. Mushulatubbee et al. to Congress, Feb. 18, 1825, in *ASP: Indian Affairs*,
2:553–54; NA, OIA, LR, M 234, Choctaw Agency, McKenney to Secretary of
War, Oct. 17, 1827, Ward to Barbour, Apr. 15, 1826.

71. McKee to Chiefs, n.d., McKee Papers, box 4, no. 130. NA, OIA, LR, M
234, Choctaw Agency, Ward to Barbour, Aug. 9, 1826; *Missionary Herald* 26
(Aug. 1830): 251–52. G. Harkins to P. Pitchlynn, Dec. 20, 1827, Pitchlynn
Collection.

72. *Missionary Herald* 25 (May 1829): 152–53. NA, OIA, LR, M 234, Choctaw Agency, LeFlore to McKenney, May 3, 1828, Ward to Barbour, Apr. 15,
1826. Tuttle, *Choctaw Missions*, 2:47. *Missionary Herald* 25 (Feb. 1829): 61.

73. *Missionary Herald* 25 (May 1829): 152–53; ibid. 21 (Jan. 1825): 6.

74. Ibid. 25 (Apr. 1829): 121. Ibid. 26 (Jan. 1830): 11, 21. Ibid. 25 (Nov.
1829): 346–47. Ibid. 25 (Sept. 1829): 282. Ibid. 27 (Dec. 1831): 384. It should
be emphasized that the number of Choctaws who actually became members of
the churches was much smaller. On the eve of migration west, 360 Choctaws,
or less than 2 percent of the nation, belonged to the American Board
churches. Ibid., *Monthly Paper* 3 (June 1832): 12.

75. DeRosier, *Choctaw Removal*, pp. 96–98, 100–1; *Missionary Herald* 25
(Dec. 1829): 379–80. Young, *Redskins, Ruffleshirts and Rednecks*, p. 29.

76. *Missionary Herald* 26 (Nov. 1830): 347. Cushman, *History*, p. 167. Tuttle, *Choctaw Missions*, 2:47. *Missionary Herald* 25 (May 1829): 153.

77. Cushman, *History*, (Stillwater, 1962), p. 159.

78. *Missionary Herald* 25 (Dec. 1829): 377–79. Ibid. 26 (Aug. 1830):
250–53. Ibid. 25 (Apr. 1829): 251. Ibid. 27 (Dec. 1831): 384. Ibid. 27 (Nov.

1831): 353. Ibid. 25 (Feb. 1829): 62. Letter of David Folsom, Dec. 14, 1829, in ibid. 26 (Mar. 1830): 80. Cushman puts most of Folsom's support in the borderlands. (*History* [Stillwater, 1962], p. 279).

79. NA, OIA, LR, M 234, Choctaw Agency, Letter of Mushulatubbee, Oct. 12, 1830. The tables and discussion that follow rely on the Armstrong Census.

80. *Missionary Herald* 25 (May 1829): 153.

81. *Niles' Register*, July 31, 1830; Nuttall, *Travels*, p. 240.

82. Hawkins to Dearborn, Dec. 18, 1801, "Letters of Benjamin Hawkins," 9:410–12. Treaty Journal, Dec. 15, 1801, in *ASP: Indian Affairs*, 1:662. NA, RG 75, OIA, Armstrong Census. *Missionary Herald* 25 (Feb. 1829): 61.

83. NA, RG 75, OIA, Armstrong Census.

84. *Missionary Herald* 25 (Feb. 1829): 61. Tuttle, *Choctaw Missions*, 2:47. In areas such as the Sixtowns the prohibition on liquor was never complete. In 1828 a missionary reported that a local chief "gave notice that he intended to drink whiskey for two moons, and granted permission to do the same. Much whiskey was brought into our neighborhood." *Missionary Herald* 25 (June 1829): 188. On the whole, however, the reduction in the trade was marked. Ibid. 25 (Feb. 1829): 62. Letter of David Folsom in ibid. 26 (Mar. 1830): 83–84. Ibid. 23 (Sept. 1827): 28. Ibid. 25 (May 1829): 152–53.

85. Marriage within the *iksa* was still banned in 1820, but by 1837 the clans had virtually vanished. Hodgson, *Letters*, 1:243. John Stuart, *A Sketch of the Cherokee and Choctaw Indians* (Little Rock: Woodruff and Pew, 1837), p. 39.

86. NA, RG 75, OIA, Armstrong Census (see entry under Major LeFlore, Western District [Chief LeFlores], 2a).

87. NA, OIA, LR, M 234, Choctaw Agency, LeFlore to McKenney, May 3, 1828.

88. NA, OIA, LR, M 234, Choctaw Agency, Ward to McKenney, May 22, 1828; Mushulatubbee to Jackson, May 16, 1829, Ward to Porter, Feb. 6, 1829. NA, OIA, LR, M 234, Choctaw Emigration, Mushulatubbee to Eaton, Sept. 28, 1829.

89. NA, OIA, LR, Choctaw Agency, Ward to Eaton, Nov. 4, 1829; Folsom, LeFlore, and Garland to Ward, Nov. 7, 1829. *Missionary Herald* 25 (Dec. 1829): 377–83.

90. NA, OIA, LR, M 234, Choctaw Agency, Ward to Eaton, Dec. 29, 1829; *Missionary Herald* 26 (Aug. 1830):252–53. NA, OIA, LR, M 234, Choctaw Emigration, Letter of David Folsom, Feb. 7, 1830.

91. DeRosier, *Choctaw Removal*, p. 104. *Missionary Herald* 26 (Aug. 1830): 253.

92. NA, OIA, LR, M , Choctaw Agency, LeFlore to Mushulatubbee, Apr. 1, 1830.

93. NA, OIA, LR, M 234, Choctaw Agency,LeFlore to Mushulatubbee, Apr. 1, 1830. DeRosier,*Choctaw Removal*, pp. 113–14. Much of the account in DeRosier contradicts that in the *Missionary Herald*. DeRosier follows accounts in the Mississippi papers, but the missionaries were by this time far more knowledgeable about Choctaw politics than any other whites. *Missionary*

Herald 26 (Aug. 1830): 253. NA, OIA, LR, M 234, Choctaw Agency, Ward to Eaton, Apr. 19, 1830, McDonald to McKenney, Mar. 22, 1830.

94. Foster to Pitchlynn, Apr. 10, 1830, Pitchlynn Papers. *Missionary Herald* 26 (Aug. 1830): 253–54. Gaines, "Reminscences," pp. 196–98.

95. NA, OIA, LR, M 234, Choctaw Agency, Mushulatubbee and Nittakachih to Ward, Apr. 17, 1830; Choctaw Council to Eaton, June 2, 1830.

96. NA, OIA, LR, M 234, Choctaw Agency, Mushulatubbee and Nittakachih to Ward, Apr. 17, 1830; Choctaw Council to Eaton, June 2, 1830. Cushman, *History*, (Stillwater, 1962), pp. 275–85. Gaines, "Reminiscences," pp. 189ff. NA, OIA, LR, M 234, Choctaw Emigration, Ward to Johnson, Aug. 7, 1830. Cushman's account is a later, much romanticized version of this encounter.

97. NA, OIA, LR, M 234, Choctaw Agency, Council of West to Ward, Aug. 10, 1830; Ward to Eaton, Aug. 19, 1830; Donly to Eaton, Aug. 14, 1830. DeRosier, *Choctaw Removal*, pp. 117–19, gives the federal reaction to events in the Choctaw nation.

98. NA, OIA, LR, M 234, Choctaw Agency, Eaton to Jackson, Sept. 18, 1830. Choctaw Commissioners to Eaton and Coffee, n.d., Pitchlynn Papers; DeRosier, *Choctaw Removal*, pp. 119–21.

99. DeRosier believes that the mass of the nation consented to the treaty, but Mary Young, in her account, disagrees and appears to be correct. The Choctaw commissioners admitted that the large majority of those present at the council opposed any cession, and DeRosier, as well as Young, cites reports that many Choctaws had left the treaty ground by the time the treaty was signed. The major evidence DeRosier cites to the contrary is a statement by the interpreter Mackey, a man whose dismissal the Choctaws themselves had previously tried to secure. DeRosier, *Choctaw Removal*, pp. 123–27. Young, *Redskins, Ruffleshirts and Rednecks*, pp. 31–32. Choctaw Commissioners to Eaton and Coffee, Sept. 25, 1830, Pitchlynn Papers. For the reaction to the treaty, see *Missionary Herald* 27 (Jan. 1831): 18. NA, OIA, LR, M 234, Choctaw Agency, Ward to Jackson, Oct. 11, 1830. J. B. Hancock to P. Pitchlynn, Oct. 20, 1830, Pitchlynn Papers. NA, OIA, LR, M 234, Choctaw Emigration, Captains of Sixtowns to Eaton, Dec. 24, 1830, Gaines to Eaton, Dec. 1, 1830; D. Folsom to Eaton, Dec. 24, 1830. NA, OIA, LR, Choctaw Agency, M 234, Declaration of Electors of Western District, Oct. 23, 1830.

100. De Rosier, *Choctaw Removal*, p. 132. Treaty with the Choctaw, Sept. 27, 1830, 7 Stat. 333, Kappler, *Laws and Treaties*, 2:315–16. NA, OIA, LR, M 234, Choctaw Agency, Ward to Eaton, Oct. 14, 1830.

101. NA, OIA, LR, M 234, Choctaw Agency, Gaines to Eaton, Dec. 1, 1830; Declaration of Electors, Nov. 3, 1830. NA, OIA, LR, M 234, Choctaw Emigration, D. Folsom to Eaton, Dec. 24, 1830.

102. NA, OIA, LR, M 234, Choctaw Agency, Letter of Mushulatubbee, Oct. 12, 1830. *Missionary Herald* 27 (Jan. 1831): 18–19. NA, OIA, LR, M 234, Choctaw Emigration, LeFlore to Richard Johnson, Nov. 19, 1830. NA, OIA,

LR, M 234, Choctaw Agency, Mushulatubbee to Eaton, Dec. 30, 1830; Nail et al. to Eaton, Apr. 23, 1831.
103. For quote, see Cushman, *History*, (Stillwater, 1962), p. 287. For the last months, see NA, OIA, LR, M 234, Choctaw Agency, Choctaws of Northeastern District to Eaton, Jan. 16, 1831; Haley to Coffee, Mar. 10, 1831. NA, OIA, LR, M 234, Choctaw Emigration, Petition of Captains, Mar. 24, 1831. P. Pitchlynn to Cass, July 10, 1832. For removal, see De Rosier, although he is much stronger on American policy than internal Choctaw politics *(Choctaw Removal*, pp. 129–47). For LeFlore, see Cushman, *History*, (Stillwater, 1962), p. 347. For the Choctaws west of the Mississippi, see Angie Debo, *Choctaw Republic*. Debo's work on the Choctaws in Mississippi is based largely on secondary materials and is not reliable, but her work on the Oklahoma Choctaws is a pioneering model of Indian history. For Pitchlynn's career, see Baird, *Peter Pitchlynn*.

CHAPTER 6

1. The essential climatic research for this reconstruction may be found in R. A. Bryson and W. M. Wendland, *Tentative Climatic Patterns for Some Late-Glacial and Post-Glacial Episodes in Central North America*, Technical Report 34, Nonr. 1202 (07), Department of Meteorology, University of Wisconsin (Madison, 1967). Good summaries of its uses on the Central Plains can be found in Reid A. Bryson, David A. Baerreis, and Wayne M. Wendland, "The Character of Late-Glacial and Post-Glacial Climatic Changes," in Wakefield Dort, Jr., and J. Knox Jones, Jr., *Pleistocene and Recent Environments of the Central Great Plains*, Department of Geology, University of Kansas, Special Publication 3 (Lawrence, 1970), pp. 54–73. An excellent critique and modification of dendrochronological techniques is found in Merlin Paul Larson, *The Climate of the Great American Desert: Reconstruction of the Climate of Western Interior United States, 1800–1850*, University of Nebraska Studies, n.s. no. 46 (Lincoln, 1974), pp. 7–32.
2. For significant interpretations of this period, see David A. Baerreis and Reid Bryson, "Historical Climatology and the Southern Plains: A Preliminary Statement," *Oklahoma Anthropological Society Bulletin* 13 (Mar. 1963): 70–75; Donald Lehmer, "Climate and Culture History in the Middle Missouri Valley," in Dort and Jones, *Environments*, p. 121; Waldo Wedel, "Some Environmental and Historical Factors of the Great Bend Aspect," in Dort and Jones, *Environments*, pp. 137–38; Bryson, Baerreis, and Wendland, "Climatic Changes," pp. 64–67; Lionel Brown, "Pony Creek Archeology," Smithsonian Institution, River Basin Surveys, *Publications in Salvage Archeology*, no. 6 (Lincoln, 1967), p. 53; W. Raymond Wood, "An Interpretation of Mandan Culture History," *Smithsonian Institution, River Basin Surveys Papers*, no. 39 (Washington, D.C., 1967), pp. 132, 138–39, 152–53, 166–67; Warren Caldwell,

"The Middle Missouri Tradition Reappraised," *Plains Anthropologist* 11 (1966): 154; Donald Lehmer, "The Sedentary Horizon of the Northern Plains," *Southwestern Journal of Anthropology* 10 (Summer 1954): 147–49; Donald Lehmer, *Introduction to Middle Missouri Archeology*, Anthropological Papers no. 1, National Park Service (Washington, D.C.: Government Printing Office, 1971), pp. 111–15, 124–28; Carlyle Smith, "Archaeological Investigations in Ellsworth and Rice Counties, Kansas," *American Antiquity* 14 (Apr. 1949): 292–300; Susan Vehik, "The Great Bend Aspect: A Multivariate Investigation of Its Origins in Southern Plains Relationships," *Plains Anthropologist* 21 (Aug. 1976): 203–4.

3. George Dorsey, *Traditions of the Skidi Pawnee*, Memoirs of the American Folklore Society, vol. 8 (Boston: Houghton Mifflin, 1904), pp. xiii–xiv. Jack Hughes, *Prehistory of Caddoan Speaking Tribes*, ICC Docket 226 (New York: Garland, N.Y., 1974), pp. 103–4, 108–307. Lehmer, *Middle Missouri*, pp. 114, 163. J. J. Hoffman, "Molstad Village," River Basin Surveys, Smithsonian Institution, *Publications in Salvage Archaeology*, no. 4 (Lincoln, 1967), pp. 63–65. Roger T. Grange, *Pawnee and Lower Loup Pottery*, Nebraska State Historical Society, Publications in Anthropology no. 3 (Lincoln, 1968), p. 126. John B. Dunbar, "The Pawnee Indians: Their History and Ethnology," *Magazine of American History* 4 (Apr. 1880): 251–53. NA, OIA, LR, M 234, Pawnee Agency, D. H. Wheeler to Col. E. B. Taylor, Sept. 15, 1866. Waldo Wedel, *Prehistoric Man on the Great Plains* (Norman: University of Oklahoma Press, 1961), pp. 107–11. Gene Weltfish, *The Lost Universe* (New York: Ballantine, 1965), p. 4. George Dorsey, *The Pawnee: Mythology*, pt. 1 (Washington, D.C.: Carnegie Institution, 1906), pp. 8–9.

4. Skidi or Skiri was the aboriginal name of the Pawnee tribe sometimes called the Loups by the whites. For the South Bands, I have used anglicized names. In Pawnee the Republicans were the Kitehaxki (Little Earthlodge), the Grands were the Tswai or Chaui (Asking-for-Meat), and the Tapages were the Pitahawirata (Man-Going-Downstream, or East). Weltfish, *The Lost Universe*, p. 6. The best discussion of Pawnee origins is in Grange, *Pawnee Pottery*, p. 71, and a more recent article, "An Archeological View of Pawnee Origins," *Nebraska History* 60 (Summer 1979): 134–60. See also Waldo Wedel, "The Direct Historical Approach in Pawnee Archeology," Smithsonian Miscellaneous Collections, vol. 97, no. 7 (Washington, D.C., 1938), p. 11; Waldo Wedel, *Prehistoric Man on the Great Plains* (Norman: University of Oklahoma Press, 1961), pp. 122, 124, 125; Lehmer, *Middle Missouri*, p. 163; John L. Champe and Franklin Fenega, *Notes on the Pawnee*, Indian Claims Commission, Prepared for Department of Justice, Lands Division, Indian Claims, Aug. 1, 1954 (New York: Garland Press, 1974), p. 52. For some origin legends; see Dorsey, *Traditions of the Skidi*, pp. xiii, xiv; Dunbar, "The Pawnee Indians: Their History and Ethnology," pp. 251–53.

5. Throughout, the Skidis, Republicans, Grands, and Tapages will be referred to as tribes. The Pawnees as a whole will be called a nation. George Bird Grinnell, *Pawnee Hero Stories and Folk-Tales* (Lincoln: University of Ne-

braska Press, 1961), pp. 223–27. James Murie, "Pawnee Indian Societies," *Anthropological Papers of the American Museum of Natural History*, 1, pt. 7 (New York, 1914), p. 549 (Murie was himself a Skidi). Rev. John Dunbar, "Missionary Life among the Pawnee," in *NSHSC* 11:276. Weltfish, *The Lost Universe*, p. 4. Dorsey, *The Pawnee: Mythology*, pp. 8–9. George Hyde, *The Pawnee Indians* (Norman: University of Oklahoma Press, 1974), p. 178. Reuben Gold Thwaites, *Edwin James' Account of S. H. Long's Expedition*, in *EWT*, 15:161. Grange, *Pawnee Pottery*, pp. 142–43. Wedel, "The Direct Historical Approach," p. 3.

6. Grange, *Pawnee Pottery*, gives the most complete list of Pawnee and Lower Loup village locations, pp. 17–34. For an earlier list, see Wedel, "Introduction to Pawnee Archeology," pp. 25–42. Thwaites, *James' Account of Long's Expedition, in EWT*, 15:141.

7. Grange, *Pawnee Pottery*, p. 30. William Duncan Strong, "An Introduction to Nebraska Archeology," *Smithsonian Miscellaneous Collections* 93, no. 10 (Washington, D.C., July 20, 1935): 273–74.

8. Strong, "Nebraska Archeology," pp. 63, 273–74. Wedel, *Prehistoric Man*, p. 124.

9. Waldo Wedel, *An Introduction to Kansas Archeology*, Bureau of American Ethnology, Bulletin 174 (Washington, Government Printing Office, 1959), pp. 634–36, 598–99. Alfred B. Thomas, *After Coronado: Spanish Exploration Northeast of New Mexico* (Norman: University of Oklahoma Press, 1935), *Mexico, and New Mexico* (Norman: University of Oklahoma Press, 1935), pp. 19–20, 31, 74. Frank Secoy, *Changing Military Patterns on the Great Plains*, Monographs of the American Ethnological Society, no. 21 (Locust Valley, N.Y., 1953), pp. 6–10, 3–31. Wedel, "Direct Historical Approach," p. 19. Wedel, "Archeological Remains in Central Kansas and Their Possible Bearing on the Location of Quivera," *Smithsonian Miscellaneous Collections* 101, no. 7 (Washington, D.C., June, 1942): 10–18.

10. Henri Folmer, "French Expansion toward New Mexico in the Eighteenth Century" (M.A. thesis, University of Denver, 1939), p. 138. Thomas, *After Coronado*, pp. 19–20, 74. George Hyde, *The Pawnee Indians*, p. 24. Reuben Gold Thwaites, *Josiah Gregg's Commerce of the Prairies, in EWT*, 20:91. Edwin Hemphill, ed., *The Papers of John C. Calhoun*, 12 vols. (Columbia: University of South Carolina Press, 1959–79), 8:533. Secoy, *Military Patterns*, p. 30.

11. For various locations and movements of Pawnees, see Noel N. Loomis and Abraham Nastir, *Pedro Vial and the Road to Santa Fe* (Norman: University of Oklahoma Press, 1967), pp. 400–401. Secoy, *Military Patterns*, p. 23. Abraham Nastir, ed., *Before Lewis and Clark: Documents Illustrating the History of the Missouri, 1785–1804*, 2 vols. (St, Louis: St. Louis Historical Documents Foundation, 1952), 1:126, 2:615, 2:709. Dunbar, "Pawnee History and Ethnology," p. 260; Grange, *Pawnee Pottery*, p. 119. Thwaites, *James' Account of Long's Expedition, in EWT*, 15:209; Kinnaird, *Spain in the Miss. Valley*, 2:223. Reuben Gold Thwaites, ed., "The French Regime in Wisconsin," *Collections of the State*

Historical Society of Wisconsin 18 (1908): 88–89. Reuben Gold Thwaites, "The British Regime in Wisconsin, 1790–1800," *Collections of the State Historical Society of Wisconsin* 18 (1908):359–63.

12. George R. Brooks, ed., "George Sibley's Journal of a Trip to the Salines in 1811," *Missouri Historical Society Bulletin* 21 (Apr. 1965): 180. Donald Jackson, ed., "Journey to the Mandans, 1809: The Lost Narrative of Dr. Thomas," *Bulletin of the Missouri Historical Society* 20 (Apr. 1964): 184. NA, OIA, LR, M 234, St. Louis, W. Clark to James Barbour, Dec. 8, 1825, and B. O'Fallon to W. Clark, May 7, 1824, Statement of Locations for Posts, Nov. 28, 1831. Hemphill, ed., *Calhoun Papers*, 7:23. Lela Barnes, ed., "Journal of Isaac McCoy for the Exploring Expedition of 1828," *Kansas Historical Quarterly* 5 (Aug. 1936): 255, 351–52. "Yellowstone Expedition: Notes on the Missouri River and Some of the Native Tribes . . . ," *Analytic Magazine* 1 (May 1820): 348, 352. Thwaites, *James' Account of Long's Expedition*, in *EWT*, 15:91–92.

13. Secoy, *Military Patterns*, p. 71. NA, LR, OIA, M 234, Council Bluffs, J. Dunbar to T. Harvey, Aug. 22, 1845. Thwaites, *James' Account of Long's Expedition*, in *EWT*, 15:87–88, 94. Strong, "Nebraska Archeology," pp. 7–25, 272. Nasatir, *Before Lewis and Clark*, 1:148.

14. Herbert Eugene Bolton, *Spanish Exploration in the Southwest: Original Narratives of Early American History*, vol. 18 (New York: C. Scribner's Sons, 1916), pp. 200–201. Louise Barry, *The Beginning of the West* (Topeka: Kansas State Historical Society, 1972), p. 4, says the 1593 expedition may have been destroyed on the Kansas or Smoky Hill River. Nasatir, *Before Lewis and Clark*, 1:29. Donald Jackson, ed., *The Journals of Zebulon Montgomery Pike*, 2 vols. (Norman: University of Oklahoma Press, 1966), 2:148. Thomas, *After Coronado*, pp. 183, 229, 278–79. Henri Folmer, "French Expansion," pp. 123, 173, 174. Luther North to Grinnell, June 21, 1928, Luther North Collection, Nebraska State Historical Society.

15. Loomis and Nasatir, *Pedro Vial*, p. 393. Nasatir, *Before Lewis and Clark*, 1:148. Frank Secoy, "The Identity of the Paduca: An Ethnohistorical Analysis," *American Anthropologist* 53 (Oct.–Dec. 1951): 525–40. Jackson, *Pike's Journals*, 2:36. Thwaites, *James' Account of Long's Expedition*, in *EWT*, 15:157, 211.

16. Murie, "Pawnee Societies," p. 549.

17. Brooks, "Sibley's Journal," p. 183. Jackson, *Pike's Journal*, 2:41. Thwaites, "French Regime," 18:88–89. NA, OIA, LR, M 234, Upper Missouri, J. Dougherty to Wm. Clark, Oct. 29, 1831.

18. As an example of how tenuous even population estimates made by actual observers are, three members of the Long expedition of 1820— Stephen Long, Edwin Jones, and John Bell—visited and made estimates of the Skidi village near present Palmer, Nebraska, on the same day. Long put the population at 100 lodges and 2,000 people; Jones said it contained 145 lodges, which George Hyde extrapolated to 3,500 residents; and Bell guessed at 120 lodges and 3,000 people. Thwaites, *James' Account of Long's Expedition*, in *EWT*, 15:161, 17:153. Hyde, *Pawnee Indians*, pp. 294–95. Harlan Fuller and

LeRoy Hafen, eds., *The Journal of Captain John R. Bell: Official Journalist for the Stephen H. Long Expedition to the Rocky Mountains*, 1820, The Far West and the Rockies Historical Series, 1820–1875, vol. 6 (Glendale, Cal.: Arthur H. Clark, 1957), p. 118. For other estimates, see Brooks, "Sibley's Journal," p. 183; Paul Wilhelm, Duke of Wurttemberg, "First Journey to North America in the Years 1822–1824," *South Dakota Historical Collections* 19 (Pierre, S.D., 1938), p. 433; Grange, *Pawnee Pottery*, pp. 119–20; NA,OIA, LR, M 234, St. Louis Super., B. Fallon to W. Clark, Dec. 8, 1825, and Statement of Locations of Posts for Trade, Nov. 29, 1831.

19. Dunbar, "Pawnee History and Ethnology," p. 256, mentions an epidemic in 1825, but Dougherty, their agent at the time, reports the 1831 epidemic to have been the first since the 1790s. Dunbar apparently thought the 1831 epidemic came in 1825; NA,OIA, LR, M 234, Upper Missouri, J. Dougherty to W. Clark, Oct. 29, 1831, Nov. 20, 1832. For other accounts of location and population, see Gottlieb Oehler and David Smith, *Description of a Journey and Visit to the Pawnee Indians . . . April 22–May 18, 1851* (reprint from Moravian Church Miscellany of 1851–52, New York, 1914), p. 29; *Annual Report of the Commissioner of Indian Affairs for* 1864 (Washington, D.C.: Government Printing Office, 1865), pp. 383–84; G. Warren, "Explorations in Nebraska," in "Report of the Secretary of War," *SED*1, 35:2 (serial 975), p. 667; NA,OIA, LR, M 234, Northern Superintendency, Memorandum of Benjamin Hallowell, Secretary of the Committee of the Friends on the Indian Commission, Jan. 11, 1870; "The Quaker Report on Indian Agencies in Nebraska," *Nebraska History* 54 (Summer 1973): 156; NA,OIA, LR, M 234, Council Bluffs, George Hefner to Col. A. Cummings, July 5, 1855; NA,OIA, LR, M 234, Pawnee Agency, J. B. Maxfield to B. F. Lushbaugh, Oct. 1, 1864; J. Henry Carleton, *The Prairie Logbooks: Dragoon Campaigns to the Pawnee Villages in* 1844 . . . (Chicago: Caxton Club, 1943), p. 69; "Letters Concerning the Presbyterian Mission in the Pawnee Country, near Bellevue, Neb., 1831–49," *Kansas State Historical Society Collections* 14 (Topeka, 1919): 617.

20. See Grange, *Pawnee Pottery*, pp. 17–34, for village sites on Loup and Platte. The Pawnee village sites at McClaine and Leshara were on the Platte east of Skull Creek, almost at the Elkhorn (Wedel, "The Direct Historical Approach," p. 13), but these villages were built only during the 1850s when Sioux raids had forced the Pawnees east (Grange, *Pawnee Pottery*, p. 18). By the mid-nineteenth century, Shell Creek was the eastern boundary insisted on by the Pawnees in land cessions to the United States. For disputes on boundary, see NA,OIA, LR, M 234, Otoe Agency, M. Izard to Col. Cumming, Oct. 28, 1865; John Ricky to G. Manypenny, Dec. 1, 1856; Council at Pawnee Villages, Apr. 21, 1857.

21. Grange, *Pawnee Pottery*, pp. 32, 153. The range of both sites is from 10 to 100 acres, but the Lower Loup sites average between 50 and 60 acres, while historical Pawnee sites average 38 acres in size. For positions of villages at various times, see Paul Wilhelm, "Journey," p. 432; Philip Rollins, ed., *The Discovery of the Oregon Trail: Robert Stuart's Narratives* (New York: C. Scribner's

Sons, 1935), pp. 220–21; Carleton, *The Prairie Logbooks*, pp. 63–64, 69; Fuller and Hafen, eds., *Journal of Captain Bell*, pp. 114–18; Oehler and Smith, *Visit to the Pawnees*, p. 24; Thwaites, *James' Account of Long's Expedition*, in *EWT*, 15:149.

22. For a description of Pawnee hunting grounds, see Rollins, *The Discovery of the Oregon Trail*, p. 213; Allis to Greene, May 12, 1835, "Presb. Mission," pp. 697–99, 708; John Dunbar, "The Pawnee Indians: Their Habits and Customs," *Magazine of American History* 8 (Nov. 1882): 327–28; NA,OIA, LR, M 234, Council Bluffs, George Hefner to A. Cummings, Dec. 31, 1855; Harrison Dale, ed., *The Ashley-Smith Explorations and the Discovery of a Central Route to the Pacific, 1822–1829* (Cleveland: Arthur H. Clark, 1918), pp. 122–23. For a fuller description of Sioux expansion, see Richard White, "The Winning of the West: The Expansion of the Western Sioux during the Eighteenth and Nineteenth Centuries," *Journal of American History* 45 (Sept. 1978): 319–43.

CHAPTER 7

1. J. E. Weaver, *Native Vegetation of Nebraska* (Lincoln: University of Nebraska Press, 1965), pp. 16, 33–34, 37. J. E. Weaver, *Prairie Plants and Their Environment: A Fifty-Year Study in the Midwest* (Lincoln: University of Nebraska Press, 1968), p. 131. Contemporary travelers repeatedly remarked on the scarcity of timber along both the Loup and Platte. Rollins, *Discovery of the Oregon Trail*, pp. 217–18. John C. Frémont, "A Report on an Exploration of the Country Lying between the Missouri River and the Rocky Mountains . . . ," *SED 243*, 27:3 (serial 416), p. 75. "Expedition of Major Clifton Wharton in 1844" (journal), *Kansas State Historical Society Collections* 16 (1925): 289. Thwaites, *James' Account of Long's Expedition*, in *EWT*, 15:239, 17:137. NA,OIA, LR, M 234, Council Bluffs, J. Dunbar to J. Hamilton, Oct. 1839; Brooks, "Sibley's Journal," p. 180. NA, OIA, RG 75, Field Notes, 1859, Pawnee Reserve Survey, p. 36. Melvin R. Gilmore, "Uses of Plants by the Indians of the Missouri River Region," *Thirty-third Annual Report of the Bureau of American Ethnology . . . 1911–1912* (Washington, D.C.: Government Printing Office, 1919), p. 85.

2. Brooks, "Sibley's Journal," p. 180. Samuel Parker, *Journal of an Exploring Tour beyond the Rocky Mountains . . . in the Years 1835, '36 and '37* (Ithaca, N.Y. 1842), pp. 51, 56, 58. Paul Wilhelm, "Journey", pp. 418–19. Thwaites, *Bradbury's Travels in the Interior of North America, 1809–11*, in *EWT*, 5:81. Weaver, *Prarie Plants*, pp. 10, 36, 128. Wedel, "Introduction to Pawnee Archaeology," pp. 4–7. Weaver, *Native Vegetation*, pp. 28, 41, 54.

3. Waldo Wedel, "Contributions to the Archaeology of the Upper Republican Valley," *Nebraska History* 15 (July–Sept. 1934): 170. Weltfish, *Lost Universe*, pp. 439–40, 463–65. Gilmore, "Uses of Plants by Indians," p. 75. Wedel, "Introduction to Pawnee Archaeology," p. 30. Carleton, *Prairie Logbooks*, p. 75.

4. Dunbar to Green, May 15, 1839, "Presbyterian Mission," p. 637.

NA,OIA, LR, M 234, Council Bluffs, J. Dunbar to J. Hamilton, Oct. 1838. *Report of the Commissioner of Indian Affairs, 1863*, p. 251.

5. Grange, *Pawnee Pottery*, p. 21. Dunbar Journal, p. 617, and Allis to D. Greene May 12, 1835, p. 697, both in "Presbyterian Mission." Brooks, "Sibley's Journal," p. 180. NA,OIA, LR, M 234, Otoe Agency, Allis to Cumming, Oct. 28, 1856. NA,OIA, LR, M 234, Pawnee Agency, G. Howell to E. P. Smith, Nov. 30, 1874; Burgess to Barclay White, Jan. 9, 1874; Barclay White to E. P. Smith, Dec. 18, 1874; Barclay White to G. Howell, Dec. 11, 1874; G. Howell to B. White, Dec. 16, 1874. John Treat Irving, *Indian Sketches* (Norman: University of Oklahoma Press, 1955), p. 150. "Minutes of Councils between the Pawnee and Their Agents," typed transcript in Nebraska State Historical Society, pp. 13, 44, 74.

6. John Dunbar, "Pawnee History and Ethnology," p. 276. *Report of the Commissioner of Indian Affairs*, 1837, Sen. Doc. 1, 25:2 (serial 317), p. 548. Oehler and Smith, *Visit to the Pawnees*, p. 29. Fuller and Hafen, eds., *Journal of Captain Bell*, p. 111. Carleton, *Prairie Logbooks*, p. 75. John Irving, *Indian Sketches*, pp. 138, 180. Samuel Allis, "Forty Years among the Indians and on the Eastern Border of Nebraska," *Transactions and Reports of the Nebraska State Historical Society* (Lincoln, 1887) 2:154, 159–160. NA,OIA, LR, M 234, Pawnee Agency, Henry DuPuy to Harrison Branch, July 30, 1861. *Report of Commissioner*, 1863: p. 251. "Quaker Report," *Nebraska History*, 54:155. NA,OIA, LR, M 234, Pawnee Agency, Testimony of G. Howell, May 14, 1873. Dunbar to Greene, July 10, 1843, p. 653; Nov. 14, 1843, p. 662; Apr. 29, 1844, p. 664; Jan. 25, 1845, p. 672, all in "Presbyterian Mission." NA,OIA, LR, M 234, Council Bluffs, G. Hefner, Annual Report, Nov. 1, 1855. Mrs. E. G. Platt, "Some Experiences as a Teacher among the Pawnees," *Kansas State Historical Society Collections* 14 (1915–18): 785.

7. I have closely followed Gene Weltfish, *The Lost Universe*, here and elsewhere. For assignment of land by the chiefs, see George A. Dorsey and James R. Murie, "Notes of Skidi Pawnee Society," *Field Museum of Natural History Anthropological Series* 27 (Chicago: Field Museum, 1940), p. 75.

8. Weltfish, *Lost Universe*, pp. 144–49. Carleton, *Prairie Logbooks*, pp. 75, 105, 106. Rev. Dunbar, "Missionary Life," *NSHSC* 16:280. George F. Will and George E. Hyde, *Corn among the Indians of the Upper Missouri* (Lincoln: University of Nebraska Press, 1964; reprint of 1917 edition), pp. 306–8. There is some dispute over whether the watermelon is indigenous; Melvin R. Gilmore, however, cites considerable evidence that it is ("Uses of Plants by Indians," pp. 122ff.). Dunbar to Greene, July 10, 1843, "Presbyterian Mission," p. 653.

9. Weltfish, *Lost Universe*, p. 119. Will and Hyde, *Corn among the Indians*, pp. 306–8, 69.

10. Weltfish, *Lost Universe*, p. 144. Carleton, *Prairie Logbooks*, pp. 75. Thwaites, *James' Account of Long's Expedition*, in *EWT*, 15:217. For a discussion of the Missouri Basin agriculture that includes all tribes, see Will and Hyde, *Corn among the Indians*, pp. 77–91.

11. I have followed Weltfish, *Lost Universe*, pp. 288–306, and Dunbar, "Pawnee History and Ethnology," pp. 276–77, in this account of harvesting. See also Hyde and Will, *Corn among the Indians*, pp. 115–33.

12. Allis to Greene, May 12, 1835, "Presbyterian Mission," p. 703. Will and Hyde, *Corn among the Indians*, pp. 75–76.

13. Jackson, *Pike's Journals*, 2:35. Allis to Rev. D. Greene, May 12, 1835, "Presbyterian Mission," p. 703. Dunbar, "Pawnee History and Ethnology," p. 276. *Report of the Commissioner of Indian Affairs*, 1837, SED 1, 25th Cong., 2nd sess. (serial 314), p. 547. Dunbar to Greene, July 10, 1843, "Presbyterian Mission," p. 653. *Report of the Commissioner of Indian Affairs*, 1838, SED 1, 26th Cong., 1st sess. (serial 354), p. 503. Hyde and Will, *Corn among the Indians*, pp. 108, 141.

14. NA,OIA, LR, M 234, Pawnee Agency, Testimony of Stacy Matlock, May 14, 1873. In 1835 John Dougherty estimated that between 4,000 and 5,000 Pawnee women worked in the fields; NA,OIA, LR, M 234, Upper Missouri Agency, J. Dougherty to Wm. Clark, Apr. 9, 1835. "Life and Experiences of Major Frank North," typescript, Edward A. Ayer Collection, Newberry Library, Chicago, p. 32. NA,OIA, LR, M 234, Pawnee Agency, Henry DuPuy to H. Branch, July 30, 1861. *Report of the Commissioner of Indian Affairs*, 1863, p. 251. NA,OIA, LR, M 234, Pawnee Agency, D. H. Wheeler to E. B. Taylor, Sept. 15, 1866.

Archaeologists have posited a decline in Pawnee agriculture on the grounds that cache pits are smaller in the nineteenth-century sites than they were in Loup Focus sites. Such a comparison is misleading, however, since, as we shall see, the horse changed the Pawnees' hunt patterns, causing them to spend less time in their villages and probably causing them to carry more food with them instead of storing it. Wedel, *Prehistoric Man*, p. 122.

15. Here I have largely followed Grange's account of historic Pawnee sites (*Pawnee Pottery*, pp. 19–27). There may have been brief abandonments of either the Horse Creek or Cottonwood Creek site or both during the 1820s because of the Republicans' return to Kansas between approximately 1825 and 1832, which few archaeologists take into account. The Clark Site, which Grange and Wedel date 1820, was probably not occupied until about 1832, since the Grands apparently were still on the Loup up to that time. Trading licenses in 1825 and 1831 specify two Pawnee villages on the Loup and one on the Republican but mention no village on the Platte. Any Grand village on the Platte would almost certainly have had a trader. NA, OIA, LR, M 234, St. Louis, Dec. 8, 1825, Nov. 28, 1831. Wilhelm, "Journey," p. 432. Rollins, *Discovery of Oregon Trail*, p. 222. Dunbar Journal, in "Presbyterian Mission," p. 617.

16. Long in 1820 said the Skidi Palmer site consisted of 100 lodges with a population of about 2,000 (Thwaites, *James' Account of Long's Expedition*, in *EWT*. In 1839 missionaries put it at 64 lodges with a population of 1,906 people. (NA, OIA, LR, M 234, Council Bluffs, J. Dunbar to J. Hamilton, Oct. 1839; Dunbar to Greene, July 13, 1840, "Presbyterian Mission," pp. 641–42).

Other estimates made in 1820 by Edwin James and John Bell put the village at 145 and 100 lodges, respectively (Thwaites, *James' Account of Long's Expedition*, in *EWT*, 15:161; Fuller and Hafen, eds., *Journal of Captain Bell*, p. 118).

17. Louis Pelzer, ed., "Captain Ford's Journal of an Expedition to the Rocky Mountains," *Mississippi Valley Historical Review* 12 (March 1926): 556. Irving, *Indian Sketches*, p. 150. NA, OIA, LR, M 234, Council Bluffs, J. Dunbar to J. Hamilton, Oct., 1839. The village of Capot Bleu identified by Dunbar in this letter is almost certainly the Dick Johnson Site (25 PK 3) heretofore unidentified by archaeologists. Grange, *Pawnee Pottery*, p. 23. Annie Abel, ed., *Tabeau's Narrative of Loisel's Expedition to the Upper Missouri* (Norman: University of Oklahoma Press, 1939), p. 69.

18. Thwaites, *James' Account of Long's Expedition*, in *EWT*, 15:196, 225–28. Brooks, ed., "Sibley's Journal," p. 182. Harrison Dale, *The Ashley Smith Explorations*, p. 118. Paul Wilhelm, "Journey," pp. 366–67. Parker, *Journal of an Exploring Tour*, pp. 50–51. Woodland game in the Missouri bottoms, especially below the Platte, was far more abundant, for it was on the better-wooded rivers to the southeast, and the conclusions reached here about the Pawnees do not necessarily apply to neighboring tribes.

19. Dunbar, "Pawnee Habits and Customs," p. 332. Rollins, ed., *Discovery of the Oregon Trail*, pp. 218–19. Weltfish, *Lost Universe*, p. 210. Douglas Ubelaker and Waldo Wedel, "Bird Bones, Burials, and Bundles in Plains Archeology," *American Antiquity* 40 (Oct. 1975): 445. Allis, "Forty Years," 2:144. "Presbyterian Mission," 14:706.

20. Gilmore, "Uses of Plants by Indians," pp. 54–55, 137.

21. Ibid., pp. 111–12.

22. Ibid., pp. 54–55, 137.

23. Dunbar to Greene, July 10, 1848, 652; Dunbar to Greene, Apr. 29, 1844, in "Presbyterian Mission," p. 664.

24. Weltfish, *Lost Universe*, pp. 94, 190, 503–4. Dunbar Journal, in "Presbyterian Mission," p. 611. Gilmore, "Uses of Plants by Indians," pp. 94, 62, 109. Dunbar, "Pawnee Habits and Customs," p. 323.

25. Weltfish, *Lost Universe*, pp. 180, 503–4. Allis, "Forty Years," p. 140. William Clayton, *William Clayton's Journal* . . . (New York: Arno Press, 1973; reprint of 1921 edition), Apr. 21, 1846, p. 88. Gilmore, "Uses of Plants by Indians," pp. 71, 87–88. Dunbar, "Pawnee Habits and Customs," p. 323.

26. Dunbar, Journal, p. 611, and Dunbar to Greene, Apr. 29, 1844, p. 664, both in "Presbyterian Mission," NA, OIA, LR, M 234, Council Bluffs, Miller to Harvey, March 20, 1848. Clayton, *Journal*, Apr. 21, 1846, p. 81. Allis, "Forty Years," p. 140. Weltfish, *Lost Universe*, pp. 503–4.

27. Weltfish, *Lost Universe*, pp. 503–4. See Gilmore, "Uses of Plants by Indians," passim, for wide variety of species used for medicine by Pawnees. Ibid., pp. 131, 95–96.

28. Wedel, "Introduction to Pawnee Archaeology," p. 86. Frank Collins Baker, "The Fresh Water Molluscs of Wisconsin," *Bulletin 70 of the Wisconsin Geological and Natural History Survey*, pt. 2, Pelocypoda (Madison: University of Wisconsin Press, 1928), pp. 244–46, 286–89.

29. Weltfish, *Lost Universe*, pp. 194–95, 504–5.

30. Weaver, *Native Vegetation*, pp. 101–2. J. E. Weaver and F. W. Albertson, *Grasslands of Great Plains* (Lincoln: University of Nebraska Press, 1956), pp. 16, 193–94. J. E. Weaver and W. P. Bruner, "Nature and Place of Transition from True Prairie to Mixed Prairie," *Ecology* 35 (Apr. 1954): 117–26.

31. Weaver and Bruner, "Transition," pp. 117–26. In the past, depending on rainfall, the transition area could have shifted east or west. This mistake has been made by most students of the buffalo. Even Frank G. Roe, *The North American Buffalo: A Critical Study of the Species in Its Wild State* (Toronto: University of Toronto Press, 1970), pp. 492–500, does not question the number of buffalo the tall-grass prairies supposedly supported. See also Wedel, *"Introduction to Kansas Archeology,"* p. 18. Tom McHugh, *The Time of the Buffalo* (New York, Knopf, 1972), pp. 16–17. David Dary, "The Buffalo in Kansas," *Kansas Historical Quarterly* 39 (Autumn 1973): 321. For travelers and explorers asserting recent retreat of bison from tall grass, see Paul Wilhelm, "Journey," pp. 343, 369; Dunbar Journal, in "Presbyterian Mission," p. 608; Rev. Dunbar, "Missionary Life among the Pawnee," p. 277; NA, OIA, LR, M 234, Council Bluffs, Capt. H. Wharton to Major D. C. Buell, Jan. 31, 1851; NA, OIA, LR, M 234, Upper Missouri, J. Dougherty to L. Cass, Nov. 19, 1831.

32. For some examples of the sighting of the herds around the forks of the Platte, see P. St. George Cooke, *Scenes and Adventures in the Army; or, The Romance of Military Life* (Philadelphia: Lindsay and Blakiston, 1859) pp. 299–300; Alden Brooks, "Grand Trip across the Plains," 1859, Ayer MS 111, Newberry Library, Chicago; Parker, *Exploring Tour*, p. 61; F. A. Wislizenus, *A Journey to the Rocky Mountains in the Year 1838* (St. Louis, 1912), pp. 44–45; Francis Parkman, *The Oregon Trail* (Madison: University of Wisconsin Press, 1969), pp. 66, 79–80, 87.

33. Fuller and Hafen, eds., *Journal of Captain Bell*, p. 125. Roger L. Nichols, *The Missouri Expedition of 1818–1820: The Journal of Surgeon John Gale with Related Documents* (Norman: University of Oklahoma Press, 1969), p. 82. Brooks, "Sibley's Journal," p. 178. Sibley makes no differentiation between the size of the herds of buffalo and elk he encountered, indicating they were small groups; George P. Hammond and Agapito Rey, *Narratives of the Coronado Expedition, 1540–42* (Albuquerque: University of New Mexico Press, 1940), p. 303. Jackson, *Pike's Journals*, 2:10. Rollins, ed., *Discovery of Oregon Trail*, p. 219. Thwaites, *James' Account of Long's Expedition*, in *EWT*, 15:206, 227–28, 234, 239, 256. Dunbar Journal, in "Presbyterian Mission," p. 608.

34. NA, OIA, LR, M 234, Council Bluffs, Notes of Council with Pawnee, June 11, 1845, Maj. Harvey; Harvey to Crawford, June 17, 1845. Clayton, *Journal*, p. 86. Oehler and Smith, *Visit to Pawnees*, p. 28. Hiram M. Chittenden and Alfred Richardson, eds., *Life, Letters and Travels of Father Pierre Jean de Smet, S. J., 1801–1873* (New York: F. P. Harper, 1905), 2:723. Stansbury, "Expedition to Salt Lake," *SED 3*, 32:55, p. 29. NA, OIA, LR, M 234, Upper Mo., J. Dougherty to Wm. Clark, Nov. 20, 1832.

35. D. G. Peden, et al., "The Trophic Ecology of Bison L. on Shortgrass Plains," *Journal of Applied Ecology* 11 (Aug. 1974): 489–97.

36. Gilmore, "Uses of Plants by Indians," pp. 67, 88, 98. Strong, "Nebraska Archeology," p. 272.

37. Charles A. Murray, *Travels in North America*, 2 vols. (London: Richard Bentley, 1854), 1:219. Gilmore, "Uses of Plants by Indians," p. 92. Dunbar, "Pawnee Habits and Customs," p. 332. Weltfish, *Lost Universe*, p. 194. Waldo Wedel, "Notes on the Prairie Turnip *(Psoralea esculenta)* among the Plains Indians," *Nebraska History* 59 (Summer 1978): 154–77.

38. Here I follow closely the chronology given in Weltfish, *Lost Universe*. I differ only in giving a slightly later date for the Pawnee return from the winter hunt on the basis of observations by nineteenth-century agents and missionaries. See NA, OIA, LR, M 234, Upper Missouri, J. Dougherty to Wm. Clark, Feb. 20, 1820; Rev. Dunbar, "Missionary Life," p. 281. For other references to Pawnee economic and ceremonial cycles, see Dunbar, "Pawnee Habits and Customs," pp. 327–28; Dunbar, "Pawnee History and Ethnology," p. 276; Oehler and Smith, *Visit to the Pawnee*, p. 29; Wedel, "Introduction to Pawnee Archaeology," p. 57; Ralph Linton, "The Thunder Ceremony of the Pawnee," *Field Museum of Natural History Anthropological Leaflets*, no. 5 (Chicago, 1922), p. 9.

39. Ralph Linton, "Purification of the Sacred Bundles: A Ceremony of the Pawnee," *Field Museum of Natural History Anthropological Leaflets,* no. 7 (Chicago, 1923), pp. 21–22. Weltfish, *Lost Universe*, pp. 92–104.

40. John Dunbar, "The Pawnee Indians," *Magazine of American History* 8 (Nov. 1882): 741.

41. Weltfish, *Lost Universe*, p. 99.

42. Ibid., pp. 97–106, 129–43.

43. Alice C. Fletcher, "The Hako: A Pawnee Ceremony," *Twenty-Second Annual Report of the Bureau of American Ethnology to the Secretary of the Smithsonian Institution, 1900–1901* (Washington, D.C.: Government Printing Office, 1904), pt. 2, p. 46.

44. Weltfish, *Lost Universe*, pp. 129–43.

45. Ibid., pp. 157–58.

46. Brooks, "Sibley's Journal," p. 190. Murray, *Travels*, 1:294, 316–20; Dunbar, "Missionary Life," pp. 279–80. Allis, "Forty Years," p. 139. Weltfish, *Lost Universe*, pp. 254–55, 243–51.

47. Paul Wilhelm, "Journey," p. 407. Annie Abel, *Tabeau's Narrative of Loisel's Expedition to the Upper Missouri* (Norman: University of Oklahoma Press, 1939), p. 72. Dunbar, "Pawnee Habits and Customs," pp. 329, 331. Murray, *Travels*, 1:294. Weltfish, *Lost Universe*, pp. 241, 91.

48. Preston Holder, *The Hoe and the Horse on the Plains: A Study of Cultural Development among North American Indians* (Lincoln: University of Nebraska Press, 1970), p. 44.

49. Ibid. Weltfish, *Lost Universe*, pp. 157–59. George Dorsey and James Murie, "Notes of Skidi Pawnee Society," *Anthropological Series, Field Museum of*

Natural History 27 (Chicago, Sept. 18, 1940): 112.

50. Holder, *Hoe and Horse*, pp. 42, 46. Andrew Lesser, *The Pawnee Ghost Dance Hand Game: Ghost Dance Revival and Ethnic Identity* (Madison: University of Wisconsin Press, 1978), pp. 107–8, originally published in 1933 by Columbia University Press as vol. 16 in Columbia University Contributions to Anthropology.

51. Holder, *Hoe and Horse*, p. 46.

52. Rev. John Dunbar, "Missionary Life among the Pawnee," p. 277.

53. For references to the power of the chiefs, see Holder, *Hoe and Horse*, p. 109; Dunbar, "Pawnee Indians: History and Ethnology," pp. 260–61; John Williamson, "Autobiography and Reminiscences," MS, Nebraska State Historical Society, pp. 30–31; Paul Wilhelm, "Journey," pp. 432–33. For the *nahikut* and the *raripakusus*, see Linton, "The Thunder Ceremony," p. 4. Dorsey and Murie, *Skidi Society*, p. 113. James R. Murie, *Pawnee Indian Societies*, Anthropological Papers of the American Museum of Natural History, vol. 11, pt. 7 (New York, 1914), p. 557.

54. Murie, *Pawnee Societies*, p. 557. Weltfish, *Lost Universe*, p. 24. Holder, *Hoe and Horse*, p. 51. Dorsey and Murie, *Skidi Society*, p. 113.

55. Dunbar, "Pawnees: History and Ethnology," p. 262. Williamson, "Autobiography, and Reminiscences," p. 30.

56. Linton, "Purification of Bundles," p. 21. Weltfish, *Lost Universe*, p. 8.

57. Weltfish, *Lost Universe*, p. 47.

58. Ibid., pp. 24–46. Holder, *Hoe and Horse*, pp. 42, 57–58.

59. Dunbar, "Pawnee: Habits and Customs," p. 745. Rev. Dunbar, "Journal," Oct. 22, 1834, in "Presbyterian Mission," p. 600. The exception to this seems to have been horses. This will be discussed later. Also see John Williamson, "History of the Pawnees," MS, Nebraska State Historical Society.

60. Dunbar, "Pawnee: History and Ethnology," p. 261. Fr. Vivier to Father Superior of the Society of Jesus, Nov. 17, 1850, in Reuben Gold Thwaites, ed., *The Jesuit Relations and Allied Documents*, 73 vols. (Cleveland: Burrows Brothers, 1896–1901), 69:223–29. Manuscript of John Dunbar, p. 6, in Dunbar Papers, Nebraska State Historical Society.

61. Weltfish, *Lost Universe*, p. 119. Holder, *Hoe and Horse*, pp. 54, 60–65. Allis to Green, July 15, 1836, pp. 705–6, and Rev. Dunbar, Journal, pp. 609–10, both in "Presbyterian Mission."

62. Holder, *Hoe and Horse*, pp. 64–65.

CHAPTER 8

1. For the basic discussions of the horse, see Clark Wissler, "The Influence of the Horse in the Development of Plains Culture," *American Anthropologist* n.s. 16 (Jan.–Mar. 1914): 1–25; Francis Haines, "The Northward Spread of Horses among the Plains Indians," *American Anthropologist* n.s. 40 (July–Sept. 1938): 429–37; F. Haines, "Where Did the Plains Indians Get Their Horses?"

American Anthropologist n.s. 40 (Jan–Mar. 1938): 112–17; A. L. Kroeber, *Cultural and Natural Areas of North America*, University of California Publications in American Archaeology and Ethnology, vol. 38 (Berkeley, 1939), pp. 76–88; Symmes Oliver, *Ecology and Cultural Continuity as Contributing Factors in the Social Organization of the Plains Indians*, University of California Publications in American Archaeology and Ethnology, vol. 48, no. 1 (Berkeley, 1962), pp. 7–9; Frank Roe, *The Indian and the Horse* (Norman: University of Oklahoma Press, 1955); John C. Ewers, "The Horse in Blackfoot Indian Culture," *Bureau of American Ethnology Bulletin 159* (Washington, D.C., 1955).

2. Weltfish, *Lost Universe*, pp. 168–69, 513–15. Thwaites, *James' Account of Long's Expedition*, in *EWT*, 15:79. Dunbar Journal, in "Presbyterian Mission," p. 602. Murray, *Travels*, 1:225.

3. The basic data on the spread of horses have been taken from Haines, "The Northward Spread of Horses," pp. 429–37, and "Where Did the Plains Indians Get Their Horses?" pp. 112–17. The tribe Haines identifies as Pawnees (p. 432) were actually Wichitas. The Wichitas as well as the Arikaras were often called Pawnees by early travelers, and the villages Haines refers to were in present-day Oklahoma, which was Wichita territory, not Pawnee territory. Marcel Giraud, ed., "Exact Description of Louisiana," *Missouri Historical Society Bulletin* 15 (Oct. 1958): 16.

4. Thomas, *After Coronado*, p. 37. Folsom, "French Expansion," Diary of De Bourgmond Expedition, 1724, Speech of Big Chief of Panimahas, pp. 173–74. Brooks, ed., *Sibley's Journal*, p. 185. Dunbar, "Pawnee Habits and Customs," pp. 321–22. NA, OIA, LR, M 234, Council Bluffs, Maj. Dougherty to John Jameson, Mar. 2, 1840. Roger Nichols, ed., *The Missouri Expedition 1818–1820: The Journal of Surgeon John Gale with Related Documents*, pp. 84–85. Thwaites, *Josiah Gregg's Commerce of the Prairies*, in *EWT*, 20:21, 337. Jackson, *Pike's Journals*, 1:320–21. Dunbar to Greene, Apr. 29, 1844, in "Presbyterian Mission," p. 664. Thwaites, *James' Account of Long's Expedition*, in *EWT*, 15:207. NA, OIA, LR, M 234, Documents . . . Ratified Treaties, Treaty 181, Treaty Journal, Nov. 2, 1833, p. 17. Rufus Sage, *Scenes in the Rocky Mountains* (Philadelphia: Carey and Hart, 1846), p. 152. Pelzer, *Ford's Journal*, p. 567. NA, OIA, LR, M 234, Council Bluffs, Maj. Dougherty to Wm. Clark, June 8, 1836, May 31, 1838. NA, OIA, LR, M 234, Pawnee, J. Gillis to A. B. Greenwood, Sept. 1, 1866, Henry DuPuy to C. Mix, July 5, 1861.

5. Thwaites, *James' Account of Long's Expedition*, in *EWT*, 15:215, put the Pawnees herd at 8,000 in 1820, and Dunbar speaks of the Grand-Republican-Tappage Group as having 6,000 animals (dogs and horses) on their winter hunt in 1836 (Dunbar Journal, "Presbyterian Mission"). By 1861 the Pawnees had only 1,200–1,500 head (NA, OIA, LR, M 234, Pawnee Agency, H. DuPuy to Charles Mix, July 5, 1861).

6. Weltfish, *Lost Universe*, pp. 168–73. Murray, *Travels*, 1:291–92.

7. For distribution of horses and social standing, see Dunbar "Pawnee History and Ethnology," p. 252, 265–66. Weltfish, *Lost Universe*, pp. 169–72.

Murray, *Travels*, 1:291–92; Allis, "Forty Years," p. 159. For the begging dance, see Dunbar, "Pawnee History and Ethnology," p. 738.

8. Weltfish, *Lost Universe*, pp. 169, 173.

9. Allis, "Forty Years," p. 140.

10. NA, OIA, LR, M 234, St. Louis, Wm. Clark to James Barbour, Dec. 8, 1825. Carleton, *Prairie Logbooks*, pp. 70, 75, 106. "Expedition of Maj. Wharton," p. 282. NA, OIA, LR, M 234, Council Bluffs, T. Harvey to L. Crawford, July 25, 1845. Fuller, "Bell's Journal of Long Expedition," p. 122. Lt. John C. Frémont, "A Report on an Exploration of the Country Lying between the Missouri River and the Rocky Mountains . . . ," *SD 243*, 27:3 (serial 416), p. 16. Oehler and Smith, *Visit to the Pawnees*, p. 29.

11. Weaver and Albertson, *Grasslands of Great Plains*, pp. 36–37, 38. John C. Frémont, "A Report of an Exploration of the Country Lying between the Missouri River and Rocky Mountains . . . , *H.D. 166*, 28:2 (serial 467), p. 289. Weaver, *Native Vegetation*, p. 63.

12. Weaver, *Native Vegetation*, p. 63. Weltfish, *Lost Universe*, p. 495.

13. Jackson, *Pike's Journals*, 2:35. Weltfish, *Lost Universe*, pp. 495–96.

14. Dale, ed., *Journals of Ashley-Smith*, p. 122. See also Dunbar Journal, in "Presbyterian Mission," p. 608.

15. Thomas, *After Coronado*, p. 183. Folsom, "French Expansion," pp. 173–74. Weltfish, *Lost Universe*, pp. 508–9.

16. Dunbar, "Pawnee Habits and Customs," p. 332. Thwaites, *James' Account of Long's Expedition*, in *EWT*, 15:215–16. Sage, *Scenes in the Rocky Mountains*, p. 97. Rev. Dunbar, "Missionary Life among the Pawnees," p. 281. Lt. G. K. Warren, "Report of Lt. G. K. Warren . . . of the Sioux Expedition of Explorations in the Dakota Country, 1855," *SED 76*, 34:1 (serial 822), p. 17.

17. For a fraction of the literature generated by this debate, see Carl Sauer, *Land and Life* (Berkeley: University of California Press, 1974), pp. 23–31, 288–300; Omer Stewart, "Why the Great Plains Are Treeless," *Colorado Quarterly* 2 (Summer 1959): 40–50; Omer Stewart, "Burning and Natural Vegetation in the United States," *Geographical Review* 41 (Apr. 1951): 317–20; Roger Clouser, "Man's Intervention in the Post-Wisconsin Vegetational Succession of the Great Plains," (M.A. thesis, University of Kansas, 1974); Waldo Wedel, "The Central North American Grasslands: Man Made or Natural," *Studies in Human Ecology*, Joint Publication of the Anthropological Society of Washington and the Pan-American Union, Social Science Monograph 3 (Washington, D.C., 1957), pp. 39–70; Philip Wells, "Historical Factors Controlling Vegetation Patterns and Floristic Distributions in the Central Plains Region of North America," in Dort and Jones, eds., *Pleistocene and Recent Environments*, pp. 211–21; Frederick Clements and Ralph Chaney, *Environment and Life in the Great Plains*, Carnegie Institution of Washington, Supplementary Publications no. 24 (Washington, D.C., 1936), p. 33; Philip Wells, "Scarp Woodlands, Transported Grassland Soils, and Concept of Grassland Climate in Great Plains Region," *Science* 148:3667 Apr. 9, 1965): 246–49; Weaver, *Grasslands of the Great Plains*, pp. 161–62; Philip Wells,

"Post-Glacial Vegetational History of the Great Plains," *Science* 167:3925 (Mar. 20, 1970): 1574–81. Conrad Moore, "Man and Fire in the Central North American Grassland, 1585–1890: A Documentary History" (Ph.D. diss. U.C.L.A., 1974), found the great majority of fires set by Indians to have occurred in the tall-grass areas.

18. J. E. Weaver and N. W. Rowland, "Effects of Excessive Natural Mulch on Development, Yield, and Structure of Native Grassland," *Botanical Gazette* 114 (Sept. 1952): 1–19. T. L. Steiger, "Structure of Prairie Vegetation," *Ecology* 11 (Jan. 1930): 217. R. L. Hensel, "Effects of Burning on Vegetation in Kansas Pastures," *Journal of Agricultural Research* 23 (Feb. 24, 1923): 631–43.

19. Lorenzo Sawyer, "Way Sketches: Containing Incidents of Travel across the Plains . . . " (New York: Edward Eberstadt, 1926), pp. 32–33. George Catlin, *Letters and Notes on the Manners, Customs and Conditions of the North American Indians*, 2 vols. (London: Tosswell and Myers, 1841), 2:16. Clayton, Journal, Apr. 21, 1846, p. 88.

20. Paul Wilhelm, "Journey," p. 427. Dunbar Journal, in "Presbyterian Mission," pp. 608–9. Lela Barnes, "Journal of Isaac McCoy for the Exploring Expedition of 1828," *Kansas Historical Quarterly* 5 (Aug. 1936): 227–77. Sage, *Scenes in Rocky Mountains*, p. 34. Nichols, ed., *Missouri Expedition, Journal of John Gale*, pp. 74, 76. P. St. George Cooke, *Scenes and Adventures in the Army*, p. 297. James Little, *From Kirtland to Salt Lake City* (Salt Lake City: J. A. Little, 1890), p. 160. Rollins, ed., *Discovery of Oregon Trail*, p. 217. "Report of Secretary of War," Appendix L, Capt. J. Dickerson to Col. J. J. Abert, Dec. 15, 1856, *SED 11*, 35:1 (serial 920), p. 528. NA, OIA, LR, M 234, Pawnee Agency, S. Warner Green et al. to C. Delano, Oct. 14, 1872. NA, OIA, LR, Otoe Agency, J. Ricky to G. Manypenny, Dec. 1, 1856. Fred Perrine, ed., "Hugh Evans' Journal of Colonel Henry Dodge's Expedition to the Rocky Mountains in 1835," *Mississippi Valley Historical Review* 14 (Sept. 1927): 196. Irving, *Indian Sketches*, p. 203. Thwaites, *James' Account of Long's Expedition*, in *EWT*, 14:263, 15:139. Pawnee burning conformed to the general plains pattern; see Moore, "Man and Fire," p. 8.

21. Howard Stansbury, "Exploration and Survey of the Valley of the Great Salt Lake including a Reconnaissance of a New Route through the Rocky Mountains," *SED 3*, Special Session, March 1851 (serial 608), p. 32. Thwaites, *James' Account of Long's Expedition*, in *EWT*, 14:263, 15:139. Most travelers report tracts of burned land, and such areas might encompass several days' travel. A survey of the Pawnee reservation in 1872, a year in which the reservation was burned over, found that some areas remained unburned. NA, OIA, LR, M 234, Pawnee Agency, S. Warner Green et al. to C. Delano, Oct. 14, 1872. The surveyors, for instance, reported portions of one township so burned over that vegetation could not be judged, but in another township they reported good grass. NA, OIA, RG 75, Survey Field Notes, Pawnee Trust Lands, 1872, vol. 164:180, p. 249.

22. Reuben Gold Thwaites, Maximilian, Prince of Wied's *Travels in the Interior of North America*, in *EWT*, 22:268. Perrine, *Evans' Journal*, p. 186. Sage,

Scenes in the Rocky Mountains, pp. 36–37. NA, OIA, LR, M 234, Council Bluffs, J. Dunbar to J. Hamilton, Oct. 1839. NA, OIA, LR, M 234, Otoe Agency, J. Ricky to G. Manypenny, Dec. 1, 1856. Lt. G. Warren, "Explorations in Nebraska," in Report of Secretary of War, 1859," *SED 1*, 35:2 (serial 975), p. 658. NA, OIA, LR, M 234, Pawnee Agency, Petition for Removal of Pawnee, Jan. 16, 1869; Inquiry of Specie and North, Dec. 4, 1875. *Explorations and Surveys for a Railroad Route from the Mississippi River to the Pacific Ocean* (Washington, D.C., 1855), 2:12–13. Moore, "Man and Fire," p. 121.

23. Brooks, "Sibley's Journal," p. 190.

24. Dunbar, "Pawnee Habits and Customs," pp. 330–32. Allis, "Forty Years," p. 139. Murray, *Travels* 1:318–20. Murie, *Pawnee Organization*, pp. 567–78. Weltfish, *Lost Universe*, pp. 243–54. Rev. Dunbar, "Missionary Life," pp. 279–80.

25. Dunbar, "Pawnee Habits and Customs," pp. 327–28. Allis, "Forty Years," p. 139. Murray, *Travels*, 1:304.

26. Allis, "Forty Years," p. 130. Dunbar, "Pawnee Habits and Customs," pp. 330–32. Weltfish, *Lost Universe*, pp. 248, 258–69. Murray, *Travels*, 1:245, 279.

27. The figures on animals killed in an attack are from Allis, "Forty Years," p. 139, and Dunbar, "Pawnee Habits and Customs," pp. 327–28. The number of attacks per hunt has been taken from Weltfish, *Lost Universe*, pp. 243–82. In 1865 the Pawnee agent reported a total yield of 1,600 hides from the summer hunt. This included deer, elk, and antelope, but the bulk of the skins were buffalo. The agent considered this a successful hunt. NA, OIA, LR, M 234, Pawnee Agency, D. Wheelis to E. B. Taylor, Sept. 15, 1865. For Republicans hunting separately in 1803, see Jackson, *Pike's Journals*, 2:8.

As mentioned previously, the Grands traded 120 packs of buffalo robes in 1813, a kill of 1,200 animals for trade alone, indicating that they must have been near the upper limits of the 1,800 to 4,000 kill range. If the three South Bands traded at least an equal number of skins in the 1830s (and they probably traded more), a time when they numbered 600 tipis, then their total annual kill can be figured as follows. Each tipi contained at least eight hides and lasted an average of twelve years; therefore, their minimum requirement for skins for tipis and trade can be computed as $1,200 + (8 \times 600)/12 = 1,600$. When the hides used for containers, clothing, robes, etc., is added to this, the large number of buffalo required becomes clear.

28. Dunbar, "Pawnee: Habits and Customs," pp. 321–22. For early mention of the Pawnee trade in furs, see Marcel Giraud, ed., "Etienne Veniard De Bourgmont's 'Exact Description of Louisiana,' " *Missouri historical Society Bulletin* 15 (Oct. 1958): 16; Thomas, *After Coronado*, p. 183; Nasatir, ed., *Before Lewis and Clark*, 1:73, 364, 2:694, 709, 758–59; Folmer, "French Expansion," pp. 173–74; George Windell, ed., "The Missouri Reader," *Missouri Historical Review* 41 (Oct. 1946): 96–97; Reuben Gold Thwaites, *Journals of Lewis and Clark*, 6:86–87.

29. The pack was a standardized unit weighing about 100 lbs. It contained 10 buffalo robes, or 14 bear pelts, or 60 land otter, or 80 beaver, or 80 raccoon, or 120 fox, or 600 muskrat. See Rollins, ed., *Discovery of the Oregon Trail*, n. 152, p. 233. In the same year the Omahas traded 126 packs of beaver, deer, buffalo, and stag, three times as much as the Grands, but their skins were valued at 5,100 livres, 400 less than those of the Grands.

30. For Pawnee solicitations, see Pierre Chouteau to Secretary of War, Dec. 14, 1809, in Carter, *Territorial Papers of the U.S., Louisiana and Missouri*, 14:344. For the Curly Chief story, see James Murie Papers, Kansas State Historical Society, Murie to A. B. Warren, n.d. For quote, see Paul Wilhelm, "Journey," 19:348.

31. NA, OIA, LR, M 234, Upper Missouri, J. Dougherty to L. Cass, Nov. 19, 1831. "Message . . . Concerning the Fur Trade," Joshua Pilcher's Report, Dec. 1, 1831, in *SED 90*, 22:1 (serial 213), pp. 13–14, 47–48.

32. For presence of traders, see Rollins, ed., *Discovery of the Oregon Trail*, p. 232; NA, OIA, LR, M 234, St. Louis Superintendency, B. O'Fallon to Clark, Dec. 15, 1824; Clark to Barbour, Dec. 8, 1825; Locations of Posts, Nov. 28, 1831. Dougherty to Cass Nov. 11, 1831, typescript, Kansas State Historical Society.

33. Allis to Greene, May 12, 1835, pp. 700–701; Allis to Trent, Jan. 16, 1849, p. 740; Ranney to Greene, Oct. 2, 1846, p. 780, all in "Presbyterian Mission." Murray, *Travels*, 1:228. *Friends' Intelligencer*, July 10, 1869, letter of S. Janney, June 18, 1869. Thwaites, *James' Account of Long's Expedition*, in *EWT*, 15:49. For a rare assertion that the Pawnees were drunkards, see Chittenden and Richardson, eds., *Life, Letters and Travels of Father Pierre Jean De Smet*, 2:722. De Smet had had relatively little personal contact with the Pawnees, however.

34. Loomis and Nasatir, eds., *Pedro Vial*, pp. 401–3.

35. Dunbar to Greene, July 10, 1843, "Presbyterian Mission,"p. 652.

36. Dunbar, "Pawnee: History and Ethnology," pp. 260–61. Holder, *Hoe and Horse*, p. 109.

37. Allis to Greene, Feb. 14, 1842, 726; May 13, 1842, 728, "Presbyterian Mission," Oehler and Smith, *Visit to the Pawnees*, p. 31. *Friends' Intelligencer*, July 10, 1869. Brooks, ed., "Sibley's Journal," p. 182. Rollins, ed., *Discovery of the Oregon Trail*, p. 222. Nasatir, *Before Lewis and Clark*, 2:799. NA, OIA, LR, M 234, St. Louis, B. O'Fallon to W. Clark, Dec. 15, 1824.

38. NA, OIA, LR, M234, Upper Missouri, J. Dougherty to Acting Commissioner, June 28, 1838; Speech of Big Elk, chief of Omahas, June 24, 1828; Petition of Omaha Chiefs, Oct. 4, 1833; J. Dougherty to Wm. Clark, Nov. 12, 1834.

39. Few scholars have given the Pawnees much credit for shaping their world. For example, Clements and Chaney, *Environment and Life in the Great Plains*, p. 31, wrote, "It is improbable that these [Indians] uses produced any significant effect on the composition of the prairie as a whole."

40. Gilmore, "Uses of Plants by Indians," pp. 59–60, 129, 136–37.

41. NA, OIA, LR, M 234, Upper Missouri, J. Dougherty to Wm. Clark, Oct. 29, 1831. Wedel, *Introduction to Pawnee Archaeology*, pp. 60–61; Gilmore, "Uses of Plants by Indians," p. 78.

42. Thwaites, *James' Account of Long's Expedition*, in *EWT*, 15:196. Clayton, *Journal*, Apr. 21, 1846, p. 88. Samuel Allis, "Forty Years," p. 140. NA, OIA, LR, M 234, Council Bluffs, Miller to Harvey, Mar. 20, 1848. Weltfish, *Lost Universe*, p. 503. Dunbar Journal, "Presbyterian Mission," pp. 611, 703. Clements and Chaney, *Environment and Life on the Great Plains*, p. 31.

43. Gilmore, "Uses of Plants by Indians," p. 79. Ferdinand V. Hayden, "Botany," in Lt. G. K. Warren, "Explorations," in "Report of Sec. of War, 1858," *SED 1*, 35:2, p. 730.

44. Gilmore, "Uses of Plants by Indians," pp. 87, 88, 60. Brooks, "Sibley's Journal," p. 180. Weltfish, *Lost Universe*, p. 202.

45. Hayden, "Botany," in Warren, "Explorations," p. 737. Weaver, *Prairie Plants*, p. 110. Moore, "Man and Fire," pp. 121, 130–31.

46. J. E. Weaver and N. W. Rowland, "Effects of Excessive Natural Mulch," *Botanical Gazette*, 114:1, 3, 16–18. Sage, *Scenes in the Rocky Mountains*, p. 154. Parker, *Exploring Tour*, pp. 56–58. Paul Wilhelm does complain about the lack of variety in the prairies around the Otoe villages, but he traveled in the fall when the tall grasses would have overtopped and shaded out the mid-grasses and forbs of spring and early summer ("Journey," p. 418).

47. Weaver, *Prairie Plants*, pp. 10, 36.

48. Ibid., p. 39. Overgrazing, according to Weaver and Albertson, is the consumption of over one-half the foliage produced (*Grasslands of Great Plains*, p. 23).

49. Most of the literature on overgrazing is concerned with cattle. Although many plants are indicators of overgrazing, their mere occurrence is not sufficient proof that this has taken place. See Weaver, *Prairie Plants*, p. 202; J. D. Weaver and R. W. Darland, "Changes in Vegetation and Production of Forage Resulting from Grazing Lowland Prairie," *Ecology* 29 (Jan. 1948): 1–29; Lincoln Ellison, "Influence of Grazing on Plant Succession of Rangelands," *Botanical Review* 26 (Jan.–Mar. 1960): 1–78; F. W. Albertson et al., "Effects of Different Intensities of Clipping on Short-Grasses in West Central Kansas," *Ecology* 34 (Jan. 1952): 1–20; Weaver and Albertson, *Grasslands of Great Plains*, pp. 21–24, 197–203; H. L. Shants, "The Natural Vegetation of the Great Plains Region," *Annals of the Association of American Geographers* 13 (June 1923): 90; F. W. Albertson et al., "Ecology of Drought Cycles and Grazing Intensity," *Ecological Monographs* 27 (Jan. 1957): 27–44. For contemporary accounts, see John C. Frémont, "Report on Exploration," *SED 243*, pp. 80–93; Hayden, "Botany," in Warren, "Explorations," pp. 740, 742.

50. For comparison, American hunters alone killed an estimated 1.5 million buffalo in 1873. See Roe, *North American Buffalo*, p. 438. Roe estimates an annual increase of 3,240,000 animals in the herds in 1830. Dunbar, "Pawnee Habits and Customs," p. 330.

51. NA, OIA, LR, M 234, Upper Missouri, J. Dougherty to Wm. Clark, Nov. 20, 1832. James Little, *From Kirtland to Salt Lake City*, p. 166. NA, OIA, LR, M 234, Pawnee Agency, Barclay White to Commissioner, Feb. 22, 1873.
52. Lt. G. K. Warren, "Explorations in Nebraska," in "Report of Secretary of War, 1858," p. 631.
53. NA, OIA, LR, M 234, Council Bluffs, Captain H. Wharton to G. Manypenny, Jan. 21, 1854. NA, OIA, LR, M 234, Pawnee Agency, Henry DuPuy to W. P. Dole, Jan. 2, 1862.

CHAPTER 9

1. Dunbar to Greene, Apr. 29, 1844, p. 664; Jan. 25, 1845, p. 672; Aug. 18, 1845, pp. 679–80; Allis to Greene, May 12, 1835, all in "Presbyterian Mission." Dunbar, "Pawnee History and Ethnology," p. 276.
2. John Ewers, *Indian Life on the Upper Missouri* (Norman: University of Oklahoma Press, 1968), p. 46. See also Symmes Oliver, *Social Organization of the Plains Indians*, p. 4; Kroeber, *Cultural Areas*, pp. 83–87; Strong, "Introduction to Nebraska Archeology," pp. 297–99; Wedel, "Introduction to Pawnee Archaeology," pp. 97–98; Holder, *Hoe and the Horse*, p. 111.
3. Allis, "Forty Years," p. 139. Dunbar, "Pawnee Habits and Customs," pp. 330–32. Weltfish, *Lost Universe*, pp. 248, 258–69. Murray, *Travels*, 1:245, 279.
4. For Sioux expansion, see Richard White, "The Winning of the West: The Expansion of the Teton Sioux during the Eighteenth and Nineteenth Century," *Journal of American History* 65 (Sept. 1978): 319–43.
5. NA, OIA, LR, M 234, Council Bluffs, D. Miller to D. Mitchell, Dec. 23, 1843; H. Wharton to G. Manypenny, Dec. 1851; G. Hefner, Annual Report, Nov. 1, 1855. Allis to Greene, May 31, 1837, p. 714; Allis to Greene, Sept. 1, 1841, p. 725, both in "Presbyterian Mission."
6. Dunbar to D. Greene, Sept. 9, 1844, p. 667; Apr. 29, 1844, p. 664; Allis to D. Greene, July 14, 1836, pp. 707–10, all in "Presbyterian Mission." Cooke, *Scenes and Adventures*, p. 290. "Expedition of Colonel Dodge," *ASP: Military Affairs*, Class V, vol. 6, 24:1. Dunbar, "Pawnee Habits and Customs," pp. 327–28. Rev. Dunbar, "Missionary Life," p. 277. Frémont, "Report on an Exploration," *SD 243*, 27:3, 13; Frémont, "Report," *HD 166*, 28:2. NA, OIA, LR, M 234, Council Bluffs, Miller to Harvey, Mar. 20, 1848. Robert Trennert, *Alternative to Extinction: Federal Indian Policy and the Beginnings of the Reservation System, 1846–51* (Philadelphia: Temple University Press, 1975), p. 154. But even after 1840 the distance had considerable annual variations. As late as 1874 buffalo were within 200 miles of the villages. NA, OIA, LR, M 234, Barclay White to E. Smith, July 3, 1874.
7. Sage, *Scenes in the Rocky Mountains*, p. 50. Donald Jackson, ed., *Letters of the Lewis and Clark Expedition with Related Documents, 1783–1854* (Urbana: Uni-

versity of Illinois Press, 1962), p. 528. Thwaites, *Maximillian's Travels*, in *EWT*, 22:284–85. Thwaites, *Journals of Lewis and Clark*, 6:88. NA, OIA, LR, M 234, Upper Missouri, J. Dougherty to Clark, Nov. 12, 1834. The Arikaras never actually located permanently near the Skidis; rather, they hunted with them for several years. See "Presbyterian Mission,"p. 701; "Expedition of Col. Dodge," *ASP*, 6:133–36.

8. Fletcher, "Hako," p. 173. Emphasis added.

9. Weltfish, *Lost Universe*, p. 451. Dunbar, "Pawnee: History and Ethnology, pp. 268–69.

10. "Minutes of Council between Pawnees and Their Agent," copy in NSHS, pp. 14, 17, 20.

11. Dunbar to Greene, Jan. 25, 1845, p. 672; Dunbar to Greene, June 8, 1838, p. 632, both in "Presbyterian Mission." NA, OIA, LR, M 234, Council Bluffs, Capt. H. Wharton to G. Manypenny, Jan. 21, 1859; G. Hefner, Annual Report, Nov. 1, 1855. NA, OIA, LR, M 234, Pawnee Agency, H. DuPuy to W. Dole, Jan. 2, 1862.

12. Alfred Crosby, "Virgin Soil Epidemics as a Factor in the Aboriginal Depopulation in America," *William and Mary Quarterly* 33 (Apr. 1976): 289–99. Karen Ordahl Kupperman, "Apathy and Death in Early Jamestown," *Journal of American History* 66 (June 1979): 24–40. Dunbar, "Pawnee: Habits and Customs," pp. 755–56.

13. "Minutes of Councils between Pawnees and Their Agents," copy in NSHS, pp. 18, 58, 70.

14. For climatic cycles, see Merlin Paul Lawson, *The Climate of the Great American Desert: Reconstruction of the Climate of the Western Interior United States, 1800–1850*, University of Nebraska Studies, n.s. no. 46 (Lincoln, Dec. 1974), pp. 32, 97–98.

15. Dunbar to Greene, Apr. 29, 1844, p. 644; Dunbar to Greene, Oct. 9, 1844, p. 688, both in "Presbyterian Mission." NA, OIA, LR, Council Bluffs, Miller to Harvey, Mar. 20, 1848, Mar. 29, 1848; Wharton to Manypenny, Jan. 21, 1854. Trennert, *Alternative to Extinction*, p. 154.

16. For just some of the numerous mentions of battle losses and raids, see Dunbar to Greene, Nov. 14, 1843, p. 659; Allis to Greene, July 21, 1843, pp. 730–31; Allis to Greene, Sept. 1, 1841, p. 725, all in "Presbyterian Mission," Hyde, *Pawnee Indians*, pp. 226–36; Sage, *Scenes in the Rocky Mountains*, p. 50; Wisilenzus, *Journey*, p. 138; NA, OIA, LR, M 234, Council Bluffs, Miller to Secretary of War, Jan. 20, 1848; NA, OIA, LR, M 234, Pawnee Agency, DuPuy to Mix, Dec. 29, 1861. For hunger as a spur to horse raiding, see Dunbar to Greene, Apr. 29, 1844, "Presbyterian Mission," p. 664. For census, see Jackson, *Pike's Journals*, 2:41. NA, OIA, LR, M 234, Otoe Agency, Dennison to Robinson, July 16, 1859.

17. Lesser, *Pawnee Ghost Dance*, pp. 106–8. Dunbar, "Pawnee," pp. 740–41. For how the ghost dance provided the Pawnees with a new means of restoring lost knowledge and ceremonies, see Lesser, *Pawnee Ghost Dance*, pp. 53–123.

18. For quote, see Dunbar, "Pawnee," pp. 755–56. For a discussion of

similar incidents, see Kupperman, "Apathy and Death," pp. 24–40. For another mention of the despair of a chief brought by the loss of his heirs, see Dunbar to Greene, June 8, 1838, "Presbyterian Mission," p. 632.

19. By the early 1870s the Pawnees, apparently to explain their situation, believed there were two Gods—one for whites and one for Indians (Williamson, History of Pawnees, John Williamson Papers, NSHS). See NA, OIA, Documents Concerning the Negotiations of Ratified Treaties, M 494, no. 2, Treaty 181, Treaty Journal, p. 15, Nov. 2, 1833; NA, OIA, LR, M 234, Council Bluffs, Miller to Harvey, May 2, 1844, Harvey to Crawford, June 17, 1845, Harvey to Medill, June 5, 1847; NA, OIA, LR, M 234, St. Louis, Harvey to Medill, Oct. 17, 1847. Treaty with the Pawnee, 1833, 7 stat. 448, Kappler, ed., *Laws and Treaties*, 2:417.

20. MS of John Dunbar, p. 6, Dunbar Papers, NSHS.

21. John Williamson, Autobiography and Reminiscences, John Williamson Papers, NSHS. NA, OIA, LR, Pawnee Agency, M 234, Troth to Janney, Oct. 29, 1870; Janney to Parker, July 10, 1871; White to Clum, Oct. 27, 1871. Luther North to Fowler, Mar. 8, 1924, Luther North Papers, NSHS. "Minutes of Councils between Pawnees and Their Agents," copy in NSHS, pp. 3, 28, 31, 33, 68–72, 89–90.

22. Williamson, Autobiography, p. 27.

23. For an evaluation of the attitudes of the various first chiefs of the 1860s and 1870s toward acculturation, see Journal of Barclay White, 3 vols., Friends' Historical Library, Swarthmore College, (microfilm) frames 150–51. Also Dunbar, "Pawnee," p. 755.

24. White, Journals, frames 150–51. NA, OIA, LR, M 234, Pawnee Agency, Speeches at Council, n.d. (council held June, 1874, reel 663, frame 201).

25. NA, OIA, LR, M 234, Pawnee Agency, Janney to Parker, Feb. 17, 1870. Dunbar, "Pawnee: History and Ethnology," p. 344.

26. Luther North, Pioneer Recollections, typescript, Luther North Papers, NSHS. NA, OIA, LR, Pawnee Agency, White to Smith, May 25, 1874; Speeches at Council, n.d. (council held June, 1874, reel 663, frame 201). "Minutes of Councils between Pawnees and Their Agents," copy in NSHS, pp. 83–96.

27. NA, OIA, LR, M 234, Pawnee Agency, Petition of Republican Chiefs, Aug. 21, 1874; Pawnee Chiefs to E. P. Smith, Aug. 21, 1874, Speeches at Council with the Quakers, n.d. (council held in June); Petition of Pawnee Chiefs, Oct. 8, 1874. Also see David J. Wishart, "The Dispossession of the Pawnee," *Annals of the Association of American Geographers*, 69 (Sept. 1979): 382–401.

CHAPTER 10

1. James J. Hester, "Early Navajo Migrations and Acculturation in the Southwest," Museum of New Mexico Papers in Anthropology no. 6 (Santa Fe·

Museum of New Mexico Press, 1962), pp. 75, 81, Ruth Underhill, *The Navajos* (Norman: University of Oklahoma Press, 1967), pp. 4, 5, 18. *Apachu* is a Tewa word meaning "stranger" or "enemy" (Underhill, *Navajos*, pp. 4, 19–23).

2. Hester, "Navajo Migrations," pp. 24, 95. Donald Worcester, "Early History of the Navaho Indian" (Ph.D. diss., University of California, Berkeley, 1947), pp. 64, 72. Underhill, *Navajos*, pp. 42–54.

3. Worcester, "Early History," pp. 91, 109, 121–22, 129–30, 249. Underhill, *Navajos*, pp. 55–56, 59, 63–64. J. Lee Correll, *Through White Mens' Eyes: A Contribution to Navajo History, a Chronological Record of the Navajo People from Earliest Times to the Treaty of June 1, 1868*, Publication no. 1 of the Navajo Heritage Center (Window Rock: Navajo Heritage Center, 1976), pp. 22–23, 27–33, 36–37, 43. Thomas, *After Coronado*, pp. 13–14. Hester, "Navajo Migrations," pp. 22–23, 75, 77. Frank Reeve, "Navaho-Spanish Diplomacy, 1770–1790," *New Mexico Historical Review* 35 (July 1960): 202. Frank D. Reeve, "The Navaho-Spanish Peace, 1720's–1770's," *New Mexico Historical Review* 34 (Jan. 1959): 20. Clyde Kluckhohn and Dorothea Leighton, *The Navaho* (Garden City, N. Y., Doubleday, 1962), p. 6. Willard W. Hill, "Some Navajo Culture Changes during Two Centuries," Essay in Historical Anthropology of North America, *Smithsonian Miscellaneous Collections* 100 (Washington, D.C., Government Printing Office, 1940), p. 409. For the quote, see Alfred B. Thomas, *Forgotten Frontiers* (Norman: University of Oklahoma Press, 1932), pp. 349–50.

4. Correll, *Through White Mens' Eyes*, pp. 72–80, 93–94. Underhill, *Navajos*, pp. 74–84. Hester, "Navajo Migrations," p. 84. David Aberle, *The Peyote Religion among the Navaho*, Viking Fund Publications in Anthropology, no. 42 (New York: Wenner Gren Foundation for Anthropological Research, 1966), pp. 25–26. Meade Kemrer, "The Dynamics of Western Navajo Settlement, A.D. 1750–1900: An Archaeological-Dendrochronological Analysis" (Ph.D. diss., University of Arizona, 1974), p. 149. James Hester stresses slave raiding by the Spanish as the critical element in prolonging these wars. James Hester, "An Ethnohistorical Reconstruction of Navajo Culture," *El Palacio* 69 (Autumn 1962): 130–38.

5. Howard Roberts Lamar, *The Far Southwest, 1846–1912: A Territorial History* (New York: W. W. Norton, 1970) p. 60. Underhill, *Navajos*, p. 91.

6. Underhill, *Navajos*, pp. 116–17. For quote, see Edward Sapir, *Navajo Texts* (with supplementary texts by Harry Hoijer), ed. Harry Hoijer (Iowa City: University of Iowa, 1942), p. 347.

7. Underhill, *Navajos*, pp. 121–26. In 1865, the worst year, 2,321 Navajos died of smallpox. Edward Spicer, *Cycles of Conquest: The Impact of Spain, Mexico, and the United States on the Indians of the Southwest, 1533–1960* (Tucson: University of Arizona Press, 1967), p. 220.

8. Spicer, *Cycles of Conquest*, pp. 220–21, Aberle, *Peyote Religion*, p. 30. Underhill, *Navajos*, pp. 154–55, 159–63.

9. Fr. Anselm Weber to C. F. Hauke, Apr. 29, 1911, in U.S. Senate, Subcommittee of the Committee on Indian Affairs, Hearings, *Survey of Conditions of the Indians of the United States*, 74th Cong., 2nd sess., 1936, pt. 34, p. 17557. National Archives, Record Group 75, Records of the Bureau of Indian Affairs, Office Files of Commissioner John Collier, Collier's Navajo Documents, fifty-five, Portion of Hearing before the Committee on Indian Affairs, United States Senate . . . July 3, 1937, p. 372. These files have a great amount of material on the Navajos grouped under different categories. Hereafter, the largest set of files will simply be listed as Colier's Navajo Documents with a file number when appropriate. Other categories will be listed as NA, RG 75, BIA, Collier Papers, with a file name when appropriate.

10. *Annual Report of the Commissioner of Indian Affairs for the Year 1883* (Washington, D.C.: Government Printing Office, 1884), p. 119. *Report of Commissioner*, 1884, p. 133.

11. *Report of Commissioner, 1878*, p. 108; 1885, p. 155; 1888, p. 191.

For a discussion of the executive orders, see, Lawrence C. Kelly, *The Navajo Indians and Federal Indian Policy, 1900–1935* (Tucson: University of Arizona Press, 1968), pp. 7, 20.

12. See the letters of Fr. Anselm Weber, in *Survey of Conditions*, 34:17553–75.

13. Kelly, *Navajo Indians and Federal Policy*, pp. 20–23.

14. Ibid., pp. 23–25. Sanford Mosk, *Land Tenure Problems in the Santa Fe Railroad Grant Area*, Publications of the Bureau of Business and Economic Research, University of California (Berkeley: University of California Press, 1944), p. 20.

15. Kelly, *Navajo Indians and Federal Policy*, pp. 22–23, 124, 128, 131.

16. *Report of Commissioner, 1888*, p. 191.

17. Denis Foster Johnston, *An Analysis of Sources of Information on the Population of the Navaho*, Bureau of American Ethnology, Bulletin 197 (Washington, D.C.: Government Printing Office, 1966), pp. 66–127, 138.

18. Aberle, *Peyote Religion*, pp. 30–32. I agree with Aberle on the unreliability of published figures before 1930, but my interpretation of these data differs from his. *Reports of Commissioner, 1883*, p. 122; *1871*, p. 378; *1874*, p. 307; *1880*, p. 131; *1886*, p. 203; *1887*, p. 171; *1890*, p. 161. The 1891 census lists 118,000 horses (*Report of Commissioner*, 1891, p. 161).

19. *Report of Commissioner, 1893*, p. 109. Plummer to Walker, Oct. 24, 1894, E. H. Plummer Papers, State Records Center and Archives, Santa Fe, New Mexico. *Report of Commissioner, 1895*, p. 118; *1900*, pp. 191–92; *1901*, p. 180; *1902*, p. 156; *1903*, p. 125; *1905*, p. 180. NA, RG 75, BIA, CCF 46869–1907–916, Navajo, Harrison to Commissioner, Sept. 11, 1907. Aberle, *Peyote Religion*, pp. 31–32, dismisses the drought estimates as too low. I obviously think that he is wrong.

20. "Justification for . . . consolidation of privately owned and Indian lands in certain townships of New Mexico, 1920," in Albert B. Fall Papers,

Huntington Library, San Marino, Cal. Aberle, *Peyote Religion*, p. 31. *Reports of Commissioner, 1886*, p. 203; *1891*, p. 309; *1899*, p. 157; *1905*, p. 108. Kelly, *Navajo Indians and Federal Policy*, pp. 108–11. *Survey of Conditions*, pt. 18: 9277–79.

21. *Reports of Commissioner, 1893*, p. 109; *1894*, p. 99; *1899*, p. 157; *1903*, p. 126.

22. W. W. Hill, *The Agricultural and Hunting Methods of the Navaho Indians*, Yale University Publications in Anthropology, no. 18 (New Haven, Conn.: Yale University Press, 1938), pp. 18, 50. Kluckhohn and Leighton, *The Navaho*, pp. 72–73. In the 1950s Navajos in even a sheepraising area such as Shonto still centered their lives on farming (Adams, *Shonto*, p. 123).

23. As will be discussed later, much of the income from livestock went toward purchasing food, which raised the actual subsistence value of stock. But in the 1930s figures show home-produced food still made up the majority of the Navajo diet in most districts.

24. For a typical statement of Navajo nomadism, see J. W. Hoover, "Navajo Nomadism," *Geographical Review* 21 (July 1931): 429–45. For two refutations, see Hill, *Agricultural and Hunting Methods*, p. 18; Kluckhohn and Leighton, *The Navaho*, pp. 38–39.

25. *Report of Commissioner, 1878*, p. 108. See, for example, Soil Conservation Service, Navajo Service, "Land Report of the Sociological Survey, Unit 11" (Aug. 1936), p. 1; SCS, NS, Land Management Unit 5, Tolani Lakes, "Report of the Human Dependency Survey" (Apr. 1937, rev. 1938), p. 3; SCS, NS, Land Management Unit 10, "Sociological Report, Chin Lee" (Nov. 1937), all in Special Collections, University of New Mexico Library. SCS, NS, Land Management Unit 18, Defiance, "Report of Human Dependency Survey" (Nov. 1936, rev. Nov. 1938), p. 3; SCS, NS, Land Management Unit 9, "Report of the Human Dependency Survey," Section of Conservation Economics, Navajo District, Region 8 (Feb. 1939), p. 3, both in Navajo Tribal Museum, Window Rock, Ariz.

26. Hill, *Agricultural and Hunting Methods*, pp. 20, 24–25.

27. Ibid., pp. 20, 26–33, 34, 39–47.

28. Ibid., pp. 20, 48–50.

29. Ibid., p. 37.

30. Kluckhohn and Leighton, *The Navaho*, p. 39. For the wide variation in movements, see SCS, NS, Land Management Unit 1, "Range Management Report" (May 1937), pp. 20–22; Land Management Unit 4, "Range Management Branch Report" by W. R. McKinney (Dec. 1936), p. 19, both in Special Collections, University of Arizona Library.

31. Leonard Fonaroff, "The Navajo Sheep Industry: A Study in Cross-Cultural Administration" (Ph.D. diss., Johns Hopkins University, 1961), p. 59. Downs, *Navajo Sheep Husbandry*, pp. 31–34. William Zeh, "General Report Covering the Grazing Situation on the Navajo Indian Reservation," p. 7, in Soil Conservation Papers, University of New Mexico Library; SCS, Land Management Unit 17, "Range Management Report," p. 14; Land Manage-

ment Unit 1, "Range Management Report" (May 1937), p. 25, both in Special Collections, University of Arizona Library.

32. J. W. Hoover, "Navaho Land Problems," *Economic Geography* 13 (July 1937): 281. H. E. Gregory, *Geology of the Navajo Country*, United States Geological Survey, Professional Paper 93 (Washington, D.C.: Government Printing Office, 1917), p. 11.

33. Gregory, *Geology of Navajo Country*, p. 12.

34. Ibid., pp. 12–14. NA, RG 75, BIA, Collier Papers, Nav. Documents 1–13, "Report of the Conservation Committee for the Navajo Reservation," July 1933. Kluckhohn and Leighton, *The Navaho*, pp. 47–48.

35. Hoover, *"Navaho Land Problems,"* pp. 284–86. SCS, NS, "Annual Report of the Navajo Project, 1935," p. 11, Special Collections, University of New Mexico Library. Kluckhohn and Leighton, *The Navaho*, pp. 47–48. Gregory, *Geology of Navajo Country*, p. 14. NA, RG 75, BIA, Collier's Navajo Documents, 1–13, Report of Conservation Committee for the Navajo Reservation, July 1933.

36. Yi-Fu Tuan, "New Mexican Gullies: A Critical Review and Some Recent Observations," *Annals of the Association of American Geographers* 56 (Dec. 1966): 573–82; Hester, "Navajo Migrations," p. 11.

37. Hoover, "Navajo Land Problems," pp. 287–88. Gregory *Geology of Navajo Country*, pp. 130–31.

38. Gregory, *Geology of Navajo Country*, pp. 130–31. *Report of Commissioner, 1883*, p. 121. John Landgraf, "Land Use in the Ramah Area of New Mexico: An Anthropological Approach to Areal Study," *Papers of the Peabody Museum of American Archaeology and Ethnology*, Harvard University, vol. 42, no. 1 (Cambridge, Mass.: The Museum, 1954), p. 59.

39. Gregory, *Geology of Navajo Country*, p. 131. *Report of Commissioner, 1888*, p. 190.

40. Tuan, "New Mexican Gullies," p. 573. For a late statement of this position, see Hoover, "Navajo Land Problems," pp. 281–300.

41. Gregory, *Geology of Navajo Country*, pp. 119, 131–32.

42. Tuan, "New Mexican Gullies," pp. 573–74, 581.

43. Ibid., pp. 582–83, 593–94, 595–96.

44. Ibid., pp. 596–97. For an example of simple identification of overgrazing and gullying, see "Problem of Soil Erosion on the Navajo Indian Reservation and Methods Being Used for Its Solution," Navajo Soil Conservation Project, 1936, copy in Coronado Room, UNML.

45. Fonaroff, "Navajo Sheep Industry," p. 58. Aberle, *Peyote Religion*, pp. 32, 53. Aberle, for example, dates overgrazing from the 1880s on the basis of agents' reports, which cite gullying in 1883 and poor grass in 1892, but gullying was not the work of sheep and later agents attribute the poor vegetation to drought. See *Report of Commissioner, 1883*, p. 121; *1897*, p. 106; *1900*, p. 191; *1892*, p. 209. For indications that the damage did not seem permanent, see *Report of Commissioner, 1903*, p. 125; *1897*, p. 106; *1905*, p. 167.

46. *Report of Commissioner, 1905*, p. 180; *1885*, p. 155; *1890*, p. 161. For the beginning of this competition in the 1890s, see Riordan to Sanchez, Jan. 31, 1884, Riordan to *Durango Herald*, Feb. 1, 1884, Riordan to Willet, Feb. 8, 1884, all in Richard Van Valkenburgh Papers, Arizona Historical Society, Tucson.

47. For accounts of the disaster in the checkerboard region, see *Survey of Conditions*, 34:17553–75; Fr. Anselm Weber to Fall, Jan. 9, 1920; "History of Crownpoint"; Fr. Anselm Weber to E. B. Merritt, Aug. 9, 1920; McKinley Board of County Commissioners to Fall, Mar. 8, 1918; New Mexico Cattle and Horse Growers Association Resolution, Mar. 1918, all in Fall Papers. NA, RG 75, BIA, Collier's Navajo Documents, "In the Depredation Area of Northwestern New Mexico," May 29, 1936. Also see "Memorandum on Eastern Navajo Jurisdiction, History—Navajo Tribe, Public Domain Situation . . ." and "Report of the Survey Made of Destitute Navajo Indians outside Proposed New Mexico Boundary Extension," pp. 22–23, both in Van Valkenburgh Papers.

48. *Report of Commissioner, 1886*, p. 203. *Navajo Yearbook*, 1957, p. 328.

49. *Report of Commissioner, 1885*, p. 155. The reservation was not yet its present size in 1885, of course, but by far the largest additions had been made. See Kelly, *Navajo Indians and Federal Policy*, pp. 18–19.

50. NA, RG 75, BIA, CCF, 46869–1907–916, Navajo, Harrison to Commissioner, Sept. 11, 1907.

51. *Survey of Conditions*, 34:17554, 17564–67.

52. NA, RG 75, BIA, CCF 82974–1922–916, Navajo, Paquette to Commissioner, Oct. 13, 1922, Wingfield to Commissioner, May 28, 1923.

53. Underhill, *Navajos*, p. 181.

54. See, for example, *Report of Commissioner, 1893*, p. 111. For a summary of these programs, see Kelly, *Navajo Indians and Federal Policy*, pp. 104–31.

55. Kelly, *Navajo Indians and Federal Policy*, pp. 54, 69, 115–27. Young, *Political History*, pp. 48–56.

56. Kelly, *Navajo Indians and Federal Policy*, pp. 106–8.

57. For sheep improvement and later evaluations see ibid., pp. 111–14. NA, RG 75, BIA, CCF, 18841–1938–031, Navajo, "Annual Report of Condition and Activities at the Southwestern Range and Sheepherding Laboratory, Ft. Wingate, New Mexico, Nov. 1, 1936, to Oct. 31, 1937," pp. 1–3. NA, RG 75, BIA, CCF, 37010–1935–916, pt. 4, Navajo, "Characteristics and Production of Old Time Navajo Sheep" by Cecil Blum. Also see "Sheep Management on the Navajo Reservation," by J. M. Cooper in *Navajo Service Land Management Conference Proceedings, 1937*, Special Collections, University of Arizona Library.

58. Kelly, *Navajo Indians and Federal Policy*, pp. 104–5. NA, RG 75, BIA, Central Files, General Services File, 20204–1930–054, Navajo Council Proceedings, Nov. 12–13, 1928, p. 7.

59. NA, RG 75, BIA, CF, GSF, 20204–1930–054, Navajo Council Proceedings, Nov. 12–13, 1928, pp. 15–33.

60. Ibid., NA, RG 75, BIA, CF, GSF, 24619–1930–054, Minutes of the Eighth Annual Session of the Navajo Tribal Council, Held at Fort Wingate, New Mexico, July 7–8, 1930, pp. 38–40.

61. NA, RG 75, BIA, CCF, 82974–1922–916, Navajo, Merritt to Paquette, Oct. 21, 1922. For sketches of Dodge, see Kelly, *Navajo Indians and Federal Policy*, p. 66; Young, *Political History*, pp. 43–45; Underhill, *Navajos*, pp. 208–10, 231–32; Donald Parman, *The Navajos and the New Deal* (New Haven, Conn.: Yale University Press, 1976), pp. 17–18. For the extent of Dodge's commercial sheepherding, see SCS, NS, "Range Management Report," Land Management Unit 17, p. 12, Special Collections, University of Arizona Library.

CHAPTER 11

1. Louise Lamphere, "Symbolic Elements in Navajo Ritual," *Southwestern Journal of Anthropology* 25 (Autumn 1969): 280, 282; Gary Witherspoon, *Navajo Kinship and Marriage* (Chicago: University of Chicago Press, 1975), p. 8.

2. Gary Witherspoon, *Language and Art in the Navajo Universe* (Ann Arbor: University of Michigan Press, 1980), pp. 76–77.

3. Witherspoon, *Navajo Kinship*, pp. 126, 15–18, 20, 94. James F. Downs, *Animal Husbandry in Navajo Society and Culture*, University of California Publications in Anthropology, (Berkeley and Los Angeles: University of California Press, 1964), pp. 56–59.

4. Witherspoon, *Navajo Kinship*, p. 119.

5. Kluckhohn and Leighton, *The Navaho*, pp. 111–12. Aberle, *Peyote Religion*, pp. 113–23. Witherspoon, *Navajo Kinship*, pp. 15, 21–22.

6. Witherspoon, *Navajo Kinship*, pp. 74–76. Aberle, *Peyote Religion*, p. 119.

7. Witherspoon, *Navajo Kinship*, pp. 87, 68.

8. Ibid., p. 100. Kluckhohn and Leighton, *The Navaho*, pp. 109–11. W. Y. Adams, *Shonto: A Study of the Role of the Trader in a Modern Navajo Community*, Bulletin of Bureau of American Ethnology 188 (Washington, D.C.: Government Printing Office, 1963), p. 104.

9. Aberle, *Peyote Religion*, p. 106. Robert W. Young, *A Political History of the Navajo Tribe* (Tsaile, Navajo Nation, Ariz.: Navajo Community College Press, 1978), pp. 15–19, 26–28. Adams, *Shonto*, pp. 65–66.

10. Kluckhohn and Leighton, *The Navaho*, pp. 305–6.

11. Walter Dyk, ed., *Son of Old Man Hat: A Navaho Autobiography* (Lincoln: University of Nebraska Press, 1967; 1st ed., 1938), pp. 75–76.

12. Ibid., pp. 32–33. Kluckhohn and Leighton, *The Navaho*, p. 70.

13. R. Hobson, "Navaho Acquisitive Values," *Papers of the Peabody Museum of Archaeology and Ethnology* 42 (Cambridge, Mass.: The Museum, 1954), pp. 9–12, 25. Dyk, *Son of Old Man Hat*, p. 103.

14. Dyk, *Son of Old Man Hat*, pp. 32–33. Downs, *Navajo Animal Husbandry*, pp. 91–92.

15. Hobson, "Navaho Acquisitive Values," pp. 17–21. Dyk, *Son of Old Man Hat*, p. 357.

16. Aberle, *Peyote Religion*, p. 48.

17. *The Navajo Yearbook, 1957* (Window Rock, Ariz.: Navajo Agency, 1957), p. 331; also in Aberle, *Peyote Religion*, p. 32. *Report of Commissioner, 1897*, p. 175; *1885*, p. 153; *1881*, p. 137.

18. *Report of Commissioner, 1871*, p. 378. Underhill, *Navajos*, p. 181.

19. Adams, *Shonto*, pp. 162–63. W. W. Hill, "Navajo Trading and Trading Ritual," *Southwestern Journal of Anthropology* 4 (Winter 1948): 374–76, 379–83, 388–90.

20. Underhill, *Navajos*, pp. 182–83. Adams, *Shonto*, pp. 152–53. Plummer to Walker, Oct. 24, 1894, Plummer Papers.

21. Hobson, "Navaho Acquisitive Values," pp. 11–12. Frank Reeve, "The Government and the Navaho, 1878–83," *New Mexico Historical Review* 16 (July 1941): 275–78, 291–94, 299. Frank Reeve, "The Government and the Navaho, 1883–88," *New Mexico Historical Review* 18 (Jan. 1943): 45–47.

22. NA, RG 75, BIA, Collier's Navajo Documents, "Navajo Trading Report" by B. Youngblood (1935) p. 10.

23. *Report of Commissioner, 1886*, p. 203; *1890*, p. 256.

24. SCS, NS, "Statistical Summary, Human Dependency Survey, Navajo Reservation, 1940," table xxx, in Special Collections, UNML. Underhill, *Navajos*, pp. 184–85.

25. Kemrer, "Dynamics of Western Navajo," pp. 148–50.

26. Hill, *Agricultural and Hunting Methods*, p. 96.

27. Kemrer, "Dynamics of Western Navajo," p. 149.

28. Underhill, *Navajos*, pp. 166–67, 152.

29. *Report of Commissioner, 1884*, p. 134. *Navajo Yearbook, 1957*, p. 222. Kemrer, "Dynamics of Western Navajos, p. 117. Hill, *Agricultural and Hunting Methods*, p. 96.

30. Some minor raids did occur. In bad years, for example, Navajos might kill the cattle of neighboring whites. Plummer to Walker, Oct. 24, 1894, Plummer Papers.

31. By 1899 the wool clip had fallen to 1 million pounds, making the trade in blankets and rugs more important than that in wool. *Report of Commissioner, 1899*, p. 156. Agent Plummer in 1894 stressed the importance of trade in averting starvation during the drought. Plummer to Walker, Oct. 24, 1894, Plummer Papers.

32. H. Schweizer to Jesse Nasbaum, Apr. 9, 1930, enclosed with H. Schweizer to Mary Austin, Apr. 8, 1930, box 19, Mary Austin Papers, Henry Huntington Library, San Marino, Cal. Underhill, *Navajos*, pp. 185–90. Adams, *Shonto*, pp. 153–54.

33. Adams, *Shonto*, pp. 153–54.

34. For complaints about horses, see *Report of Commissioner, 1883*, p. 122;

1887, p. 171; *1893*, p. 109; *1901*, p. 180; *1905*, p. 180. Also, Kelly, *Navajo Indians and Federal Policy*, pp. 108–10.

35. *Report of Commissioner, 1899*, p. 157; *1903*, p. 126; *1905*, p. 180. *Survey of Conditions*, 18:9278.

CHAPTER 12

1. For the construction of Boulder Dam, see Norris Hundley, *Water and the West: The Colorado River Compact and the Politics of Water in the American West* (Berkeley: University of California Press, 1975), pp. 17–51.

2. NA, RG 75, BIA, CCF 52368–1937–021, Navajo, Annual Report of the Navajo District, 1937, pp. 51–52.

3. SCS, NS, "Problem of Soil erosion on the Navajo Indian Reservation and Methods Being Used for Its Solution, 1936," Special Collections, UNML. Original emphasis. The dam figured in reduction discussions well before 1936–37. See NA, RG 75, BIA, Collier Papers, Navajo Documents, General Working Plan for the Navajo Project, by Hugh Calkins, Mar. 1, 1934.

4. SCS, NS, General Report Covering the Grazing Situation on the Navajo Indian Reservation, by William Zeh, Special Collections, UNML.

5. Ibid.

6. Ibid.; "Working Plan Report of the Grazing Resources and Activities of the Southern Navajo Indian Reservation, Arizona and New Mexico," by Donald E. Harrison, Dec. 24, 1930, in *Survey of Conditions*, 18:9204, 9209.

7. *Survey of Conditions*, 18:9268–93. For Post's drastic recommendations, see p. 9289.

8. Ibid., 18:9785–86, 9829, 9736, 9117–20, 9193–96, 9478–79, 9559. Aberle, *Peyote Religion*, pp. 53–54.

9. This calculation differs from later ones, in which one cow equals four sheep or goats, and is thus not strictly comparable. NA, RG 75, BIA, CCF 62000–1935–301, pt. 1, Navajo, Report to Ickes, June 14, 1938, pp. 6–8. Kelly, *Navajo Indians and Federal Policy*, p. 114.

10. The decline in lamb sales is important because some analysts have misinterpreted Navajo actions during this period, picturing the Navajos as small businessmen waiting for the market to rise before they sold their sheep. (See Kelly, *Navajo Indians and Federal Policy*, p. 114, and Aberle, *Peyote Religion*, p. 54.) This was not the case. The sale of lambs on a significant scale had begun only after World War I and was still not well established on large sections of the reservation in the 1930s, while in other regions the Navajos refused to sell any ewe lambs. (Adams, *Shonto*, pp. 157–58; NA, RG 75, BIA, CF, GSF, 7957–1936–054, Minutes of Navajo Council, Keams Canyon, July 10, 1934, p. 75.) Those who did sell lambs depended on a booming market, since the Navajo lamb crop, virtually always scrawny and underweight, was the least desired by buyers. (*Survey of Conditions*, 34:21122–23.) When demand fell, wholesalers were unwilling to take these lambs, and traders in turn re-

fused to accept them from the Navajos in payment for debt. Lack of water during the drought and the resulting inability of the Navajos to move their stock exacerbated the problem. It was not the refusal of the Navajos to sell but the refusal of the traders to buy that was the problem. (The Zeh Report is ambiguous about the causes of the failure to sell lambs, but later government efforts show that in the 1930s the Navajos were willing to sell part of the lamb crop when there was a market. Zeh Report, p. 18. Also see *Survey of Conditions*, 18:9305.) For the winters, see Parman, *Navajos and the New Deal*, pp. 23–24; NA, RG 75, BIA, CF, GSF, 7957–1936–054, Minutes of the Special Session of the Navajo Tribal Council held at Fort Defiance, Arizona, March 12 and 13, 1934, pp. 40–41; John Collier, *From Every Zenith: A Memoir* (Denver: Sage Books, 1963), pp. 152–53.

11. Kelly, *Navajo Indians and Federal Policy*, p. 158. SCS, NS, Annual Report of Navajo Project, June 1935, Special Collections, UNML. *Navajo Yearbook, 1957*, p. 328. There is some confusion in the accounts of these two winters. Parman and Collier place Collier's lobbying in 1931–32 following the storms of 1931–32; Kelly says his efforts came the next winter.

12. For drought, see Parman, *Navajo and the New Deal*, p. 33; *Navajo Yearbook, 1957*, p. 323. For the quote, see Collier, *From Every Zenith*, pp. 172–73. For Navajo reaction, see NA, RG 75, BIA, Collier's Navajo Documents, 49–56, Reasons Why Navajos Do Not Cooperate with the Government, Aug. 14, 1936 (history of stock reduction section). The best study of Collier is Kenneth Philp's *John Collier's Crusade for Indian Reform, 1920–1954* (Tucson: University of Arizona Press, 1977).

13. Kelly, *Navajo Indians and Federal Government*, pp. 157–58. NA, RG 75, BIA, Civilian Conservation Crops, Indian Division, file 22916–1933–344, Western Navajo, Collier to Balmer, May 10, 1933, Balmer to Commissioner, July 12, 1933. NA, RG 75, BIA, CCC-ID, 74638–1940–344, Detailed Statement of Improvements Made on Indian Reservations under Emergency Employment Act of Mar. 31, 1933; NA, RG 75, BIA, CCC-ID, 21341–1933–344, Southern Navajo, Hunter to Collier, June 10, 1933.

14. For accounts of Navajo reaction, see NA, RG 75, BIA, CCC-ID, 21341–1933–344, Hunter to Collier, June 22, 1933; NA, RG 75, BIA, CCC-ID, 21341–1933–344, Southern Navajo, Hunter to Collier, Aug. 12, 1933, Aug. 27, 1933, Nash to Collier, Aug. 4, 1933, Millington to Collier, May 22, 1934; NA, RG 75, BIA, CCC-ID, 22196–1933–344, Western Navajo, Balmer to Commissioner, Sept. 25, 1933. NA, RG 75, BIA, CCC-ID, 21341–1933–344, Western Navajo, Forrest Parker to Collier, Aug. 3, 1933. LaMont to Hunter, Oct. 20, 1933. Collier to Hunter, Oct. 25, 1933.

Wage labor first occurred on a significant scale during the drought at the turn of the century, when Navajos began working on the railroads and in beet fields. See, for example, *Report of Commissioner, 1904*, p. 141; *1903*, p. 125; *1899*, p. 157; *1900*, p. 191; *1901*, p. 180.

15. NA, RG 75, BIA, Collier Navajo Documents, 1939, Memorandum for Secretary Ickes, Dec. 25, 1938. NA, RG 75, BIA, CCC-ID, 19414–1933–344, Memorandum for the Secretary of Agriculture from Henry Knight, June 9, 1933.

16. NA, RG 75, BIA, CCD, 19414–1933–344, Memorandum for the Secretary of Agriculture from Henry Knight, June 9, 1933; NA, RG 75, BIA, CCC-ID, 74638–1940–344, Collier to Knight, June 10, 1933. NA, RG 75, BIA, Collier's Navajo Documents, 1–13, Report to the Navajo Council by the Conservation Advisory Committee for the Navajo Reservation, July 2, 1933, NA, RG 75, BIA, CF, GSF, 00–1933–054, Minutes of the Eleventh Annual Session of the Navajo Tribal Council . . . Fort Wingate, New Mexico, July 7 and 8, 1933, pp. 18–21.

17. NA, RG 75, BIA, Collier's Navajo Documents, 1–33, Report to the Navajo Council by the Conservation Advisory Committee . . . , July 1, 1933.

18. NA, RG 75, BIA, CF, GSF 00–1933–054, Minutes of the Eleventh Annual Session of the Navajo Tribal Council . . . Fort Wingate . . . July 7–8, 1933, pp. 18–22.

19. Adams, *Shonto*, p. 67.

20. Kelly, *Navajo Indians and Federal Government*, pp. 65–67. Parman, *Navajos and the New Deal*, pp. 17–21.

21. NA, RG 75, BIA, CF, GSF 00–1933–054, Minutes of the Eleventh Annual Session of the Navajo Tribal Council . . . Fort Wingate . . . July 7–8, 1933, p. 22. Kelly, *Navajo Indians and Federal Government*, p. 42. Young, *Political History*, p. 81. NA, RG 75, BIA, Collier's Navajo Documents, Navajo Stock Reduction, Why the Government Is Trying Navajo Grazing Cases in the Federal Courts, Feb. 8, 1941, p. 5.

22. Text of speech is in Minutes of Navajo Tribal Council held at Tuba City, Ariz., Oct. 30–31, and Nov. 1, 1933, pp. 16–19, Interior Department Library, Washington, D.C.

23. Ibid., pp. 36, 37–38.

24. Francis Paul Prucha, *American Indian Policy in Crisis: Christian Reformers and the Indian, 1865–1900* (Norman: University of Oklahoma Press, 1976). An excellent study of the dilemma of reformers is Graham D. Taylor, *The New Deal and American Tribalism: The Administration of the Indian Reorganization Act, 1934–45* (Lincoln: University of Nebraska Press, 1980).

25. Minutes of Navajo Tribal Council held at Tuba City, Ariz. Oct. 30–31, Nov. 1, 1933, pp. 44, 47, Interior Department Library, Washington, D.C.

26. Parman, *Navajos and the New Deal*, pp. 45–48.

27. NA, RG 75, BIA, Collier's Navajo Documents, pp. 1–13, The Economic Rehabilitation of the Navajos by Walter Woehlke.

28. For quote, see NA, RG 75, BIA, Collier's Navajo Documents, Soil Erosion Service, General Working Plan for the Navajo Project, submitted by Hugh Calkins, Mar. 1, 1934, pp. 1–7. NA, RG 75, BIA, CC-ID, 22196–1933–344, Western Navajo, Collier to Navajo Superintendents, Mar. 31, 1934.

29. *Survey of Conditions*, 34:17987.

30. *Navajo yearbook*, 1961, p. 153. *Survey of Conditions*, 34:17987–88. The Collier administration contended that it had always intended big owners to bear the brunt of the reduction, but this was hardly clear at the council meeting and certainly no provisions were ever made to insure it. NA, RG 75, BIA, Collier's Navajo Documents, pp. 56–62, The Monopoly of Tribal Resources, n.d.

31. NA, RG 75, BIA, CF, GSF, 7957–1936–054, Minutes of the Special Session of the Navajo Tribal Council held at Fort Defiance, Ariz., Nov. 11–12, 1934, pp. 21–27.

32. Ibid., pp. 38–51; NA, RG 75, BIA, CF, GSF, 9659–1936–054, Minutes of the Navajo Tribal Council held at Crownpoint, N.M., Apr. 9–11, 1934, pp. 52–68. NA, RG 75, BIA, CF, GSF, 7957–1936–054, Minutes of the Meeting of the Navajo Tribal Council, Keams Canyon, Ariz., July 10–12, 1934, pp. 63–86.

33. *Survey of Conditions*, 18:9204, 9248, 9556, 9559, 9585–86, 9829, 9121, 34:17801. Zeh Report, pp. 7–8, 16–17.

34. *Survey of Conditions*, 18:9120–21, 9204, 9247, 9556–59. NA, RG 75, BIA, CF, GSF, 7957–1936–054, Minutes of the Meeting of the Navajo Tribal Council, Keams Canyon, Ariz., July 10–12, 1934, p. 75.

35. NA, RG 75, BIA, CCC-ID, 21341–1933–344, Southern Navajo, Millington to Collier, May 22, 1934. NA, RG 75, BIA, CCC-ID, 22196–1933–344, Western Navajo, Balmer to Collier, July 20, 1934.

36. *Survey of Conditions*, 34:17988. Parman, *Navajos and the New Deal*, pp. 62–66.

37. For Navajo and official accounts of reduction, see Ruth Roessel, *Navajo Livestock Reduction: A National Disgrace* (Chinle: Navajo Community College Press, 1974), passim, esp. pp. 95, 155; *Survey of Conditions*, 34:17445, 18014, 17789, 17792, 17785, 17749, 17540, 17754, 17766; 37:20971, 20944, 20995, 20997, 20998. For quote, see New Mexico Association on Indian Affairs, *Urgent Navajo Problems: Observations and Recommendation Based on a Recent Study by the New Mexico Association on Indian Affairs* (Santa Fe, Aug. 1940), p. 8.

38. *Survey of Conditions*, 34:17988. Roessel, *Navajo Livestock Reduction*, pp. 155, 181. Also see Parman, *Navajos and the New Deal*, p. 64, and Aberle, *Peyote Religion*, p. 57, for slaughter of goats.

39. New Mexican Association on Indian Affairs, *Urgent Navajo Problems*, p. 8.

40. Ibid., p. 12, 13.

41. Ibid. Parman, *Navajos and the New Deal*, p. 35.

42. *Survey of Conditions*, 34:17467, 17543, 17801–2, 17550–80; 37:20971. For quote, see Richard Van Valkenburgh, Report of the Survey Made of Destitute Navajo Indians Outside the Proposed New Mexican Boundary Extension, Richard Van Valkenburgh Papers, Arizona Historical Society, Tucson.

43. W. W. Hill, quoted in Kluckhohn, "Participation in Ceremonials," p. 369; also see p. 364.

44. Ibid., p. 359. Navajo beliefs about the drought come out strongly in the senate hearings of 1936. *Survey of Conditions*, 34:17911, 17958.

45. Elizabeth Ward, *No Dudes, Few Women: Life with a Navajo Range Rider* (Albuquerque: University of New Mexico Press, 1951), p. 133. NA, RG 75, BIA, Collier Papers, Navajo Stock Reduction, Roosevelt-Smith, Why the Government Is Trying Navajo Grazing Cases in the Federal Courts, Feb. 8, 1941, by E. R. Fryer, p. 2. Kluckhohn and Leighton, for instance, after acknowledging that the Navajos were not entirely passive toward nature, assert that they resisted conservation because of their distaste for tampering with nature. Kluckhohn and Leighton, *The Navaho*, pp. 308–9.

46. NA, RG 75, BIA, Collier's Navajo Documents, 56–62, The Monopoly of Tribal Resources. For other Navajo attempts to confront directly the problems facing them—particularly through water development and reservation expansion—see *Survey of Conditions*, 18:9244, 9559, 9792; 34:18020, 18029. For an activist interpretation of Navajo thought, see Franchot Ballinger, "The Responsible Center: Man and Nature in Pueblo and Navaho Ritual Songs and Prayers," *American Quarterly* 30 (Spring 1978): 90–107.

47. Kluckhohn and Leighton, *The Navaho*, p. 239.

48. Edward H. Spicer, "Sheepmen and Technicians: A Program of Soil Conservation on the Navajo Indian Reservation," with a comment by John Collier, in Edward H. Spicer, ed., *Human Problems in Technological Change: A Casebook* (New York: Russell Sage Foundation, 1952), p. 207.

49. NA, RG 75, BIA, Collier Papers, Navajo, 1940, From Hill's Final Report on the Navajo, p. 8. *Survey of Conditions*, 34:17478–79.

50. SCS, NS, Navajo Project Range Management Policy Statement, July 8, 1935, p. 12, Special Collections, UNML.

51. For various attempts by Navajos and others to explain the Navajo position, see NA, RG 75, BIA, Collier Papers, Navajo, 1940, From Hill's Final Report on the Navajo, p. 15. NA, RG 75, BIA, CF, GSF, 7957–1936–054, Minutes of the Navajo Tribal Council . . . Fort Defiance . . . Mar. 1–13, 1934, p. 39. *Survey of Conditions*, 34:17757, 17916. NA, RG 75, BIA, CF, GSF, 7957–1936–054, Minutes of the Navajo Tribal Council . . . Keams Canyon . . . July 10–12, 1934, p. 79. NA, RG 75, BIA, Collier's Navajo Documents, 49–54, Reasons Why Navajos Do Not Cooperate with the Government, Aug. 14, 1936.

52. NA, RG 75, BIA, Collier's Navajo Documents, 1–13, Minutes of the Meeting of the Administrative Staff for the United Navajo Jurisdiction, Nov. 5–6, 1934, pp. 5–6. NA, RG 75, BIA, Collier Papers, Memorandum on Navajo Problem, Mar. 27, 1936 by W. V. Woehlke.

53. For an excellent account of the background of the IRA, see Lawrence Kelly, "The Indian Reorganization Act: The Dream and the Reality," *Pacific*

Historical Review 46 (Aug. 1975): 293–309. Also see Taylor, *The New Deal and Tribalism*, pp. 1–38.

54. Parman, *Navajos and the New Deal*, pp. 68–77. Young, *Political History*, pp. 84–86. For a sample of identifications of the IRA with stock reduction, see NA, RG 75, BIA, Collier Papers, J. C. Morgan Correspondence, Collier to Editor of *Christian Century*, Nov. 2, 1934; Catherine Sturges to Collier, Mar. 18, 1935, Collier to Faris, June 21, 1935.

55. NA, RG 75, BIA, Collier Papers, J. C. Morgan Correspondence, Collier to Faris, June 21, 1935.

56. NA, RG 75, BIA, Collier's Navajo Documents, Navajo Policies and Programs, May 1, 1935. Parman, *Navajos and the New Deal*, pp. 92–93. Parman does an excellent job on the administrative history of the reservation during the New Deal. A detailed discussion of the various administrative arrangements and quarrels here could add little to his account.

57. See n. 56. *Survey of Conditions*, 34:17986. Parman, *Navajos and the New Deal*, pp. 98–99.

58. SCS, NS, Annual Report of the Navajo Project, 1936, Special Collections, UNML. NA, RG 75, BIA, CCF, 9055–36–344, Navajo, The Agricultural and Range Resources of the Navajo Reservation in Relation to the Subsistence Needs of the Navajo Indians, May 12, 1936, by W. G. McGinnies. There are also copies in the Collier Papers and in Special Collections, UNML; *Survey of Conditions*, 34:17453, 17538–39.

59. NA, RG 75, BIA, Collier's Navajo Documents, Regulations Affecting the Carrying Capacity and Management of the Navajo Range, Nov. 6, 1935.

60. NA, RG 75, BIA, Collier's Navajo Documents, McGinnies to Collier, Jan. 6, 1935.

61. Parman, *Navajos and the New Deal*, pp. 81–106. SCS, NS, Annual Report of Navajo District, June 30, 1936, pp. 17–19, 28–60, Special Collections, UNML. NA, RG 75, BIA, CCF, 52368–1937–021, Navajo, Annual Report of Navajo Distirct, 1937, pp. 32–34. NA, RG 75, BIA, CCC-ID, 22196–1933–344, W. Navajo, F. J. Scott to CIA, n.d., D. E. Harrison to Commissioner, Feb. 6, 1935. NA, RG 75, BIA, CCC-ID, 21341–1933–344, Southern Navajo, J. D. LaMont to Hunter, Oct. 20, 1933; *Survey of Conditions*, 34:18016.

62. NA, RG 75, BIA, CCF, 57055–1936–933, Navajo, Commissioner to Murphy, June 22, 1935; Trotter to Murphy, June 22, 1935; Collier to Faris, July 3, 1935; Memorandum to J. G. Hamilton, June 26, 1935, by E. D. Eaton.

63. SCS, NS, Annual Report of Navajo Project, 1935, pp. 163–68. SCS, NS, Annual Report of Navajo District, June 30, 1936, p. 20. SCS, NS, Range Management Plan, Kayenta Demonstration Area, all in Special Collections, UNML.

64. SCS, NS, Annual Report of Navajo District, June 30, 1936, pp. 19–20. SCS, NS, Annual Report of Navajo Project, 1936–37, p. 23, both in Special Collection, UNML. *Survey of Conditions*, 34:17460–61, 18021, 18028. SCS, NS, Annual Report of Navajo District, 1937, pp. 19–31, Special Collections,

UNML. NA, RG 75, BIA, CCF, Navajo, 80320–1936–301, Navajo, Henry
Dodge to James Stewart, Apr. 20, 1936.

65. *Survey of Conditions*, 34:18021, 18014, 18017, 18028. NA, RG 75, BIA,
CCF, 62000–1935–301, Navajo, Report to Ickes, June 14, 1938, p. 21. NA,
RG 75, BIA, CCF, 62000–1935–301, pt. 6, Navajo, Dodge to Collier, Aug. 30,
1938. All these sources cite instances of noncooperation. For claims of growing cooperation, see NA, RG 75, BIA, CCF, 52368–1937–031, Navajo, Annual Report of Navajo District, 1937, pp. 26–31. For cause-and-effect argument, see Fonaroff, "Navajo Sheep Industry," pp. 67–69.

66. Parman makes this same point (*Navajos and the New Deal*, p. 88).

67. Morgan attacked these inequities repeatedly, and in the fall of 1935
the Indian Rights Association, whose real objection to Collier was his abandonment of cultural assimilation as the government's official policy, had published an article in its magazine, *Indian Truth*, attacking the Collier program
for, among other things, destroying the Navajo subsistence herds. M. K.
Sniffen, "Navajo Chaos," *Indian Truth* 12 (Oct. 1935): 1–8. For the rationale of
the Navajo Service, see NA, RG 75, BIA, Collier Papers, Navajo Grazing, Use
of Authority to Establish Range Control on the Navajo Reservation, Oct. 5,
1936.

68. Parman, *Navajos and the New Deal*, pp. 104–6.

69. McGinnies Report. SCS, NS, Problem of Soil Erosion on the Navajo
Indian Reservation . . . 1936, Special Collections, UNML. Parman, *Navajos
and the New Deal*, pp. 100–10.

70. NA, RG 75, BIA, CCF, 9054–36–341, PTA, Navajo-Hopi, Memorandum on Unified Navajo Program, Apr. 10, 1936.

71. McGinnies Report.

72. Ibid.

73. Ibid., pp. 1–5.

74. Figures are from the McGinnies Report and SCS, Statistical
Summary—Human Dependency Survey, Navajo Reservation, 1940, Special
Collections, UNML. Since McGinnies did not give an income estimate per
acre of agricultural land, I averaged together his estimates for irrigated land,
dry land, and lands irrigated by natural runoff to derive the $19.60 figure.

75. In fact, this figure probably overestimates family income, since the
number of families increased between 1936 and 1940. NA, RG 75, BIA,
Collier Papers, Navajo, 1940, Fryer to Collier, Oct. 9, 1940. SCS, NS, Statistical Summary—Human Dependency Survey . . . 1940, tables 1, 2, 3, Special
Collections, UNML.

76. NA, RG 75, BIA, Collier's Navajo Documents, Marshall to Collier, May
22, 1936.

77. Parman, *Navajos and the New Deal*, p. 121.

78. *Survey of Conditions*, 34:17445–69, 17472–17959. NA, RG 75, BIA,
Collier Papers, Jake Morgan's Activities, Navajo's Meeting, Ganado, July 7,
1936. Parman, *Navajos and the New Deal*, pp. 121–23. Dodge made a speech at
Pinon in late 1936 which Fryer would quote approvingly at the Navajo Land

Management Conference in 1937. "Opening Remarks" by E. A. Fryer, Navajo Service, *Proceedings of the First Annual Land Management Conference*, Mar. 26, 1937, Flagstaff, Ariz. (Window Rock: Navajo Service, 1937), Special Collections, University of Arizona.

79. NA, RG 75, BIA, Collier's Navajo Documents, 49–54, Reasons Why Navajos Do Not Cooperate with the Government, Aug. 14, 1936; and The Monopoly of Tribal Resources.

80. NA, RG 75, BIA, Collier Papers, Navajo Grazing, Use of Authority to Establish Control on the Navajo Reservation, Oct. 5, 1936. C. E. Faris, the deposed superintendent, still held out for cooperation, especially with the large owners. NA, RG 75, BIA, Collier Papers, Navajo Grazing, Suggestion as to the Methods of Reduction, Navajo Livestock by C. E. Faris, Oct. 9, 1936.

81. NA, RG 75, BIA, CCF, 51727–28–054, Navajo Council Regulations, Haile to Fryer, Nov. 7, 1936; Fryer to Collier, Nov. 9, 1936; Haile to Fryer, Nov. 6, 1936. NA, RG 75, CCF, 59227–1936–054, Navajo, Navajo Tribal Council Meeting of Nov. 24, 1936, Summary. Parman, *Navajos and the New Deal*, pp. 160–61.

82. All of this is covered in much detail by Parman, *Navajos and the New Deal*, pp. 160–72. Also see NA, RG 75, BIA, CF, GSF, 30853–1937–054, Navajo, Minutes of the Meeting of the Navajo Tribal Council at Window Rock, Ariz. on Apr. 9, 1937, pp. 14–38. NA, RG 75, BIA, CCF, 5927–1939–030, Fryer to Commissioner, Jan. 23, 1939.

83. NA, RG 75, BIA, CCF, 52368–1937–031, Navajo, Annual Report, Navajo District, 1937, pp. 12–13, 25, 52–53. NA, Federal Regional Archives, Laguna Miguel, RG 75, USDI, BIA, Navajo Office, Forest Surveys, Branch of Forestry, Report on Land Management Unit 17, Aug. 1936, p. 10, and Report on Land Management Unit 9, July 1937, p. 14. SCS, NS, Land Planning Report for Land Management Unit 7, Nov. 1937, pp. 22–23, Special Collections, UNML.

84. For a typical recitation of complaints, see SCS, Range Management Report for Land Management Unit 17, pp. 13–15, Special Collections, University of Arizona.

85. SCS, NS, Land Management Unit Survey, Unit 3, Woodland Survey Report, Apr. 15, 1937, pt. 3, Special Collections, UNML. NA, FRA, Laguna Miguel, RG 75, BIA, Nav. Office, Branch of Forestry: Land Management Unit Survey Unit 12, Woodland Survey, Dec. 27, 1937, p. 31; Land Management Survey Unit 18, Forestry Report, p. 11 Land Management Survey Unit 4, Forestry Report, Dec. 15, 1936, pp. 11–12. Hereafter Land Management Unit (and variations) abbreviated LMU. NA, RG 75, BIA, CCF, 52368–1937–031, Annual Report of Navajo Project, 1937, pp. 77–81. H. E. Holman, "Forest Resources on the Navajo Reservation," *Navajo Land Management Conference Proceedings*, Special Collections, University of Arizona. H. E. Holman, "Range Management for the Forest Resources on the Navajo Reservation," *Navajo Land Management Proceedings*, Special Collections, University of Arizona.

86. NA, RG 75, BIA, CCF, 52368–1937–031, Navajo, Annual Report of Navajo Project, 1937, pp. 40–43.

87. E. R. Fryer, "Looking Ahead," *Navajo Land Management Conference Proceedings*, Special Collections, University of Arizona. "Fundamental Aspects of Range Management," *Navajo Land Management Proceedings*, Special Collections, University of Arizona.

88. NA, RG 75, BIA, CCF, 52368–1937–031, Navajo, Annual Report of Navajo Project, 1937, p. 66. This emphasis on agriculture did not suddenly develop in 1937. Collier, for instance, had mentioned it in his 1936 testimony before the Senate Subcommittee on Indian Affairs. It did, however, grow stronger as the severity of the range problem and the dependence of the Navajos on wage income became apparent. *Survey of Conditions*, 34:17541. For an example of Navajo Service calculations of replacement of reduced livestock income with increased subsistence farming, see SCS, NS, Integrated Report of Land Management Surveys, LMU 1, pp. 58–62, Special Collections, UNML. Such calculations are duplicated in virtually all the surveys. For Fryer's advocacy of the plans, see NA, RG 75, BIA, CCC-ID, Conservation Working Program, July 1, 1937–June, 30, 1938; Fryer to Commissioner, May 12, 1937.

89. The land management units caused great confusion. For an example of the complaints made against them, see New Mexico Association of Indian Affairs, *Urgent Navajo Problems*, p. 11. The government tried to adjust these boundaries to meet such complaints; for Fruitland, see *Survey of Conditions*, 34:17847–48: NA, RG 75, Cf, GSF, 24619–1930–054, Navajo, Minutes of the Eighth Annual Session of the Navajo Tribal Council Held at Ft. Wingate, N.M., July 7–8, 1930, pp. 101–5.

90. *Survey of Conditions*, 34:17857.

91. Ibid., p. 17841. For Fryer's position, also see NA, RG 75, BIA, CCF, 44151–1938–054, Navajo, Fryer to Collier, Oct. 15, 1938. Fryer could also on occasion cite plans to irrigate 250,000 to 300,000 acres.

92. Tom T. Sasaki, *Fruitland, New Mexico: A Navajo Community in Transition* (Ithaca, N.Y.: Cornell University Press, 1960), pp. 39–40. For quote, see *Survey of Conditions*, 34:17475. See also *Survey of Conditions*, 34:17488–96.

93. NA, RG 75, BIA, CCF, 44151–1938–054, Navajo, Fryer to Collier, Oct. 15, 1938. Sasaki, *Fruitland*, pp. 11–15, 34–51.

94. The following account comes from Sasaki, *Fruitland*, pp. 52–69, and Tom Sasaki and John Adair, "New Land to Farm," in Spicer, *Human Problems in Technological Change*, pp. 97–111.

95. Sasaki and Adair, "New Land to Farm." James A. Krug, *The Navajo: Report to the President by the Secretary of the Interior* (Washington, D.C.: Government Printing Office, 1948), p. 18.

96. NA, RG 75, BIA, Collier Papers, Morgan-Palmer, clipping from *Santa Fe New Mexican*, Feb. 19, 1938; Collier's Navajo Documents, pp. 56–62, The Monopoly of Tribal Resources. For an example of sympathy with large owners, see Senator Chavez's comments, *Survey of Conditions*, 34:17829–30. For a

formalist critique of reducing the big owners, see Gary D. Lipecap and Ronald Johnson, "The Navajo and Too Many Sheep: Persistent Overgrazing on the Navajo Reservation," (unpublished paper, obtained from authors, Economics Department, University of New Mexico).

97. For Collier's attitude toward Dodge, see NA, RG 75, BIA, CCF, 62000–1935–301, pt. 6, Navajo, Collier to Dodge, Sept. 8, 1938.

98. *Navajo Yearbook*, 1961, pp. 154–55. Dodge made the point of dependence of the very poor on the *ricos*, but Collier dismissed it by noting that the *ricos* could not support all the Navajo poor, as indeed they could not. NA, RG 75, BIA, CCF, 62000–1935–301, pt. 6, Navajo, Dodge to Collier, Aug. 30, 1938, Collier to Dodge, Sept. 8, 1938.

99. Parman, *Navajos and the New Deal*, p. 172. For a copy of the regulations, see NA, RG 75, BIA, CCF, 62000–35–301, Navajo, Report to Ickes, June 14, 1938, pp. 15–16.

100. Parman, *Navajos and the New Deal*, pp. 173–74. NA, RG 75, BIA, Collier Papers, Navajo Grazing, Collier to Indian Rights Association, Feb. 7, 1938.

101. Parman, *Navajos and the New Deal*, pp. 173–74; NA, RG 75, BIA, CCF, 62000–1935–301, Navajo, Report to Ickes, June 14, 1938, pp. 15–16.

102. Parman, *Navajos and the New Deal*, pp. 172–73. NA, RG 75, BIA, Collier Papers, J. C. Morgan's Activities, press release, Feb. 25, 1938. NA, RG 75, BIA, CCF, 62000–1935–301, Navajo, Report to Ickes, June 14, 1938, p. 18.

CHAPTER 13

1. The sources for Land Management Unit 1 are SCS, NS, LMU 1. Land Planning Report, Jan. 1938, Special Collections, UNML; SCS, NS, LMU 1, Report of Human Dependency Survey, Navajo District, Region 8, Jan. 1939, Navajo Tribal Museum; SCS, NS, LMU 1, Range Management Branch Report, May 1937, Special Collections, University of Arizona; SCS, NS, Agronomy Branch Report on LMU 1, Nov. 1937, Special Collections, UNML. For a description of the region, see George Boyce, *When Navajos Had Too Many Sheep: The 1940's* (San Francisco: Indian Historian Press, 1974), pp. 62–91.

Information on Land Management Unit 18 comes from SCS, NS, LMU 18—Fort Defiance, Report of Human Dependency Survey, Nov. 1936, Revised Nov. 1939, Navajo Tribal Museum; SCS, NS, LMU 18, Range Management Report, Revised Mar. 1938 by D. G. Anderson, Special Collections, University of Arizona. SCS, NS, LMU 18, Agronomy Division Report, Nov. 1937, and SCS, NS, LMU 18—Ft. Defiance, Integrated Report, Nov. 1936, both in Special Collections, UNML.

Information on Land Management Unit 11 is from SCS, NS, Report of Sociological Survey, Aug. 1936, and Integrated Report of Land Management Survey of Unit 11, both in Special Collections, UNML.

2. SCS, NS, LMU 1, Land Planning Report, pp. 32–35, 77–79, Special Collections, UNML. SCS, NS, LMU 1, Report of Human Dependency Survey, pp. 4–8, 21, Navajo Tribal Museum. For 500-sheep unit subsistence estimate, see Boyce, *When Navajos Had Too Many Sheep*, pp. 72–73. Also, see him for failure of water development, pp. 71–72.

3. For per capita income and dependence on wages, see SCS, NS, LMU 18—Ft. Defiance, Report of Human Dependency Survey, p. 9, Navajo Tribal Museum. For sheepherding and farming, see SCS, NS, LMU 18—Ft. Defiance, Report of Human Dependency Survey, pp. 20–23, Navajo Tribal Museum; SCS, NS, LMU 18 Range Management Report, pp. 30–35, Special Collections, University of Arizona, and SCS, NS, LMU 18—Ft. Defiance, Integrated Report, p. 30, Special Collections, UNML.

4. SCS, NS, LMU 11, Report of Sociological Survey, Aug. 1936, pp. 13–15, 25–26, Special Collections, UNML.

5. NA, RG 75, BIA, Collier's Navajo Documents, 65–72, Report of Field Representative (Morris Burge) of American Association of Indian Affairs, 1937.

6. NA, RG 75, BIA, CCF, 18037–1937–056, Navajo, Executive Committee to Collier, Mar. 16, 1937.

7. For Morgan's and Palmer's activities, see NA, RG 75, BIA, Collier Papers, Morgan-Palmer, Fryer to Collier, July 28, 1937; July 29, 1937; Aug. 7, 1937; Woehlke to Collier, July 26, 1937; Palmer to Chavez, Aug. 6, 1937; Memorandum to Collier from Shevky and Woehlke, Aug. 7, 1937; Department of Interior Memorandum for the Press, Aug. 14, 1937; Collier to Senator Thomas, Aug. 9, 1937. For a fuller narrative of this period, see Parman, *Navajos and the New Deal*, pp. 173–83.

8. For quote, see NA, RG 75, BIA, Collier Papers, Navajo Grazing, Fryer to Lindley, Feb. 7, 1938. Also see NA, RG 75, BIA, Collier Papers, Navajo Grazing, Preliminary Report on the Navajo Situation, Aug. 11, 1937. Woehlke to Editors, *Albuquerque Journal*, June 4, 1938. Parman, *Navajos and the New Deal*, p. 183.

9. NA, RG 75, BIA, CCF 00–1938–032, Navajo, Fryer to Collier, Feb. 1, 1938—Conference with Morgan and Associates.

10. Downs, *Navajo Animal Husbandry*, pp. 12–13. For Collier's stress on only the largest horse owners, see NA, RG 75, BIA, Collier Papers, Morgan-Palmer, Collier to Hon. J. Murdock, Jan. 14, 1938. For examples of districts that allowed only five horses, see SCS, NS, LMU 3, Range Management Report, Mar. 15, 1937; LMU 4, Range Management Report, Dec. 1936, both in Special Collections, University of Arizona.

11. NA, RG 75, BIA, Collier Papers, Morgan-Palmer, Collier to Fryer, Aug. 6, 1937; Aug. 7, 1937. Parman, *Navajos and the New Deal*, p. 183; NA, RG 75, BIA, Collier Papers, Collier to Navajo Indians, Feb. 19, 1938; Morgan-Palmer file, Memorandum to Collier from Shevky and Woehlke, Aug. 7, 1937.

12. NA, RG 75, BIA, CF, GSF, 24809–1938–054, Proceedings of the

Meetings of the Navajo Tribal Council and the Executive Committee, Window Rock, Jan. 17–20, 1938, pp. 77–115.

13. Ibid., pp. 109–11, 121–22. For lower horse limits, see Navajo Service, LMU 3, Range Management Report, Mar. 15, 1937, and LMU 4, Range Management Report, Dec. 1936, both in Special Collections, University of Arizona. Maria Chabot made this same point in 1940. See New Mexico Association on Indian Affairs, *Urgent Navajo Problems*, p. 29.

14. Parman, *Navajos and the New Deal*, p. 189; For changes in the government, the abandoned constitution, and new by-laws, see Young, *Political History*, pp. 107–17.

15. NA, RG 75, BIA, Collier Papers, Morgan-Palmer, Preliminary Report on Navajo Situation, Aug. 11, 1937; Fryer to Collier, Aug. 12, 1937.

16. NA, RG 75, BIA, CCF, 00–1938–032, Navajo, Memorandum, Watson to Fryer, Feb. 1, 1938; Parman, *Navajos and the New Deal*, pp. 190–91. NA, RG 75, BIA, CCF, 00–1938–058, Navajo, Fryer to Collier, Sept. 7, 1938.

17. NA, RG 75, BIA, Collier Papers, Navajo General, 1938, Holman to Fryer, Mar. 1, 1938. NA, RG 75, BIA, CCF, 26205–1938–301, Navajo, Collier to Ashurt, Apr. 30, 1938. NA, RG 75, BIA, CCF, 65440–1939–031, Navajo, Division of Extension Industry, Narrative Summary, Navajo Reservation, 1938, p. 7. NA, RG 75, BIA, CCF, 60775–1935–301, Navajo, Dodge to Collier, Feb. 8, 1938; Dodge to Collier, Aug. 30, 1938; Collier to Dodge, Sept. 8, 1938.

18. NA, RG 75, BIA, CCC-ID, 4235–1937–346, Navajo, Fryer to Collier, Nov. 4, 1937. NA, RG 75, BIA, CCC-ID, 59055–1936–334, Navajo, Fryer to Collier, Jan. 18, 1938. NA, RG 75, BIA, CCC-ID, 59055–1936–334, pt. 5, Navajo, Murphy to Fryer, Aug. 5, 1940. NA, RG 75, BIA, CCC-ID, 59055–1938–349, Collier to Fryer, Dec. 31, 1937. Parman, *Navajos and the New Deal*, pp. 185–86.

19. NA, RG 75, BIA, Collier's Navajo Documents, 1939, Memorandum for Secretary Ickes from Commissioner of Indian Affairs, Dec. 28, 1938; Collier to Fryer, Oct. 25, 1939. Parman says expenditures declined from $830,000 to $300,000 in 1940 but also mentions a more drastic cut of an unspecified amount after 1940. Parman, *Navajos and the New Deal*, pp. 270–71.

20. NA, RG 75, BIA, CCF, 62000–1935–301, pt. 1, Navajo, clipping from *Albuquerque Journal*, June 1, 1938. NA, RG 75, BIA, Collier Papers, Navajo Grazing, Memorandum to Mr. Burlew from Collier, June 24, 1938. It is unclear whether the original suits were later reduced to three. Fryer mentions selecting three prominent men in the western reservation as the focus of prosecution early in 1939. NA, RG 75, BIA, Collier Papers, Navajo Stock Reduction, Roosevelt-Smith, Why the Government Is Trying Navajo Grazing Cases in the Federal Courts, Feb. 8, 1941, by E. R. Fryer.

21. Phelps-Stokes Fund, *The Navajo Indian Problem* (New York: Phelps-Stokes Fund, 1939), p. 10.

22. Ibid., p. 5. Parman, *Navajos and the New Deal*, pp. 236–37.

23. For part of the decision, see NA, RG 75, BIA, CF, GSF, 9659 E-1936–054, pt. 3, Navajo, Proceedings of the Meeting of the Navajo Tribal Council, Window Rock, Ariz., May 15–19, 1939, p. 72. Ward, *No Dudes, Few Women*, p. 94. Parman, *Navajos and the New Deal*, pp. 237–38.

24. NA, RG 75, BIA, CF, GSF, 9659E-1936–054, pt. 3, Navajo, Proceedings . . . Navajo Tribal Council . . . May 15–19, 1939, pp. 70–81, 89–91.

25. Ibid., p. 93.

26. Ibid., pp. 94–112.

27. Ibid., pp. 112–20, 141–50, 203.

28. NA, RG 75, BIA, Collier Papers, Navajo Stock Reduction, Why the Government Is Trying Navajo Grazing Cases in the Federal Courts, pp. 11–12. Parman says 10,000 horses were removed. Parman, *Navajos and the New Deal*, pp. 244–45, 249–50. Fryer puts the figure at 14,000. NA, RG 75, BIA, CCF, 62000–1935–301, pt. 2, Navajo, Fryer to Collier, Mar. 25, 1940. Roessel, *Navajo Livestock Reduction*, pp. 120, 131, 162, 200.

29. NA, RG 75, BIA, Collier Papers, Fryer to Bowra, July 2, 1940. *Gallup Independent*, n.d., 1940. Parman, *Navajos and the New Deal*, pp. 252–53.

30. NA, RG 75, BIA, Collier Papers, Navajo Grazing, Brophy to Collier, May 28, 1940; Brophy to Attorney General, May 10, 1940. NA, RG 75, BIA, CCF, 62000–1933–301, pt. 2, Navajo, Fryer to Commissioner, Mar. 25, 1940; Apr. 3, 1940; Brophy to Attorney General, July 6, 1940. The decision itself, in the District Court of the United States in and for the District of Arizona, Civil Number 37, Prescott, *USA* v. *Jake Yellowman . . . Lucy Yellowman*, is also in this file, as is the decision to institute contempt proceedings and the results: Chapman to Attorney General, Dec. 6, 1940; Fryer to Collier, Aug. 26, 1941; Nov. 3, 1940. Also see NA, RG 75, BIA, Collier Papers, Navajo Stock Reduction, Fryer to Collier, June 10, 1941, and NA, RG 75, BIA, CCF, 6200–1935–301, pt. 4, Fryer to Samos, Aug. 19, 1941.

31. Parman, *Navajos and the New Deal*, pp. 274–75.

32. NA, RG 75, BIA, CCF, 63261–1938–054, Navajo, Memorandum from L. Arnold, July 31, 1940. NA, RG 75, BIA, CCF, 69000–1935–301, pt. 2, Navajo, Fryer to Collier, Apr. 3, 1940.

33. Roessel, *Navajo Livestock Reduction*, p. 140. NA, RG 75, BIA, CF, GSF, 9659 E-1936–054, Proceedings of the Meeting of the Navajo Tribal Council, Window Rock, Ariz., June 3–6, 1940, pp. 137–38, 142–43.

34. NA, RG 75, BIA, Collier Papers, Navajo, 1940, Fryer to Zimmerman, May 6, 1940. Parman, *Navajos and the New Deal*, p. 253. For a text of Morgan's speech, see Collier Papers, Navajo, 1940, Fryer to Collier, Nov. 20, 1940—"Jake Morgan Broadcast."

35. NA, RG 75, BIA, CF, GSF, 9659 E-1936–054, Proceedings of the Navajo Tribal Council, Window Rock, Ariz., June 3–6, 1940, p. 142. See Roessel, *Navajo Livestock Reduction*, pp. 90–91, 178, for Navajo memories of council actions during the period.

36. NA, RG 75, BIA, CF, GSF, 9659 E-1936–054, Proceedings of the Navajo Tribal Council, Window Rock, Ariz., June 3–6, 1940, pp. 123–24.

37. Ibid., pp. 123–56.

38. NA, RG 75, BIA, Collier Papers, Navajo, 1940, Fryer to Collier, Oct. 9, 1940. NA, RG 75, BIA, CCF, 62000–1935–301, pt. 3, Navajo, Maggie Totdechine et al. to Ickes, n.d. (read July 18, 1940).

39. NA, RG 75, BIA, Collier Papers, Navajo, 1940, Fryer to Zimmerman, May 8, 1940. NA, RG 75, BIA, Collier Papers, Navajo, 1940, Burge to Harper, Aug. 5, 1940.

40. NA, RG 75, BIA, Collier Papers, Navajo Stock Reduction, American Association of Indian Affairs, "Fundamentals of the Navajo Problem," May 1, 1941. The relief load in 1940 fluctuated between 8 and 20 percent of the nation.

41. NA, RG 75, BIA, Collier Papers, Navajo Grazing, Woehlke to Collier, July 13, 1940. NA, RG 75, BIA, Collier Papers, Navajo Stock Reduction, statement for A.P. News by J. C. Morgan, July 16, 1940.

42. NA, RG 75, BIA, CCF, 62000–1935–301, pt. 3, Navajo, Fryer to Collier, Nov. 3, 1940. F. A. Pollack to R. Van Valkenburgh, Nov. 11, 1940, in Van Valkenburgh Papers, Arizona Historical Society.

43. NA, RG 75, BIA, CCF, 62000–1935–301, pt. 4, Navajo, Fryer to Commissioner, Feb. 3, 1941; Memorandum for the Commissioner from W. Woehlke, Feb. 1, 1941.

44. NA, RG 75, BIA, CCF, 62000–1935–301, pt. 4, Navajo, Memorandum to E. R. Fryer from Navajo Rights Association (submitted by Henry McQuatters, its attorney) n.d.; Memorandum for the Commissioner from Woehlke, Feb. 1, 1941.

45. Ibid. NA, RG 75, BIA, CCF, 62000–1935–301, pt. 4, Navajo, Fryer to Woehlke, Apr. 21, 1941.

46. NA, RG 75, BIA, CCF, 62000–1935–301, pt. 4, Navajo, Memorandum for the Commissioner from Woehlke, Feb. 1, 1941.

47. NA, RG 75, BIA, CCF, 62000–1935–301, pt. 4, Navajo, Collier to Fryer, May 23, 1941; Fryer to Collier, Aug. 6, 1941; Fryer to Chapman, Aug. 27, 1941. NA, RG 75, BIA, CCF, 62000–1935–301, pt. 4, Navajo, Memorandum for the Commissioner from Morgan and Gorman, Feb. 25, 1941. Gorman apparently never realized that the initiative for this whole charade came from Washington and that he was being used as a tool against the NRA. See his account in Roessel, *Navajo Livestock Reduction*, pp. 56–64.

48. NA, RG 75, BIA, CF, GSF, 9657 E-36–054, Proceedings of the Meeting of the Navajo Tribal Council, Window Rock, Ariz., Apr. 8–11, 1941, pp. 22, 27, 29–30.

49. Ibid., p. 32.

50. Ibid., pp. 48–51. The regulations had actually already been modified before the council even met. See modifications in NA, RG 75, BIA, CCF, 62000–1935–301, pt. 4, Navajo, "Title 25—Indian Code of Federal Regulations . . . signed by Oscar Chapman, Mar. 21, 1941"; Collier's order imple-

menting the regulations is in the same file, Order, Apr. 8, 1941, by John
Collier. Parman, *Navajos and the New Deal*, pp. 273–74, 278–80. Ahkeah's
position was close to that of the NRA. See his letter to Chavez, which Fryer
contended was actually the work of an Anglo attorney, Purl Willis, who
wished to become counsel for the NRA. NA, RG 75, BIA, Collier Papers,
Navajo Stock Reduction, Ahkeah to Chavez, June 18, 1941; Fryer to Collier,
Aug. 12, 1941. Also see NA, RG 75, BIA, Collier Papers, Navajo Stock Reduction, Résumé of Meeting, Teec Nos Pos, Ariz., May 22, 1941; statements
made by Deshna, Frank Manuelito, and Don Gleason at a meeting held at
Burnhams.

51. NA, RG 75, BIA, Collier Papers, Navajo Stock Reduction, Fryer to
Collier, June 10, 1941; July 31, 1941; Résumé of Meeting at Teec Nos Pos,
Ariz., May 22, 1941; Adams to Collier, July 21, 1941; Fryer to Collier, Aug.
12, 1941. NA, RG 75, BIA, CCF, 62000–1935–301, pt. 4, Navajo, Memorandum for Commissioner, H. M. Critchfield, July 28, 1941.

52. NA, RG 75, BIA, Collier Papers, Navajo Stock Reduction, Fryer to
Collier, Aug. 12, 1941.

53. Ibid., NA, RG 75, BIA, Collier Papers, Navajo Stock Reduction, Fryer
to Collier, Aug. 14, 1941.

54. NA, RG 75, BIA, Collier Papers, Navajo Stock Reduction, Lorenzo
Hubbell to Collier, Sept. 12, 1941; Memorandum for the Commissioner by
Ward Shepard, Sept. 12, 1941; Memorandum for Collier by Woehlke, Sept.
12, 1941.

55. NA, RG 75, BIA, CCF, 62000–1935–301, pt. 4, Navajo, Commissioner
to Zeh and Lenzie, Sept. 12, 1941.

56. NA, RG 75, BIA, Collier Papers, Navajo Stock Reduction, Roosevelt-
Smith, Memorandum for the Commissioner from Zeh et al., Oct. 9, 1941.

57. NA, RG 75, BIA, CCF, 62000–1935–301, pt. 4, Navajo, Fryer to Collier, Nov. 10, 1941.

58. Aberle, *Peyote Religion*, p. 67.

59. Parman, *Navajos and the New Deal*, pp. 285, 287. "Navajo Tribal Resolutions," pp. 234, 252, Bancroft Library, University of California, Berkeley.
NA, RG 75, BIA, CCF, 62000–35–301, Navajo, Stewart to Collier, July 21,
1943; Collier to Dodge, July 30, 1943. Aberle, *Peyote Religion*, p. 77. For a
Navajo account, see Roessel, *Navajo Livestock Reduction*, pp. 31–38. There were
477,000 sheep units in 1945. Carrying capacity equaled 513,000 sheep units.

60. Parman, *Navajos and the New Deal*, pp. 287–88. *Navajo Yearbook, 1961*,
p. 156.

61. Krug, *The Navajo: Report to the President by the Secretary of the Interior*,
pp. 2–3, 6–7. *Navajo Yearbook, 1961*, pp. 157–62.

62. Harold Steen, "Grazing and the Environment: A History of Forest
Service Stock Reduction Policy," in James Shideler, *Agriculture in the Development of the Far West* (Washington, D.C.: Agricultural History Society, 1975),
pp. 238–42. The Navajo livestock figures are from Aberle, *Peyote Religion*,
p. 70. They are slightly distorted, since the 1932 figure includes the Hopis,

Bibliographical Essay

The notes contain a complete bibliography of the sources used in this book. Discussed here are the works most commonly cited in the notes and what I regard as the most influential books consulted in the preparation of this study.

In a sense there are three separate bibliographies for this study, one for each of the case studies. There were, however, also other sources that influenced the larger themes of this work even though these books appear only sporadically in the notes. The works of Karl Polanyi and Marshall Sahlins on precapitalist, nonmarket economies greatly influenced my perception of Indian economies, while the work of Immanuel Wallerstein helped provide a sense of the historical context in which such economies had to survive during the years of European expansion.

I began this study of environmental and social change with a preference for rather simple materialist models, but as the research proceeded I grew increasingly aware of the significance of culture for the problems I was examining. Clifford Geertz's *The Interpretation of Cultures* and Marshall Sahlins's *Culture and Practical Reason* both proved very useful to me in this respect. Although I eventually found much of it reductionist, Marvin Harris's *Cultural Materialism* remains the most ambitious attempt to address problems of cultural change similar to the ones considered here. As reductionist as Harris, but still notable for their attempts to examine both culture and environment, are works by two other anthropologists: Julian Steward, *Theory of Culture Change*, and Andrew P. Vayda, ed., *Environment and Cultural Behavior*. Finally, the work of a geographer, Carl Sauer, particularly his collected essays, has influenced my perception of the changes that occurred in Indian societies.

American historians have provided fewer theoretical works on the relationships of culture and environment than have social scientists. James Malin's *Grasslands of North America*, despite its reactionary conclusions, remains a milestone in environmental history and deserves a wider influence than it has attained. Alfred Crosby is another historian who has looked at the relationship between societies and their environment. His brief article "Virgin Soil Epidemics" is, I think, more useful than his well-known book because it provides the crucial link between social disruption and the huge death rates from epidemics that afflicted so many Indian peoples. Insofar as this book is an attempt to write "new Indian history" with the emphasis on Indian actions, the essay by Robert Berkhofer "The Political Context of a New Indian History" also deserves mention.

THE CHOCTAWS

There still is no satisfactory history of the Choctaws before their removal. Patricia Dillon Wood's recent *French-Indian Relations on the Southern Frontier* makes use of French archival material, but it lacks a sense of Choctaw culture or politics and makes basic ethnographic mistakes. Charles Paape's excellent doctoral dissertation on the Choctaw Revolt is useful, but it covers only a brief period in Choctaw history. Angie Debo's chapter on the Choctaws in Mississippi, unlike her work on the Oklahoma Choctaws, is derivative and riddled with errors. Horatio Cushman's *History of the Choctaw, Chickasaw, and Natchez Indians* is most reliable when speaking of the events, customs, and people Cushman witnessed or knew. Often, however, the book is garbled and inaccurate, and it must be used with caution. Works on removal are stronger but problems remain. Mary Young's treatment of the Choctaws, although brief, is often more reliable than Arthur DeRosier's book on Choctaw removal, but both fail to deal adequately with the internal politics of the nation. General works on Indian-white relations in the region are somewhat stronger. Verner Crane's *The Southern Frontier* remains an excellent work, and R. S. Cotterill's *The Southern Indians* covers the entire era. An older work covering a briefer period and a narrower area, but still very useful for the Choctaws, is Nancy Surrey's *The Commerce of Louisiana*.

The basic ethnographic sources for the Choctaws are the works of John Swanton. These remain useful but must be used critically since many of Swanton's generalizations are unsubstantiated or outdated. In the journal literature two articles by William Willis are interesting but overstated. A series of early articles by Henry Halbert are often antiquarian in emphasis, but his work on Choctaw towns is very valuable. Also useful is T. N. Campbell's "Choctaw Subsistence." Charles Hudson's recent *Southeastern Indians* provides a comprehensive overview of the cultures of the region. There has been relatively little archaeological excavation of Choctaw sites, but a fine discussion of the environmental influence of the Mississippians is available in Bruce Smith's *Middle Mississippian Exploitation*, while some information on Choctaw sites is available in the work of John Penman.

There is no master work on southeastern ecology. The literature is scattered in professional journals. There is, however, a useful collection of articles on the white-tailed deer in *The White-Tailed Deer in the Southern Forest Habitat.* The reader can consult the notes for the numerous sources I have used.

The major printed sources of documents on the French period are the collection of documents by Pierre Margry and the three-volume collection by Dunbar Rowland and A. G. Sanders, *Mississippi Provincial Archives: French Dominion.* Two more volumes in this series, edited by Patricia Galloway, will soon be published by the Louisiana State University Press. Also important is a brief memoir edited by John Swanton and published under the title "An Early Account of the Choctaw Indians." I believe this dates from the 1730s, but Swanton dates it later. The Loudoun Americana at the Henry Huntington Library contains manuscript materials from the French period, in particular the letterbooks of the Marquis de Vaudreuil. A letter of De Vaudreuil to his brother was captured and published by the English under the title *The Present State of the Country and Inhabitants, Europeans and Indians, of Louisiana . . . .*

Major English sources on the Choctaws during the French period are James Adair's *History of the American Indian* and Edmond Atkin's "Historical Account of the Revolt of the Choctaw Indians in the Late War from the French to the British Alliance . . . ," the original of which is in the British Museum (Lans. 809), but a copy is in the John Carl Parish Papers at the University of California at Santa Barbara. Adair tends to exaggerate his own role in the events he describes, and Atkin is a useful corrective. Basic documents are available in A. S. Salley, ed., *Records in the British Public Record Office Relating to South Carolina, 1701–1710*, and his *The Colonial Records of South Carolina: Journals of the Commons House of Assembly.* Also see William L. McDowell, Jr., ed., *Colonial Records of South Carolina: Documents Relating to Indian Affairs*, and his *Journals of the Commissioners of Indian Trade, September 20, 1710–August 29, 1718.* Allen Candler, ed., *The Colonial Records of the State of Georgia*, is not as helpful for the Choctaws. Another basic source, although less useful during this period than after 1763, is the collection of papers of the Colonial Office in the British Public Record Office (PRO, CO 5), which are also on microfilm at the Library of Congress.

The documentary sources for the period from 1763 until the end of the American Revolution (with some material also relevant to earlier periods) include not only the Colonial Office Papers, but also a published collection by Dunbar Rowland, *Mississippi Provincial Archives: English Dominion.* Essential collections of documents are in the William Clements Library at the University of Michigan. Relevant sources are largely in the Thomas Gage Papers, but the William Petty Shelburne Papers, the Sir Jeffery Amherst Papers, and the William Henry Lyttelton Papers should also be consulted. Eron Opha Rowland also published some important documents in her biography of Peter Chester. Bernard Romans in his *Natural History* gives an account of a visit to the nation during this period, but his excellent observations must be separated from his sweeping conclusions.

The most readily available source of Spanish documents is Lawrence Kinnaird, ed., *Spain in the Mississippi Valley*, but the Bolton Papers in the Bancroft Library at Berkeley also contain valuable material. A useful secondary source on the Spanish period is Jack D. Holmes, *Gayoso*.

After 1790 the major sources on the Choctaws are increasingly American with a scattered but valuable assortment of documents by literate Choctaws. Some useful materials are in Dunbar Rowland, ed., *Mississippi Territorial Archives, 1798–1803* and his *Official Letterbooks of W.C.C. Claiborne*. Others are in Clarence Carter, ed., *The Territorial Papers of the United States*, specifically the volumes on the Southwest Territory, Mississippi Territory, and Orleans Territory. A final collection is *American State Papers: Indian Affairs*.

The basic primary material, however, is in manuscript form in the National Archives. For the Choctaws, the most important collections are the Records of the Secretary of War (Record Group 107), which are available on microfilm (M 221, M 222), and the Records of the Bureau of Indian Affairs (Record Group 75), which are also available in microfilm (M 16, M 271, M 234). The one basic source in the archives on the Choctaws that is not on microfilm is the Armstrong Removal Census.

As important as the government records are, they are often not as revealing as the reports by missionaries to the Choctaws. These reports were regularly published in the *Missionary Herald* from the time of the missionaries' arrival in the nation in 1819 until removal. The John Edwards Papers in the Bancroft Library at the University of California at Berkeley are also useful in this context. Although small in number, the preremoval materials contained in the Peter Pitchlynn Papers in the Thomas Gilcrease Institute of American History and Art in Tulsa give a valuable glimpse into the Choctaw elite. Lack of care has virtually destroyed the John McKee Papers in the Library of Congress, but some scattered materials on the Choctaws survive.

THE PAWNEES

Like the Choctaws, the Pawnees have been relatively neglected by historians. George E. Hyde's *The Pawnee Indians* remains the standard history, but it is badly biased and occasionally contains errors of fact. Two fine pieces of ethnohistory, Preston Holder's *The Hoe and the Horse on the Plains* and Frank Secoy's *Changing Military Patterns on the Great Plains*, can be used to correct some of Hyde's biases. In addition, David J. Wishart's *The Fur Trade of the American West* can be used to put the experience of the Pawnees in its proper context, while his "The Dispossession of the Pawnee" is an excellent study of their final years in Nebraska.

The lack of a good history of the Pawnees is somewhat compensated for by excellent ethnologies of the nation. The best of them is Gene Weltfish's *The Lost Universe*, a sensitive and illuminating re-creation of the Pawnee world. Also superb, even though it treats a period beyond the scope of this study, is Alexander Lesser's *The Pawnee Ghost Dance Handgame*. George Dorsey's collections of Pawnee traditional material, James R. Murie's *Pawnee Indian*

Societies, and George Grinnell's *Pawnee Hero Stories and Folk Tales* all contain valuable material, as do the specialized articles cited in the notes. Published after my basic research on the Pawnees was complete, Douglas R. Parks's edition of James Murie's *Ceremonies of the Pawnee* is a superb study that offers great insights into the Pawnee world.

The excellence of Pawnee ethnology is matched by a similar wealth of archaeological studies. The various works of Waldo Wedel stand out, but the direct historical approach to archaeology he helped pioneer has spawned numerous studies on the Great Plains. I have cited many of them in the notes. The most valuable of these works for my purposes was Roger T. Grange's deceptively titled *Pawnee and Lower Loup Pottery* and his more recent article, "An Archaeological View of Pawnee Origins."

Sources on the Pawnees before the nineteenth century are relatively rare and scattered. An obscure M.A. thesis by Henri Folmer, "French Expansion toward New Mexico in the Eighteenth Century," provides extensive quotations from many early French reports. It is a handy introduction to the period. Louise Barry's chronology, *The Beginning of the West*, can also serve as a useful guide to available materials on the period. For the late eighteenth century, Alfred Thomas's *After Coronado* supplies Spanish documents, as does Lawrence Kinnaird in his *Spain in the Mississippi Valley*. The most useful collection of materials, however, is in Abraham Nasatir's *Before Lewis and Clark*.

In the nineteenth century there are numerous accounts of the Pawnees by travelers and military officers, but none of them deserve singling out as a vital source. They must be compared and used together. They, too, are cited in the notes. Far more reliable than the accounts of travelers and military officers passing through the Pawnee towns are the accounts of the missionaries who lived among them. Samuel Allis's "Forty Years among the Indians and on the Eastern Border of Nebraska" and the Reverend John Dunbar's "Missionary Life among the Pawnee" are first-hand accounts of this mission, but primary materials in the form of letters and diaries are available in "Letters Concerning the Presbyterian Mission in the Pawnee Country . . . ." In addition, the Reverend John Dunbar's son and namesake, who grew up among the Pawnees, eventually published a series of very useful articles on the nation. The later Quaker mission to the Pawnees came during a period when the churches actually controlled the agencies, so many of their records form part of the collections of the Bureau of Indian Affairs. Additional material is available, however, in "The Journal of Barclay White," Friends' Historical Library, Swarthmore College (microfilm), and in the "Minutes of Councils between the Pawnees and Their Agents," the original of which is in the Oklahoma State Historical Society, but a copy of which is in the Nebraska State Historical Society.

The basic primary sources on the Pawnees during the nineteenth century are the records of the Bureau of Indian Affairs in the National Archives (Record Group 75), also the Records of the Office of the Secretary of War (Record Group 107), and the Records Relating to Indian Treaties (Record

Group 11). Several other manuscript collections also hold valuable materials. The John Williamson Papers, the Samuel Allis Papers, the Luther North Papers, and the John Dunbar Papers are all in the Nebraska State Historical Society. The Pawnee Indian Papers and the James Murie Papers, both in the Kansas State Historical Society, contain useful, if scattered, material.

THE NAVAJOS

Far more than the other two nations that are the subjects of this book, the Navajos are the subject of an immense and sophisticated literature. What follows only scratches the surface.

Ruth M. Underhill's *The Navajos* and Clyde Kluckhohn and Dorothea Leighton's *The Navaho* remain the best general introductions. A collection of documents published by the Navajo Heritage Center and edited by J. Lee Correll, *Through White Mens' Eyes*, is also very useful as a source book for early Navajo history.

From among the numerous monographs on the Navajos, several works proved particularly useful for this study. Denis Forster Johnston, *An Analysis of Sources of Information on the Population of the Navaho*, handles a very difficult topic quite well, and David Aberle's *The Peyote Religion among the Navahos* is not only a classic study of its topic but also a basic study of stock reduction and a stimulating examination of the connections between social and cultural change. Among the studies of Navajo culture, two books by Gary Witherspoon stand out. His *Navajo Kinship and Marriage* and his *Language and Art in the Navajo Universe* are both clear and cogent. James Downs, *Animal Husbandry in Navajo Society and Culture*, and Leonard Fonaroff, "The Navajo Sheep Industry," provide necessary background for understanding sheep raising among the Navajos. W. Y. Adams, *Shonto: A Study of the Role of the Trader in a Modern Navajo Community*, is a fine study of Navajo commercial relations just after the reduction period, and Tom T. Sasaki's *Fruitland, New Mexico: A Navajo Community in Transition* is a useful study of the economic and social failures of a development project. Finally, Walter Dyk's recording of the classic Navajo autobiography *Son of Old Man Hat* and W. W. Hill's *The Agricultural and Hunting Methods of the Navaho Indians* both deserve mention.

Most of the history of Indian peoples in the twentieth century has been neglected by historians, but the Navajos have been the subject of two careful studies: Lawrence Kelly, *The Navajo Indians and Federal Indian Policy, 1900–1935*, and Donald Parman, *The Navajos and the New Deal*. There are basic differences between their interpretations of stock reduction and the one presented here, but both of the books provide excellent discussions of the intentions of and the constraints on government policy in the early twentieth century. One should also consult Robert W. Young's *Political History of the Navajo Tribe* for this and later periods. Two other books that concentrate, not on Indians, but rather on reformers are also important for understanding federal policy during this period: Graham D. Taylor, *The New Deal and*

American Indian Tribalism, and Kenneth Philp, *John Collier's Crusade for Indian Reform*. Some sense of the Navajo reaction to reduction can be found in Ruth Roessel and Broderick Johnson, *Navajo Livestock Reduction*, the report of the contemporary New Mexico Association of Indian Affairs entitled *Urgent Navajo Problems*, and the report of the Phelps-Stoke Fund entitled *The Navaho Indian Problem*.

Two works from the literature on erosion in the Navajo country deserve special mention. H. E. Gregory's early *Geology of the Navajo Country* provides a base mark against which to compare later, more hysterical evaluations. The most useful source, however, and one on which I relied heavily, is Yi-Fu Tuan's "New Mexican Gullies: A Critical Review and Some Recent Observations."

The primary sources on the Navajos are as abundant as the secondary literature. A broad overview of the growth of the Navajo herds is available in the annual *Report of the Commissioner of Indian Affairs* for the late nineteenth and early twentieth centuries. The condition of the Navajos and their herds is illuminated by the published hearings of the U.S. Senate Subcommittee of Indian Affairs, *Survey of the Conditions of the Indians of the United States*, particularly volume 34.

The basic sources for this study, however, remain in manuscript form. Essential documents are in the U.S. Soil Conservation Service Reports (Navajo Project) in the Special Collections of the University of New Mexico Library. This is the most extensive collection of Soil Conservation Service material, but other documents and reports are available in the USDA Soil Conservation Service materials in the Special Collections of the University of Arizona Library, and in the Navajo Tribal Museum, Files, Research Division, Window Rock, Arizona. Also of some use for the period are the Richard Van Valkenburgh Papers in the Arizona Historical Society, Tucson, and the Albert B. Fall Papers in the Huntington Library, San Marino, California.

The core of the archival materials on the Navajos is in the National Archives in Washington, D.C. The holdings of the Federal Regional Archives in Laguna Miguel, California, were disappointing, and outside of the minutes of a single important council meeting, the Interior Department Library held little pertinent material. The Navajo materials consulted in the National Archives are all part of Record Group 75. They are found in the Office Files of Commissioner John Collier (in the files labeled Navajo Documents), in the Central Classified Files, 1907–1939, Navajo, in the General Service File (Council Minutes), and in the Civilian Conservation Corps—Indian Division records.

BOOKS, AND DISSERTATIONS
MENTIONED IN THE BIBLIOGRAPHICAL ESSAY

Aberle, David H. *The Peyote Religion Among the Navaho*. Viking Fund Publications in Anthropology, no. 42. New York: Wenner Gren Foundation for Anthropological Research, 1966.

Adair, James. *The History of the American Indians: Particularly Those Adjoining the Mississippi, East and West Florida, Georgia, South and North Carolina and Virginia.* London: E. C. Dilly, 1775; reprint, Johnson City, Tenn.: Watauga Press, 1930.

Adams, William Y. *Shonto: A Study of the Role of the Trader in a Modern Navajo Community.* Bureau of American Ethnology Bulletin 188. Washington, D.C.: Government Printing Office, 1963.

Allis, Samuel. "Forty Years among the Indians and on the Eastern Border of Nebraska." *Transactions and Reports of the Nebraska State Historical Society* 2 (Lincoln, 1887): 133–66.

American State Papers: Indian Affairs, Documents, Legislative and Executive, of the Congress of the United States, from the First Session of the First to the Second Session of the Nineteenth Congress inclusive; Commencing March 3, 1789 and ending March 3, 1827. 2 vols. Washington, D.C., 1832–34.

Barry, Louise. *The Beginning of the West.* Topeka: Kansas State Historical Society, 1972.

Berkhofer, Robert. "The Political Context of a New Indian History." *Pacific Historical Review* 40 (August 1971): 357–82.

Campbell, T. N. "Choctaw Subsistence: Ethnographic Notes from the Lincecum Manuscript." *Florida Anthropologist* 12 (1959): 9–24.

Candler, Allen D., ed. *The Colonial Records of the State of Georgia.* 26 vols. Atlanta, 1904–26.

Carter, Clarence, ed. *The Territorial Papers of the United States.* 28 vols. Washington, D.C.: Government Printing Office, 1934–75.

Correll, J. Lee, ed. *Through White Mens' Eyes: A Contribution to Navajo History, a Chronological Record of the Navajo People from Earliest Times to the Treaty of June 1, 1868.* Publication no. 1 of the Navajo Heritage Center. Window Rock, Ariz.: Navajo Heritage Center, 1976.

Cotterill, R. S. *The Southern Indians: The Story of the Civilized Tribes Before Removal.* Norman: University of Oklahoma Press, 1954.

Crane, Verner. *The Southern Frontier.* Durham. N.C.: Duke University Press, 1928.

Crosby, Alfred. "Virgin Soil Epidemics as a Factor in the Aboriginal Depopulation in America." *William and Mary Quarterly* 33 (April 1976): 289–99.

Cushman, Horatio. *History of the Choctaw, Chickasaw, and Natchez Indians.* Greenville, Tex.: Headlight Printing House, 1899; abridged reprint, Stillwater, Okla.: Redlands Press, 1962.

Debo, Angie. *The Rise and Fall of the Choctaw Republic.* Norman: University of Oklahoma Press, 1961.

DeRosier, Arthur, Jr. *The Removal of the Choctaw Indians.* Knoxville: University of Tennessee Press, 1970.

Dorsey, George. *The Pawnee Mythology.* Washington, D.C.: Carnegie Institution, 1906.

———. *Traditions of the Skidi Pawnee.* Memoirs of the American Folklore Society, vol. 8. Boston: Houghton Mifflin, 1904.

Downs, James F. *Animal Husbandry in Navajo Society and Culture.* University of California Publications in Anthropology, no. 1. Berkeley: University of California Press, 1964.

Dunbar, Rev. John. "Missionary Life among the Pawnee." *Nebraska State Historical Society Collections* 16 (Lincoln, 1911): 268–87.

Dunbar, John B. "The Pawnee Indians." *Magazine of American History* 8 (November 1881): 738–41.

———. "The Pawnee Indians: Their Habits and Customs." *Magazine of American History* 5 (November 1880): 321–42.

———. "The Pawnee Indians: Their History and Ethnology." *Magazine of American History* 4 (April 1880): 241–79.

Dyk, Walter, ed. *Son of Old Man Hat: A Navaho Autobiography.* Lincoln: University of Nebraska Press, 1967.

Folmer, Henri. "French Expansion toward New Mexico in the Eighteenth Century." M.A. thesis, University of Denver, 1939.

Fonaroff, Leonard. "The Navajo Sheep Industry: A Study in Cross-Cultural Administration." Ph.D. dissertation, Johns Hopkins University, 1961.

Geertz, Clifford. *The Interpretation of Cultures.* New York: Basic Books, 1973.

Grange, Roger T. "An Archeological View of Pawnee Origins." *Nebraska History* 60 (Summer 1979): 134–60.

———. *Pawnee and Lower Loup Pottery.* Nebraska State Publications in Anthropology, no. 3. Lincoln, 1968.

Gregory, H. E. *Geology of the Navajo Country*, United States Geological Survey, Professional Paper 93. Washington, D.C.: Government Printing Office, 1917.

Grinnell, George Bird. *Pawnee Hero Stories and Folk Tales.* New York: Scribner's, 1925.

Halbert, Henry. "Bernard Romans' Map of 1772." *Publications of the Mississippi Historical Society* 6 (Oxford, Miss., 1902): 415–39.

———. "District Divisions of the Choctaw Nation." *Report of the Alabama Historical Commission* 1 (Montgomery, Ala., 1901): 375–85.

Harris, Marvin. *Cultural Materialism: The Struggle for a Science of Culture.* New York: Random House, 1979.

Hill, Willard Williams. *The Agricultural and Hunting Methods of the Navaho Indians.* Yale University Publications in Anthropology, no. 18. New Haven: Department of Anthropology, Yale University, 1938.

Holder, Preston. *The Hoe and the Horse on the Plains: A Study of Cultural Development among North American Indians.* Lincoln: University of Nebraska Press, 1970.

Holmes, Jack D. *Gayoso: The Life of A Spanish Governor in the Mississippi Valley, 1789–1799.* Baton Rouge: Louisiana State University Press, 1965.

Hudson, Charles. *The Southeastern Indians.* Knoxville: University of Tennessee Press, 1976.

Hyde, George E. *The Pawnee Indians*. Norman: University of Oklahoma Press, 1974.

Johnston, Denis Forster. *An Analysis of Sources of Information on the Population of the Navajo*. Bureau of American Ethnology Bulletin 197. Washington, D.C.: Government Printing Office, 1966.

Kelly, Lawrence C. *The Navajo Indians and Federal Indian Policy, 1900–1935*. Tucson: University of Arizona Press, 1968.

Kluckhohn, Clyde, and Leighton, Dorothea. *The Navaho*. Garden City, N.Y. : Doubleday, 1962.

Kinnaird, Lawrence, ed. *Annual Report of the American Historical Association for the Year 1945: Spain in the Mississippi Valley*. 3 vols. Washington, D.C.: Government Printing Office, 1946.

Lesser, Alexander. *The Pawnee Ghost Dance Handgame*. Columbia Contributions to Anthropology. New York: Columbia University Press, 1933.

"Letters Concerning the Presbyterian Mission in the Pawnee Country near Bellevue, Nebraska, 1831–1849." *Kansas State Historical Society Collections* 14 (Topeka, 1915–18): 570–783.

McDowell, William L., Jr., ed. *Colonial Records of South Carolina: Documents Relating to Indian Affairs*. 3 vols. Columbia, S.C.: University of South Carolina Press, 1955–70.

———. *Journals of the Commissioners of Indian Trade, September 20, 1710–August 29, 1718*. Columbia, S.C.: South Carolina Archives Department, 1955.

Malin, James. *The Grasslands of North America–Prolegomena to Its History*. Lawrence, Kan.: privately printed, 1947.

Margry, Pierre, ed. *Découvertes et établissements des Français . . . mémoires et documents originaux*. 6 vols. Paris: Imprimerie D. Jouaust, 1879–80.

Murie, James R. *Pawnee Indian Societies*. Anthropological Papers of the American Museum of Natural History, vol. 11, pt. 7. New York, 1914.

Nasatir, Abraham P., ed. *Before Lewis and Clark: Documents Illustrating the History of the Missouri, 1783–1804*. 2 vols. St. Louis: St. Louis Historical Documents Foundation, 1952.

New Mexico Association on Indian Affairs. *Urgent Navajo Problems*. Santa Fe, N.M.: New Mexico Association of Indian Affairs, 1940.

Paape, Charles W. "The Choctaw Revolt: A Chapter in the Inter-colonial Rivalry in the Old Southwest." Ph.D. dissertation, University of Illinois, 1946.

Parks, Douglas R., ed. *Ceremonies of the Pawnee*, by James R. Murie. Smithsonian Contributions to Anthropology, no. 27, 2 vols. Washington, D.C.: Smithsonian Institution Press, 1981.

Parman, Donald. *The Navajos and the New Deal*. New Haven: Yale University Press, 1976.

Penman, John T. *Archaeological Survey in Mississippi, 1974–1975*. Jackson, Mississippi: State of Mississippi Department of Archives and History, 1977.

————. "Historic Choctaw Towns of the Southern Division." *Journal of Mississippi History* 40 (May 1978): 133–41.

Phelps-Stokes Fund. *The Navaho Indian Problem: An Inquiry Sponsored by the Phelps-Stokes Fund.* New York: Phelps-Stokes Fund, 1939.

Philp, Kenneth R. *John Collier's Crusade for Indian Reform, 1920–1954.* Tucson: University of Arizona Press, 1977.

Polanyi, Karl. *The Great Transformation.* New York: Rinehart, 1944.

————. *Primitive, Archaic and Modern Economies: Essays of Karl Polanyi*, edited by George Dalton. Boston: Beacon Press, 1968.

The Present State of the Country and Inhabitants, Europeans, and Indians, of Louisiana . . . by an Officer at New Orleans. London: J. Millan, 1744.

Roessel, Ruth, and Johnson, Broderick. *Navajo Livestock Reduction: A National Disgrace.* Chinle, Ariz.: Navajo Community College Press, 1974.

Romans, Bernard. *A Concise Natural History of East and West Florida.* Gainesville, Fl.: University of Florida Press, 1962; facsimile reproduction of the 1775 edition.

Rowland, Dunbar, ed. *Mississippi Provincial Archives: English Dominion, 1763–66.* Nashville, Tenn.: Press of Brandon Printing Company, 1911.

————. *Mississippi Territorial Archives, 1798–1803: Executive Journals of Governor Winthrop Sargent and Governor William Charles Cole Claiborne.* Nashville, Tenn.: Brandon Printing Company, 1905.

————. *Official Letterbooks of W. C. C. Claiborne, 1801–1816.* 4 vols. Jackson, Miss.: Department of Archives and History, 1917.

Rowland, Dunbar, and Sanders, A. G., eds. *Mississippi Provincial Archives: French Dominion.* 3 vols. Jackson, Miss.: Mississippi Department of Archives and History, 1927–32.

Rowland, Eron Opha. *Peter Chester.* Publications of the Mississippi Historical Society, vol. 5, Centenary Series. Jackson, Miss.: Mississippi Historical Society, 1925.

Sahlins, Marshall. *Culture and Practical Reason.* Chicago: University of Chicago Press, 1976.

————. *Stone Age Economics.* Chicago: Aldine, 1972.

Salley, A. S., ed. *The Colonial Records of South Carolina: Journals of the Commons House of Assembly.* 11 vols. Columbia, S.C.: Historical Commission of South Carolina, 1951–77.

————. *Records in the British Public Record Office Relating to South Carolina, 1701–1710.* 5 vols. Columbia, S.C.: Historical Commission of South Carolina, 1947.

Sasaki, Tom T. *Fruitland, New Mexico: A Navajo Community in Transition.* Cornell University Press, 1960.

Sauer, Carl. *Land and Life.* Berkeley: University of California Press, 1963.

————. *Sixteenth Century North America: The Land and the People as Seen by the Europeans.* Berkeley: University of California Press, 1971.

Secoy, Frank R. *Changing Military Patterns on the Great Plains (Seventeenth*

Through Early Nineteenth Centuries). Monographs of the American Ethnological Society 21. Locust Valley, N.Y.: J. J. Ugustin, 1953.

Smith, Bruce D. *Middle Mississippian Exploitation of Animal Populations.* Anthropological Papers, Museum of Anthropology, University of Michigan, no. 57. Ann Arbor: University of Michigan Press, 1975.

Steward, Julian. *Theory of Culture Change.* Urbana: University of Illinois Press, 1955.

Surrey, Nancy Marie. *The Commerce of Louisiana During the French Regime, 1699–1763.* Studies in History, Economics and Public Law, no. 167. New York: Columbia University Press, 1916.

Swanton, John R., ed. "An Early Account of the Choctaw Indians." *Memoirs of the American Anthropological Association* 5 (Apr.–June 1918): 53–72.

———. *Indian Tribes of the Lower Mississippi Valley and the Adjacent Coast of the Gulf of Mexico.* Bureau of American Ethnology Bulletin, no. 43 Washington, D.C.: Government Printing Office, 1909.

———. *Indians of the Southeastern United States.* Bureau of American Ethnology Bulletin, no. 137. Washington, D.C.: Government Printing Office, 1946.

———. *Source Material for the Social and Ceremonial Life of the Choctaw Indians.* Bureau of American Ethnology Bulletin, no. 103. Washington, D.C.: Government Printing Office, 1931.

Taylor, Graham D. *The New Deal and American Indian Tribalism: The Administration of the Indian Reorganization Act, 1934–45.* Lincoln: University of Nebraska Press, 1980.

Thomas, Alfred B. *After Coronado: Spanish Exploration Northeast of New Mexico, 1696–1727, Documents from the Archives of Spain, Mexico, and New Mexico,* Norman: University of Oklahoma Press, 1935.

Tuan, Yi-Fu. "New Mexican Gullies: A Critical Review and Some Recent Observations." *Annals of the Association of American Geographers* 56 (December 1966): 573–82.

Underhill, Ruth M. *The Navajos.* Norman: University of Oklahoma Press, 1967.

United States Congress, Senate, Subcommittee of the Senate Committee on Indian Affairs. *Survey of the Conditions of the Indians of the United States.* 70th Cong., 2nd sess. (1928—hearings continued until 1939), 37 vols.

Vayda, Andrew P., ed. *Environment and Cultural Behavior.* New York: Natural History Press, 1969.

———, ed. *Man, Culture and Animals: The Role of Animals in Human Ecological Adjustments.* Washington, D.C.: American Association for the Advancement of Science, 1965.

Wallerstein, Immanuel. *The Modern World System: Capitalist Agriculture and the Origins of the European World Economy in the Sixteenth Century.* New York: Academic Press, 1974.

———. *The Modern World System II: Mercantilism and the Consolidation of the European World Economy, 1600–1750.* New York: Academic Press, 1980.

Wedel, Waldo. *Archeological Remains in Central Kansas and Their Possible Bearing*

on the Location of Quivira. Smithsonian Miscellaneous Collections, vol. 101, no. 7. Washington, D.C.: Government Printing Office, January 15–1942.
———. *The Direct-Historical Approach in Pawnee Archeology*. Smithsonian Miscellaneous Collections, vol. 97, no. 7. Washington, D.C.: Government Printing Office, October 19, 1938.
———. *Environment and Native Subsistence Economies in the Central Great Plains*. Smithsonian Miscellaneous Collections, vol. 101, no. 3. Washington, D.C.: Government Printing Office, August 20, 1941.
———. *An Introduction to Pawnee Archeology*. Bureau of American Ethnology Bulletin 112. Washington, D.C.: Government Printing Office, 1936.
———. *Prehistoric Man on the Great Plains*. Norman: University of Oklahoma Press, 1961.
———. "Some Aspects of Human Ecology in the Central Plains." *American Anthropologist* 55 (October 1953): 499–514.
Weltfish, Gene. *The Lost Universe: The Way of Life of the Pawnee*. New York: Ballantine Books, 1971; 1st ed., Basic Books, 1965.
White-Tailed Deer in the Southern Forest Habitat: Proceedings of a Symposium at Nacogdoches, Texas, March 25–26, 1969. Southern Forest Experiment Station, U.S. Forest Service, USDA, in cooperation with the Forest Game Committee of the Southeastern Section of the Wildlife Society and the School of Forestry, Stephen F. Austin University. Nacogdoches, Tex., 1969.
Willis, William. "The Nation of Bread." *Ethnohistory* 4 (Spring 1957): 125–49.
———. "Patrilineal Institutions in Southeastern North America." *Ethnohistory* 10 (1963): 250–69.
Wishart, David J. "The Dispossession of the Pawnee." *Annals of the Association of American Geographers* 69 (September 1979): 382–401.
———. *The Fur Trade of the American West, 1807–1840: A Geographical Synthesis*. Lincoln: University of Nebraska Press, 1979.
Witherspoon, Gary. *Language and Art in the Navajo Universe*. Ann Arbor: University of Michigan Press, 1980.
———. *Navajo Kinship and Marriage*. Chicago: University of Chicago Press, 1975.
Wood, Patricia Dillon. *French-Indian Relations on the Southern Frontier, 1699–1762*. Ann Arbor: UMI Research Press, 1980.
Young, Mary Elizabeth. *Redskins, Ruffleshirts and Rednecks: Indian Allotments in Alabama and Mississippi, 1830–1860*. Norman: University of Oklahoma Press, 1961.
Young, Robert W. *A Political History of the Navajo Tribe*. Tsaile, Navajo Nation, Ariz.: Navajo Community College Press, 1978.

Index